A promise made is a debt unpaid.
Robert William Service
From "The Cremation of Sam McGee"

Dave,

Thanks for all your support and help over the past four years. It was really a pleasure working with you and getting to know you. I hope we don't drift too far apart over the years. I'll definitely be coming back to SSU regularly, so I doubt that we will.

Sincerely

Steven Stratford

The Wall

The Vietnam Veterans Memorial in Washington, D.C.
In many ways it speaks through the stories in this book.
More important than seeing its representation here,
are the words of one of the contributing authors,
a Marine Corps sniper that did his job well.
His words represent insights which make
The Wall an important monument:

> There's a new wall that was erected
> in Washington D.C. that cries out
> to the American people. This wall
> tells stories of pain and death. The
> wall is filled with the names of
> friends, brothers, sisters, fathers,
> mothers, and young brave men
> who gave their lives to the
> American people. Etched on that
> wall are the names of my friends,
> over 58,000 of them. My friends
> on that wall, I salute you. I salute
> you over and over for, without you
> and the memory of what you did
> and sacrificed . . . will never be
> forgotten by me as long as I live.
> You will not be forgotten by your
> family, friends, and fellow
> comrades who fought alongside
> of you. To my fellow soldiers on
> the wall, "I love you."
> *Steven Hunt, "One On One"*

A torch of Life

Ritz Publishing
202 West Fifth Avenue
Ritzville, Washington 99169

V i e t n a m :
Our Story—One On One

Stories Compiled by Gary D. Gullickson
Edited by David "Doc" Andersen
1 9 9 1

RITZ PUBLISHING
202 West Fifth Avenue
Ritzville, Washington 99169
SAN No. 297-3588

Publisher of *Vietnam: Our Story—One On One*

First printing 1991

Although the authors, story compiler, editor and publisher
have ascertained the accuracy and completeness of the
information contained in this book, we assume no
responsibility for errors, inaccuracies, omissions or any
inconsistency herein. Any slights of people or organizations are unintentional.

Library of Congress Cataloging-in-Publication Data

Vietnam: our story—one on one : stories / compiled by Gary
   D. Gullickson : edited by David "Doc" Andersen
               p. cm.
     ISBN 0-9627904-0-0 (pbk.) : $16.95
     1. Vietnamese Conflict, 1961-1975—Personal
narratives, American. I. Gullickson, Gary D., 1949- .
II. Andersen, David A.
DS559.5.V53 1991
959.704'38—dc20   91-31414
                                      CIP

Printed in the United States of America

Editor's Foreword

The stories contained in *Vietnam: Our Story—One On One* are important to America because they represent straightforward expression about the experience of war. These are the voices of America's sons and daughters who answered their call to duty. For many of the authors, their stories represent a first telling of experiences and reactions that have gone untold for over twenty years. They offer a glimpse of life at war, and after war, that will help people understand the human side of those who fought and those who kept the war machine running.

These are not the stories of generals or policy-makers, nor are they written from the predominant news media viewpoint during the Vietnam War. They are the stories of people who, perhaps, could have won the war, had they been given the opportunity by the policy-makers, and had the media presented a different image of the war. These continue to be highly charged topics for millions of Americans. Many of the following stories contain strong opinions about such topics.

Each of these stories has been edited as lightly as possible, to retain the impact of each author's natural voice. For example, an author might write *'cause* for *because,* or use conversational sentence structure. The *'cause* remains as such, and punctuation has been added, where necessary, to aid ease of reading. The language in this book is often strong and profane, but it is not intended to offend. Both Gary Gullickson and I wanted each story to be like sitting down with the author and listening to his experience. We ask you to read each story in that spirit, as if listening, sharing in his experiences and feelings. If that happens, communication will begin, or be strengthened. That communication will further a healing process which is more important than a belated homecoming parade.

About the cover

The map of Vietnam before U.S. military involvement symbolizes the genesis of the stories in this book. The rose is meant to indicate growth and healing after the Vietnam War. The drops falling from the rose represent, according to Gary Gullickson, "The blood, sweat and tears that were caused by Vietnam." About the book's title Gullickson said, "One on one is how Vietnam was for most of us. You went alone, came home alone, and even though you were with a military unit, you were alone. Now, it is time for us to tell our story . . . one on one."

Table of Contents

Table of Contents

Introduction

There are over 2000 stories yet untold. The voices of the POW/ MIAs (prisoners of war/missing in action) may be lost to America forever. It is sad but true.

America must honor its commitment. It promised to bring home all the people it sent into the most hell-like of experiences—war. Until that promise is kept, it has a debt unpaid. This is human life we're talking about. For the American government to maintain its honor, it must answer, definitively, what happened to those people. It must bring them home.

That's why the POW/MIA symbol is on the first page of this book. After talking with the publishers at Ritz, they agreed it was important enough to open this book. They also agreed to decidate a page to The Wall. Over 58,000 people died defending American principles, American honor. To all the people whose names are on that wall, we salute you. You paid the ultimate price for your country.

Many Vietnam vets wish, now, they'd died back then. Life has been almost unbearable for many of them, living with the nightmares of physical disability and/or mental images and after-effects. I too have suffered, and as a result, caused suffering for family, friends, and strangers, around me. I'm proud I served my country. I'm proud to be a Marine. But Vietnam definitely twisted me up.

Talking about my experiences in Vietnam, telling my story and listening to others, has helped the healing process. That's where I got the idea to help others share their stories. It has not been an easy road, gathering and "living" all the stories in this book, but I felt I owed it to other Vietnam vets—my best friends in life. And maybe, once America hears these stories, it will appreciate the ultimate sacrifice these men and women made. I believe this collection of over sixty stories represents a good cross-section of experience and attitudes, then and now. I asked each person to tell briefly about childhood and high school days; to then honestly talk about their Vietnam experience; and to close by telling briefly about their current activities. Some are now doing very well, some very bad; and a lot of that seems to be directly related to the Vietnam War.

Many people say the ultimate book or movie about Vietnam has not been produced. I don't know. As Doc Andersen and I have begun to realize, this book may be it. "The book" about Vietnam may be in your hands, right now. Part of the reason may be that these stories are, for many of the authors, the first time they've told their stories. Not all of them are polished writing, but they are real. Very real. Boy, can I guarantee that.

I thank every man and woman who wrote for this book. From nothing more than a letter from me, you wrote about the darkest time in your life, for no other reason than to help someone else. As I got your chapters, I was with you, back in Vietnam. I love and respect each of you. No matter how anyone sees you, you are the best this country ever had.

Thank you, David (Doc) and Star Andersen at Ritz. Your trust and belief in us made this possible. As in Vietnam, we will not let you down.

Thanks to Kasson State Bank for the many, many copies you made for me. A special thanks to Julie deGroot for her help.

To my family, Sharon, Billy and Bobby, who lived through the creation and completion of this book with me, you put up with the good and bad in me; sometimes the very bad. Thank you.

Thank you to the people who are part of my story, and those who believed in me enough to say "Go for it."

A special thanks to those of you who buy this book. It was meant for you. It is meant to show you how terrible war is, and how it can mess up a life. Buying this book shows not only that you are interested, but also that you care. You can make a difference. I promise you, some good will come of the sales of this book.

Jerry Tisdell

I was stationed in Vietnam in 1966/67. I was a member of the 612 Tactical Fighter Squadron, at Phan Rang Air Force Base. I loaded bombs and 20mm cannons. I was also responsible for maintaining weapons delivery systems on F-100s ("lead sleds"). Although I was never a combat vet, I suffered the guilt of being stuck between Saigon and the bush. My spirit was attached to every errant napalm or round that found its way to the wrong target.

I wish to reply to questions about my Vietnam experience with how I feel. The real chapter on Vietnam is yet to be written, but the "Phantom Chapter" is close. It will, for those that served and didn't serve, bring the war "full circle." There must be an end to everything, a conclusion. If our only purpose is to bring about that conclusion, it must be done.

Like my father and grandfather, I am an American military veteran who served in defense of the ideals of our country. Like my forefathers I did not create the war, I only fought it. We wept the same; we were scared. Some of us were heroes, most of us were not. We just did our jobs and tried to survive, much like my father and grandfather.

In Vietnam the mechanics of war were different. Technologically, we were better killers. But the result was just the same as when primitive man first picked up a club to defend himself from his enemy. We did the same.

I'm forty-four years old now, and as I gaze at my twenty-two-year-old son, somehow I could never picture him in the heat of battle. He seems so young and innocent, so fragile, so pure. Yet many of my brothers from Nam had already endured a couple of years of mental scars by the time they were twenty-two. How our parents must have felt when they gazed upon these battle-hardened children.

To our parents we were the "baby boomers." The generation with great expectations. "Idealistic innovators." "Have Gun Will Travel." John Wayne, he taught us well. Mrs. Robinson, not so well! But our generation would be split by a war. We knew where French Indo-China was, but Vietnam?

The beatniks turned to hippies and hippies to yuppies. The soldiers, well they were different. Odd in some ways. We were forced to be men and yet we were children. We realized that people didn't fall over when they were shot, like in the movies. We came apart, and we screamed for our mothers. Bodies would stink when they weren't buried. We knew that death was final and our brothers would not return. These were lessons we children would learn.

I look back at the twenty-two years I spent as the Great American

Bedouin, Society's Nomad, for I wandered in despair, wondering what went wrong. How could my loyalty be a lie? Was my father's and grandfather's a lie, too? Is this truly what God would have wanted? Was our society split so that part would wander and suffer while the other gave us abortion and junk bonds? We no longer exist in the world an independent nation, with liberty and justice for all. Japan sits like a vulture, feeding off our fallen land. Europe is like a parasite or disease, and we are the host. Vietnam's final chapter is yet to be written.

For years, we wandered in no direction while others cared not about our land. They stripped us of our heroes. Our brothers still remain captive, lost souls of the fight.

I say, awaken my brothers; what was dark . . . let there be light. Soldiers of the past call us to fight. Strike not a blow, but show us your might. Go forth my mighty brothers and extend your hand. Lift up your heads, wipe away the tears. Strengthen the bond absent for years. Shout out with voices to beacon the fallen, then stand as one, America is calling. Reach out my lost children, then hold me near. Save me, my children. Lost children so dear.

Listen well, my brothers. There is still the chapter yet to be written. Our country depends on us now more than ever. Our fight ahead will truly be our hardest, but surely we are seasoned warriors, for the battles have never left us; still so vivid in our minds. Our fallen, they call us from the Wall.

Take heed my brothers, hear our plight. Make the circle full, give us purpose. Our souls, they wander. Take up our souls and fight our fight. Give us meaning so we may rest this night.

I reply, rest my brothers, rest, for we will make it right.

Yes, I served in Vietnam, and there are thousands of stories about our duty there. But it is the story today that is the most important. That's the one we can change. I'm tired of looking at the world from afar, as if I'm not a part of it. We did not create the war and we damn sure did not lose it. We only did as we were told!

Today we are still being told by the very same people who wouldn't go. We must come together now more than ever. As we truly were the finest. We must be one, all veterans from all wars. But it is up to us to bring this change. There are many veterans that are successful today. We have the power to restore dignity to our land. We must call all brothers to stand tall once more. Our brothers from all wars. Good luck and God's speed.

Jim Eichelberger

I was born August 13, 1950, the first of seven children. As a child, my formative years were normal. We were raised in the old-fashioned Catholic ways of "love your neighbor," and "help the less fortunate."

My senior year in high school was the first I really had any idea of the Vietnam War. We were taught that we were morally obligated to help the South Vietnamese. I don't know if my high school training influenced me, but I joined the Marine Corps in August 1968.

We landed at Da Nang March 23, 1969. I was assigned to the Third Marine Division; the headquarters were located in Quang Tri. We spent about a week in the rear attending classes on the "Nam."

My first look at the bush seemed peaceful enough. The battalion was winding down "Operation Main Craig." While there wasn't much action, there was still a hell of a lot to get used to.

My MOS was 0331—machine gunner. They told us at gun school we would be very important. After my first firefight I realized how important my ass was to the NVA, too. I grew up in a pretty tough area in Cincinnati, but nobody ever shot at me before. If it was possible to get your whole body in your helmet, I must have done it.

Although we had some heavy action, one sticks out in my mind. Around the middle of July 1970 we moved into the mountainous area just below the DMZ. There were stories of some heavy action in the past around this area. Those mountains were real bastards, but the worst part was that we were sitting ducks if the gooks were watchin'.

Our company was split into platoons. My gun squad was with the third platoon. We also had an 81 platoon with us. Fox 2/3 was in the vicinity and on August 8th their positions were attacked by an NVA force. We could see the bastards, but couldn't fire because we weren't sure exactly where Fox positions were. Airstrikes drove the gooks off.

August 9, one of our patrols ambushed a lone NVA in the valley above our positions.

August 10, at about 3:30 a.m., all hell broke loose. I was on watch and saw some sparks followed by some deafening noises. The 81 part of the perimeter had been penetrated by sappers with satchel charges. Those guys who could make it fought out to the other side of the LZ, where we reformed. My gun team was brought up to protect the wounded. We had moved to the platoon CP. I don't think I'll ever forget the sounds of the wounded—their cries for help, even for their mothers.

The first platoon was on a nearby hill and they too came under heavy attack. The darkness and fear of hitting our buddies kept us from using all our firepower. We tried to pinpoint the gooks from muzzle flashes. Our platoon commander called in arty to blanket the area around us. The sound of those shells hurling down around us was terrifying, and comforting. Hopefully, the shit would be too hot for the gooks and they would break off contact. The gamble paid off, because shortly the NVA withdrew, leaving seventeen dead in our perimeter.

With the coming of dawn we swept the perimeter and set up a 360. Navy and Marine fighters pounded the surrounding areas while the med-evac birds came in. Although I was wounded, my luck held. I was carried aboard the last bird to make it before 82 mortars plastered the LZ. Echo Co. lost thirteen KIA and fifty-eight WIA for a lousy fucking hill and I doubt if anybody even knew the hill number.

Twenty years have passed since that nightmare and I have some various thoughts about the players involved . . .

To the politicians, who ran the country at the time of the Vietnam War: you owe every Vietnam veteran an apology. Your asinine policies put us there and then you tied our hands behind our backs.

To the news media: you reported only one side of the war. Sure, My Lai happened. Did you bother to report what the Viet Cong did? How about their butchering of villagers? Did you ever report on the hospitals that were built? Did you ever report on the CAP teams who helped the farmers harvest their crops? You bastards did more damage to us than the VC or NVA.

To the draft dodgers: you have to live with what you did. Look at yourself in the mirror. Do you like what you see?

To my brothers and sisters who served: I have nothing but love and respect for all of you.

To the American people: the Vietnam War is not over. There are over 2000 still missing.

It's not over.

There are vets who suffer from PTSD.

It's not over. Thousands suffer from the effects of Agent Orange.

It's not over. The homeless veterans . . . get them homes. . . The sick . . . get them medical attention.

The peace accords were signed in 1973.

Why, in 1990, is the war still going on?

Ted Banta, Jr.

I grew up in upstate New York and attended Fordham University. I went into the insurance business while attending law school at Fordham. I married in my last year of undergraduate school and divorced two years later.

Due to my having received an R.A. Commission through ROTC, I was assigned to the Infantry in 1964. In 1965, after serving at Fort Devens, I was part of the first contingency of the First Infantry Division to go to Vietnam.

We were stationed forty-five miles outside of Saigon (NW) near the Cambodian border. We patrolled the area regularly, in addition to other operations, including four campaigns.

I was a member of Co. C, 1st Battalion, 1st Inf. Div. We were considered to be a good unit. We were selected for special missions on occasions. Once, we had to bury a man alive—not to be discovered.

We sent out a recon patrol on a routine road clearance operation to bring in supplies from Saigon. They were holed up in what they considered to be an abandoned bunker. In the morning they were completely overrun and only one survived. Two others were wounded and lived, I believe. We went to their assistance, only, to our surprise, we were in a camouflaged base camp of some magnitude—very elite and well trained.

One-hundred-three of us went in. When it was over the next day, thirty-three of our company came out. Company B was sent to our assistance. Later, two other units were sent in by division headquarters. Our battalion commander was killed and all officers were wounded. We all stayed. We killed 171 by body count, and wounded approximately 400, according to estimates. We were up against the Phuoc Hoi Battalion, which was actually a "Regiment" (as organized during the "French period") consisting of some 700 well-trained men. They had to have a minimum of fifteen years experience prior to entering the unit. I took fifteen prisoners, fifteen feet from my position. The next morning, we discovered that one of them was their regimental commander.

Upon return, I was greeted and not subjected to the injustice (public) that the others who followed in later years were. I became a captain at the age of twenty-four. I trained troops (basic) at Fort Dix and although I attempted to resign, I was frozen for an additional year of duty. (Total: four years, fifteen days and eight hours.)

I married and remained the same for eighteen years. I have one child, and have been divorced for over three years. I am suffering from

Post Traumatic Stress Disorder and I am receiving treatment upon request.

Borrowing two thousand dollars from my mother, I accumulated an estate of almost three million dollars. However, due to my divorce, the laws in New Jersey, and the notability of the courts concerning marital issues, I have lost almost everything I built and worked for—except my one great son.

Steven J. Hunt

I was a typical eighteen year old, still in high school, looking so very much forward to graduation, so I could begin my life. I had read and heard about a war that was going on in a place called Vietnam, a country I had never heard of, let alone thought I would be defending someday. Knowing it all at the age of eighteen, my best friend and I joined the Iowa National Guard. What an ideal way, we thought, to serve our country and avoid the draft, which seemed to be sending everyone at that time to that place called Vietnam.

I was made a cook's helper and for the next nine months I chopped salads, thinking how smart I had been to enlist. During one of my monthly choppings, I began to have second thoughts about what I was doing. I was quite aware that some of my close friends had already been killed in Vietnam and I felt that I was not fulfilling my duty as an American by chopping salads on weekends.

My older brother Richard had enlisted in the Marine Corps a year earlier and suddenly I felt guilt and fearful about what I was doing. "What if my only brother should be sent to Vietnam? What if my only brother should be killed?" How in the hell could I face myself knowing that I was chopping salads for my country?

I must explain a fact of the times, in 1965. At that time there was no running away to Canada. There were no public displays of draft card burning. Everyone knew that they had an obligation to their country. So, with my guilt and fear, I enlisted in the United States Marine Corps, something I have never ever regretted and been more proud of to this day.

August 1967: As the jumbo jet left the runway at El Toro Marine Base in Southern California, I thought back to all that I had been through the last seven months of my life. I had graduated from Marine Corps boot camp, graduated Advanced Infantry Training, volunteered and graduated from Marine Corps Sniper School, and now I was on my way to join my fellow Marines in Vietnam, a country I still knew very little about.

Hours later we landed in Da Nang, South Vietnam. I can still recall stepping down from the jet, wondering where and when I would be shot at for the first time. I wondered how I would react, how I would feel, or how I could even stand being a target. I watched everyone very closely and trusted no one who was not dressed in Marine fatigues.

I received my orders to report to the Third Marine Division Sniper Platoon, stationed at a place called Camp Carroll, just a few short miles from the DMZ. Three days later, I was preparing to go on my first night patrol. I was shown how to paint my face and become almost invisible.

I was issued an M-16 fitted with infra-red night vision and then led to our most outer lines of defense. It was raining extremely hard this night as we entered our barbed wire defense, booby trapped with flares and claymore mines. Halfway through the wire, one of the men accidentally tripped a flare. As it lit the entire area, we all made a dive for the wet ground. As I lay in wet mud, I could hear the Marine next to me praying that the VC were not watching, for we were all perfect targets in the light of the flare. Luckily, no one had seen the flare and the patrol continued. My first patrol ended eight hours later with no signs of the enemy, only tired, hungry, wet Marines ready for sleep.

During the next weeks ahead, I learned very quickly how to awaken in the night and jump for my foxhole, as we were continually shelled with rockets fired from the nearby mountains that surrounded Camp Carroll. I was given orders to participate in a search and destroy mission in the nearby countryside outside of Camp Carroll. I had lost a little of my fear by this time, since I had been on almost daily patrols and operations like this one I was about to go on. I cleaned my Remington "700" sniper rifle, wrote a short letter to home and left.

Days later, after walking through rice fields, wading through leech-infested rivers and streams, and running out of rations, I realized that it was my nineteenth birthday. As we stopped for a rest break along the trail, I was presented a can of peaches one of the guys had received from home. Minutes later we were again walking down the trail in search of the VC.

I was positioned as third man in the patrol behind the point man. As we walked, I suddenly heard a terrific explosion from behind me. I turned and saw a young Marine on the ground, screaming in pain. As I walked nearer, I could see that his entire right leg was missing as dark red blood squirted from an ugly stump. Blood seemed to be everywhere. Then the reality of the situation hit me like a ton of bricks. I had stepped directly over the landmine that had been set on the trail by the VC. The screaming young Marine had not been so lucky.

We returned to Camp Carroll days later only to find out the worst of news. One of my closest friends in the platoon, Pfc. Daniel Diaz, had been reported missing. He had been on his way by chopper to Da Nang, where he was to catch a plane for Hawaii and R&R. He was going there to meet his fiancee and parents. He had planned to marry her there and we were all so happy for him. The chopper he rode had been shot down. It had crashed in VC territory and any chance of survival was "minimum." Diaz was the first of many friends I would lose in this hellhole.

I cried myself to sleet that night.

November 1967: Weeks passed very quickly as I participated in, again, almost daily patrols and ambushes. Each patrol yielded something new and different from the previous one. Almost every patrol received some type of small-arms fire that was directed at us, but the VC were always gone before we could react and fire back.

Seeing wounded and dead Marines became my daily way of life and I continued to wonder where and when it would be my turn to take one. I grew so used to the wounded and dead that I grew into a nineteen-year-old hardened combat Marine. I felt myself knowing how the young Marines of WWII must have felt and I became proud of myself and my fellow Marines for joining their ranks in history.

The patrols were never ending as the weeks passed by. I, along with all the men, kept a daily count of our remaining days in the place. I received new orders to report to Third Marine Recon Platoon for another search and destroy mission. A day later, I was once again sitting in the middle of the jungle waiting for something to happen. The first night out, we set up camp directly across from what we called a free fire zone. Free fire zones are areas where there are to be no combat troops, no civilians (who are warned in advance of these areas), in other words, anything or anybody seen in these areas would be considered enemy.

I was preparing my foxhole for guard duty that night when I heard the familiar call of "Sniper Up." I had heard this call many times in the past few months and I knew exactly what it meant to me. I grabbed my "700" and reported to the sergeant of the platoon. He told me to stay low and look out into the area of the free fire zone. As I looked, I saw that approximately 600 yards to my front was an old white-haired man dressed in a black robe. He was for sure Vietnamese and I guessed his age to be about seventy. He was moving along at a very fast pace with a young boy, who I guessed to be about fourteen, walking behind him. The sergeant informed me that the civilians in the area had been warned of the zone and these two should be considered VC. He gave me my final instructions—"Eliminate them."

The old man and the boy did not look like any of the VC I had seen in the past, and for this reason I had a hard time convincing myself that they actually were the enemy. The sergeant reminded me again that they were in an off-limits area, and for this reason should be considered VC. I took aim at the old man, remembering my sniper training to allow for windage and distance. I put my cross hairs on his chest and with shaking hands, squeezed off one shot. I recovered quickly from the recoil and watched in my scope as the old man fell.

As he lay there, not moving, the young boy just stood there, and then, finally realizing what had happened, began to run towards a treeline that he thought could afford him cover. I took aim again at the running boy, and as he reached the treeline, I fired another shot. I watched as he grabbed his right leg and fell to the ground. Immediately, he began crawling for the trees. I aimed again and fired. As I watched for the second time, he jerked almost straight into the air, fell back down and moved no more. I had done my job.

Two men from the platoon were sent out to check the bodies as I waited and caught my breath. A few minutes later they returned with papers they had taken from the dead boy. These papers identified him as Viet Cong. I felt more at ease with myself knowing that this was the enemy I had been searching for. Later that night, as I lay in my foxhole, the sergeant came over and told me that because of the two shots I had fired, we possibly would be attacked that night by other VC in the area who had heard and pin-pointed our position.

For this patrol, I had been issued one of the new Starlight night vision scopes. These new scopes were being tested for use in Vietnam and when it was issued to me I was told that if there would ever be the slightest chance that we would be attacked and overrun by the enemy, I was to destroy it so it would not fall into their hands. After hearing the news from the sergeant of the platoon, I fired three rounds from my 45 into the scope, destroying it and the $15,000 it cost the government. That night, we did receive small-arms fire and several rocket rounds, but no attack ever came. Two days later, we returned to Camp Carroll, where I got the word to move out to a place called the Rockpile, an enormous mountain about five miles closer to the DMZ. I packed my gear and caught a transport truck that was headed for my new home. I was to remain there for the next two months, going out on daily patrols and night ambushes. My new home was to be nothing different that any other place I had been, constantly receiving small-arms fire and almost daily rocket attacks, every day seeing more and more dead and wounded.

I became even harder. I hated *this place* with a passion. I began to hate the people with a passion. I began to hate everything and everybody that was remotely connected to *this damn place*. I knew that I was in need of a break because of the horror of which I was a part. I was beginning to have nightmares. Nightmares of dead and wounded Marines. Marines screaming in pain and agony. I began to picture myself as one of the Marines and sleep was hard to achieve. I requested that I be given R&R.

I returned to the Rockpile after spending three days leave in Taipei, Taiwan. I had been no different than other Marines who had seen enough death and hurt. I spent over $500 on wine, women, and song. I did get a chance to call my parents back in The World, my world, Davenport, Iowa. I spoke with them for about twenty minutes, informing them that I was all right and that I missed them very much. They told me how proud they were of me and that they were at home waiting for me to return. I apologized for the collect call and with tears in my eyes hung up the phone. God how I missed them. I lay back in my hotel room for what seemed like hours, remembering my growing up years. The final words my father said to me on the phone kept going over and over in my mind, "Keep your damn ass down." I laughed.

My first assignment upon returning to the Rockpile was to go out on another three or four day patrol. Viet Cong had been reported in an area about two miles from the DMZ and we were to go out to confirm and make contact. I was assigned to a combat platoon and hours later we headed out. Once again, as so many times in the past, the enemy was not to be seen or heard. We set up an ambush along a trail that the VC were reported to be using. My partner and I were told to set ourselves up out in front of the ambush so we could watch a small valley from which the trail led. Taking turns with my partner to watch the valley for any movements, the hours passed by quickly. Thinking nothing would happen, we began to relax a little and eventually grew lax on our watch of the valley. As we sat in the quiet of the jungle, I began to hear faint voices coming from along the trail off to our left. I assumed that the voices were that of the patrol who were coming forward to tell us to return. I looked over to my left and saw a young Vietnamese man stick his head above the bushes that lined the trail. He was wearing a white shirt with the collar completely buttoned up. I thought that he was a civilian who had taken the trail by mistake, so I raised my hand to wave him off the trail. As he saw me, he screamed something in Vietnamese and all hell broke loose. Automatic rifle fire came at us from everywhere. I knew the sound of the rifles that were firing. Once you hear the sound of an automatic AK-47, you never forget it. Bullets began to hit everywhere. Lines of bullets marched their way toward me and my partner, spitting up dirt in our eyes. But for some strange reason, they stopped about ten yards short of us. We dove for cover behind some bushes as the bullets continued to hit all around us. Since my "700" was a single shot bolt action, I knew it was no match for an AK-47. I reached for the two grenades I always wore on my flack jacket. I pulled the pins and rose only high enough to toss them with all my might in the direction of the white-shirted man. It seemed like hours waiting for the two grenades to explode, but when they finally did, I grabbed my partner's arm and we ran at top speed back to the platoon.

Two men were sent out later to check the area, but reported back minutes later with no body count. Again the VC had eluded us. Later, as we were being questioned about what had happened, I noticed that my right sleeve, just above the elbow, had a hole in it, from front . . . to back. I felt no pain and then realized that one of many bullets had passed directly through my shirt sleeve without hitting me. I closed my eyes for a moment and thought of my family and my father's final words. I had been lucky.

December 1967: December was filled with many more patrols, ambushes and numerous operations. Marines were killed. VC were killed and I became a walking robot, constantly on alert for trouble or the slightest sound that may have meant the VC were near. Every patrol became the same as before. My platoon back at Camp Carroll was filled with replacements because of all the casualties we had suffered in the past months. I was only nineteen at this time and as I saw the new men arrive, I thought to myself how young they all seemed. I remembered my first days and wondered if anyone had thought the same about me. I'm sure they did.

My only real escape for *this hole* was the letters I received from home. Thank God for those letters. I would receive a letter from home and purposely not read any part of it for hours, savoring the envelope with my parents' writing on it. I had never been away from home at Christmas before and I wasn't sure that I would be able to make it through the holidays, but I did as we all did. It was one of the loneliest times we all had ever experienced.

The letters from home were filled with stories of what was happening back in The World. My parents sent me clippings of riots, dissent, and hatred for the war. Young men were refusing to abide with the draft. Anti-war rallies were in full swing and none of us could believe the news we were hearing from the home front. Here we were in Vietnam, constantly being shot at, constantly being shelled, and there were the people back home, more interested in the riots and dissent than us so far away. It all didn't make any sense and I was a very confused Marine on Christmas Eve. No presents were exchanged, but we did drink a little warm beer that night and sang carols together. It was a very lonely time for us all.

January and February were filled with more of the same. Dying Marines, wounded Marines, blood, death. How I hated *this place* ever more. Everyday I woke, and wondered who would get it next. My father's words still rang in my ear everyday, "Keep your damn ass down."

March 1968: Our platoon was finally moved from the Rockpile area to our new home called Quang Tri. It was located on the coast of Vietnam and was filled with many waterways, small rivers, and a lot of sand, as I recall. North Vietnamese regulars had been spotted in a small village along this coast, so I was given new orders to move out with a grunt company to check out these reports and try to make contact. We were driven by transport truck to an area approximately two miles from this village and let off to make camp for the night. Not a soul slept, knowing that the shit was going to hit in the morning.

Everybody tried to write letters home and get one final wink of sleep before the word came down to move out towards the village. It was still dark when we moved out in single column towards the unknown. We all knew that the NVA were in there and as the village drew closer, we all were on our utmost alert for the first signs of trouble.

I can still remember my first glimpse of the village as I got closer, and closer. It consisted of five or six small bamboo huts alongside three small stone buildings. It was situated in the middle of a sand tract, so surrounding it was no problem. Having accomplished this, we all lay very still and waited for orders to move out. That's when all hell broke loose. Rockets seemed to hit everywhere. We had been spotted by the NVA and they were trying to start their own offensive against us before we could attack them.

I took cover next to a stone wall and literally buried my head in the sand. As each round fell, I could feel the percussion of the rockets hitting and exploding. I knew that other Marines were being hit by these rockets because I could hear screams coming from all around me. I had not been hit yet, but I found myself screaming also. I wanted these rounds to stop, but they seemed to increase as we all lay in the sand. From out of nowhere, two Navy jets from a nearby base flew over our heads. All of us began screaming at them as if they could hear. As they came back for a second pass over the village, they both dropped napalm cannisters directly on the village. The heat from the explosion could be felt by all of us, but we didn't seem to care because the rockets seemed to cease for all time. Almost immediately after the jets left we could hear big guns going off in the far distance. A Navy ship somewhere out in the harbor was firing its big guns in support of us. The whole village was being hit by these guns. I can remember being amazed at the accuracy of the guns, which were firing directly over our heads and hitting the village. I looked at the village as the rounds came and came. I could see the NVA regulars running everywhere. Some of them were on fire and burning from the napalm. But they continued to run until they dropped.

Next to the wall where I lay was a small worship temple that the villagers had erected. I climbed up to the roof of the temple to get a better view of the village and the action. As I looked, I could see the NVA still running for cover, so I took aim and started firing. The first one fell, then the second, and, as I fired a third round, I watched my third kill also fall. The third NVA had been hit in the right shoulder by my round and since I was only about 200 yards away from him I could see his face. His face is something I will never forget. I could tell that he was in pain from my bullet, but as I watched he began stripping off his backpack and all of his clothing. I couldn't figure out exactly what he was trying to do so I just sat there and continued to watch. When he finished stripping, he slowly started to crawl towards what looked like an underground bunker. I felt like I was playing a cat and mouse game with him, me being the cat. He carefully selected his path towards the bunker, crawling very low and deliberate. Had I not been on top of the temple he would have not been seen by any of us. I waited until he was about ten yards from the bunker then placed another round into his chest. He lay still finally.

Word came that we were to move out and overtake the village, so I jumped down from the roof and took—what I can remember—two steps. That's when I got mine. It seemed to hit with the force of a locomotive. I could hear a loud ringing and felt a terrific pain in my back. The force of the impact threw me forward into the sand. The ringing seemed to increase and I felt numb all over. My partner had seen what had happened and crawled to my side. I tried to crawl towards some cover, but for some reason my left leg would not respond to my wishes. I reached for my partner's hand, but my left arm would not respond also. I looked down, fearing that my leg was missing, but it was still there, not responding to anything. My partner grabbed me by the collar and with both hands drug me to cover behind the wall. I was screaming from the pain and realized that it had been my turn to be an unlucky Marine. The pain was almost unbearable. I was aware that I had been wounded, but could not fully understand to what extent or where it had happened. My partner began screaming for a corpsman who was very busy this day with all the wounded. Finally he came to me and checked my back. He and my partner were talking as I lay there and listened as closely as I could. I had been shot directly in the center of the back just above my belt line. I continued trying to move my arm and leg, but no luck. The corpsman put a quick dressing on my back and moved out to help other wounded who lay all around me.

My partner then held me in his arms and cradled me as I cried out in pain. About ten minutes later, two Marines came to me and lifted me onto a poncho. I was half carried and half drug to the rear area, away from all the fighting, where I was laid next to a wounded Marine on my left and a dead Marine on my right. I remember looking at the wounded Marine, who had taken a round in his leg, but every time I looked over at the dead Marine, I saw myself. I will never ever forget the blood, the screams and all the covered bodies of my fellow Marines who had fought so bravely. Twenty to thirty minutes passed as I lay there in pain, when I was loaded aboard a chopper along with five or six other wounded men. The screaming from the wounded filled the air and drowned out the noise of the chopper. After a short ride we arrived at a field hospital that looked a lot like the TV show "MASH." I was taken from the chopper and placed on a table in a tent that was filled with other wounded. Two doctors came over to me and began cutting off all of my clothing. I was quickly examined and told to lay very still. I had taken a bullet in the spine and for this reason my arm and leg would not respond. As I lay there waiting, my thoughts were filled with my family. How would they take this . . . if I died? I started crying, thinking about them. Thirty minutes passed then I was again loaded onto a chopper and flown to the Navy hospital ship USS *Sanctuary*. I was rushed below to an operating room, where someone gave me a shot in my left arm. Peace at last.

I awoke four days later, as I felt people touching and poking my body. Doctors were all around me, asking me to try to move my arm and leg. I tried. I would move my arm slightly now but the leg was gone and would not respond. The pain was still there as I looked around to see my new surroundings. I was on the bottom bunk of a ward filled with wounded. Tubes filled my nose and arms. I could hear men crying faintly in the distance. I remember crying out myself from the pain as a young corpsman came to my side and told me to be quiet. He said that I was supposed to be a rough tough Marine and wasn't supposed to feel any pain.

A lot he knew! A fellow Marine in the bunk next to me got out of his bed and into a wheelchair. He wheeled himself, in pain, over to my side and took my hand in his and comforted me. He talked to me for what seemed like hours. I fell asleep gripping his hand to ease the pain. I was awakened later that night by loud voices coming from the bunk next to me. Doctors were frantically working on the Marine who had comforted me earlier. The floor under his bed was a mass of blood as the doctors walked in it. I fell back into a deep sleep. I awoke the next day and looked over for my friend. His bed had been stripped and was empty. He had died that night from massive internal bleeding. I cried myself to sleep remembering his face and what he must have gone through to comfort me.

I spent the next twenty-three days aboard the Sanctuary. I had gone from 149 pounds down to ninety-three pounds. I had not eaten solid food for the entire time and I looked like a rail. From the Sanctuary, I was flown to a hospital in the Philippines, where I spent one night. I was given a steak dinner, which I could not eat, and a telephone call home to my parents, all on the American Red Cross. I can remember speaking to my parents, who were crying as I spoke to them. I told them that I was all right and that I would be home soon. I was a little beat up, but was fine and looking forward to seeing them again.

Days later I arrived in Illinois—Great Lakes Naval Hospital—where I was examined and told what had happened to me. I had received a gunshot wound to my lower back area that severed a nerve in my spine. My left leg would be paralyzed forever. I would require the use of a long leg brace to walk as well as a cane for balance. I had also received three shrapnel wounds to my chest area, but they had done no real damage and were removed. The doctors had removed my spleen, appendix, and about half of my stomach and intestines.

During the next thirteen months I spent at Great Lakes, my parents visited me almost every week. They had to drive three hours every weekend to see me and then another three hours to return home. They watched every week as I slowly recovered. The ward that I was on was filled with brave and determined men who refused to feel sorry for themselves and their conditions. Some were missing arms, legs and some had been burned so badly that they could not be recognized. They were all so proud of what they had done and there was no pity for anyone, just pride. The American people who watched the war from TV could not have seen this part. I think they should have. Maybe they would have felt a little different about the whole thing if they could have seen these young men who had fought so bravely struggle to recover the best they could, only to return to a society that gave them nothing but trouble for what they had done.

I can remember myself, returning home and seeing some of my old friends. It seemed that the war had lasted so long that everyone had grown incoherent to it and to the returning veteran. Instead of returning to waving flags and parades, we returned to a somewhat uncaring American people. Some of us understood the ridicule and the dirty looks. Some of us understood the almost constant arguments we got involved in. Some of us became strongly fueled by an uncaring American people. Some were not so lucky. They had seen war. They had seen death. They had seen the horrors that only some can imagine. Somewhere and somehow these men refused to take it anymore. For these men, I feel sorry. The Vietnam veteran is human, not a machine. The Vietnam veteran had feelings, deep feelings about being shunned by his countrymen.

There's a new wall that was erected in Washington D.C. that cries out to the American people. This wall tells stories of pain and death. The Wall is filled with the names of friends, brothers, sisters, fathers, mothers, and young brave men who gave their lives to the American people. Etched on that wall are the names of my friends, over 58,000 of them. My friends on that wall, I salute you. I salute you over and over for, without you and the memory of what you did and sacrificed ... will never be forgotten by me as long as I live. You will not be forgotten by your family, friends, and fellow comrades who fought alongside of you. To my fellow soldiers on the Wall, "I love you."

December 1989: Twenty-one years later and it seems like it never happened, but I know it did. I continue to wear a brace on my leg, which still, after all these years, refuses to work. Daily pain is a reminder I live with of a war that no one cared for. A day doesn't go by without a small thought from my mind of Vietnam. I am constantly reminded of it by my surroundings living here in Southern California. Sometimes I feel that I am once again back in Vietnam, with all the Vietnamese people I constantly have to deal with.

I became a Design Engineer a few years back, doing design work for the aerospace industry. I have two children, Steve Jr., who is now fifteen years old, and my daughter, Sara, who is twelve. They both listen to my stories about Vietnam and ask questions concerning it and the horrors we saw. Thank God they never had to endure the memories that live with me. I am remarried for the third time and my wife is a constant light for me that always shines when I need it. The memories are still there and the horror will always be there, but my family helps to ease the pains of war. I'm just sorry that some of the men could not have returned and had the chances that I have had in life.

Tom Bartos

I grew up in Houston, Texas and was attending Jesse H. Jones High School in the early '60s. Back then, Vietnam was just a name, a word we heard about in History class or on the evening news. I think the event I remember most is the American troops being flown into Thailand.

We had no idea what we were getting into.

Back in those days a kid could do just about anything and get away with it. We weren't as populated and there were more open spaces. I was majoring in Agriculture, so much of my time was spent hanging out with the guys around livestock and rodeos. "Drugs" was a term unheard of in those days and the only "high" was sneaking behind the garage for a cigarette or "conning" a friend into buying us a six-pack. Then we'd go out hunting at night in the various cow pastures that surrounded Houston at that time, and get chased by game wardens. Looking back, it was fun, but you couldn't do that now.

I graduated from high school in June 1965 and didn't know what I was going to do. I got a job as a surveyor with the highway department and just sat there for ten months. Then one day a co-worker informed me that he had joined the Marine Corps and they had a "buddy system." By this time I had already taken my draft physical and, after seeing what kind of jerks I might be drafted with, I had second thoughts. I figured I had already gone through ten months of my free life quite fast and if I signed up, I'd be out in no time.

By now Vietnam was in the news every minute of every day and from the broadcasts, we were kicking ass. I was a skinny kid at the time and just looking at those Marine recruiting ads gave me a new kind of hope. I could look like *that*! Besides, it was only for two years and I probably wouldn't see any action. But, I'd seen two many John Wayne movies—charging up the hill, music playing . . . a hero's welcome . . . that was for me!

So, in May of 1966, I found myself in boot camp: miserable . . . hot . . . DIs screaming down my throat.

I was counting the days.

I was in for two years, guaranteed infantry, guaranteed Vietnam. Within months, I was overseas.

I reached Okinawa in October 1966 and was attached to Delta Co., 1st Bn., 9th Marines. The unit was re-grouping after being almost wiped out in Nam. That's where they got the name, "Dying Delta." After a brief training mission in the Philippines which lasted until after Christmas, we boarded the USS Iwo Jima and headed for the war.

Our "jump off" date was for January 1, but had to be postponed two days while the ship rode out a typhoon. On January 3, the first choppers took off from the carrier. It was overcast and rainy. After being let out in waste-high mud, we waddled toward higher ground. This was Operation Deckhouse V, a search and destroy mission, but all we did was burn hooches.

After about two weeks, we boarded the ships once again and headed for Okinawa. After picking up more men and supplies, it was back to Nam, this time for good.

You could smell the heat as it rose over the bleached hills with the morning sun—pungent, stifling, each breath filled with the decaying smell of . . . death.

I was attached to Delta Co. of 1/9 ever since leaving Okinawa on October 31, 1966. The unit was historic as a combat amphibious force, but Vietnam was no place for a beachhead assault, although we did manage to pull one off down in the Mekong Delta. Down there, we didn't see much action except for the insect bites and the Zippo lighters that didn't work when it came time to burn a village. Then there were the green, gung-ho officers, fresh out of school, storming every stream and swamp, only to be caught in the open as the tidewaters rose.

But now, we were in-country, and I would soon learn why we were known as "Dying Delta," having the highest mortality rate in the whole 3rd Marine Division. On March 21, 1967, the battalion moved from the Dong Ha area to Cam Lo to engage in a sweep north to Con Thien. This was known as "Operation Prairie III," having passed through I and II weeks before. It was supposed to be a routine textbook sweep, one that would flush out the enemy and push him out in the open. But Charlie was too smart for that one. Conventional warfare wasn't his game. We were on his turf now. It was third down and he had the ball.

I was attached to 1st Squad, 2nd Platoon, and we had point. With the steep hills, elephant grass, and vines, it was slow maneuvering over the terrain. We chose to stay low, crossing the narrow ravines where we could hide our movements.

Late that afternoon, as we were nearing a small valley, I noticed some people moving on the crest of a distant hill. They seemed to be moving in single file parallel to us. I sent word back to the CO, Captain Keys. As he raised his binoculars for a closer look, one of the figures turned and waved to us.

"They're ARVNs. I can see their uniforms," he replied.

A horse by a different color is still the same old horse, so to speak, and these were not ARVNs but a carefully disguised Charlie. As we started to move once again, I looked up at the ridge. The figures were gone.

We proceeded to pass through the small valley. It was open terrain covered with three-foot-high grass and that was all. Suddenly, it got deathly quiet. You could hear a heartbeat. The first shot whistled over my head, the noise circling inside my helmet as I hit the ground. There was nothing between us and the ridge but grass and it was no cover. We returned fire but saw nothing except the advancing tracer rounds that cut through the vegetation like paper. I watched a round come sailing near my feet, hitting the dirt and fizzling out.

Our field observer caught a glimpse of a muzzle flash in a wooded area overlooking the ridge. We were too close to the enemy to try an air strike at this time so 1st Platoon was called up to circle the position and push them out . . . Another tactical mistake. As 1st Platoon moved into position, Charlie moved out of his. In fact, he moved around us and we were caught in a cross-fire. Then, he moved out and left 1st and 2nd platoons, unknowingly, shooting at each other.

I was near the machine gunner and he was low on ammo. When I was told to fall back and retrieve a couple of belts, I hesitated, then proceeded to inch my way to the source. No sooner had I moved from that spot than an engineer moved up to my position and was caught in the gut with a round, his lifeless body falling on me. As he gripped my collar and screamed, I put my hand over the wound to stop the bleeding. It went all the way inside. I cried for a corpsman and tried to do what I could, which was nothing. He continued to scream in pain until he bled to death a few minutes later. By then, the shooting had stopped, 1st Platoon realizing that all those curses were coming from other Marines.

Med-evacs came in to pick up the three dead and six wounded and we proceeded to our night positions. In the clump of trees from which we were ambushed, we found the discarded ARVN uniforms. And now, we were faced with another problem . . . we didn't have any food and only limited water. We tried to dig in on the side of a hill for our night positions but the ground was so hard that my entrenching tool couldn't penetrate. It took me all night to dig down three feet. It was by now too late to have a chopper bring in any provisions like food or water and give away our position, so we bedded down the best we could and tried not to think about it.

At 4 a.m. the next morning we were awakened by a barrage of incoming mortar rounds. But before we could call in our position to "Arty," they stopped.

That morning we moved out and found ourselves trying to outrun the constant mortar rounds that seemed to be following us like a magnet. This puzzled our officers since we were now in a valley and clearly had a good view of any movement. But, we couldn't see anything and if the NVA were firing blindly, they were doing a pretty accurate job. We couldn't even bring in supplies. Each time a chopper came near us, he was either shot out of the sky or driven away.

Around 6 that evening the choppers decided to make another try, hoping to drop us the much needed C-rations. We cleared a small LZ on top of a hill and waited. As the sun started to set against a red sky, we could see those birds angled in our direction. My mouth was watering. I could almost taste that ham and lima beans.

There was a mad scramble to help with the unloading as the first chopper started its descent. Just then, Charlie opened fire, destroying any hopes of our first meal in two days. Quickly, the choppers retreated and left us to ourselves. It was a sad moment for all of us.

Day three. Our stomachs were knotted from the hunger and morale was at an all-time low. We were in sad shape. In my knapsack was one package of Kool-Aid, which I lived on for three days. I emptied it in a boiling cup of water as a sort of tea. It wasn't much, but back then it sure tasted good. That was the last of the water for me.

Staff Sergeant Moon, our platoon sergeant, came over to look at us. He was as weak and gloomy as we were, but we liked him. He was one of the few guys from the "old corps" that had a heart. As he stared out over the horizon, there was a sudden spark in his eye.

"For the last three days now, I've been wondering how in the hell those gooks have been able to dust us," he says. "Until now."

We followed his finger as he pointed to a high ridge overlooking the valley. Then, he turned and pointed to the other side. On each point, there was a tall, thin bamboo reed sticking out of the ground with a clump of grass tied at the top.

"That's how he does it. He's got his lines of fire staked out. That's why we can't see him. He's miles away," he conceded.

Quickly, a squad was sent up to pull down the reeds. We thought that by now we were in the clear, but Charlie had us right where he wanted us. Leaving the valley, we entered a vast white sandy area. It wasn't until we were halfway through and seven casualties later that we realized we were in the middle of a minefield.

To get out we merely stepped in the footprints of the fellow in front, but sometimes just the right weight would set one off. I remember getting hit in the face with a foot that had no leg attached to it after a man stepped in those same footprints in front of me. The thought that I might be next stayed with me for the rest of the war.

We reached some high ground and thought that we were in the clear. In the distance, I saw two figures running across the sand—a good 500 meters. Sergeant Nicholus shouted at me to get him. It was hard to see that far with the heat waves rising over the sand. I sent off a round and watched it land well in front of him. I then proceeded to try a little

"Kentucky windage" and cracked two more rounds, the second one hitting and sending him to the ground. I waited for him to get up, but he never did. I didn't expect him to, since I could clearly see his head explode when the round hit.

Digging into the sand, we were able to find a few unripened potatoes. When you tried to eat one, the bitter taste made your stomach swell, but it was all we had. It tasted really bad.

We moved out just as the rains came, washing out the roads and making each movement a hazard. The terrain was changing as well, going from sand to dense vegetation and banana plantations. Then we heard the sounds of gunfire. Everyone started to hustle up the road, reaching a clump of trees and five U.S. Army tanks that had been pinned down by sniper fire. We proceeded to supply security for the tanks as they tried desperately to stay on the muddy trails, some too narrow for a car to penetrate. Along the way, we encountered numerous attacks in an effort to knock out those tanks. Then we got word that we were in a nest of a whole division of NVA and they wanted those tanks. Our casualties were growing and because of the sometimes heavy rain, the choppers wouldn't land. So, we piled our dead and wounded onto the tanks, at times over-heating the machines as they covered the air intakes. Still, the NVA inched closer and we lost more men, mostly from shock because of no adequate treatment.

Finally, we reached a point where we were surrounded. There was no way out. We were now down to three tanks, the other two being destroyed by rockets. Choosing a spot, we got those wagons in a circle, each pointing it's muzzle outward, and we laid down around them, each of us praying the best we could. Though at times the rain was heavy, it wasn't nearly as heavy as our losses. From the perimeter around the tanks, we could see the NVA advancing—firing and shooting. Tracer rounds bounced off the metal of our fortress. I knew then that my number was about to be cancelled at any moment. I always considered myself to be somewhat religious, but I found that I was praying to people I didn't even know . . . and we were running out of ammo, that precious link between now and the hereafter.

Smoke began to pour out of the tank engines as round after round pierced the metal. I listened painfully to the cries of our wounded, wishing I could either help or put them out of their misery. Finally, Captain Keys ordered an artillery drop—right on top of us. It was the only thing left to do.

Those few moments seemed like hours as we waited. Then, in the distance we could hear the vague thunder reminiscent of "arty." We buried our heads in the mud as the rounds hit all around us, smashing treetops, echoing throughout the countryside. This time there were no "cheers," no jubilant gestures, only relief that, for now, it was over.

We counted 240 NVA dead. As for us, we had lost 116 dead or seriously wounded. It was decided that we would try to make it to Dong Ha, where we could regroup and care for the men that were left. There, we were recalled for numerous patrols and rescue operations that kept our numbers dwindling.

Before we could catch our breath, we were called on for another operation. It was the middle of the monsoon season and the rains had just let up enough so we could see the roads as the convoy took us to "points unknown." It seems like I stayed soaked the whole time I was in-country. After the trucks dropped us off, we started a wide sweep through the muddy rice paddies—the muck almost sucking your boots off—until we reached a position where we would stay the night. I was bushed. But wouldn't you know it? I pulled an LP, a somewhat obscure procedure known as a "listening post." I took two men and one radio and was placed about 300 to 400 meters away from the camp perimeter in a remote spot for the sole purpose of "listening." It was more like a "turkey shoot," because you couldn't fire your weapon, thereby giving away your position. You just had to listen and relay back to the command post by radio. You were all alone, so to speak. One man with me was a "seasoned veteran" like myself (that's anyone who's still alive after his third month) and the other guy was really "green." We'll call him "Burt." Well, it was Burt's turn to stay awake and somewhere around midnight I felt a tug on my shirt.

"I heard something," he pleads, this time grabbing me by the shirt, shaking.

I asked where and he pointed. We listened, but I didn't hear anything. Although it was dark, I could clearly see the contour of the grenade clutched in his hand.

"Put that thing away. You want to give away our position?" I asked.

A puzzled look clouded his face as he replied, "I can't find the pin."

My only thought was "S—!!!"

In the dark the three of us scrambled to find the pin, at the same time trying to keep poor ol' Burt as calm as possible, since he was still holding the grenade. Finally, I grabbed the radio and summoned up the courage to call in.

"Sergeant Nicholus," (grinning to myself). "Did I wake you?"

I told him the facts and after a few choice words about my heritage and career in the Corps, he instructed us to throw the grenade and "hightail it back."

Well, ol' Burt would have never made it in the majors because he took a big swing and let that sucker fly—right against a tree, bouncing back toward us. All I could think of was, "Run!" The explosion woke up about fifty sleepy Marines, who quickly took aim and fired at anything that moved, which was right at us! We crawled on our bellies and tried to keep our heads down. The closer we got the worse it got. My pal, Sergeant Nicholus, apparently didn't tell the boys that we were coming home. Moments later, they stopped shooting, finally coming to realize that no VC could curse like that. That sort of finished my tour on the LPs.

I stayed with Delta Co. until that summer, when the company was down to about thirty men. Again as a regroup, I was transferred to "M" Co., 3rd Bn., 26th Marines. I was with this unit for about two months, all the while stationed at Phu Bai, running patrols, guarding convoys. It was here that I got the first of three Purple Hearts.

On the night in question, I was on guard duty, stationed at a supply bunker. The night was unusually quiet and I was tired from being on patrol that day. Standing guard had become sort of a joke, since we were right in the middle of a Marine air base and nothing ever happened there. It was just my luck that it would be this night. So, there I was in my "Colonel Ho" shoes, no flak jacket, with only my M-16. Besides that, my relief was late—about twenty minutes late.

In the distance, I could hear some popping noises. Louder and more distinct than rifle shots, and not our tanks, since they were nearby and would have made the ground shake. Suddenly, the area around me went up in smoke. They were hitting my supply dump! The gate, being around at the other end, made it impossible for me to save my skin, so I proceeded to climb over the fence. Just then a rocket landed behind me, propelling me over the obstacle, landing me face-down in the dirt. I felt a burning pain in my back. Staying low, I made my way to the aid station, where they extracted a small piece of metal and I was sent back to my unit. I was the only casualty in my battalion that night.

It was during this time that I applied for and received a transfer into a Combined Action Platoon. It was a fairly new approach to winning the war and the civilians. It consisted of two squads of Marines, together with a squad of PFs (civilian popular forces) which lived permanently in a camp near a village, thereby, hopefully, winning the support of the villagers and making them feel safe. The strategy consisted of patrols during the day and ambushes at night. My unit, P-2, was stationed near Quang Tri. I was quick to find out that it too, had a high mortality rate.

It was as though Charlie had us pin-pointed on a map. You could only run patrols down certain routes, and so he'd wait and see which days we'd alternate, then he'd either hit us, lay booby traps, or avoid that area. We had more luck on ambushes since the dark could conceal us, unless there was a full moon. One night, our ambush was ambushed by some Green Berets who didn't know that we were in the area. Another time, we had to rescue a squad of similar Green Berets when they walked into a nest of NVA and couldn't get their bearings on where in the hell they were.

Every other night at precisely 7 p.m.—you could set a clock by it—we would get mortared. Our camp was a maze of wire, bunkers, and trenches. We had more claymores strung out than we had men, and a lot of our weapons were confiscated enemy hardware that seemed to be much more reliable than our own. For that reason, we failed to turn in such gear as required, and we found ourselves scrambling for hiding places whenever the major decided to make a surprise visit.

One night we were overrun. After a series of incoming mortar rounds, we shot up some flares and found a maze of VC coming up through the wire. When the flares went out, it was pitch black. I waited for one aggressor to crawl up to my bunker before I opened fire—a 20-round clip in the face. Then, we set off the claymores, but that didn't help. We also had trouble with the PFs throwing down their weapons and trying to escape from the camp. Finally, Sergeant Petersen ordered an arty drop. We were sitting in a clump of trees and that caused airbursts which wounded some of our own men. But we also got some of them. We counted 146 confirmed enemy dead, with only six Marines and one PF slightly hurt. Still, I was okay.

It was those particular patrols that started to get out of hand. I received two Purple Hearts there in one week, all on patrol, almost all on the same trail, at the same time of day. That was three strikes. I was out of there.

I went back to Phu Bai to await orders and while there, I found out that the camp had been overrun and the casualties were high. Again, I had lost some dear friends. I was discharged the following May, choosing not to re-enlist. I would have been headed back to Nam and by now, a lot of us had the feeling that we had been betrayed. The "no-fire zones," retaking ground you sweated for and left the day before, the lack of support from the American people, were the reasons, I guess. But, I've never regretted that I was there, and been with a great bunch of guys. "The Few. The Proud. The Marines." I guess we all left a part of ourselves back there. You wonder, whatever happened to the nineteenth and twentieth years of your life. While other people were attending college and raising families, we were fighting a war that nobody wanted to win, and we weren't even old enough to vote.

Since then, I've been divorced twice, and I still have the haunting dreams—the memories. It's a part of my life that I never want to forget, nor can I forget. I still carry the pain like every other GI that went over, and people from the other wars can't figure it out. This war was different. It was enveloped in politics, and greed and the government thought for sure we'd bring them to their knees. But, it was us, the young, recent high school graduates, that got hurt. Then, they just turned us loose to lick our wounds in private, never giving us the support and comfort we deserved. Hopefully, this was the war to end all wars; hopefully, we learned something about ourselves, about how precious freedom is and shouldn't be taken for granted. Hopefully, the brave men that went over to Vietnam will someday heal.

I've tried to find a purpose, through screenwriting and film—the arts. I'm close to getting a screenplay produced and I've had a few acting parts. I feel comfortable with that. I'm called a loner, but I guess most vets are. That's what I prefer. We all suffer some emotional disabilities and I came back with many. But, I don't regret it, not for a minute. I did what I believed in.

To the GIs with inner suffering, I can just say this: Open up and let people know what you went through and what you're feeling ... for you were the best we had. Semper Fi.

Roger G. Paulmeno

High School of the '60s in Bronx, New York was uneventful concerning the Vietnam War, but civil rights was a major event for the time. Those years were not much different for high school students, who were trying to find their identity as part of society. The cause of most rebellion in high school was the civil rights movement. At first it started out slowly, but in 1968, after the assassination of Dr. Martin Luther King, this issue came of age. This interest, more than any other, created some interest in national politics and the happenings of the nation, and Vietnam became an offshoot.

Even though my older brother was stationed outside the country of Vietnam while serving in the U.S. Navy prior to 1968, it was not a major topic of discussion. Only when a friend was drafted into the Army did I take real interest in Vietnam. He was only a year older than me, and it didn't seem possible that our government would put him in a dangerous situation. My interest was aroused even more when he had returned from Vietnam. He painted a picture of pure excitement from there. He didn't seem any the worse for wear. In fact, it seemed more like some fun house at an amusement park. Thinking back about it now, it dawns on me that he never spoke of the death and dying he must have experienced there.

Time passed by, and more and more friends were drafted. Different stories about Vietnam began to emerge that were unlike the first one. My time was coming, for I was well past eighteen, and my number had not been called. I'm not sure if I really thought about the consequence of war, but felt if I were to go, it was only my duty to country. Watching Vietnam on TV did not give you any of the true effects of it. I can't think of any media that really can. In June of 1969, it came—"Greetings" from Uncle Sam. I was caught between duty to country and my fear of the unknown.

I enlisted in the Army in August of 1969. I was initially drafted, then enlisted. I had been attending the Academy of Aeronautics at Queensboro Aviation Maintenance at night and holding a full-time job during the day. I knew that a draftee had no choice of military assignment, so I enlisted to get aircraft maintenance training through the Army. It would save me a lot of money, and as long as I was going to be trained in aviation, the military would be a good life with a lot of security. When this all happened, I was nineteen years old and had been out of high school for one year.

Initially, boot camp was tough. You had all these people screaming in your face for eight weeks. We weren't sure what the Army was all about and it seemed like constant harassment, but about midway through, you realized that they were trying to train you for your own benefit. Vietnam was prevalent in everybody's mind at that time. Once you began to understand the reasons for that training, it became more acceptable.

After basic, I spent three months at Fort Ustis, Virginia, at helicopter maintenance school. I had wanted to work on jet engines, but the commander there told me that my Army contract specified only aircraft maintenance and I had to accept that. Aviation, helicopters, the chance to fly—those were good enough. There were only ten people in my class, and the top four came out as Spec-4s (Specialist Fourth Class). I was really interested in the training, so being one of the top four was easy. Five of us got orders for Vietnam.

I had no conception of what Vietnam was like. I had seen it on TV and read about it, but it was still a place that was so far away. The trip over on the jet was one of the longest and most boring trips that I have ever taken. You were really alone, even though there were a lot of guys on the plane with you. I was going to war and not knowing what to expect. It's like a woman having a baby. Until you go through it, you'll never know the hardship and the joy.

I was doing fine until the plane started coming in for the landing at Bien Hoa. The airfield there was being shelled. That scared me. Here we had traveled twelve thousand miles and I thought that we would be killed before we even got off the plane. When we finally landed, somebody opened the aircraft door. This gust of incredibly hot, foul air rushed in, as if from a huge garbage dump. It was an unbelievably strange smell. The shelling was still going on, so we were hustled off the plane and into a shelter.

We went through initial processing at the airfield, signing forms and whatever, and then they put us on a bus for the orientation center at Bien Hoa. this was one of the safest areas in Vietnam, but the bus was screened in with heavy metal screening. I asked the sergeant in charge about the screens and he said that they were to keep civilians from throwing grenades through the bus window. That got to me. I wondered how we were going to tell the difference between friendlies and non-friendlies.

When we arrived at the orientation center, the first-sergeant told us what to expect in the next week and gave us the rest of the day off duty. I wandered around the camp. There were all these FNGs (Fucking New Guys) around, who had been in Vietnam two days longer than us, filling our heads with all kinds of horror stories and making the war sound worse than it was. I didn't take them seriously. People had been telling me stories all my life, and I tended not to believe anything unless I saw it myself. There was more partying going on than anything that resembled death.

The next morning, the sergeant ran into the barracks and said that we were being mortared. I had come all this way, and this was my first real glimpse of action. I climbed the roof of the barracks and sat there, watching the mortar shells dropping all around. It was like being in a John Wayne movie in person. I knew that I could be killed but had to see it. The shelling lasted about ten minutes. One mortar had hit a latrine and killed the two guys inside. Then the sergeant climbed up and dragged me off the roof, yelling that I was crazy. I had heard about it for so long and just wanted to see the war in person.

The first week, they sent us through jungle fighting school. It was so false. You couldn't even load your weapon. I had no idea what was happening or what was really going on. When you first arrive in a place like that, you're very intimidated and are willing to listen to what anyone has to tell you. My mind was a mass of confusion, trying to decipher all the information and stories coming in.

After the week of orientation and "jungle training," the first-sergeant came running over and told me, "Pack your bags. You're leaving on that chopper out of here." He handed me a set of orders and said to give them to my first-sergeant when I arrived. I had no idea where I was going.

The chopper dropped me off at the airfield in Tay Ninh and I walked over to a unit called Alpha Troop 1/9 Cav. When I handed the orders to the first-sergeant, he asked me what in the hell I was doing there. They didn't have any openings for my specialty. I told him that I was just following orders. There wasn't room for me, so he told me to take the bunks of guys who were on guard duty and they'd try to find a permanent place for me. He took me to a hooch and found out which guys had guard that night. I got only their bunks and lived out of my duffle bag. When the first-sergeant left, the stories started. One guy explained to me that they were a helicopter maintenance ground team. Then they started telling me about the scout platoon across the flight line.

One fellow said to me, "Whatever you do, don't volunteer to go to the scout platoon. It's a suicide squad. The life expectancy there is only three weeks." I told him, "Listen, I'm not into Scouts. My MOS is Aircraft Maintenance. That's what I'm here for. This is a maintenance outfit and that's what I joined the Army for."

For three days, I slept in the bunk of whomever had guard. Then the first-sergeant came to me and said he had found a bunk across the flight line. I looked across the flight line and all I could see were the Scouts. I asked him if I was supposed to sleep over there and work with the maintenance team. He said, "No. You're going to sleep over there and work over there." I said, "Sarge, that's the Scout Platoon. That's search and destroy. I don't want to do that." His answer was, "I'm not asking you, Paulmeno, I 'm telling you. Get your ass over there or I'll put you out in the fucking boonies for six weeks. Then you'll be kissing my ass to come back." I asked him, "Is that how you volunteer around here?" He said, "In this troop, you volunteer that way. Get over there or I'll have you on the next truck going out to the field."

So I volunteered for the Scouts. When I got there, there were twelve gunners and observers and they were totally avoiding me. Me, an FNG, was there because one of them had been killed on a mission two days before. The only one who would talk to me in those first few days was the sergeant in charge, and he was trying to teach me the ropes. Ultimately I would be a door-gunner, but the first few weeks I would be an observer, which was also the co-pilot. I would keep an eye on the left side of the LOH (Light Observation Helicopter), mark the area with smoke, stuff like that.

I took a flight physical and deliberately tried to flunk the depth perception test. The doctor thought he was doing me a big favor by passing me anyway. He told me that We would fix the papers. I went back to the Scouts and consoled myself; I would be flying, which I had always wanted to do. After six months with the platoon, I could choose reassignment to anywhere else in the country. What hadn't sunk in yet was that very few people made it through six months with the Scouts. I set up my room and hung up a short-timer's calendar and settled in. At least I was going to fly.

When I went up on my first mission, the pilot and door-gunner were telling me that it was a different ballgame out there. They finally had to open up to me, because our lives would depend on each other on missions. We were at 5000 feet, heading out to the AO (Area of Operations), when the pilot turned to me and said, "Know what happens if I get hit?" "No. What?" "You're going to have to fly this thing." I said that I had never been in a LOH before and he told me not to worry; within a month I'd know how to fly like a pilot. I was telling him how I had always wanted to fly and how nice it was to be up in the sky, like that, when all of a sudden, he yelled, "I'm hit!" I didn't know what to do. He yelled again. "Grab it!" "Grab what?" "The controls!"

There was no steering wheel or anything, just two sticks on the floor. I grabbed them and the aircraft started to respond. Once the nose came up and the ship leveled out, he told me that he was just kidding. I told him never to do that to me again. I began to enjoy the flying. The mission itself was no big thing. We made right screwing turns in the air for two hours at treetop level. The pilot and door-gunner were looking down at the jungle. All I could see was the horizon spinning around. At the end of the first day, I was sick as a dog. I vomited through the whole mission and couldn't keep anything down afterwards.

It was like that for three weeks. I used to get sick in combat. I was supposed to throw out smoke to mark the target for our Cobra gunship. All I could do was lean out the door and watch guys shooting at us, tracers coming up and all I could do was throw up on them. I went to the sergeant and told him that I was no good in the air. He told me that they would court martial me if I refused to fly. I wasn't a coward, I just got airsick. He told me that it would get better after a while and it did.

The first time I saw someone get killed was on a patrol, where we found this trail that cut straight through the jungle. It went on for miles through a free fire zone. The orders specified "kill anyone in the area." We flew back and forth over it a few times, and then saw this guy walking right down the middle of the trail. We came back around and the pilot told the gunner that we were going to waste this guy. Then he turned around and saw us. The trail was only about two feet wide, straight as an arrow, and the door-gunner opened up. You could see the ground kicking up behind him. Instead of diving into the triple-canopy jungle where we could have lost sight of him, this guy ran straight down the trail. The machine gun kept kicking up dust behind him until the bullets climbed right up his back.

We came back around to verify the kill and this other jerk ran out of the jungle and headed down the trail. I was thinking, "What in the hell is wrong with these people?" Here he was, safe in the jungle, and he runs out onto the trail. It looks like they're running a relay race. One drops, and another comes out.

He ran for a while, then leaped behind a log. We could see his body jumping up and down behind the log. We wondered what was going on and came around the back side of the log to have a look. There was a spider hole behind the log with one guy already in there. He was trying to push the other guy out, without drawing attention to himself. The door-gunner killed both of them. It didn't bother me. In fact, it was funny the way it happened. I had been around tough areas of the Bronx all my life and it was really nothing new to me. I considered Vietnam no different than some areas of Central Park.

For the first month, we took fire two or three times a day. It was like going to work in the rush hour. You knew that you were going to get it again. What bothered me about the Scouts were the guys who used drugs. The philosophy was that they needed them to tolerate all the shit that they were seeing. They were afraid of death and used the drugs to calm them down. A lot of guys had bullets with their names engraved on them. They thought they wouldn't get hit, because they already had the bullet with their name on it. My thing was that I viewed it as a nine-to-five job, even though we sometimes flew for sixteen hours a day. It was something I just had to do. But it's amazing what a man can do when he has a weapon in his hands and develops its full power. You become a god, with the power of life and death. It was a tremendous responsibility. You had come from a consistent world to a place with no rules. You had to kill to survive.

I didn't hate the Vietnamese. I didn't even dislike them. If I killed someone, it was because he was trying to kill me. I believed that they believed that what they were doing was the right thing. God isn't always on the side of the Americans, with us being the only ones who are right and everyone else being wrong. Those people were in the same boat as us. The men organizing the war on both sides were not the ones who were fighting it. It struck me as ironic that we were teenagers and trained to kill with the full backing of our government, but we wouldn't vote for the policies that sent us there. To this day, I can't understand how our government had the gall to send us over to kill or be killed, and yet fought like hell to keep us out of bars, because they thought that we would kill ourselves drinking. If the guys on the other side were willing to die for their cause and wanted to call themselves "freedom fighters," that was fine with us.

The most crucial decision that a man can make in his life is to kill another human being. One thing that the Army couldn't do was order me to kill. I killed only in self-defense, or when our lives were in immediate jeopardy. I always allowed the other fellow the dignity of firing first.

They had stressed in training never to make friends, because it's just going to make it harder when they die. I never forgot that, but you make friends anyway. The first time that I took Vietnam dead-seriously was in May, when we legally went into Cambodia for the first time, and my friend, Sly, got killed. Cambodia was really heavy stuff. The XO (Executive Officer) told us that we were going into a really mountainous area on the first day. I was a door-gunner by then, but we had only three flyable birds and they wanted experienced men to crew them. So my first mission there was as an observer.

The NVA had everything set up there like we did in South Vietnam. Everything was above ground—all the camps, hospitals, ammunition dumps. There was no problem getting a body count. My team killed forty-three VC and NVA on the first day, and that was nothing. By the third day, there were so many enemy out there that we started flying in double teams. Instead of one LOH and one Cobra, now there were two LOHs and two Cobras in a team. The shit was so heavy that a single team couldn't handle it.

We were over Cambodia on May 2, the second day, and I'll never forget it. I was an observer and Sly was the door-gunner on the next team over. My LOH was making a turn and I saw Sly's bird make a left turn, which was unusual. I thought that they might be going down into a valley to check it out, but told the pilot that something was going on. Then their Cobra called and said to get over there—the LOH had just gone down. We found it nose down in the ground. Sly was laying next to the aircraft with his machine gun pointing into the jungle, so I thought that he was alive.

I told the pilot that we should go down and get him, but he said he had to tell the Cobra first. As he radioed the Cobra, the whole mountain above us exploded with gunfire and rocket fire. It was like watching the Battle of Midway. All I saw was the whole mountain flashing, and that was 9 o'clock in the morning. I was tossing out grenades and shooting M-79 rounds at them, and the door-gunner was shooting on the other side. As we came back around, the LOH exploded. This big ball of flame came up and almost hit us, then fell back down and landed on Sly's back and started to burn. That's when I realized he was already dead. I was angry and told the pilot that we had to go down and get his body. He said, "We can't. We can't. We're taking too much fire."

The gunships told us to get the hell out of there. I asked the pilot to stay so we could rescue my friend. Then a Huey arrived with four men and a team of two CBS newsmen. There was a landing zone a few feet from the wreckage and they made a vertical decent—straight down. They radioed from the ground that there were two pillboxes between them and the wreckage. We tried to knock them out and couldn't, then, after about thirty minutes, they took the two bunkers. We were still flying around, shooting like crazy, trying to keep the NVA away from the bodies.

The rescue team finally got to my buddy, and by this time he looked like a lobster—red as a beet. They picked him up by his armpits and started to drag him into the jungle, and the meat on his arms came right off, just like a boiled chicken. This poor guy was dead. He had a wife and five kids and he had extended his tour to get extra money for his family. The rescue team finally got to the Huey and then they got shot down trying to get out. I told the pilot that now we had to do something. Our gunship radioed for us to go back and refuel and rearm, and then we could go down there.

We flew to our base, about four miles away, got gas and ammo, and went back out. Two other LOHs were already there. Airstrikes were hitting the mountain and Cobras were making their rocket runs. Then they finally got everybody out. Six hours of fighting in that one area. The 11th Armored Cav. came in with their APCs and swept through the whole area. There were supposed to be 2000 NVA in that one valley. I finally got back to base and the sergeant told me to take care of Sly's belongings, so they could be sent back to his family. That was the toughest thing I ever had to do. To sit there and inventory those things and make sure that nobody stole them. Somebody would get hit and everybody else would come down on his gear like vultures. No one touched my friend's stuff.

My last friend, Geiger, died about two weeks later. It started about a week before his death. I was now a permanent door-gunner, and this other guy, Dave, and myself became trainers for FNG pilots. On one training mission, our CO asked us to check out this new warrant officer who was having trouble taking fire. I was observer and Dave was gunner and we were explaining to the pilot the maneuvers that were necessary on missions. We told him that he had to make right banking turns at all times to create a swirling pattern, and that he should never fly in a cloverleaf pattern. The problem with cloverleafs was that the enemy could just keep firing their weapons and you'd fly right into the bullets. Our swirling, screwing type pattern prevented something like this from happening.

The pilot was doing everything by the book until we took fire and he dived. We were at treetop level and there wasn't much room for a dive. The next stop was the trees. I took control of the aircraft and pulled us out of the dive. The pilot apologized and told us he had a problem under fire. We told him that we understood. He did well until we took fire again. He dived again. The Cobra asked what was going on and I told him that the guy was new and having a hard time with the noise of gunfire. The Cobra pilot told us to keep pushing him, because we were short of scout pilots. When we got back to the base at dark, the pilot apologized for a third time and said he would practice his maneuvers that night. We told the CO that he was still freaking out under fire, but to give him more time, so we could make a fairer judgment.

The guy's whole attitude was different the next day. He told us that he was now going to tell us what to do, not us telling him. "Now listen. I'm the officer here. I'm the aircraft commander. You guys take orders from me."

I looked over at him. "Wait a minute, Sir. This is not the way it's supposed to be. We've got orders to train you and observe your actions under fire. These are training missions. Unfortunately for you, they have to be in a hostile area."

He told us to fuck ourselves. I looked back at Dave, and Dave just shrugged his shoulders. He banged the pilot's flight helmet with his machine gun, then punched the intercom button. "If you don't listen to what Roger tells you, it'll be the last time you fly." I started to laugh, because I knew Dave wouldn't hesitate to kill him.

The pilot said, "Okay, okay. You guys are serious, so I'll listen to what you have to say."

The pilot did everything right. We took fire and he didn't dive. I told him to fly over the area one more time and he told us that now we would fly his way. I told him, in that case, we would go back to the base, because my life was worth a hell of a lot more than his. He said to fuck ourselves again. I radioed the gunship and asked them to terminate the mission. The captain in the Cobra told the pilot to shut up and listen to what we had to tell him. He did all right the rest of the day.

Back at the base, I told the CO that the guy might be a good pilot, but put him on long runs, let him run supplies. He was no good for the Scouts. The CO told me that he would take him out tomorrow and see how he did. That was fine with me, as long as I didn't have to fly with him.

The next afternoon, the CO came over to Dave and me. "I don't know what your problem is, but that guy flies really well." "Where did you take him?" "I took him around the base." "Fuck, Sir. Take him out to the AO where the action is. I told you he's a good pilot. He's just no good for what we have to do. If he stays with the Scouts, he's going to get somebody killed." The CO told us to take him up one last time. We agreed, but only if Dave and I could fly the mission together.

We got out to the AO and he started the same "I'm the guy in charge" bullshit. I told him, "If you start that shit one more time, I'm going to kill you." "You shut up!" Dave pointed his machine gun right across the pilot's face and fired a long burst. "The next time I fire this weapon, it'll be into your head. We are trying to train you, but Roger can fly this aircraft. We don't need you. Take us back to base now. You have five seconds to decide."

He told Dave to shut up and I grabbed the controls. He said, "What are you doing?" "I'm just preparing. All I have to do is unstrap your buckle and you're out the fucking door. We don't need you. You're a hazard to the airways. We're getting out of here."

After very little more argument, I told the gunship that we were returning to base. I flew the ship back. I told the CO that the guy was dangerous and they grounded him for a few days. Then on May 12, we got short on Scout pilots. The CO sent him out with Geiger, who was a top door-gunner and my last friend. The observer was a kid who had been in Vietnam for a week and wanted to fly on his birthday. I told the kid to enjoy his birthday and not fly with that pilot. They were in the AO only twenty minutes when we got the call to scramble.

On the way out, we got the word that the pilot had been hit doing a cloverleaf and was nose down in the ground. When we got there, Geiger was standing on the observer's side of the aircraft, trying to rescue the kid. The LOH started to smoke, then exploded. Geiger forgot the number one rule, that you throw out all the grenades and ammo as soon as you crash. That stuff just enhanced the explosion. Geiger was six-four. We brought him back in a baggy. There was nothing left of him. There were twenty-five or thirty white phosphorus grenades on that LOH.

Back at the base, the CO came into the operations room and we both looked at him. He stood there with his head hanging, looking at the ground. Nobody had to say anything. The pilot was everything. If you had a good pilot, you might get hit, but he'd get you out of it. A bad pilot would take two helpless guys with him. This pilot hadn't been good enough.

I was the only gunner who would fly with my CO, because everyone thought that he was crazy. We were flying strictly observation, high altitude, "Do not engage, just observe," when the CO saw a herd of deer. He said it would be nice to have some venison. We went down and I shot a deer. Just as we started to land to pick it up, we got the message that a LRRP (Long Range Recon Patrol) platoon was in contact and had two wounded and that the med-evac wouldn't land in the area. Med-evac had rescued one wounded man, but now the team was taking too much fire.

We came down into the LZ and it started getting darker and darker, and this was one or two in the afternoon. It got very dark, and you could see tracers flashing by, explosions all around. We had to hover about three feet off the ground while trying to decide who was friendly and who wasn't. We were about twenty meters from the NVA. Some guys ran out of the bush with the wounded men. And I saw this fellow stand up and start firing into the jungle to cover us. You could see tracers flashing around him. Then a rocket exploded right next to him and I told the CO that we'd better get out of there. They threw the two wounded on board, and as we started to rise, so did the tracers. How we didn't get shot down I'll never know.

We were after another deer the next day when the same platoon radioed that they had a "Line One" (KIA). We came in quick to avoid an approaching rainstorm. Two guys threw a body into the back seat with me. I just grabbed his ammo belt as we pulled up. They had told us that they had just been in another firefight and there were probably still NVA around. I was firing into the treeline with one hand and holding the ammo belt with the other. We cleared the area, hit the rainstorm, and this guy started slipping out. When I looked at him, I realized that he must have been over six feet tall, because his waist and legs were hanging out the door on the other side, and his shoulders were resting in my lap. He didn't have a head.

It didn't upset me so much that he didn't have a head, but it bothered me that I never knew this guy, didn't know where he came from. I wondered if he had a wife and kids, if he had a family, and what they would think when they found out that he was dead. So I was with him for about twenty minutes as we flew a zig-zag pattern through the rain. He became a friend, even though I didn't know him. I began to care a lot, wondering what his name was and if I could write a letter to his family. I was sure this was the guy who had been killed trying to cover us the day before.

We landed at a field hospital at a firebase, parked outside the wire and watched as two guys came for the body. They pulled him out of the LOH—one has the legs and the other grabs the shoulders. Then he slipped out of their hands and fell into a mud puddle. Instead of picking him up again, they started rolling him toward the wire with their feet, just kicking him over and over. I told them to pick him up and carry him with respect. One guy turned to me. "Don't worry about it. He's already dead. He doesn't feel anything." So I took my machine gun and pointed it at them. "Pick up that guy right now, or they're going to be rolling you in the mud. I don't care if he doesn't feel anything. Pick him up and carry him into the perimeter."

The CO told them to carry the guy and they gave him the same "He doesn't feel anything" story. I cocked the machine gun and gave them two seconds to pick the guy up or be dropped where they stood. They picked him up. We covered them until they were out of sight. I wanted to write the guy's family a letter, but we never could get his name. He had been new to the unit and nobody knew him.

It started as a routine insertion by the Blue Platoon. They were an infantry platoon of about twenty guys who would destroy any ammunition or food caches that we found. They were going down this trail with an FNG lieutenant. It was basically the same situation that we had with the pilot that got Geiger killed. One of the rules in Vietnam was that you never return by the same trail you had just used. They were on this trail all day long with no contact, and then it got close to 5 o'clock, which was dinner time for them. The choppers were on their way to pick them up.

Then we got word that the Blue Team wouldn't go to the LZ. The lieutenant wanted them to go back on the same trail. When the lieutenant ordered them to go, they refused. They sat down on their asses, dropped their weapons and didn't move. So the CO came over and told them to get the hell out of there. We checked the trail and said that it looked clear, but they still wouldn't move. It was now too dark to do anything, so we left them there for the night. The next morning, they were ordered out again and refused again. They weren't going back down the same trail.

Now they wanted to sit and make demands. They wanted the lieutenant rotated out of the platoon, and until that happened, they were on strike. They sent out a negotiating team and Saigon finally got involved. Some two-star general flew out to conduct talks. So we had to fly security over them for thirty days. There were gunships covering them, tanks set up to protect them, and nobody forced them to move.

They finally got the amnesty they demanded, had the lieutenant rotated out, and everything went back to normal. Everybody joked about it— a platoon on strike for thirty days. It was funny.

It really wasn't a surprise by 1970, because it was getting hard to find anyone to obey orders. Panic was setting in. The peace talks were in progress and nobody wanted to be the last to die. Fragging officers and NCOs was common. They fragged a couple of officers in Alpha Troop, but didn't kill anyone. I wasn't involved in that. We flew all the time and were constantly tired. If we weren't flying, we were sleeping. But things were changing. By June, when we went into Cambodia, the enemy must have gone underground, because it was hard to find anybody. We found this one guy who was tied to a tree, already dead, and we needed body counts. I killed that dead guy eight times that day. We were always exaggerating body counts. There was another time when we came upon this deserted village. This hooch had eight water jugs outside and I needed target practice to keep my skills sharp. These eight jugs were counted as body counts.

We began flying into Cambodia from firebases along the border. A team would go out to a firebase for three days and then be relieved by another team. After three days at one firebase, our replacements came out, and this guy who had been in Vietnam for thirteen months sneaked back on the LOH that I had been with. He was supposed to replace me, but I ended up being out there for three more days. I went back, determined to kill him, and found that somebody had also stolen many of my personal possessions. I almost did kill the fellow. I told the first-sergeant the whole story about being left out at the firebase and then having my gear stolen. There were a lot of guys in the rear doing drugs and whatever while a few of us flew. I told the first-sergeant that, if he couldn't get men to fight or even watch my stuff, I wasn't going out either. They left me alone for about ten days.

There were few other door-gunners, because no one wanted to be trained for it. People were getting really adamant against authority. Joe was the acting line chief while the other guy was on R&R, and he came to me on July 2, after those ten days. "Roger. You're the only door-gunner I have left. I can't go on missions because I have to stay here. Do me this favor and go on a three-day mission. I promise I'll watch your stuff. Nobody will fuck with your stuff."

I told Joe that I would go because he asked me to, but I wouldn't have for anybody else. I wanted to pick the crew. I didn't need assholes up there with me. In thirty days, I would go on R&R, and then could go anyplace in Vietnam for the rest of my time. So we went to this firebase near Cambodia. It rained for three days at this rinky-dink place with 175mm cannon going off every fucking minute. You can't eat, you can't sleep. It's like lots of mini-earthquakes. I had to keep candles lit around my air mattress to keep the rats from chewing through. We were wet, tired and disgusted.

On July 4th, the captain said, "Let's go back. We have a barbecue waiting."

The rain stopped and we headed back about three in the afternoon. We were flying over Charlie Troop when they radioed that all their birds were down and could we fly a last light mission for them? We flew this mission for two hours in a free fire zone and couldn't find shit. I told my pilot to get the hell out of there. Then I saw a company bivouacking and wondered what GIs were doing in a free fire zone where no one was supposed to be. We went back around to see who they were.

We hovered above them and those guys kept eating like we weren't even there. They were big, like the L.A. Raiders. I couldn't get over the size of them. Then one guy looked up and I saw the slanty eyes and the two red stars on his collar. I thought that they looked like Chinese regulars, because of their size. It was bad enough fighting the NVA, but I had heard that the Chinese regulars were fantastic soldiers. I grabbed a Willie Pete (white phosphorus grenade) and pulled the pin, ready to drop it to mark the target for the gunship. But we were taking a lot of fire and the gunship was already making runs. I fired with one hand and held the hot Pete in the other. Then the gunship told us that it was out of ammunition and that we should get out of there. My pilot radioed the Cobra that I had this hot Pete and was going to throw it out, so don't get excited.

To this day, I swear that I threw it as hard as I could. The next thing I knew, this Pete blew back and hit me in the nuts and I wondered what in the hell it was doing back in the LOH. A little fire came out of it, and it blew into my face, partially blinding me. Everything was blurry. I kept seeing balls of flame popping out like from a Roman candle, bouncing off the fire walls, hitting me all over the place. My whole life was passing in front of me. How was I going to live being blind? What was I going to do with myself? "It's the end of my flying dreams." I could see movements of the pilot's head, but not his features. I was totally oblivious to what was happening to me.

The thing that woke me up was when my helmet started melting along the side of my face and I wondered what that warm feeling was. There was no pain. The detonator fuse on a Willie Pete is only twenty seconds long, but it seemed like hours had gone by. I saw the thing burning and tried to throw it out before we were all killed. Maybe my mind had become foggy at this point because of the trauma. Instead of throwing it out the right door where I was sitting, I tried to get it out the left door. My vision was badly impaired by now. The grenade hit the wall and fell into my box of Willie Petes. The whole thing seemed engulfed in this glow. I crawled over to it, and instead of tossing it out the left side, I went back to the right door and got rid of it.

There was nothing to do at that point but sit down and enjoy the ride. I went to sit down in my seat and it had melted away, leaving only the metal frame. When my leg and calf hit that frame, that was the only sensation of heat that I felt during the entire event. I leaned into the hole and sat on my ammo box that was always under the seat. Something was firing; my M-60 was cooking off and the ammo under me was exploding as well. Two thousand rounds of ammo from the box was popping off all around me. I took the weapon and threw it out the door, listening to it firing on the way down. Then I kicked out the ammo box and the box of Willie Petes. I wasn't going to go like Sly and Geiger.

I pealed away the gloves that had melted to my hands and stripped off the nomex flight suit that wasn't supposed to burn, but did anyway. I got everything off except my chicken plate (chest protector) and underwear. I didn't know why, but wanted to stick my head out of the door and get some fresh air. Just as I did that, every bug in Vietnam must have been flying and hit my face. That's when I felt the only pain. For the rest of the trip, I worried that people were going to see me in my underwear. I hoped it would be dark when we landed so they couldn't see my underwear.

We landed at this base and these guys came running out with a stretcher and told me to lay down on it. I did that and then sat up, thinking I had to cover myself because I was half naked and I wasn't really sick. I didn't know at the time that I had third-degree burns over thirty-five percent of my body—legs, face and arms. They ran me into an operating room with very bright lights and I saw this figure leaning over me, cutting my dogtags off my neck. The pain didn't come until a month later.

I woke up four days later and found myself on a C-141 transport headed for Japan. Then I blacked out again for another week. I woke up in a circular bed, the most uncomfortable thing I had ever been in, and tried to figure out what was happening to me. My eyes were totally bandaged and I was just imagining what they were doing to me. Somebody was telling me that I had a phone call. Who would be calling me in Tokyo? It was my parents. They had received a telegram saying that I was dying. I didn't know then that I had already died and been revived. My folks wanted to travel out to Tokyo, halfway around the world, to see me.

I said, "I'm dying? I'll be shipped back to the States in a week. I'm not dying!" After all the crying and nonsense, we hung up. I started yelling. "I want to see the guy in charge." When he came around, I told him, "I remember when I came in-country I signed a form that said I didn't want anyone notified of the injuries I sustained, only in case of death. You got my parents all crazy and worried. They're twelve thousand miles away and they want to come over here. You call and straighten this out. Let them know that I'll be coming home shortly." He must have done something, because I didn't hear from them again in Japan.

I was hungry all the time—hungry and cold. My parents were still sending letters, worrying that I was dying. I wasn't about to die. They had done a colostomy on me, a temporary colostomy to keep down the risk of infection, but I didn't know that I had one. There was just this thing hanging on my side, and somebody told me that I would be sitting in it from now on. They sent me down to the cafeteria to get food. Somebody plopped food in my plate and somebody else led me to a table. I'm eating and all of a sudden I feel this tremendous pressure in my left side. I put my hand down and the bag was inflated to the max. I thought that the thing was going to blow up on me. I had little slits in the bandages over my eyes and could see the outlines of whitecoats, assuming that they were doctors or nurses. I said, "Please, could someone come over and see what's wrong with this thing? I think it's going to explode on me."

Somebody told me not to worry, they'd take care of it when I got back to my unit. I thought that it couldn't be that bad. So I started to eat and feel the stuff going into my bag, and the bag was starting to pull away from the skin, pulling the intestines with it. I didn't know that then, but I know it now. I had this tremendous pressure, like being squeezed in the kidney.

"Somebody please come and look at this thing!" The same voice replied, "Wait till you get upstairs. They'll take care of it."

Then the bag ripped loose. It totally pulled off, and I was shitting all over. Stuff was getting under my bandages and it was burning the wounds on my legs. I grabbed the bag and said, "You guys eating?" One of them said, "Yes." "Well, eat this shit?" I threw the bag on the table. They deserved to eat shit. I went back upstairs with the stuff dropping all over the place. Somebody put me back into the circular bed.

Somebody was telling me that I had been in the burn unit for three weeks and was only supposed to be there for two. I had a fever of 105 degrees and they were afraid to move me. They were going to stick me in an ice tub. I told them I was already freezing all the time, why an ice tub? It was because I had a fever of 105 degrees and they couldn't bring it down. Nobody informed me what was going on. Nobody enlightened me. I felt like a piece of shit. It annoyed me that nobody treated me like a person.

They didn't tell me they had wanted to remove my eyes until four months later. There was a shortage of beds, so they wrapped me up and shipped me out to Brooks Army Hospital. Apparently, they were supposed to finish the job. Some eye surgeon decided to experiment with my eyes. They figured that, if they were going to take them out anyway, I had nothing to lose. They did cornea transplants to see if they would take. They did. Then they grafted on new eyelids and started grafting the burns. It started with pigskin, then cadaver skin, and then with whatever skin I had left. That went on for nine months.

Once when I came out of the soaking tank and was in terrible pain, some freakin' major or colonel wheeled me into the corridor, instead of into the dressing room. The worst thing you can do when you come out of the tank is wait. You're draped with towels, and they become stuck to the burned areas, almost like an artificial skin. The officer told me that they were going to award me the Distinguished Flying Cross. The newspaper people were there and they wanted to get the publicity all down right. The ceremony lasted for forty-five minutes. Then they wheeled me into the dressing room and the nurse tried to take the towels off as painlessly as possible.

A new doctor walked in and looked at the nurse. "What are you doing? Don't waste your time like that. Do it this way." And he ripped off the towels.

All I saw was red. I started screaming and cursing him. The nurse was crying. The doctor apologized. That was just another example of my being a non-entity with the doctors. The nursing staff, and everyone else, were terrific.

The third month, I was doing so well that they decided to send me home on leave for thirty days. That's when my troubles of adapting to civilian life began. The worst thing was going back to the real world. I didn't realize how things had changed and that people weren't going to accept me, until the day I came home and landed at Kennedy Airport. It was one of the worst days of my life and it was only the beginning of it.

For thirty days, I had to deal with accusations of baby killing and how could I live with myself? As badly scarred as I was, and with what I had been through, all people saw was the uniform. It took me a week to get civilian clothes that fit, and after that I just stayed at home and waited to go back to the hospital where people accepted me. So I went back to the hospital and started feeling better, and began talking to other soldiers, trying to help them. I began to think that since I couldn't fly anymore, maybe the best thing for me to do was to go into counselling and try to work with other people.

During all this "readjustment" my family supported me

unconditionally. I feel that they endured more than I did. They not only had to deal with my situation, but had to take the abuse of my anger and frustrations. Looking back on it now, I see the anguish they must have felt. In fact, my brother offered to donate one of his eyes for me. It was a very emotional time. I cried for days afterwards that he even considered to sacrifice his own sight for me. I don't think that he really knows how grateful I am, what the gesture meant to me. My parents', brothers', and sisters' undying devotion to me was the best medicine I could have received, for their constant encouragement and love for me was the one moving force for survival.

I still had to deal with going home, and with my relatives, who had a hard time dealing with me, as I now was, and with my experiences in the war. Vietnam was winding down and the My Lai incident was on people's minds. That picture of the little girl running down the road with napalm burns was everywhere. The GI was beginning to be the enemy, not the Viet Cong. I went home and hooked up with the VA for treatment of my eyes. The burns were essentially healed, although I would always bear the scars. I was getting so much harassment from the anti-war people that I moved out of the Bronx and stayed home for two years.

One day I realized that this was crazy and that I was bored. I couldn't stand the isolation anymore. I was tired of appeasing people that I didn't know or even care about. If they couldn't deal with me, that was their problem. So, I called the VA and told them that I wanted to go to school. They put me in rehab for a while first. They wanted me to get used to negotiating public transportation and interacting in the community despite my visual defects. That turned out to be a good idea. I went there for eighteen months, then started college. When I graduated from junior college, I met my future wife. She has helped tremendously in my personal development and has been all things to me—a great asset, a helper, a friend, a companion. After four years of schooling, I received a B.S. in Psychology and began working for the state of New York on a volunteer basis.

You get to a point in life where you stop looking at things superficially. What Vietnam taught me is that you never take things at face value, never judge a book by its cover. The best things in life really are free, and you can become anything you want. I am now employed in a vet center outreach program. One of the good things is that I have empathy for the guys who were in Vietnam. Having been in Nam myself, they can't hand me any bullshit, because I know what really happened over there. If there's such a thing as being totally happy with a job and feeling fulfillment and reward, this job does it for me. It's a very rewarding experience, and sometimes, a very frustrating one.

Being in the 9th Cav. allowed me to achieve my goal of flying, even if for a short time. Now I don't have to wonder about it, because I did it. I have since learned that, if you work inside the system, instead of alienating it, you can achieve your goals and dreams. You just cannot survive outside the system. The sooner vets realize that, the sooner they can achieve their normality and continue with their lives, with the self-respect and self-esteem that they all deserve.

Today I work for the Vet Center in Westchester, New York, a Veterans Administration program for the purpose of helping Vietnam veterans readjust to a new life.

Reprinted with permission from HEADHUNTERS: STORIES FROM THE 1st SQUADRON, 9th CAVALRY, IN VIETNAM 1965-1971, edited by Matthew Brennan © 1987 by Presidio Press, 31 Pamaron Way, Novato, CA 94949.

Walter L. Kudlacik

My name is Walter Kudlacik. I served in Vietnam from October 1970 to September 1971 with the 1st Cav. Division. I was an Infantry Platoon Leader (lst Lieutenant) with D Company, 1st Bn. 12th Cav. for approximately seven months, with the balance of my tour spent as D Co. Executive Officer and battalion adjutant (S-1).

I have never really talked to anyone about my experiences in Vietnam other than a few comments here and there.

I had a gung-ho attitude about the Army and the reason why America was fighting in Vietnam, and felt that way for a good portion of my tour. As the time of my DEROS date got closer, my gung-ho attitude changed to one of survival for both my men and myself. I truly felt it was more important for everyone to survive and return to their families than to perish in a war that was becoming more difficult to believe in.

My recollections of my tour began with the anticipation of what my tour would be like on the flight from Oakland to RVN. The flight took approximately twenty-four hours total time, with stops at Anchorage, Alaska (a foot of snow on the ground) and Yakota, Japan (hot). Every minute on the plane meant RVN was getting closer, and anxiety built up tremendously as the plane made its final approach to Bien Hoa. I don't remember who I sat next to or any conversation on the plane. The only thing I do remember was that there were no stewardesses, only stewards(!) and I thought that was odd.

We deplaned and I remember the blast of heat as I walked through the plane exit. I can only describe it as the "hottest summer" day at the Jersey shore.

Our planeload of men was shuffled into an airplane hangar that had one large section of "church pews" that was split in half by rope running down the middle of the pews. The left side of the pews had soldiers that had just finished their tour and were waiting to go home on the same jet that I had arrived on. It must have been fate, because I sat in a seat closest to the soldiers leaving for home, and the guy sitting next to me going home was Ed Loniewski. Ed Loniewski was a guy who entered the Army the same day I did, from the same town as I was—Jersey City— who sat next to me on the bus ride to Fort Dix from Jersey City. I became very friendly with him in basic and AIT. Ed and I both went to OCS in Fort Benning, Georgia, but Ed dropped out after six weeks or so and got shipped over to RVN, while I completed OCS and instructed at the Infantry School in Fort Benning.

Ed looked older than I did to begin with, but what I saw was a man much-much older than I, and I felt awkward. We exchanged a few words, but it seemed he didn't want to talk. The only thing I remember about the conversation was that he said it got very, very hot. I think Ed was dressed in fatigues while I was in khaki. After a short time, our arriving group was briefed and departed for the reception centers.

My initial orders were for the Americal Division which, at the time, was supposedly in the mountains in I Corp. Rumor had it that the Americal was a problem division, and that most of the enemy contacts occurred with the Americal. None of us really knew this to be factual, but rumors were the only information being passed along.

My orders got changed while in the reception center to the 1st Cav. Division, and the largest feeling of relief overcame me because I did not want to go to the Americal Division.

The new men, including myself, assigned to the 1st Bn. 12th Cav. were flown by chopper to the firebase where the battalion operated from. The firebase was somewhere in MR III and served as the headquarters and forward support for the battalion.

I was assigned to D Company and scheduled to replace the third platoon leader, who was out in the jungle with his platoon and not scheduled to arrive back on the firebase for three to four days. It was battalion procedure for the line-infantry platoons to spend from fifteen to seventeen days in the bush (jungle) and then return to the firebase for three to five days. This was an ongoing cyclical procedure that lasted for my whole tour.

While waiting on the firebase, the conversations were mainly devoted to A Company being interviewed by CBS news with regard to drug usage in RVN, both in the jungle and in the rear. Rumor had it that all of Alpha's officers were going to be relieved of duty because of the blatant abuse of drug usage! Rumor also had it that the new officers would replace the ones being relieved. I had been in the country approximately two weeks and hadn't seen anyone using drugs!

Eventually, after four days of waiting on the firebase, my future command, the third platoon of D Company, arrived by chopper at the firebase. I was amazed at how experienced and worn down these "grunts" looked; twenty to twenty-five men, average age nineteen, looking like average age late twenties—scruffy appearance—arriving by chopper and just assimilating into the firebase compound, not saying much of anything to anyone.

My platoon consisted of anywhere between nineteen to thirty men, depending on attrition, R&Rs, etc. The platoon was broken down into three squads and one command group. Each squad was led by an NCO (normally a sergeant) and each had one machine gun, one grenade launcher, one radio, one shovel, and the rest had rifles. An average rucksack weighed approximately seventy pounds when fully loaded with supplies, ammo, poncho, mosquito net, food, extra socks, and personal effects. Our riflemen also carried 300 rounds of bullets, two trip-flares, one to two claymore mines, two frag grenades, two smoke grenades, one machete, personal knives; some had specialty items such as extra rounds for the machine gun or grenade launcher. (And I've probably forgotten quite a few other items.)

The radios weighed approximately twenty pounds, which further weighed the grunts down. The rucksacks were specially equipped with two special straps that allowed very quick release from your back in case of an ambush or firefight.

The command group consisted of the platoon leader, RTO (radio operator), platoon medic, and senior NCO that we generally called "Top." In our case, our senior NCO was called "Super Six"—six meaning E-6, his rank.

A typical mission or operation generally took place this way: 1) platoon leaders were briefed by the company commander on the upcoming mission; 2) platoon would be combat-assaulted by chopper into a landing zone in the jungle that was prepped with artillery fire and gunship fire; and 3) once on the jungle floor, the platoon would commence searching for the VC and NVA, which meant patrolling for anywhere between one klick and five klicks (a klick was 1000 meters) in one day, depending how thick the vegetation was.

Just before dusk we would set up in a NDP (night defensive position), normally circular and spread apart in teams of two around the perimeter.

Foxholes were something dug, depending on how hard the ground was. Each person was assigned a different sector to their front (out of the perimeter), where they would have to set up trip-wires attached to flares, and claymore mines, as protective measures for their perimeter.

Artillery would be called in, bracketing our position in four directions and about 1000 meters from our location. If there was need to call in artillery quickly because of enemy contact after our NDP was set up, these preplotted fires (in four directions) would save a fire mission valuable minutes needed to get the first shot out.

One memorable NDP artillery fire happened when we were in the hilly northern portion of MR III. While bracketing our NDP fire, a round hit short, and wound up exploding just outside of our perimeter. Hot shrapnel came whooshing and zinging into our perimeter. Somehow no one got injured, but there were a few shrapnel holes in ponchos and air mattresses throughout the perimeter (we either slept on air mattresses or in ponchos set up in a hammock fashion).

Each individual would have a guard watch of approximately two hours each night and assigned times were normally agreed upon.

It was a traumatic experience the very first night in the jungle, pulling guard duty for two hours. The setting would be pitch black, with normal jungle noises sounding, but to a new guy, normal jungle noises turned into events of major catastrophe. Example: The mind plays funny tricks on everyone, especially to someone who has "humped" one to five klicks in the jungle during the day in the thick vegetation with a seventy-pound ruck on his back, and in constant fear of ambush/enemy contact. Insect noises sometimes made the new guy think that a small army of VC or NVA was just outside his perimeter moving toward him. Many a claymore mine was fired by my men over the course of six months reacting to noises heard. There was also a lizard that made a sound like the words (a very high pitched descending) "fuck you," (excuse the expression). The first time you heard this lizard—and it would only come out and speak at night!—you swore that the enemy was out there saying "fuck you, fuck you!"

Most new guys couldn't sleep for the first week or so, and really were out on their feet after the first few days—sleepless nights, extreme heat, excessive physical exertion causing exhaustion—but once you got used to it, sleep came easily.

Occasionally guards would doze off on their watches, but for the most part the guys were conscientious and guarded their positions well regardless of what hour their assigned times were.

If we came across a recently used trail in the jungle, we would set up our NDP off the trail and set up automatic ambushes on the trail. Automatic ambushes were claymore mines hooked up to batteries and trip-wire activated. If the wire was tripped, the claymore mines would explode, killing anything in its kill zone. This was a deterrent to the enemy for his movement at night.

With dawn, came the platoon coming to life for another day of basically patrolling and searching for the enemy. The platoon normally patrolled in line formation with a pointman in the lead, a "back up" man would watch to the pointman's left, right and up. The platoon leader was normally third in line, specifying the direction with his RTO behind him.

Depending on where you were in RVN, the types of terrain and vegetation varied dramatically. We patrolled through wide open areas that had been defoliated with Agent Orange, to triple-canopy jungle where it was bright daylight above the canopy and "dark" on the ground—like dusk.

The heat was almost unbearable during the day, especially in the dry season. Water supply was important for survival. We normally carried two gallons of water in the dry season, and quite a bit less in the rainy season. Heat casualties were not uncommon, but for the most part, everyone became acclimated. I think the hottest day on patrol probably got to 110 degrees or so—like a blast furnace.

Terrain. I remember that on one particular day it took us eight hours to travel approximately 1000 meters because the vegetation was so thick! Then there were days when we could travel 1000 meters in one hour. The toughest vegetation to get through was bamboo, which grew in stalks anywhere from one-half-inch diameter to six-inch diameter. If six-inch stalks grew in a wall with no gaps, it was virtually impossible to penetrate, even with machetes that were razor sharp. "Wait-a-minute" vines were also extremely frustrating. These vines would catch onto your rucksacks or any portion of your gear and hold you back. The more you struggled to go forward, the more the vine would hold you up. They were almost impossible to break so you would have to back up and untangle yourself, and your seventy-pound rucksack.

Mosquitoes were horrible, especially in wet, damp areas. Bug spray would have to be used frequently, and put on your face and around your eyes. The mosquitoes swarmed and bit the hell out of you! Leeches were also another problem. If you went through a marshy or very wet, damp area near water, the leeches would get under your fatigues, and immediately start sucking your blood out. The only way to remove them was to either spray bug juice on them, or to take a lit cigarette butt and hold it close to it, but not touching the leech.

Jungle rot and immersion foot were two of the most common injuries. Immersion foot occurred when your feet stayed constantly wet. Your feet would become raw and it would be impossible to walk. We always tried to carry three or four pairs of extra socks with us.

Jungle rot occurred when you got a scratch or cut (broken skin) and it was not immediately taken care of by the platoon medic. The cut or scratch would become infected, pus up, swell badly, and hurt like hell. Massive doses of Tetracycline had to be given by the medic in addition to cleaning the infected area at least two times a day.

Malaria was another health hazard. Two pills had to be taken faithfully or else malaria would be contracted. It was the medic's job to issue and insure that you took a "horse" pill once a week and a little white pill daily, or vice versa. Once you contracted malaria, you would never get rid of it as long as you existed, or that's what we were told.

Individual self-health care was extremely important to each person while out in the jungle. We normally didn't shave for the full time out in the bush; brushed our teeth probably once a day, provided we had enough water, and washed only when we were near water (streams and pools). Occasionally, if we were near a stream, we would take turns bathing as long as security was posted in all directions.

Water supply was critical, as I mentioned before, and I remember we ran out of water on one operation. The jungle was too thick to be resupplied by chopper, so we sent out a patrol that had to go about 2000 meters to find water. This was especially scary since there were only five of us on patrol and 2000 meters was much too far to be away from the rest of the platoon. But we really needed the water. We eventually found a stagnant puddle of water that had more scum in it than good water. We carried iodine purification tablets that killed anything in the water, but also killed the taste. It was horrible! But it did purify the water.

Resupply. We normally got resupplied by chopper about every five days or so. Resupply would consist of food, water, clothing, sometimes mail, ammo, sundries (cigarettes, candy, toilet items) and equipment if needed. To be resupplied, we had to find a clearing in the jungle big enough for the chopper to set down, or big enough so the supplies could be kicked out of the chopper and not get caught in the triple canopy. We only lost a resupply once when the chopper kicked it out in the wrong location and we couldn't find it because the jungle was so thick.

Food was an interesting experience. We were issued LRRPs or C-rations. LRRPs were the favorite—dehydrated meals such as rice and beef, chicken and rice, pork and potatoes (they called this "pork and nasties"—the potatoes were horrible). You just had to add boiling water to the dehydrated meals and voila! a home cooked meal. The guys used to carry bottles of hot sauce and steak sauce as additives. Occasionally someone would have an onion or some extra additive where two or three guys would share and make a unique meal. My wife-to-be used to send me kielbasies and other "delicacies" of which I am still grateful.

The most hated foods in the C-ration (in cans) category were fruit cake, ham, and lima beans, also called ham and "mothers" because they were very difficult to eat. One day on the firebase we had a fruitcake eating contest and the winner eventually got sick after eating only five of them (no liquid was allowed to be drunk during the contest) mainly because the fruitcake had become like cement and the guy couldn't swallow it or spit it out! The Vietnamese, who would scrounge everything they could get their hands on, would not touch the fruitcake!

On one occasion, while taking a break by the riverbank, we had a fish-fry lunch (the fish were obtained by throwing grenades into the river). When the grenades exploded under water, stunned fish floated to the surface, KO'd by the concussion. A new sport was created in RVN—"grenade fishing"!

Occasionally we would get a hot meal while in the jungle (hot meal flown out by chopper). I think this happened about two times in seven months. The rear was different—hot meals three times a day.

Mail. We received mail maybe once or twice per fifteen-day period in the bush, depending on what tactical situation we were in and also depending on the enemy contact situation. Everyone normally found time to write home. Sometimes it might only be a few sentences a day before it got dark; mostly it took a few days to write one complete letter, especially if you were in a "hot" area (enemy!). I had forgotten to write, or was too busy to write, for about twenty days and my family at home got nervous that they hadn't received any mail. It wound up that the battalion chaplain had to visit me and ask me why I was not writing home; my folks had thought the worst!

Religious Services. Approximately one time a month, the battalion chaplain would visit the bush and hold religious services. During the resupply operation, he would fly in with the initial resupply chopper (bird), hold services while we exchanged supplies etc., and get on the chopper that came in to extract the (old clothes) supplies to be returned.

The Enemy. Two Types. 1) VC (Viet Cong) guerrillas from South Vietnam fighting for the North's cause. They were poorly equipped, poorly trained farmers and local citizens by day; fighters by night. Men, women and children of all ages made up the VC infrastructure. The biggest advantage the VC had was that they knew the land, the local populace, and got military intelligence very easily. They dressed in any outfits that they could get their hands on; usually black pajamas or some sort of fatigue outfit. They were equipped with a variety of weapons, from the most antiquated, to the most modern. The VC used to "booby trap" any item that a "curious" U.S. troop would handle or touch; once moved, the booby-trapped items would explode, causing casualties. They (the VC) normally did not have any numerical strength or firepower to compete with the U.S. firepower. The VC relied on ambushes and terrorist acts to offset their weaknesses. They normally moved freely during the night. ("The night belonged to the VC," was a saying in the RVN.) We did not fear the VC as much as the NVA. 2) NVA: Well equipped, trained and organized, like the U.S. troops. Trained in both conventional and guerilla warfare; excellent jungle warriors. Most of our (my platoon's) enemy contacts (fights) came against the VC. The only time we fought the NVA occurred while we were patrolling near the Cambodian border. During early 1971, the NVA was nowhere to be found in MR III except near the Cambodian border.

Combat. It's hard to believe, but only ten percent of all (U.S.) troops in RVN were combat troops; the balance were support troops in one form or another. At the height of the troop build-up there were 50,000 direct combat troops, 500,000 support troops.

My first taste of combat happened on the first firebase that I was choppered out to. There was an enemy contact just outside the firebase perimeter with four enemy killed and no U.S. casualties. The bodies of the dead soldiers were brought onto the firebase and I remember the only feelings I had when I viewed the bodies were those of curiosity. These were the first dead people that I had seen other than at a wake, and it didn't bother me at the time.

Enemy contacts with my platoon were few and far between, I guess because of the timeframe of the war. We constantly searched for the enemy, but in seven months we only had about ten contacts.

Combat is a "funny" thing. You have a fear of the unknown, but that fear instantaneously disappears with the first sound of gunfire, explosions, etc. Adrenaline fills up inside of you and you act instinctively to the situation. Things happen very, very quickly, yet seem to take much longer than they really do. Example: a firefight might last anywhere from one to five minutes, but seems like half an hour. After the combat situation has been completed, a natural "high" sets in, and everyone has a really good feeling about themselves and their actions (if done properly). That high normally lasts a couple of days and makes men more conscientious of their discipline in patrolling, etc. Once that high wears off, and no contact occurs for a while, the men tend to get lax and bored, performing the same type of search missions daily.

The first contact with the enemy by my platoon happened on Christmas Eve; a one-day "truce" was supposed to be in effect at that time. How can you have a one-day truce in the middle of a war? Anyway, our platoon was coming down a small road toward a village at about 6 p.m., to link up with the rest of the company. As we came to a bend in the road, we were ambushed as we made the turn. It was a small ambush, probably only five to ten enemy, but as is the purpose of an ambush (and during a truce no less), they caught us by surprise.

Rifle fire and grenades were being exchanged between the VC and us, but we couldn't see them. In the middle of a firefight, a truck comes down the road behind us with two Vietnamese in it. We had no way of telling if they were enemy or not. We stopped them in the road, and guarded them under the truck.

Funny things happen in combat situations. In the middle of calling supporting artillery fire, I burst out laughing because these two Vietnamese under the truck were talking to each other almost faster than is physically possible. They must have been so nervous with the artillery exploding near their truck, that they spoke a mile a minute.

A gunship helicopter came on station overhead, and we had to mark our platoon's position by popping a yellow smoke grenade. The yellow smoke identified our position, and allowed the gunship to fire just on the outskirts of our position. The yellow must have disturbed some beehives, because our platoon was suddenly attacked by frenzied bees.

The final results of this strange contact were: two to three enemy KIA (killed in action), two Vietnamese held for interrogation, one U.S. WIA (grenade wound to wrist), and one U.S. med-evaced. A med-evac was a helicopter whose sole purpose was to take wounded men out of the field and quickly to rear aid stations. The one U.S. med-evac was a guy nicknamed "Mother," who was allergic to bee stings and got stung at least ten times on his face and arms. Mother survived and returned to the platoon later, but don't mention the word "bee" around him. All of this happened during a truce!

Most of the other contacts were similar, lasting only a short time, and normally from an enemy that became quickly invisible. The only time I felt any emotion toward the dead enemy was during our last contact. In going through the belongings of the dead VC, we found a picture of what must have been his wife or girlfriend. For some reason, that moment has stayed with me over the years—how this girl would never see this man again!

Patrolling also uncovered many, many interesting situations. Our platoon once came into a recently occupied enemy bunker complex. (A bunker was a fighting position.) The bunker complex was on the outskirts of a "mini-city" in the middle of triple-canopy jungle. The enemy must have built thirty different buildings from bamboo and other materials. These buildings were all raised above ground level on bamboo stilts, and varied in size from garage-size to twenty-by-fifty feet. This city must have been a base camp for the enemy that was still active. Kitchens, classrooms, sleeping quarters, hospital beds, etc., were all in this complex. It was amazing to behold! All this complex hidden from the air (sky) because of the denseness of the triple canopy.

This complex was destroyed the following day by U.S. Air Force planes, as our platoon sat on the other side of the hill bordering this complex. Every time a big bomb exploded, the ground would shake, which led me to think, "How can the enemy survive against all the U.S. firepower?" I guess he survived pretty well in the long run.

Firebases. A firebase was a forward supporting area and the headquarters of the combat battalion. The firebase was generally out in the middle of the jungle and would serve as the nucleus of the operations. A firebase would be created by . . . a 10-15,000-pound bomb called a "daisy cutter" being dropped from a plane and detonated at jungle level. This explosion would normally generate a hole only big enough for a chopper to deposit a bulldozer in that hole. A platoon would be inserted in that hole, first to secure the area. The bulldozer operator would then be inserted and would clear a larger area so more equipment and men could come in. Eventually, the firebase would become a mini-city, large enough for an infantry platoon, artillery detachment, HQ group, and supporting units to call "home."

We lost our first company commander on a firebase that was under construction. Bangalore torpedoes (long tubes of explosives) were used to clear the vegetation back from the cleared center. They cause huge explosions to do this. When the engineers are about to detonate the bangalores, they announce to the troops what they are about to do. Normally everyone takes cover, but in this particular instance, our CO decided to photograph the explosion. Captain Chilcote was standing in the middle of the firebase with a camera focused on the area to be cleared. The torpedoes were detonated, and the vegetation to be cleared now was "lifted" from its original spot and blown in the direction of the CO. It must have been one helluva sight in that camera sight, watching all this blown up bamboo, etc., being propelled toward the camera. The CO turned away at the last second and was struck by bamboo shrapnel. The shrapnel pierced his back and punctured one of his lungs. He fell to the ground in pain, but no one came to his aid, because the troops hated him. He was a "lifer," a strict disciplinarian, but too strict for his own good. Even I disliked the man, but I was the only one to minister to him while he was down. Even though I despised him, I felt that someone should help him until the medic arrived.

Firebase duty was a welcome respite after fifteen days in the jungle. It meant hot meals, cold showers, no humping in the heat (patrolling or searching with full gear) and in general, a more relaxed time. Depending on how far along the construction of the firebase had progressed, the amount of work to be done hinged upon the stage of construction. Thousands of sandbags had to be filled by hand to cover and protect all of the different bunkers established. Filling sandbags for ten hours and stacking them on bunkers was the most boring, physically demanding job performed during the construction of a new firebase.

If the firebase was fully completed, the five days would be spent resting, training, resupplying and acting as a ready reactionary force if some emergency arose.

Donut Dollies (American women; paid volunteers) occasionally visited firebases to raise morale by playing games, or just talking with our men. These Donut Dollies raised morale immensely just by their presence. I thought it took tremendous courage for them to apply for this job, for I felt the horrible conditions far outweighed the rewards. The girls seemed down to earth with the guys, but were never around long enough to get involved with anyone. Out of the seven months in the bush, Donut Dollies entertained my men once, and that happened while we were providing security for a base near Cambodia.

Firebases normally housed six artillery pieces, either 105s or 155s (size designation). Fire missions (a call for artillery supporting fire) were performed frequently and without notice to the infantry platoons on the bases. On one afternoon, I was walking past a 155 howitzer when it fired without warning. The sudden, tremendous, explosive sound and vibration almost left me headless and left me without hearing for about half an hour. Think of the loudest sound that you have ever heard, and quadruple it. That's the sound of a 155 howitzer fired ten feet from your ear. A 155 howitzer would fire a twenty-pound explosive projectile about ten miles.

One memory that is lasting of a firebase was the beauty of Vietnam. FSB Nace or Timbuktu (?) located in Northern MR III, was situated on top of a mountain bordering MR II. At sunset, the view was unhindered and spectacular. Green, hilly mountains on one side of the FSB, and valleys intermingled with rolling green-carpeted hills laced the other side of the FSB. Within a war, a deep feeling of serenity overcame me with this spectacular scenery.

When FSBs were evacuated (normally three to four weeks duration), the firebase was stripped back to barren earth, thanks to the efforts of the last security infantry platoon. A common tactic after the evacuation, was to leave a small residual force at the base after the last helicopter had lifted off. This residual force would "ambush" the enemy when they came to investigate and confiscate any remaining items on the FSB. Numerous enemy were killed during these ambushes. It's funny. The enemy always knew where you were, but chose their times and places for contact. Sometimes they were as foolish as some of our leaders!

Med-evac. Helicopters used exclusively for transporting of the wounded, dying and KIA from the contact site to the nearest aid station. These choppers probably saved the lives of ninety percent of the seriously wounded in the jungle! The med-evac chopper pilots were fearless. They flew unarmed helicopters that had the Red Cross sign painted on them. This sign did not deter the enemy from firing upon these choppers. I would venture to say that these pilots were probably the bravest of all the combat troops in RVN, as they constantly disregarded their own safety to pick up a man that needed immediate attention at an aid station. These pilots flew by day or night, depending on when the call came for their services.

The following people were med-evaced from my platoon for the following reasons: 1) Sgt. Dave Thompson—grenade wound (wrist); 2) Mother—allergic to bee stings; 3) Slade—had to be "circumcised" (too much pain!); 4) Skin Thompson—shot through the right thigh!; 5) ? (can't remember)—machete wound in the top of his head (hit himself with a "gook machete"); 6) Mike Kovacs—heat exhaustion or drug overdose.

All survived, to my ecstasy?! I am very proud of one fact. Not one of my men ever perished. They all came back alive, of which I am truly grateful!

Ho Chi Minh Trail. The trail was a term used to describe a network of roads or trails that stretched from North Vietnam through Laos and Cambodia, and into all portions of South Vietnam. The "trail" was constructed and maintained by the North Vietnamese civilians, and protected by the NVA. The trail was the main supply route for the NVA to filter its men and supplies down to South Vietnam. Sometimes it took the NVA two months to travel from North Vietnam to their destination in the south.

Our platoon encountered this trail once after a firefight near the Cambodian border. After this contact, we pursued the enemy into Cambodia. At the time, U.S. troops were prohibited from entering Cambodia. But with this "hot" pursuit, border limits were forgotten. Actually there were no posted signs for border limits; the jungle was the same on both sides; but based on my calculations we were in Cambodia.

In the middle of dense jungle, a huge road wide enough for a big truck was at our front. This road was hidden from the sky by the triple canopy, and had signs of heavy usage. We patrolled the road for a short time and went further over the border. The further we got, the more signs we found that the enemy was getting closer, and the more nervous we became. Nervous because the trail showed signs of heavy use by a force much larger than ours, and everyone knew it. We got a call from our CO on the radio to return back to an area about half a day's "hump" away, to link up with the rest of the company for some unknown reason. We reported that we had an "active" area of enemy troops to our front, but the orders were "loud and clear," return and link up for extraction.

"Lam Sam 719" was in effect, the South Vietnamese Army invading Laos, and we had to take their place in South Vietnam as a security force. As it turned out, the ARVNs (South Vietnamese Army) got its ass kicked in Laos, and should have stayed home to provide the security for the south, and let the U.S. do the heavy fighting (even though the American sentiment showed that we should get out of RVN).

The ARVN soldiers that I had the opportunity to work with were less than satisfactory. Their noise discipline in the jungle was nonexistent, and they were poor fighters. It was my opinion that they were out on a large "camping" trip, and didn't know the first thing about being in combat.

Combat assaults. One of the most exciting things we experienced were CAs! (combat assaults by helicopter). If you participated in twenty-five combat assaults, you got an air medal!

A combat assault occurred when the platoon, in groups of five or so, was taken by helicopters either from the FSB to a landing zone in the jungle, or vice versa. These landing zones in the jungle would either be "hot"—the incoming choppers would be fired upon by the enemy, or "cold"—no enemy presence.

These combat assaults were exciting for two reasons. 1) Four of the five members of the platoon sat on the edge of the exit with feet dangling in the open air. The weight of the rucksacks held you in. Normally, just prior to the landing, the choppers would "bank" (turn sharply to left or right on a severe downward angle and "drop" to the LZ). This maneuver reminded me of a roller coaster ride where your stomach would rise to the top of your throat during the first big hill descent. 2) The anxiety and uncertainty of what type of LZ (hot or cold), and what unknown was to be encountered on the jungle floor would keep the platoon members silent during the CA. I guess this was also a time for some soul searching, which many a grunt did during these CAs. Heartbeats increased dramatically for all involved!

Helicopters also bring to mind one instance where we captured three "suspected" VC in the jungle. Once captured, a helicopter was called in to extract the suspects and deliver them to the intelligence sector for interrogation. The suspects "refused" to board the chopper and only after some physical effort did they board. The reason for their refusal we feel stemmed from the "rumor" that some prisoners were interrogated while on the chopper and airborne. Supposedly, a suspect was pushed out of the chopper if he refused to talk, and this example caused the other suspects to recite their innermost secrets!

So much for my bush duty, unless I recall something later. My gung-ho attitude diminished as the duration of my tour lessened, but that was due to many, many factors. Before I explain these factors, here's a brief background of my upbringing. My dad had served in the Army during World War II, and I was very proud of him and his accomplishments. My three brothers and I were raised to believe that America was the greatest nation, and that when your country called, you would respond without question. I guess this philosophy held true for the majority of those who served in RVN, although now I respect both the pros and cons about the war.

I guess the first factor that started my doubts about the war were the rules of engagement. To the best of my memory they were: A) Free fire zones—anyone and anything in this area could be fired upon without question. B) Limited fire zones—only clearly distinguishable enemy could be fired upon. Anyone (enemy) questionable would have to be clearly identified before contact could be made. I had a problem with this, as I felt my platoon was at an unfair disadvantage if we had to identify prior to contact. Those few seconds lost in combat normally meant death. The enemy (men, women and children of all ages) was unidentifiable in numerous cases, and reasonable doubt could sometimes result in friendly casualties or civilian casualties. How the hell do you fight a war under these circumstances? C) No fire zones—under any conditions there cannot be contact unless fired upon by the enemy. Therefore, do we let the enemy fire first and then retaliate? I had trouble explaining these rules of engagement to my troops, who thought war was war, in all dangerous situations, regardless of the circumstances!

The unwillingness or the ignorance on the part of the ARVN soldier to fight the war. As mentioned previously, the ARVN I had experience to patrol with were less than satisfactory. It may have been an isolated incident, but in my conversations with other infantry platoon leaders the general consensus echoed my initial feelings.

"Kit Carson" scouts were "Chieu Hoi's" (Northern Vietnamese or Viet Cong) that gave up or surrendered, went through retraining, and were assigned to U.S. infantry units as scouts or trackers. I refused to have one in my platoon, as I just couldn't accept the fact that the Kit Carsons were loyal to the RVN cause or to the U.S. troops.

During our jungle operations, the second platoon of D Co. 1st Bn. 12th Cav uncovered a rice "cache" (a rice "cache" was a storage location of considerable quantity) in our AO (Area of operations). These fifty and one-hundred-pound bags of rice exported from the U.S. to supply the South Vietnamese civilians were found in a VC complex. The newfound bags of rice were tagged and dated by the second platoon, and removed from the cache sight by chopper. These bags (a couple of tons) were delivered to the local government for distribution to its hungry populace. No less than two weeks later, while on patrol, another VC cache was discovered, and the same bags of rice were found with the ID tags of two weeks prior. What the hell was going on? How could the same rice bags surface out in the jungle in less than two weeks time? How do you justify this?

The general consensus was that the majority of the South Vietnamese were farmers of some sort, and didn't care whose rule dominated them as long as they could live in peace. My troops and I truly believed this.

The city population was different, though, because these people appeared to take advantage of the capitalistic advantages of free enterprise and the black market, though it appeared that they were not willing to fight for it.

Drugs. Drugs were readily available on the FSB or in the rear. An article in the "Stars and Stripes" (the military newspaper in RVN) stated that some absurd number, approximately eighty percent of troops in RVN, had taken drugs at one time or another. My own experience estimated that approximately twenty to thirty percent used drugs at one time or another. But this number is only in retrospect. While in the bush it was an unwritten law that no one would use drugs of any sort, or alcohol. The only time this may have been violated in my platoon was the "Mike Kovacs Incident." He started moaning and screaming one night uncontrollably and had to be med-evaced.

I would say marijuana use rivaled beer drinking both on the FSB and in the rear. "Juicers" (beer drinkers) drank openly while "Heads" (pot users) did it privately. At times the heads would do it publicly, but if caught, they would be punished appropriately.

Drugs were cheap because of the old supply and demand equation.

Even though a private's pay was minimal, it was tax free and additional percs (combat pay, etc.) afforded all the enlisted people an opportunity to purchase the drugs they desired.

It was extremely difficult to justify drunkenness vs. a "high from drugs" because they both left a person in a state less-than-ready for a combat situation, even though all the troops from both sides argued to the contrary!

I never condoned drug use and never will, unless it is legalized in my lifetime.

Racism. It is sad to say, but racism exists everywhere, including the Army, which was supposedly racism free! Combat and life in the jungle (jungle warfare) erased all traces of racism. Ethnic backgrounds, color, language, differences, etc. were all forgotten in the bush, because each man depended on the other for survival. On the firebases, things were a bit different. Normal camaraderie in the bush wasn't the same on the firebases. I noticed that the groups of guys that normally associated with each other in the jungle tended to "hang out" with different people on the firebases and in the rear. These groups weren't totally segregated by race, but leaned in that direction.

The rear area was the place where total segregation seemed to take place. In the enlisted ranks, this segregation seemed most prevalent. As rank increased, segregation by race seemed to diminish.

Blacks were famous for their "dap." The dap was a special greeting given by one black to another in the form of a three- to twelve-part handshake. This ritual was extremely interesting to witness. It would start off with something like a "high five" followed by a series of slaps, taps, touches with palms and backhands in "cadence" (almost done to a rhythmical beat). This whole greeting would last anywhere from three to thirty seconds depending on the complexity of the routine. The dap was always performed on the firebase or in the rear, but never in the bush!

I remember one incident vividly in the rear where violence erupted when five blacks cut in a chow line by using the "dap" as an entry excuse. The white and Hispanic guys who had been waiting in the line for approximately fifteen minutes behind them didn't appreciate the blacks breaking into the line in front of them, and a fist fight ensued.

One other racism incident stands out in my memory. In the rear, basketball games were played after dinner meals. One night after dinner, a game between a black team and a white team was in progress when a questionable call was made in the game. An argument followed and a black GI unexpectedly hit a white guy, breaking the white guy's jaw. Doug, the victim, was due to leave RVN in five days, but instead, spent the next two weeks in the hospital with a wired jaw. The sad part of the story was that Doug was supposed to get married two days after returning to the States. Doug got in the black guy's face (confronted the black guy up close, face to face) and the rest was history. Both men worked for me, were intelligent and caring, yet this had to happen. Why? I'll never know!

I still was not disillusioned with the war, but with the policy makers and upper echelon military commanders, who were leading it. A good example of this occurred in the following manner:

Our company received orders to pull out of the jungle operation and be transported by chopper to a rear area, to provide security for that area. Our platoon was extracted from the jungle to the firebase about midmorning. My orders were to be the lead person of the company, fly by chopper to the rear area, and coordinate everything necessary for our company to accomplish its mission. I did this and had about one hour to kill before the arrival of the company. Not knowing anyone or anywhere to go, I stopped at the officer's club for a few beers. Having just arrived from a seventeen-day stint in the jungle, my appearance left a lot to be desired in the terms of rear military dress codes. I wore no rank insignia (because no rank was worn in the jungle). I had to explain to the "O" Club bartender who I was and why I was dressed like I was. After the explanation, he understood and served me a beer. Halfway through my first beer a "REMF" (rear echelon mother f——r) colonel came in and immediately questioned my appearance and reason for being in the "O" Club—really none of his business. If I remember correctly, he said, quote, "I was a disgrace to the officers corps and the Army," and that I should leave the "O" Club immediately. My response went something like this: "With all due respect to your rank, Sir, I just arrived from a seventeen day jungle operation, am a first-lieutenant infantry platoon leader with the 1st Cav., and I intend on finishing this beer. If you have a problem with that, please take it up with my battalion commander, Guy Gunsmoke Meloy!" Colonel Meloy got his nickname, Gunsmoke, partially from his reputation as a tough leader who had both military and political ties, but also from loving his grunts more than anything in the world. I found out about two days later that "Gunsmoke" found out about the incident in the "O" Club and personally flew in from the firebase to confront his REMF colonel, who was harassing his grunt platoon leader (me). Rumor had it that the REMF colonel learned firsthand the meaning of the nickname "Gunsmoke." Thank you, Colonel Meloy (Colonel Meloy eventually retired from the Army as a three-star general.)

The sad part of the above story was that our company was to provide security for this harassing colonel's men, and that would become very difficult to do based on the fact that this "ingrate" chose to belittle his protector!

Paranoia. Paranoia, or being paranoid, started to set in toward the last part of one's tour; usually starting at about ninety days before DEROS (Date Estimated Return Overseas) and becoming more intense as the tour got closer to ending. Paranoia would cause different people to act in very strange "abnormal" ways.

Topics of conversations were one visible way of noticing paranoia. While most grunts talked about what they were going to do back in The World (USA), the paranoid GI would focus on how many tour days left ... did anyone think there would be a firefight soon? Was the AO safe or questionable? Had his luck run out? Etc. These questions always earmarked the first sign of paranoia.

My only confrontation with "acute" paranoia occurred while I was battalion adjutant and had about one and a half months to go on my tour. A vacancy for Echo Recon Platoon Leader had just come about, and the job could have been mine if I requested it. Echo Recon was a platoon whose members were the cream of the crop from the battalion. This Echo Platoon would be inserted into the hottest areas of the jungle, where enemy contact could be expected immediately. The Recon was short for reconnaissance—normally observing for enemy activity, usually looking for an enemy force much larger than Echo Plt. itself! Anyway, I thought long and hard about taking the job, and was on the brink of requesting it, when I decided at the last minute that the chances of survival were a lot less than being a battalion adjutant, stationed for the most part in the rear area. I chalk that decision up to paranoia, worrying that I might not survive that duty vs. volunteering for a job that, deep down, I really wanted.

I requested to witness a combat assault by my former platoon into the jungle about one week prior to DEROS, which was totally out of the ordinary for most "short-timers." With very few tour days left, most people would opt to remain in the rear to bide their time until DEROS date. For some crazy reason, I had to observe a combat assault from the C&C Chopper (Command and Control), the battalion commander's chopper, just prior to my DEROS date. Curiosity or stupidity overcame paranoia in that instance. "Once a Pollock, always a Pollock!" The combat assault went off without a hitch, and I thoroughly enjoyed it. Colonel Meloy bumped a major off the chopper so I would be able to ride and observe. Thanks again, Colonel Meloy!

Other troops experiencing paranoia sometimes did things in one specific way, day in and day out, which they thought would help them return to The World safely. From their waking moments to their going to sleep, the daily actions and conversations of these people would be like watching a video. The same characters would routinely do the same "strange" things as a superstitious reaction to get them home (USA) safely.

My rear duty mainly consisted of the running of the administrative function of the battalion. All paperwork in the Army had to be done in at least triplicate, and I would wager that half of our own forests were converted into government-issue paper for most of this needless paperwork!

During my rear tour I was reading *Catch 22*, a novel about a fictitious Army outfit that functioned haphazardly amidst the structured triplicate-form Army of that time! This novel greatly influenced my way of thinking and my philosophy about the current rear Army. Once a grunt, always a grunt, even though I was now assigned to the rear in a staff position.

Approximately one month prior to my DEROS, a division colonel visited the battalion rear area to discuss "our" drug problem. I told him that the 1st Bn. 12th Cav. rear had no drug problem. That statement unleashed a "tiger!" (But not from my tank!) This "tiger" inquired, "How could you not have a drug problem, with 'studies' showing that sixty percent of the U.S. Army in RVN is using drugs?!" That was a tough question to answer.

The truth of the matter was, and exactly as I told this colonel, "The battalion rear area was hand-picked by the officers of each company. Each rear job for the enlisted person was a reward given to only the top five percent of that company. It was my estimate that less than two percent of this battalion's rear engaged in drug use." The main problem of drug abuse came from the transient people stationed in the rear for very short periods of time. The main drug abuse problems came from these people.

Within a very short period of time, the brigade sent an inspection team to our rear to investigate our current drug abuse problem! The results indicated that the 1st Bn. 12th Cav. rear was no different than any other equivalent unit, but that an effective program needed to be implemented in all of RVN! No new drug program was instituted while I was in the rear, but there was one initiated while I was in the bush.

GIs could turn themselves into any office and request to enter the "5-day" drug cold-turkey "clean up." They would go for five days to the rear and dry out, cold turkey, and then return to their units. MACV command issued a directive that all departing GIs had to pass a urine screening test for drugs just prior to departing for The World, or remain in the RVN until clean. Many GIs took advantage of this program, mainly to get clean for their last testing, or used the program as an excuse to go to the rear for five days and be away from the jungle and all it's hazards. I think this program was a sham, and did not address the problem of drug abuse and it's causes. There were no short- or long-term solutions to this problem. It's as if the Army hoped it would go away by itself.

Awards/Medals. In our very first firefight, two guys distinguished themselves in the fight, and I wrote them both up for Bronze Stars. One guy got a Purple Heart from a grenade wound. Awards or medals were a great morale builder for a unit who recently had combat, when given out in a timely fashion by the battalion CO. Just after a firefight, the whole unit normally shared in the proud feeling of the few who received them.

Awards were also comical at times! After taking over the battalion S-1 slot (adjutant), one of my duties was to establish an award ceremony periodically for all the different units in the battalion. At times, this became fairly complicated, because records of awards sometimes were difficult to obtain and keep current. One vivid memory was the first awards ceremony I set up for Alpha Co. on the firebase in III Corp. Fifteen grunts were to receive medals based on the paperwork I received from A Co.

The "feat" of gathering the fifteen correct grunts for an awards ceremony on a firebase at one specific time bordered on magical! After hastily gathering fifteen of A Co.'s grunts, mostly with the same last name of the guys to be awarded, instructions were given to all on the "protocol" of the ceremony about to begin. Colonel Meloy (the awarding officer) was at the time a meticulous leader, and made things happen at the time he wanted them to occur.

My instructions to the "awardees" were to accept any and all medals given at that time, even if their last name or awards did not match the ones that I read aloud during the presentation. As it worked out, half of the guys had received these awards two months ago, but came through very professionally, even though it was like a football instant replay for them.

As your rank increased, the more difficult it became to get valor medals. (This based on my individual tour 1970-71, even though the situation may have been different previous to my tour.) Everyone who served a tour normally got, automatically, certain individual awards. Medals were normally given out at the DEROS station, except for those awarded on the firebases and in the rear (a low percentage).

I received my medals at Oakland, California (out-processing station) and wore them proudly on my last trip home from the Army.

This plane ride home seemed different than most of my other flights in that no one seemed very friendly to me (was it the uniform?). I was anxious to tell people that I had just returned from RVN, but no one asked! Small talk is normally made between two passengers sitting next to each other, but in my case no one really felt like talking. I had so many questions to ask about the last year I missed in the U.S., but chose not to ask.

Our plane had a layover in L.A., which was where I decided to upgrade my ride home to first class (from coach) and enjoy the rest of the trip. I was seated next to a small boy, about nine or ten years old, who asked me quite a few questions about the Army—where I'd been, etc. He was the first person to actually hold an intelligent conversation with me since returning to The World! After talking with this boy for a while, I decided to give him all my medals, both the pin-on ribbon type for the uniform, and the actual ones that I hand-carried. I felt three things at that time: 1) The war was over for me!; 2) Medals didn't really mean anything to me at that time—getting home safely did; 3) Even though the majority of people were against the war, why wouldn't people talk to me?

I guess I always traveled lightly, and this time going home was no different—no baggage, medals—but a lot of questions!

Fifteen years later, while reading a magazine on Nam, I ordered the awards I had given away. Strange, but true, I was happy to receive them again, and I would not give them away this time. I often wonder who I gave the awards to, and what he did with them.

The only other award I distinctly remember was the Legion of Merit award I had written up for Colonel Meloy. This award was the equivalent of writing a thesis on a subject. His whole tour and results of his leadership had to be translated into something spectacular (short of greatness) which fit Gunsmoke to the T! I wrote up the award, and processed it through the proper channels, but was not around to see it come to fruition, as I was shipped home. I understand he was awarded the Legion of Merit in early September 1971, which made me truly proud, both that this deserving individual got his just due, and that my writing had passed the Army qualification for that award. Congrats Gunsmoke and Walt!

Friendships and camaraderies. First arrival to a new unit, especially a grunt platoon, is unique. The "FNG" (F—ing new guy) had no friends and wasn't welcomed by anyone except maybe his squad leaders. The new guys had to prove themselves to their cohorts before being taken into the platoon as "one of the guys." Proving themselves meant: 1) Being able to hump with a full load; and 2) Contribute to the overall good of the platoon instead of being a "tag-along," or conduct themselves like a semiexperienced veteran in a firefight.

Friendships normally occurred when the FNG was taken under the experienced vet's wing, or among the FNG's own squad. These friendships normally extended to the whole platoon as the tour passed by. Race, color, creed, etc., were forgotten in the bush. What actually mattered was the worth of your fellow platoon member in a combat situation and in "survival." Friendships became stronger as the tour progressed.

Constant daily interaction with each other further strengthened relationships among platoon members. Most platoon members had never seen each other prior to Nam, and developed their relationships from their assignments to each infantry unit.

Hometowns and tastes of grunts varied tremendously. City-slickers, farm boys, all classes were put together to form a "cohesive" fighting unit that actually cared for each other while together. At the time, closer friendships couldn't be found, but once one's tour ended, relationships ended abruptly. This was very hard to believe because, during the tour, most grunts talked about what they would do back in The World with their new-found friends. This could either mean planning something permanent (setting up a business together, working together, etc.) or temporary (just a visit). When I said abruptly before, I meant no contact with any former unit members! I think I received a Christmas card for the first two years from a former comrade after returning, but that was the extent of my contact. My three or four close friends (also Viet vets) had about the same contact with former unit members. The exception to the rule was an acquaintance (made after return from RVN) that bought a farm in Ohio with three former unit members. Two of the guys work the farm, while the other two are "silent" partners.

Memories of friends—some former platoon members—are still very vivid and warm, and I would hope someday that I could meet some of them. I doubt that will ever happen, but only the "shadow" knows!

My former roommate in OCS, who I met in RVN for one day, was a member of my wedding party in late 1971, but I haven't seen or heard from him in fifteen years. (I still consider him a close friend.)

Transition from grunt to civilian. After the plane ride home, I was picked up at the airport by my mom and my fiancee, the same two who had dropped me off on my departing trip to RVN. "Things change, people don't" was not true in this case. I thought my mom and my wife-to-be looked better than I had ever seen them look, even though you'd probably get a good argument from both of them on that!

My coming home party was very quiet, unusual for my crowd, who were party people. Unbeknown to me, I think my mom had requested to all my friends that they not ask me anything about RVN! No questions like: What was it like? Did you see combat, etc.!? My crowd thought I was very quiet. I thought they were extremely quiet. I guess party people get more quiet as they get older! My adjustment to The World was relatively easy except for a few incidents:

1. My Mom dropped a pot in the kitchen which made a sudden loud noise. My gut reaction was to hit (to dive) the floor even though I did

not, but they say I gave my mom a searing stare that actually frightened her.

2. While honeymooning in the Poconos, my wife and I followed a trail through the woods to Bushkill Falls. About one-quarter of the way along the trail, I imagined that I was patrolling again in the jungle, but it only lasted for a short time. That short period made me feel extremely uncomfortable, and I just kept it to myself.

For the past five to ten years I have read, heard, and seen stories about the Vietnam veteran not being welcomed home. I guess some of the vets really needed the welcome home. I personally did not want a welcome home from anyone other than my immediate family.

I have heard the statement that America (USA) owes us (The Vets) something. That may be true for some vets, but not for me. I was called, served, and I survived. I feel that America owes me nothing, and that I just did what thousands of other vets did in serving their country's needs.

My views on the war have changed over the period of time since my return home.

In 1975, when the NVA overran the South Vietnam on TV, I had mixed emotions. At the time of the NVA push to capture, free, and assimilate South Vietnam, a force of 100,000 vets was being formed on "paper" to go back to RVN. This 100,000-man force (without USA permission) was trying to hastily organize, and its main mission was to return to RVN and fight the NVA, who had finally come out of hiding (sanctuary) to fight. This 100,000-man force never materialized, much to my chagrin, as I felt really hopeless that the NVA would overrun the southern forces and unite all of RVN to a communistic state! Even though my feelings about the war were mixed, the battle scenes and downfall of South Vietnam on TV really affected me. I did not want the south to lose. After the NVA took over the South Vietnamese Capitol, I felt both disgusted and relieved. The war had formally ended with Saigon's capture, and also put my mind at ease that our struggle was over.

I never felt that we lost the war, even though that "tag" follows the Viet vet forever. I think the U.S. troops did more than their fair share to win, and would have won if strategy was different.

Barbara Liscomb

I hate to say that I liked being in Vietnam, but I did. There was a bonding between human beings there that I've never experienced since I left. We were stripped of all superficiality. I began a long, intricate and complicated journey when I flew to Okinawa in December 1965 to report to duty as a flight nurse. There were many adventures and situations that I believe continue to affect me today. On returning from Vietnam in July 1968, I had a sense of detachment and uncomfortableness that I know many other veterans have experienced. I would like to have gone back for a third tour in 1968, but I was afraid they would think I was "crazy."

For many years since I came back from Vietnam, I have felt totally out of sync at times, as if something is missing from my life. In a war zone, you see the very best and worst in people. Some of the senior ranking nurses I had to work with were the pits. I recall, shortly after the Tet Offensive, I was working in a casualty staging unit on the night shift. I had a young black GI from the South who had lost a leg. He was crying and very anxious during the night. I called the head nurse and the physician for the unit, who were both white Southerners. I told them I thought there was something going on with this young GI and asked them to come and take a look at him. They said they'd see him in the morning and that I was overreacting. The following morning I got chewed out for calling them. The patient was air-evac'd that morning and he died on the plane of a pulmonary embolism. For many years I was angry about this and felt his death could have been prevented. I certainly think I saw and worked with the best medical people except for a few like this.

I've never experienced the intensity and stress in civilian life that I experienced in Nam. My duty as a flight nurse was to take the wounded from Nam to the Philippines, Okinawa and Japan. There was only one flight nurse and two corpsmen in these cargo type (C-130) planes and we never really knew how many patients there would be on any given day. We would leave early in the morning and fly all over Vietnam. On one flight, I lost nine pounds.

Often I felt so alone, like I had to keep these guys alive. When the flights were over, I experienced such a great high. I felt like I had done the right thing. The sad thing was that I never saw the guys again after we dropped them off, so I never knew what happened to them. There was always some unnamed person who stuck in your mind, though.

I returned to the United States after the first tour for a month's leave, but I became very anxious to return to Nam. When I returned I got involved in the Medical Civic Action Program (MEDCAP), running health clinics in the villages. I was convinced that if we went into the villages unarmed, we would be safer and not be ambushed, and it worked.

During this period of time, there were a lot of negative feelings expressed toward me by other nurses because I was an American nurse taking care of Vietnamese people. Some people wouldn't even talk to me and I felt very isolated. The physicians were understanding and kind to me and I made some friends among the Vietnamese people. I had no ethical problems with what I was doing.

I had a difficult time re-entering society after Vietnam. Many veterans were either ignored or demonstrated against. Women veterans were ignored. I came home after two and a half years in Nam and felt totally lost. I remember landing at Logan Airport in uniform, with all my ribbons on, and all I wanted to do was leave and get to the nearest military base. I have some wonderful relatives who met me at the airport, but none of them ever mentioned Vietnam! They were afraid or ashamed. I had no one to talk to, and I went through many years of silence. It wasn't the demonstrators who made me angry, it was the silent majority, who didn't have the courage to take a stance.

After the war, many of the nurses went into hiding and many left nursing altogether. I was determined to remain in the field of nursing. I was trying to adjust back into a society that I was not pleased with and I found nursing in the U.S. weird. Most people I worked with seemed wrapped up in trivia, which was so different than the nurses I worked with in Nam.

In 1983 I got a job with a Veterans Administration Hospital in Montana. It was the worst experience I ever had! It all began when I met a former war correspondent sitting next to me on a plane. He interviewed me and wrote a story for the "Arizona Republic." The governor of Montana read the story and appointed me to the Veteran's Service Board. I was the first woman ever appointed to this board and there were some people who did not want me on the board because I worked at the VA hospital. I wasn't an advocate for the good-ol'-boy network, so they harassed me and gave me a terrible time, until I resigned from the hospital.

I was brought up in Hamilton, Massachusetts, a typical New England, patriotic town. I was a young kid when my father served in Europe in WWII, and my father was a Marine for five years. President Kennedy had a tremendous impact on me and I felt that I better do something for my country. Besides, I always liked to be where the action was and that's why I volunteered to go to Vietnam.

As to whether that patriotism has changed since returning, I have mixed feelings now. I have vacillated a lot through the years. We should have tried to win the war. At times it seemed like our lives were meaningless. All the stuff that's the result of war becomes a part of you. You miss the closeness, the life and death situations. You have to depend on others; you need people. It's difficult to develop those kinds of friends with civilians. It's wonderful to see two vets reunite after twenty-two years apart and it's like it all happened yesterday. It's a bond I'll never forget.

There are many scenes that stand out in my mind when I think of my experiences in Nam. Someday I hope to meet the young man from Massachusetts whom I picked up in Da Nang in 1966, when I flew in to air-evac the wounded. This young man had both legs amputated. Usually we stacked the litters four high and put the guys who lost extremities down low in the plane, so that we can get to them easier. Anyway, this kid was on a litter in the hot sun on the flight line. He had a big grin on his face because he was going home and he said to me, "Please put me up high so I can see what's going on." I don't know his name, but I'll never forget him.

Sammy L. Davis

Sammy Davis was born in Dayton, Ohio on November 1, 1946. Because his father was a construction worker, Sammy traveled around the country with his parents and five brothers and sisters. He lived in several states including California, Texas, Georgia, Illinois, and Indiana. In each of these states, there is a place Sammy calls home.

Sammy's family was living in Martinsville, Indiana in the summer of 1966. Sammy was working that summer in the Illinois oil fields and traveling home on weekends. At the end of the summer, he went back to Indiana and enlisted in the U.S. Army. Just a few months later, he found himself stationed in Vietnam with the 9th Infantry Division, working on a 105mm howitzer gun crew. He volunteered to go on a mission with another gun crew in November of 1967, and there took part in an action that saved three lives and changed his own.

The following is from Sammy's Congressional Medal of Honor Citation: "Sergeant Sammy L. Davis (then Private First Class) distinguished himself during the early morning hours of 18 November 1967 while serving as a cannoneer with Battery C, 2nd Battalion, 4th Artillery, 9th Infantry Division, at a remote fire support base west of Cai Lay, Republic of Vietnam. At approximately 0200 hours, the fire support base came under heavy enemy mortar attack. Simultaneously, an estimated reinforced Viet Cong battalion launched a fierce ground assault upon the fire support base. The attacking enemy drove to within twenty-five meters of the friendly positions. Only a river separated the Viet Cong from the fire support base. Detecting a nearby enemy position, Sergeant Davis seized a machine gun and provided covering fire for his gun crew, as they attempted to bring direct artillery fire on the enemy. Despite his efforts, an enemy recoilless rifle round scored a direct hit upon the artillery piece. The resultant blast hurled the gun crew from their weapon and blew Sergeant Davis into a foxhole. He struggled to his feet and returned to the howitzer which was burning furiously. Ignoring repeated warnings to seek cover, Sergeant Davis rammed a shell into the gun. Disregarding a withering hail of enemy fire directed against his position, he aimed and fired the howitzer which rolled backward, knocking Sergeant Davis violently to the ground. Undaunted, he returned to the weapon to fire again when an enemy mortar round exploded within twenty meters of his position injuring him painfully. Nevertheless, Sergeant Davis loaded the artillery piece, aimed and fired. Again he was knocked down by the recoil. In complete disregard for his own safety, Sergeant Davis loaded and fired three more shells into the enemy. Disregarding his extensive injuries and his inability to swim, Sergeant Davis picked up an air mattress and struck out across the deep river to rescue three wounded comrades on the far side. Upon reaching the three wounded men, he stood upright and fired into the dense vegetation to prevent the Viet Cong from advancing. While the most seriously wounded soldier was helped across the river, Sergeant Davis protected the two remaining casualties until he could pull them across the river to the fire support base. Though suffering from painful wounds, he refused medical attention, joining another howitzer crew which fired at the large Viet Cong force until it broke contact and fled. Sergeant Davis' conspicuous gallantry, extraordinary heroism and intrepidity at the risk of his own life, above and beyond the call of duty, are in keeping with the highest traditions of the military service and reflect great credit upon himself and the United States Army."

After Vietnam, Sammy married Peggy Jo Martin from Flat Rock, Illinois and finished his enlistment with the Army in Fort Hood, Texas. Following the Army, Sammy and Peggy moved to West Salem, Illinois, where he worked for Champion Laboratories for four years and where their daughter was born. In 1974 Sam was hired by Central Illinois Public Service in Hutsonville, Illinois. During the ten years he worked for CIPS, he and his family lived in West Your, Illinois and his two sons were born. In spite of the fact that his health grew worse as each year passed, Sam frequently accepted speaking engagements, talking to audiences about the action for which he received his Medal of Honor and the duties of all Americans toward building a better and stronger America. In 1982 his health had failed to the point that his doctors put him on full disability and he had to leave his job with CIPS.

Sammy feels he has been given this time for a reason and today he travels as many as 2000 miles a week and as far as Australia and New Zealand, speaking to audiences of five to 500,000 about the plight of our living POWs, Agent Orange, veterans' issues, and the importance of patriotism in America. His "Freedom Now" speech, first delivered to the crowd gathered on the Mall in Washington, D.C. for the concert preceding the dedication of The Wall in 1984, is remembered and requested today, has been published in several veterans' publications, and has served as inspiration to many toward the push for our POWs' return. Three other speeches made by Sammy have been entered into the Congressional Record.

His official citation lists his action at Firebase Cudgil in Vietnam as "extraordinary heroism, and intrepidity at the risk of his own life, above and beyond the call of duty." It is evident that Sammy does not believe his "call to duty" ended that night in Vietnam. He says he's not a "fancy talker," but he does speak from the heart and he touches the hearts of those who hear him. His actions today continue to reflect great credit upon himself and the Army, and upon America as well.

The following is Sammy's account of the events leading up to, during and after action for which he earned the Medal of Honor, published for the first time:

November 18, 1967. We were on a big push down the Mekong Delta. The infantry was forming a big horseshoe and our job as the artillery was, as the infantry was pushing, to provide a cover for that closed horseshoe as they ran the NVA ahead of them into artillery fire, which was very effective. The operation was to start at 10 a.m. and we arrived at a good location for our base at about 8 a.m. There was supposed to have been airstrikes and artillery preps before we landed to clear the area. That's customary in landing artillery in the field. We were planning to clear and secure the area. We got there a half hour before everything started, which was not unusual. Since we were there and not receiving any fire, they said go ahead and do your thing. So, we set up and started firing. We fired all day, sporadically. Later that afternoon a helicopter landed and a major got out and said that the possibility of us getting hit that night was pretty good. We put more sandbags around our position and broke out some more ammunition. Then, just before dark, the same major landed again and said the intelligence reports say that you will be hit pretty hard tonight. He still didn't tell us what we now know he knew, that there was a reinforced battalion of NVA in the area. In fact they had set us down in the middle of them. We went ahead and fired missions on into the night and about 10 or 11 o'clock things quieted down a bit. I laid down to rest between two-hour watches.

About 2 o'clock Marvin Hart came and woke me up because he just couldn't stay awake any longer. Could I sit up with him or just take over? I wasn't sleeping good anyway. The skeeters were bad, it was hot and I was dirty and hungry and wet. It was in the Delta and you were always wet there. I got up and got an empty shell canister and lit a sandbag. They were burlap, not the plastic like they are now. You lit it and then snuffed the fire out and let it smoulder and stuck it down in the canister and it made a smudge pot to keep the mosquitoes away and it got hot enough down in there to heat water in an empty C-ration can over it and have some almost hot instant coffee. So I did that and was sitting there and we lit a cigarette and we heard mortars slide down the tube. I asked when they moved mortars into the area and Marv said I don't think they did and then they started falling all around us. They knew exactly where everybody was and were zeroed in on our position. They worked real hard for over half an hour. Usually, if a mortar attack lasted more that two or three minutes, something big was going to happen. So, we knew something was coming and tried to get ourselves ready for it. At 2:30 the mortaring stopped. You could hear a lot of yelling and screaming. I was sitting right up on the river, an off-shoot of the Mekong River. I could reach right out and touch the water. I was looking right out across it and seeing about ten million people running at me from out of the jungle. The riverbank had been cleared out by a previous airstrike in the area. The bombs made sort of a crater and we were sitting around the edge of that. I had an M-60 machine gun in my foxhole and I remember firing it until I either ran out of ammunition or it jammed. Anyway, it wouldn't fire anymore. I threw it in the river because they always told us, don't let the enemy get your weapon. I got my M-16 and fired all the ammunition I had for it there. About that time, our sergeant said, "Let's move, boys!" We jumped up and got on the howitzer. They were getting pretty close, so we could no longer hide in the hole and fight them off. We had to do something. A few of them had reached our side of the bank, but we had picked those guys off and they were trying to swim the river. They were also coming in on our west position. They had reached the perimeter there in a couple of different places. I said, "Let's get them!" We got up and turned the howitzer around to face them directly across the river. We locked and loaded a beehive round. The dart was about the size of a pencil lead and looked like a small arrow made out of spring steel. It was an extremely devastating weapon. We fired a direct fire that had 18,000 darts in it. We could see that it did a lot of good. It cleared out a big swath. It was the first beehive that we had fired under those conditions. We had used it before at the edge of the woods and saw what it could do to the vegetation and a few people, but it was the first time that we had ever fired into a mass of people, and you couldn't believe how it got fifty or sixty people just like that.

I think we got off three rounds from our gun crew of four people. I was the assistant gunner, so I actually fired the cannon. I had my back to the shield. I was trying to hide behind the small shield at the side because they were shooting grenade launchers and other arms. When I fired the third round, they fired an RPG directly at our muzzle blast and it hit the shield that I was hiding behind. The steel was high tensile steel and when it was hit it disintegrated into millions of itty-bitty pieces and it covered my whole right side. I was blood from head to toe. That didn't really hurt me that bad, it just looked terrible. But it also knocked me out and the concussion blew me back into my foxhole. The rest of the guys thought I was dead from the way I looked and since it hit my shield they thought it hit me directly too. They fell back to the next piece. When I woke up I had been lying half in and half out of the foxhole. What woke me up was the gun next to me. Instead of firing to the west as it had been, now it had to turn and protect the position that I had been protecting. They were firing beehives right over me and I caught a bunch of beehive in my backside and, when that hit me, that was the shock that woke me up. I rolled over into my foxhole. I had a flak jacket on but no helmet. I remember the ringing in my ears. It felt like I was lying in red ants and they were biting me. When I brushed my back, there was blood all over my hand and I thought, "Well shit, I've been shot. This tops a perfect day off." So, I tried to figure out what I was gonna do—die or what. Then I felt again and I felt those beehives in my back again. I peeled my flak jacket off and I could see the shiny darts. I picked a lot of the beehive off my legs and stuff, but the flak jacket saved my life. I had a dart in my kidney among other things. By that time I was starting to come around and realized what was going on. I laid there in that foxhole and saw all these tracers going off. They were colored and looked like Christmas. They were really pretty.

I raised up enough to see the river and there were, on the other bank of the river waiting to swim across, hundreds of them swimming across with rifles on their backs, and then some were right there. I surveyed the situation. I didn't have an M-60, or an M-16, and there weren't any big rocks around. I had to do something very very quick. So, I looked at the howitzer which was burning—the tires were burning, the recoil mechanism was blown off. They always told us that you couldn't fire one without a recoil mechanism. But, I didn't have any choice but to try to fire it if I could. I crawled around on the ground and found a canister that hadn't been fired. Usually the powder bags are fastened together and you used the maximum charge of seven bags to fire a beehive. There weren't any bags left there, but I crawled around trying to find grains of powder. It was kind of like hog feed and I scooped it up and filled up this canister. That was a mistake, because when it is in bags, they took up space, so I probably had a Charge 12. I loaded the projectile and then put the canister in. The gun was at an angle because it had been hit and blown back into the edge of a creek. I finally had to pick the gun up and aim it by hand. They say one guy isn't supposed to be able to pick the howitzer up, but I guarantee, if you are scared enough, you can do it. I lined it up on where I thought most of the guys were. I was behind the gun for protection, because when they saw me moving around, they started opening their 50-calibers at me, and when it hit the gun it went *boing* and chunks of metal would fly off.

So, I was lying behind it and I pulled the lanyard and since the powder was wet it kind of burned for a while and then goes bang! The beehive round goes out and does its job. Later, talking to the guys, they said the gun jumped about seven feet in the air and then rolled backward, and rolled on me. It broke my back and ribs and cut me up, but the muddy ground probably saved my life because the gun rolled over me and didn't smash me. But it worked and I thought, "Wow, I cleared out a whole bunch!" I loaded and fired twelve or thirteen more rounds. We had two Chieu Hoi notes. They were pieces of propaganda paper. You fire it and all these little papers fly out. I couldn't find anything more except these damn Chieu Hoi note rounds, so I fired at least three of these, direct fire. The next day when we went out we found these Vietnamese lying there blown to hell with those Chieu Hoi notes. It seemed funny at the time. Anyway, after I fired those notes, I fired the gun until all that was showing out of the water was the muzzle. Finally it was just in pieces from being hit with all the 50-caliber.

About that time I heard someone calling, "Help! Help!" That was a well-known ploy of the NVA, to try to get you to stop firing so they could get closer to you. When I looked closer, I could see a black guy standing about 150 yards back, off on the other side of the river, off in the jungle. When an illumination round popped over him, I could see very distinctly that it was not NVA and I said I've got to do something about this. I was the only one there to do something about it. Because of my physical condition I didn't feel I could swim the river. So, I grabbed an air mattress. It had a hole blown in it, but I puckered up the hole and blew in it and struck out across the river. I only had my trousers on and what was left of my boots. Afterward I learned how funny it looked. When I started across the river they opened up with the 50-calibers again and they just made a tremendous spray and I could hear the thuds, so I thought I would just swim under water but I knew I couldn't let go of that air mattress. Well, I thought all my guys were dead and that I was the only one left, but my guys heard the 50-caliber let loose and they looked and saw this air mattress sticking up and going across this river like hell. They couldn't figure out what it was and didn't know at the time that it was me. So I got to the other side and hid the air mattress in the weeds and stuff at the edge of the jungle.

I started climbing up the bank and got to where I remembered the guy was. The NVA were still running up to get on the bank to swim across and they ran right by me. They were just as scared as I was and it wasn't that light, so most of them didn't recognize me. I did have to pick up a big stick a couple of times and thump them on the heads. You could tell by the look in their eyes—if they knew what I was or not. I just had to be a little bit quicker and wrestled a gun away from them once. I thought there was just one of our guys there, but there were three. One white and two black. Halloway was shot in the back, another one shot in the head and the white guy had a foot shot off. I didn't know what I was going to do. Now I got three guys. So the guy shot in the head was unconscious. I put him over my shoulder and got Halloway kind of under my arm and the other guy kind got hold of him and all four of us staggered along. They all had weapons and I can remember taking Halloway's M-16, and once in a while they'd see us and start coming toward us to bayonet us or whatever and I'd pull out the M-16 and John Wayne them and they'd leave us alone. I was so tired that I knew if I fell down I'd never get up.

Finally we worked our way a little bit at a time over to the edge of the river. I took the guy shot in the head across first and told the other two to stay on the bank and I swam across the river to deposit him on the other bank. When I got there Frank Gage and another kid with blond hair and blue eyes were there. Here I am swimming across the river and by that time I was exhausted and I didn't know if I'd make it or not. I hung on to that air mattress and I'd swim, and then just relax for a second and take off again. I'd just about had it when I came up to get a breath and here was this face right in front of me. I thought, "Oh shit, it's all over." I didn't have the strength to hit him or anything. Then, with the illumination, I could see these big blue eyes. I thought, "Oh wow!" He helped me get him on the bank and I went over and got both guys on the mattress and took them to the other side, close enough that the guys there grabbed the air mattress to pull the two guys in. When they took the air mattress away from me, I just sank to the bottom. I remember it was so cool and so quiet and peaceful. I thought, "It's all over," and then suddenly something hit me and I decided it's not over yet and I pushed with my feet and got up and got a breath and made it over to the bank and crawled up on the bank.

You hoist a couple of poor guys up that had got hit and you try to get the mud out of their mouths and the dirt out of their eyes. It's kind of silly shit, but you've got a buddy lying there that's closer than anybody in the world and you know he's dead, but he's in the mud and you try to wash it out and get him away from the river.

I crawled and found Sergeant Ghant. In training you learned that for a chest wound you used your poncho. "Your poncho" stuck in my mind, so instead of looking around for a poncho I crawled all the way back to where I originally was and got my poncho because the rule says, "Use your poncho." So I went through my duffel bag and got mine and crawled back to Sergeant Ghant and put it on his chest and tied a rope around it and Sergeant Ghant never did say nothing. Me and him didn't get along too good. I respected him as a soldier because he was greatly responsible for us surviving that night and many other days and nights—because he was a good soldier. But as person to person, we didn't care for each other. I think mainly because he was from Detroit and I was from the South. And just our common heritage, you know, black against white, that was a real grind. I can remember after I applied the poncho to his chest, he opened his eyes and he looked at me, all that bullshit that I had ever heard or thought about black versus whites— that all melted. I looked into his soul and he looked into mine and he held up his hand and I just held his hand for a while and we didn't have to talk. I thank God that that happened, because it helped me a lot.

It was almost daylight. By daylight we had run the enemy off. We picked up the rest of our guys. We packed them up, for when grave registration came to pick them up and put them in the little green body bags and everything. Just down from us was a little bamboo bridge— just one stalk of bamboo that they had made a bridge out of, with hand ropes. Then, that's when we found out just how devastating the beehive rounds were. When you would try to pick up one guy, there would be two or three just stuck together because they were running at you and the beehive would just stick them together. If they were carrying a weapon, it was just like it was nailed to them with hundreds of tiny nails.

Reports didn't say there were many killed that night, but I remember there was over 300 in front of my gun that were killed by beehive. These are things that come out hundreds of years later. Then, this helicopter landed and a major got out and was taking pictures. And it pissed me off highly—the same major that was there the day before and said, "Hey, you might get hit tonight." I grabbed a gun and was gonna shoot him . . . and they thought I shouldn't shoot the major. So, I had to go to the bathroom. We just had a little bench with holes in it and that was our latrine. I walked over to where that had been. It had bullet holes all in it and there had been thirty-two of us and there were only eleven of us left. So instead of dealing with what really was, we were saying look at all the bullet holes in our shitter.

We talked about everything except what we really should have talked about. I picked it up and it was full of holes and beehive and I walked in there and said, "I got to shit all night." That's what I said. So, I dropped my trousers and sat down and we had a magazine there and I looked at all the holes in the magazine and Delbert Colson from Beaumont, Texas walked up to me and said, "My God, Davis, look at your leg."

I leaned over to look at my leg and passed out and woke up in a hospital. I spent a few days down at Dong Can and then went to 3rd Field in Saigon for a while. The reason I remember Halloway's name so well is that he was there in 3rd Field hospital. I got kidney infection from being hit in the kidney amongst everything else. They said at the time it lowered my resistance and I got malaria. So there I was lying there with malaria and kidney infection and all shot to hell, so I got real sick and ran an extremely high temperature. I ran in excess of 105 for over a week and it dehydrated me. They'd give me a complete blood transfusion and within twenty-four hours the blood would be like buttermilk. I was so dehydrated that it sapped the moisture right out of it. After running that high temperature for so long, they figured if I even made it, and they didn't think I was going to anyway; that I would be an idiot (which I am!). So they put me out in the hall to open the bed up for someone who would need it. (These things I don't remember, but have been told afterwards.) Halloway, one of the guys that I swam across the river with, was in the hospital.

He told the doctor, "You take blood out this arm and put in that arm."

The doc said, "We can't do that. It's against the rules. You may not be the same blood type, etc. etc."

I don't know what he did or what he said—he may have had a hand grenade or something—but he laid down right beside me in the hallway and put a hose in his arm and into my arm and gave me some blood. Within just a few hours after I got the real blood my fever broke and they decided I was going to live, so they shipped me to Japan. I was in Japan about four days.

Here I have to back track a little. On my birthday, November 1, 1967 we'd been out on an operation and General Westmoreland had been out on one of his famous, just-flying-inspections, and we were firing. We couldn't quit firing all at once, so when he came up to our gun, we would quit and then, when he went on, we'd start up and the next one would quit. He'd go down the line and ask if we were getting letters from home, were we getting the services of a priest or rabbi or chaplain, or what our requirements were, and of course you knew what to say. "Yes, Sir!" So he got to me and I remember how big he was. He said in a real kind voice, "Are you getting letters from home," and I said "Yes, Sir. Got 'em right here in my pocket."

Then, "How's the chow?" and, "Great, Sir." Then he looked down at my feet, and because it was always so wet down there, you looked like a prune from your knees down. The leather rotted real easily and my feet were just hanging out the sides of my boots and he said, "Son. Is that the only pair of boots you have?" and I said, "Yes, Sir." He turned around to say something to my captain, who had a brand new pair of boots on that didn't even have mud on them. He said, "Son, what size boots you wear?" I said, "Nine W, Sir." "Captain, what size boots are those?" he asked. Captain said, "Nine W." So the general said, "Take those boots off and give them to this boy." So the captain sat right down in the mud hole, and that boy sat down right beside him and put his brand new boots on. So that's how I got to know General Westmoreland.

Back to the hospital in Japan. I was there about four days—not very long. I regained my vitality very quickly. When you are nineteen you bounce back fast. They were going to send me back home. I just felt a real need to be with those eleven men. It was like part of me had been taken away and if they took away the rest of those guys, I wouldn't want to make it. I didn't know what to do and evidently I must have thrown a real shit fit. The colonel of the hospital let me call General Westmoreland in Saigon and I don't really remember what I did or said, but I do remember talking with him. I told him about how I felt and I related the boot story to him.

He said, "Oh, yes. I remember you. How are you doing?" I said I was in the hospital and they wanted to send me home, but I didn't want to go home, I wanted to go back to my guys. What I do know is at that time, right there, the citation for the Medal of Honor was on his desk, and he had just read it and put it down when the phone rang. And in talking to him years later he said, "Son, if you had asked for the world I'd of gave it to ya." I didn't want the world, I just wanted to go back to my guys. The general said as soon as you can walk you can go back to your unit. I said, I want to go back to Vietnam today. And he said, I don't think you can do that. I said I really want to go back today.

The next day I thought that I was going back to Vietnam. He made a deal with the colonel that as soon as I could walk, I could go back to my unit. What I had to do was go down from the third floor where I was, walk down the stairs to the arms room, clean an M-16 and walk up and report to the colonel and walk back upstairs. When I could do that three days in a row, I could go back to my outfit. They didn't figure that I was going to do it too quickly. Well, I was there just a few days—a week or so.

Halloway was a real eager beaver. He wasn't that little, but he was considerably smaller than me. He would pack me down the stairs piggyback, and take me to the arms room, where I would clean the M-16, and then pack me right up to the big glass window. I was all bandaged and patched up and on crutches and everything. When he let me down on the floor, God it just hurt so bad. I'd straighten up real tall and walk in to that orderly room. "Private Davis reporting, Sir." "All right, Private Davis." I'd turn around and back and I'm sure that the minute I got out of his view I just folded. Halloway would carry me back upstairs and put me to bed. I can remember waking up at night and Halloway would be there. I did that three days in a row and I had a note from General Westmoreland that when I walked three days in a row, I could go back to my unit and I went back to my unit.

They took me back to Can Tru. Where the helicopters landed it was probably about an eighth of a mile, or maybe less, to where the artillery battery was. I was still all bandaged up and on crutches. My right leg was tied up because of muscle damage, so I couldn't even use it. It was real dusty and hotter than heck. I remember seeing the dust fly as I put my foot down. I would look up and see how far I had to go yet and it seemed just as far as when I started, or so it seemed. Well, since I had been gone in hospital, we had gotten a bunch of new guys in and as it usually goes, there are a lot of war stories told. They had made Sammy Davis into a larger-than-life type person. You know, nine feet tall and had machine guns hanging off me everywhere. All these new guys that had heard my name—they didn't think I would ever make it back. Most of them didn't know if I ever lived or not at that time, and here I come plopping down the road. Everybody standing around—they couldn't believe it—all these new guys. Then I saw one of my buddies and he ran over to me and we started hugging each other. Then there was a lot of screaming and hollering and all the rest of the guys came over and picked me up and carried me in, and they made me a cook. That's how you become a cook in the Army!

John Fields

I did, literally, go into the Marine Corps with a flourish and a shout. The "Angeleno Platoon." We were all from the immediate Los Angeles area. The swearing in took place on the lawns at City Hall, complete with marching bands and speeches and politicians and media on hand. All our families were really proud. After the ceremony we had about ten minutes to say good-bye to our families and then board the buses bound for Marine Corps Recruit Depot, San Diego. While hugging my girlfriend (who dumped me while I was in Vietnam) and my mother (who did not), a reporter for the "Los Angeles Times" took our picture, which appeared on the front page of the next morning's paper. A flourish and a shout. What a send off.

Yellow footprints. Marine Corps Recruit Depot. February 1964. Reality changed forever. My reality.

I landed at Qui Nhon July 1965, and my world started turning upside-down. It had been a long boat ride over, lots of time to think. How clear I remember standing on the deck at night and looking out over absolutely vast blackness, with no real point of reference, wondering "what will be happening . . . whether I will live, get blown into bits and pieces or be able to perform as I need to" and remembering when I first told my mother that I was joining the Marine Corps. Once she could breathe again, she said, "Do you have any idea what you are getting yourself into?" With the self-assuredness of an eighteen-year-old, I believed I did. Out there on the ship, I realized I had no concept.

Landing at Qui Nhon, with thoughts of our training, and having no concept of what was going to happen, I pictured landing in full assault—Iwo Jima-Guadalcanal. As it was, the landing was uneventful, with no real highlights except, we set up around an Army supply depot. "If we were the first series of combat regiments to land," I thought, "what the f— was the Army doing there and who were they supplying?"

That was the first of many questions to come. It took a couple of days to get all the gear and equipment from the ship to a temporary storage area. After that we started fanning out to secure the area, surrounding the sight selected for our base camp. My group went, roughly, northwest. We set up on top of a hill and dug in. The first couple of days seemed like a training exercise. Dig in, fill sandbags, and be hot, sweaty and generally miserable.

Late one night while on watch, I saw two shadow-like figures walking up the hill towards us. They were moving slowly, almost like they were strolling along. After waking the guy in the foxhole, we looked at the two walking towards us. There was an eerie kind of quiet.

We took aim and fired a couple of shots each. They fell and all was quiet again. Neither of us was really excited. We just did it and that was that. A little later he went back to sleep and I was alone with my thoughts again. It was too easy, almost like target practice. Why didn't I feel something, anything? Too easy. Killing should not be that easy. It's preposterous I have to refer to the person who was with me as some "guy," because I don't remember who it was. There's lots of things that have gotten forgotten along the line.

In the morning several of us went down the hill to check it out. A couple of farmers. No guns, no grenades, nothing. A couple of farmers. Oh well, hunting season had opened.

July closed out without too much else happening. There were a lot of patrols and we secured and extended the areas around our base camp. I turned twenty, but that didn't seem to matter much. As August came in we started to move, going on numerous "extended patrols" lasting several days. I came to a new understanding of the meaning of stress. As the month progressed, we all started getting quieter and quieter. Conversations were short. No one was expressing anything about what was starting to eat away at us. "Extended patrols," "counter-insurgency operations," "suspected resistance" all meant we were going into a village or hamlet and "clearing it," which meant killing anyone who even flinched at our presence. And we did.

After returning from one such excursion, we had several days of back mail waiting. It was then that we learned of the riots taking place in Watts. My, our stomping rounds. "Stomping" used to mean playing; now it meant killing. Funny how things change. There was a different kind of quiet that came over us. All of us were trying to come to grips with this new twist in our lives. One day we did talk about it. Once. Several of us were sitting around talking and someone mentioned how angry he was with all the bullshit that was going on back home. The dissension, protests that had started up about the war in Vietnam. "The G-damned protestors" and "the fucking niggers" . . . "we should go back and take care of all of them." Silence. Anger. Hatred. Racism. Here or there, it was all the same.

A few days later we went on another "search and destroy" mission. We were to search out and destroy the "enemy." When we moved into the village we encountered some small-arms fire. Basically, that meant that the village was "fair game."

Going in and doing a village like that is such an incredible rush of energy and emotion. The whole world seems different for that moment. It is different. It's pretty bizarre. We went through and cleared the thatch roofed huts and captured some hiding in the nearby brush. It really was an organized sort of chaos. I was dazed. Some of our guys got hit near the far end of the rice paddy. (An old rule of thumb when rescuing people is to pick up the first one you come to. You might not get a chance to save anyone else.) As we were moving through the paddy and coming to our guys we all started to pass by the first person, a black man named Eddy (I think). We looked at each other and his eyes simply said, "So, what else is new?" I stopped and carried him back to dry land. He died. So did I.

Shortly after that, a lieutenant told me to clear a "cache," a small hole in the ground where people would hide during such an onslaught. The problem was that some of our guys had gotten blown up while trying to get people out of these caches. Sometimes there would be innocent people there, sometimes not. The now-accepted method of clearing was to toss a grenade or two in and sort out the pieces afterwards. I couldn't do it. Someone else did.

Things had started to quiet down a bit.

I had gone over to the rice paddy where I had brought Eddy. Anderson was busy taking pictures of a "gook" lying in a "paddy skimmer" (boat) with three-quarters of his skull missing. People were laughing. The guys clearing the cache were starting to bring people out. Two guys were carrying a very pregnant woman who was bloody from head to toe. Part way to the area set up for the corpsmen (medics), she aborted. A well developed baby. They dropped her. Shot her. Shot the baby. Several times. Anderson took pictures.

I want to stop writing now, much like I wanted to stop participating in the "art of war." There is no such thing. It's not "art." It's carnage. How in the name of God could we do it? We were told it was for God, Country and the American way. Fuckers.

My family began cautioning me about writing about what I was experiencing, what was going on, what I was seeing, because it was causing too much pain. Pain. Pain! Ha. You don't even have a concept of pain. I was writing about the light stuff.

Lots of things were happening. The build-up was all around us. The 1st Cav. came in with a flourish and a shout and got their collective tits caught in a ringer in the Ia Drang Valley. 101st Airborne came in and didn't do much better.

Ia Drang. We had to go in and play pick up. It was a clearing operation; we went in to clear the valley of any living thing. We went in, going over the top of the mountains, trying to catch the VC by surprise. After several days we had a bunch of kills and about twenty prisoners. We took the prisoners back to the base camp outside of Qui Nhon after some "field interrogation." When we got back to camp the prisoners were held in a large dug out area that was our garbage pit. The ones that were trouble were put in a four-to-five-foot wide and ten-foot deep hole with barbed wire around it. It was normal for us to urinate on them while we were guarding them. I was on watch when the interrogators wanted the "next one." I held a short rope down to him and he climbed out of the pit. His whole being was hatred towards us. We then took him inside the tent for interrogation. After several questions and no responses, three of us held him down while the Vietnamese interrogator started torturing him. His eyes.

His eyes.

Once we were done with them, they were turned over to the South Vietnamese Police, who really went to work on them.

All of our time was spent out in the bush. We had set up in a place called Phu Thai 4. Not much happened. We had some line incursions, but no real big deal. We got really bored. One day as we were sitting there, thinking about how we never get to see what really happens with an 81mm mortar. We decided, for lack of anything better to do, to take a mortar up on top of the hill and waited until sundown when the farmers and their families would be walking back in from the fields. When they were in close enough range we readied a couple of white phosphorus rounds. We set them for air detonation and fired, just to see what it would do. What it does is explode about fifty feet off the ground, showering those below with a phosphorus powder that burns upon coming in contact with moisture—on the skin, in the lungs—painful. They started running around "like ants" and fell and died. So for lack of "anything better to do," we caused these innocent people to die a very hideous death, just for our entertainment.

For some time we knew that we were going to make an amphibious assault on Chu Lai. The word came down that we were going to do it on the Marine Corps birthday, November 10. Our commanders kept telling us how great it was going to be; no other landing had taken place on the Corps birthday since WWII. With a great deal of trepidation, I listened to their hype. I had believed before, but I was younger then. So, with much ado, we boarded ship and left Qui Nhon, sailing for Chu Lai. On the way up there we were joined by several ships loaded with new guys. This was to be their first day in Vietnam. *Surprise.* The landing was nothing. There was nobody around. It was almost like a training exercise. After a lot of standing around, things got organized and all the separate groups started heading off in different directions to set up. Then we got hit.

We weren't the only ones who knew about the landing. Somewhere along the line someone called in Navy artillery. The Navy started pumping in all sorts of shit. The problem was that their rounds weren't hitting front of us where they should have, but they were coming in behind and "walking" towards us. Welcome to Vietnam, new guys! Good job, Navy. White Beach was no longer as clean as it may sound.

After the debacle at White Beach, our unit set up camp in an area outside of Chu Lai. From there we ran numerous operations to clear and secure the surrounding area. I had gotten an infection in my eyes and was choppered to a ship offshore. In a letter to my mother, I told her that after two days there I was going goofy; I needed to go home, back in the bush. I was not comfortable anywhere else. After much ado, the doctor gave me a set of welders goggles to keep the sun out of my eyes and he sent me back. So for the next couple of weeks I had restricted duty and lived in my goggles. Some idiot had decided that what we needed was movies, so they erected a movie screen, in the middle of a combat zone. The war was changing. Naturally, with such a perfect siting device as a movie screen, we started getting mortar attacks.

Light years and a lifetime ahead, December 18, 1965—Harvest Moon. The operation was supposed to have been over. We came out of the hills and a bunch of helicopters were called in, once we reached the flatlands, in order to remove all the guys with immersion foot (their feet were rotting). We had the old issue leather boots and walking through jungles and rice paddies made fertile ground for rot. After the choppers left, we started walking towards a convoy of trucks that was supposed to pick us up several miles down the road. As we were passing through a village we got hit, and hit bad. We were three-quarters encircled and rapidly running out of ammunition, and hope. Nimeroski and Frontella had gotten blown up in front of me. I was lying in a rice paddy with leeches all over my body, mortars coming in, out of ammunition, helpless. There was a strange kind of calm, almost dispassionate, that I felt, accepting that I was going to die. That didn't seem all that important, probably because I was already dead. By the grace of God, with the help of Marine Corps artillery, and by the sheer guts and determination of Fox and Hotel companies, the encirclement was broken. Death was everywhere. Life was not. And I still had eight months to do.

Shit.

Christmas came and went. Ho Hum.

The ability to love and feel joy to the world had come and gone also. Survival!

I'm not really sure what all happened in January of 1966, except we all knew the Christmas truce was bullshit, just like everything else. We had gone on an extended patrol, going about thirty miles into Laos. Simply put, we went in, dumped a village, and went back. Not that what we did was so unusual, but when we returned to base camp, waiting for us was our mail, including the recent "Stars and Stripes," the official newspaper of the U.S. Military, with a picture of LBJ pounding his fist saying, "My boys never have been and never will be in Laos or Cambodia." It was my second trip into Laos and we had also previously been on patrol into Cambodia. Just more lies to make it sound good at home.

And then in February, we hooked up with Ky's Marines. It was a joint operation. A detachment of South Vietnamese and U.S. Marines. Our mission was to "quell the Buddhist uprising." The highway leading into Hue was lined with small pagodas, portable personal shrines, individual places of worship. In the town, people everywhere. No idea how many. We were in our six-by, trucks and jeeps.

A Buddhist monk set himself on fire. Our drivers started heading for the crowds. Another monk. People running. Running everywhere. We chased in our trucks. Some shots. Not many. The trucks and our presence were enough. Somewhere in the midst of the panic, I realized that we had just broken up a peaceful protest to the carnage of war that had invaded these people's homeland. Leaving the town, our truck drivers followed the lead of the South Vietnamese in running over the small shrines lining the road. There we were, desecrating temples of worship, representing God, Country and the American way. That day we broke every law that God has set down.

And through it all, children running. Some away. Some to us. A group of about eight or ten little ones asking, begging, for food, candy—anything. Someone tossed a grenade.

The war lost any justifiability for me that day.

I had four more major operations that I participated in and I honestly do not recall much of it. I had ceased caring, didn't matter if I ended up dead 'cause I already was and it didn't matter if I got killed. I had gone beyond. Such is war.

On July 2, 1966, I landed at El Toro, Marine Corps Air Wing, California. After deplaning and a bunch of BS, I had my orders and forty days leave. In twelve days I would turn twenty-one. To say that I was "home" would be incorrect. "Home" was the bush, not L.A. Yes, I was raised in L.A., but home was not there. Home is where you are comfortable, where you feel secure. My whole entire being was not at ease away from the bush and still, in part, isn't. Once I was ready to leave El Toro I hooked up with someone who, for five dollars, would give me a ride to the L.A. bus terminal. He was quick to point out that I should get out of my uniform and into some civvies. Simply, I told him to get fucked. I was not going to hide. Besides, I had my duffel bag and it was obvious that I was in the military. He persisted in saying that times had changed and that I was going to get hassled. My response was simple—fine, let some asshole hassle me and they will find out, personally, what killing is all about. I had come home prepared to kill Americans. Don't fuck with me, period. Fortunately, no one did.

How sorry I feel for my mother—no dad, he split when I was a couple years old—when she first saw me. Her baby boy was dead. She was greeted by a shell. No love, no life. That had been taken out of me. Instead she had a son who was tormented and cold. I do wish that it could have been different. The next morning when she opened the door of my room to awaken me I almost killed her. It wasn't her. It was solely the difference of voice. A female voice was out of place for my reality. The terror that I brought home. I'm sorry, Ma.

Fourth of July stories, you bet. Bang, pop, watch John drop. We were going to surprise my brother and sister-in-law. My mother would not let me drive. On the way there was a firecracker explosion, and automatically my six-foot-three-inch skinny body was curled up under the dashboard of the car. The pain for her son. I truly cannot describe it. Hopefully one day she will write her story.

My pain. I chose to hide with alcohol-induced oblivion. It was not a fun time for anyone.

Remembering the pictures of the returning WWII vets as happy, smiling, rejoicing. Reunions were a long way off from my reality. Mine was a time of lies exposed, and degradation. Our government had, on purpose, lied to us. Over and over. When I went to Vietnam, I so believed in God, Country and the American way. When I returned from Vietnam, I believed none of it.

In trying to sort out my life . . . basically, I got married, had a daughter and got divorced. Interesting that the man who talked me out of killing her first boyfriend after our separation, is the man she ended up marrying and who adopted our daughter. She couldn't talk about anything that I needed to talk about. Fortunately, a couple of years later, I met a woman who could and did really help me in becoming human again.

In 1977, I met the most wonderful woman there is. What she has put up with through the years is phenomenal. Very importantly, perhaps most importantly, she understands and feels. She experienced it all. A year after we met, through a whole series of circumstances, while we were living in the central highlands of Mexico, I started having a series of what they call moderate to severe flashbacks. Knowing that drinking was my oblivion and feeling that the only way beyond the flashbacks was to take them on, I knew I had to stop drinking. I did. And I went just full-goose bozo. Flashbacks that would knock me cold. Flashbacks where I'd jump in the bushes for three minutes to three days.

After divine intervention, I am here, and alive, and learning to live again. For the first time I asked the questions and needed the answers. It took really earnestly asking the questions and a willingness to change within upon receiving the answers.

Today Cher and I have two young children and live in South Minneapolis. Since returning to the U.S. more than ten years ago, we have constantly been working on issues relevant to veterans and their families. Currently, we have started an organization called the Veterans Incentive Project to begin addressing some of the long-term problems of veterans, especially of Vietnam, and their families, who are homeless or near homeless.

Alan L. Fuchs

I was raised in Queens, New York. I attended Delehanty High School, and worked after school to help pay the tuition of this private school. I was the youngest of two brothers and one sister. No other member of my immediate family was in the military. My father was too young for the World War I and too old for WWII. The only person who I had contact with that war in the military was my Uncle George. He had come to America after the Nazis killed his parents, and joined the U.S. Army when the war broke out.

The last year of high school, I already knew that my marks were not good enough to get into college, and the school already had given me "commercial" courses. I figured that my draft status would be 1-A as soon as I turned eighteen that August of 1966, so a friend and I decided to push up our draft when the time came.

I graduated in June of 1966, turned eighteen in August, and was drafted in September. I was eventually sent to Fort Hood, Texas for basic and AIT. I was assigned to a number of artillery battalions. The final assignment was with the 1st Battalion, 14th Artillery, which at that time was connected to the 2nd Armored Division. A year later it was assigned to the newly formed 198th Lt. Infantry Brigade, and the newly activated American Division, or the 23rd Infantry Division.

We already had our orders to go to Nam. We were to be shipped over as a unit. All we knew was that we were going north, to I Corp. We shipped out in early October 1967 on the *USS Gordon*, an old WWII liberty ship. We stopped at Subic Bay in the Philippines, and then on to Da Nang. The ship anchored in Da Nang Harbor sometime in late October 1967. We boarded an LST, and went south to Chu Lai Base.

We disembarked on a bright sunny day on a sandy beach. I had visions of storming the beach, but that never happened. We strolled up like we were on a tour. But it would soon seem different.

The first thing that struck me was the stench in the air. The second was the heat. We made shelters in what was an artillery installation. We took our ponchos and made lean-tos, in where ammunition was formally stored. That afternoon I saw the dark gray clouds that were to come, at first gradually, usually at the same time of day, and watched as the rain lasted longer and longer, until it rained all the time—monsoon.

We had to wait till the equipment was unloaded and be picked up at the dock. About three days later, we moved three klicks north of Chu Lai Base on Highway 1, by truck. We had to wait till the road was swept for mines, a daily routine. We drove through a village of thatched huts. Everybody was dressed the same, in black pajamas and straw hats. The huts each had a dirt floor, and only one square room. Some of the people carried pigs in baskets to the market. The hooches were either on one side of the street or the other. No back alleys.

As we drove on Highway 1, a dirt road, the landscape was flat. The animate mountains rose sharply in the background. The lush green color of the vegetation was vivid. Old men with water buffalos moved slowly by, and young children bare from the waist down played in pools of water alongside the road, while their mothers washed the laundry in the rice paddies.

We turned on a road toward a gently sloping hill. This had been the "home" of the 196th Inf. Brigade, who recently moved further north. It was called simply "Hill 35." It was to be our base camp. We were positioned there to be supporting artillery for Chu Lai Base, infantry on patrol, and other artillery batteries within our range.

We had to rebuild everything, after setting up the gun. The gun was a late WWII vintage 105mm howitzer-towed, meaning it was not self-propelled. Everything had to be sandbagged—endless hours of a back-breaking work. The bunker was a hole in the ground about three feet deep. The room was eight by ten feet. It held seven men. The sides were supported with wooden timbers driven into the ground at the four corners and crossbeams. We were fortunate to get PSP (metal sheets used to make pre-fab aircraft runways) and then four layers thick of sandbags on top, as well as the sides. Since we were an artillery battery, we were always subject to 122mm rocket attacks.

The last time I knew, it was supposed to be "field" artillery. Until I got to Nam. We were Air Mobile. The "shithooks" (short for Chinooks) would pick up the 105, and a plate of ammo, and transport it to a new location. We were on Hill 35 for about two weeks, just long enough to get settled. Then we got orders to occupy a hill fifteen klicks northwest of Hill 35. I don't remember the name of the operation, but I was picked to go as part of an advance party.

The choppers came in and picked us up, and then the gun and the ammo was transported to a hill. It looked like a tiny mountain. It came to a point, and had no vegetation on it. It came to a point at the top, with steep sides. The chopper laid the gun down, and it sat at a forty-five-degree angle. We had to blast holes near the top to create "steps" in the side of the mountain, to have the gun rest straight. We used C-4 to do the blasting. "Fire in the Hole!" was all we heard the rest of the day. By night we had the gun in position. That's when we found out we didn't have any ammo for the gun. What we thought was ammo, was a case of beer. There were seven of us, and an FO and radioman. The infantry never got to the position around the hill because they got lost. The maps were really bad. So, seven men sat down and had a beer. We didn't think anything of it since nobody shot at us anyway. That was probably the only all-night sleep I had during my tour of duty. If I had only known.

That was about November 1967. Monsoon was well underway, and the clouds were dark gray, and low. It rained in torrents for hours on end. The hill turned to mud. When we did get a fire mission, some of the guns would slide down the hill. Then it took every man to try to pull it back into position. The mud was over our knees. We couldn't light fires, and the resupply choppers couldn't get out to us. Sometimes they did. But nobody ate what they brought. It looked like melted animals. Gray and fluid. We ate C-rations instead.

Nobody ate the ham and eggs.

I lived on cheese and crackers, beans and motherfuckers (we didn't quite know what those other things were mixed in with the beans) and canned bread. I loved the metal taste they had. I got very constipated. After exposure to the rain, the skin on my body was wrinkly, like I stayed in a bath too long when I was a kid. The skin cracked, and the dirt was in the cracks. We never dried out. At night we would try to get out of the rain. We had makeshift bunkers. Not so elaborate as at base camp. Of course, every living creature had the same idea as us. We had to literally fight the rats for the high ground. The rats were big as tomcats. The centipedes were twelve inches long; when we cut them in half, the halves would go in two different directions.

One afternoon, the rain let up. We received sniper fire. One lone sniper sprayed the area from a hill across the way. I fired back. I was the only one that did. The LT came over and asked who fired back. I told him I did. I said any dumb son-of-a-bitch that shot at me and missed would hear from me. Nothing was said about it.

We didn't do very much there, and about five or six weeks later, it started to wear on us. I needed to take a shit in the worst way. We had toilet paper in C-rations packages, and I would hold it tightly in my hand, and sit on a wooden ammo crate used as a toilet seat, getting splinters in the downpour, and praying to God to take a shit. I never asked God for something like that. I wondered if he'd grant such a thing.

It was getting near Christmas. We were told that we would return to base camp for a Christmas dinner. General William C. Westmoreland had ordered it. Every man was to receive a turkey dinner, with cornbread dressing, cranberry sauce, hot rolls, mixed vegetables, and on and on. We packed up and returned to base camp. We received a card that said "A Merry Christmas Vietnam 1967." It had a prayer, and a message from General Westmoreland, and listed all the goodies. God bless him. I never forgot that. That raised the morale, and moved more than a few mountains.

We settled back in on Hill 35. As December was almost over, and the monsoon rains started to move south, there was talk of peace in the air. There was supposed to be a cease-fire for the Christmas holidays. Right after dinner we got shelled. The firefight lasted about fifteen minutes—mortars, and small-arms fire. We had casualties. I don't remember how many. One mortar, three AK-47s and an old Japanese rifle, and some RPGs were captured, and three VC dead.

At the end of December, getting on towards New Year's (ours) we heard of another cease-fire. I had been transferred to "A" battery. Twenty-one minutes after midnight the cease fire was broken by the sound of mortars. We got hit hard. Besides the usual small-arms and mortars, we got it with 122mm rockets—about a dozen, I think. They really ripped us up. We called in for a dust-off (med-evac choppers) and we had gunships all over the place. My gun shot illumination rounds. High Angle. Straight up. I loaded the gun on my knees.

It was also feared that the upcoming Vietnamese New Year's "Tet" would bring some trouble. We knew it too. All units were put on alert. "Condition Red." Intelligence had an NVA battalion just out in front of us. Or in the area somewhere. Things were tense. I was transferred back to B Battery. We were on alert. Nobody left the gun, or the phones. Ammo was stored, guns cleaned, fuses were checked and rechecked. M-60s were brought into position. Sandbags were added. Nothing to do but wait. We ate at the guns, and nobody slept. We didn't want to get caught napping. There was constant communication on the phones, checking and rechecking. The people in the village at the base of the hill thinned out. We braced ourselves. We knew it was coming.

And wham! Six 122mm rockets slammed us. It almost took out FDC (Fire Direction Control). Mortars followed, with automatic weapons fire. We could see the rockets being launched from a hill not far away. At the same time, Chu Lai Base was getting hit, and the infantry on patrol drew fire. Fire missions came down. Fire Mission! We had to split the battery up two ways. One, to shoot the fire mission to protect the infantry, the other to stop the rockets heading towards Chu Lai. A guy (I don't remember his name) and I put the gun in direct fire at the location. Locked and loaded one 105 round and fired. We fired again and drew secondary explosions. Then we swung the gun around and set the coordinates for the fire mission.

Bullets were as thick as flies. We had our orders to "Fire at will." We were taking a lot of fire, and I knew that if things got that bad, we were within range of another artillery battery that could walk the rounds into us, or fire on our position if things got that bad. I didn't think of it then, but later thought, "I hope not." The night sky was lit up like the Fourth of July. Med-evacs were in and out. Gunships were trying to protect us. The noise of guns and the explosions were deafening. People screaming, guns blazing. I don't remember how long it lasted. It seemed like forever. The ammo dump at Chu Lai Base got hit. The fireball rose very high in the sky behind us. By morning, everything was quiet. Nobody talked. We sat there and lit up. Behind me was a pile of expended 105 canisters four feet high. The gun was still red hot.

We moved like zombies. I don't remember eating. I just sat there leaning back on some sandbags smoking a cigarette and staring off into space. I didn't know if I was dead or alive. We spent the next two weeks repairing the damage. We weren't cheery anymore. Our faces looked different. We had sort of a blank eye stare about us. No more FNGs. I felt strangely different. I felt old. The only sound I heard was the first-sergeant's voice. Even he seemed different. The mist hung in the valley in the early morning. Everything seemed peaceful.

In February of 1968 I was transferred to "C" Battery. I didn't like the idea because of it's location. The village at the base of the hill was built on top of railroad tracks once used to go from Saigon to up north. It ran along the coast. It was called Nuc Mau, I think. It was said to be a "Pinko" Village. The battery itself was set in a straight line against a mountain. It seemed like a death-trap to me. We got hit several times while I was there. The last time I remember something about a command of "Beehives." Those were 105 rounds with tiny nails in them. When fired, the gun went off like a shot gun. The nails went flying. It pinned everything in front of it together. Trees, people, everything.

All I remember, it was night.

Loading the gun, with the black pro-joes (projectiles).

I was transferred back to "B" battery to find out that some of the men on my gun were killed. They had gone out on an advance party. They took a jeep down a hill and hit a 250-pound land mine, killing everyone. I remember one of the guys in my gun section telling me that and saying, "I heard Charlie Battery got overrun."

I said, "Yeah."

By the time March came along, it was my turn to go on R&R. I chose Bangkok, Thailand. Pure heaven, I thought. I hitched a ride on a chopper back to Chu Lai Base. In the meantime the guy gets into a firefight. We finally landed at the base and I took a C-127 to Da Nang. Next, I remember sitting at the welcome station in Bangkok sipping on a beer that was said to be twenty-five percent alcohol. The guy next to me didn't drink, so I traded my empty glass for his full one. I was flying. I could have drank that with a spoon.

The first place I headed for was the hotel. The Express Hotel in downtown Bangkok. The second place I went was to a high-class bath house. We got to choose the girls through a window, who would give us massages. This was not a whorehouse. I sat in a steam cabinet for a while, and then she put me in a hot tub of water and bathed me. She then dried me off and walked up my back, massaging my back with her toes. After that I went to eat at a local restaurant. It was outside, with a small brick wall with wrought iron fencing. There were plants on the side. The air was warm with a slight breeze. There was a French air to the building. The man that owned it came out with his family, and welcomed me. He offered me that delicious beer, and a plastic bag with a face towel that was cooled in a refrigerator. I feasted on fried minced pidgeon and rice, prawn, sweet and sour sauces, some too hot to describe. It must have been the best Tai Cuisine in the world. I spent four days and five nights there. I went to the beach and saw the sights.

April of 1968, the weather got hot. It was the dry season. We were shooting a lot of fire missions, and we had to constantly receive ammo. Each ammo box was wooden. It weighed 110 pounds. We had four guys on the gun now, and one FNG. We had to hump those rounds up a small hill and break them out of the cases and put them together. We humped for hours in 120-degree heat. Two cases on my shoulders. Two-hundred-ten pounds on a 127 pound frame. My shoulders bled under the towels.

We were taking ten salt pills a day. Our skin was dry. Infection rate was three minutes. We took anti-malarial pills (big brown ones) once a week and a Dapzone (small white ones) everyday until the Army stopped them. I had gotten jungle rot on my ass. The skin was a whitish gray, and raised about an inch off my usual contour. The skin would just scrape off in handfuls.

It smelled bad. I would pour a disinfectant over it that would burn like hell. It didn't help. The flies landed on it, trying to lay their maggots on it. The thought of having my skin rot off my living body freaked me out.

One guy I remember we called "Stumpy" contracted everything. He was always willing to share what he got with everyone else, like ringworm. Every unit should have a guy like that. Real generous.

In the heat, the subterranean termites were really active. I was lying down in the bunker. I was in a half sleep, when I realized that something had found a meal of me. I was covered with termites that were determined to take me home. The termites' nests were about three feet wide. The local ants—we called them piss ants because they bit the piss out of you—loved them, so too, they covered my body . . . in my ears, nose and another place I don't want to mention. At about 4 p.m. the flies were active. About 6, the mosquitoes came in droves. About 7, the wild boar would run through the barbed wire and trip the trip-flares. And about 8 p.m., the local sniper shot at us. Same time every day. Never hit anything. We fired a 105 round at him once. He answered us by a single shot.

In between the boredom, we'd get hit. Nothing big. It seemed to be slacking off towards June. In July, General William C. Westmoreland stepped down. The military command of South Vietnam (MACV) was turned over to General Wheeler.

I started to get "short," because I ETSed in September of '68. I kept a short-timers calendar like everybody else. I was in the field when orders came down to go home. I had mixed feelings. I wanted out, but didn't know what I was heading into. They tried to get me to re-up, but I didn't. The last memory I have of Vietnam was going to the village and buying some carved statues. They said it was "tiger bone." I often wonder.

I got to the end of the village, and looked back—something I don't always do—and thought to myself, "Nothing is ever the same. Nor will it ever be."

I grabbed a chopper out. No time to turn anything in. It had all been destroyed a long time ago. Got my papers at Chu Lai Base and took a C-127 to Cam Ranh Bay. Stayed overnight, and boarded a Continental Jetliner—the living on top, the dead below. I met a friend on the plane—the guy who pushed up his draft with me—the friend who I met in the fifth grade of grammar school. The friend I went to Nam with. The friend who I protected with my artillery fire. He was in the infantry. We sat together. We smelled. We were dirty. We were alive.

The captain of that Continental jet loaned me his electric shaver. It made me feel like a human being again. I thank him, whoever he was. The flight attendants were wonderful. They put up with a lot, but all in good fun. To them—thank you. The flight was long. We landed in Fort Lewis, Washington. It was fifty-two degrees. I still had my jungle fatigues on. I froze. The first thing I did was to take out clean sheets—heaven.

They offered us a steak dinner on our return, but I refused.

The day I turned in my sheets, I met a young LT who was just going over. He sought my advise. I told it like it was. I hope he came back alive. I'll never know. I never got his name.

We were in Fort Lewis three days.

I signed the book, and put the reason as ETS. I saw a phone booth and thought of calling home. I didn't want to. I wanted to go to California, and continue my life. But I called home. I never forgave myself for that.

I went to the Seattle airport and bought a ticket to New York. The flight stopped at Chicago. A group of us, all heading east. About twenty-five of us. When I landed at Kennedy, it was just the two of us. My friend and I. All along the way, we vowed to see each other again. But we never did. Just me and my friend did. Vietnam was behind us now. Things were different. We went from one war to another, and didn't even realize it. We were alive, or so I thought.

I have had twenty-one years to look at the war. I've looked at it from every angle. I find I cannot look at the world through innocent eyes. I don't have that childish hope, and my outlook on life is more critical.

I went to Vietnam for a sense of adventure. I went to prove my self-worth. I am satisfied. I know what I'm made of. But there was a price. Fame or fortune doesn't mean the same anymore. My outlook and values have changed. Intangible things mean much more to me. They can't take that away.

We came home from one war to another. The war the American people and the American government waged against us. But we endured. We wouldn't go away. We will never go away. This is our land. We paid for it with our blood—our brothers and sisters. We love our land, and our own. But thanks, America. You've taught me something—faith. My soul was tempered in the fires of hell, and quenched in the reality of what America had turned to.

All this headshrinker BS doesn't provide answers. Answers will come when we reach out to other vets. People who were there also. People who understand.

There has been a lot of negative stuff said about Nam vets. Most of it worthless bullshit. The fact is that I was proud to serve with men and women like them. For the brothers and sisters reading this, Welcome Home—We are ONE.

I think the inscription I saw on a statue in the Georgia State Capitol in Atlanta is true: "He who saves his country, saves himself. Saves all things, and all things saved do bless him. He who lets his country die lets all things die. Dies himself ignobly, and all things dying curse him."

To My Vietnam Brothers and Sisters: the road for us has been hard and long. We have had to endure much just to be who we are. In that process, however, We have become closer. I find the real enemy to be indifference and silence. We must speak out—together. I love you. Your Brother, Al Fuchs.

I sit here twenty years after the war. I watch war movies about places I've been. Things I have seen, and I don't wonder why. I was there. I realize now, that twenty years of my life have come and gone. Most of it in solitude. Shut out of my own country. Left to Die. We did not dishonor ourselves or the dead. We must remember them. We fought for a cause. Maybe our own. But we fought nonetheless. We stuck our asses on the line. We proved we were made of the right stuff. Soldiers. We belong because we earned it. We have a right to be proud. Not because we won or lost. Because we were there. We were called and we went.

Coming home was not the easiest. No victory parades. No welcome home. Just silence. But that is all gone now. We have our own legacy to live. We must rise above it. Somehow, somewhere, sometime we must.

I think to myself, what a brother wrote: "When things get you down, and you feel like your going to lose it, Remember them guys. The guys you left behind. Remember you promised." Then it all makes sense.

Now there making movies about us. It took so long to let it go, now they want their heroes. Now they write books about us. I never really realized until today, just how my life had been affected by it. Now I'm the old man of the mountain.

Reading about places I've been is strange. I read a name like LZ Bayonet, and I can picture it in my mind. I know what it looked like. The strange part is, it reminds me of a place like home . . . at least for a while. A familiar place.

So, the big-shit war protester is dead. Abby Hoffman commits suicide. That's where all this shit stems from. The "Immoral War," they called it. The American people believed it. The Nam vets believed it. But it wasn't so. Any warrior knows, you fight for yourself.

I tell you I know the ending. I wrote the book. I know what happens . . . I was there.

Frank G. Erwin

We were always moving from place to place as my father was an asbestos worker—mostly on powerhouses being built by TVA. I attended three different high schools in four years. My freshman year, we lived in a little town called South Pittsburg, Tennessee, located at the foot of Mount Eagle near Chattanooga. This was the best year of my life. I made friendships that have endured many years. My best friend lives there. His name is Rusty Addock. He served in Nam as a Marine officer after I came home.

We moved to Rogersville, Tennessee and then to Old Hickory, which is right outside Nashville. I was a fairly typical teenager, I suppose—played sports, football, baseball, loved history in school. I read a lot of stories about the Civil War and always wondered what it would be like to actually be in combat. My great-grandfather fought with the 1st Tennessee Regiment as a foot soldier. We even have the rifle that he carried. He survived many major battles, the worst being Franklin, in Tennessee, where over 6000 men died in battle in less than four hours of fighting. I used to drag his rifle over the hills at my grandfather's farm in Columbia and make charges into the Yankee lines. Of course, I always won when it was make believe.

After high school I got to go to a little school outside Nashville in Lebanon, Tennessee called Cumberland College. I stayed in school about a year and a half. I remember hearing about a little place called Vietnam, where America was fighting Communism. This grabbed my attention and I saw a chance to go to war. I certainly wasn't going to miss out on the action. My head was full of stories that I had read about, how tough rebel soldiers were, and since I was a grandson of a rebel soldier, I felt it was my duty to join the cause of freedom and do my part to stem the red tide of Communism. Boy, was I in for a surprise!

After being brainwashed about the Marine Corps by a "reservist" at school, and with a few beers under by belt, I went to Nashville and joined the United States Marine Corps. I went to boot camp at Parris Island, South Carolina, and was in Platoon 150. We won drill competition and all the other ribbons except rifle range. I barely qualified as a marksman on the last day at the rifle range. This was the first time I had ever fired a rifle. It had always been make believe. Do you get the picture? I was a little boy who was full of make believe, with dreams of glory in my head, on my way to the slaughter of Vietnam, with no idea of what I was getting into.

Infantry training at Camp Gieger and off to Camp Pendleton, California for more training, and then on the bird to Okinawa. We arrived about the second week in August. I went to Camp Hanson. The base was in an uproar because the commandant was coming (General Green). Work details every day. It was boring, so when I had a chance to go to Nam ahead of schedule, I jumped at it.

I was separated from all the guys that I had trained with, so I arrived in Da Nang really all alone. (I found out later that most of them went to the 7th Marines.) I stayed there a day or two and was put on a plane to Phu Bai. I had a chance to be an office page there at headquarters. Still wanting to see action, I turned it down. Next morning I was on a 'copter to Dong Ha.

I was nineteen years old and when I jumped off the 'copter at Dong Ha, little did I know that my life was going to change drastically in only a few short hours.

Almost immediately I didn't feel so good. A first-sergeant met the 'copter and took me and a couple other new guys across the clay runway. The heat was bad, but the humidity was almost unbearable. Mix that with the dust and grime and what I saw next and I got a real sick feeling in the bottom of my stomach. I saw green plastic bags being unloaded from a 'copter and put into stacks of two. I asked the first-sergeant what that was and he told us. "Dead motherfuckers." Then it hit me. These were dead Marines being unloaded like cordwood. The ball in my stomach was getting worse by the minute. I wanted to run and hide, but there was nowhere to go.

I followed the sergeant over to a big tent that was full of 782 gear and big flies. The odor was like something dead was inside. He told us to pick through the gear and find as many magazines as we could carry and to get at least four canteens. I noticed a lot of the gear had flies on it and dark spots, with holes in many items. I then realized this gear had come off the dead and wounded Marines that I was fixing to replace. Really *bad* feeling now. This was not the way it was supposed to be.

After this ordeal I was issued my rifle, my M-14. The rest of the gear was secondhand, but my rifle was in perfect condition and it felt good in my hands. We went by the company office and signed some papers and before long I was waiting in line for a 'copter. I had no idea where I was or where I was going. I just sensed I was going where the Marines in the bags had come from.

Several of us loaded onto an old 34 'copter and headed north. That's when the door-gunner told me. He said we were going to the Rockpile. Sure enough, before long I could see this huge rock just rising up out of the jungle floor. It looked real strange; there were hills around it, but it just appeared out of nowhere.

We landed on a hill near the rock and jumped off, completely covered with dust from the 'copter. I was scared now, as I could hear a lot of gunfire coming from a hill close by; 81mm mortars were on the hill where we landed and they started to fire after the 'copters pulled away. The heat, humidity, the smell of gunpowder, the roar of engines from the 'copters—all of these sights and smells going together to make my first day in the field one I would never forget.

Something else happened that day, too, that I will never erase from my mind. While I was waiting for someone to tell me what to do, I noticed a ball of big green and black flies on something near me. I threw a rock at them, and when they rose up I saw a green high-top tennis shoe with a piece of leg still in it. There was a part of a man's leg laying right there in front of me! I turned away from it and said to myself, "Oh, my God! What have I gotten myself into now!" This was real; no more playing games. Men were dying real close by, and now I was really scared.

Before long a small Hispanic Marine came and got me and assigned me to a fire team. At that time I was so scared I didn't even know what company or platoon or squad I was with. I did notice no one was friendly or even bothered to introduce themselves. The squad leader just said I was a new guy. That's how I was addressed for the next few days. "New guy do this, new guy do that." I did what I was told.

The first night there was a lot of firing going on down in a valley under a high cliff a couple of hills over from where we were. Word was a squad was pinned down and a Marine radio was talking to CP asking for help. Later that night the firing stopped and we were told that we were moving into that valley in the morning.

Actually, we didn't move for another two days. I prayed all night that I wouldn't be killed and finally, a couple of hours sleep right before daylight. Hole watch was two hours on, two hours off that night.

When we finally moved out, my squad was put on point and guess what. I was told to get up on point. Less than a week in Nam and I was being put on point! I knew now why nobody wanted to know my name. Let the new guy get shot first, then we'll know where the gooks are.

So many things raced through my mind, trying to remember my training and be brave. I did notice something happening to me. As the adrenaline was pumping I was getting somewhat calm. I also found out that day that God had blessed me with a special ability to see things that others didn't. It saved my life that day and many times more as the weeks stretched into months in the field.

As we went into the valley where the squad was supposed to be— all were dead, we figured, but we were going to get the bodies—I moved along at point, soaking wet with sweat. I knew I was alone up there and nobody but me cared if I lived or died. I was going to live, I decided. About then I saw a North Vietnamese soldier up above me in a recess in the side of the cliff. He was well hidden, but I could see him as plain as day. This was the enemy and he was waiting on me. My heart was pounding so hard I could hardly control myself. He was a sniper that was in place for when we came after the other Marines' bodies. I moved around a bit to get a better view of him and then raised my rifle and just like at the rifle range, took a deep breath and let the air out as I squeezed the trigger. The bullet hit him in the neck and tore a huge piece of flesh from his head. He never made a sound; just flopped back and then fell over in the strangest position. After the shot the squad leader was raising hell and wanting to know what was going on up there. I yelled to him that the new guy was okay, and it was okay for him to come up to the point. After that, all the other Marines wanted to know my name.

We found the lost squad of Marines shortly after that. The odor of dead bodies rotting and the huge number of flies that were on them made a lot of the guys sick. I had blood and maggots all over my shirt so I took it off and got cussed out by some officer for it. "Still a new guy." We really had to struggle to get the bodies up on the next ridge in order for the 'copters to pick them up. I was totally exhausted from being on point and then dragging bodies out of the valley and up on to the next ridge. I noticed several people taking pictures and later realized that one was of me dragging one of the dead Marines up to the top of the ridge.

Most of them had been wounded and then shot in the face by the gooks. The radio operator I found, and I wrote his name down in a small Bible I had. I wanted to remember the name of the first Marine I saw dead in combat. His name was Paul Reed.

Since I was a PFC, I got the detail to put the bodies in ponchos and wrap them up as best we could. I had so many feelings going through me that day. I was so afraid, yet somehow I had survived my first real test in combat. Was I really a Marine yet or still a new guy?

As night set in, I wrote a Catholic priest a letter and told him I didn't think I would make it through this ordeal. I still don't understand why I was spared and so many others died.

This ends the account of my first day in combat in Vietnam with a Marine rifle company. For unknown reasons the events of that day are still very clear to me some twenty-three years later. I know that much combat was still in front of me, many real friends were killed. Some of their names I remember, some I don't. I do remember all their faces. I still see them right now as I write this account for you. I remember Patrick Gallagher, the bravest Marine that ever wore the uniform. He was so proud the day General Westmoreland presented him with the Navy Cross. We had our picture taken together. I remember the day I crawled to him, rolled him over and saw that horrible stare of death on his face; a hole in his head and his brains running out and me trying to push them back in, somehow thinking he would come back to life.

I remember Waltrich, killed on his first patrol. He was so handsome. I remember Price, who got the Dear John letter and then had his head blown off at the shoulders by a grenade. I remember Pettus, a cool dude. He looked like he was asleep with a slight smile on his face. So many more—Stroudt, Oldfield, Thomas, Armstrong, Dennison, Snyder, Morgan, on and on for what? Nothing! They all died for nothing, just like all the other Marines I was with.

This has been the toughest part for me. Trying to find some reason for all the insanity. There isn't any reason. I know now war has nothing to offer but pain, suffering, death, and insanity. War is truly hell on earth. We went to that hell and the only lucky ones are the ones whose names are on the Wall. I lived, but I really died in Vietnam. I went to war a nice all-American kid and came home a totally destroyed old man.

For years I have run from Nam with alcohol, but the time came when I had to make a stand. Either kill myself or get sober and face life. I'm able to do this today by the grace of God and by living one day at a time in the program of AA. I now work at a drug and alcohol treatment center, staying straight and helping other Vietnam vets cope with life on life's terms. It's by no means easy, but I've come to realize God didn't bring us this far to let us down now.

I firmly believe that all of us that made it home have a duty to help each other in any way we can. I love all vets and will "walk point" with any of them any time, any place. Hang in there and don't let the war claim you too! We have lost too many of our brothers now. No more! Remember that a power greater than us understands and has a special place for the Nam vet. He wants us to have peace at last!

Frank Erwin received six combat decorations, including two Purple Hearts. Frank was the lone survivor of an ambush on 30 March, 1967, during which all the members of 1st Squad, "H" 2/4 were killed in action, including Navy Cross recipient Patrick Gallagher, Silver Star recipient Clyde Matthews, Jr., and Robert J. Waltrich, who, with valor and courage, selflessly gave his life so that Frank Erwin could live.

Leon Guerra

Guerra: This means War.

My name is Leon Guerra. In Vietnam my friends called me "Groucho."

It's no coincidence that I'm in chapter thirteen in this book. I asked for it. Perhaps you are wondering why I would do that. Please let me explain. Since birth it was predestined that I go to war. My last name means "war" in Spanish or Italian. I have also been at war with myself ever since I left the service. I simply feel it can't get any worse than it is, so why not ask for the unlucky chapter. I'll tempt fate. I'm not afraid of bad luck. If it wasn't for bad luck, I wouldn't have any luck at all. I hope you enjoy my chapter. It's written for you, but it's really written more so for me. . . .

It's 6 p.m., Friday, September 29, 1989. It's raining out and raw cold. A good night to begin this chapter. It's not an easy one and please understand, for me to write about this is a walk back into depression and hell on earth in my mind.

My high school days were "normal." I was an average student and I somehow managed to graduate. One of the things I really enjoyed out of my four years of high school was the fact that I played in the band. I played clarinet and sax in a forty-five-piece school orchestra. We traveled all over New England, New York and even made an appearance at "Expo 67" in Montreal, Canada. Those were fun days, days without a care in the world. I thought life would go on forever like that. (Was I ever lame or what?) After school I would go to Louie Toupins Auto Body and work on wrecked cars to earn spending money. I always enjoyed auto body work. Back then I restored a 1961 Austin Healey "Bug eyed" Sprite, a 1954 Nash Metropolitan convertible, a 1954 MGTF and a 1929 Buick. These cars were all part of a collection I had. I no longer have them.

At this time in my life I am restoring a 1956 Morgan. (It's in my apartment).

I would also like to add that I did not drink or do drugs in high school.

When I graduated from high school in 1969 (Mount St. Charles in Woonsocket, Rhode Island) I drove out to Spartan School of Aeronautics in Tulsa, Oklahoma. After five months of school I got homesick and dropped out. I was eighteen and when I left school I lost my draft deferment. When I returned home the government came out with the draft lottery system and my number was sixty-six (born on Nov. 12,

1950). I knew my goose was cooked and there was no way out. In April of 1970 I went to my local Army recruiter and signed up for two years. On the fourteenth of that month I boarded a bus in Providence, Rhode Island and headed for Fort Dix, New Jersey. Little did I know that my life would never be the same after that day.

I must stop here for now because I'm in a depressive state just thinking of it. I will continue another day. My mood must be a happy one for me to write. (It hurts.) How I wish I could change it all; how I wish it didn't happen—the rage, the anger, the depression, hatred, numbness of emotion. I wish I could go to sleep and wake up and realize it was only a bad nightmare, a big fuckin' nightmare.

I hate them bastards—the government. I was fuckin' brain-raped and no one cares. At this time I could kill, kill, kill, kill and go on killing, but I can't kill the government for brain-raping me. Who the fuck could I kill? The entire government system? It's fuckin' impossible. Fuck you, bastard government pricks, stand on the other end of my M-16. I'll show you what it's like to get fuckin' brain-raped, you bastards.

I can't take these depressions anymore. Fuck them government cock-suckers. I need a rest from all this shit. I'll continue another day on this chapter. Please excuse the previous four-letter adjectives. It happens when I get depressed and angry. (Fuck them bastards.) Good night.

Wednesday night, 11:30 p.m. October 25, 1989. It's cold out, the sky is clear and I can see many stars. The wood stove is lit and my cat is sleeping next to it.

I can't sleep. I feel like a madman who must get this chapter done. I feel like I'm in Nam writing letters home again. I think I'm ready to continue on with this chapter. I don't know what the end result will look like, but the sad part about it all is that it is all true and I feel like a character who stepped permanently into the twilight zone.

For many years I put the war aside. I think I even forgot that I went. I even mentally denied the war or the fact that I went to it. It was a great mental defense mechanism that worked for the first few years. Now it no longer works like that. Flashbacks, depressions, suicide attempts and suicidal thoughts, tears, emotional numbness, anger, rage, confusion and alcohol misuse are all part of my life. I was never able to hold a male-female relationship together. I destroyed every one of them because of what happened in the service. I would love to have a wife and child, but that seems like it will never happen. I could never hold a job more than two to three weeks, so I have to work for myself, and that is tough at times because it's not easy working alone and constantly thinking about Vietnam.

It's on my mind every day.

When this book gets published I can never tell anyone I know that

I wrote this chapter. I don't want anyone to really know what I am or was like. Who would understand unless they were there? People that think they are close to me don't even know about this and what I have been through. Many would think I am sick.

I have three questions for all the people who were not there. What would you have done? How would you have reacted if you were there? How would you cope with it?

Please don't pass judgement on me when you read this chapter.

I knew many people who died over there and sometimes I wish I were one of them. I never knew life would be like this when I came home. I wonder if I ever did come home.

Let's begin with basic training. Here I am, nineteen years old, on a bus to Fort Dix, New Jersey. I'm scared shitless and alone, especially not knowing what to expect when I get to basic. I found out as soon as I got there. The bus stops and some big guy in a green Army uniform starts yelling at me and everyone else on the bus. What did I do to be yelled at? I started to feel fear and from that day on fear was with me. Fear grew to paranoia. It was all part of the brain raping. (Fuck them.) As we got off the bus we were shown how to get in formation and get our balls busted. This ball-busting was to be done for the duration of my time in the service. I actually thought that after basic it would stop. I was wrong; it just got worse. Whenever there was a formation we would get our balls busted. (I felt castrated at the end of basic.) I was in constant paranoia about making formations. It went to the extent that I hid under beds or in trash containers to avoid them. The guys would do anything to get out of the service; they all hated it. One guy, Hainesworth was his name, hurt his knee and he couldn't walk, so that night before he went to the medics he did at least 300 deep knee bends. His knee swelled up the size of a basketball. He was one of the lucky ones. They let him out. All through basic you were under pressure and told to kill and shown how to kill, how to make people suffer, how to kill and not feel guilt because the "gooks" (slang for Vietnamese) were not people, they were lower than that, they were lower than whale shit. I actually grew to hate these poor people that I never even knew. They were really just simple good people on the other side of the world who wanted to live as much as I did. Why did I hate them? Why did I want to kill them?

The Army turned me, a "normal" nineteen-year-old kid, into a living example of hatred, anger and rage, toward poor people in a faraway land. I was driven insanely into hatred. I wanted to kill. I lost all respect for life and what I learned in Catholic schools all my life. I totally forgot about the Ten Commandments, especially the one, "Thou shall not kill." I was brain-raped and the only thing I knew was what the Army wanted me to do, and that was kill. I was scared, but that didn't seem real anymore. I was turning numb to that. I wanted to kill and see a "gook" die. I wanted to fire rockets and squeeze a trigger on an M-60. I wanted control over life and death. I was the modern version of Dr. Jeckyll and Mr. Hyde. Threats were constantly yelled at us in basic, screaming and yelling at us. Physical abuse and exhaustion were everyday occurrences. We were denied sleep. We were all brain-raped the same way. It was a long slow process and a very thorough one. I congratulate the Army because they successfully turned me into what they wanted of a GI. I was so fuckin' brain-raped that I could no longer think on my own. I could only obey what my superiors told me to do. Maybe that's why I can't hold a job or a relationship today. I swore no one would ever control me again. One good brain-raping in life and you're all fucked up. (FTA = Fuck the Army.)

Basic was eight weeks, but when I came home on leave my family felt there was a change in me, especially when they woke me up unexpectedly in the morning. I would recite to them four-letter words they never heard from me before.

They knew something was up.

I went to Fort Rucker in Alabama for AIT for eleven weeks or so. I actually thought, and I was told, that AIT was better than basic. Those fuckin' government bastards lied. AIT was ten times worse than basic. We were under even more pressure. At that point I decided that there was no way out. I attempted suicide three times in AIT. I hated the Army. I was brain-raped and mentally abused so many times I could no longer control myself. Nothing mattered anymore. Dorothy and Mary were women I loved before I went in the service. Now they were only another human life to me. I was the survivor of a brain-raping and I was no longer my old self.

I was nineteen and scared.

One day after pulling guard duty all night and being kept awake for twenty-four hours, I received a letter from home saying that someone stole my younger brother's bicycle. That was the straw that broke the camel's back. I went into the first-sergeant's office and I started crying and yelling at him, telling him I wanted to go home: "I just can't take it anymore." I fell onto the floor and I hyperventilated and my whole body shook as I cried. My breathing sped up more and my knees pulled themselves to my chin and my arms and hands curled by themselves to my chest. I also became physically numb and very dizzy. Four sergeants picked me up and threw me into the front seat of a pickup truck. My body was kicking out of control and as it was doing this I kicked the dashboard. When we arrived at the hospital on base they took me and literally threw me on to a stainless steel table. I passed out. When I came to I was totally numb and could not move. They started yelling and screaming at me, telling me to get up. I couldn't move. After one hour or so I started coming back to "normal." I was leaving the hospital and walking home when I realized my cap had fallen off in the pickup truck; a GI is considered out of uniform without a cap. As I continued to my company a major came out of one of the buildings and started yelling at me about being out of uniform. I had to explain to him that I just came out of the emergency room. Three other officers attacked me the same way in twenty minutes and each time it put incredible pressure on my mind. I went to my company and attempted suicide again. I ended up at the hospital having my stomach pumped. I was sent to a psychiatrist after that and they still would not let me out of the Army.

I want you, the reader, to realize that pressure is how the Army brainwashes you (or brain-rapes you) to turn you into an Army machine. I was under incredible pressure twenty-four hours a day. I had turned into a machine, an Army machine. "Yes, Drill Sergeant. I want to kill, kill, kill, and go on killing (fuck you, Drill Sergeant)."

My training in AIT was in helicopter repair and learning how to be a machine gunner so we could fly and kill and kill and kill and fly. While I was at Fort Rucker it dawned on me that I was going to be sent to Vietnam. I just didn't care. I was so emotionally numb I wanted to go and get it over. I didn't have my own mind anymore. I was just a machine and a machine has no feelings and no mind, it just does what it is told and if it doesn't it is repaired (or brain-raped), reprogrammed again or destroyed. That's where I was at. I'm very very ashamed to write some of these things, but they are real and it did happen to me. If I lived or died it just didn't matter. "Work me or destroy me, I only want to do what you want me to do, Drill Sergeant. That is my only desire." Love was gone. I didn't even know what it was anymore. "Fuck you, Drill Sergeant, and if I ever saw you today, I wouldn't hesitate to kill you. I would enjoy every moment of it. Fuck you."

It's 3 a.m. I'm tired. The fire went out in the wood stove and my cat is giving me a funny look, like, "How come you're up later than me?"

I can't believe this abuse all happened before I went to Vietnam; and I'm on the American side. What did I do to deserve this? Why do they hate me? (Fuck them.) Does God forgive? Maybe I can't forgive myself. Oh well, I'm tired. Good night.

8:30 p.m. Nov. 6, 1989: Hey reader, how does it feel to be reading a chapter written by a brain-raped veteran who is pissed off at the American government?

One nice thing about America is that I can say all these things and I don't have to worry about being sent to jail because I said them.

Enough of that for now. Let's get back to the insanity of reality. Tomorrow. Good night.

9 p.m. Nov. 8, 1989: It's cold outside and warm in here. The woodstove is lit and I'm sipping on herbal tea.

I can't believe it's been almost nineteen years since Vietnam and I still have difficulty sleeping at night. Last night I was up all night just because thoughts about Vietnam kept me awake and scared. Just writing about Vietnam depresses the shit out of me. Inside I tell myself to keep on writing because another Vietnam vet may read this and it somehow may help him. I feel every Vietnam vet is my brother and I would do anything to help my brothers. That is the reason I'm writing.

I'm scared too, because these depressions are bad and I'm afraid that someday I may be at the wrong end of a weapon or hanging from a rope by my neck.

After I completed AIT at Fort Rucker, Alabama I was sent home for two weeks leave. That was one of the strangest times (other than Vietnam) in my life. I was totally—mentally and emotionally—numb; feelings were gone. All I had in my head was that I wanted to go to Nam and get it over with. I wanted to do what I was trained to do. Kill. I couldn't think on my own anymore. Leon no longer existed; he was gone forever, never to return. The Army created a new person. I was a killing machine who only knew anger and rage and all the other things I learned in basic and AIT. At that point in my life I could of walked up to anyone that looked like an Asian, pointed my weapon and squeezed the trigger and loved every moment of it. I would of laughed like an insane man while doing it because I enjoyed it. Sick, isn't it? You would never do that, you say. I learned never to judge a person until you wear his shoes. You don't know those feelings until it happens to you. I'm very ashamed to admit to you all these things, but it is true and I never told a soul until now.

My family and friends will never know that I wrote a chapter in this book because I am still too ashamed to tell them.

I was like a robot when I was on leave. I went to see all my friends in the daytime and at night I got drunk. My face never showed any emotion. I was like a rock; my thoughts were gone and my eyes were hollow. I actually felt I was a machine and I was out of place because I should be with the Army and not at home. The night I left to go to Vietnam I told my parents, with no emotion, that I would see them in one year. My friend Eddie Perolli, who came back from Vietnam six months earlier, drove me to the airport. Dorothy and I were together that night in his car. To this day, that was one of my fondest memories ever. I guess I wasn't that far gone because I do remember certain emotions that night that I hadn't felt for many months before.

I boarded the plane in Providence, Rhode Island, and flew to Oakland, California. I stayed there for five days. I received all my clothing for Vietnam in Oakland. While in Oakland I was in such a state of paranoia that I was in constant hiding. I did anything to avoid formations. I feared being yelled at again. One day I grabbed a fire bucket and walked around with it. I looked busy and no one bothered me; they thought I was assigned some detail (project) so they left me alone. That bucket and I were very close the next few days (fuck the Army).

One morning they woke us up and we had to stand at attention in front of our bunks so they could take roll call and after that we filed out in single file to make a formation in front of the building. As we filed out I hid under my bed. It was the last one in the far corner. I had suitcases all around it. I stayed under it looking through the suitcase cracks at the drill sergeant down the hall. He started to walk to my bunk; I was scared; but I felt like laughing and giving myself up. He didn't see me. (The stupid bastards.) He was standing eight inches from my face, looking out my window picking his nose. He didn't even know I was there. When he left I crawled out and grabbed the fire bucket and walked around the rest of the day looking busy. No one bothered me.

My third day, there I was, standing in a group of GIs and some captain called us over to do some detail. I just walked the other direction, pretending not to see or hear him. He started yelling at me, but he didn't know my name or number. I was actually thinking to myself, "What is the worst he'll do if he gets me? Draft me? Send me to Vietnam? What the fuck, I'm going there anyway, so fuck him." He never found me.

We boarded the plane to go to Nam. Words can't describe the feeling on the plane. I felt like I was being sent to a Nazi death camp. Guys were puking, drinking, crying, passing out and others were crying for Mom. I was in the twilight zone with a faraway look in my eyes and no feeling in my soul. We flew from Oakland to Alaska, then to Japan, and on to Bien Hoa, Vietnam. I think it was a total of nineteen hours in the air flying to Nam. It was nighttime when the plane landed and, as the door opened, I got my first whiff of Vietnam. I thought we landed at the city dump. It stunk terribly. Little did I know that in one month I would smell like that.

From Bien Hoa we were taken by military bus to Long Binh. As we drove through the streets I saw a lot of funny looking cars and people. We arrived at Long Binh in about thirty minutes.

That first night the sky looked like the Fourth of July. There was so much action going on and explosions all over that I thought to myself that people are actually dying here tonight.

The next morning I looked outside and saw my first Vietnamese person in the daylight. I started to laugh insanely, thinking to myself that I am actually here at the place I saw on TV and read about in the papers. This is it—the real thing—and I'm here. How did it happen? I stayed in Long Binh for four days, then I was assigned to the 25th Combat Aviation Co. in Long Binh. I would have my chance to do what I was trained to do. Kill, kill, kill and go on killing, and become a good Army machine, do the things they wanted me to do, and as long as I thought like them ("which for my part is not to think for myself") I was perfect for the job. "Yes, Drill Sergeant, give me more abuse. Brain-rape me again. I love the Army. I am the Army. I eat, sleep, and shit the Army. Brain-rape me more, Drill Sergeant."

When I got to my company, I felt very strange, like I didn't belong. My clothes were very green and theirs were all faded. Everywhere I walked people yelled out "Newby" (meaning I just arrived). They would yell out, usually when drunk, to bust my balls, "Short" (meaning they had a few days left in-country). I would go out and get drunk and yell out "Short" and we would all laugh. There were some good times in Nam, even if the movies didn't show it that way. (I'll tell more about the good times later.) We were all brothers and we helped each other. I wish I could see my buddies today and know how they are.

My first job in Vietnam was to repair helicopters and be a machine gunner/crew chief, fly around and do my thing. As a crew chief I would have to make formations (which I hated) and take more grief and pull guard duty along with staying up all night. This would add a lot to my paranoia about the Army. (My paranoia was at it's limit.) I heard that my friend, Luigi Rienzi, was going home. Luigi was a cook. I went to the mess-sergeant, Robert Burkett, and told him I knew how to cook. (I didn't know how to cook.) He took me into the mess hall and I was now a cook. Isn't that like the Army to take a mechanic and make him into a cook?

The reason I volunteered to be a cook was because a cook didn't have to pull guard duty or make formations. All I had to do was cook, get drunk and sleep. Also I would have every other weekend off and as an added benefit I became friends with everyone in the company because, as a cook, I met everyone when I served them food.

There were many mixed feelings in me at the time because I was brain-raped to kill people and now I wasn't doing that. I was cracking eggs and cooking roast beef instead. Somehow I felt I was out of place, so I volunteered to go up north—they were in need of help and I wanted to go help them out. "Up north" was getting up to 200 rockets fired at them every few hours and they needed assistance. The first-sergeant wouldn't let me go. "Why not," I wondered. "They train me to kill, they brain-rape the shit out of me to kill. I want to kill. It is my job and now I can't do it. Something's wrong. I don't feel right inside. Things aren't matching up anymore in my head and it doesn't make sense. Why can't I kill? You want me to kill, don't you? You trained me to kill, didn't you? Well, why can't I do it? This is fucked up. It doesn't make sense."

All of a sudden I get this crazy urge to start killing anyone around me (I'm now scared). I wanted to put a full clip into my M-16 and just squeeze the trigger and kill anyone—anyone will do. I didn't understand anymore. I was over the edge and stressed out. I just wanted a body count. Then I got this crazy urge to shoot up my room and fill my bed with lead. I don't know why, but I just wanted to shoot my bed. "I've got to get out of here," I thought to myself. "I'm going to hurt someone."

I go tell the first-sergeant I feel like killing and I want to turn in my M-16. He gives me this funny look and sends me to a psychiatrist. The doctor asks me why I want to kill. "Who the fuck is he to ask me why I want to kill? Doesn't he know I was only brain-raped one fuckin' million fuckin' times to kill and now I can't kill because they won't let me? What the fuck is wrong with these people? They make me a 'normal' kid from Rhode Island who loves fishing and homemade apple pie, turned into a fuckin' killing machine maniac insane bastard killer and now they won't let me fuckin' kill. What the fuck is wrong with this picture, Doc? I want to fuckin' kill. Don't you realize, Doc, I'm fuckin' insane now and you are keeping me here? Why the fuck don't you send me home or send me up fuckin' north? Let me kill. I want to kill, kill, kill."

Needless to say he did send me back to my company with a note, and the note said to the first-sergeant to, "Keep this guy away from the weapons. He might kill someone."

Isn't that what I was brain-raped for? "Don't they understand? What the fuck is going on?"

I was the only guy in Nam without a weapon.

A few weeks later I get this crazy urge to shave my head (why, I don't know). I go to this Vietnamese barber and tell him I want a haircut, "Same-same Buddha." He starts laughing and clips it all off. After that he rubs my bald head for luck. I started laughing. I went back to the company bald as an egg, an egg with a big moustache. When I returned to my company they threatened to give me an "Article 15" (a fine and punishment) for ruining government property (my hair). They let the charge go, then they slapped my wrist and told me not to let it happen again. (Fuck them.)

One night (after a few glasses of Jack Daniels) at the club I decided to walk back to my company with a few of the guys. We were all laughing on the way, then all of a sudden I tripped and fell into the river on the side of the road and passed out. The guys pulled me out and revived me. I got to my room and fell asleep fully clothed on top of the sheets. I forgot that the Vietnamese used the river as a toilet. I woke up in the morning with this massive hangover. I also found out I was covered with shit, piss, bugs and worms. "No wonder the guys were laughing at me last night."

By the way, I should mention that I had to cook that morning for the troops. (This is disgusting). Yes, I did take a shower before I cooked.

I want you, the reader, to know that every night was like the Fourth of July. Everywhere you looked you could see tracer bullets being fired. Just look up and you could see and hear action all over. Bombs and rockets were all around, and loud. As they got louder you knew they were coming for you. It was just a matter of time before you got it. This all led to incredible pressure and tension on me and everyone else. I felt my mind was gone after only a few months there. I was very depressed and drained. I attempted suicide again. I almost succeeded at it. I hated that place and so did everyone else there. We were all fed up and depressed.

One guy named Doane got drunk and told everyone he was going to kill himself. The sergeant yelled at him and told him to go to his room and sober up. He did go to his room. He also tied a rope to the ceiling and hanged himself to death. It was a sad moment. I felt bad for his family. We were all brain-raped and that was the result of it.

Please understand, it wasn't easy, never knowing when the VC would attack. That put incredible pressure on everyone.

Early one morning I heard rockets come in. In two seconds three had hit us. (I couldn't move). Five GIs died instantly—body parts all over. These GIs just got in-country two days before. "Why did they die and not me? Take me. I want to die." They didn't deserve it. They just got there. They were only kids—eighteen and nineteen years old. "God, what the fuck is going on? Why does this shit happen? We can't even go get Charlie, because he is gone as soon as he sets off his rockets. He runs like hell and you'll never find him. He smiles at you in the day and kills you at night. You don't even know who he is."

Maybe that's why Lieutenant Calley wiped out My Lai. They could of all been VCs. He didn't know.

Sadly, I grew to hate all Vietnamese. I'm sorry now, but that's what happened then.

Till it happens to you, you'll never know.

Drugs were a bad problem in Vietnam. One day I was closing the back doors to the mess hall and I heard a shot. I re-opened the doors and I saw a buddy of mine on the ground shaking and spazzing out. I thought he was fooling around, pretending to be shot. He wasn't fooling around, he was shot. He got it in the chest and blood was coming out all over. Within two minutes a helicopter was there with the medics sticking needles into his body. They took him to the field hospital. I never saw anything go so fast in my life. The medics were great.

You ask who shot him. A person of drugs did and he was as high as the sky at the time. They sent him to LBJ (Long Binh Jail). Who am I to say anything about him when I was mostly drunk over there.

I went to the hospital to see my buddy who was shot. He had tubes coming out all over his body. He lived, but was sent home to The World.

I'm tired and it's 2 a.m. I'll continue later. Writing all this brings back a lot of hurt and it's hard to deal with at times. I have to write it all and tell what it was really like. That is the only way people will know. This must never happen again. It was all so insane. I was only a kid and I had to do all this shit. What did I do to deserve this treatment? Good night.

9:30 p.m., November 13, 1989: I'm sitting at the table in my apartment looking at the car I'm building in my room. Yes, I'm restoring a car in my apartment. The cat is sleeping in it and I'm ready to continue on with this chapter.

Here I am using a lot of four-letter, offensive words to describe my feelings about what went on over in Nam, and I feel bad about that, I really do. I don't want to offend anyone. I also notice that after I write it all out and say how I really feel about what I went through, I feel better inside. It seems to help me. Since I've been home (about nineteen years) I think only three people have asked me what it was like over there. Two of the three were psychologists and the third was not a member of my family. No one else ever asked. I felt like a freak, like I did something wrong by going to Vietnam. I never really expressed how I felt and so I held it all in and because of that things got strange after I came home. I'll explain later. So if you don't understand my anger and why I use all those four-letter words, please be patient. Maybe you will understand in time.

I have mentioned and I will mention more about drinking in Vietnam because I was there thirteen months and I was drunk for about twelve months. Please keep in mind I never drank before I went in the service.

One night after a few hours of drinking at the club, a few of my buddies and I went to Doanes' room (the guy that hanged himself). I decided to write a note on the ceiling where he hanged himself. The note said, "Doane hung around here."

I know you think it's sick that I did that, but that's okay, because I was mentally gone.

One morning, after an evening with Jack Daniels on the rocks, I woke up and the room was still spinning. I only got two hours of sleep. I woke up drunk and I felt like the living dead. I also felt very ill. I was supposed to cook breakfast for the GIs. I was too sick to do it. I just couldn't look at raw eggs that early, so Floyd Daniels (no relationship to Jack), the other cook, served it. He also prepared lunch with the understanding that I would be in to serve it. I agreed. So here I am at two minutes before lunch with this urge to puke again. I run out the backdoor and get on my hands and knees and start puking like a dog. As I'm doing that the lunch whistle blows and the guys are coming in to be fed. The way into the mess hall was by the back, where I was. Everyone saw me puking and they all knew I was the cook. Needless to say no one showed up for lunch that day.

I remember a company party one day when we were all at a BBQ that the cooks set up. I was cooking and drinking up a storm. We were all having fun. All of a sudden two roommates break out into a fight, over what I don't know. I do know that one was from Alabama and the other was from Georgia. The captain broke it up and sent the one from Alabama to his room to sober up. He goes to his room and pisses on his roommate's bed then he drops his pants and shits on the floor. After that he passes out on the bed he just pissed in. About a half hour later the other roommate goes to his room and sees the shit on the floor and notices the other guy is passed out cold in his bed. He wakes him up and they start fighting again. They both slipped on shit and fell on the floor and were rolling around fighting in it. They were covered with it. After a while of fighting they realized what had happened. They both started laughing about it. They went arm-in-arm to the showers, and as they scrapped off the shit they had a shit fight with it. There was shit all over. They threw it on the walls, mirrors, ceiling and floors. The place stunk really bad.

Vietnam was not like anything I ever experienced at home. People just let it all out and didn't care.

Good night.

11 p.m., Friday, November 17, 1989: I just had a few beers with Nancy and I decided to come home and write a few more lines. (Authors note: Nancy = nice girl; too bad she is engaged to Walter.)

There were many times in Vietnam that I would get into this homesick mood. I would go to the runway and stretch out on the ground at night. I would just stare at the sky, watch the fireworks, listen to the action going on and I would daydream about home. Helicopters would fly over me and land upwind. That runway strip was a mental escape for me. I was only nineteen years old, 10,000 miles away from home, and I wanted to go back. Why did they have to take kids eighteen and up and send them to Vietnam to grow up so fast? What's wrong with the American government? Didn't they realize they were creating monsters out of us by doing that? Some guys that lived wanted to die.

Those that died wanted to live and everyone else was confused. I hope the government has learned a lesson out of all this. I hope no one has to go through it again.

Loneliness and depression were a major force in Nam. It was one of the "biggies." You just wanted to go home. The only way out early was in a body bag or with a Purple Heart. That's a heavy price to pay, and it happened too many times. I felt like a caged lion. I was trapped, confined. I felt like it would be an eternity before I got out. Hope was gone. (Imagine that it was only thirteen months and it felt like an eternity.) The pressure built up tremendously within me. I knew I couldn't go AWOL because the VC would get me. Even if they didn't get me I would have to cross an ocean to get back to America. It was hopeless. I can't swim and I fear water. A lot of good a raft would do. I gave up again. I went to my room and took a lot of pills and booze. I hoped never to awaken again. Another suicide attempt failed. I somehow pushed on even though I felt hopeless. I don't know where I got the strength to continue.

At one point I met a medic in Vietnam. He explained hypnosis to me. He showed me how to use it to relax and put things in perspective. I feel hypnosis saved my life over there and to this day I still use hypnosis, only I use it to help others to relax, stop smoking, lose weight, etc. I never would of thought anything good could have come out of my experience over there. I have to say that Vietnam is where I met my profession (hypnosis). I may have divorced it a few times since Nam, but I always went back to it.

One weekend I volunteered to take one of my buddy's place as a door-gunner (machine gun operator) on a "Huey" (UH-l Helicopter). As we flew out we had the radio piped into our helmets. I can still hear Michael Jackson singing "Never can say good-bye" as we flew. To this day that song still reminds me of Vietnam. (I guess everything reminds me of Vietnam, because it's on my mind daily. It's like a big monster chasing me around in my everyday life. I hope it never gets me. I'm scared.)

Anyway, as I was saying, we flew out on a mission to a faraway base. As we landed I became paranoid. I knew they were Americans, but they looked like they just walked out of hell. They were all tired looking and unshaven. Their uniforms were faded, torn and very dirty. Many of the men were bandaged. It scared me just looking at them. They didn't look like the American Army I knew. None of them smiled. I really felt bad for these people. I'm not sure, but I think I saw body bags off to the side. I remember feeling fearful and paranoid. I wanted to help them, but I knew I was as bad off as they were. I wanted to run. What could I do? Nothing. To this day that image has never left me. We returned to home base that afternoon and I felt a little more secure.

One day I was in the mess hall baking bread. Bread must rise twice before you bake it. When it first rises you shake it and let it rise again. Not too far from the mess hall was the ammo dump (where all the ammunition is stored). A VC rocket came in and hit the ammo dump while my bread was on it's second rise. There was an explosion like you never heard before. It shook the earth. A huge mushroom hit the sky and my bread rise dropped for the second time. (It doesn't rise three times. I had to make new bread.) I was pissed off and the bread was ruined. Fortunately, no one was hurt. Life goes on (I hope).

There were times I used to stare at the sky and look at the Freedom Birds or airplanes that brought the guys into and out of Vietnam, and wish I was leaving on one of them. Whenever a GI saw a Freedom Bird, he would yell it out and everyone would look up and point at it and yell out the number of days they had left. If you had less than ninety-nine days you were a "Two-digit Midget." If you had nine days or less, you were a "One-digit Midget." I never thought I'd make it to one-digit.

2 p.m., Sunday, November 19, 1989: It's thirty-four degrees out and sunny.

I left early this morning to go to the ocean and relax for a while. The beach is nice when there is no one around. It's a good place to meditate about life. I often go to the ocean and think about my existence and wonder why I am still living when so many others died over there. What is my purpose? There has to be a reason I'm still around. Maybe I'll find it, maybe I won't. Who knows.

There were too many things that happened to me in Vietnam and I could probably write a series of books about it all. Maybe this is all I'll say about it. I would like to say that one thing that really sticks out in my mind is the day I left that place (my body left, but my mind didn't). We boarded the Freedom Bird and, as the wheels left the ground, everyone went wild. They clapped, yelled, screamed, hugged each other, and some cried. I was just quiet and emotionally numb. I stared blankly into space. I didn't really feel safe till I was many miles over the Pacific. I felt they still had rockets that could hit the plane that far out.

When we landed in Oakland, California, some guy had a hangover and they thought he had a tropical disease, so the troops were ordered to stay on board the plane for a few hours more, till he got checked out. Two hours felt like an eternity.

We left the plane and boarded a bus to go to the processing center to get processed out of the Army. (I felt like processed meat.) As the bus left the airport there was a war protest outside of the gates. Hundreds of people were protesting our involvement over there. Didn't they realize I was like them. I didn't want to be there. I wanted the war stopped as much as they did. Why were they calling me a rapist and baby killer? I didn't do that sort of thing. Didn't they understand everything was so crazy over there—anything could of happened at any time. How would they have reacted if they were there? "Don't yell at me. Tell President Nixon about it. Don't take it out on me. Just leave me alone. I want to get the fuck out of the Army and get away from here."

We entered the processing center and I processed out of the Army. I was on my way home the next day and, as I went to the airport in Oakland, California, some girl walked by me and the first thing that made me feel home was the fact that she had this great perfume on. I'd forgotten what it was like. (Talk about being brainwashed.)

I landed in Boston at midnight and hitch-hiked into Rhode Island. My family did not know I was coming home and I wanted to surprise them. On the way home I had the driver drop me off at my friend "Fat Bob's" house (it was 2 a.m.). I wanted to see him. His family was sleeping, so I climbed up to the roof of his house and tapped on the window to his room on the second floor. When I left to go to Vietnam he slept on the second floor. I didn't know he now slept on the first floor. In the meantime, his father hears me on the roof and thinks someone is breaking in. He comes out with his shotgun and starts firing shots at the roof over my head. I actually thought I was back in Nam again. I can't believe it. Is this how I'm going to get it, on a roof in Rhode Island? I finally convinced him it was me. As I came down we all hugged and laughed. I stayed there for about half an hour. After that I walked home to meet my family.

The next day I went to see Mary, a girl from my past. It was nice seeing her again.

I was twenty years old when I returned from Nam. It was November 2, 1971. That meant I could not legally buy a beer. Crazy, isn't it? I could go to Nam and legally kill people, but I couldn't legally have a beer with my friends when I came home. It just didn't make sense.

From the time I came home till now my life has been one of great searching.

One of the things I noticed when I came home was that I couldn't think for myself. It was almost impossible to make any decisions. I had to be told what to do. I was still in the Army mentally. I got up early each day. I made my bed and shined my shoes. I got a haircut every three weeks. It was like being on automatic pilot. That went on far about nine months.

In December of 1971 I entered Johnson and Wales College and dropped out one year later. In January of 1973 I entered Roger Williams College. I dropped out of Roger Williams in June of 1973 because the college was too close to a very high bridge. Whenever I felt pressure from school my thoughts would be of suicide and jumping off the bridge. I went back to Johnson and Wales in September of 1973 and finished my degree in business.

While in college and for a little while after, I worked at Louie Toupins Auto Body doing auto-body work. In the evenings after I graduated from college I went back to school to study hypnosis. Shortly thereafter I opened up an office and started my professional practice. I was very busy. There were days I would see up to thirty people a day. What I didn't realize was that all these people put an incredible pressure on me. The pressure was so great that one day I fired my secretary and closed the office. I said to myself I would never practice hypnosis again (my first divorce from hypnosis).

In the early days of my practice I met this beautiful woman. Diane was her name. She had long dark hair and beautiful hazel eyes. She was very gentle. We got along great and shared many wonderful moments together. I was twenty-four and she was twenty-one. We were talking about marriage and a life together. We were both very, very happy. One morning as she left work to go home—she worked all night for the phone company—a drunk driver hit her car and killed her instantly. It was Mothers Day 1974. I miss her greatly and I have never forgotten her and the beautiful person she was. I hope she is experiencing happiness in her other life, wherever she is.

I think the pressure of her death and the pressure of the business is what caused me to close my practice. I went to Europe after that to relax, sight-see and meet some of my relatives in Italy. It was great. I loved it. I also spent time in England and while there I opened up an export business. I bought old Jaguar automobiles and shipped them to America for resale. It was a fun business.

I just got tired of it and closed up.

I returned to the States with no goals or purpose in my life. I thought to myself that there has to be a reason for living. There has to be a plan for it all. I made it home alive from Nam, not just to exist and waste my life away. I've got questions and I'm looking for answers. One day a close friend of mine, Richard Ayotte, suggested that I might find the answers to my questions at a monastery, living with the monks. He said it might help to look in that direction. I moved into a Trappist Monastery and stayed for a while. It was a mind opening experience—a very unique and special experience. I highly recommend it to anyone who is soul seeking.

I left the monastery and went back into the hypnosis business. I would try again.

In the summer of 1976 I met Fran. She was a special soul to me. I loved her dearly. We were mentally one together. I also knew she was seeing someone else at that time. It got to the point that I wanted her for myself. I felt that if I was to let her go and she was to come back she would be mine. If she didn't come back she never was mine. I let her go and she never came back. I was deeply hurt, but I feel that was the best way. I hope she is happy in life and I wish her well.

I continued my hypnosis practice till about 1979. I was then ready for something new. I opened up a restaurant. It was called "Leons Sandwich Cafe." It was a good thing but I felt empty inside. I didn't feel complete with that business, so I closed it. I then opened up an auto-body shop and used car lot. The auto body and sales were good but it put an incredible pressure on me.

Since my experiences with the Army I have never been able to take pressure. I closed the business and took a year off. During that year off I earned my pilots license. I also returned to college for a few years and received a degree in electronics. I had the intent of repairing computers after I graduated, but I never did because I realized I couldn't have a boss above me telling me what to do. I think I would have had flashbacks of Army life and I didn't think I could handle that pressure.

The next few years were spent in and out of the hypnosis business. I also entertained in many night clubs as a hypnotist. I worked at a few radio stations as a DJ along the way. I must say that that was an experience I'll never forget. I could act totally insane and get away with it. It was great, but the pressure and responsibility got to me, so I quit.

At this time in my life I am back in the hypnosis business again. I have two offices. I am also working full-time towards a degree in psychology at the University of Rhode Island. I received the inspiration to write this chapter from an English class at URI. We were studying novels about Vietnam. I decided mentally that it was my time to write about the crazy war that has been haunting me for years.

I hope you can accept or understand what I have written. You don't have to like it, but please try to understand it.

I'm young and I look forward to learning more about life. Every night I get on my knees and thank God I'm alive. I also thank him for all he has shown me. Try it. It's nice.

6:02 p.m., Sunday, November 19, 1989: The chapter's finally done, and yes, it is raw cold outside and about to snow. Not the End.

They showed me how to go to Vietnam, but not how to come back. I'm still in Vietnam and I'm afraid to leave.

Robert W. Hecker

I went to high school in Okinawa between 1960 and 1965. That was probably the impetus that got me started thinking about Vietnam. My father was commandant of the Usur Pack Intelligence School on Okinawa at the time. A lot of the students who would come from Pakistan, Korea, India, Thailand and Vietnam had a great influence on my life. I got to talk to a lot of the Vietnamese students in those days and I got a little more insight into the problems there than most Americans back in the States were getting. Especially since it was in the early '60s, everything I heard and read about Vietnam in those days had a great impact on me. That was probably the time that I made the decision to join the Army upon graduation from high school, and to go to Vietnam.

The only thing that I hoped for at that time was that the war wouldn't wind down and that it would keep going and going and going until I graduated so I could get there in time to fight in Vietnam, like my father did in WWII and Korea. I felt it was a macho thing to do at the time. My country needed me and I was raised in a John Wayne image to fight for my country and to defend it right or wrong, and that is what my plans were. However, when I came back to the States in 1965, I went to work at the Vaughn training school for the mentally retarded as a summer counselor and there I met the person who would turn out to be my future fiancee and future wife. My first wife. And I kind of waylaid my plans and decided to go to college for six months, and got a college deferment. The Army had tried to draft me while I was in high school. When I got back in the States I still had half a year to go. I notified them that I was still in high school and had a semester to go to graduation and that I was going to continue on to college. I made that decision because I didn't want to worry my fiancee at the time and I wanted to see if I could suppress the feelings of Vietnam by going off to school.

When I got to college, I found it very boring. I hated it. All that I could think about was Vietnam. The following summer I went back to work at the Vaughn training school again and started a relationship with my fiancee, and decided to enlist in the Army. I did it against my father's wishes, but at that time I was eighteen and he really didn't have anything to say about it. I signed up for the infantry, airborne infantry, in fact, and was sent to Fort Gordon, Georgia. There I took my basic and eventually went to Airborne AIT, which is also at Fort Gordon. Upon completion of this training, I was supposed to go to Fort Benning. However, I was tired of being a trainee and, with some of my other friends, Emmett Anderson, Doug Gershol, and Alvin McCarthy, we decided, "Hey, forget Airborne—we're going to Vietnam." Upon graduation from infantry, we got direct orders for the 199th Flight Infantry Brigade. However, after a fifteen-day leave at home, we were assigned to Fort Lewis, Washington at a holding company, where we stayed for a month.

We missed most of the '68 Tet Offensive. However, we still had direct orders to go to the 199th and, upon entering Vietnam, we were sent directly to our unit. We spent two weeks in a training outfit teaching us the ins and outs of Vietnam, which amounted to nothing. Next thing I know I was assigned to Charlie Company 2nd & 3rd Infantry Battalion as a rifleman. I guess that's where my story begins.

My feelings of being in Vietnam—the first day as I walked with my platoon—were scary. I didn't know anything about Vietnam and didn't know what to expect. The old guys, seeing a new man arrive in-country, were apprehensive about talking to me. In fact, nobody talked to me. It was probably the most alone feeling I ever had in my life. I didn't know how to load my rifle, how to take it apart, or how to bend the pins back on a grenade. I remember, as soon as I arrived in my platoon, the lieutenant said," Hecker, come here. Your outfit is going on ambush. Get your stuff together and hurry up. They are walking out of camp now."

I wondered, "My God, what the hell did I do? What the hell did I sign up for? This is the way it's supposed to be?" In all the movies, man, all the guys rally round you, try to help you, try talk to you and I remember that night on ambush, a Spec-4 next to me said, "Look, Hecker, it's your turn on guard duty. When the guy calls in and asks if you are okay, just break squelch."

I sat there wondering what the hell does "break squelch" mean. He didn't even bother to show me. I remember the guy calling us three or four times saying, "Are you okay on ambush? Are you okay on ambush? Break squelch if you are okay. Break squelch if you can hear me." I kept thinking, "What the hell does 'break squelch' mean? What am I supposed to do?" The next morning nothing was said about it, so I figured that they assumed we had fallen asleep on duty or, since they had a new man, he didn't know what he was doing. But that night I didn't even bother to waken the next person for guard duty. I just stayed up all night because I was too embarrassed to ask what "break squelch" meant.

Getting back to my base camp after that ambush, I just felt so alone. I remember coming back and all my hand grenades falling off my web gear and the guy looking at me and saying, "You fucking idiot. Man, what the hell's the matter with you?" I remember thinking, "What did I do?" He showed me that the grenade pins were not bent back—not attached properly. I stood there with my grenades around my ankles.

"Am I ever going to be able to catch on?" I made one promise to myself, that if I ever got enough in-country and ever mastered the art of being an infantryman, and that if I ever had the opportunity with any new men that entered country, I would take time out to try to help them. I made that promise to myself and I kept it to myself, because I didn't want anybody coming to Vietnam as hopeless and scared and lonely as I did the first couple days.

The lieutenant for my platoon was also new. His name was Lt. James Clark. I remember, we were on a sweep south of Saigon and nobody would talk to me. This was the third day in-country and nobody would talk to me. I didn't talk to anybody else and I just kept waiting and waiting for someone to come up and start a conversation. This day we had been airlifted to the Delta and we had gotten off the chopper and were running the sweep and I remember the scared feeling and I was so intent on doing all that the platoon sergeant said. We were by this hooch and they were scouting around the area. The platoon sergeant said, "Hecker, get over there and cover that side of the building." I was so scared as I went over to that side of the building and sat down on top of a knoll. I remember feeling this biting sensation on my legs and my back. I looked down and I was sitting down on top of a red ant bed. I was so scared. "The sergeant said to stay here." And in my mind, when the sergeant said stay there, you stayed there regardless if you were sitting on an ant bed or whatever else was happening. Your position was there and that's where you had to stay. I remember sitting there for five minutes, like an idiot, waiting for the sergeant to say "come on back here." I know it sounds stupid now, thinking about it; I know it sounds ridiculous. Probably people can't even conjure up the feeling of why some asshole would sit on an ant bed. But, being in-country, being in an atmosphere like it was right there in the '68 Tet Offensive, being the new guy in the platoon, I wanted to impress—I wanted to show the sergeant that I could do everything possible to try to be a good soldier. Just so he would talk to me, just so he would say, "Hecker, we accept you now."

I remember a day later I was called back to the rear because of some bullshit that had occurred before I had gotten out of my platoon. One of the fellows in our training brigade before we went out to our original infantry had been arrested for stealing a radio and I was implicated in it and I had to go back to the rear. The CO wanted to talk to me and I had been back there two days. One day the first-sergeant—"Top"— called me into his office. I walked in and he started yelling at me. "Hecker, it should have been you! That should have been you! That should have been you!" I sat there thinking, "What the fuck, man. What the hell is going on? What did he mean, it should have been me? "Well, Hecker," the Top was stating," the man that took your position on point where you should have been, was killed and Lieutenant Parks was killed. They were walking point for the company and came upon an enemy bunker and were gunned down by machine guns. I think it was a 51-caliber. Lieutenant got it in the chest and the other fellow that took your place (number two man behind the point man, which is where I started out because they wanted me to learn how to walk point, had taken my position) he was killed also."

I just kept thinking, "My God. I mean, how am I going to be accepted now? Here the Top is yelling at me. I have only been in-country two to three weeks. When I go back to the squad they are going to be on me because I wasn't there, because a fellow who had been in-country four to five weeks had been killed in my place, when it should have been me. My God, the country says it's going to take care of the boys—their sons it sends over to Vietnam. When the hell is somebody going to take care of *me*? When the hell is someone going to explain to me what the hell my position is here? What the hell am I supposed to be doing? When the hell is somebody going to train me so I can be the best soldier I can be?"

It just became such a harrowing experience. It was like nothing that I'd seen in the movies. It's almost like I became so dumbfounded about everything that was going on to me that I just closed into a shell. I went back into the tent and sat there for a day and a night just thinking, "What the hell is going on?" I just wished to God at that point that I had never signed those papers, that I never felt, "Hey, this is the macho thing to do." I kept thinking that the sergeant that signed me up for the infantry must have felt like, "I've got a real dumb ass here." Man did I feel like one. I felt so lonely because the only person that had taken time out to speak to me during that sweep before he was killed was Lieutenant Parks.

I remember, he stopped to talk to me for a minute. The conversation was too casual and brief. It probably wouldn't mean anything to anybody talking on the street, but he asked me where I was from and I said, "Sir, I am from New Jersey." He mentioned that he had gone AWOL a couple times in Ocean City and sat on the beach and I told him that me and my fiancee liked to sit on the beach, that I missed it there. He smiled at me and helped me over this little stream. Just the fact that we touched hands in itself was such an insignificant thing. The conversation, two hands touching, but it was the feeling of warmth, that somebody cared for a moment. It made me feel like a human being again. It made me feel like he was willing to give me a chance. Then the only person in the world that would talk to me or I felt like would give me a chance, because even he was new in-country—he needed a chance—was suddenly killed and taken away from me. It was probably the worst feeling in my life. If anything had to happen my first two weeks in Vietnam it didn't need to be this. I just wished over and over again that it had been me that had been killed or been shot or if I could have been med-evaced out of the country back to the States. I would even have taken an arm blown off, just to get out of that predicament. All I kept thinking was "Why, why, why did I do it?" The best way I guess to sum up how I felt at that moment was that I hated my mother for bringing me into the world. I remember thinking, "Why did that fucking bitch bring me into the world? Here my parents are supposed to protect me, help me and my mother brought me into the world and sent me off to fight a war." What was my purpose in life?

I felt alone. I felt tired. I felt drained. I felt sick to my stomach. It was like I felt utter contempt for my mother for bringing me into my world and for my parents for creating this war. It wasn't like it was supposed to be in the movies. People can't understand when you tell them something like that. Maybe another Vietnam veteran can understand when I say I hated my mother at that moment. But I doubt if other people can really understand, because I know—my children—I will protect them to the day I die. I will protect them from war. I will protect them from whatever I can. I just feel the need to protect them, I guess, like I should have been protected at that time. But, I remember writing my mother a note, my father a letter and stating what the situation was in Vietnam and how scared I was and stuff—how I wished I could come back to the States. I remember getting a letter from them, and maybe it was his old World War II sentences stating that this is war, this is the way it is. Well, I kept thinking, "You know, Dad, this isn't the way it was in WWII. This isn't the way it was in Korea. This is a fucked up war. I've only been here three weeks and I am already understanding what Vietnam is all about. It's a fucked up place. It is a fucked up war. It's just a place for young guys to get fucked up."

I don't know how else to explain it other than at that moment I felt like I was the loneliest person on earth. All I wanted to do was talk to my girlfriend on the phone. I just wanted somebody to be my friend. What happened was that a couple of days back in the rear, I signed up for a LRRP detachment. I wanted to go to the 71st LRRP outfit. I wanted to be Special Forces, but after I dropped out of Airborne at Fort Benning and was sent to Vietnam, I was told that I could go into a LRRP outfit and that would be as close to Special Forces as I wanted to get without going through the training at Fort Bragg. So after about a week back at the rear, after talking with the CO, I was transferred to the 71st LRRP detachment. I never did see my friends back . . . I thought of them as my friends, but I knew if I ever went back to my squad it would be even worse than when I left. I would stay with the 71st LRRP detachment for three months and I went on seven, maybe eight LRRP missions with my team—number was sixteen—and I remember my sergeants, Sergeant Danzer and Sergeant Piper. I'll never forget them. They were first-class soldiers. They took time out to teach me and I think that was possibly what saved me—helped me to understand Vietnam—helped me to make me a better soldier.

It was being in that LRRP outfit. I remember the first mission we went on, on the Cambodian border up by Tay Ninh. We were assigned to an infantry company that was running a sweep along the Cambodian border. I remember that morning, we woke up and I was so proud to be a LRRP because the LRRPs were distinguished by their camouflaged uniforms, and just having the uniform made me feel like a soldier. And being in a team of six guys, there was a closeness, a camaraderie that you couldn't get initially in a infantry platoon, until you made friends with everybody in the outfit. Whereas here, all six guys depended upon each other and we needed each other, so familiarity became a necessity.

That morning I remembered waking up after clearing the LZ the day before. The NVA came across the Cambodian border and set up mortar positions and were firing into our LZ and I remember we took five, six or seven rounds, and I remember sitting there mesmerized. I couldn't believe what I was seeing. They were actually firing at us. I was in this foxhole looking out and the rounds were going off around me, landing fifty, sixty, seventy yards away from me. They were just circling the perimeter. I was thinking, "My God, this is exhilarating." The feeling was there that I should be scared, but I was so mesmerized by what was going on.

They stopped firing mortar rounds and I remember Sergeant Danzer, who used to be with Special Forces, but was now with our LRRP outfit as a team leader, told the captain he wanted to go out into the woodline and search out the area, to see if he could pinpoint where the mortar fire was coming from. I remember we walked out of the base camp and my friend Al McCarthy said good-by to me—one of the guys in AIT that decided to go into Vietnam with me and decided not to be a trainee. Well, as soon as we hit the woodline and walked twenty, thirty, forty meters into the woodline, all the sudden all hell broke loose. Bullets were going over our heads. Suddenly the infantry behind us was firing into the woodline. Sergeant Danzer said, "Get down! Get down!" So we got down in a crouching position.

There was this big hole. We walked into the woodline about forty meters and there was this hole. It was like God had placed this hole there. We were in this hole and were sitting there and bullets were going over our heads. We could hear the AK-47s and we stayed there for about fifteen minutes. I listened to Sergeant Danzer talking to the captain, stating that we needed help. The captain said, "If your ass isn't out of there in another ten to fifteen minutes, we're going to call artillery fire in on your position." He said we were taking too many hits within the base camp—I think six guys were killed about fourteen or fifteen guys were wounded.

I remember this guy by the name Sherman. He was our pointman. I remember Sergeant Danzer saying, "Sherman, you got to get to the other side of this woodline," and he called in for choppers and they were going to be waiting for us over there. He pinpointed our position— where we should be for the chopper pick up, and I remember Sherman— it was unbelievable, it was like he was gliding through the jungle. I remember walking, three or four men behind, and thinking—you know, the bullets going over our heads and behind us, and this is the way it should be, the camaraderie and the guys. "Six guys in an outfit and here we are depending on one another." I remember getting to the other side of the woodline and we got there and huddled together and had a team meeting, and Sergeant Danzer saying, "Hecker, I want you twenty yards on flank. I want you facing this way until the choppers come in. I'll call you back."

I remember feeling so proud that he picked me to go out on the flank and take a position there. It was like he trusted me. It was like Lieutenant Parks all over again. It was like he trusted me and I felt good about the situation. The scariest part about it was that I sat there for about ten minutes till the chopper came. They finally picked us up. When we finally got up in the air, I remember circling over the area about 200— 300 feet up over the area, and we could see the North Vietnamese running back out of the woodline. I remember seeing ten or fifteen NVA running right up and into the position, on the flank where I had been asked to stay by Sergeant Danzer. I remember thinking, "My God, there were sixty or seventy, running out of the woodline, back over to Cambodia."

And you could see them running, and I remember the pilot telling us not to fire at them because they were in Cambodia. And I kept thinking, "My God, if they'd been late, if they hadn't picked us up in time, what the hell would I have done with fifteen NVA running at me?" They would probably have found my fucking head in Cambodia, my balls stuffed in my mouth.

Man, it was exhilarating, but it sent a shock through me that, "Hey, this is no more bullshit. The games are over. You are going to have to deal with this, son."

I just kept thinking, "Thank God, man." When this happened I was in the LRRP outfit with six guys. Six guys that I felt comfortable with. Like I said before, if it hadn't been for the LRRPs, I never would have developed the instincts that I needed to continue to survive in Vietnam.

I stayed with the LRRP outfit for another two months after that. I went on another six or seven missions. Nothing was as eventful as what happened on the Cambodian border up in Tay Ninh. I left the LRRP outfit because at the time, my friend Emmet Henderson, who had also gone to Vietnam and had dropped out of Airborne school with me, had also transferred to the LRRP outfit. He had been put in for the Silver Star, and about two weeks after he had been put in for the Silver Star for heroism, he was suddenly kicked out of the outfit for some stupid-ass reason—'cause he wouldn't get a haircut. I remember thinking, "Hey, here is a guy that is a soldier—here is a guy that killed three goddamned gooks on his own—saved his LRRP outfit. And here is the thanks, man." They took away his fucking Silver Star and they were going to send him back out to an infantry outfit.

I had orders for Nha Trang, to go up there for reconnaissance school. I thought Emmet Henderson would be going with me. Then I learned he was being dismissed from the outfit. "They're kicking him out for a fucking hair cut." Suddenly the bullshit of the Army, the bullshit of Vietnam, the bullshit of everything started coming into play and I started realizing even more what a fucking game this was. You could be the best soldier in the world, but if somebody didn't like you, you were shit.

Well, when Emmet was kicked out of the outfit, I remember the sergeant of our outfit, Sergeant Overpeck—I told him I'm not going to reconnaissance school; I'm going to an infantry outfit with Emmet. I remember him putting up a stink. I remember Sergeant Piper talking to me, trying to talk me out of it. I said if this is the way this outfit is run, I don't want any part of it. I also figured I had learned a lot from this outfit and that I could go back out to an infantry outfit—"I know I can survive, and if Emmet's going out there, I am going out there with him."

I remember about four or five days later, our orders came in and we were assigned to E Company, 4th and 12th Infantry Battalion. It was a recon platoon and I remember our first area. We were assigned to a little town outside of Chu Lon called Betri Dahn. We were assigned there to work with the popular forces. We were to help them run ambushes at night and also to help set up a defensive perimeter. They had a little base camp there with a defensive perimeter we helped them set up, with barbed wire. We'd gotten a 50-caliber machine gun and we really fortified their camp. We worked about three or four months helping the PFs and training them. I remember, after training them, going back there about four or five months after we'd left the area. The VC had waited for us to leave, and after we had left they came and they completely destroyed what we had tried to build. It was the most depressing feeling in the world 'cause we'd made good friends with the popular forces. I felt a close camaraderie, even though they were Vietnamese, because they had been nice to me and I always tried to be nice to them. When I saw the destruction of the camp and what we tried to accomplish, it made me sick. However, when I got to E Company 4th and 12, I think that was what suddenly caused me to become even more bitter about my stay in Vietnam. Probably the last experience that I had caused me to feel that Vietnam was fucked up.

This young fellow by the name of Ralph Lee Bouville was from a little town right outside of Chicago. I can't think of the name. I think it's Deerfield, Illinois. He was eighteen years old. He had been assigned to Vietnam as a desk clerk. The thing I always wanted to ask his parents was why, when they got the notice of his death, didn't they question the Army about how their son, who was sent to Vietnam as a desk clerk, could have been killed as an infantryman. He had no formal training as an infantryman, had no understanding of being an infantryman. He had gotten in some sort of trouble back at the rear with one of his sergeants, which happened with a lot of guys, and he was assigned to an infantry outfit. I think because of the problems that he had with the sergeants, he probably asked for assignment with an infantry outfit.

I remember asking Ralph, "What the fuck are you doing here, man? Like, why the fuck are you here? We are all trying to get back to the rear and here you are trying to come out to the field." And I remember his exact words were, "I want to be out here where the men are." I can still see this kid. He had a baby face. He looked like he was thirteen or fourteen years old. It went back to my initial thoughts when I first got in-country—"I am going to help Ralph. I am going to help any guys who come out to my unit who are new. I am going to stay with them and try to protect them, like I wish somebody had tried to protect me when I first got in-country."

About two months after Ralph came to our outfit, I remember we were sitting around base camp. We had just come off a sweep that morning, a patrol. We had walked about five or six klicks and we'd come back and the lieutenant, Lieutenant Lamberson, who was killed after I left Vietnam, got a message that they were flying over our area with one of the colonels, and they had spotted signs of what they thought were VC. They called us and said to get our gear ready and go back out on a patrol, out around the area we had already covered. I remember just two days before, we had gone on ambush in this area and we were walking on a dike and I was walking point, and I remember thinking, "You know, should I?" because the rice paddies were filled with water and it wasn't the right thing to do—because I was tired of being wet. I was tired of being uncomfortable.

I didn't give a shit. I decided to walk on top of the dikes, which we did to our ambush site. I remember thinking, "Should I go this way or that?" and I decided not to go along the woodline. "I'll walk this way," and we set up our ambush that night.

Getting back to Ralph. We'd gone out to the same area that we had gone out to the night before. He walked on the same dike that I'd decided not to walk down. I remember my friend, Emmet Henderson, walking point and I was right in the middle. Somebody yelled "Stop!" I looked down and saw this splash of water. Emmet and I were running down the dike and just before I got there, there was the sickening feeling and I wondered, "My God, what am I going to fucking see when I get to the end of this dike?" I was not prepared to look at Ralph dead and I wasn't prepared to look at the worst thing that could happen to him. I remember getting there and looking and he was lying face down in the water and I saw him floating in the water and I picked him up and I held him in my arms.

There was a Vietnamese not twenty yards away from us and— "Why the fuck couldn't you warn us, man!" Here's a kid—eighteen years old. He was sent to Vietnam as a desk clerk, had gotten in a little bit of trouble, was sent to an infantry outfit, should have never even been in this area, should have been back at base camp drinking beers and having a good time, or back home going to the movies and eating pizzas. Eighteen years old, man. What the fuck was he doing in this goddamned place! The side of his head was blown off from the Chi-Com grenade that he had tripped. I remember putting his body on the chopper when it came down; it was blowing water all around. Me and Emmet tried to pick up his body and put it on the chopper and it kept sliding off and I remember the look of the helicopter pilots and the gunners. They looked at us with pity, like, "You poor fucking slobs." You know, I always felt proud about being in the infantry, but the look on their faces—I can't even explain. Maybe they were reacting to the look on my face, which probably made them feel pity for us, I guess. I'll never forget loading Ralph's body on that chopper and I just kept thinking, "I've got a month left in-country."

Two nights later Emmet Henderson went out on ambush and he was in a non-restricted fire zone, where the Viet Cong were firing from. He asked permission to fire back. Higher-up came down, told the lieutenant, and the lieutenant contacted Emmet and his squad—told them you can't fire into that area, it's a restricted fire zone. I remember thinking, "You know, this war is really fucked up. It has gotten to the point of being ridiculous. Here we are being fired at and we can't even fire back because it is a restricted fire zone. What the fuck will they be asking us next?" I kept thinking, "You know, for guys eighteen years old, man, I only thought this would be a short year. A year I could just take," and at the end of the year I could just forget about it. It was ridiculous. I suddenly hated my country. I suddenly hated the Army. I suddenly hated everything I believed in, everything I thought everything stood for. I thought, "This can't happen to me."

And a couple days after Ralph was killed, and a couple of days after Emmet was ambushed—but luckily, no one was hurt—we caught this kid running down this rice paddy dike. He stuck something under a bale of hay. I was walking point. I fired my rifle up in the air three or four times. The funny thing was that when I fired the warning shots up in the air, I didn't notice how close the rifle was to my head. I almost shot myself. Like a fucking idiot, trying to warn this kid to stop. I shouted, "Come here, come here—lai dy, lai dy," and the kid kept running down the dike.

All the sudden all hell broke loose. There was a squad of eight or nine guys behind me and all of them started shooting at the kid. One of the guys, Crew, was shooting a 45 and Emmet Henderson was running down the dike shooting his M-16, and everybody else was shooting their M-16s at the kid. I was looking at the kid through the bell of my rifle and I kept thinking, "Look, this is crazy. We are turning into fucking animals. I don't want to be this fucking way, man." I shot over his head to miss him. You know, missing him on purpose, while everyone else was shooting at him, hitting him. When he finally fell at the end of the dike, I remember walking up and looking at him.

He asked for a cigarette. His brains were protruding out the side of his head—just pulsating. He had been shot in the back, and in the arms and elbows and legs, but he was still surviving. I looked at this kid and thought, "If this is the fucking enemy, man . . . If this was me, I'd be yelling my fucking guts out. But this is the enemy we're fighting. It's like there's no winning this battle. If the guy is unable to show his pain and he's able to hide his feelings and his emotions, man, these people are unbeatable."

Then I thought, "We need to get rid of this kid. We need to waste him. If he talks—if he's not a VC, if he's just a peasant—he can indict all of us."

I took a bandage and dipped into cow shit.

There was cow shit all over the rice paddy, where the cows had been pulling, helping the Vietnamese farm the rice paddies.

I dipped the bandage in cow shit, then bandaged his head.

We were going to put a bullet through him but the chopper was coming and we didn't want to get caught.

So we dipped the bandage, applied it, and wished him good luck with his cigarette.

We knew it was only a matter of time before the cow shit infected the brain.

We learned later that he died. They told us he was VC, but knowing the Army, they'd say fucking anything, and I didn't fucking care. I felt respect for this individual, but I also felt hatred for this individual. I felt respect in that I couldn't pull the trigger on the rifle to kill him, but when I thought about Ralph after I got to him at the end of the dike, I felt hatred for him. That's when I dipped the bandage in cow shit and wrapped it around his head. I said "Good luck and good-bye" and that was the last we saw of him.

From that point on I decided that I had two weeks left in Vietnam and that I was getting the fuck out. I had hurt my legs earlier and I went back to an aid station. I was sent back to the rear, then they sent me to the 93rd Med-evac. Eventually I was airlifted out of Vietnam. I remember, the lieutenant was back at 83rd Med-evac and he asked me how many days I had left, and I told him I had two weeks left in-country. Right before that some fellows had been brought back from the 9th Infantry Division down, way down in the Delta, and he was upset and he was angry at the whole war. He said, "We are sending you home. You have two fucking weeks and we are sending you home. I am sick of this fucking place. I'm sick of this fucking war. I should send you out to the field, but your legs are swollen, man. Fuck it. You're going home. You have enough of a disability. Go home."

I was air med-evaced back to The World and I remember saying good-bye to my buddies in Vietnam. I wanted to go but I didn't want to go. Everything came to a head. I just couldn't take Vietnam anymore. Everything I felt was honorable was suddenly disgraceful in my eyes.

Upon my return back from Vietnam to The World, I spent another year and a half in the Army, stationed at Fort Dix, and also Germany. While I was at Fort Dix I got to see firsthand how the Army treated it's returning soldiers. A lot of the guys who had been in the 199th and other outfits, I noticed, had been put in the stockade for disorderly conduct. They were unable to adjust to military life. I always wondered why the Army didn't try to help these guys. Why didn't they try to help them with their drug problems? Why didn't they try to help them with their emotional problems? The only answer the Army had was putting them in jail, putting them in a stockade and treating them like animals.

I also noticed, while I was working at a basic training brigade at Fort Dix after I came back from Vietnam, that I was condemned by the sergeant for trying to be too nice to the guys. I felt nothing but compassion for these trainees. I knew what they were in for, what they were headed for. I felt they needed someone to talk to and all I was getting was flak from my first-sergeant for being too nice to them. One time, a fellow went up on the water tower and was threatening to jump and the sergeants at the bottom yelled, "Jump! Jump!" and I remember thinking, "All this kid needs is someone to talk to."

I remember kids committing suicide in the barracks. I remember going into the barracks and finding kids who had killed themselves in the barracks—found them hanging in there. Why didn't the parents of these kids, why didn't the country, stand up for their sons? Why didn't they try to help these young people, like they should have helped us, those who went to Vietnam?

It was like, out of sight, out of mind. I hated my country. I hated the Army. I hated everything. I even hated myself for being part of the system. Even to this day, I still hate this country.

You told me to dump it, Gary. You told me to let it hang out . . .

I'll never get over what happened in Vietnam. I'll never get over the fact that when I came back I asked for help and I got no help from the VA. I've been married three times. I've had drug-abuse problems. I attempted suicide once by stabbing myself in the leg. The frustration and anger is there, and it will always be there.

I'm married to a wonderful wife now. I have a beautiful daughter and I'm expecting a son. I feel sorry for the hassles that they've had to put up with because of my temper tantrums and my getting out of control emotionally when I think about Vietnam. Vietnam was a twenty-four-hour-a-day occurrence for me and I'll never get over it. If I had to do it all over again, I never would have gone to Vietnam, and I never would have joined the Army.

I feel that The Wall in Washington D.C. should be bigger, and include all the veterans that committed suicide after Vietnam, or were injured coming back to Vietnam, and died from injuries incurred in Vietnam. I feel all these names should be added to the wall. Not just the ones who died in Vietnam, but the ones who suffered after they came back.

Vietnam has left an indelible impression in my mind. I'll never forget it, just like I feel the parents of the children that were killed in Vietnam have never forgotten Vietnam or their sons. The government says put Vietnam behind you. How can you put something behind you that was so intense and severe and critical during such a young portion of your life? Their asking us to do the impossible.

I'll never trust my government again, and I doubt if I'll ever trust anybody else again outside of my family.

Frank Jowers

I was born in 1947 in a very rural town in northern Florida. The county was *so* rural that it only had three towns, and a population of seven thousand. Time completely stopped in this area. It was a world to itself, completely ignorant of events taking place in the outside world.

I attended Baker County High School, played football and dreamed of leaving Baker County and seeing the world. We were only fifty miles from the Navy base at Mayport, Florida and the Navy seemed like it was my ticket out of this small place.

I saw the news reports of the fighting in Vietnam, but never dreamed of going there. In 1965 our graduating class consisted of ninety kids, and our prom was in the school cafeteria. We danced to the monkey and listened to songs like "Louie Louie," but, you know, what impresses me most now about our music? The number of songs about death. It almost seems like a premonition of what was coming.

After graduation I goofed off all summer and joined the Navy on August 10, 1965. The Navy sent me to Great Lakes Recruit Training Commands. I arrived there at 3 in the morning in a cold pouring rain and began my four years of Navy life. Our company commander told us that nobody forgets their company commander. I still remember his name and face. Still, I had no idea of going to the South China Sea. On graduation day he was the one who handed us our orders. He told me I could throw my peacoat away, that I was going to the South China Sea.

After two weeks of boot leave, I flew from Jacksonville to Travis Air Force Base, San Francisco. There we caught a converted cargo plane to the Orient. I was the only sailor on the plane. The rest were grunts bound for Nam. From Travis we went on, bounced off Midway and finally, to Clark Air Force Base, Philippine Islands. From Clark we were bused overland to Subic Bay, where I caught the ship.

The Turner Joy was finishing her Far East deployment. We pulled fairly easy duty, consisting mainly of plane guard for carriers operating in the Gulf of Tonkin. Plane guard is a tedious and boring assignment spent in chasing carriers as they launch and retrieve their planes. When on plane guard, a destroyer is to help retrieve downed planes and *most* constantly have a boat crew ready at all times. A boat crew consisted of five men and a fourteen-foot motor whale boat. The lucky men attached to the boat crew got to perform their regular duties plus stand two four-hour watches. During these watches you were stationed in an area topside, to watch for downed planes, which was usually a hot, boring job.

Usually, when a plane was down, the carrier could retrieve the pilot with one of it's helos known as "Angles." The daylight watch tried to stay out of the sun, which kept the deck hot and the night watch tried to stay awake. The USS Turner Joy, DD 951 (we used to joke that DD meant Damn Destroyer), saw action in the South China Sea from the beginning to the end. She was attacked in the Tonkin Gulf by PT boats. While on routine patrol, Turner Joy and her sister ship, the Maddox, were attacked by North Vietnam's PT Boats. This was the Tonkin Gulf Incident, which allowed the U.S. to enter the war. Turner Joy received credit for sinking two PT boats.

Destroyers are the workhorses of the fleet. They are small, fast and maneuverable. Turner Joy was 418 feet long and forty-five feet wide, with a draft of only thirty-two feet. We were able to come in as close as one quarter of a mile from the beach. It was a very unsettling feeling when the screws began to churn mud from the bottom or when the captain called for the lead line. (A lead line is a weighted rope used to measure depth of the water.) Her fire power consisted of three five-inch dual purpose guns which were capable of firing sixty rounds a minute, one twin three-inch rapid-fire mount, plus anti-submarine weapons.

These five-inch guns were our main armament and considered by the Navy to be automatic, because the powder and projectiles were loaded mechanically, but that was only into the gun. The hoist had to be loaded by hand. The gun hoist resembled the cylinder of a revolver stacked two high. The top cylinder was for the projectiles, which weighed sixty-five pounds, and the bottom was for the powder canister, which weighed thirty-five pounds. The loader deck crew had to keep these full at all times. Usually sixty rounds were loaded before firing started. After that it was a race to keep up with the gun. The loader deck and magazine were located directly below the gun mount and below the waterline of the ship. They were constantly filled to capacity with stacks and stacks of explosives. In several cases we had more shells on board than we were safely allowed to have. Working the loader deck you were constantly aware of the Willie Peter shells in their racks, held securely against the pitch and roll of the ship.

While on a firing mission in 1965, gun mount No. 53, located on the fantail of the ship, had a hang fire; a projectile lodged in the barrel. (Hang fires are a result of slightly oversized shells.) While trying to cool the gun barrel down with streams of water from fire hoses, the round exploded. The resulting explosion killed five men in the gun crew and completely wrecked the gun. Water was sprayed on the gun, because while firing, the gun barrel would become so hot as to scorch the paint off. The plan was to cool the barrel, open the breach and remove the projectile, which could then be thrown over the side, a distance of about fifteen feet, which doesn't sound far unless you are carrying a damaged sixty-five-pound explosive shell. But then we were young and foolish and still felt we were invincible. Unfortunately, this time the plan failed and five boys died. The smell of gun powder and burnt flesh clung to the ruined gun mount like an evil cloud. The crew was thoroughly spooked.

We departed the 7th Fleet in time to spend Christmas of 1965 in Long Beach, California, until the ruined gun mount was removed from the ship. In dry dock you could feel it's presence. Late at night, standing the lonely after-lookout watch on the fantail, you could feel it behind you like a living presence.

We were stateside for nearly a year. This was probably the best time in the States. The attitude of the people had not turned against the war. We spent this period training for our next deployment, with numerous gunfire exercises and general quarter drills.

In boot camp the drill instructor told us the military would make us into what they wanted, and this process continued. We became fleet sailors. Beyond fleet sailors, we were "Tin Can Riders." Tin Can Sailors were the meanest, drunkenest, wildest sailors in the Navy. We didn't need Marines to stand security watch, like carriers; we were the top of the heap. They trained us to react without thinking. Our actions became instinct.

A destroyer has an alarm bell that sounds like nothing God ever created. It is capable of raising the dead. You never forget the sound of that bell no matter how long you live. It is burned into your brain. A destroyer's berthing compartment (sleeping quarters) consists of bunks three layers high, capable of being folded as a unit and called a rack. A rack has an aluminum frame with canvas stretched across it and with a thin mattress on top. The bottom rack is about a foot off the deck. The second rack is about two foot above the bottom and the top is two foot above that. Only the man on top has room to sit and then only if he sits in a hunched-over position. In between each stack of racks are the lockers, three high. These lockers, containing all your worldly possessions, were about three feet wide, two feet high and three feet deep. The stacks were divided by a narrow isle about three feet wide. When the GQ alarm was sounded at night, you had six men waking up at once and diving into a three-foot-wide isle and dressing on the run. In my four years I never saw one pile up or collision. We had three minutes to get from our bunks to our general quarter stations. You were dressed and running before you were awake. The song from the movie "Sink the Bismarck" had a line, "We hit the decks running and we swung the guns around." That is just what we did. Life on a destroyer.

We left Long Beach for our East deployment on November 18, 1966. After stops in Pearl Harbor and Kaohsiung, Taiwan, Turner Joy arrived II Corp South Vietnam.

Naval gunfire support missions are a study in exhaustion. Even if the ship wasn't on an active firing mission, we were in "Condition Two" watches. This meant one gun mount was manned and loaded twenty-four hours a day. A call for fire could come in at any hour and when it did we were expected to have all stations manned and ready in three minutes. When the gun mounts came on line they began to move and alarm bells rang for people outside to stand clear. After all stations reported manned and ready the ship would maneuver into firing position.

My general quarters station was one of our 50-caliber machine guns. We had two 50s mounted directly over the wings of the bridge. Each gun had a three man crew—gunner, loader and one phone talker. Because of our location we were in the open with no armor. We were constantly exposed to the concussion from the guns and we got to see what was happening. Our phone talker had a line to the bridge and could hear all reports coming to the bridge. Often we were only a quarter of a mile from the beach, firing at targets a short distance inland, so we could see the contact of our rounds.

Firing missions might begin at 2200 hours and last until 0300 hours. With reveille at 0600, they were bad. Then we had to replenish, refuel and rearm and maintain the ship. There were days when we would secure from GQ and go meet a supply ship. Then we had H&I missions (Harassment and Irritation fire), one gun on the line firing spasmodically every few minutes all night long. We never could figure just who the hell this was supposed to harass and irritate, us or the enemy. If a meal was due while we were at GQ we were fed what the Navy called battle rats, greasy fried chicken and apples. The burnt gun powder hung so heavy in the hot humid air waiting to settle on the greasy chicken that a new taste was created, greasy gritty chicken that tasted like gun powder. Most of the time we ate the apples and left the chicken.

Replenishing at sea is an art! The bridge crew would approach and overtake the oiler. Once we were alongside, our bridge crew would match speed with the oiler. Then, with both ships steaming side-to-side with only about 100 feet of white water separating them, the line would be thrown and shot across. If we used a thrown line, it was attached to a bolo, then the small line pulled a larger one across. We had a line handling party consisting of ten to fifteen men that pulled the fueling hoses from the tanker to us. This was accomplished using a series of pulleys. Line handlers were on the main deck amidships, on the 01 level mid-ship, and on the fantail. To get these giant hoses on board we had our hands full. Once the fueling hoses were coupled securely, we began to drag the food, ammo and stores across. Food and stores came across on pallets in cargo nets. Powder and projectiles came across in special metal baskets. Projectiles were twenty-four per pallet and powder came in forty-two per lot. Once they were on deck the pallets had to be opened and the contents carried piece by piece by hand to the location for which they were intended.

Now I am talking about 1000 projectiles weighing sixty-five pounds that had to be carried down narrow ladders in 100-degree heat; hand-down ladders too steep to carry them down. When we looked up we never knew whose sweat was running in our eyes. After a few hours of this a human body tends to go on automatic pilot and instinct takes over. Some oilers had helos which would ferry the ammo over. They would hover over the tossing deck of our destroyer and lower the pallets. Once they were low enough we had to grab these swaying pallets to steady them and keep them from crashing into a gun mount. We were young and crazy destroyer sailors—Tin Can Riders.

If somebody was to tell me to do that now I would have to tell them all about their family tree.

When all the work was over, all the lines secured, the old man would play "Anchors Away" over the speakers. Usually there was another destroyer on the other side of the oiler. After the last notes of "Anchors Away" faded he would play "Charge." Both destroyers would go full speed ahead, black smoke boiling out the stacks. The back ends of the ship would sit down just like a car when you pop the clutch. Once clear of the oiler, both destroyers would make hard turns and throw water everywhere. The feeling this gave was a shot of adrenaline; we were the best; we were invincible; we were young, convinced that what we were doing was right!

Even as many times as this was repeated, we only had one accident. We came directly off a firing mission to meet the supply ship. This particular supply ship had an electric wench to pull the lines. The line handlers were no match for mechanical wenches and the line got loose. We were refueling at night close into land, with only red lights to see by. The call "loose line on deck" will chill anyone's blood. The books say stand still and don't move until the other ship slacks off. The line could be heard slapping against the deck. Then one man moved and it caught his leg and was dragging him. Before we could get the white lights on and someone cut the line with a fire ax, it had torn his foot off.

Our corpsman was sharp and packed the foot in ice on the reefer deck where perishable foods were kept. The captain passed the word that we were going into Cam Ranh Bay to take the injured man to a hospital. Our class destroyer was only rated at thirty knots, but when we went in we were turning thirty-three knots and pouring black smoke. Due to the quick thinking of our corpsman the foot was saved. We departed the gun line January 17, 1967 after one month on the line and arrived at Subic Bay, Philippine Islands, two days later.

Olamgapo City, Philippine Islands was a wide open city. No Wild West town, Dodge City included, could compare to this city. The city was in walking distance of the main gate at Subic Bay Naval Base, separated only by the Olamgapo River. The main street was a two-mile stretch of bar where anything went. Whorehouses were off-limits and there was a midnight curfew, but you could buy a girl out of a bar for about five dollars, go to a hotel for a dollar and maybe give the girl another five. After a month at sea, every man had two things on his mind. One was to drink yourself into a stupor, then the next night find a girl. We rated the bars as high class if they had table cloths on the tables.

Filipinos are great people and when they like you they are extremely loyal. My steaming buddies and me made friends with a mamasan at the Alamo Bar. I have no idea how many times she personally got us back to the base when we were too drunk to get there on our own. No sailor is ever too drunk to get back. We had a saying, "I might get so drunk that I have to crawl home, but by God I will crawl home like a sailor." You know, to this day, twenty years later, I can still see her face and remember her name. I believe Olamgapo was a safety valve for us, especially in the latter years. It allowed sailors to blow off steam and tensions. We departed Subic Bay January 31 and went to Hong Kong, China for a week. From Hong Kong, we returned to the gun line. This time we would be in I Corp. We were on station in I Corp from February 10 to March 3, again firing support missions wherever we were needed. We again departed the gun line and spent a week in Sasebo, Japan, then returned to Vietnam.

This time we were in operation "Sea Dragon." We were operating above the DMZ in the waters of North Vietnam. The purpose of Sea Dragon was to disrupt supplies moving by water and to destroy enemy gun sites. North Vietnam had coastal artillery sites equipped with radar. Our intelligence knew where the guns were located, but we could not fire on them until they fired on us. Two destroyers usually worked together. One would stay back while the other approached close to land hoping to draw fire. Constantly watching for hostile fire created extreme stress and strain on the crew. We often drew fire, then both destroyers would return fire until the gun emplacement had been silenced.

Then came the unthinkable. We were operating along on Condition Two watches. We were chasing what we called IBGBs (Itty Bitty Gook Boats). They were running for a cove and we went in after them. When we were about a quarter of a mile off the beach, Charlie started firing at us with his version of our 105 Howitzer. The first round hit directly aft of Mount 53, destroyed the supply office and penetrated MT 53's magazine. Luckily the sprinkler system activated and prevented any fire. They had us set up good. They knocked out our fire control radar, surface search radar and MT 53. We proceeded to get the Hell out of there. Every gun mount was firing and the stack blowing black smoke. The ship was peppered with shrapnel holes and luckily, only one man had been injured. He was struck on his butt by a large piece of shrapnel. The cure proved to be worse than the injury, because he had his whole backside bandaged and had to soak in a pan of water nightly.

After repairs were made, we joined a group of ships led by the St. Paul (heavy cruiser) with her eight-inch guns. We were supposed to attack and silence a gun emplacement on what was known as Tiger Island. In the exchange that followed, the St. Paul took a direct hit as well as did several destroyers. Even as much as we fired, Tiger Island remained a constant threat.

During our last deployment we were again working Sea Dragon. We were relieved by the Australian destroyer, *HMS Hobart*. We then proceeded to Subic Bay for shore leave. On our first day in port the Hobart was hit by a missile fired by an Air Force fighter. We were ordered back to the gulf. Getting underway that morning was an experience, because two-thirds of the crew was either still drunk, hung over and sick, or just hung over. How we made it out to sea that day, I will never know. We learned that there were thirty-four men killed on the Hobart.

I was separated from active duty August 9, 1969 and returned to a home that had changed more than I could stand. Even today I can close my eyes and go back to those days. I can almost smell the gun smoke and feel the heat of the deck.

How can it be? Twenty-six years have passed since I left the Turner Joy for the last time. Even now I feel I could still go anywhere on that ship. I can close my eyes and bring back every detail. Those four years still live behind my eyes! Every face and every smell have been burned into my soul.

Time is supposed to heal all. Well, after a quarter century, the old feelings are still alive, smouldering like coals. Maybe they have been pushed a little farther beneath the surface by the press of daily living, but it does not take much to make them boil to the surface.

At the time of my separation I was twenty-two years old, drinking too heavily, confused and full of hate. I felt the country had turned its back on us, had sent us to a foreign land to kill it's enemy, and when we got good at it, when we were master of the day and night, our country lost its heart and turned against us. I hated, *hated* the civilians of America—felt my only friends were military. Somehow, some part of me knew what I was sinking into was wrong. I decided to get out of the Navy and go home. In basic they say, "You can never go home again." Boy, is that ever true.

Four years before, I had left a small town lost somewhere in the '50s, juke boxes in the drug store, hot cars, and carefree days. Days where you could hunt or fish anywhere you wanted. When I came home I found the rich and powerful of the country had kept their sons out of the services, bought their way into schools; some had even gone as far as to become men of the cloth. Now I was no longer so sure that what we were doing in Nam was right, so it didn't really bother me that they had stayed home. What ate at me was, they had sold my home (not my parents' house), but my home I was coming back to. Virgin forestland, clean rivers and no development. In four years, they had sold my youth to the people fleeing the cities. Now, "NO TRESPASSING" signs were thick as trees. Mobile homes were everywhere and these city people were dumping their trash in rivers that I once drank from. These draft evaders now ran the county, the bank, the law, even the churches.

I tried for two years to fit in here. I went to junior college on the GI Bill and even went to church. Even trying to fit in, words like "baby killer" and "drug addict" drifted to me from people that had known me all my life. The media had done a real good job of painting us and I began to become what they painted. I let my hair grow, grew a Vandyke and acted crazy. I earned my AA degree, but I could never fit in with these college kids.

August 12, 1971 I got married and moved to Orlando, Florida to work for Walt Disney World. The early years at Disney were marked by constant rush to get things done on time. It seemed Disney was always building something new. Here at Disney I met my best friend, another vet, Clem Cave.

Clem had been a medic in Nam and could have gone into medicine, but his experience in-country had cooled him to that field. So Clem, like myself, was working in a warehouse driving trucks and forklifts. Clem and I often spent hours talking, arguing about things other people couldn't understand and did not want to hear about. Clem was a black man and he touched and helped me more that anyone else I have ever known. I do not believe Clem met a single person that he did not touch in some way. Clem was exposed to Agent Orange in Viet Nam and was constantly fighting a lingering cold or some problem with his health.

During my tenth year at Disney, my wife left me with two small children to raise. At this time my supervisor was a gung-ho exMarine that lived, ate and slept for the company. All my anger and frustrations were directed against him. Clem had his hands full keeping me calm and straight. He really helped me hold it together during this trying time. With two small children to take care of, I was pretty well locked in at Disney, so we worked together and somehow made the best of it. Sometimes I feel they thought they were taking care of me. They are eighteen and nineteen now and are really good kids, even though they still can't understand why I will not let them watch any movies with Jane Fonda in them.

In 1987 the local Vietnam veterans formed a group, and we became heavily involved in community affairs. Our group was called on several times to help search for missing children, especially in the swampy areas of Florida. The local radio stations would even allow one of the members, who had been a pilot in Nam, to fly their chopper. One of our most moving experiences came when a local business man had a tribute to Vietnam veterans at his night spot. It was almost like he took the whole place and moved it back into the '60s. He had '60s rock bands and everyone was saying welcome home and thank you. Then at midnight all the lights were turned out and everyone lit candles for the POWs and MIAs. I believe this was a powerful moment for everyone present. We are trying to attract people's attention to the fact there are still 2500 Americans in Vietnam, men who were betrayed and deserted by Henry Kissinger and his peace plan.

Thanksgiving weekend of 1988, Disney moved into a brand new state-of-the-art warehouse, and Clem Cave, who was now a Disney supervisor, was diagnosed as having colon-rectal cancer. Clem had really been working hard on this project, looking forward to seeing us working under the same roof again. They operated on him and gave him three months to live. Bob Brown, another Vietnam veteran, and I went to see him every night he was in the hospital. Clem refused to take chemotherapy or radiation treatments and they allowed him to go home. Bob and I continued to go see him every day after he got home and even when he began to look bad and everyone else stopped, we continued. Clem had always been a real strong family man and wanted to be home with his family when his time came. Clem passed away a week after my birthday the following year, 1989. Even though I knew it was close, I just could not accept it when they called me. The closest friend I had since Vietnam was gone, and even now I still miss him. His wife still calls me once in a while just to talk about him.

I have found a lady now. One who wants to worry about me and take care of me, one I can really love. We went to visit Clem's family recently and they are doing well. His oldest son looks so much like him that it is shocking to see him. Cindy is a great lady and is trying hard to understand me. I am sure we will make a great future.

I would like to dedicate this chapter to the memory of Clem Cave, my best friend.

N. Frank Brookman

On August 11, 1968, I, Corporal Norman F. Brookman remember this as being true facts about this incident concerning Henry L. Bradshaw. On the above date, I and several other soldiers returned to base camp, Charlie Hill. We had been on short patrols north of Qui Nhon, South Vietnam. The Viet Cong had hit Charlie Hill hard in January and February, 1968, during the Tet Offensive. It was known by many that Charlie had been building forces in this area for a takeover of the hill. The hill was the backbone for communications for all of Southeast Asia. I had been assigned to the 81mm mortar squad along with Henry and two others. Henry was getting pretty short, so I took most of his patrols. I felt much safer in the bush than in base camp. In late afternoon our squad returned from patrols. We had not observed any Viet Cong in the area for several days. After returning, some of the guys gave me a small birthday party. The next day was to be my twenty-first birthday. The guys gave me a pair of boxer underwear (we hardly ever had underwear) and a cold beer, along with a hot shower. I guess the guys had stolen the water and ice. After the shower, Henry came to me and advised me that I was on the guard roster that had been posted for the night. I was assigned to the main gate along with a soldier that I did not know very well. Henry told me that he would take my post and that I could take his some other time. We agreed on this and at about 0120 hours our post was hit and overrun by Viet Cong. The reports are that Henry, who had taken my post, was the first person to be killed.

Henry was alone when attacked in his bunker. The Viet Cong first threw a grenade in the bunker at him. He was able to kick it from the bunker before it exploded. After the grenade was thrown, Henry was shot in the chest area by an AK-47. He was killed at that point. I was sleeping at that time. I heard the blast and jumped for cover. The Viet Cong were all around the camp and had caught us off guard. They were hitting every place they could. We knew we were in deep trouble. The fighting lasted until sunrise. We could not get any support because of our location and the foggy weather. The mortar squad fired over two hundred rounds of mortar shells in and around the camp, trying to keep the Viet Cong out of the camp. At sunup we had been hit hard and had lost a lot of men. The body count was 101 Viet Cong killed.

Henry Bradshaw died for me that night. If he had not seen the Viet Cong, we all may have been killed. I dug the bullet that killed Henry out of the bunker wall and have kept it for twenty years. I think it should be placed to rest along with all the other memories of fallen heroes like Henry.

Henry is always being thought of.
His dedication and memory will live in my life forever.
The cause was painful.
Now rest in peace.
—Norman F. Brookman 8/88

Dear Henry,
Today makes twenty-one years since you lost your life. There is never a day that goes by that I don't think of you. I have tried to shake these feelings that I have locked deep inside of me, but have an awful time doing so. I have wished since August 11, 1968, that I would not have allowed you to take my guard post that cost you your life. I guess if it had been your twenty-first birthday I would have done the same for you. The price of friendship was high. You did me a good deed that cost you your life.
Henry, I will never forget you. I share your name with other Vietnam veterans that I meet. I know you would tell your friends if my name were on this wall and not yours. You gave me the best birthday gift that anyone could ever receive, twenty-one more years of life. I wish I could rest in peace as you do now. I know you are in God's hands, so maybe you could tell him to help me with this pain and guilt that I feel so deep inside my heart.
Rest in peace my brother.
Thanks forever, Henry Norman F. Brookman
12 August 1989

My name is Norman Franklin Brookman, born August 12, 1947, in Lynchburg, Virginia. I lived with my grandparents until the age of eleven. The next eight years were spent with my parents in the east end of Newport News, Virginia. There I attended grade and high school. I was the oldest of four children. After school, I went to work as a laborer for the city of Newport News. During this time, the Vietnam War, or even going into any branch of the service, never occurred to me.
On June 26, 1967, I found out what the U.S. Army was all about. I remember meeting a black man at the bus station in Newport News. He looked at me and asked me if I had my toothbrush with me. I thought that was a strange question at the time, but I later found out what he meant. After we had gone through test after test and physical exams in the Army center in Richmond, I thought we would go home and report back at a later date. I was wrong. We left right then and ended up at Fort Benning, Georgia, one of the toughest basic training centers in the country.
After finishing at Fort Benning, I was sent to Fort Polk, Louisiana,

the second toughest training center. The Benning boys were matched up against the Polk boys to see which basic training post had trained the best. A dozen or so of us proved that the Benning boys were the best that the U.S. Army had produced at that time. All the Benning boys scored between 450 and 500 on the physical testing.

After finishing jungle and AIT training at Fort Polk, I received orders for a special school located at Fort Gordon, Georgia, which lasted about three weeks. This caused me to be a month behind going to Vietnam with the men I had trained with. They had since been sent south to II Corp while I went to the upper parts of II Corp. There I joined with the 3rd Battalion of the 503rd Infantry, 173rd Airborne Brigade.

I arrived in-country on the nineteenth day of December 1967 and by the end of January, I had become an 81mm mortarman. By this time the Tet Offensive was in full swing from Dak To, Bong Son, and Qui Nhon. I was in Charlie Company—the "patrol moles"—and we conducted the patrols along the Ho Chi Minh Trail for most of the tour there. I was then sent down south to Phan Thiet for about two months and was a gunner for the 1st of the 501st Infantry, 101st Airborne. I saw here a distinct difference between the troops in the north and those in the south, which I attributed to the heat and Delta rains. Now, looking back, it may have had something to do with the pressures resulting in emotional release.

During the short time that I spent in the south, we were overrun by Viet Cong twice. The troops fought as true Americans, displaying great pride, toughness and honor in the face of death, serving their country well. I am proud to have served in such a hell-hole in order to have protected this country I love so dearly. Thanks to veterans, we live in freedom today. I will always remember being with the guys on the 4.2 mortars on an outpost near Phan Thiet.

The aftereffects from this war left many combat veterans hardened emotionally as a result of the loss of close friends. There is a refusal to allow anyone to get close to them, and they will not allow closeness in themselves for fear of losing this closeness. It becomes a built-in safety mechanism that closes out anyone who cares about you. I am guilty of this because of the buddies I lost in Vietnam and I hold inside of me much guilt and sorrow that I made it through and they did not. I lock out my family and friends to keep myself from showing my true feelings. After two failed marriages, I came to the conclusion that there must be a way to make life worth living for myself and for so many veterans who have this problem and don't know where to turn for help.

I had been a police officer for eleven years before realizing the problem. After my marriage failed a second time, I took a hard look at my life and faults. I was hard, aggressive, distant, and striving for perfection. I saw the strain this placed on my family, and the need to put

Vietnam, my dead buddies and all of these feelings of guilt behind me before I could go on with life and make peace with my past. The past was part of my life that I was not willing to let go, and it cost me two families.

I think I am not alone with these feelings. One has to make peace with one's self before going on with life. I carried a burden of guilt with me from August 12, 1968, until August 12, 1989. My friend on the mortar squad had taken my guard duty for me on my twenty-first birthday. He was killed. This twist of fate made such an impact on my life that I tortured myself with guilt, thinking of him daily. I found the AK-47 bullet and shell that had taken his life and, in an effort to ease my guilt, kept these items until August 12, 1988, when I placed them, along with a letter, at The Wall on the twentieth year of his death. I felt I had finally made peace with myself. I was wrong. This only made me think and feel more guilt and finally my family slipped away from me.

On August 12, 1989, I started my healing process. I made another trip back to The Wall and knelt at my friend's name. Part of the problem was the fact that I could not remember what his face looked like. I fought the battle deep inside myself, trying to resolve this, but his face would not appear to me as he had looked then. The more I tried, the harder it became to remember. It was important for me to remember. Because I could not accept what had happened to my friend, I blocked it out mentally.

He had been shot, his head cut off and taken by the Viet Cong, and I found his body after the fighting was over. This was what I had blocked out. This is what had haunted me for the last twenty years, and by going back to The Wall to sit, look and cry, I felt release from the fallen heroes whose names appear there. I finally made peace with myself and have put that part of my life behind me, and thanked my friend for giving me the best birthday gift that I have ever received—twenty-one more years of life.

There are so many untold true stories like mine that have made Vietnam a war of all wars. I am not saying that Vietnam was worse than any war before or that Vietnam veterans are any better than others. I am saying these men are different because they fought alone. The public did not support them. They were outcasts. Over the years the American public's lack of feeling toward Vietnam has changed for the better and I thank these people for helping him feel he is no longer a baby killer or someone that killed just to be killing. Thank you, Americans, for thanking me.

In combat, honesty and dependability are of utmost importance. The bond that we share is greater than any friendship that I have ever experienced.

I now have begun to tear down this wall that surrounds my feelings and get rid of some of the guilt I have felt for my dead friends. The reason I have felt this guilt for so long is that in combat I was not in a position to be able to save my friend's life.

I was honest and very dependable, but was not able to save their lives.

Friendships last forever in war.

My friends, rest in peace.

Lorence W. Blackburn

I went to school in a small town in the north woods of the Midwest, lived on a farm, was involved in sports, and worked hard to keep the farm going—before and after school, and on weekends. I was an above-average student who had problems with the school system—I felt the teaching was not fast enough. So, I quit school and enlisted in the Marine Corps two days after my seventeenth birthday.

I was sent to Marine Corps Recruit Depot, San Diego, California to become a boot. Upon completion of boot camp I was assigned to the 1st Mar. Div., which, two months later, was deployed to Okinawa for the next thirteen months. During this tour we went to Mount Fuji, Japan for cold weather training.

On a Thursday night, about 0200 hours, the battalion sergeant major ran through the area, waking everyone up, telling us to tear down everything and pack it up. By 0730 we were at an airstrip, loading up into C-130s, being given ammo, grenades and other combat gear. We were told that this move was secret. After a short flight we landed at Cubi Point in the Philippines, set up a camp, and waited. Upon purchase of the "Stars and Stripes," I found the headlines to read, "2nd Battalion, 3rd Marines makes move from Mt. Fuji to the Philippines." Some secret move.

The second day, all our combat gear was collected. We were then told this was just a "regular" move. The temperature difference—ten below zero to one hundred and ten above, in a couple of hours.

We stayed in the Philippines for the next three months, with daily bullshit such as rigorous combat training, PT and some "Cinderella" liberty.

After returning to the U.S. I was assigned to the 2nd Marine Aircraft Wing, Cherry Point, North Carolina, where, lo and behold, the Cuban Missile Crisis occurred. I saw people who were supposed to get out of service extended against their will until completion of the crisis.

It seemed like only a couple of days when "Nam" broke out. By this time I was a sergeant. I was sent over with a rifle company that landed near Chu Lai and moved inland, secured the area and set up a base camp.

LSTs and LSDs unloaded more troops and equipment. Before long it seemed we had a small town set up, with its own airport. My company had the perimeter at the start. This is where I saw my first American casualty. A wireman went out to find a break in the wire and didn't return. I was to take a patrol out and see if I could find him.

We found him floating face down, his hands and feet bound behind his back, with his private parts cut off and stuffed in his mouth, in a stream. He had bled to death, not drowned. Welcome to the Vietnam Conflict. Everyone on my patrol, including me, was in a state of shock. We fished the body out of the stream, untied his hands and feet, carried his body back into camp, letting everyone see it. We deposited his body in front of the CO's tent. We did not know what to do with it, where to take it, or anything like that. His CO didn't really know how to take care of the body, either. Finally, two corpsmen came over and said they would take care of the remains.

Our first casualty and no one knew what to do, including the man's CO. I learned a lesson from this experience—these were the facts of war: Death. A death that would occur at any time, any second, to anyone, including myself.

About an hour after this, reality really hit me. I went off by myself, cried, threw up and cried some more. From the way this man died, I was glad I was not an enemy that could be captured by myself or any of these young men in my unit. The talk was of nothing but revenge, hate and anger, in everyone, from senior to junior men. No one was exempt from this anger. I still feel some of this anger today. The questions still linger in my mind: "Why was he allowed to go out alone?" "Why didn't I, as an NCO, send or take my squad out for security?" "Was it my fault?" I've been told, "No, it wasn't your responsibility." Who the hell's responsibility was it? No one could ever answer that question and never has, so I guess I still feel some guilt about this.

We stayed on perimeter duty for the next three or four weeks and then moved out on the first of many search and destroy operations I was involved in. I saw many men get shot on both sides. Many of my friends went home either to a hospital or a graveyard. But a strange thing happened to me. I no longer felt personally responsible for any of these new casualties.

Then a new phenomenon happened. We were involved in a large firefight in Happy Valley, with us taking heavy casualties—ambushed. All of a sudden I found myself in command of what was left of our company. The CO, XO, first sergeant, company gunnery sergeant and First Platoon sergeant were history—dead, gone, departed. I was senior man alive—God help me. I prayed that I would and could make the right decisions to get us out without anymore casualties. We stayed engaged in this area for another hour when help arrived by means of another Marine rifle company coming in by choppers and gunships, blasting the hell out of Charlie. A casualty report told me that God had indeed helped me. I had lost no more men during this hour. I pulled what was left of my company together at a "secured" landing zone and counted what was left. We suffered thirty-two KIAs and fifty-five WIAs—eighty-seven casualties out of approximately 155 men.

While regrouping, another chopper came in. Aboard were seven stars—two generals—one Army and one Marine. They asked for the "senior" man to give a report on what had happened. I reported in this capacity and was told, "Good job, Captain," to which I replied, "Staff sergeant." The Marine general responded, "No. Captain. Congratulations."

I then had to get the next two senior men to meet with the generals. One became an instant first-lieutenant and the other, first-sergeant. I was then instructed to give battlefield "promotions" to anyone I felt could handle the other authoritative positions in "my" company. The Brass Balls left my position, leaving me, a twenty-four-year-old, with only a GED, as company commander. I felt very proud of this responsibility and made my other picks for jobs, and promoted them on the spot. I told them to make proper assignments from their platoons to handle what was left of their squads, which they did.

We were airlifted back to Chu Lai base camp, where I had to report to the battalion CO on what had transpired in the bush. He gave me the assignment to start writing letters to next-of-kin of the deceased. As a lot of deceased were friends, I wanted to write personal letters and was instructed to use "form letters" with just a personal note. I had lost my first battle, I thought, but as I think of it now, had I written personal letters, I would still be writing those letters.

Our replacements started to arrive and new operations started. I did my damnedest to avoid casualties, which I felt pretty good about and still do. I felt that in my five months as a CO I kept my killed and wounded down to less than fifteen percent when a lot of outfits were suffering fifty percent or more. I still say "Thank you God" for this.

One of my more traumatic experiences was when I had to go to Graves and Registration to ID a casualty. Upon walking into this cold, impersonal building, I was met by a sight that pissed me off. The two attendants were in the process of playing "catch" with a human head. I really blew my cool, screaming, hollering, wanting to strangle them and all those neat things that one wants to do when pissed off. I walked through the lines of body bags and made my ID of one of my "boys" and started to leave. As I walked outside and into the head, and closed the door, I stopped. It had dawned on me that these two young men, approximately nineteen years of age, had to do this in order to retain any sanity they still had. My feelings changed from anger toward them to feeling sorry for them. I went back inside again, seeing the rows of body bags in the building, and told them both that I was no longer "mad" at them, but told them to use a little more care in any future "football games" they decide to have.

About two days later some new officers arrived on the scene. A real captain, first-lieutenant and second-lieutenant, along with a real first-sergeant. I was allowed to keep my commission and was transferred to FLSG-B (Force Logistics Support Group-Bravo) where I was assigned to the Korean Marine Corps as an advisor. I completed my first tour of duty in this capacity.

Upon receipt of orders to the East Coast, I departed Nam and went home on leave. This was in late November. I went back to my farm without knowing a strange thing. While I was sleeping, at about 0630, I heard lots of shots being fired. I jumped out of bed and dove through the window. Thank God there was a lot of snow on the ground, as I had dove from the second floor. The "strange thing" was only the opening of deer hunting season. The shots were from hunters. God, it was cold, lying half awake in the snow in only my shorts. My family actually thought that I was crazy, as the shots didn't wake them up. But my going through the window and the storm window did. I politely told them I thought I was still in Nam.

I continued on leave until the twenty-eighth day, when I received a telegram ordering me to report back to the West Coast for further reassignment within the next five days. Upon my arrival at Camp Pendleton, California, I was told I was being sent back to Nam to continue as an advisor to the Koreans.

I reported to Staging Battalion and became the officer-in-charge of a planeload of young Marines—both enlisted and officers—flying into Da Nang. These young men were laughing and giggling all the way about there being no real problems in Nam. Upon arrival at Da Nang, the officer-in-charge of air freight asked me if I could give him some people for a working party. I asked, "What for?" He stated to me that he needed help to load a refrigerated aircraft headed for Travis Air Force Base. I agreed. For the next two hours I had all these young men load "green bags" from refrigerated trucks to refrigerated aircraft. When this was done I had all these young men gather round and I asked them if they knew what they were loading. I was told, in unison, "No." I then told them they had loaded up the bodies of the Marines they were replacing. All of a sudden there was no more laughing and giggling. Before me stood 150 very sober-faced Marines. Within the next hour all these men went to their prospective units and I flew back to Chu Lai, where I rejoined FLSG-B for assignment to the Koreans.

Upon reporting to FLSG-B I was indeed assigned to the ROKs. I flew out of Chu Lai to Tam Ky, where I joined the ROK staff, who were preparing for an operation. I was greeted by the ROK general like a long-lost brother. I was given the U.S./Korean call signs and a PRC-10 radio to carry—hopefully we wouldn't need it—to call in close air support, if necessary.

Two hours later we were flying out on operation. The Korean "sweep" was very uneventful in the beginning. The first day and a half went by without any enemy contact at all. Then we got reports of heavy fighting involving one of our Korean flank units. The main body moved out on the double over the three-quarters of a mile to the west. Upon arrival at the firefight area, I was appalled at the number of casualties the Koreans had taken. The unit was ninety-five men—there were sixty-three killed, twenty-eight wounded, and four escaped unscathed. Even though they suffered this many losses, the wounded and unwounded held their ground. Charlie heard us coming and di-di-ed out of the area, leaving dead and wounded behind.

The CG's bird came in and he, some of his staff and I flew out to the medical battalion in Chu Lai, where all of the wounded—both Korean and Cong—and dead Koreans were taken. Upon arrival at Chu Lai, we went into the Med. Bn., where the general talked to every one of his wounded men. Then the general, his Vietnamese interpreter, and two Korean MPs bodily carried a wounded Cong the short walk to the Graves and Registration Building. Seconds after they went in, the Americans working in the building came outside. Their faces were ashen in color. About twenty minutes later the general, interpreter and MPs exited the building—no Cong. The general's hands and arms were covered in blood. I did not ask what happened inside the building, but was later told the general had taken his revenge out on the Cong by skinning him alive and letting him bleed to death.

The general had told me, "No one lives that had killed one of my men."

I have no reason to believe anything different about this.

General "P," as I had heard him called, showed no pity on Charlie or his own troops. When his troops were on perimeter duty, every night he would personally check them for alertness. I remember many cases where he came back in and sent replacement guards to certain bunkers. The next morning a stretcher was sent out and came back with a blanket-covered body on it. Who was it—Cong or Korean? Your guess is as good as mine. It seemed he had General Court Authority and used it to the fullest extent he could—Judge, Jury and Executioner.

General P treated his American advisors like they were gold, as we were his main source of communications with American Forces.

For the next couple of months things were rather quiet for me as I did not have to go out on operation. General P sent patrols out all the time, and they very seldom, if at all, got into any trouble. One of the patrols captured a young woman who appeared to be half French and half Vietnamese. She was carrying an AK-47, 100 pounds of ammo and three Chi-Com grenades. She was brought back for interrogation. The answers she gave were not believed, so she was stripped naked and tied spread-eagle on the ground approximately 125 meters away from the camp. One of the MPs with orders from the major doing the questioning, got a long piece of twine. He took a hand grenade, tied one end around the grenade, went over to the woman, forced the grenade up into her vagina, pulled the pin and ran back towards us, to safety. The major, lying behind some sandbags pulled the twine taught, hollering questions at her. This woman told everything she knew. When the questioning was done and all the answers were believed, the major slowly pulled on the twine until the grenade fell to the ground, with the spoon flying off. I just turned away until after the explosion. When I looked back at the woman, all that was left was shredded meat. I just could not believe I had seen what I had seen. The Koreans were now just laughing about the "stupid broad." I walked away, went behind some buildings and got very, very sick again. I really wanted to know what kind of "madness" this conflict was.

Another incident I recall—a suspect buried up to his neck in the ground and watching them literally kick his head off his shoulders.

After completing an operation, the Koreans decided to widen the road through a ville so we would have two lanes of traffic. All the villagers were told and agreed to allow this to happen. All was going well until we got to this area where we had to take about three feet of an old woman's rice paddy. She came out screaming at us not to touch her property. She got in the Korean colonel's face, the one who was in charge of this road widening, and just yelled and screamed. The colonel had the major try to tell her it was necessary to do this. She would not listen. After telling her to shut up five times, the colonel told the major to tell her to be quiet or he was going to shoot her. The major told her once again—she continued to scream. The major told her again and then a third time. She would not quit. The colonel pulled out his 45. Had her told again. She spit in his face, so he quickly raised his pistol and shot her in the forehead, blowing out the whole back of her head. Her body was rolled into the rice paddy and buried by the bulldozers making the road wider. The road was completed without further incident.

This incident was the last straw in my mind I thought I could tolerate, so I went to see General P. I told him I had to protest the brutality I had witnessed. He replied these were "required Acts of War." I requested transfer back to an American unit, which he granted with a statement, "I do this with great reluctance." I had been with them for nine months. Three days later I was back at FLSG-B, where I was assigned to the Battalion S-2 as an assistant intelligence officer. I saw no more enemy action during the rest of my tour, but we did have a young Marine who, on drinking whiskey bought in the village of Anton, went berserk, shooting and killing six Marines. He looked like he was dead upon our entry into the tent where this happened. The bottle was full of formaldehyde, which drove him nuts and, to this day, as far as I know, he has never spoken a work to anyone. He was med-evaced out to Chu Lai, to Japan.

Then I got my orders home. I was on my way back to The World. My orders read "2nd Marine Aircraft Wing, MCAS, Cherry Point, N.C." Upon leaving Nam, we flew into Okinawa, where I spent three days watching the Marines on the way home being herded around by young troops whose only duty station was Okinawa. The way the troops on the way home were handled, like they were only trash, instead of men on the way home after surviving battle, made me upset with the officers who ran this program, and I let them know it. I got sent up to the lieutenant-colonel in charge, told him my feelings and got my ass chewed out royally, but I felt I had done the best I could to protect these men.

Upon leaving Oki I flew commercial air to Los Angeles International. Upon picking up my luggage and departing I heard this voice state, "Look at that, a *baby killer!*"

I looked around for someone in handcuffs behind me. There was no one. The person was talking about me. I really got pissed, wondering what gave this long-haired bastard a right to call me that. I still can't figure it out. I wanted to break this guy's face open so bad I could taste his blood. Finally I cooled off enough to leave the airport, without waiting outside for this guy, to beat the hell out of him.

When I arrived home on leave, I started to really drink heavily. I don't think I drew a sober breath all the time I was home. I stayed drunk. Being from a small town, I knew everyone, so drinks were not a problem to get. Then on the twenty-eighth day at home, I got another telegram to report back to the West Coast within five days. My worst fears had been realized. I knew I was on my way back to Nam. I was to report to Travis AFB. I really wanted to just not report and stay drunk. My family sobered me up and put me on a plane back to California. I reported to Travis and was sent back to Nam. Back to the Koreans for another tour.

I landed in Da Nang, stayed overnight, got drunk and left for Chu Lai the next morning by chopper. I reported to FLSG-B again and was assigned, even though I protested, to General P. It seemed he never got sent back home. General P greeted me once again like I was a long-lost son. I told General P that I was very upset about this. He told me he needed me to work in his headquarters as he was having trouble with his supply system. Upon looking at his supply records I saw why. For example, his supply officer had ordered 155 cases of lead pencils. This was enough pencils to make a two-lane road from Chu Lai to Da Nang and still have some left. I thought his mismanagement was hilarious. This assignment would not be as bad as I thought it would be. Little did I know I was wrong.

I went with a supply detail to our American supply source. I met with the supply officer and NCO while the Korean lieutenant and his three-man detail went into the warehouse. Then shots rang out from inside the warehouse. Taking the safety off my weapon, the supply officer, NCO and myself entered the warehouse to see four Vietnamese women shot to hell. They were the civilians that had been hired to work in the warehouse. An explanation given by the Korean lieutenant was that he saw these women emptying out first-aid kits into a trash barrel and stuffing paper in them to make them appear full. So he ordered his men to shoot them. They obeyed orders to the fullest. A search of the trash barrels found that they in fact were full of first aid supplies. Sabotage from our own supply depot was put to an immediate stop.

How many kits had gone to the field to unsuspecting troops? No first aid kits! The total number was unknown. This incident didn't upset me. I felt that, had I seen this action, I would have shot them also. I saw this as a "war crime," thinking how many troops would die because of lack of medical supplies. I never found out if there were any.

During my previous tour an incident known as My Lai had occurred. A young Army lieutenant was charged with murder of civilians. The part about My Lai that gets to me is the number of Allied Forces it took to retake that ville. So these idiots from Washington, D.C. could dig holes in the ground looking for bodies. True, the mass grave was found, with the dead looking like they had been slaughtered by Cong, the same as other mass graves that had been discovered after a visit by "Charlie." The funny thing about the Calley case was his court-martial board stating they *did not know* that Calley could be given the death sentence after they found him guilty. My feeling was that Calley was a scapegoat through this whole ordeal.

With his conviction, Calley was out of the war, excuse me, conflict, as war was never declared. Bullshit, it was war to me and everyone else who served.

An incident occurred while we were on convoy. An American vehicle—a six-by-six—was ahead of our convoy when it ran over a mine, killing or injuring ten Americans. The Koreans found a wire leading from the mine to a small village. On order, the Koreans all dismounted their vehicles and opened fire on the ville. They did not stop until everything that moved in the ville stopped moving—men, women, children, dogs, anything. They then moved to the ville and found that the wire went around the ville to a secluded area where the mine had been set off from.

The explanation was the people had to know about the mine. Did they? No one left to question. Seventy-plus people dead, for what reason? Who knows? Who cares? I felt nothing after this—no feeling of guilt or remorse. I still can't figure out why. Had I turned to stone or had I seen so much death and destruction I didn't care anymore? Who can answer this question for me?

On operations with the ROKs I found it interesting to note that when we came upon a ville and were going to stay for the night outside of it, the major called out and told them, "We are going to camp here. If we get any action from your ville we will wipe your ville off the face of the earth." You know, I can never recall us having to do this.

Then the best thing happened to me. General P got his orders back to Korea and I got reassigned to Da Nang—Force Logistics Command—where I was assigned as CO of MP Company. For my last three months in-country, other than Marines getting in trouble in "Dogpatch" with booze and hookers, it was very quiet.

I finally got orders back to The World, knowing the new ROK general did not want me, as I had not met him. Thank God.

My orders were to report to the 2nd Marine Division, Camp Lejeune, North Carolina. Until then my drinking was "controlled." Upon reporting to Camp Lejeune I was assigned to the Division/Base MPs as assistant provost marshal. After about eight months I was sent on a Mediterranean cruise. At the end of this cruise, a new thing happened—my ship got assigned to the Suez Canal mine-sweep operation. We stayed out another three months against our will. Upon return to the U.S., I got a new set of orders. I was on my way to Hawaii for the next two years.

Upon arrival in Hawaii, I was assigned to Camp Smith as MP Company Commander. My drinking habits got worse as the "O" club was right outside my office. The club opened at 10:30 a.m. for lunch, so I faithfully went to "lunch" at 11:15 a.m. daily and got back between 1:00 or 1:30 p.m. to my office, after drinking my "lunch." Eight to ten vodka martinis, very dry on the rocks, with a twist. Some lunch. My work day was over at 4:15 or 4:30, so my next stop was the Club for supper. I left the Club at closing time and staggered to my room carrying two six-packs of beer—so I could get a good start in the morning. I consumed these beers before going to work daily.

One morning I woke up, opened the fridge, grabbed a beer and went into the bathroom. I just happened to look in the mirror and noticed that both of my eyes looked like I had been punched out. Both my eyes were black. I looked at the can in my hand and said, "Why?" I couldn't answer. I poured the can down the sink, went back to the fridge, pulled out the other eleven cans and dumped them down the drain also. Upon cleaning up, I went to my wardrobe to put on a clean uniform and didn't have one—the only thing I had clean was one set of civilian clothes. I put these on and reported to my boss at 0800. He asked me why I was wearing civvies and I replied, "Colonel, I have a bad problem and need your advice and help." He had me sit down and had the sergeant major get us some coffee. I then told him that I had a bad drinking problem. He then showed me his desk calendar. My name was on it to see him at 1030 that morning, and he was going to relieve me of my command.

He then set me up with a program to help me. During this "dry out" period I saw everything crawling up the walls. It was as much hell as Nam was. At the end of this "dry out" I resigned my commission and went back to being an enlisted man again. Shortly after doing this I got orders sending me to Iwakumi, Japan. I spent twelve months in Japan and decided I had enough full-time military in my life, and came back to the States to become a civilian again (fourteen years, eleven months, twenty-nine days active duty). So as not to throw it all away, I joined the National Guard after I got off active duty and spent eleven years there, so I can eventually receive my retirement pay.

My life after getting away from the military has been one of turmoil. I got married to a ready-made family, helped finish raising three children, went through many different types of jobs—security, cleaning, metal shop, restaurant, security again, restaurant again. I hurt my back in the metal shop and was given a permanent ten percent disability by different doctors. I am in the process now of getting a divorce, as I really was not making much money—had a sickly, nagging wife who bled me dry. I now have a girlfriend who is also getting a divorce, who I love deeply, but cannot support like I need to. My life is a real mess, but who do I turn to? My girlfriend is ready to kick me out in the street.

I am wondering if the time has come for me to finish my life by ending it. I feel I am about ready to do this. I guess the more I think about it, I really can't see any good reason to live anymore. Then someone comes in with worse problems than I have and I just try to push on. My exwife has destroyed me with my family by telling them things about me—some lies, some truths.

So who have I got left to care about me? I really don't know anymore. So, when you read this, I don't know if I will still be alive. I feel I have no reason to live anymore. With all the death and destruction I have seen, why should I still be alive while others have died? I don't feel I have any real friends in the world—just acquaintances.

So who the hell would care? No one, as far as I can tell. My life after the military is just straight fucked up.

Billy R. McFalls

I was born and raised in a small town in Tennessee by the name of Spring City. It is known now as the city by the lake. In the early '30s the T.V.A. built a huge dam (Watts Bar) about eight miles away. Therefore, the city became quite a tourist town. We go back there quite often. In fact, the general that was killed with the President of Pakistan about two years ago in Pakistan was from Spring City. I had gone to high school with him. I went there to a dedication of a new highway in memory of him.

My first experience in SEA was in 1967. I had been picked to head up a 126-man Logistics Group which had been picked from all over PACAF. Our job was to travel from our home bases into USAF bases in Thailand to identify excess USAF property and either ship it back to the States or any base in Asia that would require it. We had been pulled from all over. Pacific Air Command. My home base was Clark Field, Philippines.

In the early parts of the war a massive amount of supplies and equipment had been shipped into SEA without any knowledge of whether or not the base that received it required it or not. This was another of the government's screw-ups.

We arrived in Udorn, Thailand in July of 1967. The USAF had a small fighter outfit in place. A squadron of old WWII AIE single-engine dive bombers, with some ground support units. The Air Force's plan was to expand the base and bring in bigger A/C. After about three days we all finally got together and realized what a bunch of shit we had run into. Everywhere you looked there was tons of unidentified supplies, most of it out in the weather. So our job was to clear it out and make space for runways, parking areas and warehouses. You are looking at acres upon acres of space. We had assigned to us heavy equipment operators, down to computer operators.

About the fourth day, we were organized and started. We had been briefed on many things. One of them was poison snakes. So bigger than shit, the first day, myself and two other NCOs were walking down this little trail when I looked up and about fifteen feet ahead of us was an eight-foot cobra with his head sticking up about two feet, bobbing back and forth. We high-tailed it out of there and told a Thai worker who was with us. He caught it just as if it was a garden snake back home. Well, believe it or not, that was the one and only snake I saw in the six months we were there. We found about a four- or five-acre field all overgrown with monkey grass and full of 100-pound sacks of cement which had been out in the weather and were completely ruined. We finally gave them to a local orphanage. We also gave them a 100-by-50-foot portable building, which we later found out belonged to a civilian contractor in Bangkok. Sorry about that.

Even though we worked twelve hours on twelve hours off, seven days a week, it was one of the more enjoyable jobs I ever had. The young people were the most dedicated and loyal I had ever worked with. We worked hard and played hard. Every young American should spend some time in Thailand. During that period in the northern part of Thailand, there was an Air America Base (CIA). We were only about fifteen minutes (air time) from Laos. They were training Laotian tribesman. For a period of time I roomed with a door-gunner from Alabama. He always wore civilian clothes, but was still in the U.S. Army. He told me about one of his missions. A USAF pilot had been shot down and he was to go in and remove all of the classified equipment from the A/C. As they were doing this, they were fired on by Laos Communists. They managed to escape, but it got pretty hairy for a while. For that mission he showed me a check from Air America for $1500. Back in those days that was a lot of money. Air America was made up of a lot of nationalities—anybody they could hire. The only problem we ever had was we were hit one night by a Communist terrorist group. They blew up a C-130 and some ground support equipment. CTs were operating quite often that far north, but that was the only incident while I was there.

We pulled out of Udorn on January 30, 1968. As we were all sitting around the makeshift terminal out in the boonies waiting for our C-130 to take us to Bangkok, I noticed an Army sergeant-major pass by, leading a little boy. I thought I knew him when he first passed by. But, being in the Air Force, I very seldom ran up on any Army personnel, so I let it pass. But, in about twenty minutes this same dude came waltzing back by and just happened to look me dead in the eye and let out with one hell of a yell. "Billy Ray McFalls, what the *hell* are you doing here?!" Well, it turned out this guy came from my home town, that I grew up with him. He only lived about one mile from where I did in Tennessee. This is how crazy that damn war was. He had his wife and two kids with him and was stationed in Bangkok some damn place and was going on his R&R. We boarded the same A/C and flew from Thailand to Vietnam right in the beginning of the 1968 Tet Offensive. As we landed at Tan Son Nhut Air Base, the place was lit up like a Christmas tree. It was 0100 31 January, 1968. We had to get off the A/C for refueling. Keep in mind, here is my friend with his wife and two kids. As we were going into the terminal, one end of that sonofabitch blew up. Hey, I mean the shit flew. It had been hit with a direct hit. Charlie overran the damn place. (Can you believe this shit?) Talk about panic. Fucking crazy airmen shooting at everything. "Man, this can't be happening. I am on my way back to The World. The rest is fucking history, man." We finally got back on the airplane and we were the last plane to leave Saigon for I don't know how long. The runway was closed for a week or more. Out of all that crap, we only had one buck-sergeant that got hit with some shrapnel. He was down at the end of the building getting a coke. He was awarded the Purple Heart back in the P.I.

I later ran into an Army sergeant who was there during that time and remembered that last plane taking off. He said it sure was taking some ground fire, which we never knew about. We made it back to the Philippines just fine, with my friend and family, who went from there to Hawaii.

I shipped back to the States in April 1968, then went back to Vietnam in 1970. After leaving my family in Rayne, approximately thirty hours later, I arrived back in South Vietnam on Braniff Air Lines. Another weird thing about the war. We sat down at Bien Hoa AFB at 1300 hours, so hot you could hardly breathe. There were about 250 airmen and Army troops. As we were downloading the A/C, a sergeant came forward, as we all knew he would, separating the Air Force and Army. Air Force one way and Army to Long Binh. By the time we got into the terminal, we had heard a hundred different rumors. At that time we thought they were rumors. Charlie had come through the outer perimeter last night, they had been hit by 100 122mm rockets the night before and did we know we had just landed at Rocket City, etc. My thought: "Here I am, thirty-eight years old and back in this shit again. The military puts the shit on top every now and then." At the time I got my orders, I had nineteen and a half years in the Air Force. I had no choice really. If I didn't take the assignment, I would have to get out (with no retirement), so there I was, right in the middle of this fucking war again. As we walked around the side of the terminal, we found out some of the rumors were true. There sat, all dressed in black, with blindfolds and hands tied behind their backs, fifteen or twenty VC prisoners, with an eighteen-year-old guarding them. He told us they were caught the night before. We asked him if he was the only guard. He said a couple of buddies had gone to get a Coke. No big deal. The cat just had to have a Coke! Goes to show you the young soldiers never really took the war too serious.

Within the next hour, we had been processed and assigned to our own squadrons. My new job was NCOIC of the 3rd TAC Fighter Wing Logistics, working directly for a Colonel McDonald. I was assigned quarters in a hooch which housed about thirty men. Really not that bad. We were just getting settled in, with me laying in my skivvies, when all of a sudden it seemed the whole hooch was coming down. It sounded like a whole artillery battery was going off. I made a dive for the bunker with just my undies. I sat in the bunker for about twenty minutes all alone thinking everybody else was wiped out. During this time, the firing continued. After about twenty minutes, a sergeant came by and looked in and saw me and called out to me that everything was okay. The firing was outgoing (not incoming) from the two batteries of 105s about fifty yards from my hooch. He told me not to feel bad, everybody had to get used to it. Well, after about two nights I could determine the incoming from outgoing, but I never got used to it. We were getting hit with 122mm rockets and 145s just about every night. I will never forget the swoosh, swoosh sound of the rockets as they passed over us. Lucky for us, most of the time Charlie was not after personnel, he was after the aircraft. Most of the time he got one or two, except on one particular rainy Sunday afternoon.

Most of our Sundays were pretty slow. Believe it or not, the war just kinda stopped. Most of the birds didn't fly. The troops just kinda screwed around and drank beer. One of the things a lot of the troops would do is go back to the shack to listen to tapes and shoot the shit. On this particular Sunday afternoon all eight people, which included the three shifts at one of our control rooms, got two direct hits with 122mm rockets. All eight were killed. One of the young sergeants had worked for me back in the Philippines in '67. This control room was completely wiped out. Was it a lucky hit or was Charlie that good? Well, needless to say, after that we stopped hanging around the shack if we were not on duty.

My part in the war in 1970 was mostly made up of making reports to the 7th AF MACV HQ in Saigon. I had reports that had to be hand-carried every month. At that time we were turning over most of the flying and fighting to the South Vietnamese (Vietnamization Program). Ha! Ha! In doing this we had to write new contingency plans. That is, what we were leaving them, such as airplanes and other material and supplies, all types of support equipment, millions of dollars of goodies. Well, this was the highly classified report.

Most of our trips were very incidental. The one I remember most happened one Monday morning. We tried to leave around 0700, but on this morning the road to Saigon had been bombed the night before and was closed. We had to wait until the Army declared it safe. So we waited around for a few hours. I didn't want to leave too late, because I knew if we had to leave Saigon after 1800 we would have to join the convoy that left Saigon every night going in-country about that time. This I didn't want to do. Charlie hit it about every night. I made a couple of calls trying to wait for the next day, with no luck. The dude at MACV suggested I catch a ride with the 666th helicopter outfit stationed at Bien

Hoa just a couple of blocks down from where I was. I called down, they said "Yeah, no problem" and got us to Saigon Toot-Sweet. Well, no big deal, we were in Saigon by 1500, briefed the colonel at MACV on our latest transfers to the USAF and was on our way back to Bien Hoa around 1700. Ha! Ha! Not so easy this time. We hooked a ride back to the triple-six launching pad, but found no ride. The troop there made a few calls and found all the choppers were out on patrol up along the Cambodian border. Along about this time, my buddy and I, a black staff-sergeant, who had become one of my closest friends, were pissed off. I don't believe he was ever scared of anything. (On one trip from Long Binh back to Bien Hoa, which was about ten miles, we were passing the dump which ran along the side of the road, when all hell broke loose. Three F-4s passed over and dropped napalm on some Vietnamese about 150 yards from us, right off the road in the dump. We had noticed them, but thought nothing of it. It turned out they were VC and had been firing 122mm rockets on the base. John wanted to stop and watch. Me, I wanted to get the hell out of there. We had been to Long Binh to trade for some steaks, that's just how screwed up the war was. What a fucking waste). We waited around the chopper pad until about 2100 when, finally, a gunship landed and the crew got out, walked over and started shooting the shit with us and asked if we wanted a ride. They were on patrol, but would be glad to drop us off if we didn't mind finishing the patrol with them. Well, to say the least, Johnson was all for it, so we got aboard. What a fucking deal that was. These crazy assholes flew us all over the damn place. Up and down the Cambodian border. As far as you could see, there were campfires, about 150,000 VC and NVA troops. On one pass the crazy fuckers went down and started shooting, just to keep them awake, the twenty-one-year-old gunner tells us. This lasted about an hour and they finally dropped us off at Bien Hoa. Johnson had a ball. Me, I was scared shitless.

That was in June of 1970. Charlie had been hitting us with rockets and sapper attacks about every night. We used to hear rumors about the grunts wishing the airmen would get hit. They would stand up and cheer when Bien Hoa and Da Nang would get it. At least the grunts out in the field could shoot back. The only way we, the Air Force support people, could actually fight back was to see that the airplanes were kept in the best repair possible. I have to give all of our maintenance and support personnel the highest of praise for fighting their part of the war, whether it be mechanics, supply personnel, cooks or administrative people. Last but not least, the bomb handlers and loaders. Particularly during the invasion of Cambodia, July 1970. Everybody was in such a state of mind of not being able to follow the enemy into Cambodia after they crossed and hit the Americans. When the day finally came, it was like sitting on the bench all season and finally getting in the ball game. It was only about twenty minutes flying-time to the Fish Hook area of Cambodia, where most of the concentration of NVA troops were. The NVA had three divisions along the border—the 5th, 7th, and 9th. These were later the same divisions that made the final assault on Saigon in April 1975.

Our mission during the invasion was to give the ARVN and U.S. troops air support. That we did for as long as the invasion lasted. I never heard a complaint from our people. Particularly air flight line people. Getting any sleep was forgotten about. We could only think of one thing. "This is the biggy. Go get them bastards." Some of our A-77 fighter A/C would fly up to twenty missions a day. On some of the aircraft one of the seats was taken out and an extra fuel tank installed.

Our bomb loading crews worked around the clock. The flight crews were as though they were given a charmed life. They would fly down the barrel of the NVA Anti-A/C guns. Even Uncle Ho himself later said they were the bravest of all. I have read many books about the war, but I have never yet read much about the people, about the hard work to patch up an airplane which had been shot up the day before, waiting for parts, no sleep, scared all the time, in the most unsafe place at that time in the world. You can say that again!

But, the sad part about the invasion was this. Our intelligence as usual was piss poor. Even though we destroyed tons of rice, weapons and other supplies, we never found the Cosun HQ. That was the main objective. We only advanced twenty miles, so the NVA just moved back twenty-one miles and the same shit started all over again. We should have done what ARVN wanted to do, drop some paratroopers behind the NVA, causing a pincer move and destroying all three divisions. But, since the war was directed by the Pentagon, not the military, same old shit.

After the invasion was over and our troops pulled back, there was something that I will never forget. Refugees by the thousands pouring over the border. What a sight to see. Within weeks all the roadsides were lined with shack people trying to survive. Army trucks full of people and weapons. The Army troops would sell you a case of Chinese rifles still in boxes for a hundred dollars. Some of the airmen were crazy enough to buy them, even though you couldn't bring them back to the States. I got caught with two AK-47s—one of the crazies! Ha! On one occasion I was visiting a friend of mine, about a week after the pull-out, and when I walked into his hooch, there sat three women about half naked. I asked him where in the hell did these people come from. He told me they were Cambodian and he had bought them from an Army troop for $20 and did I want one. This guy had a whole truckload. Man,

I couldn't believe what he was telling me—he'd had them for a couple of days. But, knowing this guy, anything was possible. I had known him before in the Philippines, and if there was only one woman in the world, he would be the one that had her. I think he threw off some kind of smell! Well, to say the least, I got the hell out of there. I sure didn't want to get caught with something like that. I saw him a few days later and he said he let them go. Just like that, man. Hell, just let them go! No big deal.

Well, it wasn't long after that when the bombing for us kinda came to a halt. We weren't hit as much. The Paris Peace talks were going on. Kissinger was planning our withdrawal and betrayal of the South Vietnamese people; release of our POWs for Saigon. What a disgrace to our country this man is and yet he is still there. What can I say?

I rotated back to the States not long afterward and got back to a normal life with my wife and daughter. I forgot about the war for a while. Everybody you worked with had been there, so no big deal. I retired from the Air Force in 1975, rocked my rocking chair for a year, moved to Rayne, a small town of about 10,000, with nobody caring about me and me not caring about anybody but my immediate family either. I built my retirement home and put up a twenty-six-foot flagpole. Then I bought myself a four-by-eight American flag and started flying it. On the 28th of April every year, directly underneath the American flag, I cry and fly the yellow and red South Vietnamese flag which was given to me by an ARVN captain. The 28th of April, 1975, the day all America should mourn for the only country we fought for, but betrayed. That is why we, the Vietnam vets, must never let them, the American people, forget how corrupt our government had become, when one man, who no American had ever voted for, had such power (Kissinger).

I later went to work as a purchasing agent for the local school board. I worked for nine years and retired with 100 percent disability. I was exposed to Agent Orange and now have acute asthma.

(No more incoming.)

Carl T. Huettner

In November of 1953, at the age of seventeen, I quit high school and joined the Navy, to "see the world." As a young, impressionable man-child, I was attracted by the thoughts of travel, excitement, wearing sharp blue-and-white uniforms, and having "a girl in every port." Then years later, having served the full ten years at sea aboard destroyers and submarines, I had matured and my viewpoints had changed considerably. I had become a veteran of many little skirmishes that usually never made the newspapers: during the Suez Canal crisis, I had served aboard the destroyer that was the last U.S. combatant ship to pass through the canal, the whole trip at General Quarters, Battle Stations. We did not know if we were going to be fired upon by the Egyptian Army, or Navy, or both.

Aboard a destroyer, we stood-close offshore, to supply gun fire-support when the Marines landed on the Shores of Beirut, Lebanon. During the battle of the Gaza Strip, we were a close-in observation ship, wondering if either side in the battle would take a shot at us. The Bay of Pigs invasion in Cuba made the papers, of course, but there was no mention of the submarine that I was serving aboard, lying submerged, just offshore. During the Cuban Blockade, my sub was in the Caribbean Sea, tracking Soviet shipping, and waiting for the word to come down from President Kennedy to shoot to sink. There were the instances of near collisions with Soviet naval ships, and an actual ramming with another ship in the Mediterranean Sea. There was the time we were fired upon by an un-named, supposedly friendly foreign Navy.

As those ten years passed, all of the fun and excitement had long worn off and I had begun to feel that I had served my country well. I even had a medal on my uniform, the Naval Expeditionary Medal, although, to this day, I don't know what I did to earn it.

By 1963, I was halfway to the twenty-year retirement, and it was time to begin to settle down a bit. I had begun to wish for something solid in my life—a real home, a wife, kids . . . I met and married a beautiful girl, ten years younger than I, and put in a request for a well-earned tour of shore duty. In 1964, I reported for a three-year tour of duty at the U.S. Naval Base, Great Lakes, Illinois. My wife had given me a fantastically beautiful bouncing baby girl, and the Navy gave me the most fulfilling and satisfying job I ever had, that of a recruit company commander, training young men to become sailors. In 1965, I was promoted to Chief Petty Officer, pay-grade E-7, and we were blessed with a fine, handsome son. Within a year, a second, equally fine son arrived, and life was good. Very, very good. I re-enlisted for six more years.

During off-duty hours, I worked. I moonlighted—pumped gas in an all-night gas station, fired boilers in a local factory, tended bar in a local restaurant, and I saved. I was able to be a good provider for my young family. I bought a decent car, a two-bedroom mobile home, and good appliances that we needed. Then came the fall of 1967, and my time at Great Lakes was rapidly drawing to an end, and I knew that I would get orders back to sea duty. Maybe I could get a submarine or destroyer tender. That is good duty because those kinds of ships usually stay in port, and rarely actually go to sea. Maybe I could get a fleet oiler—"Out on Monday, back in port by Friday." Maybe I could even get a school. I always wanted to go to the Navy's Air Conditioning and Refrigeration School. The Navy gives a prospective transferee a form to fill out, listing the type of duty that they would like to have next. Sailors call the form a "Dream Sheet." I filled out my dream sheet and waited. I didn't have long to wait.

My advance orders came through: To the USS Tutuila, ARG4. Home port: San Diego, California, Ship currently in Vung Tau, Republic of South Vietnam. I was elated! I had heard of the old Tutuila before. I knew she was an internal combustion engine repair ship. That kind of ship, like a tender, spent most of it's time in port. The USS Tutuila sat alongside the pier in Norfolk, Virginia for so long that sailors referred to her as Building #4. There was a rumor that the Tutuila had a cracked keel and was condemned from the open sea by the Navy. An old sea story about the Tutuila was that she had sat alongside that pier for so long that her bottom became fouled by years and years of sailors throwing coffee grounds over the side, until there was no freeboard water beneath her keel! Some sailors said that she sat hard atop coffee grounds and didn't rise and fall with the tides! Perfect sea duty for a married man.

I rushed home that day and told my wife that we were going to San Diego, California! Beautiful, sunny San Diego, with palm trees and beaches and everything. I told her that the ship was in some place called Vung Tau, probably on a western Pacific cruise, and probably will be back to San Diego before we got there. We celebrated by having dinner at the Chief's Club that evening.

In 1967 I knew there was a war going on, in Vietnam. I had a new color TV and Walter Cronkite was on it every night, telling us how many Communists were killed that day. But, I was in the Navy, not the Army, and I was a steam engineer. My domain was the ship's engine room, not some foxhole by a rice paddy.

I didn't realize that this Vietnam thing was causing the Navy to take blue-water sailors and send them to war in a plastic and fiberglass armada, up dirty green and brown rivers. I didn't know that the USS

Tutuila was towed off of her coffee-ground throne and sent to the shipyards, where she was overhauled, refitted, and loaded with spare parts for SWIFT boats and Patrol Boat River (PRB) boats.

When the final orders came in, ordering me to fly to Saigon to meet the ship in Vung Tau, I began to have my first doubts about what kind of duty it would be. "Oh well," I thought. "I'll fly over to Vietnam, meet the ship in Vung Tau, and sail on her back to San Diego . . . at least I'll be able to see a little more of the world, and may even get to see Hawaii on the way home."

There is an old truism that has been in the Navy for years: "If you don't know, ask the Chief."

Once I had my mobile home, and my little family safely nested in a trailer park near the naval base in San Diego, I took a city road map and headed for the Chief's Club for a couple of beers and a little straight information. I asked an old chief that was sitting at the bar, just where did the *USS Tutuila* tie up when she was in port. "There, right there," the old chief pointed to the map. "She always anchors right there when she's in port."

"No way!" another chief spoke up. "The old Tutuila is an East Coast ship and has *never* called at this port!"

Slowly, as my leave time was passing quickly, I began to piece together the real picture of what was to be in store for me. The *USS Tutuila* was a SWIFT and PRB boat repair ship, permanently stationed at Vung Tau, Vietnam, and her crews were rotated on a yearly basis. I was to be in the first rotating crew to fly to Vietnam and relieve the crew who sailed her to Nam a year ago. While the ship was never in San Diego, the Navy did re-designate her home port from Norfolk to San Diego. If only I had known this before, I would have moved my family to my wife's hometown, where she could be with family while I served my year in Vietnam. Then, as if that crushing news wasn't bad enough, the front transmission seal on my car burned out, and I had neither the time, nor the money to fix it! I was going to leave my wife for a year, with three kids to take care of, and no car!

I arrived at the California Air Force base for the flight to Saigon, my mind racing and my heart in my throat. By then, I was not completely naive as to what was going on in Vietnam. I watched Walter Cronkite on TV and knew about Canada and how much closer it was than some place called Vung Tau. I do not know what drove my body to climb that ladder into the jet, take my seat and buckle the safety belt. I looked around at the other passengers—the young soldiers and Marines—and here was me, an old man, well over thirty years old, leaving a young wife with three babies in a strange city, with no friends or relative within 2000 miles, and no car to get to the grocery store or to a hospital!

We all sat there in the plane, the others laughing and joking. There was some kind of delay. I looked back. The airplane door was still open. I thought, "I can get out. I can catch a bus home. I can sell the trailer, and get my wife and babies into a car in a couple of days and head for Vancouver."

Up to that point, that was the most anguishing and painful experience of my life. I *knew* I shouldn't be there in that seat. The door closed and the engines started. The jet began to move. It wasn't until we were somewhere between 5000 and 10,000 feet that the word "Desertion" flashed into my mind. I realized that I almost deserted! But then, "Wait a minute. Just *who* am I deserting now!" It was too late. If I had had that particular thought just ten minutes ago, I wouldn't have been there.

I flew on to Saigon and to Vung Tau. I was to learn other names, like Phu Quok, Nah Ay, Cat Lo and Firebase Wildcat. There would be other moments just as anguishing and painful, but in different ways, as that day on the airplane.

I survived the Vietnam experience. Survived without a scratch, except for a nasty scar from an infected insect bite. But, the marriage didn't survive. She was young, she was beautiful, and a year is an awfully long time. Too long for a young woman who was deserted.

After my tour in Vietnam, I did get that Air Conditioning and Refrigeration school that I wanted, and remained in the Navy. I served a total of twenty-two years active duty, sixteen years of which were sea duty. In 1975 I retired from the Navy and launched a second career in civilian life. My youngest son got married. He lives in my ex-wife's home town in Georgia. I will drive down from Minnesota and attend the rehearsal at the church. I am picking up the tab for the rehearsal dinner afterward.

My wedding gift to my son and his bride is? What else? A cruise in the clean blue waters of the Caribbean Sea. At the reception after the wedding, my son said that there will be a prescribed seating arrangement and that I'll be seated next to my ex-wife.

When the music finally starts, will I ask my ex-wife for a dance? You'd better believe it.

Nathan B. Werner

South Minneapolis was the "cameo" of Midwest Urban America. Conservative and traditional values held sway in the predominantly middle, upper-class neighborhood, although the social fabric at the time was being torn in several directions. The assassinations of several key leaders in the nation seemed to signal the shaking of cultural institutions and radical fringe groups fermenting civil disorder breathed an air of uncertainty into the late '60s atmosphere. However, Washburn High seemed insulated to major cultural change. An ivory-tower mentality isolated us from the percolating events of that time, and high schoolers' focus was on the environment of school, social activities, sports, cars, clothes etc. Dramatic events didn't touch us. These events happened and we were aware of them, but they had little or no impact on us. Consequently, Vietnam was a fairy tale, a fantasy, something so isolated and far away that it had no real influence on our lives. We saw it and heard about it, but most high schoolers were graduating and going to college, so little feedback came from individuals we knew. Dating, going to dances, and romance were far more necessary and important and had precedence in our lives over a small remote war.

1968 exploded on the scene with a fury and yet it failed to wrench us away from our small scope and tiny concepts of the world. The prevailing attitude about social issues and about Vietnam was detachment. We played the mental gymnastics games with the issues, but our lives were unchanged; scoring with girls was what motivated our lives.

Graduating from high school and going to college was a revelation. Suddenly social issues were only the boiler plate of everyone's agenda. Opinions, activism, demonstrations, political turmoil rocked the campus populace. It was impossible to be uninvolved or unopinionated. A tidal wave of social unrest was roaring on the U of M campus and no detachment was possible. Most students were spectators and intrigued by the events, yet somehow they were uninvolved and part of the whole milieu.

One year of college came and went, then came the raging paradox of military life in the USMC. From a bubbling cauldron of civil unrest to the rigid military mentality of stoicism. They seemed two different cultures rather than both part of the same. My journey into a vortex of warfare and violence had begun, the changing life of a benign high schooler into a combat Marine.

Five months of basic training was unable to prepare me for what I found in Vietnam. Marines had all heard stories, but reality makes the true believer and I quickly was involved with reality. Upon arriving at Da Nang I was issued orders for the 5th Marine Regiment, operating out of a combat base called An Hoa. "You'll be sorry" was the cryptic statement I heard from those who knew. I was choppered out to An Hoa over a beautiful countryside, emerald green mountains bordered by the quilt work of lowland rice paddies, interspersed with small villes. It was a wonderful, breathtaking sight.

When disembarking at An Hoa, combat life was introduced quickly as batteries of artillery unleashed salvo after salvo of rounds. The booming report and the bouncing earth offered no opportunity to even think. Rather, the cacophony overwhelmed you.

Orders were issued for 2nd Battalion. "You'll be sorry" followed these orders also. Further orders were given me for Echo Company. "Hell, they're on the *road*. You will be sorry!" More obscure remarks left me truly puzzled and uneasy. I would join my new unit in a few days.

My first stop was to the chow hall. "Better enjoy it while ya can, ya won't be seein' it for a while."

Inside a large screened hooch was the chow hall. Hot food and warm Kool-Aid was served by disinterested mess Marines. Through the air flew huge insects. Praying mantises ruled the chow hall as they flitted back and forth from screen to screen. As I sat with my meal and took my first mouthful of food a large praying mantis landed on the side of my face. Bewildered and revulsive, I grabbed this tormentor and threw it away. From then on I watched with one eye on my food and another on the buzzing insects.

That first night I was at An Hoa, Charlie rocketed and mortared the compound. A short, intense time of explosions, running, confusion and anxiety. There was no pattern, but general chaos until the attack was over.

The next evening a small outdoor movie screen was used to show a movie. Incredibly, the movie was in the projector upside-down and we had to watch it lying on our backs. Still more bizarre was an attack by the gooks that sent tracer rounds zipping through the makeshift theater and over the heads of the upside-down Marines.

The following day I was shipped out to my unit by a huge convoy which would pass Echo Company. The lead truck in the convoy was destroyed by a mine in the road. The smoking hulk was pulled off the road and off we went. Scattered blasted hulks of old vehicles dotted the surrounding area as our convoy passed on by, heading back toward Da Nang.

At Liberty Bridge I disembarked to the 3rd Platoon of Echo Company. The other two platoons had occupied tiny compounds along Liberty Road; our Company had road security. Ostensibly we had to keep the road open from the bridge to An Hoa, twelve miles of Bad Bush called The Arizona— "Arizona" because it was Indian country, a reference to the days of the Old West.

The Marine Corps platoon is made up of three squads and then a fourth gun squad. Two M-60 gun teams are assigned to each platoon. These squads were primarily the basic unit of brotherhood and interaction. Each squad carried out military functions such as patrols, ambushes, convoy security, etc. Each squad became a family, a small intimate collection of men interdependent on each other. Quarreling, horseplay, personality conflicts, deep concern in all aspects—it became a genuine, functioning family unit. Every man became involved with one another and the humanness of everyone was accepted by each other.

I became a member of Bravo squad, and as its most junior member I was taught and trained by the experienced Marines—cautioned, corrected, convinced and eventually . . . co-equal.

My first patrol was a large platoon-sized "rover" along the edge of The Arizona. The squad seemed to take this as a "skate"—"just toolin'" through the boonies, "no big deal." I was placed in the back of the column in front of our "tail-end Charlie." Smiles flitted across my squad members' faces as they watched my diligent behavior. I was super vigilant; my head was swiveling around like a robot's, looking for gooks. My squad just sauntered along in a column, bored with the heat and drudgery.

Kaboom! An explosion rocked the front of the platoon. We "hit the deck." Something was flying in the air through the cloud of dirt and smoke. Quiet. No shooting. Booby trap! What I saw flying through the air was a body, now detached from two legs and an arm, yet still alive.

"Corpsman up!" Our platoon radio operator was the one hit by a command-detonated booby trap. VC had ambushed us with a booby trap and they had popped it when he passed over it. Incredibly, he called in his own med-evac chopper before he went into shock, his oozing stumps being wrapped by the corpsman.

Reality came roaring in like a freight train. The tough, hard John-Wayne perspective had gone fluttering away. It was replaced by an awesome knowledge about the frailty of life. The actual world of warfare slams you square in the chest and naivete gets quickly swept out of your life. Suddenly death has stepped beside you to be a constant, unwanted companion.

Life in and around The Arizona settled into a numbing pattern of patrols by day and ambushes or LPs during the night. Weeks passed without action or incident until spontaneous, furious firefights would erupt and shatter the calm.

One incident was indeed poignant. My platoon had been moved up

Liberty Road within two miles of the combat base of An Hoa. Nearby was a orphanage operated by Vietnamese Catholic Nuns. The children from the orphanage would often come to our compound and beg for food. They became tiny little brothers and sisters to us, for somehow their innocence had yet been untouched by the warfare around them. They needed and sought our companionship and our resources.

On a very dark evening our position and a nearby ARVN compound were mortared. While explosions rocked us, NVA entered the orphanage among the sleeping children and walked through tossing grenades. The carnage among these helpless children was horrific. A dozen died, scores were wounded, and many of those were traumatic amputees.

Why? Why brutalize children—helpless, innocent children, for fraternizing with the Imperialist Americans?

We came to understand what the NVA already knew—cruelty and barbarity insure power, and power wins no matter how mighty the opponent. Winning counted.

Seething hatred emanated from every Marine toward the cowardly NVA. Each Marine wanted an opportunity to engage Charlie and do him "a job"—"Make them bastards pay." The dualism of sympathy and hatred became an odd mix of emotions. The principles of justified warfare had been violated by the gooks and we needed to see justice done, and we were the judge and jury. Added to the situation was an odd lack of press coverage about this atrocity. The press had let the whole world know about the horrible massacre at My Lai, yet the world would never hear a whisper about An Hoa. A deep cynicism toward the biases of the media made us very wary about a balanced view being reported of Vietnam.

Death, real death, always was near. Many times it came calling unexpectedly at inappropriate times, in uncommon ways and with no warning. The situations where you knew events would be hazardous were truly frightening. Hearing and seeing conflict and then knowing you would be involved in it gave you time for quiet reflection. Uneasiness. Things seem normal, events flow in their normal pattern, yet there is a discernible unsettling. It's palpable. The edges of your existence seem distant and ethereal, floating and anchorless. Fear starts stirring, creating tiny flutterings and anxiety drifts around inside your chest.

A company-size operation through several hostile villes in the Arizona—I'm "tail-end Charlie." Easy. A snap. No sweat. I finally got "some slack." Moving slowly for several hours, finally in the distance, a firefight erupted. Another Marine company had been hit—stiff resistance and radios for help, asking us to be a blocking force while they try and push the gooks against us. Our CO orders us "about face" and back toward the ville. But now I'm "point" for the company. In the distance we can hear the firefight and I get to lead Echo Co. to it.

"Yes, Louise. The gooks are really bustin' caps."

Moving toward the sound of gunfire resurrected those fears which lay below the surface of normalcy.

"Man, please di-di, Charles!"

Closer we came. The firing slackened. Carefully I crossed a "blue." The first Marine utterly unprotected and defenseless. My eyes furtively checked the opposite riverbank, and my skin tingled as I expected shots to ring out at any moment. Cautiously I crossed and then climbed out of the water, alone in foliage. Quietly I proceeded over the bank toward a treeline which was at the back of our objective. Two more Marines fell in behind me. Flat, open field to cross. Suddenly the treeline erupted with shooting. Charlie had three Marines in the open, unprotected. We hit the deck, trying desperately to melt our bodies into the hard-packed earth and become invisible. Bullets were snapping by, so close you're surprised you're not hit.

Our CO was screaming for us to fall back. Miraculously, we crawled backwards, fell over the bank into the blue. "Move it, move it," our CO screamed for us to run and envelope the ville. Sloughing out of the water we begin to lead our platoon in a run to circle to the side of the ville. Running in full combat gear wasn't exhausting if you ran twenty feet, but after 100 meters you thought you'd run a marathon. Our run diminished to a fast shuffle—each Marine gasping for air. We were limp with fatigue. Immediately, in another treeline, a machine gun opened fire at the platoon. Bullets swept the line of Marines. Every Marine dived over a paddy dike as heavy-caliber rounds smacked the protective earthen dike—remarkable nobody was hit. The air filled with whining lead. We stayed in the paddy until the other Marine company swept through the ville. They found empty shell casings and nothing else. Charlie had vanished, leaving us in frustration, with nothing to show for all our efforts.

Several weeks later Echo Company, along with 5th Marines, was pulled out of An Hoa and relocated to the east, to another combat base, LZ Baldy. We also had a different AO, the infamous Happy Valley and the dreaded Que Son Mountains.

In Happy Valley our company had an operation when a typhoon approached from the South China Sea. Choppers were grounded, forbidden to fly, and the line companies were left in the bush to fare for themselves. Our platoon commander ordered us to bury all our gear in our fighting holes, then we were to "buddy up" so two Marines could cling to each other and fight the weather. Rain deluged us. Terrific winds buffeted us as we held on to each other against the raging typhoon. For eighteen hours we were tormented, unable to move, lashed by the storm. Hygiene was impossible. Eating was limited to soggy wet food from C-rations. Sleep was fitful.

After the tropical storm, gaunt, hollowed-eyed, weary, wet-cold Marines stood and stretched, looking for their buddies. Everyone weathered the typhoon yet misery was a common denominator among the platoon. Each Marine was bankrupt of energy. Vitality was lost as we moved about like specters.

The Que Son Mountains loomed in the distance, a sanctuary for the NVA, with triple canopy-jungled mountains, rugged and fierce. The thick vegetation was seemingly impenetrable, rising to enormous heights, choking and smothering tropical heat within. No cool breeze, just hot, humid, stagnant air. Worst of all, death waited there. The NVA were serious about keeping their presence in the rough jungle, and one platoon of Marines could hardly push the battalion of NVA out. Yet we were being sent to find them.

Operating in the Que Sons became exercises in futile exhaustion, climbing up treacherous slopes and slipping, sliding and falling down others. Clinging to rocks, shrubs and roots was the only way in which to move and secure footing.

The monsoon season fell upon us with dark, dank, wet, cloudy weather—an endless season of misery which made our life wearisome. Choppers often could not fly because of the inclement weather, consequently resupply was often delayed, much to our anger and discomfort. Gnawing hunger became a new twist to our existence—six days without food was the longest stretch—until the weather broke, allowing choppers access to us. These days of hunger became routine and single days of late resupply were common. Slowly we became nutritionally depleted, then we were susceptible to various diseases and maladies—dysentery, ringworm, gook sores—became an added dimension to our misery. Dysentery was severe diarrhea which could result in dehydration. Ringworm was a fungus which grew on the skin as a result of poor hygiene. Gook sores were open, ulcerous skin sores which could slowly eat through flesh. Lack of proper restful sleep also added to our generally run-down condition. At night every Marine had three hours of watch either on ambush, LP, or standing in a hole. Legions and hordes of mosquitoes attacked each Marine with malice. Energized as if in a feeding frenzy, mosquitoes would assault without pause. Their passion was to torment humans.

Surviving the jungle became our primary focus, not the NVA. The NVA were the added nuisance indeed, the reason why we were trudging around through that bleak existence; yet living day to day took our collective energy to endure. However, in spite of the despairing conditions, we did stumble into a large NVA base camp. Scores of hooches, bunkers and tunnels were laid out before us, empty and absent of the NVA. We stood in the midst in a kind of awe and wonder that we indeed had found where the elusive Charlie actually lived. Yet there was also an eerie feeling of being somewhere where the imminent return of the owner was present, as if invading a lion's lair. A strange silence, a creeping dread permeated the air. Tension was thick as Marines all moved with extra caution. Charlie was close, perhaps even watching. Evidence abounded that the NVA were just there and left quickly.

It soon became evident that we had a real military find. We found explosives—mortars, bangalore torpedoes, weapons like 30-caliber machine guns, discarded rifles, documents, utensils, etc., all kinds of items which Charlie couldn't take with him. Consequently each cave, each tunnel, each hooch had to be searched carefully for any valuable military material. This search would take one full week, not only for looking, but also disarming an incredible number of booby traps. Booby traps of mortar rounds, bangalore torpedoes, and toe poppers. Toe poppers were a C-rat can buried underground on a blasting cap. Stepping on the ground detonated it. It had enough explosive power to blow off a foot and shatter the bones in a leg up to the hip—very insidious. However, the caves and tunnels presented daunting problems, for these were the areas of black terror and dark dread, usually unseen. Searching caves and tunnels was done with as little light as possible because light could be the element by which gooks detected you. Light made you vulnerable. Many caves and tunnels were searched as much by touch as by sight.

Checking caves and tunnels was a strangely exciting experience because it was frightening, but also it provided a time of intense awareness. It was a time of being on the edge and encountering danger. The essence of the experience was one of total awareness—each sense was acutely tuned and tingling with energy—seeking to the limits of its capability. These tunnels became a universe solely isolated—time became a nonentity and wariness with alert caution became the mode of operation. Touch, smell and hearing become a "tunnel rat's" eyes.

Searching the base camps also gave us a new perspective on Charlie—living in an uncompromising jungle, in dug-out holes, existing underground without any relative comforts, and yet still they were dedicated and fierce fighters. Morale must have been high because the commitment was sure obvious.

Operating in the mountain jungles lasted for several months. Occasional firefights, ambushes and booby traps punctuated the drudgery of our existence, but no large-scaled, pitched battles resulted. The NVA had seemed to melt away.

The Fifth Marine Regiment was pulled out of Vietnam in 1971. I was reassigned to the First Marine Regiment, where I became a part of S-2

Scout Unit. This unit became a fill-in for all different needs and operations as twelve Marines were used as Recon, Special Operations, Base security, Quick Reaction Force, whatever needs arose. Initially we were assigned to an old French fort by the Marble Mountain area south of Da Nang. Here we primarily provided security for the small village of Noui Ken San. The area was relatively pacified and there was little or no action. We accidentally killed two ARVN soldiers who tried to pass through a roadblock after dark. They were drunk and didn't stop for inspection.

Next I was sent alone to an abandoned combat base at Hill 3 outside of the village of Dai Loc. Two Marines and four Army personnel manned this huge post, which was the home of a battalion or more of troops. We were there to coordinate calls for artillery support from ARVN units to American artillery units. It was a bizarre and audacious assignment because the gooks could move in with impunity if they wanted or needed to and take the whole base. We were the token sacrificial lambs.

Two weeks after I left Hill 37, it was attacked and ARVNs had over 200 confirmed kills in and around the compound.

After I was sent back to my S-2 unit, we were sent to a refugee ville, a ville populated by peasants pulled from free fire zones and relocated there. A small compound of PFs (Popular Forces) were stationed there and we were on an operation to bolster defenses. Intelligence reports stated that the compound and ville would be hit by VC. Amazingly, Intelligence was correct and we were hit by the gooks—1 a.m. in the morning until dawn a constant barrage of rocket and ground attack. Sappers tried to penetrate the wire, but somehow died trying. Every Marine, all twelve of us, had run out of ammo. We were all down to our last magazine. We had no more frags, no more ordnance. The PFs with us all had most of their full complement of ammo left. They had all merely hid in their bunkers, occasionally sticking their M-16s over the sandbags to unleash a wild volley of shooting.

We'd saved the compound and the ville, but only for that night. We pitied the poor villagers because we knew Mr. Charles would be back when we were gone. The PFs wouldn't be any kind of deterrent; their fate was sealed with their ineptitude and timidity.

My tour wound down by being attached to S-5 civilian affairs. It was a job of watching the civilian work force on base during the day— supervise the burning of human waste, and supervise the collection of rubbish and refuse by the civilians. It was a time of an odd perspective since I saw the Vietnamese not as enemies, but as victims. Victims of the war, indeed, but more so victims of their poverty and the U.S. wealthy. Our garbage was their livelihood.

My tour ended as if on a downward sloping curve. Less and less combat, less and less bush time, but more and more perspective of the larger picture of Vietnam and the destroyed lives of the civilian population. I was sorry that I couldn't alleviate their suffering, yet I knew that titanic forces created the environment in which they now had to live, and only the slow powerful wheels of politics and economics could restore any semblance of order for them. Little did I know that the Vietnamese would yet suffer immeasurably from the military forces still locked in the war. The political solutions after the conflict would merely embroil them in a deeper morass and leave them in utter despair.

Release from the Marine Corps was in itself an exhilarating experience. It was an escape from a heavy, foreboding, structured life. Service life was a limiting life, further limited and restricted because of a major conflict in Vietnam. The freedom of civilian life is not a paradise, rather a system of making wise and appropriate choices. The military makes choices for you. However, the emotional effect of being a part of the Vietnam experience was astounding. Being loose from the practical life of the military didn't insure an emotional health. Men from the service were very often dysfunctional human beings.

When I arrived home from my service career, I was enrolled at the University of Minnesota. I was chagrin at campus life and the relative absence of political thought at the university level. The absolute naivete of the campus population about Vietnam and the nuances of the conflict there angered me. I was furious at their ivory-tower mentality that failed to see the realities of geo-politics but also the realities of war and warfare in general.

Admittedly the military had a great deal of blame concerning ineptitude, waste, and mismanagement, but they were locked into a war which was inevitable. However, the federal government, both the legislative and executive branches, insisted on fighting a conflict in an absurd and illogical way. In spite of the glaring inefficiencies of the military and the federal government, the principles of justified warfare did exist, yet liberal campus politics lost sight of this and insisted on an alternative agenda—an agenda not rooted in practicalities. This ignorance infuriated me and left me with a bitter outlook toward political activism. Coupled with this was the calloused way in which veterans were ignored, as if we had been misguided children who had gotten involved in an inappropriate adventure. This anger I felt worked it's way out in a behavior which I can only term as bitter. Bitter toward ignorance and bitter about behavior towards vets.

This anger manifested itself in a kind of "shutting-down" emotionally. A denial kind of syndrome which would then work itself out in behaviors and poor attitudes. I became confrontational and hard, insensitive and calloused, unable to be a truly tender, caring individual.

Although through the years this anger became less of an issue, yet ignorance about events in Vietnam still irritates me because often this naivete doesn't take into account the horrendous loss of civilian life— because we gave up and left. Millions of people died because we weren't committed and gave up. Cambodians, Laotians, and Vietnamese were murdered because of our need to quit and leave them to fend for themselves against a determined aggressor.

   The effect of the Vietnam episode in our nation's history is yet to be fully written, but I think it becomes a landmark in a decline of our nation's greatness. Principles of absolutes became compromised and the essence of the moral fiber of our culture became adulterated. Consequently as a culture we are in decline. Vietnam became the high water mark of our U.S. and from there we have slipped and then slid economically, politically, morally. Whatever yardstick of measurement you wish to use, we have sadly become a shadow of what this nation was and stood for.

Howard E. Campbell Jr.

I grew up in rural Pennsylvania and was raised for a short time by my aunt and uncle. They were two of the best parents that a growing boy could have. To me, they will always be Mom and Dad. Both Hazel and Harvey died when I was still in grade school. I never met my mother while growing up. I know her only by a picture. When I was just two months old my mother was institutionalized, leaving myself, my dad, and an older brother and sister on our own. Dad felt that because of my age he could not work and raise a two-month-old baby, thus bringing about the situation of me being raised by my aunt and uncle. Upon their deaths, the rest of my growing-up years were nurtured by older cousins who lived in the same house. We grew up as brother and sister and that relationship remains the same to this day. Times were tough back then and trying to make ends meet was not easy. I started working on nearby produce farms until I was old enough to get a real job during my junior and senior years of high school. Finally, I came of age and got a job at the local cigar plant, walking from school to work and putting in an eight-hour shift. There was no time for after-school activities. For as much as I dreamed about playing basketball, it was a dream that never came true.

My high school days were spent at Berwick Area Senior High, nestled in the rolling green hills and mountains of northeastern Pennsylvania. The small borough of Berwick is situated along the Susquehanna River.

I couldn't wait to get high school "out of the way" so I could get on with the rest of my life. As an average student, my grades were not too bad, but on the other hand, they were not great either. In 1968 I attended my high school graduation.

I had two chances to go on to some type of schooling after high school. But as I look back, they were not chances at all, nothing more than wishful thinking and my dreams once again came crashing down. But, after all, I had a full-time job. By this time I had left the cigar plant and started working for a supermarket.

It was at that period in history that higher education versus the military and the draft board were working on a number system. The lower the number, the higher your risk of being drafted. If you were attending college, your number could have been 1 or 2 and still have gotten a deferment from the draft. If I had been able to fulfill my dream, I would have been exempt from military service. As it was, I did not go on to college and my draft notice arrived in the mail. I tried enlisting in the Navy, but was rejected because of an anemia problem. Several weeks into basic training, I discovered that with the number system I would have been drafted anyway.

One year after graduation, when it seemed as though the whole world was preparing to go back to school or on to higher education, I was preparing for pre-induction into the Army. I have a cousin who lives close by and he received his notice at the same time—it just worked out that way. He failed because of some problems with the vertebrae in his back. Wayne was the type of person who really felt cheated. For him it was a personal defeat. He wanted to do his part in the military. Another friend who lived close by and was my age opted to join the Marines. Bob just happened to be one very lucky Marine that was never sent to Vietnam. At the time of my physical and several years before that, I was receiving Vitamin E shots for anemia. However, I passed my physical. The rest is history. After boot camp and AIT (Advanced Infantry Training) and one week's leave in between, I was shipped off to Vietnam.

I can remember leaving Pennsylvania from Wilkes-Barre International Airport. I arrived in California on March 24, 1970. During my week-long stay that seemed to last a lifetime, we had three formations a day. As a name was called, that individual would line up in front of the sign indicating their next duty station. My heart was lightened as the line labeled "Vietnam" was seemingly being ignored. I thought for sure my prayers had been answered and I would escape Vietnam. By week's end there were only a handful of GIs standing in line for Vietnam. I happened to be one of them. I also remember seeing a sign that read "Free Steak Dinner to All Returning Vietnam Vets."

After boarding the plane in California at Travis Air Force Base, we sat and waited nervously during the pilot's preflight check. Finally taxiing down the runway and trying to look back out the windows, back to the safe and secure coastline of California, it seemed as though my mind was spinning in a whirlwind and I was desperately trying to comprehend the fact that I was on a flight that was going to take me and desert me in a place called Vietnam.

Looking back at the coastline was like detaching oneself from everything that said I was safe. At that point in time it seemed as though any one of life's obstacles that happened to come my way became, all of a sudden, meaningless. I was leaving myself on the California coast that day because no matter how I came back home, or if I came back home at all, was a complete unknown. The person that was left behind on that coast would in no way, shape, or form be the same person that re-entered The World, when and if that time ever came. "The World" is what I and every GI in Vietnam would eventually and affectionately call the U.S.A.

We had three layovers during the flight. The first was Hawaii, that being a three-hour stop. I never realized that three hours could last so long or fly by so fast all at the same time. Finally leaving Hawaii, we were headed to our next destination, Wake. It was a small, and what seemed at the time, desolate island in the South Pacific. With just a short stop to refuel, we were allowed to get off the plane and stretch. Our bodies were stiff and cramped from all the hours we had spent in flight thus far. Our next stop was Guam—another short stay.

Boarding the plane once more for our final destination, we settled in and accepted our fate—that life had so coldly handed to us. By this time everyone was starting to feel that they hadn't seen water to wash with, or even take a shower with, to get rid of the hot, sticky, sweaty feeling that was starting to set in from all the hours in flight. Little did we know that it was a feeling that would never go away. The rest of the flight to our final destination was pretty much routine. I watched the clouds when it was light enough and the sunrise or sunset when it was not, and in between desperately trying to sleep, but couldn't. But most of all, wishing we could look back and still see the California coastline. That was in the past and if we saw it again depended only on the future.

A special occasion happened on my flight. I should have been celebrating with family and friends. If I had a choice, I would have not, without a doubt, chosen this type or party. It was my twenty-first birthday. I didn't even remember or think about the date with all else that was happening. At the last minute I realized it was my birthday, as the sun came up on the horizon. March 29, 1970. My only thought, my only celebration was, "Will I see twenty-two?" (Happy Birthday.)

Unfortunately, that would not be the end of my twenty-first birthday because as we crossed the International Date Line a day was lost. As we were in flight on our last stretch to the Republic of Vietnam it was still March 29, 1970. It was my birthday all over again. But at this point it did not matter. No one knew, no one cared, so what's the big deal anyway?

Our final approach to Bien Hoa Air Force Base in South Vietnam was unforgettable. The pilot announced that he would be cutting the engines to lessen the signal of our arrival. I watched as the runway came closer and closer into sight and off in the distance, beyond the airport, I watched white puffs of smoke rise from the ground, realizing without a doubt that the enemy had been engaged. Finally it seemed as though we had forgotten how to breathe, and the tires of the plane squealed and grabbed hold of the runway, bringing us to a halt.

Fortunately, we had avoided any sniper fire from the ground. At last the door opened and we began to disembark. We didn't waste any time getting off the plane, for two reasons. One, to get off the airstrip as soon as possible. Two, to get the plane back in flight after refueling and reloading. Leaving a plane is not a difficult task but that day it was one of the hardest things, mentally and physically, that I had ever done.

Stepping down off that United Airlines plane that day was my last physical connection with The World. Also, as we departed a line of GIs waited to take our places to go home. I wanted to be able to read their minds, but I only heard their shouts of "you'll be sorry" echoing in my ears. That was my first feeling of defeat. As I look back to that time and that dramatic flight, I don't remember ever having the feeling of being afraid or was it, in fact, that I was too afraid to realize it?

We spent hours, long hot hours that seemed to suck the strength and life right out of your body, processing and getting greenbacks exchanged for MPC. Sitting around waiting to go from one processing station to the next, my mind already started to wander back to how it all began.

The following are excerpts from my first letter home that I wrote during my stay at the 90th Replacement Station at Long Binh, Vietnam. They read as follows: "Wayne just doesn't know how lucky he is at this very moment. If he had to go through what I've been through so far he would just die. He used to always tell me that I had it made. Well, I know for at least this one time in my life he is the one that truly has it made... I wish you could see the villages over here. I could live in our barn back home and it would be a palace compared to this place... You know, after being over here for a short period of time (and maybe it's dumb, but) it kind of makes you feel proud to be here, knowing that when we get back home people are going to look up to you and say good things about the sacrifices that the guys are making and dying for."

Oh, what a cherry boy I was, and I didn't even know it. We spent enough time during our processing to meet a stranger and actually become friends. Many I have forgotten, with the exception of Joe McMahon from Berwick, Pennsylvania. His uncle owned and operated Dalo's Pizzeria, which is still in business today, and growing stronger. We made plans that day to take our R&R together and look each other up during our tour of duty. Unfortunately, it never came to be. After that day and our lengthy conversation, we never saw each other again. On April 2, 1970 I was assigned to the 48th Transportation Group in Long Binh.

I remember wishing my life away each and every day, and seemingly waiting forever for a letter from home. I had landed in-country March 29, 1970 and by April 12 I was already having nightmares. One was of a plane crash that I was in. The memory is vivid to this day. The plane crashed to the ground and I tried to crawl away before the plane exploded. There were many others that I could never write home about—always waking up and finding that in all reality I was in Vietnam. That same day there was a twenty-two-year-old GI that died from an overdose of drugs. Maybe that is what triggered the nightmares that particular night. I don't know.

By the end of May 1970, I realized that if I allowed it, there could be someone special in my life in Vietnam. First you must understand that after only two months in Vietnam I was very lonely and very homesick. We were already becoming friends and for all I know it may never have gone beyond that point. We didn't see a lot of each other, mainly because of the surrounding circumstances. But when she was there she always made me smile. "My" (that was her name) was very friendly and polite, and concerned about my well-being. Looking back at it now, I probably was not the only one feeling this way. Nonetheless, promises started being made. Promises that would never be fulfilled. She even got me to try nuoc-mam, which is a strong-smelling fish extract used by Southeast Asians to add flavor to rice. My said to me on several occasions that she wanted me to go home. I thought she wanted to get rid of me but when I asked why, she said because she liked me and didn't want anything to happen to me. That's when the promises of taking her home with me started. But come my DEROS date, I left, not looking back or even considering her feelings. I will never know what happened to her. Guilt set in to the highest degree.

June 2, 1970, I wrote a letter home. This is one paragraph taken from that letter. It puts my feelings in perspective as to what Vietnam meant to me, at least for that particular moment. It reads as follows: "If there is anything I wanted so bad, it is to make it over here. I've never done anything important in my life before. Maybe this will make up for it— I hope. But, I just can't give up now. I've got to make it. I am finally doing something I never dreamed possible."

October 23, 1970, I got a letter telling me my dad was in the hospital. There was a chance at the time that he would not make it. At least that's what I was told. I guess I was concerned. You must understand—there was never any love lost between us. The truth is that his other women came first before his own kids. He wanted us around only when we could be of use to him. He never went out of his way to make us feel wanted. The fourteen months I spent in Vietnam, he managed to write only one letter.

Vietnam is a place that has many descriptions of what it is in each individual's eyes—what it is and what it is not. But, in general, it was a place I went to with pride and fear. Proud to be a part of the military and what it stands for, proud to be called upon to do what the Army had trained me to do, and to have reached a readiness to prove myself to the Army and to America, I thought.

War has its many friends, but more important, war has its enemies. The easiest of the two would seem to be the enemy to be detected. But that was not the case. Soon it would be found that there were too many friendly enemies. The only friend to count on or rely upon when it was truly called for was the soldier, the GI, the guy next to you. One hoped to survive the next twelve months or whatever more time was spent in Vietnam. More important than anything, war was never fair. It is without a doubt the most unfair situation that life has to offer.

My stay with the 48th Transportation Group was a short one. During that short period the 48th Transportation Group was dismantled and sent home, leaving us there, feeling like a deserted child. We then became the 4th TG, but that was once again a repeat performance of the 48th Transportation Group. Starting to feel unwanted in a hot, dry and uncaring country, I finally got my feet planted in a more permanent situation—the 506th Transportation Detachment in Long Binh, Vietnam. Even though that was to be my base to report to, little time was spent in the safety of its environment. I was very fortunate to become a part of the group of guys that were assigned to the 506th. In a very short period of time we became friends. We worked together, slept together, played together and yes, at times we even cried together. Friends were easy to come by, but oh, so hard, and sometimes impossible to give up.

Being a part of the 506th Transportation Detachment was my final assignment and it would be my home for the remainder of my time in Vietnam. The 506th had many functions. The one that me and my friends were involved in was convoys. Their destinations, their departures and, if need be, traveling with the convoy to collect the information of convoy trailers, the information that could only be gathered by scouting the country and jungles of Vietnam, to determine the location, condition and retrievability of that trailer for future convoys. Convoys were the main pipeline to fire support bases.

I spent every day that I was in Vietnam on the road going to and coming from somewhere. I could never begin to calculate the miles traveled or the time spent in a jeep or convoy. Some destinations were at such great distances that it was impossible to return the same day. The reason for the layover was to avoid nighttime travel, hopefully avoid the enemy, and avoid casualties. Not only was my main purpose on a convoy to gather the information that the 506th needed, but it would also serve as an extra person, and one more weapon if it were needed.

There were convoys every day. So every day I, along with Max G., had to be at the convoy staging area before the sun was on the horizon. I waited for the Bob Cat trailers and gathered information to make sure everyone was present and accounted for. That in itself took several hours and we couldn't leave to start our day on the road until all necessary information was gathered.

Beyond the security gates of Long Binh there was another world waiting, a world of unfamiliar smells, noise, and a culture that was hard to fit into. Danger could be anywhere or it could be nowhere—not knowing where or when was harder than coming face to face with any of the dangers Vietnam had to offer. War was in all phases and in all situations unfair. It always left you with that nagging unforgettable question of "Why?" There was one of the many convoys that had returned home, home being back at the compound in Long Binh. The convoy didn't return from its trip whole and attached as it had left. I didn't know the condition of the entire convoy. What I did know was on that particular day there was a Lt. Dale Johns that had accompanied that convoy. The entire convoy got into some heavy fighting or land mines, I'm not sure, and had taken some heavy damages. But most importantly, the LT came back with life-threatening injuries. He was married and had two small children, and a wife waiting for him back home. I never did find out the end result, which was not unusual in most situations over there. What I did know for sure was that if he made it home alive it would have been a life-altering return. On that convoy he lost both arms, one leg, and for the rest of his life he would never be able to father children again. Why is it that someone who has so many positive things going for him, in the end, loses so much?

There was another convoy that left the staging area one day that I was supposed to be on. Instead, Maynard, a buddy of mine, took my place. Once again they headed up north and were gone for several days. The rest is history. The convoy was hit by VC. The damage was not as severe as it was to the previous convoy, but the injuries were more personal. My friend had been injured with shrapnel to the head. He was not seriously injured but mentally, it affected him greatly. As time passed, the other guys and myself could not trust his uncontrollable anger and violence. The events of that day caused a change in him that even to this day is still unanswered. I was spared the pain and suffering because my friend had taken my place. My only and ever-present question is, why? Why was it him and not me, and would I be next?

Convoys were a part of my life in Vietnam. But not the only part. As I stated, I spent many long hours in a jeep traveling everywhere. One trip that I remember was with Jim H. and myself to a fire support base called Song Be, home of the 199th Inf. Bde. It was situated deep in the heart of the jungle and war, and was not but an eye's view from the Cambodian border. Song Be was deep, thick, endless jungle—flat with nothing but a mountain jutting out of nowhere. There were two ways to get to Song Be, at least two relatively safe ways. One was by convoy, if for no other reason than there was safety in numbers. The other was by helicopter. The one thing I remember is that everything was covered with a thick red dust, which was the case throughout most of Vietnam. The look on the men's faces was one of being tired and just glad they were having a chance to rest. Song Be was an endless scene of bunkers, barbed wire and artillery. The sun was extremely hot that day and a white haze surrounded everything.

Di An was another one of my destinations. It was the home of the 11th Armored Cavalry Regiment. Approaching Di An gave you the impression that no one was home. It was flat and dry, barren and dusty. I got out of the jeep, asking myself, "Why am I here?" The answer to that question was always the same, the mission as always was convoys, the trailers and their locations. Looking off to the right in our search (we traveled in two's if possible) for abandoned Bob Cats (trailers), something caught our eye. It was tiny American flags waving in the hot humid air. The flags, each and every one, singly attached to a tank. The sight of these flags at any other time would not have meant as much, but at that particular moment the sight was breathtaking.

Di An and Bear Cat had two things in common. During the day it looked deserted and lonely, but at night it could become an unbelievable place of fireworks (not the Fourth of July kind). At this point in time I reached my twenty-second birthday. Bear Cat was home of the 3rd Bde., 9th Inf. Div. in Vietnam. I remember turning off the main highway onto a dusty dirt path. As we approached a junction of dirt roads, there, standing alongside his jeep, was a sergeant dressed not in the normal jungle fatigues, but in his khaki shirt and pants. We were concerned, yes, not knowing if the sergeant's jeep had mechanical trouble or if he was being used as a decoy by the VC to ambush our jeep. In any case, Easterday and I stopped as he indicated that we should. The following events are still strange to me and thinking back to that day gives me a chill in my spine. We were asked by the sergeant if it was necessary for us to travel any farther. We indicated that it was and told him why we were out on that particular road. His warning to us at that point was, "If you must travel on, be sure you are back out and off this road before nightfall." The reason being, when dusk fell and night covered the road, it became a free fire zone. During the day, travel was risky, but at night it could be deadly. The VC would cover that particular road with land mines or booby traps, and getting caught would be sure death. We thanked the sergeant and traveled on. Dusk was setting in as we traveled back on that very same road.

Approaching that same junction of dirt roads where the sergeant had given us his warning of danger, the road was abandoned. It was as if he had disappeared. Nothing was said, but thoughts and imaginations were running rampant.

By this time, the end of my fourteen months was approaching, ever so close. My time to leave Vietnam was quickly closing in, just as it was for the GIs waiting at the plane at Bien Hoa Air Force Base a lifetime ago. I had done what the Army asked of me. I spent fourteen long months of my life in what was another world away, Vietnam, a world that was torn apart and blown apart by many years of war. The Army was proud of me, indicating it in words, with medals and citations, proving I had accomplished that which I set out to do. I had proven myself to the Army.

Then I came home to an America that could have cared less, and was very unconcerned. Because ... all I had gone through did not count in the eyes of the people back home. I believe to this very day, that because I was not wounded physically, that no one cared enough to ask about that part of my life that I gave away. The fourteen months I spent in a war zone, another world away, were wasted. It is true that I was lucky. I did not shed any blood and guts in that war, but what I did took blood and guts to do. I was home, my tour of duty had ended. So what? By the end of May 1971, I was home with my family. The friends I left behind can never be replaced by anyone. I lost all contact with them and still do not know if they made it home. I took a trip several years ago to see the Vietnam Memorial and it did not have their names on it. My transition back into civilian life was almost flawless. The difficulties never surfaced until many years later.

I took on the same job at the supermarket I had left one year and eight months earlier, falling into the same old routine of going to work, doing my job and coming home at the end of the day. All the experiences I left behind in Vietnam just a few weeks before seemed forgotten. Very few people asked me about it and by this time I was feeling as though the subject was taboo. So, instead of any kind of response to any questions, I just kept burying it deeper and deeper inside until I myself no longer believed it ever happened.

Several months after returning to work, and with some friendly persuasion from fellow co-workers, I met and asked Linda out. She was another employee working part-time at the market. Our first date was September 1971 and she became my bride in August of 1972. I was so wrapped up in living and loving that remembering the past no longer belonged in my life. Looking back now to that time, those following years were power-packed. In September of 1973, my first daughter was born. The thrill of having Lisa, with blonde hair and blue eyes, was more than I could comprehend. It was just nineteen months later, in April of 1975, that Wendy, my second daughter, was born and became part of our family. My life by this time was definitely in full swing, and having a beautiful wife and two very lovely daughters was more than any man could hope for. The years passed by and raising our girls had become routine and a very happy way of life. Those two little girls are now both very beautiful teenagers. From their birth to this day they never allowed us to have a dull moment in our lives.

Two years ago, approximately seventeen years had passed since I left Vietnam. My youngest daughter Wendy was working on a report for school. Oddly enough, she chose to write about Vietnam. I, being the helpful father that I was, volunteered to help her. One week later her report was complete and I was an emotional basket case. I had at that point remembered what had been forgotten for seventeen years. From that point on, things went downhill emotionally, succeeding in everything that I could think of to punish myself for all the guilt that I was feeling—guilt for coming home and not knowing where my buddies were or how they were. I vowed never to let that strong of a bonding friendship happen again—guilt for having no physical wounds to prove that I was in a war zone, guilt for leaving a girl by the name of "My" behind and not fulfilling my promises to her, guilt for not having gone through the hell that tens of thousands of other GIs had gone through, because relatively speaking, I had it easy. Several months had passed and I was literally drowning in memories of guilt, sinking and not even wanting to pull myself back out. After all those months and all the torture I put myself through, I decided I had to tell my wife what I had kept inside for all these years.

Hours passed, trying to talk between all the tears that I was releasing, and they left me with a head that I thought for sure was going to explode. The conversation we had that night helped, but not to the extent that I thought it would. I was still being overwhelmed by memories I couldn't forget and, most importantly, didn't want to forget. It was at that point that instead of trying to forget those memories, I started to put them down on paper in poetry form, poetry about Vietnam. The poetry finally made me realize that all these things that were buried so deep inside were memories that I had to live with and cope with. Don't get me wrong. There are things about Vietnam that still hurt and occasionally the nightmares occur. But now, at last, Vietnam is not so hard to cope with.

I am currently working for Bloomsburg Carpet, Inc. in Bloomsburg, Pennsylvania. I am a loom operator, and am making carpet for several major airports in the United States. Working there brought me in contact with Tim Derr, an exMarine and Vietnam vet. We have become working companions and friends. The conversation of Vietnam comes up occasionally, but nothing real heavy.

To date I have written approximately thirty poems, not only of my experiences, but of experiences of other vets and the opinions of other people about Vietnam. I heard someone say once and I quote, "Vietnam was here before you came, it will be here when you leave; take from it what you want and leave the rest behind." They are pleasant words to hear. Too bad it is not that easy.

Arnie W. Sundberg

My high school days were short. I lasted two years. For me, school was a prison. I hated school. I left after two years and joined the Marines. On 10 June 1958, I joined the Corps. I served four years as a PFC. On 30 June '66, I rejoined the Marines. I went through training at Camp Pendleton, California. In November '66, I was sent to Vietnam on my request. I joined FCO, 2nd Bn., 7th Mar., 1st Mar. Div., FMF. I held different jobs, first as an ammo man, machine guns, then as admin-man (radio operator); next to gunner on the M-60, team leader, squad leader, all in Weapons Platoon.

My first job was as tower guard for Chu Lai airstrip. We ran patrols and stood tower watch. My first contact with the enemy came on our first company patrol. The company was walking along some paddy dikes. All of a sudden guys were jumping into the paddies. I heard buzzing and thought we were being attacked by bees. No way was I going to jump into the muddy paddies for some bees. About then, my captain swung his rifle at my legs, knocking me into the paddies. He undoubtedly saved my life—we were being ambushed. Just another FNG.

My first big operation was Desoto. We were up against the NVA this time. My company was almost wiped out in an ambush. We were moving across the paddies in a valley toward a ville. There were two hills, one on each side, that were loaded with VC, and NVA. They caught our company in the open. The enemy were mowing us down with automatic weapons, some rifle fire too. The command group was in the ville. First Platoon was up forward. Second Platoon and 3rd Platoon were in the rear. I was with the first platoon. We for the most part got back into the ville. Second Platoon and 3rd Platoon were trapped in the open between the two hills. They took the most casualties. We fought until dark, with some air support. We were some pretty scared troops, lying in a big circle that night. We had lost a lot of guys to KIA and WIA.

Other operations were Deckhouse VI, Pueblo, Arizona I and II. Too many things happened on those operations to give a full report. On 2 September '67, I was wounded by a 82mm mortar round. I felt we were to be mortared, so I went around and warned the company. I set my guns up with plenty of ammo. I was going to be with my 50-cal machine gun in our bunker. I never made it. After warning the company, I went to my rack and lay thinking of home. All of a sudden I heard incoming AK fire. I rolled over to grab my helmet and flak-jacket when BOOM! the first mortar round got me. I was med-evaced out to 1st Med. Bn. in

Da Nang. From there to Japan and then to The World. After about sixteen months I was okay and sent to Hawaii with E Co., 2nd Bn. 26th Mar. I requested duty in Vietnam again and on 28 October '69 I was in the Nam. I was assigned to the Combined Action Program. After school in Da Nang, I went to the second CAG, and from there to my CAP, 2-9-2. Being as I was now a sergeant, I was the CAP Leader. I had around nine Marines, one Navy corpsman, and twenty to thirty PFs. Wounded again on 4 April '70, I spent a week in in-country hospitalization. On June 15, 1970 I was sent to The World and a discharge.

Thought I was the good guy until I was walking down the street. The civilians soon set me straight.

I again joined the Marines in '72, but no more fighting. I was discharged in 1976.

Vietnam was the big happening when I joined in '66. I was going to fight for my country, mom's apple pie, and free the Vietnamese people from the Communists. "Bullcrap." I fought for survival.

To me Vietnam was a very deadly game. The politicians and our generals could not agree on anything. Public opinion saw to that. The games we played. You could shoot the Vietnamese on one side of the road, but not on the other side. We would take a hill at a costly price, then give it up, and be back in a few weeks or months to take the same damn hill again. The body count was a big bunch of crap. Everyone lied about the body count of enemy dead. Reports of our own KIAs were not told to the people correctly by the upper command. This was so the people back home never knew the real truth. The Vietnam War was very unpopular back home. The upper command, and LBJ especially, did not want the news of too many American KIAs to leak out. How would we continue the war, and get more troops, if the people knew the truth? News reporters were another problem. Some were good, others wanted the big story: killing of civilians by U.S. troops, the whorehouses, dope used by U.S. troops, fraggings of U.S. personnel by other U.S. personnel, and other stuff which made news in quiet times. They made the United States and the world believe we were a bunch of animals.

I served as a CAP leader for eight months. This was my most rewarding tour while a Marine. I learned to like some of the Vietnamese people. We lived in the villes with the people. We were involved in civic action, gathered intelligence, got them clothes and other supplies, built schools and wells. My CAP was on ambush every night. We ran patrols during the day. I truly believe that this was the way to win the people over to our side.

As for my life since the Nam, I have moved from job to job. Sometimes I was fired and other times I just quit. No job at this writing. I have been unemployed since December of '87. At this time I am filing a claim for PTSD with the VA. I never thought that I was blighted by my time in the Nam. That was before. Now I know I suffer every day with thoughts of the war. Hopefully, I one day can learn to live with my thoughts of Vietnam. I drank heavy for years, but finally gave it up over five and one half years ago. I still use pot now and again to put myself in a less hostile mood.

I try to help other Nam vets with their problems, and by doing so I also help myself.

The reasons we failed in Vietnam are many. I sometimes wonder if we were supposed to win.

1. *Body Count.* These were the count of enemy dead. Almost always over-estimated by our officers. Due to the body count, I know many non-combatants died. The pressure that platoon and company commanders were under to produce enemy KIAs, led to over-estimating the enemy KIAs. This over-estimating went all the way up command. Instead of a body count, there should have been a weapons count. No weapon—no enemy KIA.

2. *Rotation/End of Tour.* The twelve-month rotation (thirteen months for Marines) was bad in that by the time an infantryman was proficient, his ETD was up. Plus, when an infantryman was short, he was less effective. The rotation of officers was bad also. By the time an officer was a good leader in combat, his time in the field was up.

3. *Tunnel Systems.* The enemy had many tunnels. They could pop out of a tunnel, fire, and pop back into the tunnels for safety. There were many large tunnel complexes. These had hospitals, ammo storage, food storage, sleeping quarters, cooking quarters, and more. Regular underground cities. The enemy could move undetected for miles, all underground.

4. *Search and Destroy.* These operations were a farce. They were developed by General Westmoreland and his J-3, Brig. General DuPuy, to search out the enemy and destroy him. The NVA/VC knew we were coming. Many artillery rounds/bombs were dropped into the area of operations. We moved in by helicopters. Then a battalion/company would run around all over the place looking for the enemy. Very noisy. You could not surprise the enemy using these tactics.

5. *South Vietnamese Forces.* Most were very unreliable. You could not trust them to stay and fight.

These are a few of the reasons we failed in Vietnam.

Vincent Matthews

The first trauma that I was exposed to was the death of my father when I was nine years old. Then, during my first year of high school, President Kennedy was shot and killed. I grew up in New York City in a tough Irish neighborhood. Going to a Catholic high school from September 1966 to June 1968 was a very rewarding part of my life. By going to high school, I was shown values and discipline by the Irish Christian Brothers who taught there. Rice High School was a Catholic school located in Harlem, which was mostly a black population. Throughout high school, there was little said about the war in Southeast Asia. We started to be more aware of the war in the neighborhood when a couple of the kids came home dead.

I enlisted in the Marines when I turned eighteen. Upon graduation in June 1966, I entered Marine boot camp at Parris Island. Now it was time for me to go and serve my country with the fightin' force of the USMC. I could not imagine what I had gotten myself into. I had never been exposed to such rigid training and physical training. But looking back on it now, I thank God that I was able to withstand all the discipline because it probably saved my life in the jungles of Vietnam. After the training in the States, we boarded the ship in Toro to depart for Nam on the *USS Entinge*, a troop carrier, crossing the Pacific Ocean on ship with two thousand Marines, all of which were as sick as me for twenty-five days. We arrived in Okinawa and I was assigned duty with Bravo Co., First Battalion, Fourth Marines of the Third Marine Division. Destination—DMZ. My first exposure to Nam was an assault off the *USS Iwo Jima* (LPH2), a helicopter assault ship. The operation was Deckhouse VI; there were many more operations after that. A total of fifteen. I was very proud to have served with 1/4 in Nam; because of all the fighting with the NVA we went through, we always came out ahead.

The most significant event in my Vietnam experience was on October 27, 1967. The operation was Granite. We were traveling Northeast about ten miles west of Camp Evans, when the point platoon came under heavy small-arms fire. I was a rocket man. I fired light anti-tank assault weapons. With all disregard for my safety, I ran forward to where the NVA had our Marines pinned down. I fired all my rockets at the enemy positions, killing the soldiers in the bunker. Having expended all of the LAWs, I ran down the trail and gathered more and began an assault. Picking up an M-60 machine gun from a dead Marine and firing at the oncoming NVA, we began moving our wounded down to a safe area. For this life saving and heroic action, I received the Silver Star.

At the present time, I am married to a wonderful wife, Alice. We own our own home in the country. I work for the Vietnam Veteran Outreach as a counselor.

I hope that this story can give some inspiration to others like myself and all that read it.

Frederick Locke

It was around the middle of June when I received a call from my father in St. Louis, Missouri. I was in the Job Corps at the time and living in Grants, New Mexico. My father told me that I had been drafted and had a reporting date of July 15, 1966. It took about a week for the papers to go through channels before I was able to go home for a few days, before I had to report to the induction center. It was about 7:30 in the morning when my father dropped me off in front of the center. I handed my letter to the sergeant at the desk. From there I was directed to a room where I was told to strip to my shorts and socks. There were about sixty of us at the time and more coming in when we were told to form a line at the door. First they took blood, then X-rays, eye test, hearing test, and then came the doctor who had us bend over and touch our toes and walk like a duck. From there we went to another room where we were given tests and the oath was administered and we were in the Army.

It was about 3:30 or so when we were loaded on buses for the trip to Fort Leonard Wood, Missouri, where we started basic training. The first week was just orientation and medical and dental examinations, and issuing our uniforms. After the first week, we were assigned to our units for training. I was assigned to Echo 2/2, where we spent eight weeks training to become one of the Uncle Rocket killing machines. From the rifle range to the gunnard range, hand-to-hand combat, bayonet practice, marching and drilling day and night for eight weeks. Then graduation and a new duty assignment. My next stop was Fort Sill, Oklahoma, home of the field artillery. For eight weeks I trained on 105s, 155s, and eight-inch artillery pieces. After eight weeks we received our orders, assigning us to our next duty. We were not surprised to see Vietnam on our orders.

I was hoping they would have sent me anywhere but Vietnam. A few of the others did receive orders for Germany, but the rest of us were headed to the vacation capital of Southeast Asia. First, it was two weeks home with the family, then off to Fort Ord, California. It was December when I arrived at Fort Ord. I heard on the radio that Walt Disney had died. His picture was on TV and in the papers. I was kind of sad. I had always wanted to see him and visit Disneyland as a kid. But, at the present time, I couldn't even go to Disneyland. I was at Fort Ord for three days when we were loaded on a commercial airliner like cattle in a cattle car. Our first stop was Hawaii, where they fueled up, and then it was on to Clark Air Force Base. We spent about three hours there before heading on to our final destination, Saigon. It was about 10 o'clock in the morning when we landed. I didn't know quite what to expect once we landed. I guess we were all kind of nervous. We were taken from the plane and put on buses and then to a processing area for a briefing on Vietnam.

We were loaded back on the buses and taken to Long Binh, where we would be assigned to our divisions. While there, I had a chance to see Billy Graham from a distance. Martha Ray came to the camp and entertained us and afterward I had a chance to speak with her for about fifteen minutes. It was great. The first time I ever had a chance to speak with a star.

After about three days there, I was sent to the 1st Infantry Division. The Big Red One. I was processed in and received my pay after four months. My first stop was the barber, even in combat. From there I went to the club to have a few beers. It was a small place that held about thirty people or so. There was only one other person in the club at the time and he was waiting to be sent to this unit too. We spoke for about five minutes when Martha Ray came over and told me to scoot over and she sat down and handed us a six-pack of beer. We spoke for about an hour and the club started to get crowded. Martha Ray went up to the stage and entertained us for twenty minutes or so before moving on. She told us to look her up when we got back to the States. She is a great lady.

I was drinking one of the beers Mrs. Ray gave us when I heard someone call out my name. When I answered he told me to come on, we were moving out. When I got outside, I found my gear in the back of a jeep and was told to get in. I was handed an M-14 rifle and a clip of ammo and told to insert the clip but not to chamber a round. I could tell by the tone of his voice what he meant. We drove for what seemed like hours before we came to the town and camp of Phu Loi. They dropped me off at battalion HQ. I went to hand the rifle back and was told to keep it and they drove off. At battalion they assigned me to Charlie Btry. 8th Bn. 6th Field Artillery. Once there I was assigned to the 1st Gun Section, a 155 towed Howitzer. I was glad. I didn't want to work on a 105 even though they were smaller and easier to handle. The rounds weigh about forty-five pounds with canister and the 155 rounds were about ninety-five pounds with no canister. Two of the guys in the section were from St. Louis, Jones and Shipp.

There were about seven of us assigned to the first gun and there had to be at least four people on the gun at all times. Each section had a shack with four cots in it. The ones not assigned to work on the gun that day would go on other details like latrine duty. There were fifty-five-gallon drums cut in half and placed under the latrines and had to be taken out and burned out every day using diesel fuel. After the details were completed we would return to our sections and complete any duties there before we were given passes to town for a little R&R. You had from about noon until about 4. That's when the MPs would start chasing everyone back to camp. I was there about a week when we were told to pack up and get ready to move out and it was a rush to get the truck loaded with powder and ammo and then hook up the gun to the truck and throw our personal belongings on top of the truck. The CO would take the lead, with the maintenance section bringing up the rear to pick up any stragglers. Once we arrived at our location it was a mad dash to get the gun set up and the ammo stacked before we could start setting up camp. After the gun was secured it was time to fill sandbags and set up camp. We didn't have tents. We used crates from the powder racks to lay across the sandbags with ponchos on top. Foxholes would be dug and planks would go across them with sandbags on top of them for protection.

Once the camp was secured and the infantry had set up security around our position, it was just a matter of waiting. There were two words an artillery man hated to hear, "Fire Mission." It usually meant someone was in deep trouble and needed help fast. My first combat mission came during one operation when an infantry unit was to move into the Hobo Woods. For two hours we fired into a given location to try to clear out any enemy activity before they moved in. Once they were in, we fired support around them to discourage any enemy activity to come. We heard that they had found a hospital underground with three stories of wounded and dead Viet Cong soldiers. I had a chance to see my first VC when two guys from the 1st Infantry Division were escorting three Viet Cong soldiers back to their unit. Their hands were tied together and placed on top of their heads, their eyes were covered with rags and they were dressed in pants, no shirt or shoes. They had been found in one of the tunnels in the area.

Early next morning we were ordered to pack up and move out. I found it much easier to empty the sandbags than it was to fill them. We had a quick breakfast, loaded the truck, and were off again. While on the road headed for our next area of operation, we would pass through these villages and the children would stand out there and wave to us. We would take the candy from our C-rations and throw it to them. We could give them candy, but no food. Then after a while we were told to stop giving them candy. They would take it and give it to the enemy.

Once we had reached our new location it was another mad rush to get the gun set up and the ammo stacked. Then it was back to the sandbags. One of the guys said that when he got home, he was going to buy some sandbags and have his wife and kids build a bunker in the backyard. We all kind of laughed. After things were set up and the chow served, it was time to clean the gun. But first, we had to get permission from the CO. We couldn't have the gun down too long. The gunner and assistant gunner would tear down the breach while the rest of us swabbed the tube and greased the crank at the front of the gun. It took around forty-five minutes. The breach took the longest because it had to be dismantled to clean. Once the gun was cleaned, the next section cleaned its gun until all six guns had been cleaned. After everything was taken care of, we would rest and try to sleep. We never knew when we would be called out, but we did know that we had to fire harassment fire all through the night. Just before dark, for forty-five seconds, every small-arms weapon from a 50-caliber to the M-14 opened up fire on the woodline. If there was anything out there, it would be gone, or at least we hoped. After dark we would get up and fire at a designated area for about an hour, then back to sleep for an hour, then fire again for an hour all night long, one round every ten minutes. This lasted until about 5 in the morning. Then we would go back to our sandbag hotel until morning formation.

The mess tent would start breakfast at 6 for those that wanted it. One thing about the artillery, they usually had hot meals. The infantry unit that set up around us would go to our mess tent for chow and then head back to their foxholes. We always tried to warn them about walking in front of the guns during a fire mission. With their rifle on their shoulder and mess kit in one hand and hot coffee or juice in the other, they would walk right in front of the guns. The muzzle blast from one of these guns was enough to knock a person off their feet at fifty feet. The concussion alone had been known to cause bleeding from the eyes and nose. I found that out the hard way. We could always tell the ones that had been around the guns before. They would either walk behind the guns or off to the side until they were far enough in from where the blast wouldn't effect them. But there was always a few that had to learn the hard way. We would fire. Their mess kits would go one way while their coffee would go another. They would pick themselves up, show us their IQ finger and use words not fit for man nor beast and head back to the mess tent and try it again. We knew they were mad and I felt sorry for what happened, but when you have to fire, you have to fire. Usually they would make their return trip behind the gun and we would apologize. Most of them would laugh about it and go on their way. Others didn't appreciate it one bit. In a way, I didn't blame them. I know it scared the heck out of them.

After the morning briefing it was time to clean up from the night before, replace the ammo used, gather up the extra powder bags to be burned and clean up around the area and wait for the next mission. Sleep was almost impossible. It was so hot, sweat rolled off your body. We had to wear jackets that weighed about forty-five pounds along with a helmet, and you didn't get caught without it on. The CO got very upset if you were out of uniform. After a couple of days there, it was time to pack up and move out again. We packed up the truck and hooked up the gun and we were off. For about five weeks we were jumping from place to place. We finally settled down at the base of what was called the Black Virgin Mountain. The 101st Airborne rangers on top, us on the bottom, and Charlie in the center. We set up camp like usual and were getting everything ready when we were told that we had to move the whole battery. Not far, about 300 yards. We were too close to the mountain. So we hooked the gun up and moved it to the new location. We went back and picked up the sandbags. There was no way we were going to fill them again. After we finished securing the camp and cleaning the gun, it was time to relax. We were sitting around the gun when we heard the sound of shells going over our heads. The section chief said it was just a mortar unit firing support. About that time a round landed behind our truck and we all headed for the bunker. The section chief yelled for us to man the gun and prepare to fire into the woodline. We fired about three rounds when a fire mission was called down. Our sister unit, a 105 battery, was under fire and needed support. We were ordered to keep firing into the woods while the fourth gun section fired support for our sister unit. A round had dropped in and hit the powder cannister of Number 3 Gun, causing a fire. The gun crew rushed over and put out the fire as quickly as possible.

That morning while we were cleaning up the mess, a helicopter landed with General Westmoreland. He went around inspecting the damage and awarded the Bronze Star to the section chiefs of the first and fourth gun section. We felt kind of left out. We were out there under fire along with them. That afternoon a chopper brought in supplies and the mail and it was a lucky thing he did. A jeep was coming across the field behind the guns when it hit a mine, blowing the driver from the jeep, causing serious damage. Our medic rushed over to him and did what he could, then rushed him to the chopper to be taken to one of the hospitals.

The next day, we received orders to pack up; we were going back to base camp for a rest. When we returned to camp, it was business as usual. First came the gun, getting it set and ready to fire, then unloading the truck and setting up the ammo. After everything was squared away it was time to rest and try to recover a lot of lost sleep. Four guys were stationed on the gun as usual, while the rest went to the barracks or the club for a few beers. I was still one of the new kids, so I stayed with the gun and rested in the hooch until we received a load of ammo. Then I went out to stack it. While I was stacking the ammo I noticed a group of officers and photographers walking toward the gun. They were taking pictures of someone. I couldn't make him out at the time, so I jumped up on the back of the gun to get a better look. It was Henry Fonda. I tried to get closer, but with all the officers and press, it was impossible. He looked around for a few moments. Then he was on his way. I figured at least I had an opportunity to see him.

The next day we were told that new guns would be arriving, M-109 Self-Propelled Howitzers, to take the place of the outdated 155-towed. When they arrived we hurried up and moved the towed gun out of the way and the new one was moved into position. After the gun was put into position and made ready to fire, we were given a short briefing on the operation of the gun. That took about two hours. The rest was trial and error. After a few days we were getting the hang of it. After lunch I returned to the gun to check to see if the mail came in yet. The section chief stopped me and told me he had a new position for me, truck driver. George moved from the truck to the gun as the driver, a position I was hoping to get. About a week later the order came down to move out again. We wondered where we were headed this time. We packed the truck with ammo and powder as usual, except this time the personal gear was loaded on the gun along with the guys in the section, except for one other that was to ride shotgun with me. It was late afternoon when we pulled into a field just outside a Vietnamese village. All the trucks pulled in far enough behind the guns, so as not to interfere with the setting up of the gun. I parked the truck and ran over to help get the gun operational and ready to fire before unloading the ammo. After the gun was laid and the ammo was stacked it was time to set up camp. That meant filling sandbags and digging our foxholes. A couple of guys from the commo section were stringing barbed wire along the road line where the infantry were dug in. Our first night there we were hit with mortars and the small-arms trailer took a direct hit, throwing grenades and rockets and scattering ammo all over. The medic had been wounded, along with one of the crewmen of the second gun section. The medic received a Bronze Star for his actions under fire. I, for one, was glad to have him around. We were up the rest of the night waiting in the foxholes for first light. We weren't about to leave until the rest of our men could see us and not mistake us for Viet Cong and open up on us.

At first light, a chopper landed to pick up the wounded. We gathered ourselves together for the clean-up and went to work. An ordnance disposal unit came in and retrieved the ammo, rockets, and grenades and disposed of them. They dropped off another ammo trailer. We had a few fire missions that day. Nothing that lasted very long. Around 5 that evening, we were sitting behind the gun when they hit us again, and again they hit the ammo trailer. We couldn't return fire because of the village, so we stayed in the holes until it was over. Then we came out. The ammo trailer had been parked in the same spot as the other one. The next morning the ordinance people were back to clean up and drop off another trailer. This time the CO decided it was too dangerous around there, so we packed up and moved on. Our next stop was Loc Ko, where we moved into A Battery's position, a sister unit of 155s/M-109s, and set up camp. There wasn't much to do since everything was already there. The guns were pulled into their areas and set up just as if we were back at our own base, but in a way it felt strange being in another unit camp. Their barracks were locked up with signs informing us that traps were set and not to enter the area, but one of the guys pushed open the door and went in anyway. There were no traps found, but I for one wasn't about to take any chances. Some of these guys were just crazy enough to set up traps.

At formation we were told that the barracks were off-limits and tents would be provided for us. The only building we were allowed to use was the club. We received two tents and the section chief told us to set them up at a safe distance behind the gun. I asked him if back in the States was safe enough. He said not where he was from. After the tent was up it was time for the sandbags. We had to go just outside base camp, where we found a mound of dirt. We had started filling the bags when a group of kids came over and started helping. I was glad for the help. Once the bags were loaded on the truck the kids came over and wanted to get paid. We knew we would have to give them something when they started, so we all threw in a few bucks and gave it to them for there help and we thanked them and headed back to camp. Once we returned and had the sandbags stacked around the tent and the cots dug in, I took the truck to a stream I found to wash it. As I was pulling in, four kids that were playing in the creek came over and started washing the truck almost before I could get it stopped. I yelled at them to get away but they were on the truck faster than I could get the words out. About that time another truck pulled into the creek and two of the kids went over to it. After I thought it was clean enough I gave them about a buck each and headed back to camp, where the section chief was waiting for me. I had to take the truck and go with the ammo section to the main ammo dump at Long Binh, and we wouldn't return until later the next day. We went about a mile when I noticed a flash from the woods and I saw what appeared to be a rocket just miss the back of the truck in front of me. I grabbed my rifle and laid it on the door, pointing in the direction of the woods and opened up and hit the gas. The trucks behind me did the same and we got out of there as fast as we could.

When we arrived at Long Binh the ammo sergeant came back and wanted to know why we were firing our guns. We told him about the rocket just missing the truck. He went into the office to get the paperwork taken care of while we waited at the truck. When he came out of the office he waved for us to move up and he climbed on the side of the truck and we drove on in to be loaded. Once we were inside and around all that ammo I wanted to get loaded as fast as I could and get out of there. The ammo dump was one of Charlie's targets and it had been hit on a number of occasions and I didn't want to be in there if he decided to pay it a visit tonight. When we finished loading the last truck we went out to a waiting area where we parked the trucks for the night.

We were up early the next morning and had our breakfast in a can and were on our way as soon as we received word that the roads had been cleared—Charlie liked to go out at night and set little surprises in the road for us. The sergeant called back and told the CO about the rocket and he said he would report it to battalion and I guess he did. As we were passing the place where the rocket came from there was a patrol going over the area. When we arrived back at camp they were in the middle of a fire mission, so I parked my truck and went over to help. A grunt unit had run into a few VC that were giving them a little trouble so they called for a few rounds to kind of shake them up a little before moving in to clean up. After it was over I dropped off the ammo behind the gun, where it was stacked and sandbags placed around it. We were still on alert until the infantry had secured the area and we cleaned up around the gun and prepared for the next mission. When we finally received the all-clear I went to my tent to lie down and get a little sleep. I didn't get much sleep at the ammo dump. As I was headed to the tent someone yelled formation and I headed for the assembly area and joined my section. After they went through all the military stuff the CO informed us that we had to turn in the M-14 rifles and be issued M-16s, which a lot of us really didn't want after we heard about the Marine unit being wiped out because these guns jammed up on them. But we didn't have any say in the matter, so we reported to the supply area, where we received a bundle of wax type paper that, when you unrolled it, had a rifle covered in grease that took over an hour to scrape off. Once we had them cleaned we were taken out to an area where we could test-fire them. They were a much lighter weapon than the M-14, but they were kind of funny looking, with all that plastic on it, like something you would find in a toy store for your kid.

Jim Kramer

I recall hearing about a place called Vietnam from the news stories early in the '60s and it became more personal when a college buddy was drafted into the Marines and sent there in 1965. There were always jokes about it and I remember feeling a bit awkward when friends from home got back and asked me what I was doing. I was of course in college and temporarily deferred. One guy, a Korean War Navy veteran, would always give me hell for not serving my country with, "When the hell are you going in the service?!" Well, when I graduated from North Dakota State University in December, 1967, I was to be drafted in February, 1968. Lots of stories were floating around about college graduates getting "the good jobs" even if they were drafted, but there were also those of college graduates humpin' the bush.

Being somewhat of a coward, I checked out the various services and decided that if the Army would guarantee me a job as a medical lab technician, I'd enlist, even if it meant serving another year. Little did I realize that, due to my color blindness, I couldn't qualify. In fact, I almost didn't pass the physical due to my poor eyesight (minus 20/400). My older brother, an optometrist, told me he could write a letter and, maybe, get me out of it. But I said, "No. I feel I owe a duty to my country."

You see, about a year and a half before all of this, my hometown experienced its first loss to the war. A young guy I had known only in passing, enlisted in the Marines and was killed in Vietnam. Word came as a real shock to all of us. About a week earlier one of my high school buddies failed his draft physical due to high blood pressure, yet he was fit to play professional football!

I wasn't going to try and get out of it.

I was engaged to a young gal at the time I went to Fort Lewis, Washington for basic and we were married when I reported to my first duty station following AIT at Fort Sam Houston, Texas. I was trained as a dental assistant and spent six months at Fort Rucker, Alabama. It was a real shock when I came down on levy for Nam, and Pat and I cried about it the first night, but came to accept it more and more as time went on. I came home for thirty days leave before I was to report back to Fort Lewis for processing to Nam. It seemed like a dream, but as time got closer I got real scared. Nixon was in office by the time I left for Fort Lewis and everyone in my family said, "He'll have the war over by the time you get there."

The ride to the airport in January, 1969 was a long one, and very sad for my parents and wife. I just wanted to get it over with and get on the plane, but it seemed like the last few hours were some of the longest of my life. As the plane arrived and was ready for boarding, I got this gut-level feeling of despair and felt lower than a snake's belly. As I shook my dad's hand and kissed my wife and mom good-bye, tears came even though I tried my best to choke them back. Once I was on the plane, and the snow blew around the terminal, I felt like I had never felt before— a lot of despair.

Once I got to Fort Lewis, I felt better. I was with a whole bunch of guys in the same situation. We were all going to Nam, some for a second time and a lot of us for the first time. I called home the night before my plane left and it was hard to keep my voice from cracking, knowing that I might be talking to my wife and parents for the last time.

The flight to Nam took about twenty-four hours. We stopped in Hawaii and the Philippines. It was so warm there, of course. Back home in North Dakota, it was below zero. One of my seat mates was going back for the second time. He was a Spec-4 with the 4th Infantry Division and I picked his brain a lot. As we approached the Vietnam coast, it got real quiet in the plane. Those of us who were close looked out the windows. It was dark and I was scared as hell.

We landed at Cam Ranh Bay and I spent my first day working in some supply room. That night we left aboard a C-130 to somewhere else called Bien Hoa and Long Binh's 90th Replacement Depot. The ride to the 90th was scary. It was dark and hot and I don't think I'll ever forget that smell! The bus had wire on the windows, just like they told us they would have.

At the 90th I spent a few hours doing something, I'm not sure what, anymore, but then I heard my name called and I hustled to the open field. The sergeant was calling out units, "1st Air Cav., 25th Infantry Division," "199th Light Infantry Brigade," and then a long list of names. I felt like crawling in a hole, but my name never came up. I really don't recall hearing my name for sometime, but I remember being called up later and a smiling black Spec-4 telling me to throw my bags into his jeep. As I climbed in I said, "Where the hell are we going?" He said, "Just down the road aways to the 93rd Evac. Hospital."

After spending some time checking into the hospital company, finance and all the usual paper work, I was assigned to the dental clinic of the hospital. The oral surgeon was a major by the name of John Jones. We called him "The Red Baron" because of his red hair. The general dentist was named Majestro, the NCOIC was a Spec-6 whose name I don't remember, and there were two Spec-4s named Rick Raddox and Roger Fruhwirth. Rog, as he was called, said to me, "Hey, where the hell you from back in The World?" I said, "North Dakota." He said, "You're kidding. I was born there!" Turned out he was living in California at the time his reserve unit was called up, but his roots were in North Dakota.

I remember asking him, "What do you do around here for excitement?" He said, "I drink a lot." "Hell of a deal!" I said.

I remember being in an argument about the war with one of the corpsmen in my hooch. I was a "hawk" and he was obviously a "dove." In fact, I think he was a CO. Later my attitude would change. I began to get OJT in the operating room and clinic, assisting the Red Baron as the Spec-6 ended up in LBJ for being AWOL. Things were quiet for a while but when Tet of '69 hit, all hell broke loose. I remember, it was early in the morning when the sirens went off and it was Red Alert. I put on my steel pot and headed for the OR (hospital operating room). As I came around the corner of a building I looked down Highway 1, which ran within 100 yards of the hospital, and there was a gunship laying down a lot of lead. Red tracers were coming down in a red stream and I said, "Oh shit, what am I doing here?"

We didn't have any cases (patients) to work on and I remember the Red Baron telling me to go in a back room and sleep. How the hell do you sleep when every few minutes the place rocks and shudders? I don't think it was incoming, but I was scared as hell.

A few hours later the real thing happened. Jonsey and I were working on the head and face wounds of a Thai soldier and then the gas-passer (anesthetist) said, "Forget it Jonsey, he's dead." I couldn't believe it. How could this be? I started to cry in disbelief, but Jonsey said, "You better get used to this."

I guess the best way to describe how you get used to it was, you never got close with any patients. They were just bodies, which seems inhumane, but that was how I did it. Sometimes we were so busy in the OR, all eight tables were being used to help the wounded. It was a mess, arms and legs coming off, multiple frag wounds, burns and everything under the sun. I recall walking in water and blood ankle deep during the real busy times. One time when I wasn't busy assisting the Red Baron, I scrubbed and assisted a surgeon do a tracheotomy on a guy. Sometimes I would help out wherever I could and then not feel a damn thing afterwards.

Most of the doctors were real heroes that no one really knows about. They were some of the best and worked under trying conditions and stress. We got in a dog handler one time and he was peppered from head to toe with frag wounds. He was conscious before they put him under, but he arrested (cardiac arrest) and died on the table. The surgeon tore off his mask and stomped out crying. He just put his head in his hands and wept.

There was a lot of trauma and death but, "You got used to it." Which really means you stuffed your feelings, but later in my life I learned they come out, sometimes at an angle that hurts others when they are innocent.

I had the distinct pleasure of working with four oral surgeons during my tour. They were all gifted men and very skilled at their profession. Perhaps the most horrible case I assisted with was a young Vietnamese woman who had been shot in the face. The bullet entered her lower left jaw, came across her nose and literally laid her face wide open. An oral surgeon by the name of Maj. Matt Horrigan and I worked thirteen hours on her. When we were done, she was no beauty queen, but he no doubt saved her life.

I also worked with a Lt. Col. Robert A. J. Olson. What a neat man he was, and I enjoyed him as a person and was simply amazed at his skills. He extracted twenty-four teeth from one person, including all the pre- and post-extraction work, in forty-five minutes. He had a delightful sense of humor and was truly an officer and gentleman.

I didn't realize it, but all the trauma and death was weighing very heavily on me, and alcohol numbed it very well. Once my replacement arrived and I didn't have to be to work on time or even have day or night guard duty, I followed the pursuit of intoxication.

I also had learned from an American civilian we treated in our clinic that one of the largest contractors in Vietnam was RMK-RBJ, owned by Mrs. Lady Bird Johnson. I was absolutely furious! How could we be betrayed, used as puppets for some damn politician who had sent many young men to their death and made countless millions at their expense!

I also recall hearing that Mrs. Richard Nixon had visited a hospital ward at the 24th Evac. Hospital at Long Binh. All she saw were GIs with tee-tee frag wounds. I wish to hell she could have been in the OR when things were tough.

Col. Olson was the first person to call me a drunk. I of course denied it, but he was right, as I would come to find out later on in my life.

Getting short was tough. I was under ninety days and I remember the last Red Alert on Long Binh post. I literally flew from the hooch to the bunker with my steel pot and flak jacket, scared as hell that I'd be one of those "double-digit midgets" who got it with only a few days left.

Well, obviously, I made it home and was extremely grateful to finally meet my wife at the airport in Fargo, North Dakota. It was about thirty-five below zero, with a thirty-mile-per-hour wind and blowing snow. It was probably around 100 degrees above when we took off from Bien Hoa Air Force Base. What a shock.

Readjustment is sort of foggy, but I know my old friend alcohol numbed the pain for many years. I completed Graduate School at North Dakota State University and went back to my old government job. We had a son by then and was I proud of him. Later on we adopted a baby girl and, on the outside, we were the all-American family—good jobs, three-bedroom house with the two cars, and necessary toys. We went to church every Sunday.

My drinking was getting worse and I always blamed it on Vietnam. How wrong I was, as I found out later. It was just an excuse to drink. But my wife finally had enough and told me to get some help or get the hell out of the house.

I had gone to one "Vet's rap group" before I got sober but it didn't make sense, because I was still drinking. I have been in several since finding sobriety and they made a lot of sense, but I still couldn't get to all those feelings shoved so deep inside of me. I was ashamed to be a vet. I was ashamed I received the Bronze Star medal for my work in the hospital. Why did I come back and others from my hometown and others who died in front of me didn't make it back?

A divorce five and a half years ago was perhaps the toughest thing I have ever gone through, but there was some real healing with the grief. As I grieved and cried and sobbed for my lost relationship, I began to grieve for the countless people we lost in the hospital. I could see their faces and they were so real. However, I found that the more I allowed their faces to appear in my mind and grieve for them the better I felt.

I really have put a lot of the death behind me now, but every once in a while it will come back, especially when I hear a "Huey." I think, "Casualties." Diesel smoke makes me think of Highway 1 and I don't think I will ever forget the smell of Nam.

I'm really grateful to have come as far as I have today. My life is much better sober, I have a host of real friends and I know what it's like to hurt. Today I'm proud of my service in Nam. I'm not proud of what our country did in that war, but I'm proud of what I did. I know in my heart that anyone who was given the set of circumstances we were given, would have done as we did. The key was to survive.

I'm a charter member of Chapter 150 of the Bismarck-Mandan Vietnam Veterans of America and organized the chapter's color guard. We march in a lot of parades and present the colors at athletic events. I recall being in one parade and the applause from the crowd brought tears to my eyes. And another vet—it was so different—they were finally saying, "Welcome home, boys!"

I'm proud to do that, but it took a lot of talking, hurting and crying to reach this point. I'm so grateful to have had all my experiences to date. Because of them I can relate to so many people who have been where I have been and I always enjoy trying to be a good listener to others.

If you can relate to my story, especially the alcohol addiction, please get some help. It's available just about everywhere. Remember, you don't have to walk it alone.

Jon T. Johnson

I was born February 19, 1947 in San Bernardino, California. I lived in that area until I was twelve or thirteen. My folks decided that was no area to raise kids, so my family moved to the Northwest. First Oregon, then to Kelso, Washington, where I went to school. My high school days were rather uneventful. I really didn't like it. I would cut class every chance I got. I graduated in 1965. My main problem was that I was very skinny and underweight. I tried sports for a while, but couldn't stand being the bench warmer all the time, so I gave that up.

During my freshman year, I had this friend, an older kid I looked up to, who dropped out of school. He was very frail also. He enlisted in the Marine Corps, and when he came home on boot camp leave, I couldn't believe how much he had developed muscularly. I decided I was going to be a Marine, just like him. (I'm still in touch with this individual today. He spent twelve years in the Corps, with two tours in Vietnam—wounded twice. His name is Sergeant Arnie Sundberg; ed. note, see page 199 for Arnie Sundberg story.) In April of 1966 I shipped off to boot camp. I only weighed 115 pounds when I got there. When I came home on my boot camp leave, I was a solidly built 145 pounds, the best physical shape of my entire life. During my leave I showed up and got even with a few guys who used to pick on me in school.

I lived it up good for thirty days, for I knew it could be my last. In October of '66 I was shipped out with WestPac ground forces, MOS—rifleman. I was transferred to the 1st Battalion 4th Marines, 3rd Marine Division—Bravo Company, 2nd platoon—where I did my full tour of duty in Vietnam.

My second day in-country I was under fire. We'd ridden tank security, taking some tanks to Con Thien from Dong Ha. We got ambushed. I was so confused. I wasn't familiar with all the new faces yet. The squad I was originally assigned too, was the one I stayed with during my first firefight. All the while I didn't know that I had been transferred to another squad. The Marine Corps is known for not getting out the word. Well, it turned out that the squad I was supposed to be with, got wiped out. One man, who came over with me, received a punctured lung, and was sent back to The World the very next day.

Con Thien was occupied by Korean Marines. That was when I first heard of their awesome reputation in battle. Truthfully, they were great. A few weeks later, after only standing perimeter watch around the Dong Ha airstrip, my battalion got to go afloat. We would make landings off ship to shore in Vietnam, return back to the ship, go to places like Taipei, Okinawa, or the Philippines, where me and my guys had some fantastic times. I was on Operation Deckhouse V and VI during our time afloat, and our last major landing, into the DMZ, was Operation Beacon Hill, which was the very worst operation I had ever been on. My whole platoon was wiped out. After only three days, only seven of us walked out. B Company, my company, got the worst of it, and 2nd Platoon, my platoon, got the worst of it as well.

On operation Beacon Hill, the very first mortar round that hit in the morning (we had been mortared all night long) hit my parapet. It ripped out a fellow black Marine's throat as he was sitting up cleaning his weapon. Even to this day, I do not know who he was. He was an attachment from Weapons Platoon. Also, in that very same mortar burst, shrapnel from that mortar round hit Michael T. Boston of Branden, Vermont right in the temple. Blood was just gooshing out of his head. Me and some other Marines had to push Boston on the med-evac helicopter. As badly wounded as Boston was, he was refusing that he be med-vaced. He was the most caring and the best small unit leader I ever came across in Vietnam. I would follow him into Hell. I was really worried whether or not we'd ever see Boston again, because a serious head wound like that could be fatal later on. Boston is still alive today and well, I'm glad to report.

After carrying and half pushing Boston onto the chopper, I returned to my foxhole. The black Marine who had his throat ripped out by the mortar blast was there with a tracheotomy tube inserted in the ripped-out hole in this throat. The senior corpsman had placed the tube there. He was so busy with all the other casualties that he couldn't attend to this Marine. He instructed me what to do and had me striking his chest to keep his heart going, keeping the tube inserted and I kept him alive for almost an hour. (Boston often referred to this act as my unrewarded heroism.) Since I worked the hot LZ for the entire morning, I sustained this man's life right up until he was med-evaced by the chopper. It was rumored that this man died on the helicopter because once on the chopper, no one was available to keep the tube inserted in his throat and he finally died. Ever since that time, I've had dreams about this man. I've been very frustrated that despite my efforts to save him, he eventually died. I wish I could meet his surviving family some day and tell them I did my utmost, risked my life under heavy mortar fire to save his and I didn't let him down. He was black, I'm white. I hope his family wasn't racist in any way. I shined rather well on Beacon Hill. I was recommended for military decoration, though I never was decorated. Our lieutenant hurt his back and couldn't come on that one with us, so he wasn't there to evaluate my performance.

When we finally moved out of that position, we had lost so many men that we had to take their weapons and gear and put it in a foxhole and set a charge to it and blow it up so the Cong couldn't get it and use it against us. As we moved out in a column, we got caught in the middle of rice paddies. The NVA opened up on us from all sides. During the confusion, five of our guys went running the wrong way and ran right into the middle of a gook base camp. We were separated and forced to retreat. I distinctly remember Captain Ramsey calling to Lt. Col. Jack Westman, our battalion CO, and saying, "We've got five guys trapped down in an enemy base camp. They are probably dead. We can look for them in the morning."

From where I was, I could hear Colonel Westman (Black Jack) yelling loudly, "No one in the 4th Marines is to be left behind." So we lined up. I gave myself the sign of the cross, for I figured I would die that day. We advanced up the hill, taking it rice paddy dike by dike. We got to the top and had actually forced the NVA to retreat, then they regrouped and probably 1000 of them came charging out of this treeline. We held them, as our five trapped men came running to our position one by one. Collura, Maybou, Hayes, Gambino and the last one was Hall. He was shot through the legs by a 50-cal machine gun. A black sergeant, Stanley Smith, the bravest man I ever saw under fire, ran over the paddy dike, picked up Hall (all the while under fire) and brought him to safety in our lines. He received a head wound from a bullet, but refused to be med-evaced.

Just after that, an enemy machine gun nest opened up on us from the rear. We were caught out in the open paddy with no cover. Everyone that could returned fire. Many were still fighting from the front assault. Our machine gunner, Bill Curran, whipped around, went to fire his machine gun, but it had run out of ammo. I immediately rushed over to cut off 200 rounds from his backpack, which was out of his reach. He loaded his machine gun, aimed and completely wiped out the enemy machine gun nest. Bill Curran received the Silver Star for his actions. He recommended I be decorated also for answering the ammo call for, if I had not cut that ammo off his back, it would have gone unused at a very critical time. That machine gun nest may very well have killed us all. Again I was recommended for a distinguished award, but I never received one. After a fierce half-hour battle where my whole platoon was wiped out, the third and first platoons finally arrived, giving us re-enforcements. We could not med-evac our casualties, for the fog had set in deep and helicopters could not find us. We had no air support either, but we did have artillery support.

The next morning when the fog lifted we med-evaced our casualties, but during the night they mortared us again. A mortar round landed right in the middle of our casualties, wounding them all over again. They bled all night long, but we were faithful. We took care of them the best we could under the circumstances. After this there were only seven of us left from the second platoon, so I was split off and attached to the third platoon. Some of the other guys were attached to the first platoon. There was no more Second Platoon. We pulled in ragged assed, into a firebase at Gia Linh. Then to Con Thien, then back to Dong Ha. The very next operation, in April of '67, they decided to build McNamara's wall across the DMZ, known as Operation Firebreak. The strategy was to clear a strip of jungle across the DMZ to stop infiltration of NVA from the north to the south. At Dong Ha, we had traded our M-14s for the new M-16 rifle. So, on the first day of the operation, we had new, untested weapons.

The break was supposed to clear from Gia Linh to Con Thien, and clear across the DMZ. We started that operation at Gia Linh. I was wounded in action on this day, April 12, 1967. We started out early in the morning. We had Seabees with us with bulldozers, clearing the jungle. We were only 100 yards outside the compound at Gia Linh. Because it was early in the day and the gooks always attacked at night, the captain thought it would be a good idea if we all got the feel of shooting our new M-16s. He had us line up and recon a hill by fire. After that, as we rounded a bend, my team of three guys was the front fire team, and we were security for a tank that was with us.

The captain said, "Let's stop for chow." I sat down, was cooking my ham and lima beans ("ham and muthers") and I turned and saw a rocket RPG round literally skipping across the ground headed straight towards me. It knocked over my can of beans as it passed and hit the tank alongside us. The blast blew Welch into this hole where an abandoned bomb crater was. Thinking Welch had been hit, Ron Carter from New Orleans and myself immediately ran to him. We had our backs turned and then I happened to glance around and saw an NVA toss a Chi-Com grenade. It landed just inches from the bomb crater hole where we were holed up. The grenade was a dud and it didn't go off. The NVA tossed another grenade. This time we ducked and the explosion strafed over us in the bomb crater. I heard our platoon sergeant, Martinez (from Pasco, Washington) yell, "Carter, Welch, Johnson, get out of that hole. You're all bunched and the gook is trying to get all three of you."

All the while we were returning fire with our new M-16s. We got out of the hole, set up a hasty defense, spread out and all the while RPG rockets were being fired into the tank, blowing the track off and destroying it. By this time, one tanker was killed and several hurt. The tank finally got its turret maneuvered and started firing back. But this team of gooks was fierce. They didn't budge an inch. In fact, they still advanced on us. We sent a rocket team of our own up front. Their rocket misfired and they all got shot up by enemy small-arms fire. The corpsman that we sent up got shot in the head. The bullet miraculously had ricocheted off his skull. He was immobile, paralyzed, but alive. The more guys we sent up the more we lost. We had something like eight wounded men in the kill zone. My team was ordered around the right flank. We were already up front, to set up around the casualties so the gooks would not capture them. Carter, Welch and I moved out one by one, set up a good defense. But we were caught out in the open and a barrage of mortars rained down on us. I heard them coming in, put my head down and a blast landed right in front of me. I had my forearm out front to protect my head. A blast shot clean through my right forearm. I had a big gaping hole going clear through my arm that I could look down into. My arm was knocked clear underneath me.

It took me about three seconds before I realized I was hit. Then I was afraid to look down for I thought my arm could be blown clean off. When I finally looked down, I saw I still had a thumb and fingers. I was overjoyed and turned to Carter and said, "Look, I still have my hand!" He was also hit, but I didn't know it. He looked at me and said, "It's all over for me, Jonny." I then looked around and here was a gook with another Chi-Com grenade in his hand about to throw it straight at me. I was hurt and helpless. I never saw anyone with a more sadistic look on his face as that gook had that day. He had a real satisfied look as though to say, "I got that motherfucker now." He was talking in Vietnamese. His next grenade landed right next to me but it also was a dud although I rolled away from it and fell into another bomb crater. In there I was bumbling with my one good hand, trying to get a battle dressing out. Sergeant Stanley Smith came to the rescue again. He wrapped up my arm and I said, "Carter and Welch are wounded also." He replied, "Don't worry, Jonny, I will take care of them," and he did. This is the same black sergeant I had mentioned earlier, who rescued Hall on operation Beacon Hill.

Smith told me to get to the rear. I forgot to mention—after that gook threw his last dud grenade at me, he started to throw another one, but Finley got there first with his M-60 machine gun and killed him. He laid down plenty of firepower, to turn the tide of the battle in our favor, for a change. After that they put us casualties on another tank that was with us. I had one of our rocket team guys, Joe Lynch, in my lap, with his head partially blown off. The corpsman, wounded as well, kept telling me to hold his hands, yell in his ear and tell him he will be "Okay!" so he won't go into shock. I did that, then the tank we were riding on hit a land mine. It blew some of our casualties off the tank, killed another tanker and wounded some more. It couldn't be repaired, so they radioed for another tank from Gia Linh to come and tow the tank in. Once in, almost two hours later, the casualties finally got to an LZ, where we were picked up by helicopter. With my one good arm left, I loaded casualties. My right side, although full of blood, was on the blind side of the chopper door-gunner. He couldn't see I was wounded as well and the chopper almost took off without me. I remember Sergeant Martinez tapping me on the shoulder, telling me I did a good job. The door-gunner of the chopper grabbed me and I was half hanging out the door as the chopper lifted. There was so much blood on the floor I was slipping in it, and almost slipped out of that helicopter.

They landed us at D Med in Dong Ha. I remember being mad, throwing off my flak jacket in a fit of rage. Moultrie came to comfort me. He was a black rockets man who had been recuperating from his own wounds from an earlier battle. They laid us on these slabs. Corpsmen were cutting off our clothes and we waited our turn for surgery. Carter was hit in the ass, cut some nerves which paralyzed his foot (and he got to go home). He and Welch and Lynch were all shipped to Da Nang. Lynch was unconscious. I had several hours of surgery. They left my wound open to drain for ten days before closing it. About the fifth day, as I was lying in my hospital bed, Dong Ha came under rocket attack. I jumped out of my bed, with drainage tubes still in my arm. Instinctively I grabbed a sandbag with both arms and felt excruciating pain then passed out. They found me lying a few yards outside the hospital in a pool of blood. They hooked my drain tubes back up and eventually closed my wounds. I spent four months healing and then was sent back to combat.

I saw Welch again. He said Carter had been sent back to the States. Joe Lynch had been sent stateside also and he had suffered some brain damage. When I got back to the platoon, Second Platoon was at Gia Linh, the firebase that had come under very heavy artillery fire. I was in the hospital and missed that.

McNamara's wall had been built, then abandoned by the ARVNs that were supposed to man it.

My first day back, halfway down the strip across the DMZ, a Seabee unit had come under heavy fire. Seabees are engineers, not infantry. They were getting their asses kicked. My squad had to go out on the strip to rescue them. This is the very first time I ever suffered from the severe emotional trauma of being wounded. As we got to the Seabees, the NVA had really opened up on us. We were caught out in the open by enemy mortar fire. At that point I realized, after being wounded by a mortar, how traumatized I was by the sound of them again. We took up hasty positions alongside the strip. I was up against a mound of dirt. A mortar round came whistling in, landed about two feet away from my head. A new guy, Lakin, was behind me. I literally freaked out. I was numb all over, mostly from fright and nerves, I think. This is where I have trouble remembering. Other guys related to me that I was mumbling and out of my head. I was running with mortar rounds following me. I was completely out of control. My team leader couldn't get me back to my senses. A couple of guys tackled me. When I was about to be med-evaced, they said I was in shock . . . but then I snapped out of it.

Then I was marching along and my mind started playing tricks on me again. I went into it again and I was put in the back of a jeep and rode back to Gia Linh. I was ashamed of myself. "How could I come apart at the seams like that?" But, my guys kept telling me it was nothing to be ashamed of, being gun-shy during a mortar attack, especially after I had been so severely wounded by mortar fire. We were taking incoming artillery and mortar and rocket fire every day. B Company 1/4 stayed at that firebase for forty-three days, longer than any other Marine unit ever stayed there. After that, they only kept them there for ten days at a time. It was just too hairy.

After my return from the hospital, I stayed there for twenty-three of those days. After leaving there, I started to realize that I was getting shell-shocked. From Gia Linh we went to Camp Evans outside of Hue. We manned surrounding hills in the area. From there, we went to the A Shau Valley. We were the first Marines to set foot there. Army Special Forces had been there earlier.

Things were pretty mild for a while. Then we were called back to the DMZ in a hurry. B Company 1st Bn. 9th Marines had been annihilated. Ninety-five KIA and only five survivors. We had to abandon our base camps hurriedly to go back to the DMZ. We swept the area where 9th Marines were wiped out and made virtually no enemy contact. C Company had one casualty from a booby trap device. But when we got back to the positions we had to abandon in the A Shau Valley so hastily, we got ambushed the first night on the road. Our positions had been booby-trapped while we were away at the DMZ. The next day we lost a man, Corporal Zamora. He had only thirty days to go to rotate back home. We named our base after him, Camp Zamora. A Shau Valley wasn't rice paddy terrain. It was more wooded, with thick undergrowth. We had built a long winding road to get to our firebases. Truck convoys started getting ambushed every day. My squad had to rescue the very first truck ambush that occurred. A mortar crew riding on the truck barely got away with their lives.

We were taking casualties, not heavily, but with regularity. We had set up a firebase with artillery positions and patrolled the area every day. While here, I took my R&R to Hong Kong. I got myself laid and drunk. Then I stayed at China Beach for a while in Da Nang. Shortly after that, we moved to Quang Tri and turned a graveyard into a base graveyard. This, I always felt, was a major mistake of ours, not treating the people with consideration. We were always taught "All gooks are bad"—"Only good gook is a dead gook." We didn't have the support of the local populace.

We ran daily patrols out of Quang Tri. We got our share of mortars also while there. It seemed like the short-timers were the ones always getting hurt. Instead of sending the short-timers out to the field for their last days, they put them in a tent, and on mess duty. The Seabees had built a chow hall there. A mortar round hit the short-timers' tent. Breedlove, with only three days to go, was paralyzed from the waist down. Arthur Gray, a black kid from Philadelphia, a machine gunner, volunteered to go out on one more patrol one day before rotation. He stepped on a landmine.

I was really getting nervous. Finally I rotated out of there on my last day in-country. They hit bases at Da Nang, where I was, just to prove to us they could hit us during the elections we had set up.

After Nam I went home on leave. Then I was transferred to 5th Marine Regiment, 1/28, B Company. I was transferred to H&S Company. My arm was still in pretty bad shape. I couldn't do rope climbs anymore, with ruptured muscles in my right arm, so they made me ammo technician in the S-4 office. I was a good one too. My boss was a Major Voyer, and also Sergeant Fryeri.

My weight dropped to 120 pounds in Vietnam. While at the 28th Marines at Camp Pendelton, the 27th Marines were reactivated. They were sending many men back to Vietnam twice. Congress overruled that drunken cowboy Lyndon Johnson and ruled that a man must at least be back in the States one year before being sent back to Vietnam a second time. Johnson wanted all that wavered. So, for a year and a half, I stayed stationed at Camp San Mateo at Camp Pendleton. I was discharged out four months early. The Marine Corps authorized an "early out" for economic reasons. A pay raise was authorized, so why pay more men?

I had suffered stress from it all. I began to drink heavily. I got hit by a car. I was not driving, I was a passenger, and suffered a fractured back and a broken ankle. I went to college for a year and a half on the GI Bill. I started to gain weight, by the way. By now, at the age of twenty-three, I had developed into a 180-pound man. I worked in a saw mill/paper mill, and three years in a pipe plant. I started weight lifting to help my damaged arm. I was bench pressing 300 pounds and my weight came up to 200 pounds. I worked as a night club bouncer. My arm ruptured bad from weight lifting, so I had to quit. I had surgery in 1976 to repair the damage. The VA now pays me twenty percent disability payments for my injured arm.

From there I worked as a security guard for five years, six months as a private detective doing snoop and sleuth work. Nam experiences came in helpful. I now weigh 250 pounds. Thirteen years ago I quit drinking and smoking. In 1986 I got hit by a drunk driver. I got a nice settlement out of a lawsuit. I was injured in another car wreck. The woman who hit me was also a veteran with prior drunken arrest.

I honestly think that one of the biggest mistakes I made since Nam was joining these veterans organizations and clubs like the American Legion and VFW. They were turning me into an alcoholic. For three years after discharge I hit the booze hard. They way overdo it with the booze in these clubs. I would tell any vet getting out today, beware of those places. They mostly consist of a bunch of drunks.

I never did marry anyone. I just had too many ups and downs. The VA declared five years of my life "lost time" due to all the surgery I've had, and considering healing time as well. My VA disability is for my arm injury only. I was turned down for a stress claim.

I just try to survive from day to day. Since Nam I've got an attitude, "Don't make long-range plans."

I'm looking forward to a reunion of my old Nam comrades.

I've gotten in touch with several of them since Nam.

Last job I had I was working for a Japanese firm, but I was fired for insulting a Jap on the job.

I don't particularly like the way they are buying up America.

Earl Woodall

I was born September 11, 1947 in Paragould, Arkansas, the child of alcoholics who were poverty-stricken. My father, Richard Coyle, made only seven dollars a week as a fisherman. I entered the world on a boat on the St. Francis River and was named James Coyle. When I was a child, my brothers and sisters and I were removed from the Coyle family due to neglect. I entered the social services system, only to find much worse abuse and mistreatment.

On October 28, 1958 I was fortunate enough to be adopted by the Woodall family—Lucy and Aubrey of Little Rock. I considered this to be one of the happier events in my life. I was a very old child, chronologically, to be adopted, though my experiences gave me more age than my eleven years.

As I matured and the turbulent Vietnam years began, the words of my parents, to bring honor to the country if the need arose, resulted in my enlisting in the United States Marine Corps on November 7, 1967.

First there was boot camp in California, and then on to Vietnam with the 27th as a grunt. Vietnam was a whole new world. No words can reflect the shock to one's senses. I actively try to suppress all that I saw, smelled, heard, and especially what I felt. My letters written home show the confusion and fear I felt.

"Dear Mom & Dad, We lost six more men in the field the other day and it sure makes me feel worse about being over here. This will be a short letter. We are going back out in the field at 4:30 so I will have to get ready. I'm sending some pictures home. See if dad can take the negatives and make some pretty good pictures out of them. The gooks over here don't do too good a job. If he can I want him to send them back. I will take pictures and send them to him and he can keep the negatives and send me the pictures if he doesn't mind.

"Mom: will you get in touch with Red's mother and send me his address? She lives at 320 S. Valmor and she works at the Seventh Day Adventist on University.

"The sand over here is about a foot deep and the VC plant booby traps almost in every spot. Every time you take a step all you can do is pray there isn't a trap in front of you.

"Well guess I better close. Don't forget about the pictures and Red's mother. I love you, Earl"

While on operation Allen Brook we were to take three treelines. The morning we were to leave I had a fever and my company left without me. When I was flown out later, my whole company was wiped out— *DEAD.*

"Dear Mom & Dad, We just got back off an operation. It seems like everywhere we turn there is a load of gooks. We really got our butts kicked. There are only three men left in my platoon and only twenty-eight in our whole company. We lost over 200 men in less than five days. If anyone tells you that there isn't much going on over in Vietnam you tell them your son was one man out of twenty-eight that was left in our Co. that God was looking over. Mom! You can't imagine how things are over here, when you walk along and someone that you know steps on a booby trap and when you get to him he hasn't got any arms or legs and he is just laying there screaming, I just hope I will get out of here okay.

"Mom! Send me Red's address if you can. I'm sorry about messy letters, but I'm lucky I can still write.

"I'm mailing a camera home, the part that rolls the film is broken. See if dad can fix it and send it back to me along with some color film.

"Well guess I better close. I will send 200 dollars home this month if I can get a money order.

"Remember I love you and Dad very much. Your Son Earl P.S. Write real soon"

"Dear Mom & Dad, Everything is a little better now we are finally off that operation called Allen Brook and I sure lost a lot of friends. This will probably be a short letter I have to go on patrol in a few minutes and I better get ready.

"Mom: I'm trying to make some tapes and send them home to you and dad so you can hear my voice. Doesn't that sound like fun? Will also send you around two hundred dollars within the next few days, then with the hundred dollars that I will get back off my income tax I shouldn't owe dad but about $150 dollars. Does that sound about right? Then I can start sending money home to save for a car when I get home. I sure wouldn't come over here for just the money because it doesn't mean enough to risk my life for.

"I was just watching it rain and it sure made me homesick to be home where I could sit there and listen to it rain and not have to worry about getting killed. Well, better close. Write real real soon. I love both of you and dad and God Bless you for everything you've done for me. I guess now I'm grown up enough to see and appreciate everything you have done for me. I can look back on some of the things I've done and just see how much of a kid I really was, but when you have to fight for your life I guess it just makes you grow up. Love your Son Earl"

"Why God chose me to live, I don't know. All that day I picked up pieces of bodies and the remains of my company and close friends. It just so happened that the first treeline we were to take was an R&R

center for the NVA. When we attempted the maneuver, well, you know the rest.

"As a squad leader, I had nine Marines and six ARVNs (South Vietnamese Soldiers) I was responsible for while on patrol. One of the Marines discovered a booby trap. As I attempted to use the straps from my rifle to blow it up (we didn't have any C-4), another soldier hit a trip-wire and I was sprayed with shrapnel. I was med-evaced to the First Med and then to Great Lakes in Illinois. My parents received the following telegrams:

YOUR SON LCPL EARL WOODALL 2405952, HAS ARRIVED THIS HOSPITAL. HE HAS BEEN HOSPITALIZED AS A RESULT OF FRACTURED LEFT HAND AND MULTIPLE FRAGMENT WOUNDS AND HIS CONDITION IS CONSIDERED SATISFACTORY. THE WARD MEDICAL OFFICER DOES NOT FEEL THAT YOUR PRESENCE IS REQUIRED FROM THE MEDICAL STANDPOINT. YOU MAY SEE THE PATIENT AT ANYTIME ON YOUR FIRST VISIT AND FROM 2:00 PM TO 4:00 PM AND FROM 7:00 PM TO 9:00 PM THEREAFTER. HE IS ABLE TO WRITE AT THIS TIME. HIS MAILING ADDRESS IS NAVAL HOSPITAL GREAT LAKES ILLINOIS 60088, WARD 3 EAST. YOU ARE ASSURED THAT HE IS RECEIVING THE BEST MEDICAL CARE AND THAT YOU WILL BE ADVISED OF ANY SIGNIFICANT CHANGE IN HIS CONDITION. J W ALBRITTAIN REAR ADMIRAL MC USN COMMANDING OFFICER NAVHOSP GREAT LAKES ILL.

THIS IS TO CONFIRM THAT YOUR SON PRIVATE FIRST CLASS EARL A WOODALL USMC WAS INJURED 19 JUNE 1968 IN QUANG PROVINCE, REPUBLIC OF VIETNAM. HE SUSTAINED FRAGMENTATION WOUNDS TO BOTH LEGS. BOTH ARMS AND THE GROIN FROM A HOSTILE EXPLOSIVE DEVICE WHILE ON PATROL. HIS CONDITION AND PROGNOSIS WERE EXCELLENT. HE WAS TREATED AT THE STATION HOSPITAL DANANG, AND WAS MEDICALLY AIR EVACUATED TO THE US NAVAL HOSPITAL GREAT LAKES, ILLINOIS ON 23 JUNE 1968 FOR FURTHER TREATMENT. YOU WERE NOT NOTIFIED. INITIALLY YOUR SON WAS REPORTED AS TREATED AT THE STATION HOSPITAL DANANG AND RETURNED TO DUTY. ON 6 JULY 1968 A CHANGE WAS RECEIVED TO THE INITIAL REPORT WHICH REVEALED THAT YOUR SON WAS NOT RETURNED TO DUTY, BUT WAS RECEIVING TREATMENT AT THE STATION HOSPITAL DANANG WITH HIS CONDITION AND PROGNOSIS BOTH GOOD. WE REGRET THIS ERROR AND HOPE IT HAS NOT CAUSED YOU ANY UNDUE ANXIETY.

While in-country I watched many friends become maimed and an equal number die. It became hard to care or become close to anyone because it hurt so damn bad to lose someone that you went through all this hell with. But then it was also hell to detach myself from those around me.

I truly believe there must be a purpose for me—as I recall the times I lucked out and came out alive.

My life since coming home has not been easy either. I found it was not any easier to get close to people and I had an uncanny way of destroying any relationship before it got me first (get them before they get you). I felt estranged from the world, especially those I could not understand and likewise could not understand me. Although I wanted and desperately needed love, I fought any attempt to get close, like my own private war. Even now, after three years of marriage, it is still hard to believe it won't end too. My wife Robin Kaye feels I am a hero and I find it hard to see what she sees in me. She tries to understand what I feel and have experienced by reading and watching anything pertaining to Vietnam. I guess it's hard to live up to her ideas of what I am and I worry that I cannot do it. I know many of the problems we've had and overcome are due to me still being in Vietnam. I know with her as my ally I will win my own war since we weren't allowed to win the one in Vietnam.

Wesley Voeltz

I grew up in Minnesota. We moved a lot. High school days were good overall. I played sports and did as good as I could for grades. In 1968 I graduated.

I guess as long as I can remember I always wanted to join the Marine Corps, and I finally got my chance in December 1968. Boy! What an experience that was, when I stepped off that bus in San Diego. I will never forget what went through my mind. "What in the hell am I doing here? Why did I ever think this was what I wanted? It was never like this on TV!"

From then on it was "shut up and learn how to kill." Every time you had to sound off it was "Kill VC."

Well, boot camp was rough, but I made it through and spent the first year in the States. I finally got my orders to Nam in November of 1969. I had to sign a release form to go because my brother was already there. No one knew this back home and I didn't tell anyone because it was my decision and I wanted to do this. I felt it was something I had to do. I had no idea what I was going to do there, but with being in motor transport, I figured I wouldn't be in the bush with the rest of the grunts.

Well, two more weeks of combat training and we were on our way to Okinawa. From there we waited for our orders as to what part of Nam we were going. When the orders finally came, that's when I really got scared. About 4 in the morning we boarded a flight to Vietnam. We landed in Da Nang on January 13. One of seventy, I will never forget stepping off the plane and seeing 200 or more Marines waiting to take the flight back, short-timers going home. What a happy bunch of guys, all cheering and hollering, "Welcome to Nam, new guy."

We went into the flight terminal and proceeded to check in. I don't remember if I knew I was going to Chu Lai or if I found out then, but about an hour later I boarded a C-130 to my final destination. There were six or eight of us on the flight and each one scared to death. The flight was about forty-five minutes long, but seemed like three hours. We finally landed in Chu Lai and were unloading when old Charlie decided to see if he could scare a few people by starting to shell the base. Not more than two hours in-country and already we were in the bunker. I thought, "Boy, is this going to be a long thirteen months!"

I adapted to everything pretty well, I guess. I was assigned to the motor pool and got to know most of the people there. The hardest part was being the new guy. There were a few of us with only a few months to a few weeks. Boy, when the rockets came in, those short-timers always seemed to make it to the bunker first. That is something you learn with time.

The first couple of weeks were the toughest. There were rocket and mortar rounds almost every day and every night. We spent at least half of the night out on the perimeter because Old Charlie liked to sneak in and try to blow up the planes. There is nothing worse than a new kid on watch with an M-16. You start seeing things that aren't there, or were they? Anyway, Charlie laid off and that's when we got the word that the VC were starting to gear up for a big Tet Offensive. We heard rumors that it was going to be like the one in '68. Well, nothing happened. As a matter of fact, everything was quiet right through February, on into the first of March. Then I had to go on my first convoy to Da Nang. Everything went pretty well for the first ten to fifteen miles. We passed through two or three villages up Highway 1 to Da Nang.

I don't remember the village we had just passed through, but there were a lot of Vietnamese out in the rice paddies. When we heard gunfire, we were caught out in the open without any place to hide. So, we stepped on the gas and got the hell out of there as fast as we could. I found out later that one of the trucks had been hit but no one was hurt.

We got back to Chu Lai okay and things went pretty well. I felt fairly comfortable with the idea that Charlie was on the other side of the fence and the only way he was going to get to me was with mortar rockets. He kept letting us know he had a supply of them.

Memorial day 1970! Charlie must have saved every rocket in the country for us, because he started shelling us about 6 in the morning and kept it up most of the day and into the night. He knew just where he wanted his rockets to go. He walked them up and down our flight line for about twenty-four hours. We spent this time in bunkers or out on the perimeter. When we were finally given the okay to come back into camp, we were pretty shocked at what we saw. Charlie had hit three aircraft (F-14s) and had made quite a few holes in the ground. When we got back to our hooch, that's when we discovered that just two hooches down from us a hooch took a direct hit and four Marines were killed.

No matter how much you are taught to accept death it is never easy, especially when you see and talk to these people every day and then they are gone. We sat around and talked and tried to forget what happened. It took me about two days to get over the scare and the shock of what had happened. That's when I felt my shoulder hurting. I started checking it out and I discovered there was a cut on the back of my shoulder blade. One of the other guys asked what happened and I said I didn't know. I must have caught it on a nail when I ran into the bunker.

I think it was some time in September or the first part of October I got to see Gary for the first time in about three years. We were best friends in school and he had joined the Marine Corps about a year before I did. Boy, did we have a lot to talk about. We didn't have a lot of time together, a day, maybe two, but we made the most of it. We talked and partied all the time we spent together. Gary was on prisoner runs with the Army at this time. I envied him, but knew that my chances of ever being able to do this was slim to none.

Well, Gary left to go back to his unit and things were going okay. We left Chu Lai in October or November of 1970, I don't remember exactly. From there we went to Da Nang to Mag 16. There I met up with Gary again.

Da Nang was pretty quiet, not much incoming. I still had to pull guard duty. What excitement Charlie did not give, Gary and I made up for. Gary rotated back to the States in December. I know when he left I was a short-timer just waiting out my time—days. I think I had about three weeks left in-country when my name came up for door-gunner and I said, "No, thanks. I'm a short-timer and I'm going home in one piece."

I left Vietnam with the feeling that we'd done our part, but when I got back home I (with the exception of friends and family) found out what people really thought of a Vietnam veteran. I decided the best thing to do was to forget that it really happened. Sure, it will never be forgotten, but I never cared to talk much about it. It's easier to forget it.

I didn't fight any battles and I didn't go out into the bush, but I'm damn proud of the people that did. And all the people that lost their lives over there are heroes! No matter what the public may think. Everyone that served in Vietman did more than what was asked of them. A lot of them gave their lives; some gave their minds and are still giving.

I came home, got several jobs and thought I would just forget Vietnam. I started dating Gary's sister, Mary, and we were married. We have three sons, Mike, Shawn and Brian. I love my family very much. I work for IBM and Mary and I are foster parents. She is a good, caring person.

It is easy to say I will just forget Vietnam, but it is quite another to do it. A bond was made with the guys I served with. No matter if I ever see them or talk to them, it will always be there.

Larry Underhill

I was born in Austin, Minnesota in May, 1946. I went to school and graduated in the same town. I didn't get a chance to travel as much as most other people did in those days, like on vacations. We used to go up north to Mille Lacs Lake in the summer when I and my brother and sister got older and my dad finally found a good place for us to stay and do some fishing.

While in the latter years of high school I learned about world history and we studied about the war that was being waged in Vietnam and in several other places on the small earth at that time. This was in the school years of 1962-64. I read the reports from *NewsWeek, Time, Life* and *U.S. News & World Report* about the trouble that was increasing with every year that went by. I would give my reports in Social Studies on the problems in Southeast Asia. After graduation I enlisted in the Navy and by September of 1964 I was in boot camp in San Diego, California.

While going through boot camp they prepared us for war and everything that went along with it. But it could never have taught us about the war that was happening in Vietnam. They didn't teach us about how horrible and out of place jungle warfare was. I guess they didn't learn much from the Japanese during World War II and their capabilities in jungle warfare, or they didn't think that it would be the same type of war as with the infamous Japanese warrior who virtually lived off the jungle and got to know it better than any combat troops that were sent to get them out. That is what we were up against in Vietnam. They lived off the land; they terrorized the villages that were in the countryside; most of them came from these remote areas and they had hundreds of miles of tunnels that ran from North Vietnam into the south. How could you fight an enemy that would come out of the ground at night and strike and disappear just as fast as they appeared? They used suicide squads to drive into or to drive near military installations to kill. They didn't care how many civilians got killed or wounded in doing it. It proved a point that the sooner the Americans got out of Vietnam the sooner the killing would stop for them.

A friend of mine that is living here now was talking to me about how the Viet Cong would tell them that we were bad and not to help us. But when they bought something in the markets they would always buy things that were made in the U.S.A. She told me that they would laugh under their breaths at them because it didn't make sense to them that if we were so bad, why did they buy our goods? She also told me that the Viet Cong had tunnels under most of the military bases in South Vietnam. She was from a village south of Saigon called My Tho. She was telling me that the tunnels ran underneath the military bases in Long Binh. These tunnels had food, money, hospitals and living quarters for the forces that we were trying to fight. This war was not fought to win in the first place. We were being sent to our graves and for eternal hardships before entering the country.

My story begins while in my last two weeks of Radioman "A" School in San Diego. I and four of my other classmates were sent to the XO's office one morning and were told that our orders were for Vietnam. We were one of the first to be sent to Vietnam under the rank of E-5. We didn't know what our job was going to be and were told that we could leave our blue uniforms at home because of the extreme heat.

We were not given any material to read or to study that would give us an idea of what to expect when we arrived there, so we basically went there green. This was their first great error to the American forces sent there in the early years of the conflict in 1964 and 1965. We arrived at Tan Son Nhut airbase in Saigon on 13 July 1965. We were assigned to HEDSUPACT Saigon. This was to help install a communications station in Saigon for the U.S. Navy. It was located in the old commissary building in Saigon near the MACV compound and directly across from General Westmoreland's villa. We started to install the Teletype communications networks which took about four weeks. Everything was checked and rechecked. As a seaman apprentice, my first job was to make all necessary corrections in the communications manuals that we had at the time. Later on there were more. I then made seaman and my duties changed to running off messages and also a message clerk. I then made Radioman 3rd Class and was assigned to the service desk, and monitored the Teletypes from Guam and the Philippines. After receiving approval of my final security clearance I worked mainly in the back room of the communications center. I monitored the cut tape relays and cut tape of messages that were to be sent to MAVCOMSTAPHIL. It was in Saigon that I found out how horrible war can be, not only for the troops in the country but for the Saigon population. Taxi cabs were blowing up at least once a month, homemade claymore mines were being tied to bicycles and detonated from people hiding in an alley, kids blowing up in amongst American personnel, booby traps put in fuel tanks of trucks, filled with explosives being driven into the fronts of hotels and detonated, people riding by on their bicycles and dropping a handmade grenade at you. The problem I had with this is that they didn't care how many Vietnamese they took with them when they went on these suicide missions to kill Americans.

One incident that will stick in my mind forever is the morning I got up and decided to walk over to the Kyson Hotel for breakfast. I saw a truck coming my way down Tran Hung Dau Street, which is the main street in Saigon. It seemed strange to me to see a Vietnamese truck on the road at 0500. As it passed me I heard some shooting and as I turned around all I remember is a big flash of red. Then I remember someone asking me if I was all right. I was lying up against a cement fence about twenty-five feet from the sidewalk where I was walking. I remember that all I could think about was trying to remember where my hotel was. I was staying at the International Hotel about five or six blocks from the Kyson and it was on the way if you had to go to the American Hospital, and the clinic was just across the street from the hospital with a BOQ in back of the clinic. That street broke off to a Y from Tran Hung Dau. On the way back to my hotel I was tackled by someone in an Army uniform and was told that a fifty-five gallon claymore mine was found across the street in one of the many bars. It was disarmed and I finally got back to my room and laid down for just a minute and decided to try it again. Just as I walked out of the hotel a man rode by on a bike and threw a grenade. I turned around and ran back into the hotel and hid in a closet while the MP threw a sandbag on it and the Vietnamese Con Sat (White Mouse) shot the guy in the back five times. I went back to my room in sheer terror and was told to get to the top of the hotel immediately because a bomb had been discovered in a shop on the ground floor of the hotel and it was directly under my room. I was on the third floor. This all happened in a two-and-a-half-hour period.

I remember at work in the comm. center in the mornings especially, the windows shaking. Then we would say "another bomb going off." This was the most difficult thing to deal with as a young person in that it was so congested you were not safe anywhere in that city. There was a different smell for every one or two blocks you traveled. Garbage piles were almost two stories high until the Army came in and hauled it away. They found people, babies, and kids buried in the heaps of garbage. The people didn't care about their own people no less us, the invaders of their country. The student population and the Buddhists didn't want us there. They used to write on the streets "Americans Go Home" and the Vietnamese National Police would be out on the street painting over it very quickly with tar. I told a Vietnamese friend of mine, who later saved my life while there again in 1968 during Tet, that we didn't want to be there anymore than they wanted us to be there but we had no choice; the government said we had to be there to help the Vietnamese. Looking back to that day, what a waste of time it was to try to help a people that didn't care one way or the other. The only people that cared were the military, the Vietnamese politicians and businessmen. And it did help the American economy recover. Nearly everything that was used by the civilian people and military people had to be leased from companies owned by Lady Bird Johnson. This was told to me by a civilian construction worker—that he was not allowed to take any of his personal tools over there—that they all had to be leased from a company in Texas that was owned by Lady Bird. There is another reason they didn't want the war to end. There was too much money to be made by making it last. The high-ranking officers in the different services were happy because they could get medals, rank and publicity from the only or last war that they would see or be able to participate in.

The United States had to fight according to the Geneva Convention, but the North Vietnamese and Viet Cong didn't recognize the Geneva Convention. This was what tied your hands when it came to real warfare. World War I and II had no such policy that you could only shoot the enemy if you were fired upon first, or couldn't carry a loaded weapon into a military compound. This was a total joke. War is war. You must fight by the enemy's rules if you want to ever win.

I was transferred to the Delta region for just a short time. This was probably the worst place I was ever in. There don't seem to be many documentaries on this subject that I can remember seeing. When you are traveling down a river in a river boat and there is shooting from both sides of the river, and you call for air support, they start shelling you because they see something in the water. The people along the shores in the villages were not too friendly because they had no idea what was going on half of the time. They didn't know who was the president of Vietnam at the time or any other time in their lives. Most people didn't know what their money looked like. The Delta region was a forgotten hell hole.

I remember watching General Westmoreland sitting on the veranda of his villa in the morning. He made a near fatal error in the judgment of the Viet Cong on at least two occasions. The first one was when he stated that the VC didn't have the firepower to reach into the city of Saigon. An officer that I knew and used to bring messages to was killed right after that comment, during a parade, when rockets were fired in to the center of town. The second time was when four or five rockets exploded in the trees that surrounded MACV headquarters and just about took him out.

From the Delta region, I then was assigned to Advisory Team 35, Coastal Surveillance Center in Nha Trang; and was assigned to the Communication Advisor to the Vietnamese Coastal Groups in Vietnam. There is another part of the Vietnam War that was not covered by any media. I to this day don't think that anyone knew we were there other than our direct headquarters. I was assigned to Coastal Group 27, located in Phan Rang. Actually it was on the coast at the mouth of a large bay in Ninh Chu, which was about seven miles from Phan Rang. When I landed at the airbase I asked how to get to the Navy base. Nobody knew that there were any Navy people located in the area. An Army sergeant overheard me talking to this dizzy Air Force sergeant, and told me that they had some Navy people living at their compound and that he would take me to them. This was near the end of my second consecutive tour and at the end of my third and final tour in Vietnam. The duties on the Junk Base, as it was known, was to install, maintain and improve the communications between the Vietnamese bases and the Americans. The average number of American advisors to a Coastal Group was five or six. So the numbers were very low and the total number of Vietnamese usually averaged seventy-five to ninety Vietnamese.

We had to go on patrols with the Vietnamese to patrol the coastline. We had almost 100 miles of coastline to patrol. This was one of the longest patrols in Vietnam. We checked fishing boats, trawlers, sampans and basket boats for weapons, current registration papers and ID papers. The patrols lasted anywhere from two days to almost thirty days. We would go on search and destroy missions, recon with the Marines; gunfire spotting and set up ambush teams with the Vietnamese Navy. Everything we did was with the Vietnamese and very little with the Americans. The only time we used other American forces, they came from one of the other Coastal Groups and the PCFs from Cam Ranh Bay. We were located south of Cam Ranh Bay.

I did keep a log of the activities while on patrol with the Vietnamese. I will only tell a few of the average missions that were experienced while at the base. I did travel extensively throughout the country to different coastal groups checking, repairing and installing new equipment at almost all the other groups from north of Da Nang to Vung Tau, which was near Saigon. It was once known as the Riviera of Southeast Asia. Here are but a few patrols that I participated in while in CG 27. "My first patrol—Aug. 19, 1967. We detained five people that had no papers or invalid papers. Returned to base with the detainees. Aug. 20—underway at 0800. On station 1000. Stopped four junks and detained three people that had no ID papers. 2000—had to go south and anchor due to high winds. Detainees were lost over the side. Not sure what happened to them. Continued patrolling the next day in the region near Hon Da. Aug. 25th—underway at 0600 and searched total of seven junks and took another detainee. We transferred the detainee to another junk that was called in for assistance from the junk base. We anchored for the night. Continued patrol on the 26th and 27th of Aug. No incidents to report. Returned to base on the 28th of August."

The first patrol was probably the best experience in how we were looked at by the Vietnamese. I was told that the Vietnamese would test me on this first patrol to see if I really was interested in what I was trying to do for them. At the first meal they gave me a bowl of rice and then put a fish head in it. I was then supposed to take the fish head and eat it along with the rice. It took me just a minute to decide that I would need to eat that fish head so I did, and it wasn't as bad as I thought it would be. Then it was everything. The Vietnamese didn't mind if I went along. As a matter of fact they used to ask for me to go with them. We had to buy our C-rations from the Air Force at the price of $10 a case or from the Army for $12. So we ate with the Vietnamese. I didn't care to much for C-rations that were canned in 1953. It was at this time that the Vietnamese base commander told me that to be safe in the area I should keep with the Vietnamese and not stay too close to the Americans. So I did just that. About the only Americans that were there were the Army's Advisory Team 35 and the civilians from AB&T just up the road from us.

"On September 2, 1967 we were underway at 0830 and at 1025 we detained four without proper IDs and again at 1200 we detained one more person that didn't have an ID card. We radioed the base for a boat to come to our location and get the detainees. At 1500 we were underway for Mui Dinh and at 1814 arrived at the salt flats at Ca Na. We patrolled in that area until 1910, when we noticed trucks and other vehicles being stopped on the highway. We observed two individuals taking money from the drivers of the vehicles and the Vietnamese NCO ordered the 50-cal and the mortar to be put on deck. The NCO then fired three shots into the air with his M-1. The two individuals ran up the mountain behind them. We then directed our fire at the two going up the mountain. We then went ashore and searched the side of the mountain and found the two VC tax collectors. We searched the cave and found large sums of money and food, and there were four tunnels leading into the mountain that we didn't follow. They were going in different directions from the coast. It looked as though one was going to Phan Rang and the others were going somewhere else, but they all lead to different places. They were used, I guess, to supply money to the forces in the jungle. They were all accessible from underground. We took everything and went back on board the boat. Back to base at 0730. September 4, underway again. Searched five junks and detained two suspected VC. The two were then interrogated by the Vietnamese NCO on the boat. They would not talk and eventually died from the interrogation methods. At 1340 we were underway and received small-arms fire at BC-124. One SVN was wounded with two suspected VC killed. Small-arms fire then stopped at 1800 from BC-124. At 2008 we searched BC-124 and the bodies had been carried off. We anchored at 2340 and returned to base at 0620.

"On September 6, we were underway to the bridge at Ta Hai. We heard small-arms and automatic-weapons fire and the 155s from the RVN base started firing then suddenly stopped. Radioed AT-35 to find out why they had stopped firing. We arrived on station at 0500 and waited for the VC sapper team. We exchanged fire with the VC with six casualties. We could not get an accurate body count of the VC. We then departed the boat and surveyed the damage to the two villages. The VC destroyed several houses in one village and killed several of the villagers. We returned to base at 0840. At 1000 we were underway for a two-day patrol in the area that was thought to be where the VC were being kept. The two-day patrol was without incident and we tested all the weapons on board.

"On September 8, we arrived on station to assist in a Medcap with the Army Advisory Team 35 medic, and returned to base at 1835. We were again underway at 0600 on September 10, 1967 for Tan Thanh and Mui Dinh. We arrived on station at 1048 and received automatic and small arms fire from CN-258 AB-459. We returned fire. It seemed to last forever—they are not stopping at any cost. They wanted our asses. Radioed back to base for help and air support. It seemed to take forever for help to arrive. At 1520 firing stopped. We checked our wounded and then went ashore for a body count and to gather personal data on the VC. Five males dead, three wounded and later died. Two VC women were killed, one approximately sixteen and one about thirty-five. At 2045 we were underway back to base.

"Underway again, September 11, we were going out for at least ten days on this one to patrol north to Nha Trang. We stopped several fishing trawlers that were Chinese. We were out to sea too far to draw any type of fire other than another boat.

"September 26, we are underway at 1030 for the northern patrol areas. We checked eight sampans and detained five people without proper ID at 1220. At 1320 we received five rounds of small-arms fire from a basket boat. Returned fire from the 30-cal. One VC killed; the other was wounded; he said that they were collecting money from the many fishing boats in the area. We patrolled until 1820. We anchored and had boiled squid and rice. 2000 we were underway again. At 2030 we received several rounds of automatic weapons fire and small-arms fire from the beach area. Returned fire without casualties and no body count. 0830 return to base."

This was what was happening to the Navy personnel that were stuck in these small areas in the middle of nowhere. We didn't get to see a USO show unless it was close. And even then we probably didn't know about it. We very seldom went to the Air Force base other than to get things for the house that we were building on the base. We became friends with the civilians that ran the Red Horse Division, supplying the base with ten articles—they always gave us ten requisition slips. There were nothing but numbers on them. The guards at the front gate would count the articles then the requisitions. If they matched they would let us go. It worked every time.

We went so far as to steal the colonel's ceiling tile on one occasion. We were caught once but went back and got it. The colonel asked the chief what we were doing and the chief told him we were taking his tile. The chief said that anytime they saw our jeep with the eyes painted on the hood, and we had the trailer hooked up to it, we were stealing. The colonel thought it was a joke. I guess the joke was on him in the end. We got his tile.

I remember when two Red Cross workers came to the base. They were there because of the two lieutenant JGs that were there. Nothing more. They didn't seem to care that the three enlisted people there would have liked to have talked to them too. The chief gunnersmate and I had baked an apple pie from a No. 10 can of apples and we made the dough from scratch. And we then baked it in a cake pan. We offered the two women a piece of pie and they really had a good time seeing the pie come from a cake pan. They said they were having trouble with window peekers on the hill where they lived on the air base, so I told them that we could go up there with them to make sure that it didn't happen anymore. That is when the senior advisor told us that we had better things to do outside. We never saw them again or had the opportunity to talk to them again.

I had an opportunity to go to the hospital for a few weeks when I contracted malaria. I really liked the nurses that were serving hard duty in that country. I don't think they knew what they were in for before coming in-country. They were fun to talk to and it seemed as though they knew you or had lived next door to you in the States. I was probably fortunate in that I didn't get hurt bad enough that I couldn't take care of it. The Vietnamese really looked out for us enlisted. We were good company, tried to learn their language and customs and had a great time with them on duty and off duty.

I had to go up north to Da Nang. I think it was Coastal Group 24 or 25. I was there to replace a guy that had been wounded. They didn't go on patrols too often there. The VC had come from the hills and tried to overrun the base for three days in a row. I remember it was awful hard on the 30-cal that I had to use. The barrels were burning out as fast as I could screw them on. Then it suddenly stopped. I then left Da Nang and when the C-130 was taking off there were rockets exploding in front, beside and behind the plane as it took off. I again wondered what the hell I was doing there. I did that quite a bit. I was there for three years and was ready to leave at least 300 times. I did not go on R&R because

I wasn't sure if I would come back or not. While in Phan Rang we did take some unauthorized R&R with the Australians. If they had a Caribou going to Australia they would get us on the radio and we would take the trip.

I didn't take a leave in the three years to go back home, for fear of the troubles back in the States. They wouldn't let us bring our weapons home with us, so I felt unsafe in coming home. When I did come home I did have my M-14 with me.

I remember when AB&T was trying to build another landing zone for ships on the beach and the Caterpillar driver was pushing sand out in the water. He was really moving, then suddenly the Cat was up in the air, then the front end went down in the water, and it started spraying water all over the place and the driver was trying to get out of it, and he finally got off the Cat and it went down in about six fathoms of water. That was pretty fun to watch from the junk boat.

There were many instances that come to mind, one of them was in the afternoon an LST had landed to unload some stuff at AB&T and I saw this guy dancing on a picnic table. I thought I recognized him from somewhere and sure enough it was a friend from boot camp. He was stationed on the LST. He gave me a tour of the ship and then I gave him a tour of our base. I remember him saying, "I'm glad your here and not me." The next day they were gone and I never did write to him or him to me. I used to wait up to three months for mail and some of the mail never did get to me.

I participated in an operation that destroyed a village in the southern patrol area. The name of the village was Tan An Thanh. We had boarded the junks at 0200 and we were on station at 0400. The Vietnamese landed the boats on the beach and our boat had gone in sideways and was caught by a large breaker. We struggled to get off the boat. I remember thinking to myself that I would wait until the starboard side went down to jump off, because it was too far to jump if the side was out of the water going up. So I waited for the starboard side to go down and decided it was time to go. I thought it would only be a two to three foot drop, but in fact it was about five feet into water that was over my head. I had the M-14 and 100 rounds of ammo, four grenades and a PRC-25 on my back. I went down like a rock. I got on the beach and cleaned the handset out for the radio, and helped several others get off the boat, including the senior advisor. He handed me his 30-cal carbine and the boat just about crushed me. We walked about four miles inland to the outside of the village and started firing. It was all over at 1000. We went back and started to take things off the boat, which was submerged and filling with sand. We got the armament and ammunition off the boat and had to send for a PCF to pick us up. There were five of us from that boat. The PCF could only get in so close, so we had to swim out to it. I didn't really think I could make it with everything. The only thing that I was missing was most of the ammo and the grenades. I made it to the boat and was I happy. I told myself never again. I have had a fond dislike of swimming ever since. I can't swim in a pool—I'm allergic to the chlorine. But I don't like lake or river swimming.

We went back the next day to retrieve the engine from the junk boat with a Huey. It was too much for it so they sent a CH-47 down to get it. Overnight the VC had rigged a booby trap to the boat with a wire running from the beach to the boat. We had a guy that was with the CIA that had discovered the trip-wire on the beach. If it wouldn't have been for him we would have been killed. We got the engine out of the boat and used the VC charge plus the C-4 that we took with us and blew it up. There were intelligence reports that said the VC were going into the village to get water, that the only thing left standing was the two water wells in the village. So I was ordered to go to the air base and got poison for the wells. I got about fifteen pounds of rat poison and put it into two gunney sacks, flew down in a chopper and put them into the wells. The report said that the contaminated water had stopped the insurgence of the VC to the village for the water. I have always wondered how many I killed by putting the poison in the water.

People ask me if I remember my first kill and what it felt like. My first kill was a male about sixteen years old. We were checking papers on five people of a fishing boat, and in the process of them getting the papers out of the bamboo container, the boy threw a grenade on the boat. It bounced off the deck into the water. To tell you how crazy this was, there were six Vietnamese and me on the boat. We had guns trained on them while the Vietnamese NCO checked the papers. They tried to kill us even when they were guarded. I shot the boy in the chest, neck and left side of the head. At that time I was using duplex rounds in the M-14. And we sprayed the rest of the people. It was over in a few seconds. I guess it didn't bother me too much or at all because it was over so fast and it was them or us. Being with the Vietnamese, we always shot first and fed the sharks later. If the boats didn't stop with the three warning rounds they were sunk. It was as simple as that. The second and third kills were just as easy. We had gone into a village when the night before the VC had taken the village chief hostage for the *sone*. They said if the *sone* gave himself up that they would let them go. They did. They cut their heads off and placed them belly down on their mats and placed their heads on their ankles. We went on from the beach and had to camp that night about 300 yards from the beach. We dug in and went to sleep, if that's what you called it. The next morning we had gotten up and looked around and realized that we had dug our foxholes in an old cemetery. We put everything back in where they were dug up and left. As we entered the village some children came out to greet us. One of the Vietnamese officers shot one of the older girls as they approached. We didn't know what to do and we asked him why he did it. His reply was that her tits were too big. We examined her and found two trip-wires running up her sleeves and that two grenades had been placed in her make-shift bra. Her purpose was to kill as many of us as she could. As we walked into the village we noticed four men walking out on the beach. We went to the house where the village chief and his son were lying and helped bury them. Then we set up a command post on a hill where an old temple once stood. All there was left was about one to two feet of wall. I looked for the four men that had been walking out of town and couldn't see them. Then I saw them looking at us from the other side of a huge rock from the beach. I told the guy from the CIA that they were down there watching us, so we went down after them. They were brought up to the hill and placed in four corners after they were tied to posts. I had to keep them from talking, so I would throw rocks at them if they started to talk to one another. I heard a noise coming up the hill and reacted by firing in the direction of the noise. I saw an old man flying down the hill. He was supposedly the father of one of the men we had captured. A chopper had come to the location and picked up the detainees.

The third kill came when the Army, while pleasure cruising in the gulf, had picked up a sampan with an old man in it who didn't have the correct papers. I had to take the old man to the AB&T pier, where his sampan was moored and take it to the base. I was in the bow of the boat and he was working the rudder and we were on our way to the base. It was getting dark and hard to see. I felt the boat rock and looked back and saw the old man reaching for me. I shot him point-blank in the upper lip with a 45. I realized that he had lost the rudder and was reaching for it, maybe, and I had shot him. What really made me angry is that I lost my Timex trying to get him back in the sampan.

We had caught a larger trawler off the coast and had to fire on it. The crew beached it. What was left of the crew had abandoned it. Only one got away. The rest—seven in all—were killed. We went on board the trawler and there were new AK-50s, B-40 rocket launchers, and radar equipment on board. The trawler was powered by two 2500 HP diesel West German engines and the screws were in excess of a three-foot radius and were made for speed.

I would accompany the medic from the Army Advisory Team located near our base. We would go to a village and treat the kids that had sores and were sick. I helped deliver two babies while on two separate medcaps. One village that we went to, we were told to leave at separate medcaps. One village that we went to, we were told to leave at 1800 because the VC would come down from the mountains and take the young women and drink. So we returned to the base and then we mortared the hills that night. We did quite a bit of that when I was in Phan Rang. The base commander said it was to keep the VC moving.

I went to the Air Force base in Phan Rang once to get some stuff, and left with a movie projector. The next week I went back to see if they would give me movies. The supply sergeant said "No," he could not give us the movies. He then told me if he could get a black beret like mine he would see to it that we would get movies every Wednesday. I told him that they were hard to get because you had to be affiliated with the coastal groups to get one. I went uptown in Phan Rang and bought a beret and device for it and took it back to him the next day and he kept his promise. Every Wednesday we got a movie. There was a merchant ship that used to anchor off the coast from AB&T, the MS Chevron. We would get movies from them also. The chief and I would go aboard so he could play cards and I would go up to the radio shack and talk on the radio, or listen to music. We didn't have the luxury of radio there. There was radio and a TV station in Saigon. The TV was broadcast from a Navy plane from Guam in the early beginning. It would fly around and broadcast. The thing I didn't like about radio was the guy they made a movie on, Good Morning Viet Nam. What was good about it? It was hot, raining, muddy and some gook was always trying to kill you. I remember listening to Hanoi Hanna when I was stationed in Saigon. I would tune her in on the R-390 and listen to her daily synopsis of current events and she had better music. I could tune in to stations on the west coast on certain nights. When I left Saigon the radio stayed there. I really missed it. We were cut off from everything.

I was on missions to Pleiku, into Cambodia when we weren't supposed to be there, and as far south as An Thoi and as far north as north of Da Nang. I traveled by boat, jeep, truck or plane. Even took Air Vietnam, or as we used to say, Air Nguc Mam. It was quite an experience for me. I flew missions dropping leaflets over special targeted villages telling the Viet Cong that if they would surrender their weapons they would have complete amnesty, which was only part true—they would get money but they were sent to islands off the coast of Vietnam. That's where they had their prisoner of war camps. It was almost impossible to escape from them. The waters were infested with sharks and jellyfish. You could leave but it was the swim of three miles that would kill you.

On one occasion our intelligence officer and his counterpart had gone into the village of Ca Na early in the morning to get information secretly. A PC had let them off in a rubber life boat and had them on radar when they beached. They were there for about an hour, and had them on radar on the way back, then lost them. The PC radioed us to see if we could send a couple of junks down there to help them search for them. We set out for the southern patrol zone and looked for them for almost three hours. Then the sea started to get rough and we decided if the boat went down they didn't have a chance in hell of surviving with all the sharks that were in the water. The number of sharks made us think they had capsized. The chief then looked out to sea to see if he could see anything and sure enough every once in awhile he could see this little black dot bob up in the horizon. The PC took off to see if it was them. They returned and it had been them. They were four miles out to sea. The current had gotten so strong on the way back that they could not control the lifeboat and drifted past the PC without ever seeing it. It was dark and the Swift Boat didn't have it's running lights on at the time for security reasons. They were dehydrated and sunburned but okay. It was an almost fatal mistake on the parts of the intelligence officer and his counterpart to have done that with only one boat in the area. He wasn't too swift in the first place. This stunt just confirmed it to us.

The 51st Infantry used to guard the beach area for AB&T. That's where the barges carrying bombs and shells, jet starters, etc., were off-loaded. They were not the brightest people in the world either. They had received a new 50-cal and wanted me to get a junk to take them out to sea so they could practice shooting it. So I called the LT in charge and told him I had a boat that would take us out. We took the boat to the AB&T side and they boarded with the machine gun and a fifty-five gallon barrel. We went out about a mile or so and they dropped the barrel over the side and we drifted a bit then they started shooting at it. The swells were about three feet high and they had lots of problems hitting the barrel. Either they were shooting into the water directly or into the air. I tried to show them how to do it but the sergeant knew all about how to do it and he wasted 200 rounds on the water and air. The LT didn't do much better, so the two Vietnamese and I sank it with the 30-cal that was mounted on the stern of the boat. They then had to take grenade practice because there were PFCs that had to qualify. The LT asked me to throw the first grenade and they were supposed to hit my target. I think he wanted to humiliate me because of the barrel incident. So I pulled the pin and threw that damn thing so far and high I thought it would go off in the air. The lieutenant wanted to know if I would reconsider going into the Army. I said, "What for?" The sergeant asked me how I could throw it so far and I told him it was no different than throwing a baseball. He said that the Army didn't want them to throw it like a baseball and I told him if I threw it the Army way the enemy was too close to me. He laughed and said, "You're right." And I said, "I know I am."

There were a lot of good men there. I didn't have too many friends while in the field, because as I said earlier, I went with the Vietnamese or I traveled with several Vietnamese from the junk base to wherever I had to go. I did speak pretty good Vietnamese—it was a priority of mine. It was hard to try and get them to do something if all they said was "okay" at everything you said in English. One of my Vietnamese friends traveled with two hand grenades on him. One for him and one for his wife. He told me that if the VC ever captured them they would cut his head off and rape his wife many times then cut off her head too. So he preferred suicide rather than getting caught. He was later killed in a firefight. I took his wife to Nha Trang so she could get all the paperwork completed from the U.S. Navy and Vietnamese Navy. He was killed in a U.S. Navy-led operation on a VC-held village. They gave her some money, and we both flew back to Phan Rang. She later killed herself. He was so nice and so was she. She was so pretty, just like a picture, but there was no future for her without her husband.

We had lost the Vietnamese warrant officer and our engineman in an accident with the jeep. It was run over by an earth mover on the air base. The Vietnamese call me lucky, because I had been there for so long and still survived. There are lots of moments that I say to myself how really lucky was I? Because I had a hard time getting a job, because I was there, I couldn't tell people where I had been for fear that I would get into trouble with the crazies here. I was a nervous wreck. I had nightmares all the time. I jumped into shrubs at loud noises. I can't enjoy fireworks on the Fourth of July with my children and wife. They say they can understand but they will never fully understand why I can't listen to them.

When I went to Cam Ranh Bay to come back to the States, the jet I got on had round-eye stewardesses and they asked me questions and I had a difficult time understanding them. I didn't sleep at all on the trip back. We landed in Japan and I walked around for about fifteen minutes and was ready to go back to Vietnam. We landed in Tacoma, Washington an hour before I left Cam Ranh Bay. It took twenty-three hours to fly back to the States and I asked the stewardess if it was safe for me to leave the plane. And she just looked at me and said that she was sorry for what we had gone through. She asked me how long I had been there and I told her three years and she sat and talked to me for quite a while.

We got off the plane and had to take a taxi to Pier 91 in Seattle. There were six of us that had to report there. The taxi actually charged us each $25 for the trip. Shit, we couldn't even get a free taxi ride to Seattle. I didn't have a uniform other than my Marine tiger cammies. The XO started in on me, asking me why I wasn't in the Uniform of the Day and why I was out of uniform and where my dress shoes were. I told him that I had been in Vietnam and he said that it was only a year tour of duty and that I should have had the Uniform of the Day on. I told him to take another look at my orders. He apologized to me and told me he would take me down to the DX to get new uniforms. I had to pay for them. So I wrote home for some money for uniforms. I then went to chow and discovered what milk was and what real food was, and being a petty officer, I could get seconds and thirds of everything. I grew from 160 pounds to 255 pounds in the three months I was there. They tried me as a brig guard at first. I had to guard three prisoners while they played basketball and did their exercises. The one told me that he was going to escape and kill me with my shotgun. I told him to go ahead and try. I really wanted him to try to take the gun away from me so I could blow his brains out all over the cement court. They then made me a brig runner. I would travel somewhere that had a prisoner and would bring him back to Seattle. That was pretty good. I enjoyed that. I had to pick up a kid in Idaho that had gone AWOL from San Diego. I had a good talk with the kid and we had a mutual understanding. He didn't want to go to Vietnam. Then I told him that I had been there for three years and I came back, and explained to him that four years in the Navy was easy to do. He returned to San Diego and I don't know what happened to him after that.

I remember when the U.S. brought over the PACVs. They were the air boats. These things even scared me half to death, because I had never seen or heard of them before. They would come from the sea and would go over land and end up racing across rice fields. The water was going everywhere and the Vietnamese that were working in the fields got just as scared and started running away from that monster from the sea, and would eventually get killed. It was great for flushing out the enemy in the rice paddies. They didn't stand much of a chance against that thing. They discontinued its use as far as I remember.

The other thing I liked to watch was Puff The Magic Dragon or, as we called it on the radio, just "Puff." It had great firepower and I remember the low long roar and the spiraling red tongue of the Puff. And then there was Snoopy—the rockets and mini-guns were devastating to the enemy. That was one airship you didn't want to make a mistake and shoot at. The Seabees in Nha Trang had a deuce-and-a-half called the War Wagon. This thing had no windows except for little gun ports cut out of the armor plating. The whole truck was armor plated. It had quad-50s in the back on the bed of the truck. It was quite a truck. I remember when I was in Nha Trang, shooting at the two lights on Buddha's head. There was a huge statue of Buddha on this hill and we would take shots at the lights on his head. Mainly it was for something to do while you baked in the sun all day. This was the most boring time I spent while in Vietnam. The whole town was off-limits to GIs because of the upcoming Tet new year of 1968. There were skirmishes throughout the town every now and then. I had to go to Saigon during the 1968 Tet Offensive, and was that thrilling. I landed at Tan Son Nhut airbase the day before Tet and checked in at COMNAVFORV, where I first worked in 1965. It had changed a little. Then I went to my hotel. It was the International again. That was a coincidence. I was ending my third year of duty just as I had began.

That night I was awakened by three loud explosions. I got up and looked out the window and saw rockets flying at another BOQ just down the street. I grabbed my rifle and ran to the roof of the hotel and saw three people on another building roof about two blocks away firing the rockets. I started shooting at them and realized that they would be firing them at me if I didn't stop, so I stopped shooting and immediately left the hotel. This was at about 0300. I got back to COMNAVFORV and stayed there until morning and I then went to Cholon, a suburb of Saigon. I had a difficult time finding a taxi that would take me there so I ended up paying almost $150 to get to the bridge. I had to cross the bridge on foot and I took care of my business and was coming back over the bridge and bullets started flying and whizzing around me. I ran over the bridge and ran down the street to the Vietnamese Naval Headquarters and stayed there for almost three hours until things quieted down somewhat. I then got back to my hotel room, got my things and went to the Miami Bar across the street from my hotel. A good friend of mine, who was Chinese, owned the bar and I hadn't seen him in almost two years. I went in and told him I needed a safe place to stay and that I was leaving on Friday. He then told me that I could stay with his family until I was ready to go back to Phan Rang. I flew back on Friday and was so ready to leave Saigon that I took a flight to Phan Rang on Air Viet Nam airlines. It was the only thing that was leaving early enough for me. All I remember saying to myself is that I had to leave Saigon and get back to the field where it was a bit safer.

I remember the first Tet celebration I participated in. It was in 1965, when I first got there. They were selling firecrackers and flying kites and shooting firecrackers from long sticks with rubber bands and the kids of Saigon had fun too. Some of the Americans were buying firecrackers and shooting them off. They had firecrackers that ranged from about one inch to almost six inches. I remember a guy in a jeep threw one of the big ones out of the jeep into the street and it blew up another jeep, and someone dropped one out of his hotel window and a guy down below caught it and it blew off his arm. It seems as though the

Vietnamese had been selling fireworks that were loaded with plastique. They were not used by too many Americans after that. MACV told everyone not to buy fireworks from the economy.

Tet was a day of celebration for the Vietnamese people and I remember one night the senior advisor of our coastal group went over and told his Vietnamese counterpart that he didn't want them to start shooting that night. The Vietnamese lieutenant looked at me when he left and sent 200 rounds through the 30-cal they had set up in the back of the compound just to spite what the American officer had said to him. There wasn't much love lost between the Vietnamese and American officers. The Vietnamese didn't care for them at all, especially on our base. The two officers that we had on the base very seldom went on patrol or made recon flights or anything else that may have endangered their lives. It was pretty pathetic. The Vietnamese didn't want them to be with them anywhere. We enlisted *men* were more like them and we tried to do as much as possible to include the Vietnamese in what we were doing for them. They had more desire to do things with us than with the two officers that stayed hidden. Whenever we needed something the enlisted did the job. Our senior advisor went to Nha Trang and told them that he had stepped on a pungi stake while on one of our many operations. I heard the commander say to him on the one occasion that they had flown down to Phan Rang, how his foot was after stepping on that pungi stake. I let the asshole have his moment of glory and didn't tell the commander that he had not stepped on one, and in fact that he was lying to him. I think he was waiting for me to say something to the commander about him not really stepping on a pungi stake. We did put a scorpion in his boot one morning. He did have enough sense to empty his boots before putting them on. We thought that he would just put them on and get stung. Then he would have had a good excuse for limping the next time he went to Nha Trang.

I remember another lieutenant that eventually went to one of the RAG groups in the Delta. He kind of reminded me of Ensign Parker on "McHale's Navy." He tore up a boat and took out a dock and eventually blew up a boat trying to get a VC flag from the water. It had a charge under it. He would come to Saigon looking like John Wayne and he had two pearl-handled revolvers and the grips were turned to the outside. I think he thought he was General Patton. The only thing—Patton had ivory grips on his revolvers. I'm not sure if he made it out alive or not.

I did take a trip through the Delta on a PBR. We had to go into Cambodia to check the supply route of the VC going into Cambodia. The Cambodians that lived in the villages on the river were not pleased to see us and they didn't know who we were or what we were. We stayed on the river and came back after three days on the river. I didn't care for that duty at all. I was thrilled to be going back to Phan Rang.

When I was in Phan Rang, the base was about seven miles southeast of Phan Rang. The dirt road that we would travel on was mined all the time. It was the road that was being used by trucks to carry the bombs and stuff from the beach of AB&T to the Air Force base. There was a mountain of rocks just on the way to Ninh Chu. It had an artesian well in it and the girls would fill up their two water cans there and carry them home. This mountain had to be at least 300 feet high. There was a hill of salt that was at least four stories high in Ca Na. This is where the salt was taken after it had been harvested from the salt flats all around Phan Rang.

Da Lat was the most interesting place I was at. It was like the corn belt in the U.S. They could grow everything there. That is where almost all the fruit came from. I think this was the area most needed by the North Vietnamese. There was sand on the beaches so white and fine that I was told that the Japanese would export it for grinding lenses. You could throw it in the air and it was almost like dust. I was ready to invest in some beachfront property when the war was over and to live there. I really liked it in that one area. For one reason or another the VC didn't care for that part of the country. And it was in one of our free fire zones set up by the Vietnamese. This meant that if anyone was caught in that area they were shot with no warnings.

On one of our many patrols to the southern sector we would run across big turtles in the water. They would be pretty big and so I wanted to catch one. The Vietnamese said that we couldn't because they were sacred. Then they told me about one of their early emperors, who had to escape the invading Chinese. The only place he could go was to a small island off the coast. The story goes that he was seen walking on the water to this small island when in fact he was standing on the back of a large turtle. So, the Buddhists hold the turtle in sacred esteem.

We once had to enter a village from the beach. It was located in the middle of a long narrow bay. When we entered the bay there was an old rusted tanker sitting aground in the middle of the bay. We entered the village and started talking to the village chief. That was when we found out that the tanker in the bay had been shot up by the Americans during World War II and it was Japanese. They took it into the bay to repair it but couldn't. They have been there ever since. They could never get back to Japan because nobody knew where they were. They were probably listed as killed. There wasn't much to remind them of Japan and the war except for the swords that still hung on the walls of their houses. From what we could get from the men, there were 220 men on the tanker when it went aground and there were only fifteen of the original still alive in the village. They were quite happy where they were. Besides, it would have been a dishonor for them to return to Japan. And yes, they knew the war was lost for them and had ended.

They just didn't want to leave the paradise that they had found in Vietnam. I don't remember if I wrote home about that or not. I may have because it would have interested my dad because he had been in that area during the big war. My dad used to tell me that he was in "the big one" and I kept telling him that I was in the longest one. Then we would laugh.

I was at the terminal in Saigon one time waiting for a flight out. I had to get radio parts down there and this kid came up to me and said didn't you get John Wayne's autograph? I told him no that I didn't know that he was there, and he said that he walked right past me. All I can remember is seeing this real tall person in jungle fatigues go by. I thought that he may have been an officer or something. I never looked at his face. But by then it was no big deal to me, I guess. In the back of my mind I just really didn't care to bother someone for an autograph. And to me they were just another person. I wonder if it bothers them that they are not recognized by someone when they are seen in public. I hope not.

We took a drive to Cam Ranh Bay one time from Phan Rang to pick up our pay and to get a new jeep. On the way we had picked up a Korean that was also on his way to Cam Ranh. We got behind a slow-moving truck and the Korean took his M-16 and shot at the back of the truck. The driver then moved to the side of the road so we could pass, and as we passed the truck the Korean shot the driver in the head. He told us that the trucks would move slow so the VC could get a good rocket shot or small-arms fire at us in the jeep. When we arrived at Cam Ranh we picked up our pay and went to see about a new jeep. We found some nice new lSl's that had the switch and we parked our jeep in it's place and took one of the new lSl's. Our old jeep had the motor mounts busted from the harrowing drives from Phan Rang. It was nice to have a new jeep. So we painted eyes on the front of the hood and it was unofficially ours in an official way. That's how we had to do things there because it was nearly impossible to get anything from anyone if you were in the Navy. There were so many things that happened to me while I was there. The events that I have written are not in sequence, but are written in the order that I could remember them. There are many things that I can't remember and probably will never remember that happened while I was there.

When I returned back to the States, I decided to take two weeks leave and go home for the first time in three years. My mom was waiting for me at the airport in Minneapolis. It took them a while to get there because of the dense fog on the way up. The next day I got up and there was a neighbor woman, about my age or maybe a bit older, that mom introduced me to. Her husband was one of the college people and had a good job while we were in Vietnam. I think she had this fantasy about me and the image that we had to some women. Not all the women, but the women that were married to the pencil-necks that didn't go. I think to them we were real men and their husbands were something else. I remember that every time I went outside she would go outside too and wave to me and do all kinds of things to be noticed. She always came over if she knew I was there and she wanted me to tell her all about what I had done. I think she really got off on it. She was quite a lady. I was always nice towards her and realized that she was very unhappy with what she had at home. I just didn't trust the American at all when I came home and still don't to this day. I have a real craw in the neck about college people. And the people that I work with, whether they are workers or managers, they have to prove themselves to me first before they get my attention. I've told many of the managers this—prove it to me first and I'll go along with you and then will do everything I can to help them.

I was an assistant scoutmaster and scoutmaster for one of the local Boy Scout troops. My experience in Vietnam I shared with the kids. I mainly trained them in camping, cooking, wilderness survival and winter survival. It was good for me to help these young people understand a little bit about how to survive in any type of situation, and not to panic, but to think things out. My oldest son became an Eagle Scout in 1989. It was one of the happiest times in my life. I worked with him for six years in scouting so he could reach a goal that I couldn't. My youngest son is now a Webelos and I will try to help him through scouting so he can also attain the rank of Eagle Scout.

In conclusion to this chapter, I hope that the citizens of the United States and our government come to the realization that Vietnam was a war and that we did our best with what we had and that we are not all crazed killers, but citizens of a country that has not recognized us for what they did to us. The government sent us to Vietnam. We didn't pay our own way to that country. At this time the only friend a Vietnam veteran has is his family and other Vietnam veterans. These are the only friends he can really count on for honest and sincere help.

John Samuel Tieman

At times you have wondered what it is that I recall when I think of my six months in Vietnam. I was in the rear echelon. Guerrilla warfare, in fact, changed the nature of what it meant to be in the rear, and made my base camp one unlike most bases in our military history. The war affected me not so much for anything I did as for what I saw. As an artist, I went to war; as an artist I came home; and as an artist, I now write.

I was in the 4th Infantry Support Command, Headquarters and Band, An Khe, Binh Dinh Province, the Central Highlands of Vietnam. The mountains. The An Nam Cordillera, where the nights could be cool to the point of chilly. The *way* outback. While the conditions attributed to the rear echelon are quite true for most places, and to some extent true for Camp Radcliff, my base camp, it must be pointed out that our situation was considerably more primitive. Ice cream? We had no ice cream. Nor TV, nor radio, nor hot water, but lots of red dirt and all the monsoons you can stand. The nature of an infantry division is such that nothing is altogether permanent, for it must and can pick up at a moment's notice, as indeed it did twice while I was there, three times if you wish to count the Cambodian Invasion as a move. On the other hand, we did have a mess hall, hooch maids, those half-size Japanese refrigerators, and plenty of penicillin for those who got to the point that they just couldn't stand their hand anymore. Bob Hope even visited Camp Radcliff once, and several of us were asked to play in his show, though none of us did. In a few words, our conditions were better than the "legs," but not nearly so cozy as soldiers in the city or the Air Force. My everlasting memory is one of being constantly dirty.

We were of the infantry but not in it. An article gave the impression that most people in the rear thought of the war as distant, the infantry likewise distant. That's not the way I remember it. A common punishment for us was to send someone to a line unit, which involved no more than throwing your shit on your back and walking one hundred yards to Charlie Company, First of the First. (In civvie that's C Company, First Battalion, First Infantry Regiment, Fourth Infantry Division, of course.) The only time I ever saw a "classic" engagement, i.e. our guys here and bad guys there, was when we caught about 150 "Injuns" on the first mountain outside our wire, perhaps one and three-quarters of a mile, a fight in which Charlie 1/1 got in its licks, zapping and getting zapped like troopers. "Sweeps," which were more or less patrols that cleared a base camp after attack, were often the events of every morning. When I first arrived in Vietnam, I pulled guard duty every three days; towards the end, it was every other day, about as often as we got hit. There are few more fearful events than to be on guard and hear an explosion behind you. Guard duty was twenty-four hours. On or off duty, we often slept with our rifles. And we could be quick with the trigger, for on not just a few occasions did a bandsman, a clerk or a cook get "a confirmed kill." Or get shot by a sniper, as did a trombone player in the 101st Airborne who lost his leg. Not that we were ninja material, mind you. But how well I remember the mud, the foxhole, the guard tower, the jungle rot, the ring worm, the sappers, and the rocket attacks. How I remember well all the pain.

Our base camp was considerably more dangerous. If for no other reason, this was displayed by the mere fact that this was the area through which the final offensive of the war was launched. Right down Highway 19. The area never was safe or secure; it was always "Injun Country." In my case, the first night I was in An Khe, seventeen choppers were blown up by the bad guys. I don't recall how many were killed, although I do recall seeing a hooch full of guys go up. My first two, three months in Vietnam's Central Highlands, we were rocketed every night. Either that, or we had "sapper" attacks. Sappers were these nasty little bastards who were put on earth with the expressed purpose of blowing me off of it—demolitions experts trained in infiltration. Then there were convoys. Highway 19. Then there was the Mang Yang Pass. (For years, in all my waking nightmares, that God-forsaken stretch of pass would haunt me like some spectral scene out of Hieronymus Bosch.) The pass went through the mountains leading to Pleiku, a major city, and beyond to Cambodia. At the Mang Yang, the road narrowed to one truck-length wide, with a cliff going straight up one side, and on the other a drop perhaps 1000-plus feet at points. To someone on the other side of that deep but very narrow gorge, we in fact presented a target not unlike ducks in a shooting gallery. From above on our side, a bad guy could simply drop a hand grenade. And if the enemy were not enough to shorten our lives, the slightest error on the part of the driver could send you hurtling to your death. If your engine failed, the truck behind you was under orders to push you over the cliff. Convoys never stop. (We commonly would run over civilians foolish enough to test this iron rule.) The monuments to the Mang Yang Pass were the trucks that littered the floor of the gorge, vehicles that appeared as Tonka toys to a grown man; the other monuments being the tombstones over the graves of the men of the French 100th Light Mechanized Battalion, who in 1954 were wiped out to the man in the Mang Yang Pass. Their cemetery was located on the eastern entrance of the pass, and rumor had it that they were buried standing up and facing France. But I digress. The point being the men in my outfit, the 4th Infantry Support Command, are classified by Vet Centers as "combat veterans," although I would not compare my experiences to that of the grunt, river rat or combat medic et al. Put it simply, I was a degree or two removed from the eye of the storm, as it were, but I literally could see it from where I stood. Which was fine with me. I worked very hard to be a REMF, a "Rear Echelon Mother Fucker," but my luck wasn't as good as the guys in Saigon, say, or the Air Force. Still, I lived.

Mine was not a particularly heroic war. On the contrary, when I look back upon it, there is a curiously passive quality to my war. It was a wise man who said, "War is largely sheer boredom punctuated occasionally by sheer terror." At their worst, the memories related above were the incidents of minutes, even seconds. The rear echelon was the world of "reaction," not aggression. A rocket attack would be over and done with in perhaps ten seconds, although, as a friend who lost his legs to one can tell, the effects of such an attack were often devastating.

No, it was not particularly heroic. Among the casualties of war that I recall were two young fellows, about seventeen or eighteen, who committed suicide. Then there was the fellow in Charlie 1/1 who went berserk one night and killed four of his friends before he was finally hunted down and shot dead like a mad dog. I knew of only one person who wasn't a "head" or a "juice freak." Of the friends I kept up with after the war, I know of no one who did not suffer from post-traumatic stress. But I was never afraid; attacks happened fast, as a rule, and I never had the chance to be afraid. I remember the events of the attacks with a clarity that, for all the years, is crystalline. But of heroism, of glory, of elan, these . . . of these matters I know nothing.

Coming home was not such a terrible experience for me. No one ever spit on me, although occasionally, when I'd mention that I was a Nam vet, I could feel the room temperature drop fifteen degrees. I returned to a junior college and later universities where I met a number of people who became lifelong friends. Which is to say that people were generally quite kind to me. The fact of the matter is that, unless someone was a very close friend and willing to listen, I just didn't mention it much. Even some close friends didn't want to hear about the war, and who can blame them? Hell, I spent years trying to forget: to put it metaphorically, I presumed that if I burnt the bridge then I'd forget the way back. And now. Well, now I'd like a bumper sticker, not the one that reads "Vietnam Veteran And Proud Of It," but one that reads "Vietnam Veteran And Learned To Live With It." But the years after the war . . . of those years there is little to relate other than the relatively eventless life of the student, a life I eagerly embraced, and that I look back upon very fondly. Long hours in the library. The dear friendships. The lovers. And the anger. The anger over the war. That was there for years. I remember a morning, I was at Southern Methodist University, when it occurred to me that for the first time I had gone twenty-four hours without dwelling upon the war. I had been home for over three years.

Today the war seems pretty distant. When I want to recall it, as when I'm writing now, I'm the one who has to make the effort, as the memories have become polite in that they seldom intrude except upon appropriate occasions. The memories have grown old, and like their master, don't have that youthful vigor. My concern today isn't the service, but veterans' rights. Hospitalization, geriatric care, employment, education, the homeless vets—all that. In a few words, it's become my charity, veterans' rights. And then there's the image of the Vietnam vet. The way the public perceives the Vietnam vet is something I still find barely tolerable.

Recently, not long after I recounted these experiences to a dear friend of long standing, Phoebe Cirio, she paused the next day at the Jefferson Barracks Cemetery in south St. Louis. She groped for precise phrases in relating her feelings to me, her depth of emotion displayed in recounting the scenes of row upon row of graves for eighteen-year-olds. I replied how, if I had it my way, we wouldn't have pristine rows of stones in front of which we make speeches about heroism or honorable deaths. No, each tombstone would contain a picture of that man as he was taken from the battlefield, even if that picture is just of a bit of rib cage or no more than a hand. "But John," Phoebe replied, "those are just horrors. And horror teaches only fear. And we don't learn from fear as much as from the other emotions."

And with that wisdom of Phoebe in mind, I ask myself what emotions I now have, what emotions beyond the memory of horror? I no longer feel guilt, for I have long since forgiven myself for the sin of being twenty, but I do feel regret in having been one agent of so much suffering. I regret that I once killed someone; I regret that I feared going to jail more than I ever feared the enemy, and for this reason seldom spoke out against a war that even then I knew to be wrong; regret, yes, regret... And pity. Wilfred Owen once said, "My subject is war and the pity of war. The poetry is in the pity." Pity, and the depth of pity. The weariness of pity, how it doesn't go away, how it forever evokes a sigh, a line from a poem, then the quiet.

And, in recent years, a certain quiet pride. In more cases than not, Vietnam vets are stronger for their experience. Fifteen or twenty years ago, we learned the lessons of a war that society is only just beginning to come to grips with. And we learned it on our own. And we were seldom helped, but often hindered. And from this we grew strong. We learned to quietly carry on throughout the years; just as some of us learned to take abuse, most of us learned to be misunderstood; all of us learned to carry on. My society finally learned what I learned a long time ago, that it's silly to even try to forget. So society has finally looked over its shoulder, as it were. It's learning that it squandered the finest army that it ever fielded. Society is learning only now that it lost a war when its fighting men never lost a battle. Society is learning that it's twenty years behind its veterans, that far from asking itself the how or why questions, most people cannot simply recount what happened during the Vietnam War. But I can. And so can my buddies. And I take pride in having done something that most people simply read about, and, not that I'm any hero, but having the utmost respect for those who were truly conscientious objectors and had the courage to take an anti-war stand, one I supported when I came home; I have a slight contempt for the wimps of my generation. The times called upon one to take a stand. I don't think it was fair to ask that of a nineteen year old, nor do I think it was fair to kill those who chose bravely. But I take quiet pride in counting myself among the men, women who simply did their duty. (Me, the guy who can't change a light bulb without instructions; believe it or not, I originally joined to be a helicopter pilot.) I might add that I volunteered to join the Regular Army, that I lied to get in, and that at any time I could have gotten out. Allergies, slightly color blind, I'm allergic to wool, I have hay fever. Imagine being in Vietnam during hay fever season, and not being able to discern green from brown as you march along in your woolen socks. My youth. As society in general, and in particular men of my generation, turning to their vision of yesterday, where some find regret now I find quiet pride. In one sense, to put it simply, I can always say that, though I have my faults and my regrets, being a wimp has never been one of them. The war, my experiences after the war, and the lessons I learned, the way in which I faced all that, in these I take quiet pride. For what it's worth, I paid my macho dues.

Lessons? I learned confidence. I learned it by staring down the barrel of a gun and not flinching, so to speak. I learned that there's not really that much in life to be afraid of, that there is deep wisdom in the notion that "a coward dies a thousand deaths though a brave man dies but once." I learned that even death can be light as a feather, as the poet says. I learned that it is much easier for people to rush to war than it is to rush to peace. I learned that there are those who enjoy killing. I learned the name of a torturer. I learned that never again is it possible for me to be the guilty bystander who says nothing when witnessing cruelty. I learned compassion. I learned of the school of cruelty, of the subtleties of its technique. I learned that the same bullet which strikes down a man also strikes down his mother. I learned the word "widow." I learned that the highest ideals in life are those that nurture, encourage, and teach that which is pacific. I learned how to vow that never again would I harm another man or woman, that in all my dealings with people I will search for that which is quietude, stability. I learned that it's possible to love your country even when its society is blind, perhaps then more than ever. I learned love before I could speak. I learned to listen for the rumor of war, and learned from the warning how to warn.

In the end, there is one certainty, one unchanging emotion. A history lesson, the feel of something larger than self, larger than nation. In my lifetime, there have been just two events which I can say with certainty that people will speak of these long after I'm dead and forgotten. One, the 1985 Mexico City Earthquake. The other, the war. I've been in an attempted coup, I've witnessed the birth of a nation, I've climbed a mountain, published widely, traveled the world.... But none of these will be more than dusty curios in a few decades. But of the war? Of the war people will speak long, long after all that I was becomes dust.

And one last fact. One last casualty of the war. Before I went into the Army, I wanted nothing more than to be a symphony conductor. The dream. After the war, I hardly ever played a note. Peace, John

Born is St. Louis on New Year's Day of 1950, John Samuel Tieman has lived in Europe, Asia, the West Indies and Latin America. At times, he has worked a wide variety of full and part-time jobs—a medic on an ambulance, an interpreter, a warehouseman, a secretary, a bank guard, a librarian's assistant, a soldier, a musician, a lobbyist, a teacher and a teacher's assistant among other jobs. His primary and secondary education were of the traditional Latin Catholic school. Tieman earned his bachelor's degree in History, English, and Education; following this, he earned his MA in Modern and Medieval British History. Both degrees are from Southern Methodist University, where he was a Graduate Research Fellow and president of the history honor society. From 1982 through 1986, Tieman lived in Mexico City, where he completed two manuscripts, one of poetry entitled Edae, the other of philosophy entitled The Selected Pessimism of John Samuel Tieman. *His eyewitness account of the 1985 Mexico City Earthquake appeared on the front page of a Sunday edition of the "St. Louis Post-Dispatch." He has published a number of guest editorials. An anthologized poet, since 1986 his work appears in such periodicals as* The Americas Review, The English Journal, The Caribbean Quarterly, *and* River Styx. *He has published translations from, and compositions in Spanish. Within the last year, Tieman has completed a play entitled "The Vietnam Requiem." A decorated veteran of Vietnam, Tieman is a senior officer in the Veterans of Foreign Wars. Though primarily a senior high school instructor, he has taught the junior high, the junior college and the university levels, as well as working with the behaviorally disordered adolescent. A certified teacher of History and English for over ten years, at present he lives in his hometown. He co-hosts "The Morning Show" on KDHX, Radio 88.1-FM. He is a frequent guest lecturer in both history and literature, and gives monthly poetry readings.*

Steven Stratford

At a very early age, I had become convinced that the world had played a cruel, dirty-rotten trick on me. The world was not the kind, coherent, sympathetic place I'd previously been led to believe.

The year was 1968 when our great leaders Bobby Kennedy and Martin Luther King were assassinated; the year that mass riots like those of Chicago shook the nation; with the massacre of innocent college students at Kent State soon to follow. 1968, the year of the surprise Tet Offensive in Vietnam; of draft card burnings televised coast to coast; the year that thousands of U.S. teenagers were escaping to Canada to save their lives. Yes, it was 1968 that I graduated from high school, graduated in "the real world."

Like hundreds of thousands of other teenage boys at the time, life and death decisions had to be made, decisions that would affect the rest of our lives—if we survived! The "future" was an abstract concept to this particular unenlightened conscript, who really could not imagine living beyond the age of thirty.

Those were troubled times to say the least. What to do had never mattered nearly so much! Before that year was up, I had enlisted in the United States Air Force to avoid the draft and the likelihood of hand-to-hand combat. The following year I landed at Tan Son Nhut Air Force Base, Republic of South Vietnam. Like a steer being herded to the slaughterhouse door, I'd been led down the garden path and into the jaws of a monster—into the jaws of WAR!

One of my greatest fears as I was growing up was that I would become a "normal" person. Normal people were those who worked at regular jobs, did the same thing day after day after day, and became faceless members of society who blended into the masses. I had never met a normal person who was happy. They all seemed to be in some sort of a trance: mindlessly doing whatever this force called society dictated; marching in step to the hypnotic beat of some universal clock; following each other like sheep from the womb to the grave.

By the time I reached junior high school I had formed my own concepts about the nature of reality. My evolving political, philosophical, sociological, and psychological views, although I could not articulate them as such at that time, were fairly well developed. Early in life, the dichotomy between what I was told and what was in fact true, became clear to me. Stories about Santa Claus and the Easter Bunny aside, most of what my parents and teachers told me about what I considered to be important was not true. The pretty picture of the world painted for me by them had holes in it big enough to drive a truck through. It seemed to me the truth was not told to me because it would be harder to control if I knew it. I despised being lied to or being told half-truths, and learned to expect nothing less. I became a pessimist who saw conspiracies behind everything. As such, I subscribed readily to theories that validated my paranoid ideas.

I saw school as being nothing more that a tool used by the perverted ruling class. By convincing masses to serve elitist institutions and to submit to elitist laws, control was maintained. I became obsessed with escaping this fate.

At school I made it my job to read between the lines and expose hypocrisy that ran rabid throughout the material we were being indoctrinated with. For example, history teachers would tell us what wonderful, altruistic fellows our founding fathers were. "Liberty and justice for all," would be quoted as their ideal, and into the minds of these docile trusting young normal people would go this "fact," so generously bestowed on them by the powers that be. What we weren't told was that this liberty and justice was only intended for white men that owned property (those same wonderful altruistic fellows). Women had no right to liberty and justice; their function in this new order was to serve men and submit to their authority. Native Americans had no right to liberty and justice; their function was to do as they were told, to relocate upon demand, to submit to even more oppressive laws that they had no say in. Slaves certainly had no right to liberty and justice; they were simply condemned to the status of property.

The reason we were being so misled was obvious to me. By brainwashing young people into believing that his system was designed and implemented by compassionate wise men with everyone's best interest at heart, little individual units of capitalistic ideology could be produced that fit nicely into the elitist-controlled, money-fueled, power machine of government that they were expected to serve blindly.

So, I would challenge virtually all of my indoctrinators as they attempted to create a normal person out of me. I saw a real need for things to be different, but it became more and more clear that it was unrealistic for me to expect to change the system. The status quo was firmly entrenched. The power and force of all social institutions were at the beck and call of the elite. I was their captive. The law required me to submit daily to their propaganda under the guise of getting educated. Without having had any say in the matter, the rules that I was ordered to follow were imposed on me. Any hope of avoiding being forced to be normal through conventional means seemed all but impossible. Frustration became paramount. I felt trapped and miserable. I tried to rebel and was subjected to punishment by authorities for doing so.

I began to hate my parents and my teachers. They would answer my questions of "Why" with statements like, "Because I told you so." They would do one thing, yet demand that I do another. "Do as I say, not as I do" seemed to say it all. Hypocrisy ruled the world I had been born into. The only alternative to being forced to act normal seemed to be— to cease to be. My fate seemed to be one of doom. At the age of fourteen, in a state of total loneliness, disillusion, and despair, I put the barrel of my loaded 7mm magnum hunting rifle in my mouth, reached for the trigger (intent on pulling it), but was unable to reach it because the rifle was too long. So, I took off one shoe and sock, placed my big toe in the trigger-guard, and put the barrel back in my mouth. Then, the absurdity of being found with the back of my head blown off and my big toe in the trigger-guard, caused me to change my mind. However, my depression and unhappiness remained and began to manifest itself in more and more antisocial behavior. Cutting school became habitual, and the authorities at school were on the verge of expelling me, when they demanded that I seek professional help.

From then on I was required to see a psychiatrist at school once a week for an hour. The system had branded me a deviant and the stigma attached to this role was mine whether I wanted it or not. However, an interesting by-product of this process was that I was no longer considered "normal." My diagnosed "mental disorder" (borderline personality), made me different. In a sense I relished my new-found uniqueness. My antisocial act toward self-destruction paid high dividends. People now saw me as being different. They treated me differently. They took me more seriously. The psychiatrist would listen closely for more clues to help him specifically categorize my form of madness. My parents would listen closely for clues to possible future behavior problems. My teachers and fellow students would listen closely for further evidence of my insanity. I was being heard! I began feeling different. I became comfortable in my new deviant role. It worked.

As if to prove to myself and my observers that this assessment of my defiance were correct, I began displaying further evidence of my uniqueness. I started spending my time in the local pool hall hustling amateur pool players for cash, instead of going to school. I began dressing differently (pegged Levi's, pointed toe boots, etc.), wearing my hair differently (greased back to a ducktail); and talking differently (using slang and curse words). I would go to school for tests only, and managed to get reasonably satisfactory grades anyway. I began seeing those normal people as suckers.

This behavior eventually led me to being expelled from high school, which really set me apart from normal people. I went to continuation school for a few hours a day and took some correspondence course through the mail. I not only graduated with the rest of my class in 1968, but I graduated in the upper half of my class scholastically. This to me was just further evidence of how dumb normal people were, and of how I could beat the system, my way.

Unfortunately a war was waiting for nice young high school graduates in 1968. My options were limited—jail, Canada, college, or war. College seemed like the easiest alternative, so I gave it a try. My adopted deviant role, however, was not popular among the University of Montana administrators. I was on academic probation for my grades when I got caught having a coed spend the night with me in my dorm room, and was expelled.

My options became more limited. I joined the United States Air Force to avoid the infantry. It was real hard to be different in the military without going to the brig, but I found a way. A Vietnam veteran gave me a get-rich-quick scheme and assured me I could lead a wanton lifestyle in Vietnam, so I volunteered. Being different had become an obsession with me. My deviant identity became more important to me than any ideology. I became unprincipled. Any means became justified to attain my goals. To be free of government control, autonomous, and wealthy seemed to me to be necessary to realize my greatest potential. If I could attain this power over my own life, I would be free to bring about a better world. So, for me to beat the system by whatever means, would be for the greatest good. Serious crime by society's standards seemed benign compared to the legal manipulation of the masses by the political and economic elites.

My deviant career took a huge leap when I arrived in Vietnam. I became a black-marketer and drug smuggler. To me the war started out being a big game. A game where few rules, if any, applied. The whole thing was immoral, so how could individual acts of immorality be judged apart. It was an anything-goes atmosphere. But I soon discovered that without regular doses of narcotics the horror of the war was more that even I could endure. My time was divided between participating in mass genocide, and wheeling and dealing in an underground illegal culture. My deviance had progressed to depravity. I had become an assassin and a pillager for the system I despised. I suffered from a self-inflicted, total, moral collapse. Another suicide attempt failed to kill me (an intentional overdose of heroin), but it snapped me back to my senses. From the moment of my recovery on, I refused to cooperate with the military in any way, shape or manner. For taking this stand, I was declared insane, put in a straitjacket, and locked in a padded cell.

I eventually cut a deal with my tormentors, signed some ludicrous statements absolving them of any responsibility for my condition, and was released from the military. But my deviant career was far from over.

I learned plenty over there, more than I was equipped to deal with. I learned that countries (even ours) intentionally lie to their people, that our leaders were not to be trusted, and that the war we were waging was immoral and unjust. Daily I was ordered to commit crimes against humanity under threat of execution. Under the guise of nationalism, I was forced to participate in the murders of innocent men, women and children.

The fifteen months that followed my arrival in Vietnam were a living nightmare, a nightmare that has affected my life to this day.

After I was discharged on August 26, 1971, I was unemployed and addicted to heroin. I wandered around in a daze. I was full of hatred towards the military and the government for what they had made me do, and done to me. I could not deal with the fact that the madness going on over there was allowed to continue. As long as I was full of heroin I was at least able to continue to exist. It made me numb. It made me not care as much. But, it also made me do things I would not have otherwise done. My morals deteriorated. Keeping the drug pumping through my veins became my exclusive goal. However, the cost of a heroin habit stateside was astronomical compared to what it cost in Nam. The only way to keep up a habit was to commit crimes. I stole from everyone I knew, including my family and friends. I even turned out my little brother, something I never in my wildest nightmares imagined I would do.

My primary source of illicit funds became my family's liquor store. I was stealing hundreds of dollars a week from there. Eventually I was found out by my father, and this source was subsequently no longer available. I had already burnt all of my bridges with everyone I knew. No one that knew me would even let me near their homes, and for good reason. It was time to either start burglarizing stranger's homes or pulling armed robberies. I couldn't cross that bridge. I was at the end of my rope. I started to kick my habit involuntarily. I was going crazy. Once again I seriously considered suicide. I remember clearly: it was a rainy afternoon; I was walking along the Napa River, which was swollen with newly fallen rain; I threw my outfit into the rushing water; and I was about to throw myself in too. As a last resort I decided to reach out for help. I called my father. He came and picked me up. We talked. I told him how desperate I was, and asked him what I should do. I was in tears. He told me that he saw little if any hope for me. The only suggestion he had was that I commit myself to the drug program at the Napa State Hospital. Shortly thereafter I entered "Our Family," a one-year residential drug treatment facility located there.

For the next twelve months I worked exclusively on my drug addiction. Twelve hours a day, seven days a week I struggled to come to terms with my haunting past. I tried to learn how to function in what seemed to me, *a world gone mad*! And the war raged on. As I reflect on those days, it all seems so foggy and surrealistic that it is difficult to be sure that it even happened.

How people managed to pretend that everything was okay was beyond me. The fact that the media was feeding us only the lies that the government fed it, explains this in part. But, nobody seemed to want to know the truth. Eventually I learned how to pretend that everything was okay, and I graduated. I got a job working for a construction company as a laborer and heavy equipment operator that lasted for about six months. After that I went back to school on the GI Bill. I studied business for one semester before getting an offer I couldn't refuse. My father had come into some "extra cash" and told me that he would back my brother and me in starting a new business.

After doing extensive research into business opportunities, I determined that due to the energy shortage that supposedly existed, the firewood business would prove profitable. So, my father fronted the start-up capital, and the deal was that my brother and I would do all of the organizing, management and legwork free, and work for free until my father recapped his cash, then the three of us would be equal partners.

The necessary equipment was quite expensive and the work very hard, but after many months of work, "Flame of the Valley Woodcutters" was a thriving business. The second contract I secured was the exclusive rights to five thousand acres of oak trees in Pope Valley, California.

This job required hiring nineteen additional men and supervising them all. After working sixty-hour weeks for about a year for nothing, I determined that my father had received his original investment back in company profits. At that time my brother and I requested that our names be added to the ownership of the company assets and that we both begin immediately to receive compensation for our work. The response that we received sent us both into shock. My father informed us that "his records" indicated that he had not received anywhere near his original investment back in profits. And furthermore, he had "changed his mind" about our original agreement. He said he had decided to keep the business himself and that if we wished to continue to work "for him" he would pay us "the going rate" for our labor from then on.

I told him in no uncertain terms what he could do with "his business," and struck out on my own. I lived by myself in a small mobile home on Tomorrow Mountain, near Lake Berryessa, and cut wood to earn a living. I had been heroin free for two and a half years when once again I became addicted.

Shortly after I began using again, I attempted suicide once more. I took several thousand milligrams of Thorazine (of all things) and was discovered four days later, still unconscious. It was my uncle who found me, and he suggested that I go to the Delancey Street Foundation in San Francisco, rather than trying to kill myself again. I did as he suggested, and for the next two years Delancey Street was my home. In order to get into that program I had to donate everything I owned, a twelve-wheel drive Army transport truck, a twenty-two foot mobile home, a 1956 Chevy convertible, several chain saws, a hydraulic wood splitter, and all of my personal belongings.

While I was at Delancey Street trying to work out my "behavior problem," I also worked full time. Therapy there is dealt with during the evenings. After I was there about nine months, I became the department head of the Procurement Department. In this capacity, I supervised from nine to thirteen employees. Our job was to provide the needs for 365 residents by acquiring donations of goods and services. The year prior to my taking this position, the department took in one million dollars in donations. After one year under my management the department took in over two million dollars.

Three nights a week for the entire two years I participated in and often facilitated group therapy sessions (The Synanon Game). I was also involved in a great deal of community service during this time. And, I also attended Century 21 Real Estate School. Before I left Delancey Street, I had acquired my real estate sales license.

When I did leave Delancey Street, I went to work for Murdock & Associates Realtors in Napa, California. I had no assets or cash when I left Delancey Street. I borrowed three thousand dollars to get started. In the beginning I sold residential property. At the end of my first year in the business I had closed fifty-two escrows and earned sixty-five thousand dollars. That was the least profitable of the three years I spent working for that company.

It didn't take me long before I was dealing in investment property exclusively. At first I managed all of my client's rental properties as well as handling all of their property sales and purchases. When the number of properties I was managing reached close to one hundred, I turned their management over to a professional property manager.

Most of the transactions I was handling were complex 1031 tax exchanges or syndication development projects. I personally formed seven limited partnerships in which I acted as a general *managing* partner. I developed subdivision apartment complexes, mini-storage facilities, and other commercial property. When I left Murdock & Associates three years later to start my own firm, I owned all or part of thirty-three properties in Napa and Solano Counties.

Investment Real Estate was the name of the firm I started in 1980. Technically it was a branch office of Investment Real Estate in San Francisco. However, I was the sole owner and general manager. I employed one other real estate salesman, two full-time secretaries, and a full-time general contractor. The management of this company was my sole responsibility. For one year the company thrived.

Unfortunately, I had become addicted to speed in the process. I was convinced that without them I could not succeed; that I needed them to become motivated; and that if I stopped using them I would loose everything. My live-in girlfriend at the time eventually gave me an ultimatum, though. Either I quit using or she would leave me. She said that she didn't care if I lost everything, that she wanted me, not my money. So I quit.

Then came the real estate crash of the early 1980s. I was overextended with three and a half million dollars worth of property and a twenty-thousand-dollar-a-month negative cash flow. When the dust had settled, I had lost all of my property and was two hundred and fifty thousand dollars in debt. I lost virtually everything I owned—vehicles, furniture, personal property. Lawsuits and bill collectors became a way of life.

I went to work for a real estate company in Fairfield, California for a year after that, but I wasn't handling my life successfully. I wasn't using drugs, but in my own eyes I was a total failure. I had gained a hundred pounds and felt like shit most of the time. I soon got out of the real estate business, never to return. Shortly thereafter my girlfriend left me and I once again started using.

For the next couple of years I managed a used appliance company in Napa (reconditioned appliances). I could have managed this business with my eyes closed, and in essence I was. My drug addiction was getting progressively worse.

My life as a dedicated deviant was resumed. I saw myself as unwilling to submit to what I perceived as an evil, self-serving, elitist oligarchy. Crime became a way of life to varying degrees throughout this period of my life and eventually led to my commitment to prison.

In March of 1984, I was arrested for many drug-related crimes. For quite some time I had been "on the run." A convicted murderer, who I had testified against in court, had put a price on my head. I was kept in solitary confinement in the Napa County Jail for nine months while I awaited trials. I was convicted of overdrawing my checking account by just over three thousand dollars and of credit card fraud. I received a three-year-eight-month prison sentence, which was suspended to allow me to go back to Delancey Street Foundation.

I stayed at Delancey Street for eleven months this time. While I was there I worked in the Research and Development Department. In addition to this job, I did volunteer work as a teacher in the Delancey Street GED Program. I worked with adults who were trying to pass the High School Equivalency Exam.

When I left Delancey Street, my probation officer "violated me" and had me sent to prison to do my sentence. During my incarceration, I spent a total of almost a year and a half in maximum security solitary confinement because of the contract out on my life.

Being locked up in a cage all by yourself is torture. All you have is your thoughts. I don't know that it is possible to convey an experience such as this.

I had plenty of time to reflect on my life and on life in general without any outside influence during this period. I can not imagine a more alienating experience than that of being locked up in a cage for years. I was bitter, resentful, and full of hate. For many months I blamed society, the military, and specific individuals for my circumstances. I would fantasize about just how I was going to get even with those responsible for my incarceration (the snitch that turned me in, the cop that busted me, and especially the D.A. that prosecuted me). I would play out whole scenarios with infinite detail in my mind: how I would kill them, when I would kill them; and then how I would dispose of their bodies.

The nightmare that had begun in Vietnam was far from over for me at that time. In fact I saw a direct relationship between my Vietnam experience and my incarceration. If I hadn't been sent to Nam, there was no way I would have ended up in prison. My nightmares in prison were full of my Vietnam experiences. In an effort to express these feelings I decided to write about it. For many months I worked at doing just that. It was a cleansing experience, a catharsis of sorts. What I ended up with expressed my feelings clearly.

Yes, there are many of us behind bars. An unbelievable number of federal and state prisoners are Vietnam veterans. Almost twenty-five percent of all Vietnam veterans are either behind bars, on parole, or on probation. Why is this? Who really cares? Wouldn't you just as soon forget that we even exist? Maybe that is part of the reason.

The average age of the Vietnam soldier was nineteen. Yes, it's the children society sends off to fight its battles. Like the Israelites during the time of kings Ahaz and Manasseh of Juday, you offered your children as sacrifices to an ideal, an ideal that these "Children" did not understand, but one that they were forced to offer themselves as sacrifices for; one that, had they understood, I believe, they surely would have resisted.

We may not have understood just what it was we were being asked to lay our lives on the line for, but what choice did we have? Our parents didn't seem to understand either, but at least they had some say in who made such decisions for them—they could vote. However, we trusted our government, like fools, and we are still paying the price. Those of us who are still alive, that is, but . . . who really cares?

No, "kids" are naive. They believe what they are told, especially by their elders. We were told that we were defending our country, and we believed it. But, you grow up quick during a war—you have to. And, as we grew up it became perfectly clear to us that we had been lied to by our government. However, by then it was too late. By then we had to defend ourselves as best we could. Survival became the name of the game.

We were everybody's enemy in Vietnam. Everybody, that is, except for the corrupt government that we were keeping in power against the wishes of the majority of its people. Oh, what fun it was to be police for tyrants; to be hated by those you thought you were there to defend. Our "friends" by day were our enemies by night. But we did our duty!

When we were told to round up villagers, like they were cattle, and cart them off to concentration camps to create "Free Fire Zones," we did it. After all, we knew what was best for them, better than they did, didn't we?

When we were told to destroy entire Laotian villages with bombing raids, because they grew their crops in rows instead of the more common helter-skelter manner, we did it. After all, everyone knew that the Laotian villagers were too dumb to grow their crops in rows, without Communist influence or assistance, didn't they? It didn't matter that Laos was a neutral country or that Congress had specifically forbidden our involvement in that country. After all, Congress didn't understand the military significance of the situation, or so we were told. So, when congressmen were sent to investigate these atrocities, we were ordered to lie to them—of course. Oh, yes, we did our duty—under threat of a firing squad!

But, the military had our best interest at heart. That's why they made sure there were plenty of drugs available to us, to help us cope. You name it: marijuana, hashish, opium, speed, and the king of drugs, heroin, were available. We could get them all, and cheap too. The fact that Vietnam's Vice President Ky was the biggest drug dealer in southeast Asia (supplied with raw, pure heroin by the CIA, as documented in *The Politics of Heroin* in Southeast Asia), assured a steady supply.

Yes, I became a heroin addict in Vietnam. This emotional pain killer eased the pain that came with being forced to commit war crimes. I don't know that I could have coped without it. Perhaps that is why it was supplied.

However, if you returned to the States after 1971, like I did, you found out the hard way that you weren't permitted to come home with your habit. Too many GIs were coming home hooked—about eighty percent of all enlisted men at that time—and that did not make for good public relations. You see, it was "OK" to use drugs over there. After all, if they busted everyone who used, who would be left to fight their war? But, once we had served our purpose, if we managed to survive, that was a different story. Then we had the opportunity to experience the wrath of our government.

I was a sergeant in the United States Air Force during my tour of duty in Vietnam, a non-commissioned intelligence officer with Top Secret Security Clearance. I also had the dubious distinction of being the seventh person in USAF history to be subjected to President Nixon's new, four-phase "Drug Program" in 1971.

Phase I of this new program was called "Detection," and consisted of a urine analysis test. Once your test came back positive, you were immediately taken into custody and flown to Cam Ranh Bay, Vietnam for Phase II.

Phase II was called "Detoxification." Here, we were held in a cluster of Quonset huts, with bars in the windows and armed guards at the doors. "Cold Turkey" was the name of that game. And they were making the rules up as they went along. The screaming was almost constant. So were diarrhea, constipation, the shakes and *pain*! These soldiers were literally "going insane." I even saw two GIs die there, due to inadequate medical attention. Being a guinea pig does have its drawbacks. To this day, when I think of "Hell," I think of Cam Ranh Bay!

Once our systems were clear of drugs, the Military Police arrived with stretchers for the next leg of our journey. First, we were each forcibly injected with 1000 mgs. of Thorazine. Next, we were strapped to a stretcher in restraints. Then, all of us were hauled out to the runway, stacked like cordwood on a cargo plane used to transport bodies back home, and away we went.

Thorazine has an immobilizing effect in such high doses, but it leaves you conscious. You are unable to speak. Your mouth gets so dry that your tongue sticks to the inside of your mouth. Thirst eventually becomes intolerable. Your inability to move or call out is absolutely terrifying. Death seems preferable to your current state, but it, like relief, seems unattainable. However, somewhere out over the Pacific Ocean, another comrade of mine did die. An overdose of Thorazine was the cause of his death. This is how I was sent home from Vietnam.

When we finally made it back to the States, I was taken to Lackland Air Force Base, Texas, for Phase III, "Evaluation." This phase was supposed to take twenty-one days and it consisted of every kind of psychiatric test imaginable. They called it a hospital ward, but the bars and guards were still there. Each of us had a psychiatrist assigned to him, and it was their job to determine whether or not we could be rehabilitated. They wired our heads to machines, showed us ink blots, had us put odd shaped pegs in odd shaped holes, play with colored blocks, take tests and answer questions from sunup until long past sundown, day in and day out.

As I began to recover from my drug-induced state, the enormity of the crimes I had been forced to commit by my government again began to haunt me. I decided that prison, or suicide if necessary, would be preferable to continuing to contribute to that corrupt insane war. At this point I made it perfectly clear to "my" psychiatrist that I wanted no part of the military. My experiences in Vietnam had made a conscientious objector out of me. I had been a part of that madness long enough, and I just would not go along with it anymore.

The Air Force had invested hundreds of thousands of dollars in my training and security clearance. Because I was now a known heroin addict, both the training and the clearance were worthless. I was able to convince them that any further expenditures would also be wasted, because I would not cooperate with the military in any way, shape for form. I refused to wear my uniform, to answer their questions, or to even make my bed. I was finished with them, whether they were finished with me or not.

My twenty-one days came and went, and I was still there. Everyone who came before me (all six of them), and many who came after me, were gone. I had studied Nixon's new law well. It stated clearly that we were only to be held in Phase III for a maximum of twenty-one days. We were either to be discharged by then, or sent to Phase IV, "Rehabilitation." If they could not be convinced that we could be rehabilitated, they had determined it was cheaper and easier to discharge us.

On my thirty-first day I cornered "my" psychiatrist and demanded to be told why I was still there, in violation of the law. What he told me will remain vivid in my memory until the day I die. The first thing he said was, "Oh, haven't you been told? You're leaving tomorrow!" At that moment, as you might imagine, I was elated. I was finally going to exit this nightmare. My adrenaline flowed freely. Then, he got right up in my face, almost nose to nose, and said, "Yes, they will be taking you to the mental ward tomorrow. You're insane!"

By the time what he said had registered, he had spun on his heel and made his way through the door. It's probably a very good thing that he was out of reach, for both of our sakes. I was in shock, and there is no telling what I might have done.

The next morning, sure enough, two orderlies arrived with a straightjacket and a stretcher to cart me off. Once they had the jacket on me, another 1000 mgs. of Thorazine were injected into my ass before I was strapped to the stretcher. Then, they took me to a padded cell. No, the nightmare wasn't over yet; far from it. And, there was certainly more than ample time to reflect on the year just past:

March 28, 1971, 2130 hours. Tu Do Street, Saigon Vietnam . . . Several buildings are already ablaze as the third and final rocket strikes on one of the many bars that line this street. They call this part of town Sin City. Tonight it is Pandemonium. Across town, on the second story balcony of a house in an alley off Tru Mihn Ky Street, Sergeant Steven Stratford stands in the shadows watching, with tears in his eyes. This is his twenty-first birthday and his girlfriend, Flower, works in that bar. It was to be a special evening for them. It was a night that he will never forget. Although he often wishes he could.

Yes, there was plenty of time to remember all the top secret reports I had read and prepared—so full of incidents I would have found impossible to believe a year before. They haunted me.

My Lai was not the only, nor the worst, massacre of its kind to occur in Vietnam. It was just the only one the civilian press got hold of. Atrocities were commonplace. Prisoners were tortured as a common practice. Neutral countries were bombed every single day that I was there, while at the same time, the American public and Congress were being lied to. Believe me, I know, it was my job to provide targets for pilots to bomb in Laos, and to confirm their destruction. We devastated nearly a third of that entire country. It looked like the face of the moon when we were through with it. How many hundreds of thousands of innocent Laotian civilians were killed in the process? Who knows? And, at the same time my "co-workers" were doing the same thing to Cambodia.

By Nuremberg standards, I and thousands of other American soldiers should have been tried for the war crimes we committed. The mass killing of innocent civilians in neutral countries certainly meets that criteria, as does torturing and executing prisoners of war, and burning down the occupied villages of your allies.

Maybe I was crazy. A person can only handle so much reality of this type, before going over the deep end. But it soon became apparent that my sanity was not the U.S. Air Force's primary concern.

Shortly after I was incarcerated in the mental ward of Lackland Air Force Base's hospital, I was offered a deal. I was told that I only had two choices. The first was, that I could continue to refuse to cooperate, in which case I would then be discharged as a mental case. My other choice was, that if I would sign two documents, they would give me a General

Discharge under Honorable Conditions within thirty days, and that in the meantime I would be transferred from the mental ward to the convalescent ward, where I would be free to come and go as I pleased.

So what do you suppose these two documents consisted of? Well, the first one was an affidavit whereby I would swear that I would not divulge any of the top secret information I was privy to. The second document was a sworn statement in which I was to release the USAF of any responsibility for my drug addiction. Oh, I signed them, all right. But, I was a "mental patient" at the time, so I can hardly be held responsible for what I signed. *Can I?*

I finally did get out, but the nightmare did not end. I still had to live with all that I had seen and done *in* that war. Every time I saw the news I was reminded that the war raged on; that the lies were still being told; that the dead were still coming home. The networks posted the body counts like they were the score to a ball game—daily!

I told my story to anyone who wanted to hear it, but they were few and far between. No, what we had to say, you did not want to hear. I guess that's why you didn't want to hire us. You did not want to know. I'm sure you had your reasons for wanting to forget about the war, but it wasn't even over yet!

Maybe that is why the war went on so long. Nobody wanted to deal with it. I'm guilty too. I tried at first. I went to demonstrations for a while. But, the frustration made me angry and the guilt haunted me. So, I ran off to the mountains to hide from it all. That didn't work though, and nothing else did either. The war finally ended, but not for many of us. Hardly a day goes by that I don't think about it. At times these thoughts have overpowered me and I've "gone back," back to a bunker at Pleiku with flares drifting down out of the sky as wave after wave of VC charge to their certain death, screaming; back to the main gate at Tan Son Nhut as the man standing in front of me has his brains blown away by a sniper; back to Tru Mihn Ky Street on a sunny afternoon as a firefight breaks out between the VC and an Australian Courier, passing through the crossfire, unarmed, unable to help, scared to death of dying.

When I've "gone back," it's all been there: blood, fire, smoke, gun flashes, and bodies blended together in a kaleidoscopic panorama; screams, explosions, hollering, the sounds of death abound; the stench of burning flesh, offal, gunpowder, and sweat envelop me. I wish the war could end for me; many of us do.

There are still hundreds of thousands of us that have somehow managed to survive. Unfortunately, many of us haven't been able to recover from the war, though. Some of us are not the same as we were before the war. We find it much harder to accept the party line; we're not nearly so naive as we once were. We may look like anyone else, but we are not the same inside anymore. War, especially an immoral war, tends to damage the survivors. We tend to have a harder time liking ourselves. We tend to lose faith in society's institutions. We don't find it as easy to trust people. And, we are not treated like we were before, either. Our government abandoned us in our time of need.

Perhaps you have a better understanding now as to why so many of us are behind bars; why so many of us are addicted to drugs; why so many of us are in mental hospitals; why so many of us are unemployed; why so many of us wander the streets homeless; and why we are discriminated against. But, does that really matter? I mean, who really cares? Our government sure doesn't.

It would have been so much easier for you if we had all come home in "body bags." We are a constant reminder of the dark side of our government; a side you do not like to think about; a side that seems too hard to change.

Well, here is another dark side of it to think about! Our government still refuses to accept responsibility for the war-related problems of many Vietnam veterans. From Agent Orange poisoning to stress-related disorders, the U.S. claims that military service in Vietnam was not a mitigating factor, despite the overwhelming evidence to the contrary. When you consider the hundreds of billions of dollars the government wasted on that war, you would think that they would have no qualms about spending a fraction of that amount repairing the ruined lives of the survivors. But, unfortunately, such is not the case. Instead, the money is spent on such necessities as "Peace Keepers," "Freedom Fighters," and "Star Wars." And, Reagan continues to cut back on veterans' benefits every chance they get!

The Vietnam War cost millions of lives and hundreds of billions of dollars. Over three million Vietnamese people were killed, most of whom were civilians. Hundreds of thousands of civilians in Laos and Cambodia were killed. Over 58,000 American lives were lost. And thousands of Korean, Australian, Filipino, and New Zealand soldiers were killed too. WHY?

If our nation had learned something of great value from this war, perhaps it would not have all been in vain. But, unfortunately, this is evidently not the case. Our leaders still finance terrorists to overthrow elected governments. Devices capable of destroying all of mankind are still provided funding. Ridiculous presidential fantasies of space umbrellas still gobble up billions of dollars. "Hire more cops, and build more prisons," is touted as a solution to our nation's drug addiction. And yet, every day, Vietnam veterans die from war-related injuries that the government refused to help them with. Is it really any wonder that more Vietnam veterans have committed suicide since the war, than Americans were killed in action during the war? Think about that for a while!

However, something changed as the time I was doing progressed. I gradually began to realize that by blaming others, I gave them a sort of retroactive control over me which would assure similar control in my future. I figured out that I had to take back control of my life, from those I'd given in to. And, that to do this would require taking responsibility for all of my actions and all of my circumstances. Suddenly I found myself on the right track.

This realization prepared me for what was to follow. Before long I found myself in a minimum security situation at San Quentin. Then I made the most significant discovery of my life. I got involved in a spiritual growth movement of sorts (A Course in Miracles) that has changed my life to a degree that I would have thought impossible. This discovery (of my spiritual self) taught me more than I knew there was to learn. I learned how to perceive the world in different terms, how to actually see things differently. My perspective of life broadened. The "history" of the world did not change, but the significance of the events that took place did. I began to perceive a deeper meaning in life than I had ever imagined. I began to realize that my individual perception of reality had become twisted by my intense desire to have things be as I thought they should be. Who was I to know how things should be? Were my ideas so much better? Look what I had done to my life and with it! Had I not made matters worse rather than better with my feeble attempts at rebelling against what I perceived as a corrupt society? In essence, I came to terms with myself and recognized that inner peace is all I could ever hope to really accomplish. And, that in accomplishing this I would truly become a being worthy of emulation.

Realizing that I am a part of something that is ultimately good and much greater than myself has helped me to make great strides towards true inner peace. Seeing the events of history and of my life as necessary steps in the unfolding of a more beautiful and glorious future has made my life much more meaningful.

I am no less aware of the deviance that is prevalent in the world. Having experienced first-hand delinquency, war, insanity, criminality, and addiction, I am all too aware of these problems. I am also acutely aware of the elitist deviance that takes place daily throughout the world. The difference is that I have discovered how to best deal with this information in such a way as to help myself and the world, rather than cause harm. If this makes me normal, then so be it!

While I was still at San Quentin two other very significant events took place. I decided that acquiring a college education was important to me, in order to accomplish the goals I had set for myself. Since I decided that I wanted to change many of our social institutions such as the prison system, our public education system, the way our nation deals with its drug problem, and the way the media is used by our government and big business—an advanced education would be necessary. So I applied to Sonoma State University, and believe it or not, I was accepted.

I also decided that it was of utmost importance to me to find a woman to spend the rest of my life with, someone to give all my love to and to be loved by. I had never had such a relationship. I'd never been married. I had never been willing to make such a commitment to any woman, probably because I hadn't been willing to give that much of myself to anyone. However, within weeks, while still a prisoner at San Quentin (of all places), I met the woman that was to become my wife. There was no doubt whatsoever in my mind when I met her that this was the woman meant for me. I know, beyond a shadow of a doubt, that the Course in Miracles made our meeting possible. And it wasn't but another week, when he tells her, "I wanna marry you." "Yes," she said, "what took you so long?"

I was released from prison on June 21, 1987. On July 4, 1987, I got married. On August 31, 1987 I became a full-time student at Sonoma State University.

I finally have my life and my mind together to a degree I never thought possible. At least sufficient enough to resume a more or less "normal" life and to seek the help that I need, and believe I deserve. One thing I have yet to accomplish though, is getting the military to accept responsibility for my war-related injuries. In the process of doing just that I have filed a claim for a service-connected disability due to Post Traumatic Stress Disorder. While I was stationed in the Republic of South Vietnam (July 24, 1970—July 6, 1971), life was like a nightmare (as I have already gone into detail about). It has been eighteen years (almost to the day) since I returned, but the nightmare still has not ended. The latest episode in this nightmare had been my dealings with the Veterans Administration.

My job in Vietnam was to provide pilots with targets to bomb in Laos. The U.S. was not even supposed to be involved in Laos. That is what our President was assuring our Congress. What I was ordered to do on a daily basis was commit war crimes. Thousands of innocent Laotian villagers were murdered by us and I was ordered to participate. How does someone live with such a legacy? I stayed high on heroin. It worked. At least I could then do what I was ordered to. I am ashamed of having participated in the genocide of the Laotian people. I know the time will come when I will have to answer to God for what I did and I dread it. Now I am told that I must "prove" that the incidents that took place while I was there actually occurred. "We regret that we are unable to establish service connection for PTSD. The evidence we have shows you were not exposed to a valid in-service stressor," is what the letter I received in response to my claim said. "The evidence we have"—what the hell does that mean? I can just see some Army private at the U.S. Army and Joint Services Environmental Support Group researching records to substantiate my claim. Whoever it was, if they could not find any record of Tan Son Nhut or Saigon being rocketed or mortared during the entire year that I was there, they were certainly derelict in their duty ("The U.S. Army stated there were no recorded rocket or mortar attacks on Tan Son Nhut Air Base..."). There are tens of thousands of GIs who witnessed these attacks. In essence, I am being told that I am either a liar, or that I imagined the whole thing. Talk about adding insult to injury!

Many of the life threatening situations I found myself in while I was in Vietnam were only witnessed by people in the immediate vicinity. However, when rockets and/or mortars hit military installations or major cities, there can hardly be no record of it. On at least six occasions, Tan Son Nhut Air Base was rocketed or mortared while I was stationed there. And, on at least three occasions Saigon was rocketed or mortared while I was in town (not to mention the numerous sapper bombings, drive-by shootings, buses and taxies being fragged, etc.). All but one of these attacks occurred at night, and the night sky could be seen alight for miles around by anyone who happened to be outside. The sound of the explosions could hardly be ignored, as they would wake anyone nearby from the soundest sleep.

Exact dates, places and names from eighteen years ago are very difficult to recall, much less verify. When I filed my PTSD claim I was obviously naive. I actually thought that the Veterans Administration was an agency that existed to assist veterans, not one that exists to protect the government from valid veterans' claims. For me to be told that there is no record of rocket or mortar attacks in the Saigon area while I was there is absolutely absurd!

So, they put the burden of proving that I experienced "stressors" on me. Well, I may not be able to "prove" all of the incidents that happened to me took place, but I can certainly prove a significant number of them did.

In an effort to find documented records of specific incidents that I experienced, I began reading books written by GIs who were there and books about the war in general: while researching *The Vietnam Experience*, published by Boston Publishing Company, Copyright 1983; in the volume entitled *Fighting for Time* I found a story, "Saigon's Warriors" by

Brian Nicol. Brian was stationed in Saigon at 27A Vo Tanh Street, just a few blocks from the main gate of Tan Son Nhut Air Base during much of my stay there. In this two-page story (pages 114-115), Brian talked about an incident that he witnessed in the month of November, right outside the main gate. I did not witness this incident, but I did hear about it, and it happened just one week before I witnessed an American GI get his head blown off right in front of me at that same gate.

I was able to track down Brian Nicol. He is the editor of *Honolulu Magazine* in Honolulu, Hawaii. Brian did not remember hearing specifically about the GI who was shot the next week, but he did say that he definitely recalled both Tan Son Nhut and Saigon being rocketed and mortared on numerous occasions. He also said that he would be more than willing to testify to that effect. Brian could not believe that the V.A. was denying that these rocket and mortar attacks occurred. "How could they even say that?" was his reaction.

Doing this research has caused me a great deal of grief. It has made me very angry and frustrated. Having to take myself back to these incidents and reliving them to recall details is a very painful process.

Because I need to find witnesses to these events, I have been reading my old copies of the Vietnam Veterans of America newsletter, "Veteran." There is a section in this periodical called "LOCATOR," where veterans can try to locate men that they served with. As I searched these newsletters for the "proof" I need, one thing that became clear is that there are many other veterans out there being subjected to this process, many other veterans who are being told that they imagined their wartime experiences or are lying about them. One example of many in the June 1989 issue is: "We are trying to find anyone who was in Ban Me Thuot during the fall mini-Tet of September—October 1968. Information is needed to verify a stressor affecting SP . . ." (Name and address listed by author Stratford, withheld by Ritz Publishing.) This sickens me. Why is the V.A. doing this to us? The V.A. is supposed to be there to help veterans, not hurt them.

My search for records of the truth also led me to the Disabled American Veterans organization. When I contacted them and told them what I was being subjected to, they were not surprised at all. They told me that "no veteran has ever been awarded a PTSD claim upon their initial request. In fact, it usually takes two or three appeals for a veteran to actually win a claim." This is disgusting. The more work I do on this claim the angrier I get. The D.A.V. also told me that the V.A. intentionally denies all claims no matter what, because most veterans get so angry and disgusted that they do not pursue their claims. "They find this to be a very effective means of saving the government money."

What kind of a country is this that I risked my life for?

Having to pursue this claim hurts, but I must finish what I have started. I was just a child when my life was entrusted to my government. If there is any justice, the V.A. will put an honorable end to this ordeal for me. Meanwhile, I am doing better than I ever imagined I would be. This is my fifth continuous semester at Sonoma State University. I am now a senior, and I have completed ninety-nine units. My GPA is 3.98.

During my tenure at this institution I have been extremely active in the campus community. I have been a student representative on the A.S. (Associated Students) Board of Directors for five semesters now. This year I am the elected Vice President of the A.S., and Chairman of the Board. This is my second year as a director on the Enterprise Board (the campus corporation with a monopoly on all money-making ventures on this campus), and my first year as a director on the Student Union Board (the campus corporation that owns the Student Union Building and operates most of the services in that building). Other positions that I currently hold on this campus are: Chairman of the A.S. Interview Committee (which makes the recommendations for all student positions on this campus); student representative on the Personnel Board of the A.S. (which oversees all A.S. employees); student representative on the Student Equity Board of the A.S. (which ensures that the A.S. adheres to Affirmative Action regulations and actively recruits minority students); student representative on the Community Service Committee of the A.S. (which encourages students to become involved in community service volunteer work in the community); student representative on the Student Union Goals Committee (which interviews students for positions of the Student Union Board and sets the goals for the Student Union Corporation); Vice President of the Young Democrats Club; and Vice President of the Reentry Students Association.

Positions that I have held in the past on campus are almost too numerous to list. However, a few key ones are: Editor of the A.S. "Update" (the A.S. newsletter); Editor of the "Reentry Outreach" (the Reentry newsletter); and reporter for the "Star" (the campus newspaper).

My educational pursuits have not been limited to conventional academic classes either. I have completed internships in Sociology, History, and Communication Studies (and I am currently undertaking one in Political Science). I have completed Special Studies in Sociology and Psychology. And, I have completed two semesters of Community Service Program studies through the Psychology Department.

Off-campus community service work I've done includes; volunteer assistance in the GED Program at Delancey Street Foundation (1957-77 and 1984-85); Big Brother in Big Brothers of America (1978-82); Tutor Companion (helping a troubled teenager with his studies and providing him with guidance) currently in Sonoma County; Director of the Step

Into The Future Foundation (a self-esteem program for teenagers in Napa County), where I also co-facilitate quarterly four-day workshops and weekly follow-up sessions; and for about a year now I have been returning to San Quentin every three weeks, where I volunteer my services in the Pre-Release Program, informing inmates about to be released as to, how to get assistance that they are otherwise not informed of, how they can return to school, and get financial help to do so, how to get along well with their parole officers, and how to otherwise successfully turn their lives around.

I am currently a member of: Vietnam Veterans of America; the Sierra Club; the National Geographic Society; the Smithsonian Institute, the Association for Research and Enlightenment; the Endangered Animals Coalition; Amnesty International; the Church of Religious Science; and the Harley Owners Group.

I am currently a Presidential Scholar, on the Deans List, and in "Who's Who Among Students in American Universities & Colleges." I am the Ambrose Nichols Scholar at SSU (awarded to the student who contributed more to SSU than any other) and I won the William Randolph Hearst Scholarship. I was also awarded the Most Outstanding Social Science Student of 1988-89 by the Educational Support Program. In addition I have received thirteen other awards on this campus.

If I sound a bit pompous about my accomplishments, it's only because I am proud of what I have been able to accomplish. When I first considered returning to college, I wasn't even sure I could cut it. I credit my accomplishments to my willingness to surrender myself to what I call the Holy Spirit that lives within us all. By allowing my direction to be determined by this power greater than myself, I have found that there is virtually nothing that cannot be accomplished.

For any of you out there that are seeking enlightenment and empowerment, I strongly recommend the Course In Miracles, by The Foundation For Inner Peace. It has certainly enabled me to find inner peace and begin to realize my potential.

Charles A. Voeltz

I graduated in June of 1962 from high school. I worked at different jobs throughout the summer and fall, but could not find a job I liked, so I joined the Army January 24, 1963, and was sent to Fort Knox for basic training. After basic training I was sent to Fort Rucker for aircraft maintenance training. I went to three schools, ACFT Maint., Single Rotorblade Observation Helicopter Maint., and Single Rotorblade Turbine Helicopter Maint. After school I was sent to Fort Benning, where I was assigned to A Battery 377 Aerial Artillery. I was assigned as a mechanic on the ground crew for six months until I was assigned a Huey tail no. 62-2027 all my own. It was armed with the XM-11 system 48 rockets. For the next year and a half that beautiful Huey was mine. I flew hundreds of hours as a crew chief for the new pilots as they were trained to fly and shoot the rocket system.

We flew day and night, day after day, until they could fly in all kinds of weather, under all kinds of conditions. We lived in the boonies more than Fort Benning. We spent two months in North and South Carolina being tested, because we were the first Army division to use helicopters to move men and equipment. We lost our first and best pilot in South Carolina in September 1964, Jerry C. Spence, Capt. A lot of Hueys lost their jet turbine engines in the Carolina. Because of those accidents a lot of lives were saved in Vietnam. We were sucking long grass in our turbine engines, causing the compressor blades to get out of balance and blow up.

We installed filters to prevent this from happening before we went to Vietnam. We lost one Huey in Fort Steward on a night mission. Thank God no one was hurt. After all the testing, they changed our name from the 11th Air Assault to the First Cav. Div. and sent us to Vietnam. I helped fly my new Huey, No. 64-2026, to the east coast of Florida to be cacooned and put on an aircraft carrier for Vietnam. We were shipped by train a month later to Florida, where we were put on an aircraft carrier with our Hueys.

The air conditioning was not working so they just took one pilot and crew chief per Huey. As we left Florida and headed for the Panama Canal they were able to get the air conditioning to work, and the rest of the trip was a lot cooler. We went through the Panama Canal and then refueled and took on fresh water and then we were on our way to Vietnam. It took us thirty days to get there. We dropped anchor just off the coast of Qui Nhon, and started to put our Hueys together. Our company commander told us to put our duffel bags in his Huey, and then he left us.

I had trouble with my Huey—an electrical short—so they moved it off to the side, and moved on to another one. I was there for thirty days with just the clothes on my back. I washed my clothes at night and hung them up to dry. Every day I would help put more Hueys together until we got to mine. After a day of trouble shooting they decided to fly it to An Khe. When I arrived at An Khe I found my duffel bag all wet and moldy. My dress shoes were green along with all my other clothes.

We had to live in small individual tents for a month until we received larger tents. The first month was bad. The perimeter around the First Cav. was not very good and just about every night some bullets would come through our area. One morning when we got up we found some holes in our tents. As we started to check the tents we found a hole in one tent that went out the other side, then in another tent and out the other side, then in another and not out the other side. This is the Gospel truth. The bullet went in the tent, through the holster and cocked the hammer on Gary Pancake's 45 revolver. His 45 saved his life. He was in line with that bullet. His 45 was laying on top of his duffel bag by his feet.

I flew a lot of missions, over 300 to be exact, mostly around An Khe and Pleiku. We flew support for every one that needed it, from a convoy to infantry that was pinned down and needed help. I was on call, twenty-four hours on, twenty-four hours off, day or night. The flight that stands out in my mind the most is when we were called up to Pleiku one night. A convoy was ambushed one mile southwest of Pleiku and by the time we got there it was very dark and the South Vietnamese Army could not secure the area until morning, so we flew over to Pleiku and made camp until sunup. I refueled my Huey and bedded down for the night. As soon as we could see we flew over to the area to secure it. As I sat in the door of my Huey I could see no survivors at all. The trucks were burned and damaged from the mines they hit.

We flew back to Pleiku and then I refueled my Huey again. Then that following night it happened. We received a call that Charlie was overrunning a Special Forces camp about two miles southwest of Pleiku. It was a very hot and humid night. We had a hard time getting off the ground with a load of rockets, fuel, and ammo for the door-gunners. Sometimes we had to slide the skids on the grass to obtain lift I do not know how we found them. All we had was radio contact—no radar. We flew high enough to clear the highest hill according to our maps. I hoped they were right. You could not see a thing, it was so dark. When we arrived at the camp they set off a white smoke grenade. But I could not see it, so we fired two rockets and then they told us what direction, from impact, to drop the rest of them. There were three Hueys, so we took turns until the Special Forces told us to stop.

We flew back to Pleiku and I refueled my Huey and loaded more rockets and ammo for the M-60 machine guns. Then I bedded down for the night. About 2 a.m. we received another call from the Special Forces. This time I almost did not make it. As we were sliding our skids on the grass to get lift someone said, "Isn't there a power line here some place?" We turned on our landing light and the wire was right in front of us. As I sat in the door I watched the pilot quickly raise the nose of my Huey to clear the wire. I quickly keyed my mike and told the pilot we were clear, then he quickly nosed my Huey over to keep the wire out of the tail rotor. The ground crew back at camp thought we hooked the wire and were going to flip over. I do not know where the power came from because my exhaust temp was redline and the T53Lll jet turbine engine was working as hard as it could. We came down, just kissing the grass, and we were off again. We again chased Charlie away and then returned back to refuel and reload. Then I bedded down.

About 5 a.m. we received another call from the Special Forces, so we flew out there again. This time, after we emptied our rockets on the enemy, Puff showed up to help us out. I never saw him in action before. It was like a huge flame thrower. He lit up the sky and we never were called out there again. I never saw that camp in the daytime, but I was proud to be part of the crew that successfully completed three missions at night to save the Special Forces. I am very proud of those missions.

Sometimes we would pick up a Special Forces man and drop him off on a hill to live with the people in the area and try to find out if the VC were in the area. We would go back a week later and pick him up. We would usually get a mission within a week. This time we were to destroy a village that the VC was using. This night they picked my Huey, the one we had the big flood light on, and one from another company that had the 50-cal guns on. As we left An Khe the Huey with the light on was first, mine was next and the Huey with the 50-cal was last. It was a very cold night. We were flying west over a small river when some 50-cal rounds from the ground came flying by my Huey. They sounded like an M-80 firecracker going off.

We found the village and destroyed it. On our way back we used up our rockets and ammo on the riverbank. When we got back to An Khe we discussed the mission and wondered how they could see us when we had our lights taped so you could not see us from the ground, and all we could figure out was that we got between them and the moon and became a silhouette in the sky. I carry a 50-cal round on my key chain to remind me of a mission that almost cost me my life.

I spent seven days in Saigon on R&R and had a chance to see how the people lived. I was surprised how backward they were, but the city was interesting. There was a lot of French architecture in the buildings left over from the French when they were there. I had a chance to see the new 1966 Chevy cars in the showrooms, and spent some time at the zoo. Eddy Fisher was staying in the same hotel I was, and I was able to take some movies of him. I also have some movies of Bob Hope. I went to church in Kennedy Square and the mass was in Latin. A lot of kids lived in the streets. They had no homes. The city was very dirty and sewer water was in the streets.

I received the Air Medal for twenty-five aerial missions. I received the First Oak Leaf Cluster for 100 aerial missions. I received the Second Oak Leaf Cluster for 100 aerial missions. I received the Third Oak Leaf Cluster for 100 aerial missions. My call sign was Armed Falcon.

I left Vietnam on January 22, 1966, on a Freedom Bird and returned to civilian life. I work as a mechanic and am married and have five children. I just wish the war had ended differently.

Floyd R. Stringer

High School here is tenth through twelfth grades. I started school year 1964-65 at Alamogordo High in late August. I was an average student in accelerated classes for three years, during which I was in orchestra and dance band (on string bass). No sports; didn't excel at anything. Just cruised, stayed out of trouble. Priorities were friends, work, girls, and cars, not necessarily in that order. Enjoyed my middle-class white upbringing—first one in my family on both sides ever to graduate high school in any generation. Consequently, I also felt compelled to attend college, make my father proud, etc. So I applied to Eastern New Mexico University and majored in Drafting/Engineering with a minor in Music because I was on a partial music scholarship. I passed (barely).

But I was wasting time. Came home for Christmas break and told my dad I was gonna drop out and join the Army so I could get what I wanted instead of being drafted. That was December of 1967. He said he thought I would be making that decision soon. So, by February 28, 1968, I was in basic training at Fort Bliss, El Paso, Texas. Having failed the hearing-test part of my physical, I couldn't be a helicopter pilot, but because of my mechanical aptitude I signed up for helicopter mechanic.

I graduated from basic on April 25, 1968, and reported to Fort Eustis, Virginia, Transportation School on 9 May 1968; 67N20 MOS School was eleven weeks—Single Rotor Turbine Utility Helicopter Repair. At about five weeks, some guy came in and asked who thought they wanted to be instructors after graduation, so I said, "What the hell. It'll make my mother happy if I don't go to Vietnam right away," so I put my name in the pool. Three days before UH-1 school graduation, I got my orders—Instructor School, Fort Eustis, Virginia.

After graduation (1 Aug 68) and two weeks of Instructor School, I was teaching helicopters. In November 1968, I got notification of my receipt of orders for Nam. December 10, 1968 I left Virginia for thirty-five days of leave before reporting to Oakland Army Base for shipment to Nam; reporting date 15 January 1969.

Upon arrival at Oakland, I met three old friends from UH-1 school. We got our shots, processed, got drunk, got tattooed, and shipped from Travis AFB, California, on 19 January 1969. Made stopovers at Juneau, Alaska, and Yokota AFB Japan, before landing at Bien Hoa Replacement Depot, RVN, 20 January 1969 about 0300.

About 0730 we had a formation where guys' names were called. The heat and the smell of the country were starting to make an impression on me. I got a ride over to the chopper pad and was told to wait for my ride. It came soon enough.

On only my second helicopter ride, I was on my way to Dong Tam, Mekong Delta, HQ for 9th Inf. Div. After a stopover at the now famous Soc Trang, we arrived at my ultimate destination, 162nd Aslt. Hel. Co., 12th Grp., 1st Avn. Bde. Upon meeting the CO and reporting, I requested a ship of my own. I wanted to be a crew chief and a door-gunner. (Oh, out of the mouths of babes.) All I wanted to do was fly. I didn't know about the rest. How could I? I was twenty years old. My father was too young for WWII. My uncle was in Korea, had a bullet hole in his shins, but wasn't around to talk to. So, the CO told me I'd be on a preventative maintenance (PM) crew for a while and, if my performance was satisfactory, I'd be moved to a flight platoon later.

In the meantime, I was bunked (billeted) in the maintenance platoon hooch, shown around the compound, introduced around, met my platoon sergeant, who happened to have the same last name as mine, and met my co-workers; they showed me where the bunkers were. They said they had just moved down to Dong Tam from Phouc Vinh in September 1968 and my PM duties were 100-hour inspections on UH-IH birds and emergency repairs. We were expected to fly twenty-four birds a day—sixteen slicks, eight UH-IB or C gunships. Our depot kept flying, even to the point of flying scavenger missions, that is, carrying parts to downed birds with minor mechanical problems that could be flown out with the installation of a part or two. These were rarely hairy, but as you know, any time was party time in RVN. So, not wanting to miss anything, I volunteered for as many as I could.

As portrayed in that damned movie *Platoon*, there were two distinct groups, the Heads and the Juicers. Being into rock 'n' roll music, I fell in with the Heads, and like our hero in that flick, started to smoke a little—a lot—even on duty, only at night, out on the flight line, in groups around the birds that were crewed by the Heads. Had some really good times, good vibes. Sat in a bunker one night during a rocket attack and watched Spooky (C-47 w/7.62 mini-guns) kick Charlie's ass. Good times. Good friends. Good memories.

After two months of PM crew duty, the shop OIC told our crew to go out to the flight line and retrieve a disabled bird—815. Seems its crew chief, a Head, was late for "crank" (engine fire up) that morning, hadn't cleaned his air filter (somebody sabotaged the filters by opening them and dropping in one M-60 round and closing them back up) and lost an engine on lift-off. No injuries, but the turbine engine T53-L13 was scrap metal. So the ship's OIC says to me, "Stringer, we fired the other chief. When this one goes out, it's yours!"

"WHAT A TRIP—WHAT A DEAL—WHAT AM I DOING!"

So I moved my gear over to Flight Platoon hooch, upstairs (downstairs was Gunship Platoon, I was slicks) White Tails, Vultures.

I got a bunk next to my door-gunner (he was responsible for the operation of our two on-board M-60s) whose name was Mike, from Montana, if memory serves. Five foot seven inches or so, 120 pounds, blond, small but tough (seems he had already spent a year in the bush with the 101st Airborne and extended five months to get a five-months drop in service) and he says, "So what do I call you?" "How about Floyd? That's my name." "Nope. Father-in-law's name is Floyd." "My middle name is Ray." "Nope, no good. How about Fuzzy?" "Okay with me." "That's cool."

So that was my new nickname in the flight platoon—Fuzzy. Made me feel welcome and a part of the outfit. I started playing crew chief and right-side door-gunner as soon as my ship came out of maintenance with a new engine. Please note that Mike and I flew left and right, respectively.

Routine missions. Learned the ropes for two or three days—how to stand up coming into an LZ and check for trip-wires on tree stumps or pungi stakes; sit down and reach for your mike button and say "Clear on right, Sir!" anytime we sat down; open the pilot's door for circulation; sit down for C-rations at Ben Tre for lunch; and back to work in the afternoon.

On my fourth day, I lost my cherry. We left a PZ (Pick-up Zone) in a diamond formation, my ship in lead. It was 13 March 1969. Upon approaching the LZ—a dry rice paddy surrounded by dikes with a large clump of brush to our left front. Almost at touch down my pilot started to wriggle rapidly in his chair immediately to my left. Before I looked to see what the problem was, I saw an NVA running down the dike away from my ship, toward a small hooch. I couldn't fire at him because my disembarking troops from Sunshine Company were standing between the NVA and me. I started whistling as loud as I could but couldn't be heard over the ship's noise, so I swung my M-60 barrel down and to the right and squeezed off two rounds. The grunts jumped around at me just as we lifted off, and I'm pointing at this dink running down the dike. As soon as my barrel clears the friendlies, I'm busting caps at this dude running for cover. He's less than 150 feet away, and the grunts open up and there's little puffs of dust flying all around. The last thing I saw was him sliding on his face into the doorway of this dink's hooch. I don't know who got him, but I claimed him.

When I swung around to tell my pilot and A/C (aircraft commander) that I'd got one, Mike, my left door-gunner, was kneeling behind the pilot's seat, fooling with those little red handles on the back of the seat. Then it dawned on me that all the commotion earlier was the pilot getting hit. I got to the seat just in time to help lay the seat back, unbuckle his belts and pull him out of the seat. We laid him in the UH-lH rear floor, cut his pants legs up the middle to the crotch and bandaged a hole in his right leg, right where it becomes buttock. The A/C is flying as fast as the ship will travel back to Dong Tam, and the pilot crooks a finger for me to come talk to him—he's laying on the floor with his head in the crook of my ankle. He says, "I think my left leg is bleeding, too!" So we split the other pants leg and sure enough, shrapnel from the bullet ricocheting off the seat had made several small holes in his left leg, way up high. So Mike bandages that one. The pilot smiles, crooks his finger again and I pull my flight helmet away from my ears and he says, "Are my balls all right?" Yeah, his love life would be great after a little hospital time.

Upon closer examination of the aircraft after a stop at the base hospital, we found no fewer than twelve holes in the left side of the ship through the rotor blades, belly, and one first aid pack behind the A/C seat. That small patch of brush was full of NVA. Unfortunately, I never heard what happened to the poor SOBs we left on that hot LZ. And it has worried me for twenty-one years.

We got back into the routine after a couple days in maintenance— patch holes, replace rotor blades, etc.—and all was calm until one bright shiny afternoon when we finished early, only to find out our aircraft commander had volunteered us for a night insertion into the Plain of Reeds, a notoriously hot swampy area WSW of Saigon—two to four ships from several companies flying together to insert numerous grunts in waves in tactical formations and areas. By the time we were lifting the third wave, it was dark. What's weird is, in Nam, no one flew with position marking lights 'cause they were just targets at night, so each pilot flew in position by watching the other ship's instrument lights! Close. Too close. Then, if you'd fire, Charlie would follow your tracers back with his green tracers. Did you ever sit almost still (100 mph at night is almost still!) and watch someone fire 51-cal tracers at you? Beaucoup Pucker Factor! As helicopter personnel, we lived through that one. I'm sorry to say a lot of grunts were not so lucky. Bummer. Back to normal regular routine, whatever that was. Flying six days a week, sixteen hours a day.

On April 10, 1969, upon leaving our base and heading out to the bush, we were told we would be flying train in the diamond formation in the last flight of four ships, extracting 9th Inf. grunts from their night position to move them to a new area. After flying out one wave, we were the last ship on the last flight in the last lift. Since we were leaving an area that was no longer secure, we had "suppression" (permission to fire) upon extraction. My gunner (a substitute, an MP who wanted to fly) and I opened up with both M-60s, to an altitude of about 350 feet. As soon as we stopped and sat down the ship shook violently once, as if hit by some gigantic hammer. We started down fast. The pilot and A/C were busy. The gunner and I started busting caps in rapid fashion and we were watching the jungle come at us. The A/C did an auto-rotation (read "controlled crash"), lost rotor speed a little early, and we crashed into a road alongside a rubber plantation. Everyone jumped but me. My M-60 was stuck between two stalks of bamboo and I was trying to free it when I realized my vulnerable position. I jumped out, hit the ground alongside one of our VC suspects, hands not tied, stripped to the loincloth, and he was giving me dirty looks—pulled my AF survival knife, put it to his throat and screamed, "Move, sucker, and I'll slit you from ear to ear!"

As the C&C ship landed in a dry paddy to retrieve us—our grunts and suspects—I grabbed my M-60 and twenty or thirty rounds in one hand and that dink in the other and sprinted the two hundred feet to the other ship. As we were running, one of our C-model gunships rocketed a small hooch 100 meters in the opposite direction "just in case." We got on board the C&C ship, which was quite overloaded, but somehow the A/C got us off and back safely. Another day in Vacationland Vietnam.

After sitting around for a couple of days, sending 815 back to depot for rebuild or salvage, getting my hair (nerve) back together, I started substituting for other crew chiefs who hadn't had a day down in a while. On my second day flying, on the way to the first PZ of the afternoon, we heard over the radio that the LZ was booby-trapped, but that the grunts had prepped the area and set them all off. All was now in preparation for our arrival. As my ship approached the LZ, we were in left wing in diamond formation. The grunts were assembled, ready to embark upon our touch-down. I stood up, surveyed my side, sat down to reach for my "mike" and all hell broke loose. The ship was pitching violently up on it's nose—my M-60 ammo was flying by me—I was being thrown forward almost out of my seat toward the pilot (except for my seat belt). Shit was happening! When things stopped moving, my right thigh was bloody and my pants were shredded above the knee. My right wrist was bloody and I was hanging partly out of my seat belt. I looked up just in time to see the pilot stepping out between the seats. As he went by, I said, "Lieutenant, I'm hit and I'm hit bad!" So he says, "Okay!" and walks out. I unbuckled my seat belt, slid across the floor to the left side of the ship and the gunner (Bart), grabs me by my arm pits and drags me out of the ship. As he sits down in this dry paddy and cradles my head and shoulders in his lap, he bandages my wrist and gets someone to tourniquet my leg. I'm lying there crying and cussing, screaming and bitching and Bart says, "Take it easy, man, you could be as bad off as him. Besides, you're going home!" As I look about three meters past my feet, there is the grunt LT with the top of his head missing. He had been standing in front of the ship when it pitched forward, permitting the rotor blade to hit him in the side of the head—*ZAP!*

While I was the only one on board a helicopter who was hurt, there were two KIAs and eleven WIAs among the grunts. Obviously, we had landed on another one of those booby traps the grunts had been clearing. As we found out later, they were U.S. 105mm rounds that a CH-47 Chinook had accidentally dropped in transit. Charlie got 'em and used 'em to his advantage.

Poor Bart, the door-gunner. He felt terrible. Ordinarily, on his ship, he would have been flying right side. But since I was the crew chief and technically out-ranked him, even though I was a substitute on his ship, I insisted on flying right seat. He wrote to me later and told me how he should have been the one who was hit and how bad he felt. Not to mention Tom! He was the regular crew chief who just wanted a day down to run personal errands! But I can honestly say that I have never had a bad thought toward either of them in twenty years. It was just fate, "The one with my name on it." It was war and no one was to blame. As would be said today, "Shit happens." After lying in that dry paddy for about fifteen minutes, we heard a UH-1 approaching. It was a scavenger— no med-evacs were available. A scavenger was one of those salvage/ emergency parts-run birds—no litters, no medics, just a way out of the bush. About half the wounded were loaded on board and away we went back to Dong Tam. And someone had put one of the KIAs on board with us. No blood, not a mark on him, but he was obviously dead and no one had closed his eyes or bagged him. Bummer. Two rules of helicopter evacuations—never mix your KIA and WIA. Never look in the eyes of a dead man.

Upon our arrival at Dong Tam hospital—wish I could remember the unit numbers—I was the last one out and into the hospital. Once inside, my clothes were cut off me, I was examined, sent over to X-ray, had two IVs installed, and an air bag splint put on my broken right leg, put back on a Huey (this time a med-evac with IV poles and a medic) and sent down to the Evac Hospital at Vung Tau, the in-country R&R site on the southern coast. There, by 2:30 p.m. I was prepped and ready for surgery. By this time I had relaxed, probably had some morphine, and wasn't scared as bad.

The next thing I knew, I was being awakened by a corpsman who said my folks were on the phone. The phone was stationary, but the beds were mobile, as mine was rolled over to where the phone was. I picked it up and said, "This is Stringer. You got my folks on?" I received some basic instructions on MARS procedure and the operator said, "Stringer? You just talked to your folks!" "No, I didn't! But I'm ready now!" "All right. Hold on." In what was an amazingly brief time, my father said, "Hello?" "Dad? It's Floyd—over?" "Where are you?" Strange voice, "You can't tell 'em." "I can't say, but I'm in a hospital in a secure area and I'm okay." "Are you hurt badly?" Strange voice, "You can't tell 'em." "I'll have to write and tell you—but be satisfied that I can write and I'm in one piece."

I could hear my mother crying in the background. She wanted to know who she was talking to on the first call, where I was and why they had her phone for a wounded GI call. Seems they got their patient order wrong and hooked someone else up to my poor mother. Scared her to death.

They didn't close the wound on my leg. The cavity on the top of my thigh couldn't be covered by several 4X4 gauze pads. Couple days later, when they decided I was stable and where I was going, they put me in a one-and-one-half spica cast—goes from my armpits to my toes on the right leg and to the knee on my left leg for support. Shipped me to Camp Zama Army Hospital, Japan on 20 April 1969. I had been in-country exactly three months.

In Japan, I was operated on to close the wound on my leg and set the bone. I was placed in skeletal traction, and told I'd be in Japan for six to twelve weeks. The morale was remarkable—ninety-five percent were bedfast and not going back to the Nam. I laid there and watched the guys from Hamburger Hill come through. I listened to a nineteen-year-old chopper pilot, who had lost his lower leg in a fiery crash, lose his mind as he slept. I saw a major come through who had been shot from behind with a .223 cal. (M-16). A first-lieutenant with no legs from the knees down. And everyone got letters, packages, presents, even phone calls. It was quite a place, Ward 2 South.

On June 9, 1969, the Army sent me out to Yokota AFB by Huey, put me on an AFC-141, and gave me the worst, scariest ride I'd ever had. Twenty-two hours non-stop to Travis AFB, California. I was there about three days and was transferred to William Beaumont Army Hospital, El Paso, on (ready?) Friday 13th June 1969. Home at last!

I was in the hospital as an in-patient for another twenty months while they figured out how to best tie the tendons back together in the back of my hand. During my first nine months there, I met my wife, who was a U.S. Army hospital medic. Although she worked on the officer's ward, she had a friend on the enlisted ward. We met in November 1969, were married on 1 May 1970 and she was discharged 25 May 1970. So, obviously, she intimately understands a lot of the problems that go along with our life since. We started off with a lot in common.

As for my homecoming before marriage, I had it good. I didn't have any bad experiences at airport or bus terminals. I was sent home on convalescent leave twice for thirty days each time. One night I was in a small restaurant with two friends who were helping me get around, since I was still in that body cast. If you can picture this, I had to try to sit in a chair (no booths), right leg stuck straight out, left buttock on the chair, trying not to slide off onto the floor. Some ragged-looking cowboy on his way out comes over and says, "What happened to you?" I just said, "Vietnam." He gave me one of those slow, small cowboy grins and said, "Welcome home, Bud." Shook my hand and walked out.

That is why, for one, no one can tell me that what we did was wasted—for nothing. Don't tell me 58,000 died and their lives were wasted. They died for what they believed in, for what they thought was right.

As a disabled Vietnam vet, in the West, I had no trouble with the VA. Got my disability started, no problem. Got my school checks. Even got an OJT program with an automotive machine shop and got the VA to pay for it.

Since I've been in the work force, I've been a mechanic, machinist, mailman, service department manager, service writer, drag racer, and track announcer. The only job I was ever fired from was because of chronic nervousness, from which I still suffer. I get nervous, get jittery, panicky, but I'm learning to control the anxiety attacks and panic. My counselor says almost none of it has to do with Vietnam. She's good and her husband is an RVN F-4 A/F fighter pilot. Maybe she's right.

I've been to the DAV National Vietnam Veterans Memorial in Eagle Nest, New Mexico (or Angel Fire) and I was trying to go to The Wall for my twentieth anniversary of going into the hospital, but I couldn't make it (financially). Maybe next year. In the meantime, I tell everyone who will listen that I was there. I have a half dozen T-shirts proclaiming my past. New Mexico issues all kinds of special license plates to disabled vets, exPOWs and now, to Purple Heart recipients. I have Purple Heart plate 0175, and the decal on the back window says, "Vietnam Remembered."

Mike Stout

When I entered high school in 1960 at Kellyville, Oklahoma, there were only about one hundred students there at the time. My time in high school was relaxed and carefree. I wasn't too serious about my studies or anything else, for that matter. I only did what I had to do to get by. When I graduated in 1964 there were twenty-nine seniors in my class (two of us would have service in Vietnam in our future). I enrolled that fall at Oklahoma State University but was unable to attend classes for more than one semester at a time. I alternated between going to college and working at the Liberty Glass Co. in Sapulpa. This plan might have succeeded except for one event that burst upon the scene— VIETNAM.

I received my draft notice in March 1966 and I reported to the Oklahoma induction center on March 9, where we were required to strip naked and form a line. Our physical exam consisted of bending over and grabbing our ankles. An Army doctor moved down the line and placed the back of his hand on the cheek of your ass—if it felt warm, you were *GONE*.

Those of us who passed our physicals were flown to Fort Bliss, Texas for basic training. After basic, I received orders to report to the Medical Training Center at Fort Sam Houston, Texas for AIT. At that time, I was relieved. No infantry for me. When our class graduated from AIT, we had a formation where they would announce where our next duty station would be. Out of about 200 men, the names of three were called. They would be going to Germany. The rest of us would be going to Vietnam.

On 22 Aug. 1966, I said my good-byes to my wife, Marty (we married right after basic) and my parents. I left Tulsa bound for California and feeling mighty low. That night I arrived at the Oakland Army Depot. Two days later my name was finally called and we were bused to Travis AFB. At 3 p.m. on 24 August 1966 I began my journey to Vietnam, with stops in Honolulu and Clark AFB in the Philippines. After a very tiring flight, the pilot announced at last that we were approaching Vietnam. We landed at Tan Son Nhut at 1:30 a.m. on 25 August. Even at that hour, the heat was suffocating. We were loaded on buses and taken to Camp Alpha, which was just next door. There I received orders for the 1st Infantry Division, the Big Red One.

The next day, after a sleepless night, we boarded the buses again. This time our destination was the 90th Replacement Co. at Long Binh. This bus ride gave me my first real look at Vietnam and its people. I was not impressed.

At the 90th they would have a morning formation so they could assign you to a detail. As luck would have it, Joe Mondragon, a fellow medic and my good friend, and I were detailed to burn the contents of the metal drums that had been cut in half and placed in the latrines. There must be better way! A week later, Mondragon and the other medics assigned to the 1st Infantry had long since left for Di An, the headquarters of the Big Red One. I was still at Long Binh and still burning shit. I could see into the future... "What did you do in Vietnam, Daddy?" "Well, son, I burned shit for my Uncle Sam!"

Finally, on 5 Sept. my name was called from the morning formation. We loaded onto deuce-and-a-halfs for the convoy to Di An. All I could think of on this trip was how strange this land was. It was if we were suddenly on another world. When we arrived in Di An we were taken to the 1st Admin. Co. It was raining hard and we were moving around in a sea of mud. I stayed at Di An for a week because there was a mix-up in my orders. The 1st Admin. Co. assigned me to be their company medic, but it seems I was needed more at Lai Khe by the 2/28th Infantry. I missed the truck to Lai Khe on 12 September. A trip to the EM club was the main reason.

It was four days before I boarded a deuce-and-a-half for the run up Highway 13 (Thunder Road) to Lai Khe. When I arrived there it was raining, but mail from Marty lifted my spirits dramatically. I was temporarily assigned the 2/28th Battalion Aid Station. The next day the battalion went to the field on a training operation. We were the first replacements in the division and we replaced the men who came over by ship when the division shipped out for Vietnam in the summer of 1965. There were so many replacements that it was felt we should be broken in gradually. Nothing of importance happened on this training operation. I spent one miserable night in the rain and mud, and that I'll never forget.

By 1 Oct. we were back in Lai Khe, so several of us medics decided to go check out the village of Lai Khe (which was in the perimeter of 3rd Brigade base camp). I discovered that Lai Khe, South Vietnam and Kellyville, Oklahoma, U.S.A. had nothing in common, except size.

On 4 Oct., the battalion surgeon, Capt. Paul Bakule, assigned me as the aidman for the second platoon, Charlie Co., 2/28th Infantry. This company had a reputation (throughout the war) as a rowdy bunch, heavy drinkers and good fighters, in the field and in the base camp. I moved into my tent on the perimeter and found the men of the second platoon a little wary of their new "Doc." In the six months I spent with them I discovered that they would do anything for me, even die if need be, to protect me. God, what a bunch! I became good friends with Sgt. Ed Greene of Lenoir, North Carolina.

On 7 Oct., Charlie Co. was on alert all day on the airstrip. We were the brigade reaction force, but I was not eager to jump on the waiting Hueys and fly off into the unknown. The next day was spent giving Charlie Co. immunizations. They didn't seem to mind too much.

We choppered to An Loc on 12 October. There we set up a perimeter around an artillery company. Our LZ was on the front lawn of a Frenchman who owned a big rubber plantation. The Frenchman and his family watched us from the balcony of their chateau.

From An Loc we went to Loc Ninh, which was very near the Cambodian border. Most of our operations until this time had been small-scale and most of the casualties we suffered were from booby traps and snipers. This was about to change in a hurry.

On 25 Oct. it was raining hard and we found a large VC base camp that we had been searching for the past two days. The VC had already pulled out. By Halloween we had returned to Lai Khe and decided to go trick or treating. The battalion sealed the village of Lai Khe, trying to catch any VC who might be home visiting. We didn't find any, although they probably were all VC.

My twentieth birthday (3 Nov.) found the 2/28th once again on alert at the airstrip. We waited all day and returned to the company area late in the afternoon. The next day we were loaded onto C-130 aircraft and moved to the Special Forces camp at Minh Thanh. The 1/26th was already there and I had a chance to visit with Bill Roye from Oklahoma City. We had met at Fort Sam. We made several patrols in the area but made no contact.

I will never forget the hatred in the eyes of the villagers at Minh Thanh. I wondered to myself, "What the hell are we doing over here when the people obviously hate us so much?"

On 5 Nov. I developed a fever and was sent back to Lai Khe. The battalion returned later in the day. The next day the battalion was moved to Soui Dau, in Tay Ninh Province. We were close to Nui Ba Den (Black Virgin Mountain). On 7 Nov. we made an assault into a hot LZ near the mountain. After we had cleared the LZ the 1/28th moved in and we moved to another clearing about a klick away. Both battalions established their NDPs, which were close to each other. This operation (Attleboro) had already turned up beau-coup VC. The next morning, the 271st VC regiment and 101st NVA regiment attacked the 1/28th perimeter in full force. Our perimeter received enough fire to keep us occupied with our own problems. Our sister battalion was catching hell and there was nothing we could do to help them. For five hours the battle raged on. One of the dust-off choppers that managed to land during the battle carried our battalion chaplain, Father Michael Quealy. He was killed while giving Last Rites to a wounded man.

As luck would have it, Charlie Co. 2/28th was lifted into the 1/28th perimeter to help mop up the remaining VC/NVA. I was on the first lift in and I was mighty scared. After the snipers and VC in spider holes were taken care of, Charlie 2/28th searched the area and found the largest VC base camp any of us had ever seen. In one bunker, our troops found over 25,000 Chi-Com hand grenades. There were tons of supplies of every kind. No wonder the VC fought so hard. We had almost spent the night in their division supply base. We remained in the vicinity of Nui Ba Den for several days, but the VC had long since slipped into Cambodia.

We were back in Lai Khe for Thanksgiving, where we had a complete turkey dinner. We also had nine Vietnamese orphans sharing our feast with us.

We left Lai Khe on 5 Dec. for an operation in the Rung Sat Zone, which was the mangrove swamps at the mouth of the Nha Be River. Travel in the Rung Sat was rough. After we were deposited on a riverbank by U.S. Navy LSTs out of Nha Be, the company had traveled only a couple of hundred meters in about two hours. Several men had collapsed with heat stroke, and getting to them wasn't easy, to say the least. After two days of ambushes on the rivers and canals of the Rung Sat, we were all wrinkled like prunes. Water. There was saltwater. On ambushes, our M-60 crews had to float their guns on air mattresses to keep them above the water. No heavy contact was made, although we did knock off several sampans. On 9 December we were choppered to a small village at the edge of the Rung Sat. There we piled our rotted jungle fatigues so they could be burned. We had to lie naked in a peanut field so the sun could dry our bodies. Between the saltwater and the large blue crabs that tried to eat us alive, our skin was in poor condition.

The rest of December we operated in the Loc Ninh-Quan Loi area. On 23 December I was reassigned to the Weapons Platoon (Mortar Platoon). On Christmas Day some of us were selected to go by convoy to Di An to see the Bob Hope Christmas show. If two Americans ever deserve to be loved by the GIs, they are Bob Hope and Martha Raye (who by the way was in Lai Khe).

Charlie Co. started off the new year on 1 Jan. by pulling road security north of Lai Khe on Highway 13. Our area of responsibility was near the villages of Bau Bang and Ben Dong So. Both villages had been bulldozed down earlier for being a little too friendly with the VC. On 2 January we were back on Highway 13 after returning to Lai Khe the night before. After mine sweepers had cleared the roadbed each morning, we would secure our stretch of highway. Late one morning, Sergeant Greene led a patrol of about fifteen men to the east of Highway 13. The patrol was on its way back to our lines when they reported finding something that looked suspicious. Those of us that were in the Co. CP group were sleeping or reading but became alert after this report. Suddenly a huge explosion was heard in the direction of the patrol. A call for a medic came in from the patrol, so I grabbed my aid bag and a sergeant grabbed his M-16 and we went racing off in the direction of the explosion. The area was mostly scrub jungle and elephant grass so we made pretty good time. But by the time we had gone a couple of hundred meters, I thought that my lungs were going to burst.

As we approached the patrol, we discovered an old abandoned rice paddy about seventy-five meters across, and the patrol was just the other side of this waist-deep paddy. How I managed to finally cross this obstacle, I can't recall. Somehow I managed to splash my way to where the patrol was located. The troops who were not wounded had formed a small perimeter, and several bodies lay inside that perimeter and they needed help fast. The first man I came to was Spec-4 Strandberg. He was quite obviously dead, as was the next man, Spec-4 Fugate. He had less than a week left in Vietnam. The next man I came to was my good friend Sergeant Greene, who insisted that I treat Private First Class Spina next. Spina was in a lot of pain because he had a sucking chest wound, which I covered with the plastic wrapper of a battle dressing. When I started to work on Sergeant Greene, I could see that his chances for survival were slim. The lower part of his body was shredded by the blast, which probably came from a VC claymore mine. About all I could do for him was to administer morphine.

When the dust-off finally came in, we loaded these wounded along with Private First Class Howe, who had shrapnel in his buttocks. They were taken to the 1st Medical Battalion at Lai Khe, and the rest of the company returned to Lai Khe before dark. Learning of Sergeant Greene's death did not surprise me, but I was shocked to find out that Spina had died. He had a sucking chest wound in the left armpit that I had somehow missed. From then on, I stripped all our wounded. I did not want to lose another man due to my incompetence.

The shock of losing these men had hardly eased when Charlie Co. and the entire division had embarked on Operation Cedar Falls on 8 Jan. The assault on the village of Ben Suc was led by the 1/26th and their battalion commander, Lt. Col. Alexander M. Haig, Jr. We (the 2/28th) were right behind them. The VC had apparently decided not to fight for the village so they went underground. Ben Suc was in the Iron Triangle and was known to be a VC village. We had no major contact during Cedar Falls, but the first night in Ben Suc, one man was walking between two of our bunkers when he stepped on what must have been a very large mine. We searched for the man who stepped on the mine, but could not find him. After daylight we placed what small pieces we could find of him into an empty sandbag. I guess these remains were returned to his family.

At the end of January, our battalion was given what amounted to an R&R. We were sent to Long Binh to help guard the huge ammo dump. We patrolled for several days in the thick scrub jungle and the only thing we found was a large population of red ants. During the night of 4 February the VC blew up part of the ammo dump. It looked like a giant 4th of July party—lots of fireworks. This was not in the portion of the perimeter that we were guarding.

Operation Junction City began on 22 February. We had been lifted to Soui Dau the day before. I was supposed to go on R&R to Hong Kong on 5 March, but it was cancelled for some reason. Instead I went to the 93rd Evac. Hospital at Long Binh on 9 March—I was on TDY status. I had just finished my first year in Uncle Sam's Army.

At the 93rd, I worked the 11-7 shift in the recovery room. There were about thirty medics at the 93rd that I had known at Fort Sam. While I was TDY I once again developed a raging fever and was admitted to the hospital. There was an old mamasan that swept the floors and she spotted the Big Red One patch on my shirt that was hanging next to my bed. She asked me where I was from (in Vietnam). When I told her Lai Khe, she said, "Ah, beau-coup VC, Lai Khe, beau-coup VC." "No shit, mamasan? Beau-coup VC, Lai Khe?" She then told me that her family had fled the north because they were Catholics and that she hated the VC. Well, I believed her anyway.

I returned to Lai Khe on 25 Mar. and was told then that I was being assigned to Alpha Co. as their senior medic. Alpha Co. had good leadership in Captain Sawtelle and First Sergeant Ford. My first operation with Alpha Co. was Operation Manhattan, in the Iron Triangle. As we were entering a VC base camp, the man directly in front of me suddenly went up in a cloud of smoke. The force of the explosion threw me several feet to one side of the trail we were on. I was stunned for just a moment. My ears were ringing and I had severe pain in my back, but at least I wasn't bleeding. The troop that had stepped on the mine was lying in the trail a few feet in front of me. He was minus one foot. The missing foot, still in his boot, was sitting upright just off the trail. After we had requested a dust-off for our wounded man, we were informed that BG James F. Hollingsworth, the assistant division commander, was in the area in his command chopper. General Hollingsworth's ship sat down in a small clearing not far from our position, and the general walked into where we were. A litter was made from a poncho and the wounded man was carried to the waiting chopper, one of the men carrying the litter was BG Hollingsworth. This did not go unnoticed by the other men of Alpha Co.

On 20 May (my first wedding anniversary) we were on Highway 1A, south of Phuoc Vinh, pulling road security. We had some fancy bunkers, mainly because every day about 4 p.m., a local VC put a few rounds of 60mm mortar into our perimeter. We named him Milton the Mortar Man. We could set our watches by him. We were still short of medics in the battalion and I was still hoping to get out of the field sometime soon.

The battalion left Lai Khe on 14 June to begin Operation Billings. We were forty-five klicks from Lai Khe and only two klicks from the Cambodian border. Almost immediately, we began to encounter small groups of VC. I think we were the first American troops to operate in this area. On 16 June we had just finished preparing our NDP, when we heard the report of the mortar tubes. Everyone made a mad dash for the bunkers. I was there waiting for them. One of the new men, who had just gotten off the resupply bird a few minutes earlier, made the mistake of sitting in his bunker with his back to the entrance. Shards from one of the mortar rounds took off the back of head. He had been in the field for maybe ten minutes and he was already dead. If you get killed in the first ten minutes of your tour, or if you get killed in the last ten minutes of your tour, what difference does it make? You are just as dead.

The next day, 17 June 1967, the 1/16th Infantry and the 2/28 Infantry (minus Charlie Co.) moved out of our NDP for a clearing about a klick away. When the lead elements of the 1/16th (their recon platoon) entered the clearing, an ambush was popped by a battalion of the 271st VC Regiment. Alpha Co. 2/28th was just outside the clearing when the ambush was started. Our riflemen had to maneuver so they would not be firing into the 1/16th lines. By that time, all hell had broken loose. Cries for medics came from every direction. I found and treated as many wounded as I could, but every time I would move, VC snipers would shoot at me. Besides my regular aid bag, I carried a large waterproof bag that was about two feet square. This bag was full of nothing but battle dressings. Our battalion commander, who had in his personal gear some sheets, at my request, tore the sheets into strips that I could use for bandages. After numerous airstrikes and what must have been hundreds of rounds of artillery, the VC broke contact after five hours.

Soon the casualties were coming to our makeshift aid station faster than we could treat them. After things had settled down, 222 VC bodies were counted around the perimeter. American losses were thirty-eight killed and 155 wounded. I was near total exhaustion as was my fellow medic, Jim Callahan. During the battle (later named the Battle of Xom Bo) there were film crews from CBS and a reporter from AP, Henri Huet (later killed in Vietnam), who were taking photographs. Many of the wounded I treated were from the 1/16th. We had no idea what happened to their medics but it made no difference; we would go out and drag out of danger any American who needed help. At last the wounded and dead were taken from the field. There was nothing else we could do for them.

The next day I spent most of the time in the Alpha Co. CP bunker. That afternoon I was told to report to the Battalion CP as there was someone who wanted to talk with me. To this I replied that I didn't want to talk to anyone. After I was told that the visitor was MG John H. Hay, the division commander, I thought it might be a good idea to go after all. General Hay spoke with me for several minutes and then presented me with the Silver Star. I am proud of this for only two reasons. I did the best job I could and there were some Americans alive that day because I was able to help them. My wife and family back home in Oklahoma saw me on the CBS "Evening News," with Huntley and Brinkley.

On 27 June, we were back in Lai Khe to meet our new battalion commander, but I was more interested in meeting another replacement that came in that day—*mine*. The first week in July I went on a three-day R&R to Vung Tau and also made Spec-5. I was feeling pretty good about this time and I was getting pretty short. I moved back to the battalion aid station on 8 July. I really hated to leave Alpha Co. but we had several new medics that the battalion surgeon was sending out to the line companies.

My last few weeks in Vietnam were spent in a variety of ways. I made several trips to Di An and Long Binh by hitching a ride on either a dust-off or a slick that happened to be going that way. I even rode shotgun on a convoy down Thunder Road to Di An. Life at the aid station was bullshit.

On one trip to the airstrip at Lai Khe to pick up some newly-arrived medics, I stopped to offer a ride to a couple of men from the 1/16th. They climbed into the back of my ambulance jeep and I continued on my way. All at once one of these guys calls me by name and asks me how things are back in Sapulpa, Oklahoma. When I turned around, there sat Carl Bell. I had gone to school with him years before at Blue Bell, a little one-room school west of Sapulpa. I hadn't seen him in a long time and here we run into each other 12,000 miles from home.

It finally came time for me to leave Vietnam. About the middle of August I left Lai Khe. My first stop was Di An and the 1st Admin. Co. I had orders to report to Fort McClellan, Alabama as my next duty station. We were bused from Di An to the 90th Rep. Depot at Long Binh and on 23 August 1967 I left Vietnam from Bien Hoa AFB. In my mind I can still see that big green Braniff 707 coming into Bien Hoa to take me home. We made a stop to refuel at Yakota AFB, Japan and from there it was nonstop to Travis AFB, California. Good-bye Vietnam; hello California.

After leaving the Army in March 1968, I returned to my old job at the Liberty Glass Co. in Sapulpa, Oklahoma. In a couple of months I decided to take the Civil Service Exam. I went to work for the U.S. Post Office in Tulsa, Oklahoma in June 1968. I worked as a letter carrier until July 1977, when I was retired on disability. I had a lot of problems while working for the post office and I realize now that most of them were the result of my Vietnam service. I worked at several jobs over the next few years, none of them for very long, until June 1981, when I went to work for a company in Perry, Oklahoma. I was employed there as a personnel clerk until December 1987. Four back surgeries have taken their toll and I am unable to work any longer. I am now totally disabled and have been told that I will need further surgery on my back.

It has now been twenty-two years since I returned home from Vietnam. In those twenty-two years there has not been one single day that I have not thought of my time in Vietnam, and the one question that I've never been able to answer—WHY? Why Vietnam? America, can you answer this question for me? Why were we in Vietnam in the first place? I've read most of the answers given by the so-called experts and their answers are all bullshit! Why did our people send their sons off to fight and die in Vietnam, in a war that was never meant to be won? Didn't we learn anything from Korea? How much American blood will it take to get your attention? Why did you send us there and then turn your backs on us? When we came home, why did you act as if we had done something wrong? Remember, you sent us there. Why do you now treat us as your bastard children? America, why have you forgotten the POW/MIAs from Vietnam? I guess it's easy for you. You don't even want to think of the ones like me who survived and came back home. Why worry about some poor bastard pulling a plow in some rice paddy in Vietnam or Laos? After all, that's all behind us now, right?

I wish I could sit down with the men who were in Washington in 1965 and ask them to explain a few things to me. Maybe somehow it would make some sense. Some of those men are now dead and I believe they better have had some good answers, because their day of judgment has already come. As a nation, our judgment has not yet been rendered. The jury is still out.

Jim Stewart

Of course I did not know what to expect, and I never thought I would stay in Vietnam for four years.

I volunteered for the Army in 1965 and all I knew was that I didn't want to be a cook. There had been policemen in my family, so I thought that when I qualified for the military police that joining would be the honorable thing to do.

Basic training was at Fort Jackson, South Carolina, and the Military Police Academy was at Fort Gordon, Georgia. I was really square and a virgin, and never got into the scene of going off base. My free time was spent playing ball, golf, and hanging out with my other square friends.

Once we graduated from the academy we were sent to Fort Benning, Georgia, but our assignment was kept confidential. After a long bus ride through Georgia we arrived to find everyone at our new duty station wearing green T-shirts, not the regular white issue. But we still didn't grasp the meaning. We were never told of our next destination, but we were now welcomed to Counter-Guerrilla Warfare Training School. After six weeks of combat training we were given three weeks leave and told we would be put on a troop carrier headed for Vietnam.

In August of 1966 the 552nd MP Company was loaded onto the *USS Buckner* with thousands of Marines and sent off on a twenty-one day "cruise," and I would forever hate ships and the Navy. We finally stopped in Okinawa and the Marines were given shore leave. Drunk Marines were everywhere, throwing up and swimming on beaches clearly marked "NO SWIMMING, CONTAMINATED WATER." Mostly we just stood around and watched the drunkenness, never giving any thought that many of these young men would never return home. The next day we were at sea again and were told we would be landing in a few days.

On disembarkation day we climbed down nets onto landing crafts with unloaded rifles and pistols and headed toward the beach. We landed in Vung Tau, the in-country rest and recreation center. The beach was beautiful and I could see a sharply dressed MP directing traffic. All looked quiet. I don't recall being scared, and I don't recall the stifling heat that all the vets talk about. As a matter of fact, I thought it was pretty neat.

From there we got on a C-130 cargo plane for a flight to Bien Hoa. We all had to sit down on the floor with our legs straight out and cargo straps were braced across our legs to keep us from sliding all over the plane. It was very uncomfortable. Once in Bien Hoa we loaded into buses with windows covered with mesh wire. This was to protect the occupants from grenades that might be thrown at the bus, but at the same time many girls were waving at us from the street corners.

Our final destination was the large military post of Long Binh. It would become the largest military complex in the world. Bien Hoa would also become the busiest airport in the world.

At Long Binh, all we had was a chow hall sitting on top of a barren stretch of dirt. No showers, no latrines, no tents, no perimeter fence, nothing. We ate and got to work. We had thirty days to make our compound inhabitable. It would be thirty days of hard, tedious, boring labor. When asked what was to stop the VC from coming into the compound at night, we were told there was nothing but us. We went out in teams of two, dug in, sat, and watched. I must have seen about fifty VC moving about, but I'm sure there were none. We wanted to shoot every bush that moved in the wind, but we of course didn't. There was a hamlet about 300 yards away that was sympathetic to the VC, so why shouldn't we be attacked? That night I was truly scared for the first time in my life. I was nineteen.

The monsoons, which I always loved, meant we could bathe. It would be 100 degrees and sunny, and then the rain would come. There would be enough time to strip, lather up and rinse off. Each day became more boring, a repeat of the day before. I had my big toe nail removed at Fort Benning and it got infected. So I went to sick call and an Army doctor took a pair of scissors and opened the skin where the nail had been cut out of the toe. This was to "drain out the infection," he said. I hurt so much that I had tears in my eyes, and I really hated this doctor. I couldn't walk for a couple of days, but at least I didn't have to fill sandbags.

Daily letters from girlfriends and moms arrived, and at the time really were sanity savers for all of us. One day we came upon a letter from one of the guys lying on top of his bunk, so of course, we read it. He told his girlfriend how scared he was because every day he had a brush with death from the nightly firefights along perimeter. We couldn't figure out where the hell this guy was pulling perimeter duty. Certainly not with the rest of us. We had by now built reinforced sandbag bunkers along the perimeter that the teams would sit in at night. To kill the boredom we would throw rocks at the motor scooters that drove by in the dark on the paved road that ran parallel to our perimeter. It was very dark and all you could see were headlights, so you had to lead them just right to hit one of them. The only action we heard at the perimeter was the cursing of the one or two Vietnamese as the rocks ricocheted off the pavement. Obviously our counter-guerrilla warfare training was not paying off.

As I recall, part of the 716th MP Battalion was responsible for the security of Long Binh. We, the 552nd, were to take their place, but first the Inspector General (IG) had to inspect our compound. One jeep in the motor pool wouldn't cut inspection so the lieutenant told me and Tom Likely, my friend from the Bronx, to take it off base until the IG left. We were ecstatic. After thirty days of drudgery we were finally being freed. Until that time, no one had been allowed off base. Off we went toward the town of Bien Hoa—armed, but assured the road was secure. It appeared to be that way. Who could set up an ambush on a road that was completely lined with car washes all the way to town? We decided to pool a couple of dollars to get the jeep washed. Little did we know that the car washes were simply fronts, and I was about to become a "man."

A kid, I guess about ten years old, greeted us with an old rag in one hand and a hose in the other. I don't know if the hose even worked. He wanted to know if these GIs wanted a "short time" and kept hitting the palm of his right hand with his left fist. This, we were about to learn, was the universal symbol for getting laid. I couldn't believe it was so easy. I had gone with the same girl back in the States for about three years, and in those days you were permitted to wander no further south than the breasts, unless you promised marriage—and this was only going to cost five dollars. I was led merrily to the back of the car wash to a small room with one wooden table and a bamboo mat on top of it. I don't remember what the girl looked like. All I knew was that she was young and naked. That was enough for me. As she laid on her back she fanned both of us. Actually I think she was only fanning herself. I'm quite sure I set a land speed record, got up, and politely left. My knees were raw from the mat and I'm sure she had bamboo marks all over her back, but what the heck.

Once back at Long Binh, Likely let everyone know my adventure. I was really razzed. Had I worn a rubber? No, and just where were you going to buy a rubber at that time? Hadn't I paid attention to those VD prevention films we were made to watch? Yes. I wasn't feeling real well right then, so I was given a bottle of whiskey and instructed to go bathe my "thing." The alcohol would of course "kill the germs." I was really paranoid now, as my "thing" just didn't look or feel right. Was I going to wind up in an asylum some place in the Philippines with incurable syphilis? I don't know how many days passed before the yellow pus began its discharge. I was in deep shit now. I faked having a cold and went off to sick call. A cotton swab and a microscope confirmed my fear—gonorrhea. One more trip had to be made to the dispensary for the second penicillin shot. No one would ever be the wiser. Of course my company commander found out about my "cold" when he got his copy of the monthly sick call recap from the dispensary. Lucky for me, he wasn't a lifer. I was admonished and sent on my way. Of course, being a "man," the letters from my girlfriend weren't that important anymore. I slowly stopped answering her letters and finally wrote her a "Dear Jane" letter. What a cad.

Occasionally Long Binh would be mortared. The favorite target was the ammo dump, which was located just to our south. Once hit, it would explode for several hours. We'd grab out steel helmets, flak vests and M-14s and hit the perimeter.

The base never did get a ground assault while I was there. One night I was awakened to a bunch of commotion in our tent. Guys were walking in with their gear on, rifles in hand and I asked, groggily, what had happened. I had somehow just managed to sleep through a mortar attack. I got up and dressed hurriedly, thinking that sleeping through an attack would get me court-martialed. I could always sleep through anything. One night after a round of drinking, I woke up to find myself outside of my hooch. Around me were my foot locker and wall locker. It was obvious I could be carried any place while asleep, much to the enjoyment of my hooch mates. The lieutenant also got a kick out of waking me that morning. Private Gomer Pyle at your disposal, sir!

Duty at Long Binh was as boring as filling sandbags. Too many static posts. Too much "guard" duty. I thought it was going to be a long and boring year. Working the gates to the base was all right because you saw a lot of faces, but in general it was the pits. About a month after we started pulling duty, our platoon sergeant asked for volunteers for temporary duty with the First Infantry Division, the famed "Big Red One." I jumped at the chance, and so did a friend from Wyoming, John Prahl. The other guys thought we were nuts. Off we went to their base camp in Di An (pronounced Z-ahn). Finally we were near the boonies and ready for action. We were to help escort convoys of ammunition and supplies to the troops in the real boondocks.

For our first assignment, we put on our steel camouflaged helmets and flak vests, loaded our M-14 rifles and shotguns, strapped pouches holding the M-79 grenades for the grenade launchers around our chests, clipped smoke grenades and fragmentation grenades to our vests, locked the M-60 machine gun onto the tripod on the back of the jeep, and hopped on. We were ready to meet the enemy, and he'd better watch out. If nothing else, we looked bad.

As we led the convoy of trucks out of the main gate, I noticed a sharp metal bar attached to the front of the jeep. It extended straight up from the front of the jeep hood about five feet and then out at a ninety-degree angle. I asked the infantry driver what this was for and was told, to protect me, the machine gunner, from being knocked out of the jeep. It seems the VC liked to string wire across roads to knock the lead vehicle's machine gunner into the path of the convoy behind him. That's, of course, if it didn't decapitate him first. I was thrilled. As I bent over, a frag grenade fell off my vest onto the floor under the machine gun. It bounced around as I frantically tried to grab it, and finally it fell to freedom out of the back of the jeep onto the road. I don't know how many trucks ran over it. Probably fifty or so. Well, maybe on the way back we could stop and pick it up. I was ready for combat?

In all our convoys we never took fire, but I remember seeing the 11th Armored Cavalry just after their engagements, sitting on the sides of the road in their tanks and armored personnel carriers (APCs). They always looked dirty and pissed. On the way back from Lai Khe and the Iron Triangle, where heavy fighting was taking place, the convoy was split in two because one of the trucks broke down. I was dropped off at a bridge just outside of a small hamlet to secure it until the rest of the convoy caught up. Mentally I was fine, until three hours passed and it started to get dark. I hadn't seen a villager in a long time. Nothing moving now. I wondered how long I would be stuck there, and why I hadn't insisted on another MP being dropped with me. Just before total darkness I saw the distant gleam of headlights. I would be safe, but it would now be too late to find the grenade I had dropped. I hoped it would never be found.

Static duty posts at Di An were a little more exciting than at Long Binh. However, we all wanted to hear during morning line-up that we would be going out on convoy. Di An had a VC prisoner of war (POW) compound where they interrogated captured VC. I can recall the one little muscular runt that was captured lugging a 50-caliber machine gun around. This gun weighs 126 pounds, and he must have carried this over a long period of time, as the barrel had dug a perfect half circle in his collarbone. I couldn't believe the age of some of the VC women and how fragile they looked with their long black hair. They must have endured a lot. All wore black pajamas and would sit and groom one another's hair and pick out the lice.

At night we would secure the perimeter entrances to the base. Claymore mines that we could detonate from our bunker would be put out. Concertina wire would be strung out across the road about every ten feet out to about 100 feet from the perimeter. We would then take our chairs out of the bunker and sit in the road and watch the nightly fireworks of the gunships firing at the VC. You could not hear the fire, but would see a steady strip of red light up the sky. You couldn't even see the gunship. The red light would magically appear from a thousand feet in the air, make its way to the ground and then reverse itself when they stopped firing. It was a magical sight, but certainly not on the receiving end.

There was a mortar placement right next to our bunker. The three-man team would come out at night, smoke and talk until about 10:00 and then go into their small pup tent and sleep. As we sat in the road and chatted, we would later almost be knocked out of our chairs by the deafening sound of the now-awakened team that would, without telling us, get up from their sleep and fire off harassment rounds into the night, just in case anyone might be walking around inside our perimeter. Our ears would ring for an hour. We asked them to give us a heads-up before they fired so we could cover our ears, but there weren't too many grunts who liked MPs, so of course, we suffered and they enjoyed it. One night as we sat watching the show, red tracers flew over our heads. We could not hear the gunfire, but it was obvious that we needed to stay in the bunker.

One morning we went out on the road to pick up the claymore mines. They had been turned around and were facing in at us. Victor Charlie did own the night.

I liked Di An. The First Infantry MPs were bad. They would pull ambushes at night. A squad would go out just prior to nightfall and be in after daybreak. It's what John and I wanted to do, but were never given the opportunity. They were really in the war. I remember seeing dead VC thrown in the town square and always felt that justice had been served.

I saw my first person killed while at Di An, but it wasn't a VC. We used to escort a deuce-and-a-half (two and a half ton truck) into the town to pick up the local national workers and bring them back on base. They were most generally laborers, but we also picked up office staff and PX workers. We always made our run to town early in the morning. The streets were typically crowded with pedestrians, motor bikes, bicycles, and cabs. After we made our pick-up at a designated stop in town, the truck would labor through the traffic. Our jeep followed behind. One day, as the truck maneuvered a corner, a young school girl on her bike, probably about ten years old, was caught by the end of the truck and it knocked her under the rear tires. The back of her skull was ripped open and she was dragged about twenty-five feet, until the screaming people in the back of the truck were able to get the driver's attention to stop. The girl was wearing the beautiful silk dress that they all wore when going to work, school, or social functions. We went to her aid, but it was too late. She was dead, her dress soaked with blood, bits of skull and brains on the street.

I was assigned to stand over her body until the authorities arrived. In the meantime, her relatives arrived and threw themselves onto her body, picking up pieces of her skull and caressing them. My orders were to make sure the body was not moved, and I had a terrible time with the family. I didn't understand why they couldn't just pick her up and carry her off. I know that's what they wanted to do.

Help arrived and the girl's body and parts of her skull and brains were put in a plastic body bag. Off they went. I always thought there should have been more to it than that, maybe a news team, interviews, something. But this wasn't a VC, just a young innocent school girl no one would really miss, except the family. It's as if she wasn't a part of the war. She was just a Vietnamese kid with nothing to say.

We stayed at Di An for a couple of months. I even got to see the training film on VD prevention again, but I still didn't know where you were supposed to get rubbers. My big toe was infected again and I went to sick call. I was told to put peroxide on it, which didn't really help. At Di An at night it was pretty dark. We had sat through a few mortar attacks so, unlike Long Binh, it was pretty much lights out at night. On my way back from a shower my foot found its way under a tent stake and it ripped my toe open. I cussed and cried all the way to my tent. Of course, everyone thought my show of emotions was a trip. Man, it hurt, but that was the end of the infection. I wrapped up my toe, limped around for a week, and it was fine. What would I be like if I ever got shot? I had heard that many times the feeling of being shot was not as painful as ripping up my toe, but I didn't want to find out.

We were finally given our walking instructions and found our way back to Long Binh and the 552nd; the cocks-of-the-walk had arrived. We all took the patch of the Big Red One and had them sewn on the right shoulder of our uniforms. We didn't know that being temporarily assigned did not authorize us to wear the patches, but no one told us any different, so we maintained our celebrity status. I spent the rest of this tour with the 552nd on town patrol in Bien Hoa.

It was 1967 and the GI population was growing. That meant more drunks in town. Bien Hoa was a quaint little place with dirt roads and French-influenced red tiled buildings. Bars and whorehouses were everywhere. One night my Bronx friend, Tom Likely, told me we had to "raid" one of the local brothels. He wouldn't tell me why, but we were on patrol together and always stayed together for safety's sake. We made sure the brims of our shiny MP helmets were no more than an inch off the bridge of our noses, which always looked bad, and off we went. Two big MPs on a mission.

The brothels usually consisted of a big room that might have as many as ten beds in it. The privacy for each bed usually consisted of drawn curtains. Needless to say, the sound of grunts grunting was everywhere. Our presence sent everyone scrambling. Likely got to one cubicle, threw it open, said "excuse me" to the two naked occupants, and bent over the head of the bed and began searching the floor. Once he found his wallet, he stood up with an "as you were" and off he went. I followed behind. Mission accomplished. He was one funny guy.

The MPs were feared by military personnel. Unlike the Shore Patrol or Air Force Police, we were it. We were the only branch of service that had jurisdiction over everyone. To the general populace, we could be their saviors, and we were generally respected and often pampered by the Vietnamese as we kept many a drunk or redneck off their backs.

There were prostitutes in Vietnam as in any war, but the generalizations you hear from the vets today about them all being whores is the furthest thing from the truth. There was a definite distinction between a bar girl and a prostitute. (Off duty, the MPs were treated royally by the bar owners and shop owners in general, as well as the workers and girls.) Many reflections from the typical GI stem from getting "screwed" over by the girls that worked in the bars. There were girls who could be "bought out" of the bar for a price. This would mean that you could pay the owner a determined price and the girl would leave the bar with you. This usually wasn't the case as many of the girls couldn't be touched with a ten-foot pole. The typical terms of "slut" and "whore" usually stemmed out of frustration that the GIs, usually drunk, thought a particularly attractive girl would leave the bar with him at night because he had been spending lots of money on "tea" and she had been telling him all the bullshit about being handsome, a "babysan," etc., when, in fact, the girls couldn't stand these unclean rednecks who reeked of body odor and beer. Many of the girls already had Americans who they lived with, and they worked in bars during the day for, of course, the cash. Or they actually had Vietnamese boyfriends or husbands.

The trick to making the money was the con job, and they pulled it off beautifully. GIs, usually a group of them, would enter a bar and sit down and order drinks. A girl would sit with you and ask your name, where you were from, etcetera, but you would have to order her a "tea," usually a shot of Kool-Aid. As you sat and became more drunk, and she stayed sober with the "tea," she would promise you the world. Most of the time she would also excuse herself for a few minutes to go work another table out of eyesight of the table where she had been sitting. The GIs would get drunk and leave in a huff when the girl would renege on her promise (and lots of times with the assistance of MPs), or at the end of the evening the girl would get up from the table, leaving a drunk GI behind, walk out of the bar and get in a cab, or the back of a motorbike, and go home. As in the typical male fashion, these girls then became "whores" and "sluts." It's the male way of rationalizing. It was actually funny to watch—great justice. Many of the GIs were assholes with the women and I'm sure many rapes took place. The bar scene was the Ugly American at his best.

In 1967 I got word that I was being transferred to the 300th MP Company in Saigon. They were stationed at Tan Son Nhut, the airport in Saigon. I had only heard about Saigon. The 300th had responsibility for protection of the Saigon docks. My first sight of Saigon was something else. Here was a city, built to hold about 500,000 people. Three to four million must have lived in and around the city. I had never seen anything like it. Wall to wall people. In May of 1967 I was decorated for heroism and promoted to Specialist 4th Class. I was then assigned to a squad whose sole responsibility was to guard General Abrams' compound (the Commander-In-Chief) and another strategic compound outside of Tan Son Nhut. The duty was easy and the squad was able to make its own hours, so we usually worked twelve hours on and twelve hours off for four days and then took three days off. The job was boring and not what I really wanted to do, but I really couldn't complain about hours. I used to stand outside of the gate at night and watch all the people walking and going by on their bicycles. A Vietnamese girl would go by late at night just before curfew and wave to me from the cyclo she was riding in. A cyclo was nothing more than a motorcycle with a carriage on the front. It was open-air and probably the most often used form of transportation.

One night she stopped and handed me a piece of paper with her name on it and the bar where she worked. Her name was Nguyen Thi Ngoc Mai. I went to visit her at the bar and soon thereafter I was at her apartment on Minh Ky Street. I moved in and she quit work. Mai was eighteen years old at the time, and extremely shy and quiet. Mai's neighbor and best friend was named Dao. She lived with an Army guy named Smokey Beech. He and I became good friends. It wasn't long until Mai became pregnant, so I extended my tour six months to stay in-country. You actually were not supposed to live off base, but no one ever checked on you. I believe that probably one-fourth of the GIs in Saigon lived off base.

I wasn't happy with the duties of the 300th MP Company so I chose to go to Vung Tau, the in-country R&R center. Mai was not thrilled with my decision at all, but packed her belongings shortly after I got there and came down. Mai got a job in a bar in town and slept there at night with the rest of the girls. Vung Tau was small and isolated so there weren't a lot of living accommodations off base. I seldom saw her because when I wasn't working, the owner of the bar didn't want me spending too much time with her in the bar because she couldn't work the guys on R&R for teas. Of all things, I got a job with the bar band and played lead guitar for them when I wasn't working the night shift. The bar was two stories. The first floor was the bar and the second floor was the dance area, so even then I didn't get to see her much, as she was made to stay on the first floor and work for teas.

One of the other duties we had in Vung Tau was ship and tug escort. I didn't mind the tug escorts. We would load up with weapons and ride the tugs down into the Mekong Delta that took down barges of ammunition, supplies, and building materials. These tugs were operated by American firms and had mostly American and Filipino crews. They loved having us along. Our job was to fire on anything in the water that looked like it could contain booby traps or explosives that the tugs might run into, and to return any fire from the shorelines. The M-79 grenade launcher was great for this. The crews, however, were always well armed themselves, but usually with smaller caliber rifles—burp guns. We carried the big stuff with us. A usual trip would last about a week.

On the other hand, we had to pull security for the large freight ships that would come in off the South China Sea and head up to Saigon to off-load their cargo. These trips were a bitch. Some guys could spend a month on one of those ships. The trips up the canal only took several hours, but you could sit for weeks waiting for a crew to off-load you. Two MPs would ride the ship and, while in port, there always had to be an MP on duty on the water side of the ship to watch for VC frogmen. It was boring with a capital B. We usually worked eight hours on and eight hours off. It was a drain. Eat, work , sleep, and work again. It was on one of these trips that I contracted mononucleosis. I was taken off the ship by an ambulance to Tan Son Nhut and then put back on the ship when it headed down river to Vung Tau. From there I went straight to the hospital. I was in the hospital for three weeks. Mai came in to see me, and was very depressed. She was really showing her pregnancy and was not happy in Vung Tau. She wanted to go back to Saigon.

When I got out of the hospital I went to the bar where she had her few belongings packed, and we checked into a room. It was the first time we had been together alone since we got to Vung Tau. I never did understand the Buddhist philosophy or their emotions, because when they lost a loved one or were depressed they could become extremely emotional, but almost trance-like. It was a rough night and neither of us slept. I put her on the bus the next morning. We thought she would never see me again. After I reported back to the company, I got assigned to another ship and went back to Saigon. The other MP and I decided to work one twenty-four-hour shift apiece so that we could get off the ship. I had to go check with other MP companies to see if I could tie onto them for a six-month extension. I went to the 527th MP Company in downtown Saigon. They needed a man, so I signed up.

Afterwards, I went to our apartment at Minh Ky. Dao was the first to see me and let out a scream. Mai was really pregnant now. I went back to Vung Tau and spent the rest of my tour there on town patrol. Soon I would be back in Saigon, but first I would go home. My family was absolutely "thrilled" that I was going back again. I can still hear my brother screaming about what an uncaring person I was to put my mother through this again. I was never so glad to leave; a "great" visit.

I was asleep when the Tet Offensive started. Saigon had been immune to any attacks and it was the general belief that the VC wouldn't dare hit the city. The first four deaths in Saigon that night were MPs. Two were killed on duty at the embassy when nineteen VC sappers blew their way into the compound. Two MPs on motorized patrol responded to a radio call and were killed outside the embassy grounds. They were from the 527th. About twenty-five MPs from the 716th at Tan Son Nhut responded to fighting at an officer's quarters. They all crammed into the deuce-and-a-half truck, probably thinking it would be a false alarm. When they pulled into an alley near the billet a rocket propelled grenade (RPG) was fired into the front of the truck. All tolled, nineteen MPs were killed and it took a couple of days to get them out. Twenty-seven MPs were killed during the fighting to protect the city. After the 9th Infantry and 101st Airborne finally responded, much of our time was spent firing into buildings without even seeing anyone. It was a mess. Bodies lay dead all over the city, but life went on as usual. Except for the curfew at night, local civilians went on with life as they normally would. It was all very confusing.

The second Tet Offensive came a few months later. Ever since the first offensive, the VC continued to fire mortars and rockets into the city indiscriminately. As my friend Per and I patrolled the city one day, we saw about five mortar rounds walked into the city about a half mile from us. The sad thing was that wherever they landed, they couldn't miss hitting civilians. The city was that crowded.

It was early morning when the offensive started and I was at the apartment. I would have been going in for my assignment, but as I hurriedly got up I realized I would possibly be stuck; mortars were landing and the streets were vacant of cabs and cycles. I went down and stood on the street, and off in the distance I saw an MP jeep. It was Per. The MPs had been mustered earlier and he had said "Here" for me when my name was called during role call.

I met Per Christiansen when I got to the 527th MP Company in Saigon. He was a Dane form Canada who enrolled in college in the States and found himself drafted into the Army. He always marveled at how square his American friend was, and I guess I was. We would be friends there and when I came back to Washington, we would spend many a time together in Vancouver, British Columbia, where he lived. Unfortunately, he moved way up into the province and we lost touch with one another. He was a true friend.

The carrying of weapons when you were off duty in Saigon was strictly prohibited, so until Per arrived, I had nothing. The VC never really got into the city during this offensive, but we spent lots of time responding to calls of "civilians down" due to the mortars and rockets. A dead body in person is so much different than portrayed in the movies. They stink immediately because of the blood. They lose control of their bladder functions and the smell of urine and stool is nauseating. The blood doesn't look like blood. It's thick, it stinks, and looks more purple than red.

Before the first Tet Offensive, Saigon was a crowded yet lazy city. Nothing seemed to be done by the book. We worked twelve-hour shifts, noon until midnight and midnight to noon. The midnight-to-noon was a killer. We were only armed with our 45s and you were prohibited from having a round in the chamber. Around 3 a.m. your body would rebel and search for sleep. Many a night we would find a secluded area, pull over and snooze until 5 a.m. or so. The only people moving after night were the MPs, Vietnamese MPs, and supervisors. After the Tet Offensive we were loaded for bear. A security guard company of ex-infantry personnel was attached to the 716th Battalion (the 527th was one company of 716th). These guys, usually wounded once or twice from combat, would be assigned to man M-60 machine guns that were mounted on the backs of the patrol jeeps. We now also wore our flak vests, carried our M-16 rifles, and possibly a few grenades thrown in for good luck. We were still ordered not to have rounds in the chambers of our weapons, but everyone ignored this. We were not about to be caught unprepared. The streets were now patrolled combat-ready.

After Tet, I spent a short time riding shotgun for an MP who was assigned to accident investigations. All of the traffic in Saigon caused quite a carnage, especially when you mixed in the large flat-bed trucks carrying supplies with the thousands of pedestrians, bikes, cabs, and cycles. Hundreds of civilians must have died or sustained serious injuries as a result. The accident investigator did not have an enviable job.

Riding shotgun wasn't fun either. The 527th stayed in a large hotel near downtown. It was probably five stories high. The street floors were occupied by merchants, tailors, barbers, laundries and a bar that catered specifically to the MPs' needs. Our jeeps would be parked across the street from the bar once we got them out of the motor pool. One evening one of the SGs was loading the ammunition belt into the M-60 machine gun that was mounted on the back of the jeep. It was facing directly toward the bar. He slammed the carriage down on the belt and the gun went off, sending about six rounds into the bar. Two bar girls were killed and one GI was wounded. It was this kind of death and the death of the small schoolgirl in Di An that never got reported.

While working patrol we received a call of gunfire in a bar just off Tu Do Street. When my partner and I responded, there were GIs and bar girls taking cover outside the bar. I was told that there were three Vietnamese soldiers in the bar. It was rare to ever see a Vietnamese soldier in the bar. It was rare to ever see a Vietnamese male in a bar that catered to GIs. The mix of booze and the fact that there was a lot of animosity between the local males and Americans being with local girls could become volatile. About twenty GIs and girls had run into the rear bathroom when one of the locals started firing his pistol. I jacked a round into the chamber of my 45 and decided to go in, putting the 45 back in my holster. Inside, the three local soldiers were standing up at the center of the bar. One had a 38 revolver in his hand at his side. He looked pissed and the two others looked scared. I had to walk past them to get to the bathroom. When back at the bathroom, I told the GIs and girls to walk single file behind me quietly and out of the bar, which they did. When we got outside, the Vietnamese MPs had shown up and went into the bar with their M-16s and apprehended the three men. About two weeks later two other MPs responded to the same type of situation at another bar. They had to run up a stairway to get into the bar and they had their weapons drawn. When they got to the top, both of them were killed by a local with a 45 pistol. I just wonder if I had had my weapon out if I would have shared the same destiny. I was still lucky.

REMF stands for Rear Echelon Mother Fucker. That meant you were not in combat. It was estimated that for every one combat troop, there were about ten REMFs (actually support troops—cooks, clerks, mechanics, doctors, lawyers, you name it.) I was considered a REMF because I wasn't humping out in the boonies all day, even though there was danger in my job. I never liked all the grunts and jarheads calling us REMFs because it was usually the luck of the draw where you wound up. They actually called us that out of jealousy and frustration because they would have traded their position for ours in an instant. It didn't make them any better than a REMF, but the situation on the REMF was certainly a Catch 22. The biggest REMFs of all were the officers. Not the field officers, but the fat cats who had all the luxuries and did diddly-squat during the war. I would watch in wonderment when General Creighton Abrams, Commander-in-Chief, would come back to his villa for lunch every day. There would be him and three other officers, usually a colonel and maybe a major or two. They would change into their Sunday-best tennis outfits, complete with headbands, and play badminton on a blacktopped badminton court for a couple of hours. They had a ball. While GIs were being massacred, they played without care. That was the life of the REMF. No better, no worse than the grunt. Just luckier. I'm waiting today to meet a REMF, but every vet I talk to was a combat soldier, and I just don't understand it. The odds just aren't there. I want to meet a vet who was a cook and never left Tan Son Nhut air base.

The AWOL (Absent With Out Leave) situation in Saigon was out of hand. I believe at one point there were approximately 5000 GIs in Saigon who were AWOL. Drugs were all over the place. With the black market so prevalent, the AWOLs would be used to the advantage of the Vietnamese. An unscrupulous local would, for example, get a GI all the drugs he wanted, an apartment, and a girl. All this guy had to do in return was shop his heart out at the local PX, using stolen ration cards and a helpful clerk, and then turn all the goods over to the papasan. Once this GIs usefulness was used up he would be killed and we would find a dead GI in an alley.

The AWOLs even got so bold as to ambush MP patrols. Saigon was a city of thousands of alleys. The AWOLs would be set up as a jeep would come around a corner and the MPs would be accosted at gunpoint. The AWOLs would take everything—the jeep, their weapons, their boots, anything that could be sold. It could get hairy, especially at night. I often wondered what happened to these AWOLs. Troops were pretty well gone after 1972 and in 1975 all the Americans got out. Are they still there? How were they accounted for? MIAs? I'm sure they did not all turn themselves in. Records show that there are 1290 servicemen still missing from non-hostile acts. I'm sure many of these were AWOLs.

Much has been said about the beautiful "round-eyed" women who came to Vietnam to boost the morale of the GIs. I never understood the mystique. Most of them were dogs and most of them were hands off, except for the officers. I'm not saying they did not give valuable help, but they often gave the impression of conceit and were seldom seen around or with the locals. They had the reputation of being officer whores, and they acted it.

As best I can recall, Mai had a baby girl around May of 1968. She named her Tuyet. I went to the hospital the day Mai had Tuyet, and I remember walking in the room. Mai was rolling a bottle of hot water back and forth across her stomach. I guess this was to prevent stretch marks. She never did have any. Tuyet was beautiful. For a newborn she didn't have a wrinkle anywhere on her. She looked like Mai. Mai was thrilled with the baby and I was now pulling the type of duty I always wanted to pull—motorized patrol. I soon made sergeant.

The day came when I was nearing the end of my enlistment. This meant either re-upping with the Army for another two years or going home. This period of time is cloudy for me, but I made the decision that I would return home. Mai immediately moved into a very small apartment and made plans to go back to work. As I was really immature, I couldn't understand her actions at all, but after all, I was leaving her. What was she supposed to do?

The plane ride to Seattle was terrible. I was really emotionally messed up. When I got off the plane, I remember my mom and sister-in-law were there to pick me up. I didn't even smile. It was raining like hell, and cold. The war was finally over for my family, but not for me. Nothing was said about it. I was sixteen again and home. I had a room at my mother's house, but I knew that I was going back. I got a letter off to Mai and sent her some cash and broke the news to my mom. Of course, my brother Frank yelled at me to the point that I broke down and cried. He, of course, called me a baby. Here I was, a very young man who had seen more life and death than anyone around me, who was a father, who had been away for two years and who had grown up. I knew right then and there that I was the only adult in the room. My brother finally physically threatened me and left. I hurriedly obtained a passport and visa and was on my way. It didn't matter to me at the time that I didn't have a job, and it was hard to make people understand that I was trying to take responsibility for the things I had done.

When I left America in late 1968 I felt like I was going home. Once in Hawaii, I had to go through customs and it was almost disastrous. I was told by a customs agent that the Vietnamese government would not let me into the country without a round-trip airplane ticket. What was I to do? When I got out of the Army my out-pay was about $700. I recall that the one way plane ticket cost about $500. He told me to buy a ticket from Saigon to Bangkok, Thailand for about fifty dollars. This would satisfy the Vietnamese that I could get out of the country once my visa expired. If things didn't work out in Saigon I could always walk into the American Embassy in Bangkok and tell them I was broke. They would then put me on a military flight back to the States and sue my ass for the airfare. It sounded good to me. I think I had a lot of guts for someone "so young." Not a baby after all.

Once in Saigon I flagged a taxi to Truong Minh Ky Street. Dao saw me first, and let out a scream for Mai. She had no idea I was coming back and I should have known, none of my letters or money made it to her. Any American mail would be opened by whomever, hoping money would be in it. It was a corrupt city. I immediately fell ill. Mai nursed me for over a week—my entire nights spent sweating and shivering.

I was not doing anything to enhance my chances of finding a job within the time allowed on my visa. When I felt better I went to the immigration department and told them I was visiting my brother Per and wanted an extension. I showed them my ticket to Bangkok and they extended my visa thirty days. I felt very lucky. I humped the streets during the day while Mai worked at the bar. It was tough and I was getting desperate. Talking to some Filipino neighbors one night over a beer, they told me to go down to the PX headquarters and fill out an application. After doing so, the personnel department sent me to see an Army Major Oakes, a military policeman. Their security department was nothing more than him and a few buck-sergeants and he was given orders to expand. There was an Australian civilian there, whose name I can't remember, looking for work too. We were the first two civilian security specialists hired in-country and I couldn't believe it. When I was told I would be making seven dollars an hour, which figured out to be over $14,000 a year, I almost shit. In 1969 that was a lot of money for someone to be making in the States, let alone Vietnam. I was rich. I would be working out of the headquarters in Saigon and afterwards I would be assigned to the Southern Area Regional Exchange Headquarters, which had responsibility for security of all PXs in the southern area of Vietnam.

I came home from work one day and there was an old-looking lady sitting on the edge of one of our beds. She was the stereotypical mamasan, chewing away on black betelnut, her jaw protruding from the chaw. This was Mai's mother. She did not speak English and my attempt to speak Vietnamese was not going well. I never knew much about Mai's family. I knew that her father had been killed by the Viet Cong and that her mother lived in the Mekong Delta, I recall, either in Can Tho, or My Tho. I was to meet her only that one time. It was an uneasy liaison. How could someone look so weathered? I was too young to realize that if you were a farmer and humped around all day in a rice paddy and worked extremely hard all your life and had inadequate health care, your body would show the effects. Her mother's did.

I got paid once a month and I gave Mai all the money except for a small amount I would send home to a savings account. I never cared or questioned what she did with the money. I know a lot of it went to her family in the Delta. We did not get paid in greenbacks (American money). Neither did the military. We got paid with Military Payment Certificates, which looked like monopoly money. It was only to be used in the PXs, American clubs, or on base for movies, etc. If we wanted to shop in a Vietnamese store or on the market, we could exchange our Military Payment Certificates (MPC) for Vietnamese money (piaster and dong). At the time I recall that we would get about $1.20 of Vietnamese piaster for every $1 MPC. However, Mai would take my MPC and off she would go, coming back later with a ton of Vietnamese money and no MPC. She had just come from the black market. Vietnamese were not to have any MPC, but they wanted it dearly. They would give you about $2 of the Vietnamese money for every $1 of MPC, so you could almost double your income. The Vietnamese would then sell the MPC back to the GIs for greenbacks. How would the GIs get greenbacks? Simple. They would send a money order home and have their parents send them greenbacks in the mail. They could get as much as $3 MPC (depending on the demand at the time) for each $1 of American money. This money was then sent out of the country to the black marketeer's bank account. Money laundering at its simplest. We were always told that to launder money in this sense was to buy weapons for the enemy, but we all really knew that it was the Vietnamese fat-cats who were making the profit. The black market was not run by the poor class, it was run by the wealthy, who were usually synonymous with government officials, including American officials.

The civilian investigators who worked for the exchange were armed. We carried snub-nosed 38-caliber pistols. We really had no power to arrest, just investigate and make recommendations. However, this did not apply to Vietnamese. We could not confiscate obviously stolen goods from the open-air black market. The black market was not operated in dark alleys, but on the main streets of Saigon. Stall after stall of American goods, including American military equipment. Not even the local Vietnamese beat cop could touch these stalls. It was handled strictly by the customs police, who would periodically "raid" the stalls and confiscate the goods. It made headlines in the U.S., but the haul made was nothing, as these people were notified in advance of the raids so they would put out a token sacrifice that they knew would make all the American civilian and military leaders happy, plus it was good news for the folks back home. Many Americans were directly involved with the black market, and even I was involved indirectly, as I tolerated the conversion of MPC to piaster to American greenbacks. Billions of dollars were defrauded from the government. But we were running a war, not the morals of profit makers, so the market thrived for years.

The reported losses for the exchange system in Vietnam were in excess of $100,000 a month. Most losses, however, went unreported. The exchange was the single most important contributor to the black market. Luxury items, such as televisions, radios, stereos, cameras, freezers—yes, freezers, beer, wine, liquor, and cigarettes were rationed. You could buy, for example, four cases of beer a month. Every time you bought one case, the clerk (always a Vietnamese) would punch out one square on your card. Now, if this clerk was your girlfriend, she could become very adept at punching out this same hole, over and over again. Martel Cognac was treasured by the Vietnamese. It would sell in the PX for about four dollars a bottle. It could be sold on the market for twelve dollars or more. The turnover of Martel Cognac was great, however, and it would be obvious to everyone that a shipment was in as the lines would stretch for miles outside the PX in anticipation of buying a bottle. Did all these people drink cognac? Nah, but just about everyone dealt in the black market one way or another. We did quite a few investigations for ration card theft. The supplies of unissued cards were always being "stolen" out of safes. I recall one search of an apartment where this civilian must have had one hundred blank ration cards. This man was obviously making some dough. "Arrested" American civilians were sent home, nothing more, nothing else done to them. There was really no risk, so why not indulge?

More than once we would trail a convoy of PX goods through the streets of Saigon, only to see a flat truck full of goods pull out of the convoy and turn into a Vietnamese Army compound, or down an alley to be off-loaded by local police. There was nothing we could do about it but write a report. Again, no action would be taken. It was the cost of running a war.

Tuyet was now walking around. She was a good little girl. The sense of family is very tight with the Vietnamese. Everyone, including neighbors, took care of and looked after the little kids. She was always being picked up and loved by someone. Mai had become pregnant again. I had often talked to her about getting married and going back to the States, but she would not leave her family. Further more, she never had an ID card. All Vietnamese were required to have identification on them at all times. To not, would mean you would be suspected of being VC.

Mai and I did not go out in public very often as the Vietnamese men did not appreciate any woman who patronized a foreigner. One day we were in a cab together and came upon a checkpoint manned by about ten local national police. Mai had no ID, so she was carted off to jail. If I would have intervened, I would have been beaten and arrested. All I could do was go home and tell Dao. She spent three days in jail.

I came back to Vietnam to bring my family back to the States and I knew I couldn't stay there forever, so in 1969 I was really trying to get a commitment from Mai. At that time, I never understood the greatness of their family ties. Mai was adamant, so I decided to move out. This, I felt, would force her hand and she would change her mind. I found an apartment on Hai Ba Truong Street. This was an area of town where you hardly saw a GI, unlike Truong Minh Ky, which was just outside of the airport. Mai would come to work and ask for me to come back, but I was as stubborn as she was. It seemed like it was all about to end. I probably should have left Vietnam right then and returned to the States, but to what? I stayed.

We worked six days a week, ten hours a day, so I kept myself busy and went into the field on a lot of audits and investigations. Vietnam was beautiful. I was able to see a lot of the country. I can recall a fishing village, Nha Trang, that had to be one of the most beautiful, quaint places I had ever seen. The only thing to do at night in Saigon was visit the bars. I did get a basketball team organized and we would go down to the Chinese sector, Cholon, and get our butts kicked by those little guys, but that happened only once or twice a week. Television was the pits—Armed Forces Radio and Television Network. So, it was off to the bars or a restaurant. My civilian boss, Ron Halsall, was from Hawaii, and we would go together. Or, when Per was still there, we would try to go out together.

A girl sat with me in one bar and I bought her tea. Her name was

Carol. I don't even know her Vietnamese name. I brought her out of the bar and went to an officer's club for dinner. The Army officers were going nuts over her and she was really embarrassed and I was too, because they had the typical redneck attitude that they could say anything they wanted to an "un-American" woman. We ate and left. She started living with me, and never asked me for a thing. I kept working every night until 10 and then came back to the apartment. Being as uneducated as young people were back then, I told her I did not want her to get pregnant. However, saying it does not prevent it and she did get pregnant. I was going nuts. I told her she really had to leave and I didn't want the responsibility. She did leave and I remember her coming to the door and knocking one night. She wanted to know if I wanted to see my son. She named him Jim. I remember going to a very crowded building full of Vietnamese in tiny one-room cubicle. There, an old lady was taking care of a small newborn. The room was very dark and I was petrified. Not of the darkness, but of another child. I held the boy briefly and left.

Shortly thereafter, there was another knock at my door. It was Mai. When she came in, it was obvious that she had returned to work as her clothing smelled of cigarette smoke. She asked me if I would like to see my daughter. I was at wit's end and at an all-time low emotionally. Mai went into the bathroom to take a shower. I remember feeling bad because she was always well endowed, but not now. She looked at me and said, "Your baby has taken all my milk." That night I went back to the apartment. Dao and Hue were there as well as another friend I had known. I don't believe Tuyet recognized me. Phuong was in a bassinet and Mai went over and picked her up as I sat down on a bed. She must have been a few months old. Mai said, "Look at her feet. She has ugly feet just like you." It was true. They were very slim and long, with narrow toes. Phuong was lighter than Tuyet and her hair was brown, not like Tuyet's black hair. I didn't know what to do or say, but I felt like a complete failure. I asked Mai if she would move to Hai Ba Truong with me and she said she couldn't. It wasn't too long after that, that I gave my two weeks notice and left Vietnam. I was depressed for months.

Four years in Vietnam is a long time for a kid who was just nineteen years old. Typically, I should have been back in the States being as irresponsible as I could, without any pressure, other than getting a job at the Chrysler plant. Instead, I saw things in four years that most men would not experience in a lifetime. Today, I can't tell myself how I handled it. Was it innocence, irresponsibility, selfishness, or immaturity that made me walk away from the responsibility of my own children? It was a two-way street, and I'm sure no one thought the war would end, or that everyone and everything would just go away. I do know that I decided that I would not become a father again, and I probably would have been a good one. My family did not really want to hear of my years there, but they really wouldn't be able to understand it anyway. I chose to clam up and hold it all inside me. I was no combat hero. I am not the GI that is portrayed on TV every day, humping for his life. Most of us weren't. There must be embarrassment to admit that you never went on that patrol where only two came back, or withstood an ambush while on long-range reconnaissance. Maybe that's why I have never met a cook that never left Tan Son Nhut.

It was such a zoo and I must understand the mistakes I made and the people I hurt. I hear so many horror stories about the Amerasian children. I believe that Jim and Phuong might be dead. Tuyet was old enough and healthy enough to survive, but with the poor health care there, and the fact that the Amerasian children were not liked, leads me to believe if they did become ill there might not have been much hope.

I struggle with it today. I struggle with how pompous the Americans were, and still are. About how it's portrayed that the Vietnamese would not fight, even though their war losses far surpassed ours; all the stereotypes about the people, whose only fault was to have our government move in and destroy a country in a matter of ten short years. We had our heroes, but we also had our murderers, rapists, drug addicts and thieves. The rest of America seems to be satisfied with the bullshit propaganda our government feeds us about "giving our all." We abandoned a country that we alone destroyed, and if history were reviewed in other than the B-movies about Vietnam, maybe we would all see this. It was our most embarrassing moment and we won't admit it. There was no peace with honor.

I would like to know if my daughters are alive, if I'm a grandfather, and if out of all this there came some happiness and tranquility to the lives I helped create and abandoned so far away. I can't involve my future with it, so maybe I'm just being irresponsibly selfish, but maybe there would come some forgiveness and understanding. Maybe it would help put this to rest.

I am currently with the San Diego City Schools Police Department. I have been married to Marcia for seven years, no children, nine cats. Stopped drinking May 2, 1989. Just thought I'd throw that in.

Barry Stanchfield

High School—uneventful. Our graduating class of 1965 at Alexander Ramsey H.S. was over 740. Got my first car with two weeks left of school—a '55 Dodge Royal. Happy as a clam.

Not until June 1965, when LBJ called for 500,000 troops, did it occur to me Nam might be in my future. I knew how to type and wanted to be a printer like my dad, so I enrolled at Dunwoody, January 1966, for Printing.

I worked nights at Montgomery Ward for $2.41 an hour. I was 4-A until November 1967, when I graduated. Drafted. Arrived at Basic January 29, 1968. Our training NCOs were telling us all we were VC-bait after Tet that week.

I was 71-B-20, clerk-typist. Assigned to 1st Logistical Division at Qui Nhon, arriving May 8, 1969. We had some NGs with us. They told us a presidential order required that all National Guardsmen be pulled from Nam by January 1, 1970, so they were cocky, having only seven months to go. I had eight months left in the Army 'til DEROS.

I worked in the message center at Support Command, Qui Nhon—good duty. Free cartons of stale L&M cigarettes from an Ohio VFW. Some of the guys had two Asai speakers in their rooms. Warm showers next to the street, Lambrettas going by until curfew.

Pulled guard three times a week. Our AFVN radio tower was outside town near a leper colony and the city municipal well. We didn't dare eat local food, because half of us got dysentery and never tried it. Table water was polluted from all the piss tubes. In 1971 I visited Tijuana. It reminded me of Qui Nhon.

Our captain was a little tin god. He had his wife send him the newest *Playboy*, then parade past us into his office to read it after telling us how nice his wife was. The captain wouldn't allow us to remove our blouse tops and work in green T-shirts 'cause we might have made him seem lax. We ran the multi-lith machine and our uniforms became black with the spraying ink.

One Saturday the chaplain gave me four dozen blank bulletins to print his Sunday service. For some reason I printed all his bulletins so that you opened it and the service was printed upside-down. The captain called me in. He knew I detested him. I became a gate guard until he could ship me up-country.

Chaligny, one of our message center guys, brought in a quart plastic bottle of white tablets he bought at a local massage parlor. It was U.S. Medical Corps Darvon. The captain almost had apoplexy because one of us had black-market contraband in his message center.

Later on, a guy who arrived in-country with me, Bobby Singley, was taking Darvon in his upstairs barracks room. He came out onto the second floor porch, almost fainted, and went over the guardrail in a somersault. Page told me Singley hit the concrete walk and became paralyzed from the waist down.

July 6th—shipped to Army Depot, Qui Nhon at Long My in Phu Tai Valley, eleven miles up Cordillera toward Pleiku. Typed morning reports, adjutant's work, R&R clerk in a Quonset hut. Like an S-1 unit. Engineers put up our buildings; we poured cement walks, whitewashed. We had movies four times a week plus beer. We told Pop, Tran Dinh Loi, that Americans were on the moon. He called us all liars. Pop seemed happy when Ho Chi Minh died. LaPorte took Pop to our barracks to watch "Bonanza" one day, and old Pop couldn't get over the TV set.

We lost two guys at Long Mai. One guy in F Company had an E-5 friend going on sergeant-of-the-guard duty. The E-5 left his 45 on his bunk and went for a shower. The Spec-4 picked up the gun, pulled out the clip, looked down the barrel and said, "Mom told me never to do this," pulled the trigger, and shot himself through the eye.

What it was, the slide on the 45 was cocked, which had chambered a round, and he didn't know.

I still think about our other casualty, Tom Taylor from North Carolina. He got sick in November, slept all the time, weak. He was in my squad. We brought Taylor a coffee can to piss in, he was so weak. Medics examined Taylor, told Captain Jones to get him to the 85th Evac., Qui Nhon. Taylor stayed, wouldn't eat.

I went on R&R to Taipei. The following week I got back to a barracks with only the Vietnamese hooch-maids and poor Taylor inside. The maids were going to the wire to go home and one of them told me, "You get cool water on rag, put on Taylor's head. He burning up. He sick." At the time I didn't want to. I had R&R stories to tell the squad when they got back, and helping Taylor was inconvenient.

They finally got Taylor on a med-evac the following day. The platoon sergeant returned to tell us that Taylor died on the chopper. Taylor had spinal meningitis, Qui Nhon said.

Our E-6s and E-8s huddled and seemed furious. They promised a congressional investigation into why Taylor wasn't moved earlier. Nothing ever came of it.

We all had ringworm before the monsoons hit in October. Our barracks were on a sand bluff, higher than our showers. Ravines opened up, so our whole company packed sandbags to keep the erosion far from our buildings. We wore boots in ankle-deep mud to shower and got a hot water heater in December 1969. We had hot chow until snipers hit our food trucks, then dehydrated egg powder.

Developed real rage for our H&I fire from our 81mm mortars. Whenever contact was made outside our wire, our pits would fire mortars all night at irregular intervals. Shells went right over us and I dreaded that THOOP sound. Hardly slept at night from November to January.

One day at crossroad I noticed an MP with an M-14 sitting by an open green con-ex container (storage for holds of ships). You couldn't stand up inside a con-ex of corrugated steel. The MP was guarding a half-naked GI sitting on a towel inside. The GI had gotten high on grass and assaulted our CO or XO. He was waiting for shipment to Long Binh Jail. If he ran, the MP would fire, no doubt.

After that day, I didn't consider, "I'm here in Nam. What more can they do to me?" That GI found out what they could do. When I got home, I planned to stay drunk for a month.

I just found widespread despair over there. Your viewpoint becomes narrow when you're just counting off days.

From January to August 1970, I was sober maybe four or five days. Veterans Hospital, August to November 1970, for alcohol abuse and psychiatric care. Alcoholics Anonymous 1976 to the present.

I married in 1973. Check up at VA revealed my lymph nodes were the size of tennis balls. Shades of Agent Orange! Biopsy negative. Our three kids are normal, no defects.

Apprenticeship and journeyman printer at the St. Paul newspaper, from 1970-1988. U.S. Postal Service, 1986 to now.

I'm constantly amazed at how my fellow Americans can support stooges like Reagan, Bush, Quayle. Fear, greed, and the media run this country. Ask the parents of 283 Marines why they had to be in Lebanon in 1983. Ronnie can't tell you. He's not accountable. Even Clark Gable and Jimmy Stewart did their share in WWII—not Ronnie.

Our society now is frighteningly cosmetic. Appearances count for everything and the cold realities will somehow improve (later).

I'll never believe in the U.S. government again. The people, yes. I'm proud to have served with those enlisted men over there. I could support someone like John Kerry.

John A. Salgado

My name is John Anthony Salgado, born May 1, 1944 in Havana, Cuba. My parents had migrated from Spain to Cuba as a young couple to escape the Spanish Civil War. My father worked hard in a cigar factory to support my family, which included a twin brother and one sister. When I was nine years old my family traveled to Tampa to visit my mother's sister and her family, who had come directly to the States in the 1930s. It is still unknown in my mind how it came to be that of the three children, I was chosen to remain behind in the States. I was granted a student visa by the Immigration Department and soon found myself attending a local elementary school. I did not speak or write English, so consequently those first few years were quite rough. Not only was it a strange environment but I really felt very much alone. The first year was the most difficult and rarely did I make it to school without losing my breakfast.

Things smoothed out somewhat during my junior and senior high years. Even though I was very shy and basically an average student, I did excel in artistic areas, especially those relating to drawing, architecture and drafting. My baseball skills were above average and the combination brought an element of peer acceptance.

Until my family, one by one, was able to leave Cuba during the latter parts of my high school years, I lived with and was raised by my aunt and uncle. They were financially comfortable, educated people who were involved in community and civic activities. They were there for me, but had already completed raising their own three sons. My uncle was a small man in stature, but with the biggest heart imaginable. He was generous and supportive of anyone who deserved help. It was from this family that I learned the value of honesty, unselfishness and certainly never to take anything for granted. They were extremely proud to be Americans and contributing to the growth and development of their community.

After graduation I worked in a local millwork shop as a draftsman and gained some experience in the job market. While in grade school I had a fairly good sized route delivering the famous *TV Guide*—at the time it was a new magazine and everyone wanted home delivery. By 1966 I had worked for some time with a small architectural firm and completed nearly two years of basics and pre-engineering at the University of South Florida. Still uncertain of what to do with my life and with Vietnam very much in the news, I began to feel a strong sense of duty or responsibility to participate in what I then thought to be an honorable endeavor. I felt I "owed" the U.S. for affording me the privilege of an education and giving my family the opportunity to live in a free country.

Obviously not too bright at the time, I telephoned the local draft board to inquire about my status. Needless to say, I received my "Greetings" to report to Jacksonville for a physical within a matter of days. Everything happened quickly after that and my childhood fear of the unknown came back with a vengeance as I entered basic training. During my AIT training at Fort Sill I became increasingly aware of an almost intolerable guilt. As a resident alien I could not be sent into a combat area, but how could I possibly stay behind when all my friends were being shipped out? The ties were too strong and my sense of honor too great because these comrades were my family too. When I inquired about my circumstances, I was advised that if I signed a "waiver" and successfully underwent an FBI background investigation for a "secret clearance," I could indeed participate. It never occurred to me to investigate the nature of the "waiver" and I wonder to this day exactly what it entailed.

It was June of 1967 when our chartered jet touched down at Bien Hoa north of Saigon. As the door opened and we started down the ramp, I could feel my khakis soaking through the enveloping heat and could smell the scent of gunpowder in the air. We marched past a file of combat veterans who had done their time and were headed back to the "real world." The vets looked old at twenty or twenty-one and as they watched us in total silence, some shook their heads, but none said a word. I thought, "What have I gotten myself into?" It was then that my stomach knotted up and chose not to let go, as it seems for many years.

When I arrived at Lai Khe, with its semi-permanent tin roofed hooches, tents, and foxholes, it felt like an unreal world or a dream which was only too real. The next few days were spent on simple tasks, primarily filling sandbags for perimeter wall and foxholes reinforcement. We took turns manning the switchboard, which was our only real link with base camp. Assigned to Btry. A, 2nd. Bn., 33rd Arty., 1st Inf. Div. responsible for a towed 105mm Howitzer artillery unit, our primary function was to support the various First Division field operations and individual infantry battalions, down to patrol sweeps. This required the battery to be in the field with the infantry units over ninety-five percent of the time I was in RVN.

I, like everyone else my first week or two in-country, seemed dedicated to adjusting to the climate and the water, which I was sure would destroy me in an unheroic way by causing me to shit myself to death. It is amazing what our bodies eventually adapt to.

On 29 October 1967, the battery moved from Lai Khe to Quan Loi through the combined efforts of CH-47 and CH-54 helicopters. While at Quan Loi, the battery fired over 100 rounds of counter-mortar fire during a mortar attack on our base camp. Two days later, A Battery made an aerial combat assault on a fire support base five miles northwest of the besieged village of Loc Ninh. The entire night and most of the following day was spent in preparing the position for occupation, building bunkers, parapets and sleeping areas.

On the following night, approximately 0300 hours, 2 Nov., the night defensive position was struck by a heavy barrage of mortar and RPG rounds prior to a ground attack staged from three areas to hit the position on three flanks simultaneously. I was in a bunker with my section chief when the mortar rounds started popping in, and I had never experienced the earth shaking beneath me in this manner. We glanced at each other, and at that moment a bright flash passed between us. We could not have been more than three feet apart. We had previously set up a tent over the bunker and the flash resulted from an RPG round passing through from one side of the tent to the other, leaving clear cut holes on either side, and proceeding to hit an ammo dump approximately fifty yards from our position. We quickly ran to the FDC, where assistance was required by the 1st. Bn., 18th Infantry, with artillery cover.

The enemy forces consisted of two reinforced VC battalions whose intentions were to overrun the fire support base at all costs. We were able to fire four missions in spite of the intense volume of hostile fire. Fifteen hundred rounds were fired in one hour's time. Several rounds were plotted and fired within twenty meters of friendly positions, a tribute to the accuracy and precision of the men of this unit.

Occasionally, I accompanied my LT as a forward observer because my primary responsibility was the locating, plotting and providing of coordinates to the FDC for artillery or airstrikes. Possibly this was the one area where my "real world" skills assisted me in the quality of my contribution.

During this time almost all secondary roads and night defensive positions we used had been sprayed with defoliants to deny concealment to the NVA forces. We literally drove through, walked in, slept in, and ate in areas sprayed for "our protection." From mid-'67 we were increasingly exposed to sprayed areas and almost all of the personnel complained of rashes and myself and another had constant headaches and stomach problems.

At 0300 hours, 29 November '67, our battery was alerted for movement to the vicinity of the Bu-Dop Special Forces camp, which was under heavy VC attack. At 1000 hours, the battery moved to Bu-Dop by CH-47 aircraft. At 2200 hours, the fire support base jointly occupied by us and the 1st Bn., 28th. Inf., received 150-200 rounds of 82mm, 60mm, 140mm mortars and 122mm rockets. The attack lasted approximately thirty minutes. Following the mortar and rocket attack, a vicious ground attack was launched by an estimated force of 400-500 VC. We received a fire request from the infantry commander to commence direct fire to the east, across the airstrip. While still under intense ground attack, the No. 1 and No. 2 gun sections left the cover off the bunkers, leveled their guns and fired at the incoming VC at point blank range.

The VC just kept on coming. It was unbelievable. Some were tripping over their fallen comrades, but not seeming to slow them down. The direct firing continued for one to one-and-a-half hours, during which time 376 HE rounds and sixteen white phosphorus rounds were fired into the attacking forces. The commanding officer later said, "The direct firing by A battery significantly aided the defense and prevented the position from being overrun."

On 2 December '67, at 1100 hours the NDP/FSB was again hit with 82mm mortars. Myself and another FDC member were outside sitting down behind the bunker when the mortars began popping in close to us. As I crawled into my bunker I was joined by a new recruit. I cannot remember his name, only that he was the "All-American boy" type, with blond hair, blue eyes, tall and thin but muscular, a ready smile but, being new, quiet and experiencing the "feeling of the unknown" which hit us all at one time or another. Almost immediately all hell broke loose; a deafening noise; my ears ringing; sand and metal flying through the bunker. This young man, who was just there beside me, fell to the ground and with a quick glance I was aware that the gaping hole in his stomach allowed me to see through to the other side. Blood began dripping from my forehead and temple. Almost immediately I lost my sight. I could hear the section chief calling for the medic as I yelled out, "I can't see, I can't see!" As I was bandaged and carried out I remember praying to God, "Please don't let me be blind. Take my life, my arm, my leg, but don't let me be blind." I was soon advised that we had taken a direct hit from a 106mm recoilless rifle, which the VC had stolen from U.S. forces.

During this encounter the battery suffered five casualties requiring evacuation, including the battery commander, executive officer, a cannoneer, myself, and the young man who never knew what hit him. My shrapnel wounds were treated at an evac hospital and I returned to my unit within a few days. During this period I remembered a seasoned veteran telling me, "One of the first laws of survival in Vietnam is to be buddies with everyone, because you need buddies to look out for you. But be close friends with no one, because it hurts too much when he dies."

From that point on and for many years thereafter I thought of that young man, who was shoulder to shoulder with me, and wonder why him and not me. This was only one of many similar experiences which do not leave you intact, as you were before they happened.

As many others, I went to Vietnam believing there was a job to be done. Unlike most, I had seen firsthand what becomes of a people when their freedom is taken from them. I did what I believed must be done. I survived and wasn't ashamed. That is, until I came home. When I left Travis AFB I was harassed, called vicious names, spat upon and pushed aside as if I were a nonentity. I knew then where I stood in the hearts of my countrymen.

I had seen, while in Vietnam, among men, more capacity for understanding, sensitivity and love, than I had ever encountered in my life. I also experienced and appreciated a lack of prejudice and bigotry which unfortunately does exist, even today, in what we call the "real world."

I will never regret my participation in Vietnam, only that we were not allowed to succeed.

I had known that the odds of survival during my tour were not very good, but if I was going to die I wanted it to be as an American citizen. Some friends in my unit were aware of this and one of them, without my knowledge, had written to Senator Edward Kennedy on my behalf. Kennedy tried, but the immigration laws were just too strict and there was no provision in the law whereby an alien could be naturalized while outside the continental U.S., even with a Purple Heart in hand.

Upon my return to Tampa, the first person I saw was my mother. She had never been aware of my location during the time I was in RVN. Since she spoke no English, she never realized that I was anywhere but TDY in California. My family felt she had seen enough of war in her lifetime and would not be able to handle it, had she known. My letters to my brother and sister were mailed to their office and it was to them that I attempted to share my experiences and pain.

A few weeks after returning I decided to go to the Immigration Department to apply for my citizenship. My sister had heard from a friend that if a person had served honorably in the armed forces, especially in a "war zone," such person would automatically become eligible for citizenship. My sister accompanied me as I went in and stated that I had just come home from serving in Vietnam and would like to complete the process of becoming a U.S. citizen. In addition, I had completed the required five years since applying. The officer, an older, short and stocky lady, made the remark, "another alien" and proceeded to be extremely rude and unsympathetic. If she had not been a woman, I am quite sure that at that moment I would have hit her, and suffered the consequences. She stated that there was no such law, and then completely refused to talk with my sister or myself. She then called her co-worker, and by that time I just about had it. My sister was in shock and could not comprehend their responses. At that point, I didn't give a damn about obtaining my citizenship, because the injuries I had sustained and the conditions I had survived, fighting for "my country," should have been sufficient. I was told, basically, that it was not my country. I was angry, hurt and confused, suddenly not caring any longer about anything or anyone.

It was at this time that my "self-destruct" period actually began. Drinking on a daily basis was only the beginning of it. I had saved sufficient money to purchase a second-hand Ford Mustang and it was all I needed, along with frequent pints of bourbon, to begin my nightly driving and drinking. Never with a definite destination or plan in mind, I would cruise for hours, drinking until I reached a point where I knew I had to get home or pass out before I did. I was totally out of control. One night specifically, I had driven to Clearwater Beach, which was about thirty miles from Tampa on the west coast. I had drinks all night and it was about 1:30 a.m. when I started back home. Struggling to stay awake behind the steering wheel, I have no recollection of how I managed to get back into my parents' driveway or even inside the house. The next morning when I got up and went outside, the right side of my beautiful '65 Mustang was practically demolished—hub caps gone, door handle gone, dents and scratches all along the right side, both tires flat. I knew I must have hit every curb I had come close to and more than likely scraped a few telephone poles along the way. It was then that I realized that someone up above must have been watching over me, and I thanked God that I had not killed anyone.

Several attempts at returning to college were unsuccessful because I was never able to sit in a classroom and concentrate. I had begun to feel guilty for being a Vietnam vet and would also try not to disclose the fact that I had been born in Cuba. Ongoing experiences seemed to reinforce that this was the best way to handle both. Paranoia is the only way to describe my denial of my birthplace and my military experience since I felt that *everyone* was aware and unaccepting. I left school.

About a year after returning from RVN I took a drafting position with a small local consulting engineering firm. The salary was not great, but the work new and interesting. The partners in the firm treated me with consideration and respect.

In the fall of 1968 I had begun seeing a Vietnam widow whom I had met through a friend from basic training. Her husband had been killed in RVN earlier that year and she was expecting his child. I thought she was the most beautiful woman in the world and my justification for living was to be there for her and her child. I knew little about pregnancy but I wanted to be a part of whatever was to come for her and the baby. In my heart I knew this was the fatherless child of a fallen comrade and although it's difficult to explain the emotions I felt at the time, was compelled to take his place. We shared tender and never to be forgotten moments, but for reasons of which I was never informed, shortly after the baby's birth, she chose another man to share their lives.

And then there was Nancy ... the most compassionate, big-hearted, unselfish and caring person I had ever known. At this point, I have to say that if it hadn't been for Nan, I doubt I would be alive today. We had met in the latter part of 1968. She had been a roommate of Mary, the woman I spoke of above. They had been high school friends and decided, when their husbands had both left for RVN, to share the expense of a small cottage owned by a mutual friend. Nancy's husband had been killed in the fall of that year and both had returned to their parents' homes. We had become friends while I was seeing Mary and had continued to socialize with other mutual friends. She had been distressed when Mary had discontinued our relationship, and was there as a friend in many "desperate hours."

Nancy seemed to instinctively understand my state of mind with regard to Vietnam, and was ever ready to hug me and tell me she was there if I needed to talk about it. She tried to gently guide me and we became the very best of friends. She was always there when I needed someone to talk to. But frequently I pulled away, rejecting her friendship and resuming my aimless, lonely drinking patterns.

Somewhere, somehow, sometime during the period between 1970 and 1971, Nancy and I fell in love. It was tenuous and neither of us was really aware, due to our own personal fears—hers of needing and losing someone again, and mine of being too unstable for a successful relationship. Thank God and Nancy's determination, I slowly decreased my drinking and began to feel good about myself. The fact that someone like her really loved, needed and wanted to be with me provided strength I did no know I possessed. She respected and understood my feelings and I, in turn, was able to share her grief and be of help to her. She actually needed and valued me!

In April of 1971 Nancy and I were married. Within a matter of weeks symptoms of gastric and urinary difficulties, which I had been experiencing since Vietnam, increased in severity. I was vomiting blood in the mornings and the back pain which had plagued me since AIT grew worse. Over a period of eighteen months Nancy assisted me in seeing some of the finest diagnosticians in the area with no results or decrease in symptoms. In August of 1972, when Nancy was seven and a half months pregnant with our son, I found myself hospitalized on an emergency basis with congestive heart failure and early renal failure. Fortunately for me, a young surgeon felt he knew the cause, a tumor involving three of the four parathyroid glands, and potentially fatal. Fortunately, his diagnosis was correct, and with emergency surgery and a period of time in ICU for my endocrine system to stabilize, I recovered with what I thought at the time to be only a residual problem of hypertension. Unfortunately, within two weeks Nancy became severely ill and it was necessary that labor be induced prematurely. Our son was very small and very ill. We had no medical insurance, and between the two incidents and ongoing medical costs for our infant, we suddenly had nearly $30,000 in medical bills to contend with.

During the next two years Nancy and I were totally involved in the struggle to keep our son alive and healthy, pay off our debts and hold on to our home. Despite it all we never seemed to question that we would survive as long as we worked together.

In 1974 I was hired by a large consulting engineering firm in Lakeland which specialized in the phosphate industry, and my skills as well as income level steadily increased. By 1977 the recession had affected the phosphate industry to the extent that decline in production forced the near shut-down of my employer and resulted in my being laid-off for a five-month period. The financial pressures began to build up—it was almost impossible to find work in the area. Not knowing this was to happen, we had built our dream home on one and a half acres of beautifully wooded land in Valrico. The mortgage payments were becoming more and more difficult to keep up with. Nancy was doing everything humanly possible to keep us going and to this day I do not know how she managed it so well.

At that point I knew a career change was necessary and proceeded to take the civil service exam for sheriff's deputy in Hillsborough County. I really enjoyed my work in law enforcement, perhaps because it reminded me of some of the better aspects of the military—the camaraderie, etc. But also, it seemed to trigger the "flashbacks" and emotional distress I had thought were under control. It became so bad that I was concerned I might not be able to perform under pressure. After a year and a half, I walked into my wife's office in the middle of my shift and asked her to type my resignation letter. The only question she asked was whether I was sure that was really what I had to do. She knew it would just mean more uncertainty and transition, but did not try to interfere.

Since there was still no work in the area, I took a six-month assignment in South Carolina and at the same time applied to TVA in Knoxville, Tennessee. In the meantime, while I was gone, Nancy had to put our house on the market, take care of our six-year-old son, all the yard work and a demanding job.

When the house was sold, my family met me in Knoxville and I began working with TVA. We bought a home and began to settle in. Nancy was able to transfer with the corporation she had been with in Tampa, our son made the transition beautifully and all seemed to be going well. It was only about seven months later that my father became critically ill and was placed in an ICU unit in a Tampa hospital. We drove down and Nancy more or less took charge of my father's care because he wanted her with him twenty-four hours a day. After three weeks, Nancy was exhausted, we had to return to our jobs, and John, our son, needed to be back to school.

We were back in Knoxville only a matter of days when my father died. For financial reasons I came back to Tampa alone for the funeral. For some reason I became increasingly homesick and unhappy with my work in Knoxville over the succeeding four to five months. Nancy and John had made some good friends and we had all been excited to learn we were expecting twins later that summer. It didn't happen, as Nancy miscarried late in her sixth month. I wanted to come back to Tampa and once more subjected my family to a move. When we returned we built a home in Valrico.

Nancy was constantly feeling tired and ill and her doctor referred her to a specialist, who diagnosed her condition as systemic lupus. She was in and out of hospitals two or three times a year, requiring chemotherapy whenever her white blood count became excessively high, and ongoing Prednisone treatment.

Upon our return from Knoxville I had been employed by a large consulting engineering firm in Tampa as an electrical designer. I was making a good salary and there was plenty of work. But, somehow, I felt that the "war" had stolen ten years from my life. And, just when we thought life would be somewhat easier, Nancy's illness made even routine requirements more difficult for her.

In 1985 I decided to again become involved with the sheriff's department and was accepted as a commissioned reserve deputy. Due to the time that had passed it was necessary for me to go through the police academy once again. It was a volunteer position, requiring a minimum of twenty hours of patrol per month. It seemed to fit just right and I was really enjoying it, so much that I was putting in thirty to forty hours. Without realizing it, I was trying to find again that type of friendship and sharing that I had experienced in Vietnam.

On the morning of May 17, 1986 I was at my drafting table, turned to pick up a tool behind me and immediately felt a sharp pain and intense burning sensation in my lower back. I could not walk or stand up. I was taken to an orthopedic specialist who advised me that I had severely advanced osteoporosis and resulting multiple compression fractures. I laid flat in bed for about three weeks and then progressed only to a recliner. It was necessary to consult a number of specialists, undergo a bone biopsy and multiple endocrine tests to rule out malignancy and determine the causative disease process. Bone density studies indicated I had less than sixty percent of normal bone mass, and the specialists agreed that the prognosis was poor. The entire problem was resulting from endocrine imbalances occurring prior to the diagnosis and treatment of the parathyroid tumor in 1972. I was placed on long-term disability. It was necessary for me to resign my commission in law enforcement for obvious reasons of physical limitations.

I began to withdraw and avoid people, keeping to myself as much as possible and this, unfortunately, included my wife and son. As a result of my disability, our financial status changed drastically and instead of quitting work, as the doctor's had been advising Nancy for years, she was forced to increase her earning power. It just wasn't enough. We exhausted our savings and went into debt before we could sell our home and move into a smaller, more economical and easier-to-maintain location.

I had hopes of Nancy going back to college and John finishing high school with the friends he had grown up with. All that was not possible. I felt guilty that my life plans had changed and I had cheated my family. Nancy is always in physical pain and extremely tired because of her illness and John unhappy in general.

The VA, which we had been fighting for eighteen years because of my medical problems, repeatedly denied any assistance... but, we have not yet quit the fight.

I am very resentful of the VA and in general have a lot of anger and frustration to deal with. I often take out that anger on those who are closest to me without realizing it. Through the years I have gone to the vet center here in Tampa on many occasions and I have to say that it is the only place outside of my home where I have been able to open up and really talk about things that I otherwise would be unable to share. The fact that the staff is composed of Nam vets, I am sure, is the key factor. As far as I am concerned, this is undoubtedly the best service that has been provided to the Nam vet.

At this point, Nancy and I are probably going through our toughest time, not only with our medical problems, but an ongoing financial struggle which, at this stage in our lives, should not be happening. My income will remain static and it will be up to Nancy to provide for the future. At our current ages of forty-six and forty-one, our primary concerns are our son's education and planning for our older years.

We recently celebrated our nineteenth wedding anniversary and continue to be amazed that we have survived. Perhaps that is too harsh. The struggle together to mend and grow has made us strong and provided a wealth of love and understanding few ever know. We recognize that a part of our bond is a shared grief because Vietnam left us both damaged, and the emotional wounds, though shared, we will carry with us throughout our lives.

Paul Reed

I was born and raised in Dallas, Texas. I graduated from Hillcrest High School in 1966. As I recall, I had an absolute blast; seems I took nothing serious. I was the guy that rode a motorcycle through the school halls. I was also the one that got expelled my senior year for skipping class one day before final exams. If it had not been for my dear mother reminding the school principal that he would have me back again next year, I would not have graduated in 1966. Adventure was my middle name.

If it was exciting or a little risky . . . I was ready to go. So it was only natural that in 1965, when I saw U.S. combat troops on TV fighting in Vietnam, I wanted in on the action. At seventeen, I was hardly mature enough for Vietnam, but I wanted to quit high school, join the Army, and go to Vietnam. Today, I am very grateful to my father for not allowing me to do that. Anyway, I had the desire to pitch in and do my share. Joining the Army had only been delayed for a year.

On October 8, 1966 I enlisted in the U.S. Army. They gave me a Military Occupational Skill (MOS) of 11-Bravo, which is infantry. To make matters even worse, once I was in basic training I decided I wanted to be "elite" and joined the paratroopers. After all, I thought, they were even going to pay me extra each month just to jump out of airplanes. I was going to have the time of my life. At this point I still had no conception of what "Infantry" and "Paratrooper" meant. I just knew that it sounded exciting and that I was going to have a blast. Just like high school days. Yeah, right!

On graduation day from jump school at Fort Benning, Georgia, about ninety-eight percent of the graduating class received orders for Vietnam. I was sent to A Com. 2/504 Inf. 82nd Airborne Division at Fort Bragg, North Carolina and stayed there until January of 1968. Jumping out of planes was great, but time was passing and it looked as though I was not going to get to go to Vietnam. The next step was to volunteer . . . which I did. It was denied. I volunteered again ninety days later. This time I was going.

February 22, 1968 I arrived in Vietnam at Bien Hoa. One of the first things I will always remember about Nam was that blast of hot oven-heat air that hit me as the door of the plane opened. It seemed as though it could singe the hair off my arms. That was the first clue I had that I wasn't going to be fond of Nam. The second clue came when I heard all kinds of explosions, incoming artillery, and automatic weapons fire, sounds I would soon become accustomed to. One home-bound 173rd trooper asked me what unit I was assigned to. I quickly replied, "The

173rd Airborne Brigade." You would have thought I said the "Instant Death Brigade" by the depressed look on his face. I asked him why. "No need for me to say why," he said, "you'll find out soon enough!" I did find out, for sure. The 173rd had 10,041 casualties out of a total of 58,000. That's five times the losses of the 187th Airborne in Korea and more than either the 82nd or 101st Airborne divisions lost in all of WWII.

Within two weeks I was stepping off a Caribou (light cargo plane) at Kontum City airstrip. I had been assigned to A Co. 1/503 Inf. 173rd Airborne Brigade. One of the first people I met after getting off the plane was the company commander. His name was Capt. Jim Davis and he had been given the name Diamond Jim Davis by the men. As he stuck out his hand to shake mine he asked, "Where are you from, trooper?" I said, "Texas, Sir." He said, "That's where I'm from." At that point I felt reasonably secure. Just knowing someone else from home seemed to ease the tension.

Geographically speaking, the area around Kontum City and southern Dak To is some of the most, if not the most, mountainous terrain in-country. The mountains are several thousand feet tall. So tall, in fact, that helicopters had a hard time flying that high. When standing on top of some of them, we were actually above the clouds. One of the first mountains I had to climb—it took us over four days to get to the top. Seventy to eighty pounds of gear on your back, including water, ammo, rifle, and shovel, didn't seem to help things too much either. We lived like Gypsies, it seemed—carried all of our supplies with us and got resupplied when we needed it by chopper. We, being A Co., would move on company-strength search and destroy missions every day. Come early afternoon, about 3:30 or 4 o'clock, we would dig in because the sun would go down around 5:30 or 6 o'clock. That means we would dig new foxholes every night. Sometimes the ground was dry and sometimes it had rocks in it—made it very difficult to dig in. But I soon learned how to be thankful for the foxholes. The effort expended to dig them was well worth it.

The trees in this area were over two hundred feet tall and sometimes it would rain under the canopy of these trees. I am telling the truth when I say we were always wet. Wet from rain, sweat, urine, or blood. A person could get a small scratch on his hand or arm and, because of the high humidity and being wet all the time, jungle rot would set in. I had every kind of rot a body could get—jungle rot, crotch rot, and severe athlete's foot rot. The way we would get the poison from the jungle rot out of our body was to find a leech and let him suck it out. The leech would suck it dry and a few seconds later would curl up and die (ha ha!). More than one time at night I would wake up and find several leeches sucking on me. And of course, each time we walked through creek beds, swamps, or small streams, we would be pulling leeches off.

During certain times of the year monsoon rains would come. These monsoons are not just rains; this water would come down in solid sheets. If a person wasn't careful he could drown standing upright. Add this volume of water to the mountains and it would be impossible for us to climb up. We would take one step forward and slip back three or four. I went to sleep soaking wet several times, wrapped up in my poncho liner. I was miserable. Day in and day out of it—that was enough to drive a person berserk. When the rains quit the sun would come out and it would feel as though we were in a sauna. Water was sometimes very, very precious and a lot of our water came from streams or creeks.

Mosquitoes were the next most miserable thing we had to contend with. We were supposed to take our malaria pills, which I did, because I didn't want to get malaria. But there were a lot of guys that didn't because they had a tendency to give a person diarrhea. Watching some of my buddies in convulsions from malaria out in the middle of nowhere, ten thousand miles from home, made me want to sit down and cry. It was very painful, but not as painful as other things we had to see.

What made things even more difficult was an elusive enemy that we were searching for. Usually, he would be dug in and fortified on the very tip-top of a tall mountain. They had ropes tied in the trees which they could climb up and down and when we would come up the mountain they were next to impossible to spot. The pointman almost always got a round between the eyes. Airstrikes, artillery, napalm, or anything else, couldn't make them budge. They had dug in and down along the side of the tree trunks and had bunkers under the trees. The trees were so big that three men couldn't stretch their arms around. When night came there was no way to dig foxholes and we had to try to sleep on the side of a steep slope. The only way that you could keep from rolling down the mountain was to prop yourself up against a tree. At first light I felt like death warmed over.

Sometimes the enemy would be so strong that we would withdraw and try to approach them from another direction. In doing this it seems as though he knew every move we were going to make. Back down the mountain halfway, and then between some other mountains, is where he caught us. I know we lost thirty or forty men that day. The enemy was deadly accurate with his mortar. Finally, after about two more days of airstrikes and night probes, the enemy just left. Don't know if he ran out of guts or ammo, but he just left. We were now able to retrieve our two or three dead pointmen. One thing I'll never be able to forget is the stench and smell of death in the jungle. These particular guys that we were up against were from the 304th NVA Regiment. They were the ones that kicked the French butt at Dien Bien Phu in 1954. They were actually a hard-core NVA death squad. Their nickname was "Steel." The reason I know this is because I was able to get one of their diaries. It contained this guy's military ID card along with his orders and a fight song from the 304th. He was also carrying a VC flag and the NVA flag.

After about three months in the field and operations in, on, or around the Ho Chi Minh Trail, we were moved over to Bong Son. Bong Son is on the coast of Nam. We had fire support bases named LZ Uplift, North LZ Uplift, and LZ English that we operated out of. We would depend on these FSBs for artillery support and these bases were what we called the "rear area" when we spoke of the rear. They even had tents for us to sleep in, a luxury that we were not accustomed to. We felt like we were in hog heaven when we got to sleep in a tent.

The particular thing I remember most about Bong Son was the local VC. They generally were just young inexperienced kids—sometimes not, though. The most scared I ever got was at Bong Son. The terrain was nearly flat for the most part. There were no big rocks or big trees to hide behind. We were basically just out in the open. We were all digging in one evening and we got hit. Charlie would always hit you when you least expected it. I mean Charlie would *always* hit you when you least expected it. I mean, those guys were so close to us we could smell them. This particular time they were so close we had to call artillery in on ourselves. This is what I received my purple heart from. American artillery. After the artillery stopped, a voice came over a bullhorn speaking perfect English. The voice said, "American officers and men, you are commanded to leave Vietnam and go home, or die." At that point I began to worry a bit, as I thought we were going to be overrun. We called in some more artillery and the voice stopped for a while. Later on that night we were set up in a perimeter about 100 meters away from a creek bed. Two of those little guys had snuck up that creek bed and had laid their AK-47s over the embankment and began firing full automatic, raking our whole perimeter. It was pitch dark, at about 0100 hours, and you could not see your hand in front of your face. As I was startled awake I can remember I was hugging the earth like I've never hugged it before. It seemed as though the firing would never quit. Finally, one of the guys on guard found the charger handle to the claymore and blew it. The claymore was about twenty-five meters away from the creek bed and of course facing these two VC. Needless to say it put their lights out. At first light we went to inspect and found only one dead VC. Only two small beebees from the claymore had penetrated his head. One of my buddies hammered in a pair of paratrooper wings in his forehead with the butt of his knife. I said, "What was that for?" He said it was for his buddy that had been killed in an ambush by the VC. It was our usual practice to just leave the bodies where they were. On this occasion, as we were waiting for the choppers to arrive, we could hear some loud moaning and screaming coming from the creek bed. I assumed it was his mother. Apparently she had hustled on back to the village and told the others what had happened. As the choppers began to arrive we were taking automatic weapons fire. Fortunately, that was one hot LZ on which no one was hit. Looking back—to be woke up like that was traumatic, but it was common. It was also typical for the VC to use psychological warfare on us. They didn't have enough men to overrun us at that time, but they did a good job of making me think they had.

Occasionally, we would accidentally find caches of weapons and enemy supplies. While on patrol in the Bong Son area, we stopped to take a short break. One of my buddies just happened to sit down right on top of a giant cache. It contained Soviet-made 122mm rockets still in bamboo packs that the enemy used for transport over the mountains, and hundred-pound bags of rice. Also, some smaller types of rockets. Humping those out of the bush to an area where they could be picked up was difficult, to say the least. It didn't seem to bother my friend Rick. I'm very glad he was my friend. He was a big (and I mean big) Swede from Minnesota. Humping twenty-five frags and two thousand M-60 rounds along with his other gear was no problem for him. On another occasion we happened to be in a firefight on a large mountain and it's an understatement to say that I was scared to death. I just knew the NVA were going to overrun our left flank. In checking with Rick I received some real consolation by asking him if he was scared. His reply was "Hell no. When we get out of this place, Paul, I'm going to buy you a beer." For some reason it helped for the moment. He also sent his wife a pair of ears through the mail.

On another occasion, one of the tunnel rats in my company found a complete underground hospital out in the middle of nowhere. Several prisoners were brought up. They were so pale I'm sure they had been down there for a long time. The best part about that hospital was that the tunnel rat brought out an American 50-cal ammunition box full of American fifty dollar bills. All together there was $175,000. Who knows how they accumulated that much and where it came from. Probably from the black market. The money was, however, quickly taken from my buddy. But this story had a good ending. Four or five years later my buddy successfully sued the U.S. government for the money. It was even tax free. That's one person that benefited from the war effort.

Some of the operations along the coast just east of Bong Son were very enjoyable to me. Each afternoon after patrolling, the ole man would set us up in a semi-perimeter next to the ocean. Then we were allowed to go swimming in the ocean. It was just an incredible time we had, because the beaches in Vietnam are very beautiful. We even had a unit of tankers operating with us for a month and they spoiled us. You see, they were accustomed to and normally had such niceties as real potatoes and chicken eggs, of which they generously shared. They also had such things as fish nets (seines) and cooking oil from the rear area. We would get out in the ocean and seine for fish and then have a big fish fry along with french fried potatoes cooked over a wood fire in steel pots. There were times when I actually thought I was in the Boy Scouts, because sometimes we went weeks without contact with the enemy.

The other really good time that I remember was when we were outside of An Khe on pipeline guard. We were guarding this pipeline that ran from Qui Nhon to Pleiku that carried oil. We were on that detail for approximately one month. As you might guess, mamasan and papasan had a thatched hut right across the road. Well, they also had three daughters that we became friends with. My parents would send me sardines in a can and I would give them to mamasan and papasan. Before long they invited me to dinner and you guessed it, they were serving those chicken eggs that had been incubated for twenty days and the baby chick is just beginning to peck its beak out of the shell. They expected me to eat that, plus they also had nuoc-mam, which is the juice that's made from rotten fish heads, beetles and stinks like you know what. The Vietnamese culture requires that if a person is invited over to eat, he must eat everything that's put on his plate. But this was too much for me. I could feel "you know what" coming up so I dodged out the open hooch door and headed for a black market Coca-Cola. Somehow that carbonation helped calm my stomach. They also had a small dog. When I noticed him not there I asked where he was. Mama-san said, "He make GI stew." I about gagged.

In conclusion about my experience in Vietnam, I would just like to say that it's an experience that I wouldn't take a million dollars for and at the same time I wouldn't go through it again for a million dollars. It certainly matured me somewhat and, looking back, I don't know what or how I would be if I hadn't had to go through it. It's very hard to say. I know that I was damaged emotionally from seeing the kinds of things that I saw and doing the kinds of things I had to do, but putting a price tag on the damages is very hard. I have been married and divorced twice since leaving the service and I know that my Nam days' experiences have played a large part in my past marriage failures. A day seldom passes that Vietnam doesn't cross my mind.

I feel like I have learned to cope with my feelings about Vietnam over the last twenty years. Since coming home in '69, my parents have been very supportive, as well as my sister, Pam. I think this alone has been the greatest single factor in my recovery. Family support has been very important. Of course, the Lord Jesus Christ has taught me to forgive. I think that the word "forgive" is not only the greatest word in our dictionary, but its also the hardest to learn to do. Since the Lord Jesus Christ taught me to forgive my former enemy, my life has been steadily improving. I harbored hatred for the enemy that I had been taught to hate for over eighteen years, but one day the Lord showed me that the Vietnamese, either North or South, are not the real enemy. We can't see the real enemy. He is a spirit. Forgiveness is the key. Since receiving forgiveness form the Lord Jesus and forgiving my former enemy my emotional wounds are healing. I recommend this process to the Vietnam vets. Forgive, Forgive, and Forgive!

Robert W. Prichard

Growing up as a so-called "baby boomer" during the 1950s and '60s, I suppose you could say that I inherited a lot of middle class values and ideals from my parents, neighbors, and friends.

After attending a Catholic grade school for eight years, I went to the public high school in my hometown of Oak Lawn, Illinois, a southwestern suburb of Chicago. All in all, I'd describe my childhood and adolescent years as pretty much normal for the kids of my era. About all I wanted, or expected, out of life was a chance to make a decent living, have a home, a nice car and a good family. Little did I know . . .

Basically, by the time I was fifteen or sixteen I was into the normal routine of fast cars, drink a few beers and try to get laid. By my sophomore year in high school, Vietnam was starting to heat up, but it was just one of those things you just didn't worry about. Most of our fathers had served in WWII and it was just something you had to do— Uncle Sam called, you went, no questions asked.

By my senior year, I'd known a few guys that had been to Vietnam and it didn't seem like that big of a deal; do a year and come home, or so I thought. . . . A different generation, a different war, you know—you kill them, they kill us—it was the same as it had been for thousands of years. The weapons may change, but the end result is the same.

When school was ready to end in June of 1966, I knew it would be only a matter of time before the draft got me, so I checked out the different recruiters to see about the options I could get, maybe learn a trade or something on that order. Finally, the good old U.S. Army offered what sounded like a pretty good deal. My dad had served in the U.S. Army during WWII in Europe, so I guess that played a part in my decision also.

I took my oath and left 615th Van Buren in Chicago on July 12, 1966 and was put on a train with about four hundred other poor slobs headed for Fort Leonard Wood, Missouri. When I stepped off the bus that picked us up at the train depot, I felt as if I'd entered a different world— all of these sergeants with Smokey Bear hats yelling and cussing everyone. I thought, "Damn, and I've got three years of this bullshit to contend with." Stand in line, shave your head, stand in line, check your teeth, stand in line, get your uniforms, stand in line and get fed, and so it went. Most of the guys in my training company were from the Chicagoland area, with a handful of farm boys from Illinois and Indiana, so at least the culture shock wasn't too severe.

After basic training was finished and we all went our different ways, to AIT, I was duly informed that the Army, in its infinite wisdom, had decided I needed no additional training as a mechanic, as was "guaranteed" in my enlistment and, I'm just a dumb kid, just barely eighteen, so what did I know, right? They gave me this form to fill out for two choices of stateside duty and two choices for overseas. I thought to myself, "Well, give me all or nothing." So for stateside choices I put Fort Sheridan, Illinois or Fort Harrison, Indiana and for overseas I put only Vietnam. The Green Machine decided I belonged in Keaserlautern, Germany.

Upon arrival to my unit during Christmas of 1966, it became clear that everyone from the company commander on down was dead drunk. After the holiday season ended, they remained that way and then I found out that was the SOP for this duty station. I had hoped that my tenure of military service would amount to somewhat more that being a wino, so after about two months I filled out a DD1049 and requested immediate reassignment to Vietnam. At the end of March 1967, the Pentagon informed me that I'd been accepted and orders would follow directly.

By May 1 of 1967 I was back home in Chicago, enjoying a thirty-day leave before I reported to Oakland, California for processing and transportation to Vietnam. We'll let it go at saying I had one hell of a time during this leave. There was talk all around me pertaining to the war by this time. I'd say by this period, close to eighty-five percent of my friends were already wearing a uniform of one of the services. How did CCR sing it in "Fortunate Son"?

On June 3 of 1967, I showed up at the infamous Oakland Army Terminal and tried to get my ducks in a row. The Navy was loading a transport ship, a huge mother, there at the wharf. In this oversize barn they informed us that about four hundred or so of us were going by ship. Now there are maybe one thousand or so guys in this damn oversize barn, about half of them sick from getting their shot record updated; there was almost a half inch of puke on the floor and this lifer's talking boats. I think to myself, "I ain't no squid and I ain't no Marine," so panic starts to set in. They say the ship isn't leaving for about two more days, so this guy in the rack next to me comes up with an idea. We go up to this platform where this lifer is and we play real gung-ho, tell him that we're bored and we could maybe help him out with all his paperwork and such. This E-6 is happy as a hog in shit seeing two dumb-ass PFCs wanting to help him out. He ushered us behind his counter and showed us what to do, sorting files and shit like that. It took us about forty-five minutes to see how the system worked before we located our files and discreetly slid them to the top of the pile.

Less than four hours later we were strapping ourselves into the seats of a Boeing 707 and gave each other a nod as the plane became airborne and we could see "our" ship below in the bay. Being a typical eighteen-year-old PFC, I thought we'd really put one over on Uncle Sam.

June 5, 1967, we touched down at Bien Hoa or Saigon—somewhere— and were taken by bus to the replacement center. A little over a month ago I had been in the mountains of Germany and now I was in Vietnam—about one hundred degrees in the shade and the smell of burning shit covers uniforms. Everywhere I look I see OD jeeps, trucks, choppers, planes and uniforms. They said this was a secure area, only an occasional mortar or two. Luckily, I only spent one night at the replacement center before I got assigned.

My home for the next year, I learned, would be with the 2nd Bn., 34th Armor. Two guys picked up ten of us and proceeded to Long Binh, where HQ Company of the 2/34th Armor was based. The first-sergeant gave us a pep talk and we were told we'd have "indoctrination classes" for the next two days and then we would be sent to our platoon or to a line company. He informed us that there were only two actual armor battalions in Vietnam, so the line companies A, B, and C were permanently attached to different units.

After two days of classes learning "all about" our host country, I was assigned to Bravo Company in Lai Khe. Bravo was attached to the 1st Infantry Division, better known as the "Big Red One." They flew myself and another FNG to Lai Khe on a shuttle-run chopper, ash-and-trash sortie. We got dropped at the helicopter POL dump and there we sat for about three hours. From the surroundings, I thought we were back in the Stone Age. "This is supposed to be a brigade-size base camp?" At about this time a battery of 105 (towed) Howitzer down the road opens up on a fire mission and I don't know my ass from third base. We had no weapons issued yet and there wasn't a soul in sight; the chopper had departed after fueling up. We turned around as we heard a jeep coming toward us—MPs—the first time I was ever been happy to see them. We told them what was going on and that our unit hadn't sent anyone to pick us up. "No problem, hop in," they'd give us a lift.

Arriving at my company area, I couldn't believe my eyes. The motor pool was muddy red clay, almost like grease when you walked in it. There were about a dozen hooches set back into the rubber trees. Each one had wood about four feet up and then screen for the rest of the walls. The tin roofs had long overhangs to (supposedly) stop the rain from coming in when the monsoon wind was up. It didn't work for shit, but it looked good on paper, I guess.

We were greeted in the orderly room by the first-sergeant, and this dude thinks he's Super Lifer. I figured he wipes his ass with a wire brush when he wakes up in the morning. After ten minutes of his shit, we're sent to supply to draw weapons. The supply sergeant gives me three sets of jungle fatigues, steel pot, canteens, ammo pouches, flak vest, an M-14 and a pistol with a GI shoulder holster. I'm a damn mechanic. What the hell do I need all this crap for?

The next morning the first-sergeant asks me if I can drive an ACAVM113. I told him I'd never driven one before, that I'd driven a self-propelled Howitzer during OJT. He assigned me to two Spec-5s and told them to teach me all they could by 2 p.m., as the company had afternoon convoy escort to Di An. In a matter of hours, I'd managed to become fairly competent with the ACAV and by 2 p.m., we were at the convoy assembly point at Lai Khe with three ACAVs and one M48A3 tank.

We formed at the convoy assembly area with about seventy-five dump trucks from the 1st Engineers and proceeded south on Highway 13. As we passed by Ben Cat, the ACAV in front of me hit a mine and all hell broke loose. I remembered the "Herringbone Formation" and I steered left, then stopped. Everyone had opened up with the 50-cals and M-60s. We had rice paddies on both sides of the road for about a hundred yards before the bush started, so we just shot the hell out of the treeline for maybe two minutes. No sooner had we ceased shooting than this Special Forces captain comes out of the bush with about twenty-five ARVNs. He comes over to the road and starts raising hell about us shooting up his gooks. Pate, who was the ranking man in our group, walks this "Green Beanie" over to the mine crater and shows him two wires running in the direction he'd just come from. They were supposed to be securing the road and here we have a command-detonated mine. I knew then that I was in some deep doo-doo. To this day I believe that those ARVN's are the ones who detonated the mine— ARVN by day, VC at night.

As it turns out, almost the whole B Company was set to DEROS at the same time, as they had come from the States as a unit in 1966. I was one of the first replacements to come in and the whole company would be replaced in three weeks.

As I settled in for my tour, I tried to learn all I could from the short-timers. My typical evening was spent at our company area's combination officer, NCO, and EM club, a beer-hop shanty behind the supply room. All of us FNGs would listen to the war stories of the short-timers and try to separate the facts from the bullshit. I figured these had made it through a year of this and I was determined to do the same.

The next few months were spent mainly on convoy duty or road security. Every once in a while, Division or MACV or someone would come up with something hot for us to check out. Usually we'd find an abandoned base camp or a weapons cache—pretty routine stuff.

Division moved us up to the Quan Loi-An Loc area to support the grunts on search and destroy missions in the so-called Fishhook area. We were teamed up with elements of the 1/16th Infantry and 2/2 Mech. The straight-leg grunts were catching a lot of grief from booby traps and such and they figured our tanks and ACAVs could eliminate a lot of those hazards. We set up at the Michelin Rubber Plantation and by night we secured the plantation and airstrip and patrolled during the day. The "hustlers" set up an instant shantytown "ville" right outside our perimeter. I couldn't believe it at first—bars, trinket stands, whorehouses, the whole works. Those damn gooks are a thousand years behind us, but they knew how to get our bucks.

The VC mortared us about every other night but not one of those bastards in the ville knew a thing about it.

Division moved us and the 2/2 Mech south on Highway 13 to an area known as Claymore Corners. Upon arrival we teamed up with the 168th Land Clearing team. These guys had these big D-9 Cat dozers with a plow made for clearing jungle.

We stayed out for three months clearing jungle in this so-called free fire zone. We found and destroyed numerous base camps and weapons caches but only got a body count of three or four gooks. We had our command ACAV destroyed by two RPGs but never got the gooks who fired them. It was like they vanished.

Soon afterwards they informed us we'd be having a maintained stand-down at the Lai Khe base camp. Our CO, Captain Donovan, was a mustang who'd come up through the ranks, and decided we'd have a party. So he purchased a pallet of beer out of his own pocket. He came out to the formation in Bermuda shorts and one of those wild Hawaiian shirts and announced he didn't want to see a man in his bunk that night unless he was passed out. He was one of the finest officers I'd met in the Army and was respected and well liked by every man in the company.

That night Captain Donovan and Sgt. Barney Davis, the mess-sergeant, started wrestling with each other, both drunk as hell. They started shooting flares off and pretty soon we had the provost marshal down there. It was one of the funniest things I'd ever seen. Our first-sergeant had to cover for Captain Donovan because he was so loaded he couldn't walk or talk.

All in all we had a pretty tight outfit. I'd say we were probably seventy-five percent or better RA, which is pretty much the normal for a tank company. The 1st Inf. Div. took pretty good care of us as an attached unit. We had our own recon section, plus they gave us a lot of extra weapons. Some of our tanks had two 50-cal machine guns plus shotguns and other small arms. I understand from another vet of B 2/34 Armor, who was there about two years after I left, that when the company was returned to the 25th Division, the IG couldn't believe all the "extra" firepower we had.

What was supposed to have been our last two nights of stand-down turned into Tet of 1968. We had all partied pretty hard that evening and about 2 a.m. all hell broke loose. They mortared us for about thirty minutes, then the rockets started. We never had rockets used on us before, so at first we didn't know what the hell was happening. They kept it up to almost 10 a.m. before it let up. Everyone was assigned to track, mounted up, and the REMFs went for the bunkers. Finally, brigade calls us up and tells us they have NVA sighted at Chon Thanh, so we headed north on Highway 13. We'd hardly cleared the base camp when MACV "commandeered" two platoons of tanks from us to go to Saigon to defend the poges down there.

En route to Chon Thanh we took sniper rounds but nothing we couldn't handle. Upon arriving at "Chi Town," as it was called, we moved into a NDP already occupied by elements of the 2/12 Mech and a battery of eight-inch SP Howitzers. They told us we had to keep Charlie from mining the road at night, so we'd be making "thunder runs" at different times at night. We would usually use two or three ACAVs and took a tank and ran down Highway 13 wide open and recon by fire on both sides of the road to keep the gooks confused. What a rush. No lights. Just the stars and muzzle flashes from the machine guns. Let me make a point here. Highway 13, known as "Thunder Road," wasn't a highway, but a two lane road, paved in spots, gravel in other spots, filled with craters from forty years of war. It was ours during the day and Charlie's at night. From Saigon to the Cambodian border you could see the remains of French vehicles destroyed long before Uncle Sam decided we would "bear any burden . . . Oppose any foe . . ."

The next day they moved our HQ and recon section (three ACAVs and two tanks) to a different NDP about ten miles down the road. We were told to secure it to keep the gooks from booby-trapping it before they moved some more infantry and arty into it the next day. That night we were on fifty percent alert, so we had a man on 50-cal and another on the radio.

About 4 a.m. Bennett and I were on duty, waiting for marching orders to come via the radio from brigade. I'd just cranked the engine up on the ACAV to charge up the batteries when Bennett yelled at me to keep down. As I peeked out of driver's hatch I was greeted by 50-cal and 7.62 tracers as well as M-16 fire ricocheting all over the place— about 9.9 on the "Pucker Factor Scale." Bennett, thinking fast, pops a parachute flare out over HW13, where the fire is coming from, and we see the recon section from 2/2 Mech on a thunder run. Having worked with these dudes so much, we flipped our radio to their frequency and yelled, "Ronnie Recon, why are you clowns busting caps on our NDP?" Their platoon leader came back on line and wanted to know who we were. "You got Dreadnought Bravo 50 here, you asshole!" They ceased firing and he told us that the brigade had told him that all the NDPs on that section of road were vacant. Military intelligence, yes sir. This second-lieutenant, "Ronnie Recon," I can't remember his real name, was a first-class line officer, a really young dude who knew his stuff. He starts copping a plea, telling us he didn't know we were there, so just to fuck with his mind a bit, we told him we'd mined the road for his return trip—just to mess with his mind a bit.

My buddy, Tom Bennett, was a city kid like me. He came from Milwaukee and we shared a lot of the same interests. We were together almost our whole tour and ended up in the States at Fort Hook, Texas upon our return. We were informally known as the "Gruesome Twosome" by most of the lifers. He started out as the rear M-60 gunner and I was the driver. One of our crew weapons was an M14-E2 with a Starlight scope, which Bennett could use as well as anyone in the Army.

One time during a maintenance stand-down, we were "volunteered" for base camp perimeter guard by this one ignorant lifer who had a real hard-on for us after we'd put a dud mortar round under his pillow. We showed up at the guard mount post with this M14-E2, an M-60 machine gun, M-16 plus our 45s. This other lifer with the infantry, in charge of the perimeter, asked if we were John Wayne and Audie Murphy. He puts us in a bunker right between HW13 and the ammo dump for the night and goes about his business. In the wee hours of the morning, Bennie wakes me and tells me to look up through the Starlight scope. I make out three figures moving across HW13 towards the perimeter wire, so I could tell him we have movement in the wire and request permission to open fire. This asshole tells me that there's a LRRP team in our sector and not to fire. Bennie tells me these bastards are on their backs and are halfway through the wire already. I get back on the horn and tell this sergeant these gooks are coming under the wire and are almost inside the perimeter. Again this asshole refuses to let us open up. Bennie looks at me and says, "Fuck that clown. It's our ass on the line here," so we just smiled at each other and opened up, him on the M14-E2 and me on the M-60. Trip flares in the wire go off and the other two guys in the bunker wake up and start rock-and-rolling their M-16s. Next thing we know, this sergeant-of-the-guard lifer comes flying up in his jeep with some second-lieutenant and starts yelling shit like "court marshall" and "LBJ" and "Leavenworth" and shit like that. They relieved us of our weapons and took us back to our company area. About 9 a.m. we were called into the orderly room and the CO and first-sergeant informed us they found two dead gooks in the wire with satchel charges and maps of the base camp, so we we're not going to LBJ anymore. I couldn't believe this crap—I'm nineteen going on ninety.

Another occasion that comes to mind is when the ammo dump got blown up by sappers in broad daylight, while the gook laborers were on base. Brigade calls us and says they got two men trapped inside the ammo dump. They asked the CO if he could send a tank in there and rescue these dudes. To this day I wonder why Bennie and I volunteered to go in and get them out. We buttoned up the hatches and drove about a half mile to the ammo dump with all this ordnance cooking off. I couldn't see out of the vision blocks, so Bennett cracks open the track commander's hatch and guides me around all this debris in the road. We had no sooner turned into the ammo dump when they call us on the radio and tell us it's a false alarm—the two dudes had already escaped. There was all sorts of artillery and mortar ammo all over the ground so I couldn't do a pivot-steer to get out of there. It must have been one hundred and twenty degrees inside the ACAV because of the fire, so Bennie popped open the rear door and I had to back all the way out of that inferno. By the time we got back to our company area you couldn't have put a greased ice pick up my ass.

Upon our return this one lifer, Sergeant Nathan, or "Sergeant Stateside" as we called him, started giving us a ration of shit for going in there in the first place. That's when we decided to put the dummy round in his bunk. This guy was such an asshole, he wanted us to shine our boots when we were past our ankles in monsoon mud. When he was in the shower that evening we slipped the mortar round under his pillow. He comes back and flops down on his rack and hits his head on this round under his pillow, so he pulls it out and almost shits on his cot. He tries to run out of the hooch and drops the round two or three times. All of the other lifers are about to die laughing because they thought he was an asshole, too. Bennie and I were sitting on the roof of a bunker watching the whole scene through the screen walls of the hooch. As he comes screaming out the door with this dummy round, we're laughing so hard we've got tears running down our cheeks.

The next morning the first-sergeant calls Bennie and I out of formation and we're about to bite a hole in our lips to keep from laughing, and tells us we're in for serious punishment for our latest escapade. He then tells us we have to burn shit for a day, so in a voice loud enough for the whole company to hear, Bennett says, "Hell, I'd volunteer to burn Nathan any day." Everyone from the CO on down cracked up because everyone in the company knew Nathan was a class-A dickhead.

Afterwards, more of the same old grind—convoy security, road security, search and destroy and recon patrols.

What started out as a desire to do my duty for my country and help the Vietnamese people to fend off the Red Menace came to be a deep resentment of the people. The ARVN tank outfits that I saw never were in the field, never had mud on their boots or dirty uniforms. What became of Johnson's promise not to have "American boys dying for Asian boys?"

One time, as we came through the ARVN area of Ben Cat, we passed these ARVNs sitting in a roadside bar in their clan uniforms and they flipped us the bird, so we threw them a couple of CS grenades as a present. To this day I still resent those people, and my government for all they've given these gooks while they continue to screw the Vietnam veterans.

As my tour drew to a close, Mini-Tet of 1968 had broken out and we caught more of the same old crap—find 'em, count 'em, and bury 'em, business as usual. I still say, nuke 'em till they glow; it worked in Japan, it would work in the Nam.

After a forty-five day leave in Chicago, my next duty station was Fort Hood, Texas, where my friend Bennett had gone also. It was almost impossible to believe, but we ran into each other my first day on post. We pretty much picked up where we'd left off in Nam.

He'd bought a Rambler SST and I had a Camaro SS396, so we did the gearhead scene until I ETSed a year later. He married a gal from Austin, Texas and I was his best man. Unfortunately, we've lost contact through the years. If you're reading this, Tom, contact me. We've got a lot to catch up on, bro'.

Upon my return to civilian life I tried to catch up on all I'd missed and would stay up twenty to twenty-two hours a day. I also found I wasn't comfortable unless I had a firearm in my possession.

As the years progressed for the last two decades, I look back at three failed marriages, countless trips up and down the so-called ladder of success. How can you tell people that weren't there how it really was? I don't think it can truthfully be done. How can someone know what it's like to live day-in-day-out in a life-or-death situation until they've been there? The people of the United States of America have betrayed the Vietnam veteran lock, stock, and barrel. From PTSD to Agent Orange to the POW/MIA issue, we have been sold out to the lost. The Veterans Administration has screwed us every way we turn. I was brought up to believe "My country right or wrong." I can't believe that anymore because of the sorry treatment we've gotten right on down the line. For instance, the Centers for Disease Control in Atlanta, Georgia claims they couldn't get accurate results on the Agent Orange issue because they couldn't find enough vets to volunteer for the study. Well, I did volunteer and no one called me. This is nothing more than a conspiracy between the government and the big chemical companies and anyone who can't see that has got to be the most stupid person in the world. I suffer the effects of Agent Orange plus PTSD but the VA won't do a damn thing, even though I've signed up for the treatment numerous times. The government paid off for Love Canal and Times Beach for dioxin, but not for the Vietnam vets. How do the people of America tolerate such injustice? We gave all we had, and they turn us out cold, yet they bring in thousands of Vietnamese refugees and give them money, housing and anything else they cry for.

I stayed in PTSD therapy for three years and when I went in front of the VA rating board I was told I didn't qualify under their guidelines, even though both of my case doctors said otherwise. That's justice? On appeal I asked why two doctors had me in the PTSD program if I did not in fact suffer from PTSD. This so-called board consisted of one young doctor in his twenties and two obese women in their forties. What do these people know about PTSD? Probably as much as the CDC in Atlanta knows about Agent Orange.

At long last, I'd like to thank a few people. First of all I'd like to thank Gary for giving me the chance to tell my story. I'd like to thank my mom and dad for being there when I needed them and not bugging me when I didn't. I'd like to thank the "Iron Whore," my 1985 Harley-Davidson Wide Glide for being able to flow the cobwebs out of my head when most other things fail. And most important of all, I'd like to thank one special lady, my wife Rose, for being there to try and understand the pain I feel, always ready to help me get through. I couldn't make it without you, Honey. I love you.

Remember: POW/MIA!

Terry A. Potts

My high school days prior to being drafted by the Army in 1966 and actually joining the Marines for four years instead of going into the Army, were probably pretty much average for the time. During this period young males like myself were very aware of the possibility of being drafted and sent to Vietnam because you were constantly aware of those older around you who had been drafted and sent. As time went on, more and more of my close friends were either joining the Air Force, or whatever, to beat the draft and possibly avoid going to Nam as a grunt. Before long, all of us eligible males were in one branch of the service or another except for a few who got deferments.

Every evening on the news after school you could catch the so-called body counts being given—how many we killed versus how many of us got killed. It wasn't exactly the ideal way to grow up at that time, because the war was escalating and you felt your number was coming up. I received my draft papers about one month after I turned nineteen, which was to change my world. But, prior to that, me and my friends did what a lot of other kids at that time did, and that was drive our 1955 Fords or Chevys around, hanging out at drive-ins, dating, drinking beer, drag racing and getting into minor scraps with the law. It was fun while it lasted and at that age you practically feel indestructible anyway. I would say, except for the Vietnam war going on, it was a good time to grow up. Things were just less complicated than they are now. That is, compared to the way a lot of high schools are now, with the drug problems, crime, etc.

I joined the Marines in September of 1966 and went through basic at Parris Island, South Carolina. It was basically being fucked with almost twenty-four hours a day, excluding sleep. From there we went through four more weeks of intensive training at Camp Lejeune, North Carolina. That wasn't much better than boot camp. From there I went on leave during Christmas of 1966 for thirty days. Then I went on to Memphis, Tennessee for aviation jet engine school for six months. From there I got orders for Cherry Point, North Carolina, assigned to a squadron (VMA-224) where I stayed for about two years before getting orders for Vietnam in the summer of 1969. I went on leave before reporting to Camp Pendleton, California, for what is called staging. This was three weeks of extensive field training before going over. In the Marines, your MOS means nothing because you are reminded over and over that all Marines are basically grunts and could be in the field at anytime. So, for three weeks I went through humping hills in full gear, firing weapons, learning gook warfare, etc. In a lot of ways, it was similar to boot camp.

We left on a Continental Airlines jet for Okinawa, where we took a military hop into country. Upon landing in Da Nang, my first impression looking out the window was government issue caskets, stacked three high, being loaded on a C-130 with the bodies of those that didn't make it. We finally disembarked into a very hot, humid, dusty environment and eventually started processing the rest of the day. I finally got orders to go to Chu Lai, which is about thirty miles out of Da Nang on the South China Sea.

My first night in-country was spent at Da Nang in what was called a transient barracks. Some time during the night we got hit with incoming and small-arms fire, which brought home the fact that you were no longer as safe as you were a few hours earlier.

I finally got to Chu Lai the next day and processed into a new squadron, got assigned a rifle and ammo, helmet, flak jacket, etc. We were told to carry our rifle everywhere we went, and you were supposed to wear your helmet and flak jacket, which wasn't always done. You could get a false sense of security at times.

Sometime in my first few weeks at Chu Lai, about six of us Marines in an open-bed truck, stopped along the outside perimeter road. This was just because one of the guys wanted to score some dope from one of the local Vietnamese. (Vietnamese marijuana was commonly used in Vietnam.) Well, an Army guy guarding the perimeter in about a forty-foot tower fired at us with a rifle-powered grenade that just barely went over to the other side of the truck. He was a real smart-ass because he could have screwed some people up. We reported it, but I don't know whatever was done. Who was the enemy anyway? (We could have been some more names on The Wall in Washington. There were a lot of accidental deaths in Vietnam.)

Working in my squadron wasn't too bad except for the humidity and occasionally, in the daytime, hearing sniper fire and incoming rockets. Probably B-40 rockets, Chinese made. The gooks usually operated best at night, when they would occasionally send in sapper squads, trying to blow up planes or whatever. I remember a few nights lying in my rack asleep, or half asleep, and start hearing incoming walking our way. You didn't ask questions, you just jumped out of your rack with your rifle and piled into the bunker in back of the hooch. It was pretty scary at times.

One of the peculiar aspects of this war was that during the night we could be sitting on our bunker getting high and listening to Jimi Hendrix, Cream, or whoever, and watching in the hills around the base about a half mile away the firefights going on. We would be sitting there getting high, watching the tracer rounds go back and forth looking for their target, illumination flares going off, close air support, etc. It was an experience, but at least we weren't in those hills. Being in the Marines, though, the lifers would remind you that you are a basic grunt who can go to the field as needed. That was comforting to know! Even though I was a jet engine mechanic, we had fired a lot of different weapons for familiarization and had a lot of field training, learning the different kinds of booby traps used by the Viet Cong. But, I never really got to used it.

After being in Vietnam for close to six months, we fell into Nixon's withdrawal of troops and eventually were sent to Awakuni, Japan for the remainder of our tour of duty overseas. We used to get demonstrations by the Japanese all the time—for us to get out of their country. Who does like the United States anyway?

After coming back to the States from Nam, nobody really gave a shit except those that went. It was something you couldn't talk about, because nobody wanted to hear it, or they thought you were stupid for going—baby killer, psycho, dope head or whatever. I'm only proud in a personal way that I went and it has nothing to do with love of country anymore.

The years afterward have been the real eye-opener in that this country is for the rich and basically always has been, and that capitalism just uses its citizens, including sending its poor and working class sons to its fucking wars.

If I could go back in time and know what I know now, I would have gone to Canada or elsewhere, because it turns out they were given amnesty anyway. Another smack in the face to those that did go to Vietnam.

Going into the military at that time (Vietnam) has changed me, some in the ways I think about this country and this exploitative system. Needless to say now, it was an unpopular war and you almost feel used for going. Since becoming a civilian I have truly learned the exploitative nature of the private sector, specifically in the job market. I have worked rotating shifts, seven days a week for a Fortune 500 company, which is the worst goddamn way to earn a living that you can just about experience. After eleven years of that company, I had to give it up because it was ruining my health.

I have worked construction in the heating and air conditioning field in all kinds of weather, and been laid off at the end of the job because they have used you all they can. The capitalists don't give a fuck how it may affect you financially. I have seen annual ten and twenty-five cent raises for doing this type work, and rarely missing any time from work. That's capitalistic gratitude, I suppose.

As the years have gone on, affirmative action came into play and all decent jobs are now given to blacks because of the color of their skin. Now white males must pay for the sins of our forefathers. What kind of justice is that? Once again it was for and because of the rich that slaves were ever brought to this greedy country, but they say the working class must pay for it. And we all do pay, one way or another, through our tax dollar, crime, welfare babies, the inner-city drug problem. Most of them are nothing but the products of welfare mothers who didn't give a shit about them to begin with.

So now I'm a middle age Vietnam veteran who can't find a decent job and I suppose I should really love this fucking country. Far from it! Statistically, one out of eight people in this country lives in poverty. The average income is around $14,000 per year. Big bucks, if you want to live in a ghetto. The very nature of this system requires and demands a class society where one feeds off the other and the rich capitalists are loving the fucking hell out of it.

What have the rich ever done for this country? My answer is that the rich of this country have never done anything except exploit its citizens. In fact it is actually getting worse. There is an extreme lack of affordable housing in this country, decent paying jobs, more street people every year and a Congress that votes itself one large raise after another. Affordable health care is another problem in this "Great" nation.

Until the working classes get together and have one hell of a march on Washington to let these self-serving politicians know they are fed up with their greedy, impotent ways, nothing is likely going to change.

Government is supposed to be by the people and for the people, not government by a few for a few. This country needs a good working class revolution similar to things that have been recently happening in communist countries.

Newell R. Nelson

I was born September 14, 1947 in Salt Lake City, Utah. I never knew my real parents because I was put up for adoption somewhere around 1951 or 1952, near my fifth birthday. From what I have learned, my mother was seeing several men, so nobody ever knew who my father was. The police or whoever found me in an apartment, dusty, crying, with sour milk in my bottle. I, plus one or two of my brothers and sisters, were taken and later put up for adoption. From what I learned, I had at least one younger brother and possibly more. The adoption agency, which is the LDS Church (Mormon) has a law, where the records of adoption are sealed forever, so I don't think I will ever know who my parents were. I was adopted into a family with a mother from Sweden, a father who was born in Mexico by American parents, and a stepsister who was ten years older.

I started school a year later than everybody my own age. I was in school at age six with five-year-olds. During my school years I was average to sometimes just below average for grades. I made very few friends, mostly because I was overly protected. I was never allowed to go to friends' houses and I was never allowed to have friends over to visit me. It was always "come straight home" after school. At age twelve I got a newspaper route and kept it until I was drafted into the Army. I was more free to do other things without my folks knowing—going to friends' houses, etc. During high school I had average grades, but never was able to go out for any sports. But I went to most games, since all were played in the Salt Lake area. I bought my own clothes and fairly well supported myself with my paper route money. My father drank a lot, so we were never close. My mother and I were fairly close, but there were a lot of differences between us, so my childhood was not really very happy. My stepsister was ten years older, so she was never really a "sister" to me. She got married early and was never around much, so I never got close to her at all. My mother died in the '70s. My dad is still living (I think), but he doesn't want any relationship with me at all. The same with my sister. I feel that they can live their lives—I'll live mine. Since Vietnam (1968) I have not been back to Utah, mainly because of my father. (More about that later.)

I received my draft papers during the summer of 1966 and had to take tests, etc., before the Army would take me. School and mental tests. I guess I passed because I was drafted and ordered to enter the U.S. Army on November 30, 1966. I was told to report to Fort Douglas, which is very small for the Salt Lake area. My father did not want me to enter the Army, but as you know, I had no choice. The last few days I stayed at a friend's house because of the conflict me and my dad had about the Army. The last year or so at home I became friends with my parents' friends' son, who was about four and a half years younger than me. He was also adopted about the same time as I was. I didn't realize until later that this person could be my brother. I spent a lot of time at his place the last few weeks before I went into the Army.

After arriving at Fort Douglas we took a bus to Fort Lewis, Washington to start basic training. Because of the Christmas holiday coming, we spent two weeks in training and then got a leave for the holiday. I never spent one day at home, as I spent time with friends. I had never felt more free, more than ever before in my life. I spent Christmas with my friend. We talked about being brothers forever. This person was about the best friend I ever had while growing up, or until this very day. His parents and myself were also very good friends. But, during the time I was in Vietnam, they moved and nobody knows where they went to. I never heard from any of them after I got back from Vietnam. My folks also say they knew nothing. But, I felt that because I felt he was my brother, they moved. Why I do not know, but I guess they had a reason. Anyway, except for a leave before I went to Vietnam, I have never seen them again.

On or about May 15, 1967 I arrived in Vietnam. I did not go out to the lines right away but stayed back at the base. I was assigned to the 2/13, 1st Air Cav. Division. I was assigned to be a jeep driver for a company commander or whoever wanted me to drive them places. I really was not very happy with this job. I wanted to get out with my friends and men who I knew, out to the lines. Most of my driving was into a village so the officers could be with a Vietnamese girl. I always had to wait with the jeep. After about a month or so, I finally decided to try to go out with my unit. I asked the company commander my request and he said yes. After a few days, I went out by helicopter to my unit, Co. B, 2nd Bn. 1st Air Cav. Division. The first thing they gave me was a radio! I could have had a 45-pistol but I wanted my M-16. They gave me a 45 anyway. So I had to learn the radio really fast. Because I was a good-sized person they figured I could carry a radio without any problems. This was true. I could carry a lot of weight. I carried the radio for a platoon first-lieutenant for a while, then for the company commander for a while. We saw very little action during this first time, maybe a sniper once in a while, but we were always on patrol every day.

After a while I got the M-60 machine gun, had to give up my M-16, but kept my 45. I hardly ever had to use the gun at all because I had it for a short time. Towards the end of the year we moved north towards the DMZ and Da Nang. I then had the M-79 rocket launcher for a while. With the action heating up, lots of snipers, lots of minor action, a few men being hurt and killed, and we were moving more and more inland and to the north. I really wasn't too sure if I would make it out of the country.

One night in January of 1968, shortly before the Tet, a company was into a very heavy firefight, serious enough that every man was for himself! During the night men from that company were returning from the firefight one or two at a time. By morning about half of the company came back to our LZ, some hurt, others scared to death! We kept flares in the air all night so we wouldn't shoot our own men. The next day, my company went west, towards the firefight, to recover our wounded (if any) and the dead. It was about a five-mile walk. Upon arriving at the area, there were very few things standing after our bombing all night. A few trees, some hooches (Vietnamese houses), etc. We found a lot of dead Americans. I don't know the count, but it was at least thirty. We spent the whole day getting the dead out. We did not find one dead gook, but did find loads of blood and tracks leading higher into the mountains. So we knew that the gooks were hurt very bad—lost a lot of men. That day I carried several of our men who were killed, several that lost parts of their heads, arms, etc. It really was a very gross day, knowing that these men had family back in The World. This was sometime in late January, don't know the date. . .

Shortly after, we were sent to the Hue area to go on patrols and to help clean up the enemy around the city. We never went inside the walls of the city. We stayed in that area for quite a while, seeing some action, losing very few men. Shortly after the February 4 action, I was put up for a Silver Star, a Bronze Star with "V," and a Bronze Star. I also was promoted to sergeant. I was squad leader the rest of the time in Vietnam.

I learned a lot while over there. I grew up a lot over there, learned about drugs, learned about death, etc. Now that I look back, I am very glad I went over there. I didn't like the fighting or death, but I now know how other people in other countries live. I am very lucky to be from the U.S.A. If I had a chance to fight for my country again, I would in a second. As for why we were over there, I am not really sure, except to help another country. But if we ever go to war again, I hope it's for a good reason.

I flew back to the U.S.A. and received orders and pay at Fort Lewis, Washington. I received a thirty-day leave before I was to report to Fort Carson, Colorado. I received $1400 cash, back pay from my year in Vietnam. This was a great deal of money for me, as I have had very little money through my life. I went back to Utah and was planning on staying with my friend (brother?) in Salt Lake City, but they had moved, left no address, and everybody I had asked did not know where they went to. It looked like they completely dropped off the earth. I stopped to see my mother, and she was glad to see me, but my father was not. I never stayed at home, but spent time at a friend's house and also went to Oklahoma to spend a week with a friend I had met while in AIT. I went to Fort Carson a few days early since I had almost run out of money and figured its best to get settled at my new home. During my stay at Fort Carson, I was squad leader and we "played" war games my last five months. Of course, I was asked to sign up for more years in the Army, but I did not want to go back to Vietnam, so I just ended up my service at Fort Carson. During my stay at Fort Carson I did receive my medals.

After I got out of the Army, I did not know what I wanted to do. I went to visit a friend in Arkansas for a few weeks, spending Christmas there. After that I drifted around the country, working at different jobs. In 1974 I first started working at carnivals at the New York State Fair. During these times, I found a checkbook, then forged checks for several hundred dollars. At a road check I was arrested and charged for forgery in West Virginia. I pleaded guilty and was sentenced to a one-to-ten year sentence. Since I had no family or friends to help me on parole, I never got out on parole. I ended up doing just under five years, the max time a person can do on a one-to-ten year sentence without screwing up while in prison. I was released to a work release center, and then was fully released. I went back to the carnivals, since it is a very easy job to get and they never ask about your past record. I traveled all around the country from California to Maine to Florida with different carnivals. I did most of my work with the games because they pay better. I enjoyed this work because we go all over the country and see new places every week.

Up in northern Minnesota I was picked up and charged with a crime I did not do. I won't go into detail, but it was a sex crime. Since I had no money, no family or friends, was a Vietnam vet, was a LDS (Mormon) and was a carnival worker, I was guilty before I even entered the courtroom. I went through trial, which was really a joke, and was found guilty. I feel, because I was a Vietnam vet, they felt I was a baby-raper and killer, so they found me guilty. I was given a sixty-five month sentence. In this state you must do two-thirds in prison and one-third on parole.

After being released to a halfway house in St. Paul I stayed there for a month. Somebody broke into my room while I was at work and took all my new clothes I had just bought. I reported to the director of the halfway house about all my stuff being stolen. They would do nothing. So I left the halfway house and the state of Minnesota. I went to the East Coast area and worked for carnivals again. During the Christmas season I sold Christmas trees, then headed south and worked in Florida with my boss, then to New Orleans for their Winter Carnival. While selling Christmas trees during the holidays of 1988, the FBI picked me up for parole violation and I also was a suspect for a kidnapping in Minnesota. When they returned me to Minnesota, the kidnapping charge was dropped because I don't think there ever was a kidnapping, but they used that in order to find me quicker on a parole violation from Minnesota. I was ordered to finish my sentence, twenty-one months, here at Stillwater. So, I ended up doing the whole sixty-five months for something I never did. I was "sentenced" for leaving the halfway house, and leaving the state of Minnesota.

During the whole sixty-five months at this prison and at Lino Lakes prison, I have always held a job, working at Industry Machine Shop, at the Lino Lakes upholstery shop and now in the kitchen. I have had only three days where I couldn't work because I was sick and never had any write up or spent any time in seg here at the prison. I have kept a clean record here in prison and also out in the streets, except for when I forged those checks in West Virginia. I know that I will keep a good record when I am released this October, but will they leave me alone? Will I be able to start my life over again, without being charged for something I didn't do? Can I go to work without worrying that the police are watching me? Will I be able to march with a Vietnam vets group this Veteran's Day in November? I am proud to be a vet, but why have I spent eleven years in prison, six for something that never happened, because I am a Vietnam vet? It makes me wonder what am I going to do when I am released this October. They want to put me into a halfway house—again—when I am released in October. They say here that they can do anything they want with me.

My plans are not complete. I do not know what I will do. Since October is at the end of the carnival season I will not go back to that kind of work. I think I will stay away from that kind of work for now. What I really like to do is drive truck cross-country, be on the road all the time! But, I do not have enough experience in over-the-road driving. I have driven trucks with the carnivals, but most trucks wouldn't pass DOT rules and most companies wouldn't okay jobs like that. But a guy has to start some place! I would really want a truck driving job very bad. But I don't know any company who would take me.

As of now, I have no plans except to stay out of places like this.

Bernie Melter

I came into this world in the back of a hearse on the way to St. John's Hospital in Rapid City, South Dakota on a cold, winter February day in 1938. The ambulances in the city had all been called out. My father had attended the ABC bowling tournament in New York City because I wasn't expected until April. Seems that was the beginning of my never getting anything totally right. My dad, who had been a sergeant in the South Dakota National Guard's unit of the "Red Bull—34th Division," was killed during the war. As my mother was of Native American extraction, there was a bitter court fight for custody of my sister, brother and I, with my Caucasian grandparents obtaining custody of us, which, in those days, was an easy judicial decision, as Indians weren't responsible parents.

I was raised in a succession of boarding schools run by Catholic orders in South Dakota, Iowa, Florida and Oregon, when I finally became of age and was able to return to my mother's home, which was in a tiny farming community in southeast Minnesota. I attended school from 1950 to 1956 in Cannon Falls and graduated in June of 1956, one of sixty-three other students. Because of the Universal Military Training and Selective Service Act, most youths of seventeen joined a reserve unit, either the local Army Reserve Company, where you drilled one night a week, or the Navy, Air Force or Marine Corps units in the Twin Cities. The night before my seventeenth birthday I was not yet decided upon a reserve enlistment in the Navy or the Marine Corps Reserve. During World War II, I had Uncles in all branches of the military and two very close uncles in the Navy and Marine Corps. I had ruled out the Army as that is where most of my classmates had gone—the local unit where, when we graduated the next year, they would go to Fort Leonard Wood for six months of training and spend the next seven years in the reserve, drilling one night a week for fifty-two weeks of the year—at least in the Navy and Marine Corps. I would only sacrifice a weekend. I guess my infatuation with John Wayne in *Sands of Iwo Jima* and *Flying Leathernecks* as well as my lack of self-esteem at the time resulted in my applying for an enlistment in the Marine Corps Reserve. Of course, the fact that the Navy required you to pass a mental and physical whereas the Marines just needed to know that you were physically qualified (warm and breathing?) and weren't to worried about the mental test could have been a factor.

I enlisted in VMF-234, Marine Air Reserve Training Detachment, MARTC, NAS, Twin Cities on 26 February 1955. I was assigned serial number 15 37 204 and from February to June I was placed in a "rookie" platoon and treated as sub-human each weekend until I was released from high school for the summer and could attend recruit training and at the culmination of that, summer drill at MCAS, El Toro, California. Having successfully spent the summer being a Marine, I returned to high school for my senior year and the Marine Corps was attempting to make an Aviation Ordnance man, MOS 6511, out of me. They recognized my great growth potential by making me a Private First Class in November 1955. Just previous to my enlistment, regular Marines were being promoted, automatically, out of boot camp. That practice ceased in January 1955 and I enlisted in February. Staff Sgt. Larry Matrice, the Ordnance Chief at MARTC, NAS, Twin Cities, determined that I would never make a quality ordnance man and cited the example of having asked me for a phillips-head screwdriver and I had gotten some Vodka and OJ for him instead of some type of mechanical utensil.

Upon graduation from high school (sixty-fourth out of a class of sixty-three) I reported to the Infantry Training Regiment, Camp Geiger at the Marine Corps Base, Camp Lejeune, North Carolina, to undergo training. As a result of Staff Sergeant Matrice's recommendation, I reported to the base as a 9900—Basic Marine, with one stripe on my shoulder. After suffering through the ignominy of being classed as a "Q!#&*&%* Reserve" by the regular troops because I had to wear leggings, as my reserve clothing issue in an Aviation unit was for field shoes instead of boondockers (boots), I was made a squad leader as the old time WWII and Korea NCOs thought the new "pups" coming out of the post McKeon boot camp at Parris Island weren't "real" Marines. (McKeon was the drill instructor who drowned thirteen recruits in the Ribbon Creek and suffered an extensive, publicity oriented court-martial and; as a result, the old time NCOs didn't think the boot camp and the DIs were as mean [good] as prior to that time.) I lasted as a squad leader for two weeks, until one of my Polacks from Pittsburgh went AWOL. I was then reduced to BAR Man until our graduation.

Graduation day arrived at the end of August 1956 and all the Marines from Parris Island had orders, boarded buses and departed for points around the globe. I and a small handful of others had no orders. Me, because I was still a basic Marine who had orders to report to the CG, MCAS, Cherry Point, North Carolina for duty in an Aviation billet, and the personnel people in Camp Lejeune, were hesitant to have a warm body leave their base for another in North Carolina. I was given a list of six or so MOSs along with the other six Marines, and we were given a tour of the base to determine which of these MOSs we would like to "strike" for. We visited the Engineers out at Courthouse Bay, the Tankers at the Tank Battalion, Communicators at Comm Company, the Military Police on mainside, and others. By the time we returned to the

Transient Center, the other five had made up their minds. All I had noticed was that the Infantry, Engineers, Tanks and AmTracs, and communications were very labor intensive at the rank of PFC. It wasn't the gunnies who were digging up or laying mines or the staff-sergeants who were breaking treads off of tanks. I passed on them. As for the Military Police, I never had any aspirations of walking around being the target of so much abuse. As an MP you never knew whose side you were on. Finally, a Marine "gunner" (Chief Warrant Officer) asked if I could type. I lied, having flunked typing in high school, and said I was an excellent office machine operator. (These guys wore the Uniform of the Day, drank coffee, ate donuts and read promotional material [comic books). They were rarely out in the weather and had the ear of the first-sergeant and company commander. I had never seen a company clerk pull any duty either, like guard or mess duty. I took the typing test and scored an amazing five words per minute gross. I was admitted into the fraternity of the Loyal Order of the Remington Raiders.

I was assigned to Headquarters Co., Headquarters Bn., MCB, Camp Lejeune, North Carolina and worked for the Legal Affairs Office. I was mainly a "gofer" for the Legal Assistance Officers, second lieutenants waiting for instant promotion to captain so they could practice trial and defense counsel duties. I was told then that I was never going to leave Camp Lejeune and its civilian counterpart, Jacksonville, North Carolina (that great wooden sidewalked community that housed such stellar entertainment centers as Jazzland and Murphy's house of ill repute). I was able to attend East Carolina State College on base campus and settled in. Unfortunately, I still did not have a primary MOS. My MOS had been changed from basic Marine 9900 to 0100— Basic Administrative Man. In order to go overseas you needed a primary MOS. I then was assigned to a Colonel Stallings, who was called out of retirement to work with Colonel Rouse on the court-martial of Matthew McKeon to provide General Burger, the Convening Authority, with the CA's action. Again I was a "gofer." As a result of my close friendship with Colonel Stallings, he used what influence he had at Headquarters Marine Corps and, when we finished our duties, I had a set of orders for the First Marine Aircraft Wing, Japan. After normal leave, I went to the Aviation Replacement Battalion at El Toro, bypassing Cold Weather Training at Pickle Meadows, California, that most replacements had to endure because of the Chosen Reservoir experience in Korea.

When I arrived in Japan, I spent about a week waiting for someone to make up their minds as to where I would be assigned. As usual, everyone else had ultimate orders to certain destinations and jobs. I was finally assigned to an old seaplane base that housed three different

Armed Force installations across the bay from Yokosuka, Japan, the home of the Pacific Fleet's COMNAVFORJAP. I was assigned to Marine Aircraft Group 16, a helicopter group and further assigned to H&HS-16 to work at the group Headquarters for the Group Adjutant. Mostly I was again assigned to duties as a "gofer," driver for Colonel (later Major General) Fred Leek, CO of MAG-16. When I found out that besides being the Group Field Music (bugler) and guard mail driver, that I would spend all eighteen months at that facility and probably not get to go on any operations to the Philippines or Korea etc., I created such a ruckus that the Group Adjutant, Lieutenant Likens, transferred me to VMO2, which was on Okinawa—a bastard outfit commonly known as the "Orphans of the Far East" due to the fact that no one wanted them. VMO2 was under the operational control of the Commanding General, Third Marine Division and administrative control of the First Wing in Japan. When I got there, the administrative chief was a nasty old cigar chomping cook, not unlike "Cookie" of Beetle Baily fame and he almost killed me when he found out that my MOS was 0141, Administrative Man and I had been newly promoted to corporal. I worked my way up from the Mail and Files section to Administrative Chief and finally wangled my way onto a Detachment that was going to the Philippines for a week-long operation with the "grunts." We stayed in the Philippines from November to February living out of field Transport Packs.

Moved from ship to shore due to a real "incident" involving American citizens and finally Typhoon Relief operations. During our time there we really "locked and loaded" and were issued Geneva Convention Cards determining that we were possibly going into a "combat" situation. This didn't materialize and I returned to Okinawa. My reserve enlistment had expired and although I was on a two-year extended active duty period, the only way I could fulfill it was to go "regular" and drop the dreaded R for Reserve from my USMCR. I asked to be stationed in Minneapolis with the Air Reserve as a reenlistment option and the commandant in his wisdom decided I should be on Recruiting Duty in Milwaukee. Looking at the civilian employment picture in Minnesota in 1958 and all that was available was "labor intensive," i.e., manual labor in the stockyards in South St. Paul, or being a farm hand and, not having enough Indian blood at that time to qualify for a BIA scholarship, and with no funds, I reenlisted and went to Milwaukee with a short delay in Treasure Island, San Francisco to get my Blues issued. I spent four wonderful years on recruiting duty in Milwaukee and ended up getting married and having three children during that time.

In 1962 I was transferred to Marine Corps Base, Camp Pendleton, California after having turned down a set of orders to Camp Lejeune,

North Carolina. As a married man I didn't want to end up at a base that sent Marines, even Remington Raiders, to places like Guantanamo Bay, Cuba or six months out in the Mediterranean on little LSTs (Large, Slow Targets) for weeks at a time and then liberty in great places like Dijoubi, Africa, or Naples, Italy. I went to work at Support Company, HqBn, HqRegt, MCB, Camp Pendleton, a company that housed all the Marines who ran the PXs, commissaries, Enlisted Clubs, Officers Clubs, Base Photo Lab, Base Training Aids Library, Base Ranges and the Stewards at Officer Quarters. We never had the company all together at one time because we were scattered throughout the base. We also provided support services for the chaser unit for the western half of the U.S. as well as housing and administrative support for all the misfits returning from overseas for discharge. It was probably the best learning experience that I had in my career due to the variety of administration I learned. Everything from allotments to uniforms (cash sales). I was a sergeant when I arrived and by the time I left in 1965 I was still a sergeant, age twenty-eight, with ten years in the Marine Corps, when I was assigned to my fist Fleet Marine Force assignment with the grunts, or in this case, the Cannon Cockers. I thought I had it wired to go to the 11th Marines at Camp Pendleton when I spoke with the Monitor from HQMC, but ended up going to Twenty Nine Palms, to the Force Troops. My wife and then four children with one on the way traveled with our mobile home to the High Mojave Desert and a new adventure. We set up housekeeping in a drab, dreary mobile home settlement about three miles from the main gate and I reported to Force Troops, FMFPac for duty. I could have stayed at the G-3 in the headquarters, but asked to be assigned to a firing battery. When I reported to the 4th Battalion 11th Marines, CWO Clow, the adjutant suggested that I stay at the Headquarters Battery of the battalion as the Acting Administrative Chief until I made staff-sergeant, which we both hoped would be that fall, when I would take over at battalion as the S-1 chief. I asked the gunner to reconsider and assign me to a firing battery so that I could go to the field etc., rather than be stuck at a headquarters. He agreed as I had the necessary experience after support company and assigned me to Battery M. This was in April of 1965. I was ready to stick it out in the high desert for a two- or three-year tour of duty and then knew I was overdue to do an overseas tour in either Japan or Okinawa. I would lobby my monitor for a tour in Japan with the First Wing.

Unfortunately, the composition and make-up of our battery changed rapidly in the days and weeks of May as rumors of our possible involvement in some place named Vietnam became a reality, what with the 3rd Marine Division being committed to a place called Da Nang in March. Rumors from the head had it that Korea would be re-invaded and cause the Americans to supply to war zones, one in Vietnam and one in Korea. So we thought that we were destined for duty in Korea. We practiced cold weather shoots and CSMOs from one place to another. We had a change of command when Captain J.O. Black, USMCR, came aboard from the Base Provost Marshal's office. Captain Black or "J.O." as he was unaffectionately described by the troops, brought rapid changes. Our corpsman gave up his Navy dungaree's and whites, his beard and long hair to a crisp, starched Marine Corps utility uniform with a Parris Island or San Diego "high and tight" haircut. When the Battery SNCOs didn't come into the office for their usual two or three cups of free coffee I knew something was up. J.O., myself and the Btry first-sergeant (who demonstrated an abject fear of the skipper) went to Camp Pendleton for a meeting. We joined others in Regimental Landing Team-7 and found out that we were leaving by the end of the month (this was May '65) for parts unknown and that this was all secret.

On 28 May 1965, I left a bride that was nine months pregnant, didn't drive, along with our four children, to participate in a motor march to San Diego, California to hook up with ships to ferry us to the Far East. All of our equipment and tarps were covered with masking tape where our identification marks were so that the civilians wouldn't know who we were. We split into three serials, one of which promptly got lost on the way down. Let me tell you it is a long way in mighty mite, PC, or five-ton from Twenty Nine Palms to San Diego. We waited in San Diego for ships to ferry us over and didn't get aboard the USS Blatchford until 1 June 1965. We were at sea for several days when we arrived at a port. None of us knew where it was until we read Port Hueneme and someone mentioned it was just up the coast from Pendleton and was the home of the Seabees. We took on a battalion of Seabees and thought that was it. One morning we came up on shore after we had picked up the Seabees and thought this had to be Alaska or Hawaii and it turned out to be Seattle/Tacoma, Washington and we had stopped to pick up a company of Army communicators. So much for a rapid voyage to the Far East.

We arrived in Okinawa and took up places recently vacated by the members of our sister batteries in the 4th Bn., 12th Marines of the 3rd Marine Division. After about a month we departed in new LSTs for somewhere in Vietnam. We were briefed for the Da Nang Area TAOR but instead were landed in Chu Lai. Our battery distinguished itself under J.O.'s leadership. We usually fired from positions in front of the 105 Howitzers and we were an 155mm Howitzer Battery. Eventually we had twelve 155mm Howitzers as we picked up five M109 Self Propelled to go along with our towed models. I then became a gun section chief with a makeshift crew made up of my clerk, the garbage driver, one of the two cooks, a motor transport mechanic and one 0811, gun bunny to set the fuses for us and make sure we had everything correct. We were allowed to practice together at night on the towed howitzers, firing harassment and interdiction (H&Is) rounds during the night. These fires were primarily designed to keep us and the enemy awake and let him know we were watching. We fired at key crossroads, bridges, river junctions and crossings that had been sighted by aerial observers. We were given a fire mission for the whole evening, by type of round, fuze and charges, either green bag or white bag. This was how we learned. During Operation Double Eagle I and the main portion of the battery took the M109 howitzers (SP) on the road and aboard ship for a landing down the peninsula and we stayed behind to take care of the battery area while they were gone. The Battery Comm Chief, a staff-sergeant who was NCOIC, and the remainder of the troops, including my gun section, was left behind and were mostly lance-corporals, corporals and two of us were sergeants. Late one afternoon, a Force Recon Patrol that had been inserted a couple of days prior to Double Eagle called in for some fire support. Their call sign was, I think, Brandywine 2. In any event, the 105mm Howitzers of the 3rd Bn., 11th Mar. and of the 3rd Bn., 12th Mar. could not reach them. We had no 8-inch or 155 Gun assets available and no tanks that could be used for artillery. Someone remembered our three 155mm Howitzers remaining in Mike Battery TAOR (three had been given to 105mm How. Btry's as back-up) and a Fire Mission was sent to Mike Battery. Our staff-sergeant manned the Exec Pit and called the mission to the three guns. One gun crew became so excited they couldn't or didn't get a round in time. My crew was ready as well as a crew manned by 0811s and we delivered effective, timely fire as trained. The remaining gun couldn't be negotiated to reach the target. For this action we garnered some attention from the brass on the hill (I think it was BG Jonas Platt, USMC) and ultimately received a letter of thanks from the 3rd Force Recon.

The balance of my tour in Chu Lai consisted of being the Ammo NCO for the battery as well as the battery administrative chief. I made staff-sergeant on the last permanent peace-time list with a precedence number of 1175, meaning that though I was selected in November of '65 I didn't get my stripes until February of 1966. The battery was broken up in March, as we transferred people away from Mike to other batteries and units within III MAF so we wouldn't all transplace/rotate home at the same time. This was especially true because the whole 1st Marine Brigade from Hawaii was due to go home in March 1966. J.O. left us and went to regiment as the artillery liaison and picked up his Oak Leaf along with some personal decorations, including a cigar stuck in his mouth by Lt. Gen. Walt, CG III MAF after a particularly demanding mission at Tam Khe shooting from a cemetery as the only possible place to get the trails placed without shifting because of the mud and rain.

I rotated back to the States on June 18 by leaving Chu Lai with First Lieutenant Stier from Pontiac, Michigan and going to Da Nang AB to wait for a plane to take us out. When we arrived at El Toro, it was Fathers Day, 1966, a Sunday. The PXs were closed, clothing sales were closed and we were allowed to take whatever hold baggage survived the storage for the past twelve months in Okinawa to a barracks, take a shower, change into civilian clothes because none of us enlisted men had summer service uniforms and they wouldn't let us buy any.

The balance of my Marine Corps career went down hill from that point on. I reported to the First Force Service Regiment at Camp Pendleton only to be told that they were going to go down to cadre-strength by sending most of the troops overseas to Vietnam along with the Regimental Colors. I reminded the regimental adjutant, a Captain Spelioupolis, that I had not been back in the States for the requisite six months and I ended up being one of the last people transferred out of the 1st FSR to the newly formed 5th FSR to go with the 5th Marines area to train at Margarita with troops coming up from ITR. I eventually transferred to Supply Battalion as the administrative chief and activated five companies. While there we toyed with battalion administration. I made gunny in March of '69 and in February of 1970 I was called by the monitor and asked if I would like to go to Cherry Point, North Carolina for duty with the Air Station. At that time I had a wife, five children and a mobile home and thought it was funny I wasn't being sent back to Vietnam as it had been almost four years since I had returned from my first tour and some MOSs were going back in six months to Nam or Westpac. I made the journey to Cherry Point where I was assigned to Station Operations and Engineering Squadron, (SOES), the Road Runner's, as Squadron Administrative Chief in the S-1. I enjoyed my tour, but as it turned out, it was short-lived. In November 1970, after I had been there a short seven months, I was alerted to Headquarters, Marine Corps that I was going back to Nam with the 3rd Marine Division. In February 1971, with the 3rd Marine Division pulling out of Vietnam, my orders were changed to the 1st Marine Division, FMF in Nam. I left Cherry Point in February, took my family to Cannon Falls, Minnesota to live and left for the Movement Center at Camp Pendleton.

When I arrived at Camp Pendleton the Movement Center changed my orders from Staging Battalion to the Movement Center and I spent five days TAD with them prior to joining a flight draft on Easter Sunday for Okinawa. When I arrived on Okinawa I was informed that the 1st Marine Division was pulling out of Nam and that I would be sent to the

1st Marine Air Wing. I was at Da Nang and then was ordered to 1st Marine Air Wing (1st MAW [Rear) where I was assigned to Marine Aircraft Group-15 (MAG-15) and further assigned to Marine Fighter Attack Squadron 115 (VMFA-115) an F-4B Gun Squadron, as admin. chief. They had just flunked their latest A&I (IG) inspection. We were stationed at Iwakuni, Japan and "flitted" around the Far East, from Japan to Okinawa to Japan to the Philippines, to Japan to Osan, Korea to Japan and finally to Okinawa in preparation to go to Da Nang. When we were in Da Nang, Major Duffy, our XO, was killed when he took off and had a head-on air collision with an 02 Birddog flown by the SVN. It was the only casualty while I was with the squadron, other than some major hangovers, etc. I departed the squadron before they flew to the "Rose Garden" in Thailand and HQMC, in their wisdom, transferred me to MCB, Camp Lejeune and I found myself working for the Base Personnel shop as Personnel Chief. I enjoyed my tour at Lejeune. We had four-bedroom quarters on Louisiana St., in SNCO Capehart housing. I was active in youth baseball, football and scouting. I stayed at Camp Lejeune from May 1972 to June 1975, when I was transferred back to MCB Camp Pendleton for my final tour of duty with Marine Corps Tactical Systems Support Activity (MCTSSA) on the beach at Camp Pendleton. We were a sub-unit of MCDEC, Quantico, Virginia and worked for a future commandant, P.X. Kelley, then a Brigadier General. I absolutely did not like the MCTSSA assignment. I was Activity Personnel Chief and had over 140 officers all over the world, about fifty-eight enlisted and hundreds of civilians all working on "deep" research projects in the 1985-90 time. I didn't particularly get along with the "Mustang" Captain that was the adjutant, a Captain Neil Thomas, and so he and I both put in for retirement at the same time. On April 13, 1976, a Wednesday, with no hoopla, parade or any type of formation, I left the USMC and became a Fleet Marine Corps Reservist.

I returned home to Minnesota, unemployed, undereducated with a small monthly retirement check from the USMC (at that time a little over $400 per month) with my wife and five teenage children, to a small rural community, Cannon Falls, Minnesota. My wife went to work and I became a "house husband/scholar" enrolling in Inver Hills Community College. My entire twenty-one years in the Marine Corps was worth six semester credits of college experience according to the registrar at that institution. In December 1976 my unemployment ran out. I had worked at a minority position (I'm a Native American) for Northern States Power for ninety days the summer of '76 and would have stayed with NSP except the boss for power production came down from Minneapolis and said, "I did good work, for an Indian," and invited me to work at the Black Dog plant where I could, for overtime, make over $12,000 per year. I told him I was going to college to get an education and he mentioned something to the effect that I didn't need an education, I could make more money than most Indians without one. That concluded our conversation, and my employment possibilities with NSP. I considered his remarks to be very racist.

I found out a job opportunity existed within Dakota County for an Assistant Veterans Service Officer position in early December 1976. I interviewed for the job twice and was turned down both times although I finished in the top three. Shortly after Christmas, 1976, Mr. Bill Meyer, the director of that office, called and offered me the job. It seemed that the previous selectee's either didn't want the job or couldn't pass their physical. I started with Dakota County on January 3, 1977 and worked there until April 10, 1980 when I competed for and won the job as Goodhue County Veterans Service Officer. I graduated from Inver Hills Community College by attending night school and Saturdays with an AA Degree (Liberal Arts) in June of 1978. In August 1981 I graduated from Mankato State College with a Bachelor of Science Degree (Magna Cum Laude), as an Honors Student. Since that time, I have continued as the Goodhue County Veterans Service Officer. I have been active in other veterans organizations and have been awarded the National American Legion's "Good Neighbor Award for work with Veterans"; Minnesota Marine of the Year, 1987 by the Marine Corps League; Minnesota County Veterans Service Officer of the Year, 1987, by the State of Minnesota; Presidential Citation for Outstanding Community Achievement of a Vietnam Era Veteran by President Jimmy Carter and Albert Quie, Governor, June 1979. I am currently the head of Minnesota Veteran's Affairs, chosen by the Governor in 1991.

T. J. McGinley

I was the second of nine children, four of which were draft age in 1967. The oldest was in the Marines already, one in military school and another in high school. I'd just graduated, no plans for college; prime draft target; *expendable*.

I felt if I went to Nam the chances of my brothers going would be slim, so I went Airborne to assure a ticket to Southeast Asia. It worked. I went and everybody else stayed home.

I was in a line company for seven months when I had a chance to join a recon platoon known as Tiger Force. Being in Tigers was the pinnacle of my military career, because I felt I was part of an elite within and elite, the 101st.

Being in the field with this small but effective unit of sky soldiers turned out to be the safest place in Nam, for me anyway. Each man was hand picked, field experienced, and overall knew what they were doing.

I didn't take the military as seriously as they would have wanted me to. In the rear, as little as I saw of it, I seemed to attract trouble. Certainly for all who participated in the fighting, that part was a hassle to say the least. However, as much as that dominated, there was a bright side to all this madness. I learned to live each day as if it were my last, not just then, but ever since.

I've also found, through research, that all my childhood heroes were recon men. For example, Francis Marion, the Swamp Fox; Stephen Austin of the Texas Rangers; John Mosby, the Gray Ghost; and the men of the Alamo. Small units of volunteers up against, more often than not, superior numbers. "Upstarts," "rabble," "nonconformists," "misfits," lifers have been calling recon men throughout history. But, these same lifers will admit, recon men were the best in the business of out-Indianing the Indians.

Another segment of my experience that fascinated me, was the jungle. During operation Nevada Eagle, the 1st brigade of the 101st entered the jungle of the Central Highlands on May 17, 1968 and stayed there until Feb. 28, 1969. Hot, wet, green and magnificent; we were places humans have never been before, sleeping on the ground every night in a different place for months. As a young boy I was in scouts and loved camping out in the woods. Operations Nevada Eagle and Massachusetts Striker were a scout's dream—endless camping. I admit it had it's drawbacks, humping a ruck full of C-rations, but the overall testing of one's self against all odds was the ultimate challenge.

We were camped in the Rao-Nho Valley about sixty miles southwest of Hue in the Central Highlands of South Vietnam when I first saw them. A message came around that a friendly element would penetrate the perimeter in our sector—to be aware. They came out of the jungle like their name implied—silent, intelligent, cautious, deadly—Tiger Force. They were clad in Asian camouflage fatigues and each one looked like he alone could do the job they all were assigned to do.

This moment took me back to my boy scouting days, when camping in the Ozark woods of central Missouri. I was earning my Eagle, which required several survival type merit badges and I was looking forward to being accepted into an elite tribe of Indians known as Mic-O-Say, as this was the highest scouting honor in Missouri. But as life would have it, this prize eluded me for, as a teen-ager, other concerns took precedence, like my first car, girls and graduating from high school. Earning my way into Mic-O-Say was put aside and I felt deprived.

When orders came around that we were moving, we packed our rucks and left that part of the valley to the Tigers. I didn't see the Tiger Force again until three months later when we were extracted to the rear for a stand-down. Except for the first few days in-country seven months earlier, I had seen nothing but jungle and had spent endless hours walking point, setting up ambushes and being ambushed. So, I was looking forward to some civilization and, among other things, to receiving the many merit badges we had earned in a well-known hell called the A Shau Valley. That's when I saw them again.

You can't join the Tigers. They choose you. To even be considered you had to be experienced in the jungle with firsthand knowledge of ambush techniques, survival techniques, and above all, the enemy. Close to the end of the stand-down, I was approached by three Tigers. They told me they had heard I was good and asked me to join them. My company commander, Captain Tom Kinane, the smartest field officer in the Nam, said of this, "Tigers are taking all of my best men." Inside me I had finally been accepted into Mic-O-Say in the form of Tiger Force.

I'm not going to tell you all the war stories. I'll leave that for better writers. However, being hand picked by this elite unit of sky soldiers was the highest honor of my brief military career.

I gained in the end by my Vietnam experience because in experiencing the dark side of life, I now appreciate the light side and live each day as if it were my last. In closing I can say without reservation that I am proud to have served with the Tiger Force.

In conclusion, life has been very good to me, knowing I've seen the worst it has to offer. Now there's nothing but the best.

Haston A. Magnuson

I was born and grew up on a small farm fifteen miles northwest of Paris, Texas. My father was a feed mill worker and my mother worked at a cleaners as well as running the farm. My two brothers and I grew up picking cotton and hauling hay. The whole family had to work to make ends meet. I graduated from a small country school with a class of twelve in 1967.

During October '67 I joined the Army with a friend on the "Buddy System" because we grew up during the McCarthy years, when we all hated Russia and Communism and felt it was "our American God given duty to go to Vietnam to stop the spread of Communism." My friend and I joined with a ninety-day delay. One December we went to Dallas for our physicals. My buddy failed his and I woke up the next day in Fort Polk, Louisiana, having arrived via "Tree Top Airlines."

I took basic training there in the 4th Battalion Co. E and remained there to take AIT. Thirty-one out of sixty of us at AIT went to Germany, eight went to Korea, three stayed stateside and eighteen of us lucky souls went to Vietnam. I can still remember the feeling of uncertainty as I was called forward for assignments, called up out of line and told "Magnuson—Vietnam!" I had feelings of wanting to go, being proud of going to go, but already missing home and family, being homesick and knowing Vietnam would be even more so in being able to bring these feelings out in me.

I was given a thirty-day leave to go home. We really enjoyed the streets for thirty days and nights before I shipped out of Dallas on June 8, 1968 for San Francisco. We took a helicopter from S.F. to Oakland Army depot. Oh, what a joy—we got all of our shots in Oakland. On June 10 we boarded American Airlines to Hawaii, Guam and Wake Island before we arrived in Bien Hoa.

I remember looking out the plane window and seeing all the sand, tank tracks, bomb craters, mountains, and seeing planes weaving out around the mountains and being afraid we'd hit a mountain. We stepped off the air-conditioned plane to be hit in the face by 100-degree humid heat laced with the smell of garbage.

We were herded into a bus from the planes to the replacement center. Three days later they sent a truck from the 9th Infantry for us that was lucky enough to be assigned to them and were taken to Bear Cat. I was in another reception center for a week of combat training, learning the exact art of crossing rivers, digging foxholes and the ever-wonderful experience of going out on day and night patrols.

One of the things I remember most of the first night patrols I went out on, was of walking through a rubber plantation not knowing the destination and not really even caring. We set up an ambush spot in a crater hole and were paired off. One got to stay in the hole position and the other lucky sucker like me got to put out claymores. I crawled out and didn't have any earthly idea where I was going in the dark, thinking I've already messed up. I was so scared, pitch black, not knowing what or who was out there, and you remember the pair partner back in the crater was as scared as you are. I followed the cable back to the position. If I lost that cable, "I'm a gonner 'cause it's too dark out here and I don't know which way I'm headed." But it turned out to be a lucky night after all. No contact.

Lucky me, I was stationed with a S&T unit (Supply and Transportation). Even better, the first time I had perimeter guard, we had the pleasure of being hit. I remember thinking that the rockets were pretty as they exploded. Of course, I didn't know what they were, much less how deadly dangerous they were. It wasn't until later that I learned what each flash and sound meant. I stayed at Bear Cat for sixty days without much action or many firefights.

They moved me to Dong Tam in the Mekong Delta. I spent thirty days riding shotgun on a wrecker in convoys with a 50-caliber machine gun. It didn't take long before I was dreading each convoy, knowing I would be seeing guys get killed and not seeing where the shots came from and not being able to get who's doing it—knowing all I could do was spray the treelines and hope you got him. Seems like our convoys were always being hit and someone getting killed—seems like always.

Eventually, I talked the first-sergeant into letting me volunteer for patrols from Tan An, My Tho and Can Tho—a company of the 2nd Brigade of the 9th Infantry. That day, two platoons of eight men each went out, myself part of the 2nd. We walked across rice paddies and through jungles and more rice paddy dikes for about two hours, until the pointman caught a sniper round in the leg. We all hit the dirt, but it was the only round fired. With no more action, we called in choppers and med-evaced him out and we went on. We crossed more rice paddies and jungles and were ambushed. Come to find out, the sniper from before had been trying to keep us away from a small village. Three or four guys were hit but no one was killed. But they finally ran off and we chased them until we lost them, when they just disappeared into the jungle. But we still got five of them.

That didn't bother me because, when you know you are defending yourself, seeing them dead isn't such a big deal. We called for a med-evac for our wounded and their dead. The choppers came back for the rest of us. We returned to the unit and didn't go back out for another four days.

Next patrol we went on, we went out in a westerly direction from

My Tho. We stayed out two days, all night. One company of us set up ambush while the other company rested. The next night we switched over, but we didn't make any contact that night. The second day we returned to the unit and enjoyed C-rations.

I went back to Dong Tam and stayed a couple of weeks, returned to My Tho and from there I went to Can Tho. There, Intelligence got word that the VC were planning to overrun the base camp, so we had to go on guard duty around the perimeter and set out two listening posts of six men each. We had a wide range to cover and we weren't in exactly the same position, but we were in a close enough area to pair it off. We weren't supposed to make contact, only observe and listen to see what we could pick up on from the enemy. But they walked up on us, right into our position. We had no choice; we had to make contact with the enemy. It seemed like a company of them in the firefight. You couldn't see anything except rifle flashes. Afterwards, out of the six of us, there were only three of us that were left alive.

When you are sitting next to someone who gets shot, it bothers you worse than seeing a dead enemy who'd been trying to kill you. Your brain tells you that he's dead because he was trying to kill you and you were defending yourself. But seeing someone else, especially a friend that gets shot—it does something to you. It makes you realize that it could have been you just as easily. But you usually don't have time to get scared during a firefight because ten minutes seems like hours. We finally got help from another company that came out. We finally got back to camp that night—really early in the morning—but we couldn't sleep, couldn't rest, so we waited till daylight so we could go back out and get our men's bodies and four VC bodies. It looked like they'd drug some of the bodies off, but you couldn't be positive of that. Then we waited at the base camp for three days and nothing ever happened. Intelligence's attack never came, but we were never sure if it was because we had spoiled their surprise when they stumbled into our position that night or if Intelligence just had been fed false information. Either way, we lost three men because of it. I received the Army Commendation Medal.

Next patrol we went out on, we had a report of VC in a village and we went out on choppers this time. They set us down on the edge of the village in the daylight and no more had we got off the Hueys than the VC opened up on us with AK-47s and RPG rounds. One helicopter was hit and crashed but no one was killed. We started advancing through the village. I thought seeing a buddy get killed all of a sudden was bad, but seeing a buddy get hit and start hollering for his Mama—that is the worst. A lot worse than seeing someone get killed right off the bat. Knowing that there's nothing that you can do but lay there and listen to him cry and beg someone to come get him and help him out. I think through this I learned to help other people anyway I can, even if I get hurt in the process—as long as I do what I can and know I can live with myself instead of knowing that I didn't try to do anything. But, there are still times that you can't do anything. But trying to determine when you could or couldn't help in the right place, that's the difficult part. You have to use your own judgment. I took a lot of chances that I wouldn't take today. But if I had it to do over again, I probably wouldn't come back alive because there are things that I would do now that I didn't even think about doing then.

After we swept through that village, I forget how many of us were wounded—five or six—but we took a body count and had fifteen VC. We med-evaced all our guys out and they came and got us and carried us out. That's when I got my Combat Infantry Badge.

I'd been writing my girlfriend I'd left in Paris, Texas. I'd sent her a picture and she wrote back and said it looked like a bunch of boys playing games over there, playing cowboys and Indians. And I knew that was the beginning of the end of my relationship with that gal. Here my friends were getting killed and she'd say something like that. It could never be the same between us. I'd find me a Vietnamese girlfriend if I had to.

I remember being out on guard duty, lying out on a bunker looking up at the stars and wondering if the folks at home were looking at the same stars or what folks at home were doing right then the same second. I'd remember how brave I was as a kid playing cowboys and Indians, wondering where all that childish bravery went to.

I went to Dong Tam. I had about three months left in-country. I really didn't want to go back out on patrol, but it seemed like there wasn't anything else to do. Time was passing so slow. So I finally decided that I'd go out one more time. I went back to ride a convoy with some friends to Tan An with the 1st Brigade, 2nd of the 39th Infantry and stayed there. I remember waiting on patrol duties, seeing some guys sitting on top of a bunker and they picked up this little Vietnamese boy about four years old and threw him over the side of the bunker into a rice paddy head first. The kid got out okay, but just the thought of those GIs treating him like that just because he was Vietnamese still bothers me. That's something I can say I never did, was mistreat anyone. I never took any chances, but I never mistreated anyone, never slapped anyone. Today it gives me a clear conscience. If I'd shot somebody that I had any doubt about, it would bother me today. But, I can honestly say I treated all the Vietnamese people right. I helped them when I could, gave them food when I had it and they didn't. That's the most I got out of Vietnam—learning to do something for someone else.

I remember seeing this one old lady when we were on convoy. The GIs, if the Vietnamese didn't get out of the way, would run over them. This old woman didn't get out of the way of an eighteen-wheel truck hauling supplies and it ran over her. Her body got hung up in behind the rear duals on the trailer. Every few feet there was a big bloody spot in the road. That wasn't my fault, but it doesn't go away. You still think about it and I know that if it had been my fault, I couldn't live with it. I know that there are a lot of guys that face living with having done things like that every day of their lives. But at the same time, the same Vietnamese people that we were helping, that were cutting our hair and shinning our boots or whatever, could very easily be the enemy. You couldn't trust any of them. So, I can't blame anyone for what they did over there. I'm just glad that I don't have to live with it myself. But I can't blame them. The enemy was everybody from a little six-year-old kid to a ninety-year-old woman. It didn't take but one bullet and your mistake was paid for.

I wasn't in any major battles like Hamburger Hill or Khe Sanh, but they shot the same kind of bullets and it didn't take but one. But now I look back and see all the times that I could have been killed and I didn't understand it then, why it wasn't me a bunch of times. But I realize now that God had put a hedge around me to keep me safe from hurt because he had a purpose for me. And that purpose is serving Him today. I thank Him for that hedge.

I stayed in Tan An a week and finally they took us out about twenty-two klicks and set us down at the edge of a jungle. They told us that there'd been enemy activity in the area. So, we were to patrol the jungle. There were four companies of us, a good many of us. We headed into the jungle and picked up sniper fire and had a few hit. But the snipers were so scattered out that they couldn't really do much damage. We set up L-shaped ambushes at night. They took part of them back in. But two companies stayed out and kept L ambushes. The VC walked into A Company's ambush—it was about a company of VC—and they almost overran the ambush sight, but they held them off until daylight, when the VC were gone. Then we hunted them while they med-evaced our dead and wounded out. Then we hunted the VC some more through thick jungle and across streams. We set up another ambush the next night and didn't have any contact. We'd scared them back where they came from.

We left when helicopters came in and took us back to Tan An. I hadn't been back long and was fixing to go back to Dong Tam when they called us up and wanted us to go back out the next morning. They took us out to the north side of the jungle and let us down. There were two companies of us this time. It took about sixteen helicopters to set us down, right in the middle of an ambush. But they let the choppers fly out before they opened up on us. We were pinned down. But there was plenty of us to keep from getting overrun. We called in artillery on our position and pounded them for about two hours. After the artillery quit, we charged their positions and there weren't many of them left. A few stayed and fought. We killed some and some ran away. We had a body count of forty. We cleaned up our stuff, got our wounded and bodies med-evaced out. It took four hours to do all that. Then they came back and got us and took us back to Tan Am.

I went back to Dong Tam and stayed there until I had three weeks left. Then two buddies and I "borrowed" a three-quarter-ton truck and went to Phu Loi—went AWOL. We went to see my uncle in Phu Loi. We spent the night in Saigon. We stayed drunk most of the time. I don't know what kept us from getting killed, but we went to see him. He was a civilian working on helicopters. He was in the hospital with appendicitis. We stayed in the hospital all night. I slept in my uncle's bed and my buddies slept in somebody else's bed, I guess. We were too drunk to care. We went back to Saigon and got drunk. We stayed there all day and started back to Dong Tam about the fourth day. We were drunk on rice whiskey. We went out into the jungle and took pictures of each other with a Polaroid camera. We didn't know that there was anyone around, but now you can look at the pictures in the door of the hooches behind us and see a little boy standing there. We could of easily been killed, but we were drunk and didn't care. We went back to Tan An. They wouldn't do anything to us for being AWOL for four days because we were short-timers. We only had two weeks left. We stayed and messed around for two weeks. We were lucky that we didn't have to go back out.

I left there and got on a Chinook at Dong Tam. We flew across country to some other little air base in the middle of the jungle and picked up some more guys and we went to the 90th replacement center at Long Binh. Stayed there and processed out. We had to get our hair cut and they took away all the pictures that we weren't supposed to have or bring back. We stayed two or three days and they took us to Bien Hoa. We got on a plane and everybody was happy and laughing . We took off from Bien Hoa. I remember the last thing I saw as we were leaving Vietnam was a C-130 flying down below us and it got hit and crashed into the jungle—a big old ball of fire and flames. We were not happy until we got about 30,000 feet up, in the middle of the sea. Then we started laughing and being happy again. I left Vietnam on the 14th of June 1969 by American Air Lines and flew to Japan and then to Oakland.

We got to Oakland and processed out. I remember seeing protesters at the Oakland Army Depot. I got a plane to Dallas' Love Field. From there I caught a cab to the bus station. It was going to be four hours before another bus left from Paris, so I called my parents to come to Dallas to get me. It was a two-hour drive and I was ready to get home. At the bus station, a queer tried to pick me up. That was all I needed. I kept thinking my friends are dying and he's doing something like this.

My parents finally got to Dallas and we left for home. That night I was eating supper at home, twenty-four hours from the time I'd been in Vietnam. It wasn't long before I started missing the friends I had left in Vietnam. The friends I had at home before I went to Vietnam were just not the same. The one friend that I ran with in high school, his dad had got him out of going in the service. I saw him and he was not that close a friend, but the guys that are veterans that I made friends with, were. I had a lot of black friends in Vietnam and I still feel a closeness to black people today. I didn't see any prejudice while I was in Vietnam. We depended on each other.

I was to go to Fort Bragg, North Carolina after my thirty-day leave. I went to Paris and talked to the Army recruiter about getting my orders changed. He said no way could I get them changed. I then went to Dallas and they said they could not help me, but gave me an address at the Pentagon. I wrote the Pentagon and asked to get my orders changed. About a week before I was to report to Fort Bragg, a Spec-5 Scott called from the Pentagon to tell me my orders had been changed, and to report to Fort Sill, 200 miles from home. The orders arrived the day before I had to leave. I would love to meet that Spec-5 Scott someday.

After I got up to Fort Sill, I was assigned to the 2nd Battalion 36th Artillery. After I stayed a couple of months, I couldn't really hack it, so I tried to get out of the Army. I got all my senators and representatives from my district and my neighbors that had any influence, all to write letters for me. I had a stack of them. I took them to my CO and he laughed at them and said that I didn't need to get out. I still had a year and a half to go in the Army. He said I really didn't want out anyway and he wasn't going to push for it. So I signed papers to go back to Vietnam and they turned them down because by then they were beginning to reduce troops over there and I had already been over there once, so they wouldn't let me go back. If I hadn't ever been over there they'd have let me go, but they wouldn't let me go back.

I was stuck with Fort Sill for the next year and a half. In that year and a half, I did a lot of drinking, a little bit of work and got fatter than a townhouse dog. We went down to meet the girl that had become my pen pal while I was in Nam. So I went down to Odessa, Texas to visit her.

I had a boring year and a half of being drunk and trying to stay out of trouble—went to jail once, wrecked my new car, bought another one and wrecked it, drank some more, then drank some more, and stayed drunk for a year and a half. In the meantime I'd go home every other weekend, got a lot of speeding tickets, nearly had my license taken away, but there wasn't anything they could do to me. They couldn't send me to Vietnam. I'd already been there.

I finally got out on December 21, 1970 and went to Odessa and married the pen pal on January 23, 1971. We lived there for a couple of months and forgot about the Army and Vietnam. We moved back to Paris, Texas and went to work on a dairy for two years. I left there and went to work on the N.B. Hunt ranch in Fannin County for a year and a half. Then I went to work at the Flex-O-Lite plant in Paris and have been there for over seventeen years.

I got to where I couldn't sleep and I got real nervous when I got around people, a lot of people, so I started going to the VA Hospital in Bonham, Texas in June of 1989. The doctors wanted me to start going to the Vietnam veterans group they had started. Now I go once a month to see a doctor and participate in group therapy. It helps, but I still have to take two kinds of medicine for depression and anxiety. I have learned what to expect when I have to be around a lot of people. If I can get out of it, I don't get around a lot of people. Now I enjoy hunting and trapping with just my wife. I enjoy being with other Vietnam veterans that know how I feel. I also have my wife to lean on because she helps me so much. Without an understanding wife, I don't know how I would make it from day to day.

My friends that were killed in Vietnam . . . I can't remember most of their names, but if I see something that reminds me of how or where they got killed, like a tree, creek or something said, I can see their faces like it was yesterday. I am hoping to start going to the VA Hospital once every two months soon. They call it PTSD (Post Traumatic Stress Disorder).

I always thought if something like that was going to bother you, it would do it soon afterwards and I have learned since then, for some people, it did bother them as soon as they came back. It depends on how much action they saw and the type of person they were when they went over there. I didn't think it could happen to anybody twenty years later, but it's happened to me. They told me at the VA that it does that to you. That's why it's called *Post* Traumatic Stress Disorder. They've helped me a bunch. I couldn't ask for them to be any better to me. I don't ask for money or anything. All I ask for is understanding and I have found it.

It's getting harder for me to work in front of people and with people. Unless it's a certain kind of person. I can't work in a crowd. I get nervous and I really get a problem with people telling me what and how to do things. In my mind, I wonder what right they have to tell me how to do anything. They haven't been through what I have been—they haven't seen what I've seen. I don't want them telling me what to do. They don't understand your problems anyway, until they can walk in these old moccasins of mine.

I don't blame the Vietnamese for the things that happened, because they were fighting for a reason. I don't blame anyone but the politicians of that day for not letting us win that war sooner. Whenever your kids say something about Vietnam, it's the only war the U.S. ever lost. I don't feel like we lost it. I feel like the politicians lost it.

On November 11, 1989 my family and I attended the Vietnam Veterans of Texas Memorial dedication in Dallas. I was in a parade of veterans that was to march to the dedication that started from the meeting place under a bridge on the Trinity River. Some of the veterans were riding motorcycles, old pick-ups, campers, Cadillacs, all types. We marched through Dallas, five miles to the Fair Park State Fair grounds. President Bush was there—he came right by us. The Vietnamese community of Dallas joined us in the march part way and carried a wreath to place at the dedication marker that said, "From the Vietnamese village of Dallas and Ft. Worth, we thank you for our freedom, that we can live today."

It meant a lot to me, because they looked at you and smiled and said thank you. And that's more than most of the American people ever had done since I'd been back. Most of the American people called you names or asked you some weird questions that didn't amount to a hill of beans. Then this Vietnamese in the parade meant more to me than anything in the whole nineteen years since I've been back. They did more to thank me.

I have been working at the same job in Paris, Texas at Flex-O-Lite for the past seventeen years. I made it to being a leadman before I started going to the VA in June of 1989. I have started my own chimney cleaning business and I sell inserts for fireplaces. I still work at Flex-O-Lite, but I don't plan to for long. My new business is doing really well and I hope to open a fireplace store soon. I give God His part and more from the business income and He has made it all happen for me. I thank God for all he has done for me, like my wife, children, job, business, and it has all fallen together for my good. God had already had my life planned out from the beginning. I wish I'd of known Him when I was in Vietnam. It would have been so much easier.

Now I have a good job, plus my own business. I'm the Corps Sergeant Major of the Paris Salvation Army Corps. I still live on a farm and enjoy hunting and trapping with my wife. As I go from day to day, I think of Psalms 1:1-2, "He that dwelleth in the secret place of the most high shall abide under the shadow of the almighty. I will say of the Lord, He is my refuge and my fortress, my God; in Him will I trust."

Thomas C. Magedanz

Until I was ten, we lived on a farm in the northeastern part of the state, up by Milbank or outside of Revillo, South Dakota. When I was ten my dad sold the farm and went to college at Northern in Aberdeen to become a teacher, so we lived for three years on the campus up there in "married student" housing. Then he got a job teaching down at Yankton High School, where he's been teaching ever since. He's still there now. I graduated from Yankton High School in 1967 and I went to the School of Mines for three semesters during '67 and '68. I started thinking about it during '68, I guess, and later in the year I enlisted in the Marine Corps under the delayed enlistment program. I entered active duty in February of 1969.

I first heard about Vietnam in the seventh or eighth grade. Our teachers told us that we were fighting Communism and that was the thing we had to do. So all through high school I was in favor of the war. The strong protests and things hadn't quite happened yet, especially in South Dakota. At the School of Mines there was very little anti-war activity, but I read a lot about it and finally decided that I still thought the war was right and that the United States should be fighting there and stopping Communism. I was pretty much in favor of the war and believed and supported everything the government said.

I had sort of always liked the military. When I was little we played soldier and things like that. Then in high school and college too, I would look at the old *Life* magazines from World War II and read about those battles. I wasn't thinking of joining, just interested in the history of it.

I went to college at seventeen and had convinced myself that the war was right and I decided that it was wrong for me to be in college taking a student deferment while there were other people being drafted to go to Vietnam. A lot of people who opposed the war were being drafted to go to Vietnam, and I figured if I was gonna be in favor of the war, then I should be willing to go fight in it. So I joined up. I thought if I was gonna do something as crazy as quitting school to join the service, I might as well do it in style. I joined the Marine Corps. I guess I kinda wanted to go to Vietnam and serve there. If I was gonna take this kind of step, I should do it in a combat-type situation. I finally took the step in November of 1968. It was a delayed enlistment program, so I went on active duty, finally, in February of 1969.

Marine Corps boot camp was pretty crazy. I had heard all kinds of things about it, but when I got there, the physical aspects of it weren't that bad. It was hard, and I expected that. What I wasn't really prepared for was the mental aspect of it. We were all just kind of dazed for about three weeks. I know there's a method to their training, but it was just a complete, rigidly controlled existence. That's something I feel good I went through. I view it as an achievement.

I was trained as a rifleman and was sent to the school for that infantry specialty. I spent about six months, total, in training. The basic things carried over to Vietnam, but there were a lot of other things in Vietnam that were not really covered in training, and I'm not sure they could have been. We could have used a lot more on Vietnamese culture and traditions. We didn't know the first thing about their language, respecting them, what to call them. If we had known, we might have behaved a little bit better among the civilians and maybe they would have liked us a little bit more.

After we finished all our training, I had about five months in and got a twenty-day leave and went back home to Yankton. When I left, I remember my folks took me to the airport in Sioux Falls. They were both holding back tears when I left to get on the airplane. They were proud that I was doing it, but they were really concerned too.

I reported to Camp Pendleton in California, where my infantry training had been. We were set up with a staging unit and actually had garrison duty. I arrived in Vietnam on the twenty-ninth day of July, 1969. We flew into Da Nang at night. My orders were for Fox Company, 2nd Battalion, 3rd Marine Regiment, 3rd Marine Division. There were three or four of us who needed to get up there to that particular battalion or regiment. We sat for a couple of days trying to find an airplane going to Dong Ha, which was the rear for the 3rd Marine Regiment. It was about six miles from DMZ. There were signs close to the runway that said, "Gotham City" and "Wayne Manor," you know, from "Batman." Another sign said "Dong Ha International Airport, Elevation 1C."

Someone showed us how to get from the airstrip over to the 3rd Marines' Rear. They were just in tents, with a lot of sandbags around there, and lots of bunkers. Five of us walked into the Fox Company office and were told, "Well, we had five guys killed in Fox Company just a couple of days ago by an American airstrike." Whether it was an electronic mistake or whatever, five guys got killed by our own jets and we were the replacements.

We spent four days in the rear drawing gear and in classes and then we waited to get out to the bush. When we arrived there it was windy and blowing all the time. There was sand in the air almost like a sandstorm. Everything was dusty. My most vivid impressions were of the soldiers. The guys coming down off the DMZ had big packs and ragged, ripped clothes. Their jungle boots, the black leather part, was all tan like the soil. Their toes would be sticking out and the canvas would be ripped and worn and just shredded. They all had a bunch of sores and bandages on their arms. I thought they had been wounded or something, but it was just jungle rot. They all had about three or four days growth and they had kind of shaggy hair. I thought they must have been in the biggest combat of all time and was just kind of awestruck.

We finally went by convoy from Dong Ha to Vandergrift Combat Base, "LZ Stud," as it was called. Helicopter gunships escorted the convoy all the way along Highway 9. It was about twenty miles or so. We saw peoples' houses, "hooches" we called them later, with grass roofs. They were really simple, primitive things. You could see that they'd been using C-ration boxes and artillery crates and anything they could scrounge in order to build their houses. I knew they were poor people, but I really saw it there.

We flew out to the bush in the evening, going over high hills, thick vegetation, jungle and real mountainous country. We landed on top of Mutters Ridge, or "Mothers Ridge," as we called it. All five of us new guys got off with our rifles at the ready. There were four or five grunts just standing their with their arms folded and without any shirts on. They were waiting for the resupplies on the chopper. I was nervous and scared, but I was really ignorant of how dangerous it really was. I got in just at the tail end of their operation. It was called "Operation Idaho Canyon." We were only up there for about a week. I was lucky, as nothing too much happened to our platoon. I was sort of "last rifleman, last fire team." Another company in our battalion, Echo Company, got hit the night of August 10, 1969 and in one night they had twenty-five Marines killed and seventy-five wounded. NVA sappers got inside their perimeter. Because of all the activity happening in that area, the battalion command post with the colonel and first-sergeant and all their map carriers came out to the bush. They were staying with our platoon on the next ridge from the fighting. We could hear all the shooting, but we were providing security for the colonel and didn't have to walk up that hill. During my first week in the bush, I got shot at once. I was able to get down behind a log and could hear this real sharp snapping sound. The squad leader saw this happen and yelled, "Hold it! Hold it!" A fellow next to me, down the line, also a new guy, saw me moving through the bushes and shot at me from about thirty feet away. My squad leader got him too stop shooting, and he was really scared too. They had us go down and shake hands and I said, "It's okay. Don't do it again though!" (laugh).

You soon learned the daily routine of how to do your patrolling, how to do an ambush, how to pack your pack and how to ration your food and water, and how to sleep in the rain. In two or three weeks you pretty well got used to the conditions and living that way. I did my whole year in the infantry in the bush; there's nothing like it. You don't get resupplied enough. There were times we went hungry; one time I went three days without any food. It was monsoon and they couldn't get helicopters in to resupply us. They finally dropped pallets of C-rations by parachute from some cargo planes. We saw them land way off in the distance. We couldn't even get one of them, but the other one we did get. Two squads went to get them and it took all afternoon, as they had to carry these big cases of C-rations back on their backs.

One time we came across some NVA as we were moving down this little rice paddy terrace kind of thing. There were four NVA in green shirts, shorts and sandals. We didn't see them having weapons. We just surprised them. Our gunny went down and captured the two that were real close to us, but the other two ran and slipped off into the bush. One of them dropped his pack and we found it. There was some rice and a little tin can of canned mackerel in tomato sauce. We cooked up that rice and mackerel and got a few spoonfuls to go around for the four of us. We hadn't had any food and that was just super. When we got the C-rations, that was better. We never had enough water. It was rationed out and it was so hot. We'd be so thirsty and we'd sit there with canteen in hand. It had water in it and you'd open up the canteen and take a sip, then sit it down and close it and think about how thirsty you still were. I remember some guys would lick the dew off the leaves in the morning just to get water. When we went down south of Da Nang, we didn't have that problem. It was more lowlands and wells and streams, so we could get water.

During the rainy season, you slept in the rain. Most of the time you just put a towel over your face to keep the rain drops off. You curled up in the fetal position and grabbed your ankles in a ball and it was cold. You shivered when you were sleeping in the rain and you just got used to it.

The time we went without food was the start of the monsoon in October of '69 in Antenna Valley. It rained for ten or twelve days in a row, on and off, day and night. We were completely soaked all the time and out of food. The whole battalion started getting a lot of non-combat casualties—malaria, pneumonia and immersion foot (if your feet are wet all the time they get like dish-pan hands and if you walk a lot the skin rubs off in the boot and gets like a big open sore). A lot of guys were med-evaced for these reasons. In fact I got med-evaced for malaria at the end of that month.

Finally, our company commander just said enough of this, and they set us in on this hillside for four days. Normally you only stayed at a place for one or two days so you didn't get mortared. We stopped on the hillside to kind of dry out. We set up hooches out of our ponchos so we could get inside and take our boots off for an hour or so and dry our feet. The living conditions in the bush really stick in my mind. It was filthy and we were hungry and thirsty and wet or else too hot. We had to rotate watch at night, so you never got more that three or three and a half hours in a row, so after a year, that wore you down.

We moved to a new location, sometimes every day, sometimes every two or even every three days. You'd pack up all your gear, everything would go on your back in your pack and we'd move in single file. You would spread out behind the pointman, but you couldn't loose visible contact, as you didn't' have a radio and you could loose someone real fast.

The packs were heavy, probably heavier than they should have been. After a while the circulation in your shoulders would cut off from the straps. You had to be alert and be careful of the enemy or whatever. Every half hour or so we'd "Take five" and then get up and move on. Basically we 'd move frequently to a new spot so that we wouldn't get pinpointed by the enemy. We just progressively got more and more tired, emotionally tired too, and under more and more strain as time went on. By the time I got short, I was ready to go home. I really remember being pretty well drained, exhausted. With all the tiredness and mental exertion and strain, we all respected each other because we were going through the same thing. For all the hassles of it, we could say, "I'm an infantryman, and I'm a combat Marine." It was probably unfair, but we kinda looked down on everybody else, and we were proud that we were in the bush. As far as I'm concerned, that's still the best group of people I've ever been associated with. I liked those guys.

In the Marine Corps, the esprit de corps comes more from just being a Marine. But in Vietnam it went beyond that; it wasn't so much being a Marine as it was being a grunt, being in the infantry. Even in 1970, when things were winding down, there was still pride in being in the infantry. In fact, we had more respect for an Army infantryman than we did for a Marine Corps person in the rear. Being a grunt was important to us. It might have not been fair; we were kinda cocky looking back on it, because there were lots of guys in the rear who did some dangerous things. But, you couldn't have told us that at the time.

I don't know of any instances of people using drugs of any kind in the bush. In the rear there was a lot of dope. In the north, when we came down off the DMZ, there were little kids selling it. It came in packs like little cigarettes. There was something else, kind of a liquid diet from the black market that guys took so they'd stay awake on watch. Again all this was in the rear, not in the bush. We wanted to be alert and not be screwed up in the field. We could have carried it easily from the rear, but it just wasn't used in the field.

I wasn't aware of or prepared for just staying out in the countryside for weeks and weeks on end. You got used to it though; it seemed to take a week or so and then you kinda felt like you belonged out there. After a month, you really did feel like you were part of the landscape. You almost felt like you're part of the earth or in harmony with the world like the hippies used to say, like you belonged there. If you went back to the rear it'd take another week or so to get used to being out in the bush again.

In the rear it was set up so that LZ Ross was a battalion headquarters for the 7th Marine Regiment. Each company had a supply shack and a couple of big tents for the transient guys who were sleeping there. The permanent guys, like company clerk and company supply, had a different place to sleep. But transient guys, those coming back from R&R or something like that , stayed two or three days in the rear and slept in those tents on cots. They also stood lines at night on the perimeter in the bunkers. That was a little bit better than standing lines in the bush, because you did have a bunker there and there was the concertina wire out in front and it was a little tougher for the NVA to get in. It wasn't quite as scary, although it probably should have been because they were more likely to attack a base.

They did attack LZ Ross in January of 1970 and they killed fourteen Marines and wounded about seventy. We were out in the bush and we missed that. We were probably ten klicks away, up in the hills, and we could see it happening. Illumination rounds were up above LZ Ross for maybe three hours and we heard them dropping mortars all the time. We couldn't tell who was shooting who, you know, but we heard a lot of small-arms fire and a lot of mortars dropping in there. The whole thing took two or three hours, and I don't know how many gooks got killed there.

My first enemy contact was the one at the DMZ where the sniper shot at us and then our own guy shot at me by mistake. Then it was a long time before my own element had anything. The first time I really shot my rifle wasn't until November of 1969. We got a call that Hotel Company in our battalion was in trouble. They had some casualties and we were called up as a reaction force. That's really scary, because you know there's already trouble there and you're pretty sure that you're gonna run into some yourself. They choppered us over to that area and we just formed a column when we landed and started moving out. There wasn't much to it, but that's the first one that really sticks out in my mind.

I was just a regular rifleman through my first six or seven months. In Vietnam a squad averaged eight or nine men. In mid-February 1970, into my seventh month, we lost all three squad leaders in our platoon. One was killed, one went home and another was injured and went to the rear. All of the sudden we needed three new squad leaders and with seven months in, I was one of the senior guys in the platoon. I was supposed to be just temporary, but ended up keeping it. The guy on

R&R, who was supposed to take over when he came back, couldn't read a map to save his soul, so I kept the job from February of '70 to July of '70. That was a job I was proud of.

I had malaria twice in Vietnam. The first time is how I got out of Antenna Valley in October of '69. That was toward the end of my third month over there. So many guys had gotten malaria. We had run out of malaria pills for a couple of weeks, so that's why. One day I started feeling chills and felt a little sick. The corpsman gave me some pill, and I was okay for a couple of days. Then I was walking point one day. It was real thick and I was "busting trail," just cutting your way through. It was really hot that morning, so I couldn't tell if I was sick or what, but about the time we were to stop for the day, I really felt bad. Our corpsman took my temperature and said, "Holy shit." My temperature was 104.5. A fire team took me down to a stream coming down over the rocks from the mountain and put me in the water and kept dumping water over me to get my temperature down. After an hour or so the med-evac helicopter came to pick me up. I went to a naval hospital in Da Nang, NSA Hospital, and I was there for six or seven days. Before I left there I got to go out of the hospital to the movies and ate some cheeseburgers. It was really nice and I got to sleep on sheets!

The second time, I got it in Australia on the first day of my R&R. I just felt like I was getting a cold. When I got to Sydney and to my hotel room, I was feeling sorta strange and by evening I was guzzling pitchers of ice water. The next morning I was close to delirious. The hotel called a cab to take me to the doctor and he said, "Yeah, you have a high temperature. Five dollars, please." Then they called another cab that took me to an Australian military base. I then spent a week in a civilian hospital and another week in Australia in a convalescent home; it was like an old folks home. That was my R&R! I went back to Vietnam just before Christmas.

I was still in the rear and tried to get back to the bush on Christmas Eve day. I flew out in a chopper, but it was too foggy to land. Some chopper must have made it because they brought some guys back. One of them was my friend Jack Zoodsma (he got killed the next February). He had been in the bush ninety-five days straight. We went to the mess hall on Christmas Eve to eat chow. He just went crazy eating the mashed potatoes with his fingers and just stuffing them in. He was kind of a crazy guy anyway, but ninety-five days in the bush really did it. Then we went to a movie. While we were there a frag was thrown in the Fox Company office, trying to get the first-sergeant, and it hit seven guys. Nobody died. Apparently there were a bunch of fistfights and stuff going on that night, but nobody was shot or anything. The next day, Christmas, I was still on LZ Baldy and just kind of walked around; there wasn't much about Christmas.

On New Year's day we were on this ridge of mountains. At midnight, down to Tam Ky, which was one of the American Division's bases, and there were flares, green, white and red star-cluster, going up at midnight. You looked the other way and about thirty miles in the distance, Da Nang, you could see flares up over there too.

We went through a typhoon in September of '69. I was still in 3rd Marines and we'd come down off the mountains and were guarding a base at Cua Viet. We were guarding the perimeter and there were some observation towers on tall wooden poles with little shacks on the top of them. The typhoon came through, and luckily, my fire team was in a bunker right on the coast overlooking the beach and nothing happened there. Our bunker was real low to the ground, with walls about three-feet high and on a little patch of high sand. The waves got big and choppy and the water started coming all the way behind us, but we were still high enough to be dry. We just hunkered down behind those sandbags and were okay, even though we weren't concerned at this point. There were four guys in one of the observation towers and that thing blew down. They knew it was getting bad, that the wind was getting really strong. They tried to climb down the ladder, but the wind was too strong for them, so they got back inside and hoped that it would stay up. But it didn't. It blew over and two of them were killed and two of them were med-evaced back to the States. The next day we went back to where the company was staying. This was a base with hardback hooches and all of them were demolished, just leveled. It was such a strong, powerful storm, I guess it was amazing there were just two guys killed.

I want to mention guys who were killed who I knew very well, who were in my unit. First there was Frank Blas. We called him "Guam" because his mother was Guamanian and his father was a retired Air Force guy. We got to be good friends in the 3rd Marines. He was killed by a booby trap with Golf Company. The next one was Jack Zoodsma. He had long blond hair and we called him "Blondie" sometimes. It was on an ambush in Happy Valley that he was killed. Jim McClurg was the lieutenant that I mentioned being killed. He used to come around and ask where the different guys were from and got to know them. He said "Yankton, South Dakota? My brother goes to college there!" He had visited him there. He said, "God, there's nothing to do there. What do you do in a little town like that?" Then he laughed. Anytime after that, when he saw me, he'd talk a little bit about Yankton. Jim Carlin was a very bright guy, friendly and just an impressive person. We stopped in a ville one day and he was playing with the kids. They all seemed to like this handsome guy. On the way back, we saw three or four young men squatting near the village. We didn't suspect them, but they must have been NVA. Anyway, a couple of days later they shot Jim. I still wonder if those kids pointed him out somehow. Chuck Strief was hit at the same time and was in the hospital for three or four months. Carlin would have been successful in civilian life; he had a lot of good attributes. He was the closest to me physically of anyone that was killed, just ten feet away. Another guy that got killed was Gilberto Garcia. Garcia was hit by sniper fire. Rick Kirkendall and Ruben Vela hit booby traps and although injured, they did live.

The best memories I have of Vietnam are the guys that I knew. They were probably the best group of people I've ever been associated with, before or since. Old Jack Zoodsma, who was killed, was just the craziest guy. He was always making jokes and talking about how "The lifers are hassling the private." He'd say, "Wow, man, they're hassling him again." He always kept us laughing. The time we got choppered in to help Hotel Company, when we were all really scared and had that first shooting incident; when we got up to move, Zoodsma turned back and looked at me and said, "Wow, man, those gooks can fuck up your whole day!" That really broke the tension. He was a super guy and when he died, it really was a blow to all of us.

I think we had more contact with Vietnamese people than a lot of guys. We were in the lowlands and would have civilians around, but when we went to the mountains, there wouldn't be civilians. They were very poor and there were never any men in the villages below sixty-five or so. There were women and old men in the villages and there were kids under fourteen. No males between these ages. These villages would be like clusters of three or four huts. It looked like two or three families were kind of together. Bigger clusters would be a ville or town. Old women, old men, women and little kids. The hooches had grass roofs and dirt floors. They had wells where you dipped a bucked down. It was like a gallon can with a string that they dipped down. We would often get water from those wells.

If they were close to an American base, they were a lot more forward; the kids would ask for food, "Give me chop-chop." The farther out in the bush you were, the more scared they seemed to be.

We didn't try to hurt them. Some guys did some dumb things or said some dumb things, but I'm not aware of anybody actually abusing civilians or really hurting them. But I'm sure that some guys just said and did things that made people mad, that weren't very respectful.

I remember seeing some civilians up in the mountains around Happy Valley. They were absolutely wretched people. They were living under a rock in little lean-to affairs with some crooked scraggly sticks and some other sticks and leaves on top for a little roof. They were scrawny, skinny, wretched people.

At one time our company was set in around a ville trying this new program. We were there for about two weeks and were supposed to provide security for the village. In the daytime we were supposed to kind of make friends with the people. Each of us was assigned an area or a group of families that we were to get to know and be friends. That was a lot of fun. We got to know the little kids and played with them. Nobody in my company set out to be bad guys or bullies or anything. It's just that the way the war worked out, and the way that we operated, I'm sure that it caused the civilians a lot of disruption.

On one occasion, our platoon took this group of about 150 women and children from Golf Company. We were moving them to another area where they could eventually be taken to some camp or something. We were scared we were gonna make enemy contact because we made contact coming over. It was dark and it got to be 10 or 11 at night. Everybody was carrying somebody else. We were going through rice paddies that were up to my ankles and little kids' knees. I carried an old lady on my back for a klick, the last kilometer or so. She was too tired to go any further. At one point that night, there was a lady carrying a baby. They must have slipped on the mud or something and fell down. The baby's head hit a rock and the baby died that night. I remember that lady just screaming and crying and groaning. We thought we were helping, and except for that incident, we were. Our lieutenant came around and said, "These people haven't had any food, you got any C-rats?" We all kicked in a couple cans and those people ate that night.

A couple of weeks later we went to this ville where these people were taken. There were refugees there, and were in a bunch of tents. These tents were ungodly hot inside. Their hooches, with the grass roof, kept fairly cool inside. Now they were sitting there just doing nothing. I'm sure we didn't make any friends in that episode.

We saw them harvesting and planting rice. They carried these poles on their shoulders and on the ends were these big bundles. We saw a lot of water buffalos, or "water bulls," we called them. One time when we were out on patrol, there was a water bull just kinda standing across the trail. We didn't want to go by this bull. There was just a little old tiny lady there. We said, "Hey, Mamasan, get that bull away for us, please." So she just reached up and grabbed him by a little rope around his neck, and just led him off. We were big bad Marines and we were scared of a water buffalo.

We had two lieutenants that I'd consider pretty good. They were just opposite personalities. Both were willing to be themselves. Lieutenant McClure was a very outgoing gung-ho type, very gung-ho. He looked like a combat leader, and he liked that stuff. He'd just as soon be walking point as anything. He didn't, but he wished he could. We'd follow him any place, because we knew he was a good leader and we

liked him. He was sent to another company and was later killed. When
I went to Washington last fall, I met the guy from his company who put
the battle dressing on his neck when he got hit. He was a good man.
Lieutenant Malone replaced Lieutenant McClure. He was very quiet,
bookish type of guy, small and didn't look like a Marine at all. But, he
turned out to be okay too. He knew enough to listen to the platoon
sergeant and he watched out for us and seemed to be a reasonable type
of guy, and that was all right.

When it was time for me to come home, my flight was the 20th, a
little earlier than I expected. On the 18th I took a chopper to Da Nang
again. I spent two days there waiting for my Freedom Bird. We slept on
the cement floor in the transient facility waiting for the airplane to come.
We got on it early in the morning. Somehow I got an SKS rifle on the
plane without the stewardess seeing it. I had taken it to Da Nang for
Kerkendall and had done all the paperwork to take it out of the country.
We took an airliner, Continental Airlines. When we took off, I looked
out the window to get a last look; I just stared at the countryside and
tried to remember what it looked like at night and just tried to remember
the whole experience. No cheering or anything, just quiet in that
airplane when we left to go to Okinawa.

We spent a couple of days in Okinawa and then flew to California
to Norton Air Force Base. We got on buses that went to Camp Pendleton
to the separation center. We were processed for a couple of days and
took liberty in Oceanside. We got discharged at 1 in the afternoon and
hired a station wagon and went to L.A.

My friend Kirkendall was from a suburb of L.A., Pomona, and I
brought his SKS rifle to him. I didn't know where he was, but I knew his
dad had the same name, so I looked him up in the phone booth. I didn't
know if he was in a hospital or what, I just knew he'd been hit bad
enough to be med-evaced back to The World. I called up his parents,
and his mother answered and said, "Well, he's home, you know." I told
her I was at this certain motel and she said she'd come over and picked
me up. I said, "How will I know you?" and she said, "I'm in a white
Chrysler. How will I know you?" I said, "I'm the only one with a rifle!"
I stayed there one night and Rick was there with his girlfriend. His arm
was in a sling and everything, but he was happy to have his rifle and he
took me around the next day. He took me to the airport. First I had a
flight to Omaha, but then I got bumped off it, military standby. Rick's
girlfriend started chewing out the ticket man, saying, "He hasn't seen
his family in thirteen months and you gotta let him get on this airplane."
It didn't do any good so my bags and everything went to Omaha and
later I got a flight on Western to Sioux Falls. I got there at 11 at night and
called my folks to come and we drove home to Yankton. I was up all

night, smoking, which my folks had never seen me do, but it was good to be home.

My schedule got all screwed up. I don't know why I couldn't sleep at night. I wasn't having nightmares or anything like that, I just couldn't sleep. I found myself then sleeping until 4 in the afternoon. Being home where it wasn't dangerous anymore, you could just lie in bed. That was nice. I remember one thing I did. In Vietnam you had to be careful if you were smoking a cigarette. You just didn't light a cigarette at night because the snipers could see you. One night I went out at night in my folks' front lawn and lit my lighter and held it up above my head, because, "I can do this now. I don't have to worry about anything." It was a nice relief to be able to sleep and to be able to not be afraid.

As far as dealing with people, it was kind of a disappointment because nobody really knew much about Vietnam. A guy that I used to play baseball with said he hadn't seen me in a long time and "Wasn't I in the service or something for a while?" Yankton wasn't a bit different in 1970 than it was in 1969. It was like I'd never been away. Nobody asked very much about it. They might ask, "Does it rain a lot in the monsoon? Did your M-16 ever jam up? Did you ever have any dope?" That would end the conversation.

I went right back to college then after I got home. You could tell there was no respect for military things. Ribbons or medals or something like that were considered a tin soldier type of thing and were talked about with a sneer. There wasn't any respect for what you'd been through, but on the other hand, there wasn't any out-and-out abuse. There were a few people who were interested, or at least knew that you had experienced something.

It seemed so open back here. In Vietnam the next treeline was 100 meters or closer. It was into August and it was getting a little cooler. August felt *cool* to me!

I didn't have any particular incidents right away, but I did have later on at college. A guy in my fraternity was kinda drunk, I guess. Somebody had asked me something and I had said something about Vietnam. He was really against the war and he just exploded. He held and imaginary rifle with a bayonet and thrust it at my neck. He said, "How would you like it if someone did that to you?—to kill if you're actually face to face with killing, so you can really understand it?" That type of thing. He had never talked to me about what I did in Vietnam. He didn't know what I did, but he just really totally hated me. That's the only time anybody really did anything against me because I had been in Vietnam.

I went back to college at the University of SD in Vermillion in the fall of '70. All my stuff transferred from the School of Mines so I graduated in five semesters in December of '72 with a four-year degree. I went out and looked for work, but I was only twenty when I got home and was a little young for settling down. I found a job at a loan company for a while, but didn't like that. I went back to USD and got a teaching certificate and taught school for two years in Iowa. Then I went back in '76 for a masters degree at Vermillion in public administration, and I worked for the university for a while.

One thing that I did was take a trip down the Mississippi River with a friend of mine. We started in Yankton in a sixteen-foot fishing boat and went to New Orleans; it took about six weeks. That was a good time. Then I joined the Peace Cops and I spent three years in the Philippines, which was an interesting experience and interesting to compare to my time in Vietnam. I still think I'm a little more proud to have been a Marine in Vietnam than a Peace Corps volunteer, although I'm glad I did both. I got married in the Philippines to a Filipina and we had one daughter there and we had a son here, so we have two kids. I got out of the Peace Corps in 1982 and got a job with the state government, Department of Water and Natural Resources here in Pierre. So, I'm going along.

About my feeling on the outcome of the war in Vietnam. When I got back to college, I pretty much turned against the war and I guess I'm not surprised at the outcome. I feel that it was kind of a lost cause to start with. To win that war we probably would have had to make it a colony. I might be wrong on that. There's been so much that's happened in the meantime, with the killing in Cambodia, the holocaust there, and the conditions in Vietnam now, the boat people and everything, that I think any anti-war person should think twice about it. And pro-war people too should think twice about it. It was an extremely complex situation, and I still think that we should not have gotten involved and that we'd have been much better off had we not been involved. But, I'm not sure that I'm right.

I'm angry at the way things turned out and the way that some parts of the war were run, like some of the bureaucratic things and the politically expedient things. I'm angry at student deferments and at refusing to call up reserves in order to not disturb the middle class too much. Let the lower working class—coal miners' kids and black kids and Mexican kids and farm boys—let them fight the war; nineteen years old, not married—let them die. We were all really young, and I think if they were serious about fighting war, they would have asked all levels of society to sacrifice.

It seemed like in the early years of the war they tried to minimize it to not alarm the folks back home. They did it for political reasons to make it seem easier than World War II or Korea. I think that was a disservice to the Vietnam veterans. It was a "crisis" and not a war for a long time.

I'm proud that I was a Marine and I'm proud that I was in the infantry and that I did a year in the bush. I'm proud that when I was eighteen I cared enough to quit school and give away my student deferment and join up. I think that my political judgement was probably wrong at the time, but I still am proud that I did that.

As for the country, I feel that the United States, believe it or not, showed a lot of restraint over there trying to do the right thing, trying not to kill civilians and trying to abide by a set of rules in order to fight for the principles of democracy, even though it turned out to be a big mess. I think we did fight with one arm behind our back and we did it because we were trying to follow democratic ideals. We did it for reasons that were honorable, and I think taking the long view of it, that the United States' behavior in Vietnam was not all that bad except for the way it turned out. The problem was that it was a lost cause before we ever went over there. I met some real good guys over there that I'm glad I met and I'm proud I had the chance to serve with them and be one of them.

I did a year in the bush. I think that's an achievement. It took a long time for me to separate feelings of guilt as far as the political policy versus feelings of pride that I was over there, and for a while it didn't make sense. It was like trying to have your cake and eat it too, but I can separate that now. I can say I'm proud that I was over there and still disagree with the policy.

I went to college and part of my grad school on the GI Bill. I did have a deal where I lost a couple of years of GI Bill because I wasn't in the service long enough. I was twelve days short, and that bothers me a lot. I did a year in Vietnam in the bush and I think I should get full benefits. But I did get enough to finish my bachelors degree and take me most of the way through my masters, so that's okay. I used the dental benefits and had an Agent Orange physical.

Being a veteran is different than it used to be, I guess. Now it's almost gone too far the other way. When I got back to college in '70-'71, being a veteran was something to be sneered at almost. You could be accepted as a good person if you, like, repented for your evil ways before. But if you were proud of being in the military, you were an immoral person. Nowadays it's almost gone too far the other way, like these big legendary things about Vietnam now, when they make it sound almost worse than it was, like the Rambo movie and that kind of thing. Mostly I guess, in both situations, it was a case of people not really understanding the situation. At least there's some acceptance and respect now for having gone through the experience of Vietnam.

I'm proud I fought in Vietnam. Like I said, proud that I was a Marine, proud I was in the infantry. I feel that I tried to do the right thing when I was over there and in joining up. I'm not ashamed of anything I did over there, and I've lived long enough now to see the pendulum swing the other way, where people respect us again. Some delayed benefits, I guess.

By the time I got back to the States after being in the Philippines, the first thing I did was buy a couple of Vietnam books. Here I had just finished three years in the Philippines, which was a very intense experience, and I'm reading abut Vietnam again for some reason. Then I kind of stumbled across the Rap Group here. There was a seminar at the Kneip Building by an SDSU professor on the PBS Vietnam Television History and I went there. All these guys from the Rap Group were there, and you invited me to come to the Rap Group, which I did. I still don't feel that I've had any problems or anything like that from Vietnam other than that it was always real important to me. But going to the Rap Group—I don't think I ever missed—I went for a year just like clockwork and I've always really enjoyed it. I suppose it was the idea of being a Vietnam veteran and being proud of it.

I've always kind of put down my own service a little bit and I found, talking to more guys, while I wasn't in the heaviest combat around, I did see a fair amount compared to some other guys. I find myself feeling a lot better about being a Vietnam veteran. I still think that the war was wrong, but I've moved a little bit to the center on some of those feelings. It's been a growing experience that way.

Our Rap Group association organized a trip in 1984 to Washington, D.C. for the second dedication of the Vietnam Memorial for the statues. That was a good trip and was the first time I'd been to Washington, D.C. I found all the guys that I had talked about on the Wall. I think the Vietnam Memorial has been a really great thing for Vietnam veterans. It's really focused people's attention on Vietnam veterans in a reverent way, with the names of the dead on The Wall. I'm glad I got to see it and I'd like to go back again.

Editor's note: information for this story was taken from transcripts of an interview conducted on May 5, 1985 and November 3, 1985 for South Dakota Vietnam Veterans Oral History Project, Thomas C. Magedanz, Project Director, sponsored by the Vietnam Era Veterans Association, Inc. and the Robinson Museum of the South Dakota Department of Education and Cultural Affairs, Pierre, South Dakota, funded in part by a grant from the South Dakota Committee on the Humanities, an affiliate of the National Endowment for the Humanities. The opinions expressed in the interview are not necessarily those of any of the sponsoring or funding entities.

Jack Lutt

I grew up on a farm near Wayne, Nebraska. My brothers and sisters and I learned at an early age to milk cows by hand and do chores around the farm. I always liked living on the farm and will always have good memories about those days. We went to a country school, then on to high school in Wayne. Although I wasn't very big, I always wanted to play football. But, we always had to get right home after school and get to the field. I liked driving the tractor too, so it wasn't all bad. I went out for wrestling, but a kid broke his leg, and they discontinued wrestling in those years I had left. I never cared much for high school, and didn't go to any of the traditional proms or school dances. I went out and drank beer and partied. Although I had the best of parents, who tried to teach me right from wrong, I didn't listen to them like I wished I would have.

Before going to the Army, I fought in the Golden Gloves in 1968, and I'll never forget being so tired after the match, which I lost to a decision. My dad came in the dressing room and I couldn't even raise my arms to give him a hug. I'll always remember the letters from my family while I was in Vietnam as being my main inspiration, keeping my spirits high.

In April of 1969 my tour in Vietnam began when I arrived in Cam Ranh Bay. I can remember very clearly our descent. It was night and the flares, fires and smoke made me wonder what was in store for me, thousands of miles from home. Being a new guy, I didn't know yet the difference between incoming and outgoing rounds. Even though I found out they were outgoing and not to worry, I didn't get much sleep just the same. I was able to write home, but it would be about twelve days before I'd know where they would station me, so my family wouldn't be able to write back for a while. It had to be hard for them back home, not knowing what was going on.

My MOS was Equipment Storage Specialist and I was sent to Long Binh depot. I couldn't believe it was so modern there, a lot different than I had imagined. The weather was something else there, hot and humid everyday, then the nights got pretty cold. It's wasn't uncommon for it to get to 110 degrees most days. Most days I ran a forklift, loading trucks with supplies. We worked everyday. If we got caught up, we got Sunday afternoon off. The water wasn't very good there. We drank hot water in the day then, at night, if there was enough, the water was cold for showers. I felt fortunate, though, thinking of the guys in the field, who definitely didn't have it so good.

The monsoon season had started. It rained every day, but the trucks kept coming in. I didn't think a person could get so soaked. It was about mid-May. I'd been in-country a month. We'd spent some days stringing barbed wire on the perimeter. On the twelfth of May we had seven incoming rockets that killed three. Everybody tried to get to the bunkers. I definitely knew the sound of incoming!

In June we had several more rockets come in. One guy was hit by shrapnel in the company by us. Monday night was guard night for me every week, plus working everyday. It was pretty tiring. There was a great bunch of guys there. Without them to blow off steam and drink black beer with, it would have been much tougher.

The months were slowly going by. I'd never been bitten by so many mosquitoes in my life. A lot of rats and snakes were there also. A friend of mine got swelled up pretty bad by bites, but one time was a little more than other times. The doctor told him he'd been bitten by a rat.

In August we had three straight nights of rockets. Two men were killed. Sometimes I think we spent more time in the bunker than in our bunks. In September I volunteered to go on a convoy carrying explosives and 105mm rockets to different units. I really got an eyeful of different villages and saw a lot of GIs out on the bunker lines. When I got back I was put on permanent guard duty. It was hot, hard work, but I liked it better than going to the depot everyday.

November 25. I was on sandbagging detail everyday. There were B-52s bombing the Cambodian border. We also had five mortars come in. Let me tell you, the ground was rock-and-rolling around the clock. It was a heck of a way to spend Thanksgiving, but I'd been thinking for a couple of months of 1049ing out of this unit. Everybody thought I was crazy, but I felt like I wasn't doing enough at Long Binh. It just seemed too spit-shine there, and I didn't like it.

December 2. I got orders to be a door-gunner in the 1st Air Cavalry Division. First I went to take some training, then I had a physical for Aerial Gunner. On the fourteenth I got to Tay Ninh, which was located in what they called the Dog's-head, on the Cambodian border. My thinking was that I'd be on a Huey, but it would be on a Loach, or OH6A, a reconnaissance chopper with the Apache Scouts. "These guys fly at treetop level and scout out VC trails and most generally I'm told take a lot of fire." The Cobra flew above and took out the enemy position when the Scouts dropped a smoke on the position. On the 27th I went on a training flight. I'd be an observer in the left seat, with an M-16 and a smoke ready to drop if we were fired on. The machine gunner was in the back seat. Also, if the pilot got hit, the observer had to know how to get the chopper safely away. Nobody told me not to eat right before going up, and after a few steep turns and dives I lost my cookies all over my M-16. I learned the basics of flying and how to hover before landing, but the real emergency, I'm sure, would have been terrifying. It was enough when the pilot pretended he was hit and fell forward over the stick. The chopper went into a nose-dive and I had to bring it under control. "What the heck am I doing here?" I thought, then I remembered that I had volunteered.

I found out right away the guys were a real tight outfit and you had to prove yourself before they really opened up to you. I met a guy named Barry Kalletto, who asked me over to his table at chow. He was telling me some real heavy tales, from being with the Scouts. One time a bullet was shot through the Loach floor, up between his legs. He was an observer like me. I'll never forget him because he was the first to make me feel a part of the unit. Barry, the pilot, and door-gunner were killed when their Loach took enemy fire and they were unable to reach the LZ and their Loach exploded. Although I didn't know Barry that long, I'll never forget him!

January 5th. We'd been going on missions every day, spotting a lot of enemy trails. We took fire. It happened so fast, yet it seemed a long time, hearing rifle fire from the jungle. I dropped a smoke, and emptied my M-16. The door-gunner was letting them have it real good also. We went up to altitude and then the fun started. I didn't really care much for the idea of being in that bubble as a sitting duck, but I did enjoy watching the Cobras attack. Not many can experience real assaults from so close. The Cobra went up high, turned toward my smoke, hovering for a minute, then all dive, rockets and mini-guns blazing. The firepower was amazing and the pilots of those Cobras, Hueys and Loachs were the best!

January 8. Our door-gunner spotted a lone VC in heavy jungle. The gook kept circling the tree as we circled. We must have been there two hours. That tree was ready to fall on him, before he was finally chopped up like the tree was.

January 10. We started off on a first-light mission, headed over a river, then I remember a busy highway. We started going lower and lower. I wondered what the hell we were doing, then the gooks were raising their fists at us. The door-gunner was dropping watermelons on them. I remember not being too crazy about doing this to the people, but I remember, also, not liking gooks too much either. Friendlies by day, enemy by night. I didn't trust a one of them. Scouts just had to let off some steam once in a while and buzzing the highway was one way they did it. Later, at treetop level, we came across what at first we thought was a large group of NVA. We almost opened up on them, but they started waving and flagging us down. We called it in and they ended up being friendlies. I wonder if they knew how close they came to being fired on.

Apache Blues Recon Platoon was in the next hooch beside the

Scouts. I got to know some of the guys pretty well, and they thought I should get out of Scouts and into the Blues. My sergeant didn't like the idea, because they were short-handed. I had seventy-six hours of flying with them and was just assigned the M-60. I was moving to rear seat. I've got to say I did some heavy praying to get out of the Scouts. I swear a voice was telling me I wouldn't make it home if I didn't get out. I haven't kept my promises through the years that I made that day. I can only thank God, and also the sergeant of the Blues, for getting in with them.

January 20. From the Loach I could see the jungle was thick. I was really getting the test. Not a breeze to be found; so hot and muggy I could hardly breathe. The thick jungle trails wanting to scratch your face and arms, along with the mosquitoes eating us alive, made for a long day. I felt better with my feet on the ground though. If helicopters were shot down, the Blues were scrambled to get the occupants out as fast as possible. There was always a portion of our squadron that stayed at base camp in case of a scramble.

February 10. The siren went off, signalling a downed bird. It's hard to explain the feeling, knowing those crewmen could be dead, or have VC closing in on them. We'd had guys go out with half their clothes on, just as long as they had their rifle. Every second counted! A Loach was shot down in heavy jungle. Our pilot told us he couldn't land, there were VC in the area, and our door-gunner was putting out cover for us. We would be rappelling in. We put our gear on and I don't mind telling you, I was pretty scared. I didn't receive any training at rappelling like the rest of the guys did, because I'd been in-country a few months before I got to the Cav, and they figured I didn't need it. It would have helped, because I burned going down the rope pretty bad. Thanks to the door-gunner keeping his barrel red hot, we made it safely to the Loach. Going toward it, I could see the three crewmen sitting outside the bird. They had some cuts and bruises, but didn't look too bad. But, one never knew what kind of internal injuries they could have. We got them raised up into the Huey, then they came over to us and dropped lines. Up and over the jungle we were dragged. I was never so happy to get to the nearest firebase. I could see a bunch of GIs watching, probably wondering what the hell was going on.

Our rescue had been a success and we were headed for Tay Ninh. I felt real good, knowing I was contributing something more, and felt proud to be in the 9th Cav. Knowing also, that the young guy shot down in the Loach was my replacement in the Scouts, I knew it would have been me wounded.

February 16. Our platoon was airlifted close to an enemy village. We watched as a jet bomber leveled the village. One of the bomb fragments landed a foot away from me and started a fire. I thought, "Shit, that was too close!" We headed toward the ville. The fire was too intense to get too close to the hooches, so we went to check out the surrounding jungle. We saw bunkers right away and a couple of gooks went in, forgetting about their weapons outside. Our Kit Carson Scout tried to talk them out with no luck. We threw in two grenades, plus shooting a lot of rounds into the bunker. We thought, "Hell, there's no way they could have lived through that," when all of the sudden four NVA came out with their hands up. We couldn't believe it. We checked out some other bunkers, but the rest must have gone deeper into the jungle. We were ordered to get the prisoners out of there for interrogation. We put ropes around their necks, and kept them in front. I had just turned twenty years old, but these black-pajama boys couldn't have been but sixteen or seventeen. The dirt tunnels they lived in—like rats. What a life. I guess it showed their determination to defeat us.

March 11. The Loaches had been taking fire regularly. We usually got sent on missions when they received fire. We were going closer to the Cambodian border all the time. Whenever we were on an active VC trail, the brass turned us around on the border. Our Cav. units had found huge weapons and rice caches in the last few weeks. I felt we were going to catch up with Charlie one of these days.

On a mission the previous month, we were inserted on a hot LZ. The gunships were firing support for us—too damn close! Fire started eating us up from behind. I was bringing up the rear and the fire was right on my rear. I told Jim Brown, our radioman, that we'd have to get a move on. I knew we couldn't really push our pointman too fast either, but there wasn't much choice. Well, we finally had to scrub that mission. The fire was just too intense. I'll never forget that fire being so close, and the trail and jungle so thick, and not being able to get away as quick as I wanted. We almost fried that day.

March 16. The low birds spotted a downed helicopter in heavy jungle. Our platoon went in to check it out. The jungle was so thick that the VC hadn't been there. We found the remains of the two pilots and there weapons. God, that's a terrible thing to come upon. But at least the family got word of their loss. We all had lumps in our throats that day—never to forget.

March 18. I had guard duty with Mark Diorio. He was with the Scouts. I flew with him when I was a Scout. Anyway, he was different that night, talking about his kills and other gung-ho talk. He was saying he wouldn't make it back to The World. He thought he'd be killed. On this day his Loach took fire, and Mark was hit. He died soon after. We miss you, Mark.

March 19. Close to Cambodia, we came across an enemy training area, complete with replicas of tanks and helicopters. Later on, our pointman and machine gunner, Porky, came head-to-head with an NVA soldier. He started shooting his 30-caliber machine gun, but Porky got him first. All hell broke loose then. Everybody in our platoon, I thought, was doing their job, and we all worked good together. Sergeant May called for me to go down the trail aways with my M-79 and start laying rounds out at the NVA. I was using an experimental M-79 mounted under my M-16. It fired every time, but would not eject the round. So I had to use a branch to knock them out. I remember a lot of AKs going off around us, and also snipers in the trees. Jorgenson was hit in both legs, and we got him med-evaced out; the helicopter hovering above to lift him out looked like a sitting duck so we were all laying out heavy metal. Gunships were helping out a lot, giving us support fire. There were a lot of NVA I could see out in the jungle, and ended up shooting my twenty M-79 rounds plus some in a spare pouch. I think I was in kind of a shock or a daze. With everything going on, I remember the bunkers, and somebody dropping concussion grenades in them—the moaning and groaning of the almost dead being dragged out. My left ear being exposed to the grenades might have explained the daze, but a lot just could have been the heat of the battle. Six hours of fighting later, a lot of our guys had wounds from the day, but thank God no one was killed. At a debriefing later, we were told we had run into a battalion base camp. We had killed thirty-nine enemy soldiers, which intelligence later said had been the base camp for a gathering place for a massive attack on our Tay Ninh. On our chopper going back that night, nobody said anything. We were all emotionally drained. But the eyes talked.

April 10. VC had launched several offensives the last weeks, trying to get in our base camp. Lots of shooting was going on. I had orders for seven-day leave in Hawaii, caught viral pneumonia and spent my leave at 93rd Evac Long Binh. What a bum rap.

April 15. Our platoon was called to a special meeting. We were going to be inserted in close, by a reported prison camp of our guys, but the mission was scrubbed. I didn't sleep much, thinking about the mission, but I think we were all ready and willing to go.

April 29. My folks wrote and told me that my friend Bob Dongberg had been killed in-country. We'd been writing each other over there. He was with the 101st Airborne. I was getting real short and was told I wouldn't have to go to the field anymore. But the news from back home put my head in a spin. I knew it was crazy, but I asked to stay in the field. Bob and me had some good times back home, and planned on a lot more. I'll miss him.

May 2. We scrambled to a downed Scout Loach in Cambodia. It

almost made it to a clearing in the jungle. We got there and found the three crewmen in bad shape. I helped carry them to the med-evac. I'll never forget the one guy, because his head had a gash in it real deep. He asked me and the medic if he'd be all right. I told him "Yeah, you'll be okay." Doc, I think, was kind of caught up in the emotion, and told him he was in pretty bad shape. Jorgenson, I remember, chewed out Doc when we got back to base. You always try to keep spirits up in the wounded. Not as easy as it sounds, I know.

May 16. My last day in Tay Ninh, they dropped smokes on the pad and the Huey flew a final pass for me through it, which was tradition for guys going home. I still couldn't believe it. "I'm going home! Good-bye Vietnam!" But not to be forgotten.

I saw three sides—supply, Scouts and Blues—when I was in Vietnam. Truthfully, after basic and AIT training, I hoped to get orders for Vietnam, and when I got there I didn't want to be there. But I was young, and didn't really know if I could make it for a whole year. Maybe I was stupid for volunteering for 1st Cav., from a safe supply job. I liked the guys at Long Binh, but I'll never regret leaving, feeling I had to do more, that I had to do it for myself.

Being with the Scouts of 1st Squadron 9th Cav. was the scariest thing I've ever done. I was just with them a little over two weeks. I've always been bothered about asking about the Scouts, but knowing of all the Scout birds that were shot down so often, I definitely wouldn't be here now if I would have stayed. The 1/9 Cav. just had a reunion in June 1989, at Fargo, North Dakota. Art Dochter, a lift door-gunner, got hold of me the Christmas before. I hadn't heard from any of the guys, and I didn't try to get a hold of them either. I often thought of them, and wondered if everybody had made it out of the Nam all right. My wife of fifteen years and I headed for Fargo, but it was weird. The last fifty miles, I slowed the cruise down on our car, and was kind of lost in a time zone, not knowing if I really wanted to get there or not. It ended up being the best thing I've ever done. These guys are the greatest. I should have known they'd be easy to talk to. I've had trouble saying the word Vietnam, or even telling people I was there. I'd say I was overseas. Except from family, I wasn't treated real good when I came back. I even went in to my hometown VFW, where I was a member, sat down for a beer and wasn't served for at least twenty minutes. The bartender must have had a problem in his head with Vietnam vets. I told a guy beside me I didn't have to put up with this crap. I went to another tavern.

At the reunion in Fargo I found out that the three Scout men we med-evaced out May 2 died later. I was headed home and never knew until nineteen years later. A couple of the guys at the reunion told me I was smart to have gotten out of the Scouts. One Blue said he was so surprised to see so many Scouts at the reunion since so many had been killed. With the Blues, I feel now, was the right place for me. I think I worked well with the team. In Vietnam I know there were many GIs who had worse tours than mine, and before I got to the Blues they had some rough battles. I'm just telling my own story. I credit our pointmen for there expertise; being exLRRPs helped save our butts lots of times, and every single one of you guys in 1/9 Cav. . . . you guys will always be family to me! And to our friends who didn't make it, you'll never be forgotten. I'm proud to be a Vietnam vet. I'd do it all again.

I wish we could do more to get our MIA-POWs back. This bothers a lot of us in the unit. My wife's uncle, Lt. Col. Tom Scheurich, was shot down over Hanoi in March 1968 and is still missing, so we have a real concern about this issue.

Since returning home from Vietnam, I've worked at several jobs, the last eleven years as a county road employee. I was recently offered a job which pays much more, but my hearing problem, which resulted from Nam, kept me from getting it. My dad died of cancer in 1986, at the age of sixty-three. This has been tough for the family, but we're making it through. In World War II he was a belly-gunner, and he went through some tough years, too. I'm a private pilot and fly when I can afford to. Sometimes it brings back some memories up there.

In my story I didn't use many of my buddies' names. I would have liked to, but I thought maybe they wouldn't like to be mentioned in that way. But here at the end I can't help but mention a few great men. Beal, Jorgenson, Cortez, Henderson, May, Braun, Setters, Kluck, Ligette, Fox, Hamm, Gannon, Mugzy, Burns, Bloor, McCord, Esquibel, Engerbretsen, Hugele, Henry, Allen, Shider. For all the guys in the Vietnam War who were badly wounded and scarred, you deserve the best care possible, and I pray you get it. Take care out there in The World!

Darrell D. Johnson

In the spring of my last year of high school, 1966, Vietnam really wasn't a part of our lives. Kids from the country: a few got jobs around home; a few went to college; and a few of us went in the service. A friend and myself went into the Air Force, three into the Marines and of couple to the Navy. Six days after graduation, I was in Texas, in basic training. My first assignment was as Security Police, Minot, North Dakota as a Missile Security Guard. I had been there about eighteen months when the order came down—Vietnam! What little we heard or ever paid attention to, the war at that time wouldn't amount to much. Everyone was excited just to get out of the *cold*. We compared assignments—Da Nang, Tan Son Nhut, Bien Hoa, Nha Thrang—great! I got stuck at some place called Phu Cat, which wasn't even on our map. I went back to Texas for AZR training, then Seattle, Cam Ranh, Qui Nhon, and finally by Army convoy to my new home, Phu Cat.

I soon understood why it wasn't on the map back in the States. It wasn't even built yet! This was early in February, 1968. The same evening, I was assigned perimeter guard, only there was no perimeter, just a bull-dozed fire zone. No wire. Just you, the bugs, and the river, or jungle, depending what side you were on. There were flares, 16s, 60s, a radio, maybe claymores if you were considered a "Hot Spot." The K-9 was in front, LPs out—the farthest was around three klicks. At this time, Phu Cat was mainly a chopper pad for the Army. The Air Force hadn't taken over yet. The whole area was supposed to be VC or their friends and relatives. At midnight that same night, I got my first inkling of what Vietnam and the "War" really meant.

Mortars!

This would last for a week, almost always at midnight. The bunkers and sandbags held and I only got covered with dirt once. We usually switched assignments daily—SAT Team, ammo dump, LPs, or QRF. Then you would go to the club when you could. They had a few good bands, but anything was good then. It got to the point after a few months there and we had the jets in, that you could tell the in-coming. You knew they weren't ours and you'd be on the radio before the first one even hit. Experience. Now the Tet Offensive was in full swing. I was at Plu Cat approximately six months. Things were getting hot and heavy down south. A few of us "experienced" seventeen- or eighteen-year-old troopers were sent to Tuy Hoa and some to Ban Me Thuot. I got Tuy Hoa. I stayed in that AO until my DEROS. Someone was getting hit all the fucking time. ARVN. Army: "Blow the pipe line along QL-1." I got to be sergeant here. I worked with the Army MPs, National Police, Air

America and Air Vietnam. The craziest were the ROKs, White Horse Division. I made many friends there. A couple were with me and another Air Cop in Phu Heip when we ran into a VC squad. We scared the shit out of each other. They ran one way and we went the other. I got grazed just below the heart; just scraped my rib. I couldn't report it because the Air Base was in Yellow Alert and my ass would still be in Leavenworth by being three miles off base in a VC-controlled village! Our girls hid us. I went with the same one for eighteen months. She and her friends saved our asses a few times and gave us good intel. That's why I think it was kind of overlooked by my superiors when I was caught off base. Training and experience kept growing: auto-40mm canister, 50-cal, APC, Quad 50s. We had to have one qualified operator on every team. The air base was really growing now—F-100s, F-4s, Sceptor, Spooky, Bird Dogs, Huey Gunships, ROK 105s, and Navy offshore.

We had another offensive during this period. Everyone was all shook up. We worked the same tower on perimeter for 180 days, twelve to fourteen hour shifts. I got to be the best grid-map reader around. So, I got to train all the new guys. I'd just get on post, all set up for the night on top of the tower, listening to the Doors or Hendrix and I'd see the jeep coming!

First thing I'd tell him was to dump his flak jacket and helmet and take all that unnecessary stuff off. All I needed was a new kid to die of heat stroke on me. When it came to calling in quadrants for artillery or air strikes, I was very picky. I was called every name you can think of. Usually, our main problem was with the VC blowing the pipeline. I'd let the new guy handle it two, three, even four times—the grid charts, azimuth boards. While they were trying to figure it out, I'd call it in on Lima-Lima. I'd make them do it over and over and over until they got it right. You see, I had learned by experience what a tiny mistake can make. At Phu Cat we mortared ourselves. We only took two in-coming, the rest were all ours. Radio communications—every time someone would try to say "Short Rounds!"—someone else would cut him off. We made complete asses of ourselves that night. Luckily there was only a minor shrapnel wound.

During my stay at Tuy Hoa, I had many various "jobs," and at nineteen going on twenty, my whole attitude changed. I grew up *Right Now!*

There was some mission my people were to undertake—now remember, I was working hand-in-hand with Korean Whitehorse Div. and occasionally we'd be asked to make—sweeps around the base perimeter with them. If I felt anything amiss, I'd say so. "Fuck these ninety-day wonder boys and their 'book.'"

This was an entirely different type of war than what you were taught in the States. I had my ass chewed by so many new LTs and tried to keep a straight face. My colonel, because he knew I was right, would reprimand me to make things look good. The new LTs were sent back the next day.

There was another thing that I was amazed at back in late '69—early '70 at Tuy Hoa, and I'm still befuddled today. We were building a new defense control center for the air base. It's why all the "tops" chose me, just a sergeant, to man the "alternate" by my fucking self. In my thinking, "This is a job for a captain or major, and more than one person." I report, they drive me off in a jeep, dump me and say, "It's your's as soon as we make radio checks!" Twenty years old and in charge of a whole fucking air base with men, women, and artillery, not to mention birds, which were the main priority, and four or five radios to monitor, contact maps to keep track of. We made it through okay, but why? I'll never know why people do strange things like this.

Responsibility is one thing, but to just have it dumped on you all at once like this is really a traumatic experience. One mistake, even the slightest, unforeseen diabolical mishap, not only are the birds lost, but human lives as well.

Another strange thing I learned while going TDS from here to there: if only a chopper ride away, you had to learn the set up before you even went out or you'd waste each other. At one base, K-9s in front, at another, behind you. "Know were the 'Friendlies' are" and, "LPs don't move." Starlight might pick you off.

A bad experience at Tuy Hoa. ARVN ran into some VC between Phu Heip and QL-1 in paddies. Red flares everywhere. ARVN ran south to U.S. Army Compound, lit the wire and U.S. Army wasted them. VC vanished into the villages and hamlets laughing. The first time I ever saw "spooky," besides guarding it, was at Tuy Hoa. A bad night. All of us were getting hit—MACV in Tuy Hoa City, air base, Army compound, ROK Compound, Nui Chi, Nui Chap, Chap Chi. I guess "spook" came from Pleiku. We'd already scrambled all our "birds" and sent them elsewhere. I was working outer perimeter as usual. Canister 40mm, M-60, M-16, flares above. Below, 50-cal, grenades, flares, claymores. The only thing I remember about that night is that suddenly it was "daylight" and the tower vibrated like a herd of buffalo were running underneath it. Besides the WP, occasional mortar and tracers going in and out, was a solid red line coming from the sky. And the noise! I'll never forget. A mini-gun in action! That's how close it was. In the morning ROKs and ARVN would make a sweep, pick up the leftovers.

"Pacification," for my part, was through my informants, usually young kids you befriended. You worked your way up to their parents.

Cultural and language barriers really hurt in the beginning. You had to gain the trust of the people. Still, there were always hard-core VC.

As far as drugs and alcohol abuse, Nam fucked me up. Some black brothers came back from R&R and had some Thai weed. First time I ever tried it. I got sicker than shit and wanted to die. In Nam, to stay alive you were constantly on alert and this emotion carried back to The World.

I don't care what other people say, no matter how tired or wiped out you were, you were alert!

Everyone then, in the late '60s and early '70s, no matter what color, covered each other. You had to be on a constant high. The pressure and constant threat did things to peoples' *minds*. Who do you trust? Who not to trust? Our unit was *tight*, as I imagine many more were. "One for all and all for one!" Then I got hooked on "Darvon." More on this later.

Leaving Nam was a very emotional experience for me. I was working outer perimeter security. I saw the Freedom Bird land. Then the SAT team relieved me and I had one hour to pack and go. Orders— all the paper work—was done. Enough time to shower, change clothes and . . . *GONE!* I only got to say good-bye to two guys who were lucky enough to have a day off. This really hurt. To fight and live with these guys for months on end, and just say "Good-bye, you'll make it" over the radio, really hurt me. I cried and I'm not ashamed to admit it. I only hope that I taught them well.

My return to the States was really a traumatic experience. I spent a month in the Seattle-Vancouver area, just trying to clear my head. After two years in Nam, this was entirely new to me. I'd lost all track of civilization. Yes, I had to go through the "baby killer" syndrome, the alienation that I received when I finally returned home. Even friends and relatives. Yes, and family. Vietnam was something you didn't talk about. You were an outcast. People didn't know if you were going to flip out or not. Another thing that pisses me off is the media coverage—TV etc. Yes, I admit we did get ornery and extracted revenge. The My Lai Massacre was blown all out of proportion. This is something that you cannot "label" all Vietnam veterans for. There was also a war going on in the States—the protesters, Kent State, a lot of things that I never heard of until years later.

My drug and alcohol problem took effect at this time. I was totally "wasted." If you can print this, Gary, tell our brothers, "It's a bad trip, a cop out." It took me years of treatment and I'm still not over it. I was married for seven years and I lost that. I did jail time. I still have flashbacks. My moods change and I just have to get away from people.

James W. Hudson

Our Seaboard World Airline transport touched down in Cam Ranh Bay. The transport was air-conditioned, and it had been a pretty rough ride since leaving the real world. We were happy to touch down, but we were totally unprepared for what was going to hit us.

When we reached the stairs, the heat and humidity washed over my body and I broke out in a sweat. The smell was that of a garbage dump or, I thought, of dead bodies. Yes, this was Vietnam, and the smell of dead bodies went right along with my line of thinking.

My heart-feeling was that this was the place I would be killed. I used to watch this place on TV after school, and now I was there. A dream. Right. Soon I would wake up.

This was reality—I was here. "Got to make the best of it." I was sure glad I paid attention in basic and AIT.

My orders were cut: 1st Air Cavalry. I was sure to see action with this company. Their reputation was spread all over Vietnam—"Hell Raisers," "Kick Asses," "Death From Above," and all that other macho shit.

"Well, I asked for it," I thought, "by joining up. I got to just make the best of it."

Upon my arrival at the company area, I was assigned a hooch and a bunk. A lot of the "older" vets just stared. Some clapped and laughed. I could hear just about everyone shouting, "*Short!* My replacement is here!"

There was a lot of work going on in the company area. This was the Tet season, and I can remember that my first detail was filling sandbags for a bunker. This bunker had to have three sandbags from the inside out. Enough to take a rocket, or to just slow it down.

Night fell, and I didn't know what to expect. I joined in with some guys and started to put away a few beers. The Temptations were in the background, singing, "I got sunshine, on a cloudy day . . ." The memories started to come—Kim, the girl I left, my family, etc. Everyone felt the same. We all had one feeling, "I got to get back to The World." Yes, the U.S.A. was "the world" to us—the whole world.

A few nights passed, easy as far as war goes, but the heat took its toll. It would drop into the nineties at night, but you couldn't escape it. It was everywhere. The only thing we had to cool things down a little with was a fan. Tempers remained hot. It came with the oncoming of night. The sound was horrible. First a whistle and then a thunderous pounding that shook the hooches. One rocket could tear through the tin roof on a hooch, and it was all over. It was a body-bag home to sit it out in the hooches. Thank God for bunkers! A grunt's home away from home.

Sirens were always sounded to alert the base that we were receiving incoming rounds, and to take cover. The base was under attack by NVA Regulars and Viet Cong. It was time now to "mount up," as we would say. Our job now was to engage the enemy in combat. Our bunker line wasn't penetrated, so the First Air Cavalry took to the air, in an air assault. Now it was our turn to bring the max to Charlie! What nerve— to attack the Air Cavalry!

I can remember the first incident that I had my first known kill. I was occupying bunker 426, and I was the Communications Specialist (radioman) of a three-man team. Our first job was to make sure our claymores were facing outward, toward our line. Charlie would manage to turn these things around so we would use them on ourselves. Second, we had to make sure the wires were making good contact. We wouldn't set up the M-60 until dusk. That was to make sure Charlie didn't know what we had. It was all supposed to be a great surprise for him. Our M-16s were locked and loaded, and the M-79 grenade launcher was cocked, with a beehive round. Now it was time to wait. Wait for him to come.

"Echo Tower, Echo Tower, commo check, over."

"Bunker 426, this is Echo Tower. Identify RDO operator."

"Echo Tower, this is Juliet Whiskey Hotel, over."

Those were my initials in military jargon.

A short while later, "Echo Tower, Echo Tower, this is bunker 426."

"Bunker 426, go with transmission."

"Echo Tower, I have spotted movement about one hundred and fifty meters to my right."

It was a herd of water buffalo being herded by a some figure, right into our perimeter.

Echo Tower identified such incidents, and my last request was, "Echo Tower, with permission to kill."

A click of the RDO affirmed to me that my transmission was "rogered." Using Kentucky windage and Tennessee elevation, I popped off several rounds into a man I didn't know.

All of a sudden, our whole line opened up. We were in a firefight! There was hot lead that lit the night up with its tracer rounds. I looked over at the M-60 and the barrel was read. It was rock and roll time! Our '79 man left the safety of the bunker to enter the pit where he worked out of.

During the firefight, Echo Tower would call for artillery flares to light up the jungle. After a firefight like this, reality sets in. For me, I couldn't believe I had killed someone. It was like my first time laying a woman. I had done it, but it just didn't feel that good. In all this, a change came over me . . .

I wanted to kill.

I wanted to always give the enemy a chance to die for his country. I wanted to help end this war, and I knew it would come from us grunts, beating the bush.

One of my friends was killed that night. Fritz, a redhead who had only two more weeks in-country. He was "short," too short. The jinx caught up with him. A round from an AK-47 cut his throat in half. He lay there, gurgling in his own blood. Now I had good reason to hate. I vowed in my heart to pay back for this loss, any chance I could get.

Upon my return to America, I found our country in chaos. My first inclination was to join up with the friends that I had left. I found that it was going to be a question and answer period. It was like being arrested. The usual questions surfaced wherever I went. "Did you kill anybody?" "Did you kill women and babies?" "Was the weed any good?" "Where were you shot?" And, of course, "Show us."

I had come home, but some funny feelings were inside me, once I was home. I felt out of place, and I wanted to go back. Yes, go back to Vietnam. It was too quiet and eerie. When things were too quiet in Nam, something was going to happen. It usually did.

One example: after leaving a bar one night, a car backfired on 11th and Liberty Street. I automatically hit the ground to take cover. There was about a foot of snow on the ground and it covered me. My friends all had a good laugh while I brushed myself off. Thoughts of Nam went through my head, and I told myself, "I've got to stop this! I'm home now! The war is over for me!" Or so I thought. It would return daily, as if it were a shadow.

My second case involves violence. I was at a dance, and some guy voiced his opinion to me. My eyes trained on him, and I followed him to the john. When I entered the john, he was facing a urinal, taking a piss. I came up behind him and tried to piss between his legs, only to wet the back of his pants. When he cocked his head to turn around, I hit him and knocked him out. I then dragged him into a stall and tried to drown him in a toilet.

Yes, I was violent and my attitude was, "I fear no man," and I was going to prove it. I still hold this attitude today. I left Nam in 1971, but Nam is still with me today. When it rains, and on hot days, I relive Vietnam. I will never forget the horrors I've seen, and the feelings I received when engaging the enemy in combat. I was trained by the best to be a pro hit man, a killer, and I set forth in Vietnam to do a job. All our superiors wanted was a body count. Matter of fact, there were rewards for the platoon or squad with the highest body count at the end of the month. It was unreal, and some people wonder why Vietnam vets have problems.

At present I work as a supervisor for the Center for Forensic Psychiatry. I am a regular member of the 82nd Airborne Division Association, the 1st Cavalry Division Association, and the American Legion. I have received numerous awards in photography (*Photographer's Forum* magazine) and awards in poetry. I was voted one of the Outstanding Young Men of America in 1987. I hold a Second Degree Black Belt in Karate.

I quote J.F.K.: "Mankind must find an end to war, or war will find an end to mankind."

Dan Henning

My name is Dan "Go Go Gomez" Henning and I currently reside in Lake City, Minnesota. I tried growing up down in Clarksville, Iowa for the first fifteen years of my life, but since I couldn't accomplish the task in that short amount of time, my family moved to Lake City, Minnesota in 1964 so I could complete the task. I graduated from high school in 1966 and attempted to continue my schooling at Mankato State College in the fall. In January of 1967 I dropped out of college and drove to California with a friend in pursuit of the American Dream. Either it wasn't really there or we weren't looking in the right places because my friend and I returned to Minnesota empty-handed in March. He joined the Army in the spring and I followed his footsteps in July of 1967. I ran out of gas one morning on my way to work and hitched a ride down to Winona, Minnesota and enlisted in the U.S. Army, "RA-Unassigned," whatever that meant. I would soon find out what RA-Unassigned meant during basic training at Fort Campbell, Kentucky. It meant the Army would decide where they needed me the most, which, of course, was in the infantry in Vietnam. It also meant that I was *stupid*, besides being naive.

After graduating from basic training, most of us boarded a bus headed to Fort McClellan, Alabama where we would be schooled in Advanced Infantry Training and Jungle Warfare. Some of the jungle training seemed tough at the time but I never imagined in my wildest dreams what jungle warfare might actually be like. I would soon find out.

The most desperate thoughts and feelings I have ever had in my entire life consumed my mind during my two-week Christmas leave in December, 1967. My next stop, or duty station, would be Vietnam—that I knew. What exactly it meant to be an infantryman in Vietnam, I had no idea. But the sergeants who had trained us had been there and they all assured us it wasn't something to look forward to. Questions raced through my mind a million miles per hour. Would I be shooting at people who looked like my little Korean sister? Korea was over around there somewhere—I was sure of that. My geography was a bit hazy when it came to discussing the location of countries halfway around the globe. But, being nineteen and willing to learn the fine art of guerrilla-warfare, I was easily led down the path of the Red, White and Blue. My head had been filled with political PR work, believing that if we stopped Communism halfway around the world, we wouldn't end up fighting them on our back doorsteps. The fact that Cuba was Communist and a mere ninety miles off the coast of Florida never entered my mind, as I learned to refer to the Vietnamese people as gooks and dinks and other sub-human names. It was part of the political campaign to convince us that we wouldn't actually be killing other human beings, just gooks and dinks. The same type of brainwashing took place in the training of soldiers in all wars preceding Vietnam, hence the "Krauts" and "Nips" and "Slant-eyes" in WWII. We were made to believe that if we only killed these names, we weren't really killing other humans. Now we must move on to the Big One, WW-Nam. The reason I signed up for the Army was—out of boredom—and for the adventure. The adventure turned out to be much more than I had bargained for, to say the least! Maybe *unforgettable* would be a more appropriate description!

On New Year's Eve of 1967, I boarded a plane at Fort Lewis, Washington with guys I had trained with, on our way to Vietnam. We arrived in Cam Ranh Bay on the second day of 1968. At formation the following morning we were all handed orders to our new unit—Delta Company, 4th of the 31st Infantry, 196th Light Infantry Brigade, stationed out of Chu Lai. We would be going to Chu Lai for our one-week in-country training, as the Americal Division was stationed there. One other significant event happened in that formation that morning. The sergeant in charge nicknamed me Gomez, from the character in the TV show "The Adams Family." Since all of the guys in the formation heard the sergeant refer to me as Gomez, the name stuck throughout my Vietnam tour. Our week of in-country training taught us how much we hadn't been taught in jungle school stateside.

When we arrived at our company area, we were informed that Delta Company had recently been hit and we would be replacing the casualties they had sustained. We all wondered if it was a good idea to join a combat unit which had just lost thirty-plus men, but the choice wasn't ours to make. We were informed by some old timers who happened to be around the company area that this next year would be the *worst* year of our lives, even if we survived it. We were issued a rucksack and poncho and poncho liner, three canteens, a pistol belt with ammo pouches and a first-aid bandage, an entrenching tool, and our M-16s. We were told that we would be issued frag and smoke grenades and ammo for our M-16s once we got out to our company. We were warned not to take anything with us that we didn't want to carry on our backs every day. I immediately put the tape recorder that I had received for Christmas in my foot locker for safe keeping along with my dress clothes. The only other advice we got was not to write things home that might make our families worry about us. We weren't quite sure what that meant, but assured the first-sergeant that we would comply with his orders, for a while anyway.

On the 16th of January we were choppered out to our battalion's fire-support base, Hill 445 in the Que Son Valley. As soon as we got off the choppers we were assigned to our respective platoons and squads. The Old Timers looked at us like we were morons who would never make it back home. We looked at them as if they were animals, and they were, for the most part. They showed us exactly what we had to do to survive. They were the teachers and we were the students. If you didn't pay attention, you wouldn't last long here at the Vietnam Vo-Tech, out in the bush. There were certain unspoken rules in the bush that were unforgivable to bend or break. Falling asleep on guard duty at night was inexcusable—it couldn't and didn't happen more than once! There were still dead NVA soldiers tangled in the wire around the perimeter and I remember taking a good look at them to see what I would be like if I wasn't careful over here. Us *New Meat* were on probation and we knew it!

We were replaced by another infantry company on Hill 445 after a week and we walked away from the security of the firebase. Our daily routine consisted of humping all day every day with our only breaks being to search a ville now and then. Our bodies began to ache all over. The first three days we humped all day and dug foxholes. When we reached the hill we had picked for a night-logger, I was so tired that I wished that I were dead. All three nights when I was awakened for guard duty, I was still holding on to the inflator gadget on my air-mattress. I had passed out trying to blow it up. The next day the air mattress got thrown on a chopper when we got resupplied because I wasn't going to carry anything I wasn't using. We found out that New Meat got to carry all the extras like claymore mines, trip-flares and extra machine-gun ammo, in boxes, not around our shoulders like the movies. We were told the ammo would get dirty and jam the M-60s. The rugged daily routine and not receiving any mail for the first month or so weighed heavily on us New Meat. I often wondered if any of us would ever make it home.

The Old Timers were a bunch of combat-hardened veterans who knew their shit. They became our heroes for having just survived as long as they had so far. I often wondered if I would ever enter the world of being a Short Timer. They had certain privileges like not having to walk point with only a couple weeks left in-country, and we all envied them tremendously. One thing we couldn't yet understand was the look in their eyes. Now it is referred to as the thousand-yard stare. They could talk to you and look right through you, and the mountain behind you. Never a day went by between mid-January and Mid-June that someone didn't start a rumor about us going in for a rest, or stand-down, as the Army called it. All of the dreams about taking a shower, eating hot chow and sleeping up off the ground became broken promises.

Each promise was broken with the same excuse—"The Enemy Situation." That phrase eventually came to mean absolutely nothing to us, as we often thought that we might end up humping our heavy rucksacks until a chopper came out to take us to the rear to go home. Would any of us actually be alive a year from now? It sure didn't seem like it in that place and time. We were in a life-and-death situation every day.

In February our company got ambushed and we lost our commanding officer and two more wounded and one dead. They were loaded onto a dust-off (med-evac) chopper and out of our lives forever. By now everyone called me Gomez and the Old Timers had added "Go Go" so at that point I became Go Go Gomez. Go Go was a different person than Dan Henning, and I had to make some major adjustments in my every way of thinking, including turning off my emotions. A few other guys stepped on booby-trapped mines as we entered the Antenna Valley in March. During Easter weekend we made contact in a big ville on a river. We were linked up with our Bravo Company, which lost about fifteen guys as we began to sweep through the ville. That evening after we had searched the ville, as we were setting up our night-logger, our senior aid man lit some C-4 (plastic explosive) to warm up his C-rations. His fire was greeted with a burst of AK-47 rounds and he took five rounds to the neck/throat area when the NVA sprayed our hill. Doc Burroughs was the ranking medic and he came in from the ambush platoon position to assist another platoon medic with the field trach being given to our ex-senior aid man. We took turns breathing down his tube while we waited for the dust-off to pick him up. As the med-evac approached our hill we held him on a poncho ready to lift into the chopper while still taking turns breathing down his tube. The chopper knocked us over while trying to land and we dropped him but we picked him back up and loaded him on the chopper along with a couple guys from my platoon who had been hit by the same AK-47 burst. We heard later that our efforts had been in vain as the senior aid man didn't make it back to our battalion aid station at LZ Baldy.

By April us New Meat had three months in-country already and were finally getting in the shape we needed to be in to withstand the punishing daily routine that our new jobs consisted of. In mid-April we were choppered out of our Que Son Valley and flown up west of Da Nang, which was being overrun. Next we got choppered up by Hue, which was also being overrun by the NVA during the Tet Offensive. Our final move north was to Camp Evans, which is near Highway 1. We guarded a bridge and pulled sweeps around Camp Evans. Our last operation at Camp Evans was to be the blocking force for the First Cav. as they drove the southeastern end of the A Shau Valley for NVA. We were the first to talk to them as they came out of the A Shau and they told us about being fired on by a Russian tank. The siege at Khe Sanh was over now and our latest rumor said we were going back to Chu Lai to guard the airstrip. Of course that was nonsense and we found ourselves back in the Que Son Valley the next day.

It was mid-May now and we remembered Hill 445 being bombed once we left, to render our bunkers useless to the NVA in our absence. By the time we got there, Hill 445 was secured and our job was to re-take the rest of the valley. Off we went, humping up and down the hills and across the rice paddies. We were met by mortar rounds about noon one day as we cleared the top of a small hill at the far end of the valley. We had no foxholes and had to dig some deep ones quick. We called in gunships, bombers and artillery from Hill 445. We continued to get mortared for three days before our colonel decided that Bravo Company would try and take Hill 102 that night. They were down on the knoll of the hill we were on and only about 500 meters from the base of Hill 102. They would assault it that night. They did and were repelled by machine gun fire which kept them pinned down all night. The bombing continued all night and into the morning. When it began to get light out, the jets dropped a smoke screen so Bravo Company could pull back off the crest of Hill 102. Once they got off Hill 102 they were choppered up to Hill 445 to secure it, because they had suffered a lot of casualties the night before.

At noon the next day we took Hill 102 without a fight and the NVA had radio wire running from bunker to bunker and barbed wire around the crest of the hill. The following morning my platoon began a sweep off the jungle side of Hill 102 and it was my squad's day to walk point. The pointman accidentally hit a bees nest with his machete and they were all over us. We were wedged into the jungle by the trail we had cut and there was no way out. Everybody got stung quite a bit but my left eye was swollen shut and my face, neck and arms were full of stings and I even had some in my mouth from yelling for everyone to pop smoke in hopes of suffocating the bees. I went up to Hill 445 for a couple days to let the swelling go down. The day I returned to Hill 102 I was reading my mail and talking to my buddies when a mortar round landed about five feet in front of us. My best buddy and I both got hit with shrapnel in the head and a new guy who was walking up the hill behind us took shrapnel in the back and legs. My buddy, 2-2, and I both jumped on a resupply chopper, which took us to the battalion aid station at LZ Baldy to get stitched up. The next day we were sent back out to Hill 445 to rest up for five days before re-joining our company in the field. I never saw the new guy again, until next year while I was stationed at Fort Carson, Colorado. He had recovered and was doing good. My friend and I had been wounded on the 24th of May and were back out in the field with our company before the end of May. I remember writing home and telling them it was too bad you had to get hit to get a rest with our outfit.

Early in June we had re-taken most of our Que Son Valley and there seemed to be a lull in the action. We still hadn't been given a rest yet. And then it happened. On the 13th of June we were choppered back to our "Permanent" base camp for a three-day stand-down. We all thought being out in the field was the worst place in the world, but we soon found out that being in the rear allowed us too much time to think. Out in the field all of our time was spent concentrating on surviving, but back in the rear we had way too much time to think about how much time we had left in the field. It was a vicious circle. We thought we longed to be in the rear, but once we got back there, depression set in and we longed to be back out in the bush. We felt much more at ease away from the lifers and back out in the field where we belonged—out in the bush with the rest of the animals. We were at home back out humping our gear every day all day.

The biggest treat for me in Chu Lai was sitting in the USO listening to the jukebox and eating ice cream, although I did enjoy the hot chow, cots and showers, too. All the things we desired in life out in the field were things most Americans took for granted. Slowly but surely we began to question the United States' intentions, the significance of the war and our own force's strategies. We couldn't help but doubt our strategy of giving up the Que Son Valley and then having to re-take it a month later. Were the lives of our buddies being lost in vain? Were we really saving these people from Communism? It sure didn't appear that we were accomplishing our goals if, in fact, that's what our goals were. We began to feel like we were expendable and could be replaced if need be. We always read the "Stars & Stripes" KIA list and knew that a lot of guys were being replaced daily throughout Vietnam. Oh, well, we were back in the field before we even realized it and there was no time to question the politics of this war out in the bush.

The end of June finally arrived and I had been here six months already. Six months down and six more to go. Our bunch were the Old Timers now and the New Meat that arrived looked at us like we were some kind of animals. We looked at them like they were morons who would never make it back to The World.

Shortly after the Fourth of July we humped out of the Que Son Valley to a new AO (area of operation) which turned out to be in a rain forest with a triple canopy. This triple canopy was new to us and the tiny amount of daylight that filtered through seemed threatening to us. We humped around the mountains through the rain forest for a week before we were ordered to cut a trail off the western side. This trail would lead us to the bottom and a huge river. It took us four days to cut our trail to the bottom, where we found the river and a huge NVA trail running alongside of it, complete with bamboo bridges across the dry-runs coming down from the mountains. We also found a shack with spare bicycle parts but no one was home when we got there. We followed this trail for a couple weeks before we were choppered back to the far end of the Que Son Valley again. We began building a small firebase, clearing away brush, building bunkers and laying wire around the crest of the hill. We secured the hill for the artillery and mortars that were brought in by choppers while we pulled sweeps around the area each day. This hill was named LZ Gimlet.

The month of August was unusually quiet for us as we stayed at Gimlet, which overlooked a river. I went to Australia late in August and my company was still at LZ Gimlet when I returned in early September. Shortly, we were replaced by another infantry company and we humped across the valley and began building another small firebase named LZ West, which took the better part of September.

Around the first of October we were on the move again, chasing our elusive enemy, the NVA. On the 6th of October, after being out of C-rations for the third day, we got resupplied. I received a box from my mother with an Angel Food cake and other goodies for my twentieth birthday. It was the most delicious food I have ever tasted, before or after. My birthday wasn't until the next day but no one heard me complaining. We had been eating pineapples, bananas and sugarcane to keep us going. We kept on humping and following the generous tips supplied to us by our colonel, which brought us fairly close to the Laotian border. Since we only had our grid-square maps to call in support, no one actually knew where we were in reference to Laos or any other country. Our location was always a deep, dark secret, something that wouldn't interest us grunts anyway. Our job was to flush the enemy.

We were supposed to draw enemy fire and have our dead and wounded ready to load on the Dust-offs when they reached our position. Nothing more and nothing less. If this wasn't the case, why then did we walk single file across rice paddy dikes which were surrounded by perfect ambush positions? One hundred-plus American kids walking across rice paddy dikes surrounded by woods and jungle on all sides made us sitting ducks for the NVA. After we had drawn fire, or "made contact," as the Army called it, then they brought in the gunships and bombers. Once the ambush position was silenced, next came the dust-offs to pick up our dead and wounded. After we had sent our KIAs and WIAs to the rear, all that was left out in the field were the "Walking Dead" who had been lucky. The Old Timers with the thousand-yard stares and the New Meat, always in a state of shock and mystified that any of us were still alive, knew full-well that none of us had any guarantee that we would be alive tomorrow.

The first time a guy in your squad got hit was a big event. I remember when Duke, my second squad leader, hit a booby-trap up north in April. It hit me hard. I helped Duke on the chopper and as it was taking off I got my Zippo out and torched a couple of hooches in the ville. I did it for Duke. Of course it was misplaced aggression, but wasn't that what Nam was all about? I knew the people who lived in those hooches probably hadn't set those booby-traps, but I had to do something to avenge my loss of Duke. Duke was a big soul brother who had taken me under his wing and to lose Duke was a gigantic loss. After there were only two of you left out of your original squad, it wasn't such a monumental event to lose a guy or two from your squad. But losing Duke, my first, really tore me up. You knew you had to go on and the best way to be able to do that was to turn off all of your emotions and just not give a shit about anything that happened anymore. It seemed to be a natural defense mechanism.

Early in November we went back to Hill 445 to build new bunkers before the monsoon season set in again. After two weeks of building bunkers we were replaced by another company and took off humping again. Our colonel assured us that there was an NVA base camp somewhere in the mountains that would be our new AO. Once we reached the mountain range we found a big trail and began following it and getting ambushed about once a day. The farther into the mountains we humped, the more we began to get ambushed. We trudged on, hoping not to find anything, as our bunch was getting *short*.

On December 1 we were ambushed and I lost a close friend. He was a Mexican-American kid from Texas and one of our original bunch who had come to Delta Company with me. The triple canopy we had encountered prevented the dust-off from landing, so they lowered a wench through the jungle canopy and pulled his body up to the chopper. His face was black as they lifted his body up to the chopper. Even with my emotions being turned off for the past eleven months, I cried for Ray, who I believed had died for nothing in the stupid game they called war. His DEROS was the same as mine, 30 December, which meant he died with only twenty-nine days left in the country and rumor had it we were going to get a drop and make it home for Christmas. Those bullets didn't care how long you'd been in Nam or how long you had left and his death haunted me immensely.

A few days later the point squad from another platoon found two NVA shaving in a small stream and shot at them. They wounded them but they escaped up the trail into the mountains. We followed the blood trails, which split at a Y in the trail further up in the mountains. We split up and both point squads got ambushed within minutes, so our colonel told us to pull back three miles so the B-52s could come in that night and do what they should have done to begin with. All night the B-52s pounded the area where we had found the trails. It felt like an earthquake as the ground shook underneath us as we tried to sleep.

The next morning our orders were to return to the area and see if there was anything left. It was my platoon's day to walk point and my squad's turn also. As we approached the small stream where the two NVA had been shaving the day before, Fast Eddie, the pointman, stopped to listen. It was the perfect place for an ambush because the trail went straight up once we crossed the stream. I was behind him with my M-79 and as his first boot hit the water they opened up on us from above and off to our right. Our whole squad hit the dirt behind some boulders and began yelling to see if anyone had been hit. Everyone said they were okay, but I could see blood on the new sergeant's face who was behind me. After the gunships had come in and sprayed the area, we pulled back and all three of us had holes shot in our rusksacks, canteens and other gear we were wearing. The new Shake-N-Bake sergeant's face had been cut by chips of rock from the bullets hitting the boulders we were hiding behind. He didn't even know he was bleeding he was so scared, as were the rest of us. Another platoon took over walking point and we didn't get ambushed anymore on our way up to the NVA base camp. The Y in the trail went to a hospital on one side and a training camp on the other side. The NVA had radio wire running from bunker to bunker and bamboo shoots in their bunkers coming from a stream providing them with running water. None of the villes we had ever been in had running water, but the NVA were resourceful enough to have it way up here in the mountains.

We were pulled out of the area as soon as we blew up all the remaining bunkers that were left in tact after the bombing. As we continued humping to a new AO I began running a high fever at night when we reached our night-logger. A med-evac wasn't allowed to come out to the field at night for someone running a fever. So, our senior aid man, Doc Jackson, a soul brother from Frisco, finally sent me in to have a tooth pulled to get me out of the field before I collapsed in mid-stride. Later the same day, some guys who were securing Hill 445, found me wrapped in my poncho liner under a half culvert freezing to death in the 100-plus degree temperatures. They took me to the aid station and the doctor thought I might have malaria. That evening I caught the last chopper off Hill 445 going to LZ Baldy. A doctor at our battalion aid station there took a blood sample, which turned out positive for malaria. I was moved to a hospital in Chu Lai, where I was informed that I had malaria. A doctor told me the next day that I would be going to

Cam Ranh Bay for a thirty-day rest. I told him I didn't have thirty days left in-country and I sure wasn't gonna extend for a thirty-day rest in Nam! So he got my orders changed to go to Cam Ranh and catch a Freedom Bird back to The World. That seemed to be the best news I had heard in a whole year, or so I thought. I finally knew I had a chance of reaching my twenty-first birthday. I hated to leave my squad, platoon and company out in the field because they were a very big part of me. We had been *our* family for the past year and I felt closer to them than anyone else in the world—they could be trusted!

The following week in Chu Lai and Cam Ranh hospitals gave me some time to reflect on the past year of my life. I began to prepare myself mentally for finally going home. I had a hunch my biggest problem might be integrating back into society, and I was right. When we came off the plane in California we were greeted by people calling us names and I couldn't understand that. It wasn't our war. Why weren't these people in Washington yelling at the *real* culprits, the congressmen who were allowing this war to continue? At that point I wished I still had my M-79 with me, so I could lob a few rounds in their direction. I was beside myself and I came to the realization that "Coming Home" no longer had the same meaning for me as it did when I left Fort Lewis, Washington a year ago. When I went to Vietnam, the phrase "Coming Home" meant to get back into the groove, where you were when you left. But, upon actually returning to the States, it only meant to "Get Out Alive." When the definition of a phrase changes that drastically in one year, you do an about-face and never "Come Home" in the traditional sense. You are always "Still There" and never able to revert back to the person you were before you left home. Even if that phrase has been your only hope for the past 366 days (leap year). At that point, even coming home seemed to be for naught.

When your government sends you out to be killed at the tender age of nineteen and you survive the ordeal, it still makes you feel like your life is worthless. Once your country shows you that you are expendable, you begin to believe it and it makes you bitter toward the government and everyone else around you. The next step is when your feelings of worthlessness begin to merge with feelings of helplessness and despair. At this point depression sets in and the person reaches out for help. Usually to the wrong places, such as alcohol and drugs, which only deaden the individual's perception and can make them suicidal. If you don't believe me, check out the statistics for the suicide rate among Vietnam vets. The reason for turning to drugs and alcohol is simple. In combat you learned to turn off your emotions and, having never learned to turn them back on, it's much easier to reach out for a non-emotional fix rather than people, who wouldn't or couldn't understand anyway. The people who shunned us—why ask them for any help after the way they had treated us?

When I got back to Lake City, Minnesota on the 21st of December, 1968, the thing I wished for more than any Christmas presents, was for someone, anyone, to ask me what I had experienced in Vietnam. But no one seemed to think it was important. All I heard was, "Merry Christmas, I'll bet you're glad to be home. Just forget about all that stuff going on over there." Stuff going on over there. Were they referring to all the kids coming home in body bags? The political smoke screen had worked. The general public thought all that was going on over in Nam was a little police-action. The Pentagon Papers hadn't been leaked yet, so the extensive casualty rate was not yet known by the general public. They said to forget the last year of my life, so I did for a while.

This is where Post Traumatic Stress comes into play. PTSD is what is left of the human mind once the combat experience is over. Combat experience is a double-edged sword, an ordeal that can either be stuffed into a body bag with your remains, or a disgusting, revolting horror show that you take home in your mind for the rest of your life. Combat experience is half physical reaction that warns you to hit the dirt or take over, and half psychological response which allows you to turn off your emotions while you continue to fight and keep presence of mind after the guy beside you has just had his leg or head blown off. A human being can easily be trained to be a combat soldier by turning off his emotions, but the rather typical problem of turning their emotions back on once the experience is over remains to be a mystery which baffles medical experts yet today. The "Bottom Line" is: *you had to be there!*

No amount of debriefing can erase the terror and feelings of despair that combat experience leaves a person with, let alone the vivid, color pictures of your friends bleeding to death while you were unable to help them. Holding a buddy in your arms while you watch blood gurgle out of his nose and mouth and knowing there isn't one God Damn thing you can do to save his life, is the most worthless feeling any human being can ever experience—barring *none!* Half of your mind wonders how long it will take the dust-off to reach your position to take your friend back to an aid station. The other half of your mind knows you have to lay him down on the ground while you continue to hold your position so it doesn't get overrun, which would mean certain death for your entire outfit. The choice is almost impossible to imagine for someone who has not experienced it. These are the choices that young soldiers are forced to make under the most difficult circumstances. They regret each choice they make for the rest of their lives, no matter what it was.

The extreme and unbearable confusion and deafening noise of combat, including the whistling of incoming mortars and the blasts they make as they explode all around you, and the small-arms fire continually racking your brain, make thinking, as we know it, virtually impossible. The full spectrum of combat experience can be found in any veteran's cemetery, from the seasoned combat veteran to the teenager who was killed in his first firefight on his first day in the field. I saw both types die in Vietnam and they were both brave men. Once you're dead, combat experience means nothing. Neither does the Purple Heart that your family receives at your funeral.

1991 will be my twenty-third year on the run since I returned from Vietnam. I was honorably discharged from the Army in 1970 after three years of service. Since then I have had two marriages break up and many other relationships go sour and jobs too numerous to mention. I have lived in Arizona, Colorado and Minnesota, each more than once. I attended college for three and a half years during the '70s, carrying a 3.5 GPA while taking political science, psychology and creative writing. I learned all I could about the domestic and foreign policies of our government while in college and finally gave up. I drank heavy for ten years before I decided that being intoxicated wasn't gonna help me out of my dilemma. I have "almost" quit at the present time, but I still like to have a few beers and talk to a Nam vet about our individual experiences in that faraway place many years ago.

Last fall (Sept. 90) a doctor who is also a Vietnam vet recommended that I go through the PTSD program at the VAMC in St. Cloud, Minnesota, so I did. The doctor in charge of the PTSD program also diagnosed me with PTSD and I attended group therapy for three weeks. I had to leave as I had rent to pay, etc. I had filed for a PTSD disability claim in August of 1990 and was contacted by the VA administration in December informing me to come to the VA hospital in Minneapolis for a physical. I talked to a doctor who almost dozed off during our fifteen-minute meeting on January 4, 1991. I received a notice in March that I was being denied any disability compensation for my PTSD claim. I was outraged and immediately sat down and wrote a letter requesting a personal appeal hearing as soon as possible. I told them that since I had been diagnosed by two doctors as having PTSD, one of them being the doctor in charge of the PTSD program at the VAMC in St. Cloud, Minnesota, that I wanted to know what evaluation they were using in determining that I was not suffering from PTSD. I then asked if both of the doctors that diagnosed me with PTSD were wrong or they merely overlooked their diagnosis and went with the doctor who dozed off while he talked to me during my formal physical. I went on to inform them that I personally knew of cases of truck drivers and a dental technician who did *not* see combat in Vietnam, but were receiving PTSD disability payments. I told them I wanted to find out if their decisions of awarding disabilities to persons who saw no combat was consistent with denying awards to *real* combat veterans who spent their entire tour out in the bush. I went on to say that if this was the case, their priorities were severely inadequate and unfair for actual combat veterans. I then asked if anyone who had worked on my case, including "their" doctor, were themselves combat veterans?

I finally got so fucking mad that I ended the letter with this final paragraph:

"Oh, Fuck it. Just give my disability rating to some Candy-Ass, Chickenshit mail clerk who was stationed at the R&R center in Vung Tao. . . . I'm sure he had a hard time readjusting to civilian life after sorting mail and drinking beer for a whole year. Mailrooms have always been a constant source of Traumatic Stress, we all know that! *Fuck you cock-suckers!* SGT. GO GO GOMEZ"

As you might have guessed, I didn't send that letter, but I should have. I was too easy on them the second time around. To make a long story longer, I had an appeal hearing on April third, 1991 and am now waiting to see if I will have to go to Washington for my Final Appeal Hearing. Or, if they would rather deal with my problem here and now. I don't think they want a person with my attitude walking around Washington complaining about the VA administration in Minnesota. But if that's what they want, I'm *Ready To Go!* It's their choice!

I have recently located some of the guys who were in my company in Nam and am planning on going to a 196th Light Infantry Brigade reunion sometime this year.

The original chapter that I submitted for this book was a condensed version of a manuscript containing the letters I wrote home while in Vietnam. I edited out all the family jargon trying to reduce it to a chapter-size manuscript, but it was still too long for use in this book. I hope it will be published because it is so raw, so literal. It begins with complete naivete, soon to be replaced by very bitter anger and resentment. Friends of mine who have read all or part of my manuscript have commented on the daily life of a grunt (infantryman) being so drastically different from the Vietnam movies they have seen. All I can say is, "Who ya gonna believe, Me or Rambo? I was in Nam, and he was in Hollywood."

Postscript: When I was stationed in Fort Carson, Colorado in 1969, I was playing basketball by my garage one day with some friends and a big car pulled up. All I could see was the top of a black guy's head. So I walked over to the car and a familiar voice said, "Gomez, what in the hell are you doin' here?" I knew the voice well and when the driver sat up it was my Main Man Duke, who had hit the booby-trap the year before. He wasn't permanently disabled and I was happy for him. It was great to see him again and we had a nice long talk about his wounds, etc.

Denver's City Park brought my next pleasant surprise in January of 1973. I was at the park with a friend and we were taking a break from playing frisbee. A guy across the park by the lake was running wind sprints and then walking back to his car. I told my friend I knew who the guy was, but she was quick to point out that was impossible because we were too far away to see his face. I told her I knew who it was by the way he walked because I had watched him walk for six months every day in Vietnam. I walked toward his car as he was walking back to it and when we got close enough to see each other's face, he yelled, "Gomez" and came running over and gave me a big hug. It was Angie, my first teacher in Vietnam. I was so happy I almost cried. Angie had always been such a big inspiration to me when I first arrived out in the field. It was a very special moment for me that I'll never forget. Angie was an Old Timer when I got to Delta Company and that made him one of my special heroes.

One last reunion that was very dear to me was when the friend I had gone to California with in January of 1967 came to visit me in Colorado when he returned from Vietnam in December of 1969. He had gone to Nam from Germany and was stationed in Saigon as a clerk. On the 25th of May, 1968 he was typing up a morning report for an infantry company and he saw that he was typing my name as having been wounded in action. Small world indeed. He had transferred from being a clerk to being a door-gunner on a chopper and had extended in Nam to get an early-out from the Army. He and I are still close friends although he lives in Wyoming and I in Minnesota.

There is a special bond between Nam vets that is very concrete and predictable. My guess is, because we fought the unpopular Vietnam War together and then returned home only to find out that our efforts had been in vain, and not appreciated by the general public . . . whose freedom we had been told we were fighting for. We were shown *no* appreciation whatsoever and shunned, to boot! Now ask yourself, if you were in our place, how would you feel about life in general, and the United States government? Would you feel betrayed? I think so.

Richard Hawk

I was born in Washburn, Illinois July 31, 1947. I lived there for about five years and then we moved out to Sisseton, South Dakota. There my dad got fixed up with a job with the banker taking care of his livestock. There was my mom, my dad, my brother and a sister born later, in 1958. We farmed where my dad took care of the livestock on the 240-acre farm. I went to country school and graduated from there in the eighth grade. When I was on the farm at Sisseton, my mother made sure that we went to church every Sunday. I was brought up in the Episcopalian faith. We weren't a rich family, but we weren't poor. We had three square meals a day and that was all we could expect at that time. I think I had a happy childhood. My dad made sure that we all had things to do. We went to 4-H every month, so we weren't isolated from other people.

After grade school in the country, I went to Sisseton for high school. Things were different. You could tell that the kids from town thought you were different since you were from the farm. I tried out for basketball one year, but didn't make it. That was because the kids that lived in town had practiced basketball while growing up and I didn't have that opportunity in the country. There was no basketball court available and I had chores to do. That was furthest from my mind.

I graduated in 1965 as an average student. Of course, I got A's in my ag classes and belonged to FFA all four years. After I graduated, I did labor work for the school. It was cement work for a new school they were building in Sisseton. In the spring of 1966 I went to school at Brookings, South Dakota for a semester. Then they come out with the deferment. I was to go to Huron to take my test to get my deferment. I felt it was too far to go, so I didn't do it. So, my draft notice came in July or August of that year and I was inducted on October 22, 1966. The induction was at Sioux Falls, South Dakota.

From there I went to Fort Bliss, Texas. We got our haircuts, shaves and first indoctrination into the military. Six of us were drafted from my county I had graduated from high school with, but we were broken up then. After Fort Bliss I wound up at Fort Riley, Kansas, where I took my basic training and my AIT. Basic training was two months and AIT was another six months. Just before we were ready to take our tests to finish basic and start AIT, it turned very cold. They had made us almost strip down, with no gloves on, to take our final tests. A lot of the guys got frostbitten fingertips. I had been raised in a colder climate, so it didn't bother me. When we did the low crawl on the ground, there were a lot of sand burrs that would dig into your clothes and just wipe the shit out of ya. That was one of the things that stuck out in my mind about basic.

I didn't hear much about Vietnam at the time. Nobody said anything about it during basic. When I got to AIT and I got into armored training, they started to drill it into our heads that we were either going to the Middle East or to Vietnam. At that time they had that six-day war in the Middle East. My first orders for Vietnam came in May 1967. About two-thirds of us from my battalion were on the levee for Vietnam. They were starting a big build up in Vietnam at the time.

I finally got to Vietnam in late July 1967 and landed in the Long Binh airport or Bien Hoa, I don't remember which. I noticed when I left Watertown, South Dakota there was a Spec-5 in the seat across from me. You could tell he was frightened and almost had tears in his eyes because he was headed for Vietnam. To this day it bothers me wondering whatever happened to him. He kind of put me on edge, because I didn't know anything at all about what to expect. I hadn't even had contact with anybody that had been there and I think he had probably been there before.

When I arrived there I looked out the window of the plane and saw the craters from bombings all around the airport. It was hot and muggy. I had never experienced the humidity and the smells that I smelled in Vietnam.

My first duty station was at Cu Chi with the 25th Division. My first orders had said 11th Armored. The unit that I ended up with at Cu Chi, the 3/4 Cav, had been in a bad ambush in late June and I was one of the replacements for the guys killed that day. Nine were killed and twelve wounded. It was a real shock to arrive there. Our main mission was to provide road security for the road between Cu Ci and Dau Tieng and Tay Ninh, where we ran convoys during the day. That was my early mission, but we always ran into booby traps and mines. We ran convoys at night to try to make contact with the enemy. If there was any enemy activity, lots of times we would get fired at with RPGs, sometimes small arms-fire, and sniped at. This was in July and August of 1967.

We lost guys now and then, one here and one there. Many of them were able to return to the unit. Near Christmas time, the story changed. We pulled more sweeps and we started getting into more contact with the enemy. On Christmas day we were up in the Hobo Woods. We were to be a blocking force for the local force. There was a route through the bush that had been cleared out and it had grown back up to shoulder-high weeds about fifty feet off the edge of the road—there was nothing but jungle. We had a little bit of contact with the enemy forces before. We found rice caches in the bush down by the river. A couple days before Christmas the ARVNs had been down in the river. They had been down there swimming just like nothing was going on. They left us then and had left the area. On Christmas day, it was supposed to be a cease-fire day, someone had spotted some enemy activity. They had to call headquarters to get clearance to take it under fire. Just as they were getting clearance, there was an RPG fired at one of the guys that I knew. It fell short of him and then all shit hit the fan. After we thought that we had taken care of everything, we made a check into the edge of the jungle and found brand new graves and foxholes and they were just freshly dug. We didn't go back in any further to see if there was any more or anything else there. We went back to our positions along the road and about 3 o'clock I glanced out the corner of my eye. I saw the head of a Charlie sticking out above the weeds. That day I was manning a 30-caliber machine gun. I picked it up and emptied a 100-round belt right into the edge of the woodline. Without stopping, Sergeant Michaels, our platoon sergeant , called my track commander, Pete Zamora, and asked him what was going on down there. My track commander told my platoon sergeant that his observer spotted some movement. The sergeant told the track commander to get a tank down there and put three main-gun rounds in there. So we got a tank down there and put in the three main-gun rounds and then they cleared out of there.

Another guy from Florida was on the ground with me. We were going to go back in there to see if there was anything in there. I didn't hear anything myself, but I saw my other buddy move away because he thought he heard something and he was scared. I didn't go in myself to check it out and if I would have I probably wouldn't have been here today. Then it was like that until the 20th of January. Tet started and we started getting more contact with the enemy. Third Platoon of my troop was supposed to be on standby. Orders got switched around, so about 10 o'clock at night we had to leave the main gate. Everybody had gone to the club that night because we had had orders to stand down. I stayed back in my living area writing letters home. Someone came in and said we had to move out. For some reason I had a feeling down deep in my stomach that there was something up.

Up until then I had been manning a 30-caliber machine gun on my track and I told Pete we've got to get that 30-caliber back. He said we'd get it back tomorrow. We had lent it out to our ambush squad. They had used it the night before. So, we left base camp and got no more than a quarter of a mile from Cu Chi, just outside the main gate in an open area, and base camp's perimeter was just to my right flank, and there was an open field to my left, and I was on the back end of a personnel carrier. The minute that we got into the ambush site there was a personnel carrier in front of me and four or five more to the front that got hit in the gas tank just like that, and they were burned along with the crews. I was scared and the first thing that was going through my mind was getting hit by human waves. I thought they would end up coming and taking us prisoners. I stayed back with my track just in case anything would happen. These tracks were burned to the front. Then my driver goes to the front to see if he could help anyone. He said Kosel had been hit, that he took a direct hit from an RPG. We had gone through basic training and AIT together and, anyhow . . . David, my driver, says Gene took a direct hit. While this is going on two other guys had been hit and come back to the dust-off area. They had been hit pretty hard themselves. One guy by the name of Lammers, and Dandridge, and both had been hit pretty good. There was a tank to my rear and they had been putting out fire themselves. While all this was going on we had been receiving tracer rounds from base camp and base camp didn't even know what was going on. Anyhow, the headquarters sent out people to clear the area and we went back to base camp.

We couldn't communicate with anybody and weren't allowed to see anybody, so the next day, what was left of us had to go back to the field. The military didn't provide us any kind of psychiatric help or any chaplain or anybody. That's the way Vietnam was. But they took us back to base camp and after all the casualties we took, it got to be the next day and we found out there had been nine guys killed. One was named Klippen, who was a lumberjack up in Michigan. His birthday was the same day as mine and we got to talking about hunting bear and I would talk about hunting deer. We had this to support each other. Hell of a nice guy. They all were. That night, that just took the wind out of me and I've never been the same since.

In October I remember I had run across a sweet-corn patch at the edge of a village. I was gettin' lonesome for some home cookin', so I went in and grabbed me about a half a dozen ears of sweet corn and it was gettin' late in the evening. I took 'em back and threw 'em in a steel pot and put some water in it. Then I got some C-4, which is plastic explosive, and I used that to start a fire, and then I went to the cook and asked him for some butter. He was wondering what I wanted the butter for and I let him know that I was fixin' some roastin' ears for myself and if he wanted some he'd have to go get them himself. I was just gettin' homesick for some home cookin'. They were good too.

After January and the ambush it took us some time to get reorganized and get back on the ground. To that point we had all gas tracks and they had talked about replacing the gas tracks with diesels. There was always the chance of getting hit in the gas tank with an RPG because it just was an automatic explosion. Out of my platoon we had five personnel carriers and three tanks and in our troop there were three platoons. So we had probably fifteen personnel carriers and nine tanks and we had more fire support ourselves than a lot of the infantry units did. If an infantry outfit got into anything that they couldn't handle, then we had to go in and help 'em out. After Tet happened and we got new guys and got started gettin' organized—we got back on the ground a little—well, things started pickin' up in February. When Tet started, it was like forty-five days straight, out in the field. We didn't have any other clothes. We had maybe one change of clothes the whole week, if we were lucky. We had to wash them in our steel pots to try to clean 'em. We were gone constantly, for about forty-five days straight.

Then we got into Ap Cho, another village not far from base camp. Another mechanized outfit had been in this village for about fifteen days. They would take it during the day, give it back to them at night; take it during the day, give it back to them at night. And I have since found out that the day before we went in there the Catholic Chaplain had given us last rights to go into that village because this mechanized outfit had lost probably better than two-thirds of their unit in there. I remember the morning goin' in. We gave some of these guys a ride back into base camp. One of the guys on the ground when we were goin' back to base camp—the words out of his mouth—"If I see you guys back in the States the beer's on me." He was just glad to be gettin' out of there. I could just feel what he was sayin'. It scared me about what we were gettin' into that day. Anyhow, I'm on a track personnel carrier with a new TC from out of Windom, Minnesota and a new driver. The TC's name was Sergeant Tscherter. And a new guy by the name of Gilbert. He showed up in January. Anyhow, we pull in and we started goin' in on line after we soften the positions—the enemy positions. As we were goin' in on line I have a tank from the Third Platoon on my right. A guy by the name of Jim Doles was riding up on the outside of it. He was tryin' to get my attention to find out where the live fire was comin' from out front. At that time there were guys on his tank gettin' sprayed with machine gun fire. As this is all happening and Sergeant Tscherter gets hit in the chest on both sides and his hands go up and his helmet goes back and I'm in back of him and the next thing I know the driver jumps and spins around and he's comin' back at me and he is yelling that Sergeant Tscherter's been hit. So I get out of his way and he gets behind the cupola of the personnel carrier to try to help Sergeant Tscherter, but instead he should of stayed in the driver's hatch. The next thing I know this guy is lying down in the back end of personnel carrier. He'd been hit with machine gun fire. He was unconscious. I didn't know how to drive the personnel carrier. I got in the cupola and tried to get it outta there, but I couldn't get it outta there so I could get these guys to dust-off. This other new guy, Gilbert, finally gets in the hatch and he finally gets it so we can get it outta there. And while this is happening, there's a new E-6 breakin' under fire and running and ends up on my track and I got two guys down and I can't do anything for them. There were some other guys that had threatened to shoot him too. Finally we got these guys back to the goddamned dust-off area. Sergeant Tscherter—I don't know if he made it to the hospital or not, but he died later that day. The driver—I don't know if he made it or not.

Anyhow, they gave me a new guy by the name of Hogan to man the vehicle. We continue our sweep on to the edge of the village. We took a lot of casualties ourselves. To this day I don't know how many because it was havoc in there—it was just pure hell. There was a tank from Charlie troop that had been in there earlier and had been knocked out by a recoilless rifle in that village that nobody had found. So, we were lookin' for that too, because a recoilless rifle, when it hits a tank, it takes everything out. They had left the guys on the tank, the ones the Charlie troops had lost in the village. I could still see that tank sittin' there in the middle of the village, all burned out.

We continued our sweep to the edge of the village and there's guys on the ground tryin' to blow up bunkers and this, that and the other. One guy by the name of Whitey, he was from California. He was originally from Minnesota. I noticed him grabbin' at his hind cheeks because he had been blowin' bunkers and got some shrapnel in his hind quarters. I guess its just a burning sensation, but we continued on. There were gooks layin' all over—dead bodies from the days before. It was just pure hell. And then we got to the edge of the village and there was another mechanized unit in there on line. I don't know whose they were. But there were personnel carriers lined up at the edge of the village and each cupola had brass and links and all that piled up from firefight just heaped all around them. There was at least a good dozen tracks lined up and Hogan was tryin' to find a spot to get in on line. And as we get in on line I hear an RPG go over my head. And knowin' what an RPG was like, I hit the ground. I was scared. I was *frightened*.

Pretty soon Hogan orders me to get back on the track to man the 50-caliber. I'm hesitatin', but eventually I finally give in to him and I get back on. He tells me what he wants me to do. He told me he was goin' ahead to take a tank in to knock this bunker out that was to our front. Well, there was a big bomb crater just to my right front, where a big 500-pounder had been dropped. There is just nothing but rubble to our front, where it had been bombed over and over. Hogan gets on the ground and goes to try to get one of our tanks to get in there and knock him out and as he was tryin' to get the tank in there, three infantry tried to come around to my right front. They get sprayed with machine gun fire. How bad they were hit I don't know. I put down a field of fire of five-round bursts and told him to just keep his ass down, then I see this RPG comin' up outta the ground. I saw the round come up, out of the bunker where he was. And then the next thing I see are these goddamned gook heads with North Vietnamese hard hats, one with just a cold stare on his face, and I still can see that stare.

Boy, when I seen his face, I cut loose with that five-round burst.

Hogan tried to get the tank in there while this was happening, but he couldn't get the tank in for some reason or another. He got back on a personnel carrier and came back and I says I think I got a kill, and it looked like a big red spot where his head had been. He says he thought I got a kill and then Hogan starts firing M-79 grenades rounds into the bunker and we get a secondary explosion, which was probably from a rocket. If I would of had my shit together that day, I would of told Hogan to cover my ass and I woulda went in there myself and blowed that bunker, 'cause I feel it shoulda been good for a Silver Star 'cause it was holding up the whole goddamned troop and some more armor.

But after what I'd been through from the 20th of January to the 14th and all the other firefights in between, I just couldn't do the job. It was enough just to be there. Physically I was there, but mentally I don't think I was. You had to depend on these guys better than your own brothers and sisters. Like from January 20th to the ambush, there ain't a day that goes by that I'm not thinkin' about it.

There was one day in April, after the ambush, we were makin' a sweep through the jungle. Either the Ho Bo or the Boi Loi. Third Platoon had spotted some goddanged gooks trying to get around to their rear to outflank them. This is damned jungle that had been knocked down by Roman Plows, big five-pound links of chain tied between bulldozers and pulled by tracks. It was just nothin' but rubble. It had been bulldozed and cleared and the Vietnamese had dug into it. We were makin' a sweep through this. My platoon leader from the night of the ambush was there. Someone caught them trying to outflank the Third Platoon. We maneuvered into a firing position. I was on a tank this time. I was down inside loadin'. DePew, my track commander, was tryin' to get in to a position so he could get lined up with a bunker right to our left front. We were gettin' some light 50-caliber machine gun fire from it—'cause a new guy riding up on the outside got sprayed in the throat. DePew had tried to get positioned so we could knock it out in the process. He backed into a 500-pound bomb crater. It jarred the shit out of my back and everything. I thank the good Lord that he did it 'cause an RPG coulda come through the tank that day and got me, 'cause we were knocked outta commission. I tried to knock this bunker out with some LAWs, which is a light rocket for an infantry outfit. I tried three of them sun-of-a-guns and I couldn't get them to operate. We were just down in that bunker and that was it. Pete Zamora, the guy whose track I'd been in before—he was trying to get me to where this was coming from.

We finally got the fire cleared up. We started searchin' bunkers and everything and I got to one bunker and I found a brand new M-79 grenade launcher laying in one of these bunkers that had been blowed all to hell with probably a grenade or C-4 charge. Headquarters wanted to blow 27 into that bomb crater, but we had to get a tank retriever in there to pull it out, 'cause we didn't want to blow it in there. We couldn't get out of there by ourselves. It happened to be, or so I was told, that this enemy unit that we had been in contact with that day was the same unit that had hit us outside base camp on the 20th of January.

There were some more firefights that we were in, I can remember plain as day, but the locations coulda been in Cambodia, inside the Cambodian border—I don't know. Another day in May, the troop had three helicopters shot down—gunships—right in a row. I don't know why we got drug in there that day. I can remember a part of a napalm bomb laying out to the front of us that had been dropped but didn't rupture. It didn't blow up like it should when it hit the ground. As we were gettin' in there to go on line to do what we had to do in there, there were ox carts comin' by with bodies loaded on them. Body after body after body. Who was in there before we were, I don't know. I don't know if it was from what the air force had done or not. When we went in there that one day, when the three choppers were shot down, we had to go in and get the crews out. We were gettin' a lot of live fire early in the day. We got the crews out. I don't know what the casualties were. We cleared out the live fire and we went into our logger position, the normal position we went into, a wagon-wheel formation for our own protection, for night position. I was so goddamned tired and beat. I had stripped down the M-60 machine gun that I had been mannin'. Pretty soon I wake up and see a track in the middle of the perimeter burnin'. A Headquarters track. I don't know what the hell had happened. I was so drained and so tired. All I had left was an M-16 'cause my 60 was in parts 'cause I was cleaning it. Pete Zamora, my track commander, told me to put some fire out to the front 'cause there was a hooch out to the front. There were bombers coming in with 40-mm cannon fire, with loud crackin' sounds around the perimeter, to try to break up what was goin' on out there. It was just a scary damned feeling that night. Like I say, with that place, I don't remember where it was, but I remember it just as clear as day.

The first time you see death like that—I remember one guy that died on the night of the ambush. One of the remarks out of his mouth was what would you do if you saw mamasan or babysan out there with an AK-47. He was an orphan and he had a hard life himself. But after he went through that ambush and him saying what would I do if I'd seen a woman or anyone with and AK-47—or anything—like I say, I would give him a second chance. But after goin' through this ambush, if I seen anybody that looked like a threat to me, I was goin' to waste them. Without any feelings for it. To see your friends and the guy that you went through basic and AIT with together, it really hurts. Like from the night of the 20th of January, when Henry came to me and said Kosel took a direct hit, that was just like walkin' into the brick wall for me. Then goin' back to base camp and trying to get some sleep that night, they didn't give us any medication to try to calm us down or get rid of any of the anger or fear or whatever we were feelin' from it. We had to deal with it ourselves. Nobody told me to try to forget it or that you gotta put it behind ya. 'Cause I think they were too goddamned afraid and couldn't deal with it themselves.

In May to June it calmed down a little bit for us. We started gettin' a break. Vietnam was still there. It was a threat to me every day. There was no way of gettin' around that for me. Not after what I had been through in January, February, March and April, and I haven't been able to put it aside and I doubt if I ever will be able to put it aside. The military had never been able to let me understand what I was doin' there and they don't want me to understand what I've been through. Like I say, it's somethin' that I gotta deal with every day.

When I was leavin', I got orders and they took me down to Long Binh and for some reason or other I got stuck there for a week because the plane that I was scheduled to get out on had to be used some other way.

Finally there was a couple of guys from the 101st Airborne that I ended up with one night and they took us down, the three of us about 10 o'clock at night, and said you guys catch anything and everything that's able to fly outta here. That's what they told us. We cornered a major at the airport and tried to get some help to get out of there. He got us on a Carribou, a transport, cargo plane and they flew us to Okinawa. When we landed there, they told us to take our bags, 'cause this is the end of the road. We took our bags and we had our jungle fatigues on yet. We got down there and they took us to a motel and put us up for the night. They had to schedule us for another flight. The next day we were taxiing down the damned runway after we got on a military flight and there was flames comin' out one of the damned engines. They had to bring us back and check the engine out. We stayed there for another day and when we got ready to go the next day, the landing gear was all flat and they had to fix that, so it took us an extra two days just to get outta there.

When we got to Travis, there was nobody there waitin' for me. They could care less if I came home. I got to Travis and they put us on buses to Oakland to process us out. I got there and there was another guy sittin' on the bench, two from B Troop, one from Minnesota and one from South Dakota, and we'd gone through basic and AIT together and they had left Vietnam a week before I did and they were still sittin' on the benches waitin' to process out. I seen this and I got my orders and my orders said I had two more days in the military. I went in there and fell in line with these other two guys from the 101st and I was going to take my jungle boots with me and they said no I can't, so I dumped them into a bin, which really pissed me off 'cause I wanted my goddamned jungle boots. Anyhow, I fell in line with these other two guys and we got in there and processed out. They could have looked at my orders, 'cause I had two more days left and by about 10 o'clock that night I had plane tickets back to Chicago. That's where they sent me to and from Chicago I had to take a plane back to Minneapolis. When I got to Minneapolis there was a couple a drunks there that got on my case at the bus station and they wanted me to buy them beer 'cause I had my uniform on. The minute they did that I went back in and I got rid of the uniform I was wearing and got me some civilian clothes. And like a goddamned fool I went down to the theater and watched John Wayne and his Green Berets and I wish I hadn't done that, 'cause I don't think much of the man anymore.

War ain't like Hollywood tries to portray it. It's too bad people can't see it for what it is. I got a bus from the cities back to Sisseton and I got out and my dad comes in and picks me up. I think he was kinda shocked and surprised to see me alive yet. He was glad for me, but that was about it. A bed was ready for me and I went in and slept that night. My mother came in the next morning and she got me up. I didn't find out until later from my mother that my dad had come in that morning and tried to wake me up and I snapped to in bed. I don't know if he touched me or tried to grab me or what it was, but my dad was scared of me that morning. My mom came in to wake me 'cause my dad told her to come in 'cause he was scared of me. She could see the change in me because I had gotten hit from the recoil from a main gun tank and shattered an eye tooth and got a facial tic that I didn't know about myself, but my mother noticed that. Other than that I went through a whole damned year without gettin' injured. Everybody else had either two or three purple hearts and lot of 'em didn't even make it six months in the unit.

After I got home, I was either drivin' livestock truck or I worked at the school doin' cement work. I did that for a few months until I went back to school. In the spring of '69 I went back to school for another semester at Brookings. I couldn't concentrate on anything. My grades weren't very good. And the attitude I think kind of scared me off too. The way students were treating Vietnam veterans at that time. A buddy of mine who ended up stayin' at Ft. Riley, Kansas—he was a medic down there and he was feelin' sorry for me bein' over in Vietnam and him not goin', and another buddy of mine from up at Sisseton, wound up in transportation over there and he didn't see anything much on the ground. Roger and I went back to Brookings at the same time and he was getting better grades and he was goin' down to the damn bar, havin' a good old time and I'd be sittin' up in the room tryin' to study and I couldn't cut it. I don't know why. I dropped out because my dad wanted to quit farmin' and then I took over the farm.

We milked cows and my brother went into the Navy and I found out they were takin' them in the Navy for two years. I couldn't' see him goin' into the Army 'cause I figured he would end up on the ground too, and I couldn't see another life ruined because of the military, and that's just what would have happened.

I stayed on the farm there for four years. My brother came home and, after the service, my brother and I were two different people. Before, when we were growin' up, we would be huntin' and fishin' and would go to the state fair. It's a sorry thing, what war does to a person, and I think I am a good example of it. I have ancestors that have served and I figure I am the sixth generation of my family in this country. I can go back to the war of 1812, to the Civil War, and WWI and WWII. I feel that I saw more in Vietnam in just one firefight than they saw in all their conflicts. Just, nobody else has told me anything about it. I don't think I have a poor attitude towards it. It may be justified, but I don't think it was called for. It's made me more cautious about any kind of war. I have a hard time believin' what anybody tells me anymore. Because of Vietnam, it has put me on alert. Anybody tells me anything, I have a hard time believin' what they are tellin' me, even if they have a college degree. All I have is a discharge paper and I am proud of it, but a goddamned degree don't prepare you for what reality is about. The reality I saw is behind the butt of a goddamned rifle.

I never did get married. I believe a lot of this is because of Vietnam, and the country has not allowed me to deal with Vietnam in a healthy way. Until I have been able to deal with Vietnam, I'm not goin' to dump Vietnam on a relationship. I've got too many friends of mine that have been married and divorced and married and divorced. Not only that, but the birth defects and everything else. I cannot put another human bein' through that. I don't think I'm being selfish for that. Until this country starts dealing with the veterans in a just way for what we've done, even though we didn't know what we were gettin' into, it's a sorry situation.

My message to another Vietnam veteran: we got a lot of fightin' to do yet. Time may be short, but hopefully things will go for us. Maybe we can help each other; we gotta help each other, even though we don't agree 100 percent with what each other is sayin'. Because, we need each other's support. If there is any Vietnam veteran that doesn't think he's havin' problems, he's only foolin' himself. He is just as much a human as I am, even though we are made out to believe otherwise, just because of what we been through. My suggestion is to try to get hold of somebody to deal with and if you're not satisfied with what you're hearin', go find somebody else until you're satisfied.

I hope this is not an ending, but the beginning of something better.

David Harrigan

I was born and raised in the nation's cherry capital, Traverse City, Michigan. We were middle-class rural "country folk," neither rich nor poor. We were self-sufficient farmers and we got by; father was a mechanic and mother made clothes for us kids. Somehow they found a way to put seven of us through high school and helped coax me through college. To this day I don't know how they ever did it!

The oldest of seven, I attended Traverse City Saint Francis High School, graduating in 1968. I received a certificate of automotive technology from our local community college, Northwestern Michigan College, graduating with a diploma, June 13, 1969.

I will always remember May 13, 1970. That's the day I was to report, along with five other residents, to a place called AFEES, Detroit, Michigan. The other young men from the area were David Bontek, Darrly Coddington, Dirk Hughes, Phillip Lowery and Thom Wressle. Little did we know then that we would soon become a part of history—America's longest and only undeclared war. The six of us boarded a North Star bus bound not for glory, but rather our induction physicals. I had just "won" Michigan's first birthday lottery draft; my number was 128!

As our bus rolled through nearby Buckley, Michigan, the raindrops falling off the window sills resembled the teardrops running down the sides of my cheeks. I was a true "cherry." I had been raised Catholic and had never been exposed to how the other half lived; this was my first time away from home for any length of time. I had always thought that perhaps my asthma allergies or my nervous, lazy eye (my right eye does not focus properly) would warrant a possible deferment. I was wrong! They took everyone that showed either a heartbeat or a pulse, and even the Marine Corps got into the act, selecting about six or eight from our ranks, as they were low on their quota for that particular cycle! I recall only one deferment that day, the fourteenth of May, 1970—a young man from Traverse City confined to a wheelchair with polio. The rest of us that "passed" our tests were officially sworn in on or about 12 o'clock noon, 14 May, 1970 at Fort Wayne, Detroit, Michigan.

Most Michigan recruits received basic training at Fort Knox, Kentucky. For some reason that I cannot explain, I was systematically sent to Fort Leonard Wood, Missouri. (I remember my drill instructor by name from Leonard Wood—Sergeant [E-5] Juan Malave.)

My AIT training took place at Fort Sill, Oklahoma. It was there that I was given orders for Vietnam. My primary MOS was 13A10—Field Artillery Cannoneer.

I arrived in-country 6 Oct. 1970. As we were un-assing the civilian airplane at Cam Ranh Bay, the stink of that place just about knocked me unconscious, back into the plane. I never could get used to the international dateline, heat and humidity and intense stench of that place.

My buddy Duddington and I had been together, side by side, all that time. We were given different orders on or about 8th Oct. 1970.

Upon my arrival a few days later in Chu Lai, I was "drafted" for a second time, this time by the first-sergeant of HHB Div. Arty., Mr. Estel C. King. FSC King said to me, "Harrigan, I want you to be my mail clerk." I became the unit mail clerk for HHB Div Arty. 23rd Infantry.

The fellows there would always bring me things in "free" envelopes that could not be sent home for free, such as 8-track tapes, cassette tapes and camera film. I had my mom send me a bunch of stamps; that way I could put postage on anything that required it. That was my small contribution, of sorts, to the men in the field; a little something to take the edge off a very rough tour.

One quiet Sunday morning, it may have been either Easter Sunday morning or Mother's Day, I noticed what seemed to be an unusual amount of helicopter activity near our barracks and mess hall. I turned to a fellow soldier there and asked what it was all about. He told me that the choppers were bringing in the casualties to a nearby Graves Registration point. I knew that somewhere in the world, a family would soon be grieving the loss of a loved one. I wanted those brave young men and women to be remembered and never forgotten. For me, my tour was serious business from that day forward.

My DEROS date arrived one year later, 5 Oct. 1971. I will always remember that day, about 11 a.m., as we approached the Seattle-Tacoma airport. We had been in the air for nineteen-plus hours, seeing nothing more than clouds and water. I squinted my eyes; could that be land below? At almost that very same moment, a pretty stewardess voice—the voice of an angel, I think—came over the public address system: "Gentlemen, welcome to the United States of America. Welcome Home, boys." I cry every time I remember that. I'm crying now as I write it!

I finished my tour of duty with the 7th Artillery Corp Group, 2nd of the 34th F.A., Fort Lewis, Washington. I was given an early out for RVN service on my twenty-second birthday, December 18, 1971! I was discharged about 5 a.m. the morning of the 23 December; home in time to join my family for Christmas 1971 and New Year's 1972.

When I arrived home, the city had moved out to where the country had been. It all seemed to have taken place during the 600 days of my absence. The hometown I left was not the same one that I returned to.

To the best of my knowledge, all my friends from Traverse City returned safely and live near or around the area. The Moving Wall came to Traverse City May 1, 1989 and brought out some old feelings and sentiments in me that were buried real deep. I then discovered Michigan lost nearly 2,646 persons and that seventy-seven still remain missing to this day. One is from a nearby farm community—Kingsley, Michigan. I hope to live long enough to see all those classified as POW/MIA returned.

I chose to remember my friends in the lyrics of a country and western song by Johnny Cash. "The seasons come, the seasons go; we get a little sunshine, rain and snow; just the way it was planned to be."

I have been employed by Chef Pierre and Sara Lee Bakery Company since 1974. We package and ship frozen pies and cakes for the food service industry. I work as a forklift operator and clean-up person in one of the largest cold storage freezers in North America.

My friends from Chu Lai, both the living and those that did not return . . . I have not forgotten them!

Randall J. Hain

Born and raised in Milwaukee, this Vietnam veteran, like most of us, is different. I graduated from high school in 1963. My friends and I were always lifting weights, living up to our reputation as Milwaukee beer drinkers and doing enough crazy things so as not to get bored.

At that time I had one of the fastest motorcycles in the city, a 1958 Triumph with eleven-to-one compression ratio. My drivers license had been suspended and I did not stop by request of a policeman. I got away that time, but several months later, a drunk failed to yield my right of way and I hit him broadside at 50 m.p.h.

In traction for five months. That didn't work, so they screwed my femur together with two pieces of metal, ten screws, and a bone graft. While trying to rehabilitate myself in college, I got my notice to report for a physical. We all pulled down our pants for this Army doctor, bent over, and got our draft notices October 13, 1966. They drafted 53,500 people that month, which was the largest draft call since the Korean War. The lottery system was not in place at that time, and it became quite political as to who—think of people like Cassius Clay, Dan Quayle, Bruce Springstein, and Hulk Hogan—did and did not get drafted.

Why did I get drafted in spite of being permanently disabled? It seems that I went into a police station and raised some hell about a parking ticket that I paid, and of course they arrested me and threw me in jail. I called my pop and he pulled my bail. The judge fined me $10 and put me on probation for a year. Little did I know at the time, that this misdemeanor judge was also a bird colonel in the United States Army Reserve. (The same guy was suspended from practicing law in about 1984 for being caught having sex with a prostitute in the elevator of the Milwaukee County Courthouse.)

The bus trip from Milwaukee to Fort Leonard Wood and then to Fort Hood was a real dog. I kept asking myself, "What am I doing here?" The only answer I could come up with was that nothing is more important than to secure my "guaranteed Constitutional rights" in the name of freedom and democracy. I would have raised hell about the situation, but by now, after being on probation for a year, I was so intimidated and felt that unless one has money and a strong legal defense, there was absolutely no hope for an indigent like myself.

Complaining about my physical condition in basic training did no good. They took X-rays at Darnel Army Hospital. I tried to explain this awkward situation to my sergeant one day and he threw me up against the latrine wall and held a straight razor to my throat and threatened to kill me if I pressed the issue. Nothing at this point could have been more important than my guaranteed Constitutional rights, and at the time, my life.

We left from Fort Lewis in Washington after a week of rain, and landed in Cam Ranh Bay about eighteen hours later. Two things hit me like a cop with a gold badge. There were about fifty pallets of beer. I never saw so much goddamned beer in my life, and at 115 degrees, the smell of urine. Very heavy! Such a deal at only ten cents a can.

Nha Trang (tent city) was my first assignment. As a personnel specialist, my job was in G-2 intelligence and information gathering for 1FFV (First Field Force Vietnam). After being there a month, my commander asked me if I wanted more responsibility in this field, and I declined because I didn't feel comfortable with it. As I reflected on this situation, I think of the pickle jar that LTC Oliver North is in today. It could have been me.

Tuy Hoa, 6th Battalion, 32nd Artillery HHC. My work as a personnel specialist was one of the best times of my life, and probably the most rewarding. I liked it so much that I would often work Sundays, when most everyone else was off duty. I kept records for a battalion according to MOS (military occupational specialty) and submitted a bi-weekly status report. Being the classified information it was, I choppered it to Nha Trang every other week. My commanders never complained if I was going for three or four days at a time. About ten or fifteen percent of the 525,000 GIs were classified as being in transit, so no one really knew how many of us were in the Vietnam theater at any one time. This could amount to part of the POW/MIA question.

Towards the end of my duty, I was sent out to Charlie battery by truck to deliver ammunition for our eight-inch and 175mm track-mounted guns. I should not have been in the front end of the eight-incher when they fired it, but after all, I never had any type of artillery field training. I get $144 per month because my ears ring and I don't hear very well. The next day following an inspection of battalion records that I was responsible for, they promoted me to Spec-5, non-commissioned officer.

Going home was the best part of my Vietnam tour.

For the next several years, I went through many colleges, women, and places to live. I wound up with several degrees in industrial marketing and the communication arts. I supervised machine shops until 1982, when a degenerative disc disease and post-traumatic stress have kept me from working ever since.

1982 was the year that I was commissioned by Ronald Reagan to serve as a Local Draft Board Member for the Selective Service System. As an Administrative Law Judge, it was my duty to insure that all conscientious objectors could experience their guaranteed Constitutional rights. What is more important than freedom?

The Army Reserves decorated me with the Republic of Vietnam Gallantry Cross in 1984.

After several attempts to gain a service-connected disability from the Veterans Administration, I filed a civil lawsuit in U.S. District Court. They dismissed it due to the statute of limitations. The Army Board for Correction of Military Records refused to correct my pre-induction medical record. (See UNITED STATES DISTRICT COURT DISTRICT OF MINNESOTA THIRD DIVISION Civil #3-90-468.)

This chapter was supposed to be about my experiences in Vietnam. I sometimes wonder myself if I have anything to say about them at all. I have faith in our guaranteed Constitutional rights, due process of law, and yes, I do believe that some day I will be compensated for this "error of injustice." At this point it has something to do with a "private bill" before the U.S. Senate and Congress.

Wish me luck. If I loose, we all loose!

Martin J. Glennon

It was 1969 and I was a full-time freshman at a Midwestern community college in East Chicago, Indiana. When I received a grade that didn't measure up, I immediately thought, "I don't need this! Forget it! I'm pulling out." After class I quickly made my way to the administration building and withdrew from English. By dropping this class, I became a part-time student, and thus I was now eligible for the draft.

My draft number was in the forties, but I didn't really care. If I did get drafted and sent to Nam I'd just check out what was going on. Besides, it would be better than sticking around here. Just three weeks later I got my call for the induction station. On August 5, 1969 I went from Hammond to Chicago to leave for basic training in Fort Leonard Wood, Missouri. It wasn't long before we visited the barbers. We all came out with the GI haircuts. That means one inch from being bald. This is done so soldiers lose the identity their personal hairstyles express. Then they find a new identity, Army style, in Advanced Infantry Training, or AIT.

During basic we were taken to a mock Vietnamese village and shown what to look for that might be of danger to us. Little Vietnamese boys selling popsicles out of booby-trapped boxes were just one of the many hazards. This realization hit me with mixed emotion. The Viet Cong had indoctrinated the young people's minds so much, that they believed if they willfully deceived a GI to buy one of these popsicles, they would get an eternal heavenly reward. The booby-trapped boxes would not only kill the innocent, unsuspecting soldier, but would blow the child to kingdom come as well.

When we spoke with counselors and asked what we would like to do in the Army, I decided I wanted to be a medic, as my father had been during WWII. Within a couple of weeks we were assigned to our AIT. I was to go to Fort Sam Houston in San Antonio, Texas to begin Combat Infantry Medic training. My official title was Combat Infantry Medic, meaning I would be in the jungle with the infantry. Little did I know my experiences would be life changing, and forever leave an insoluble memory in my mind.

Although we were required to have twelve weeks of training, the word was out: "Only ten weeks training." Our army in Southeast Asia needed us. I thought, "It's hard to believe. They can't be going through that many medics . . . There's only one per infantry platoon?" Then one older sergeant I found told me, "Haven't you heard, the Combat Infantry Medical casualty rate is one every seventeen minutes." I drew back in silence, contemplating what he must have been through. Maybe he was joking. He was in Nam in 1968 when it was really bad, but I told myself, "It's not so bad now. Besides, I might get sent to Germany instead." Little did I know, I was to be sent to one of the hottest spots and roughest units in Vietnam.

The men who volunteered for Vietnam were not given orders for it. They probably thought these men were mentally sick to want to go there. My name was called. As I had thought, he said, "Private Glennon— Vietnam."

When the assembly was over, I called home and broke the news to my parents. They were sad, but I would have a two-week leave before I left for Nam. Within a few days, I was heading for home. Those two weeks went by fast. In no time , I was on the plane heading toward Oakland, California. This was the dispersing station for incoming GIs to Vietnam. While in Oakland, we were held over for a number of days. It was nerve racking. We would see some seasoned soldiers coming back because they were returning through Oakland as well as going out. We would ask them how it was. Usually they just shook their heads. Sometimes we got a few to say something, but there was a faraway look in their eyes, as if they had left a part of their souls back there *in* Nam. Some were very somber and looked as if they had been through hell and back. I was a robust, fun-loving guy, but these GIs that came back seemed to be more mature, even though some were my own age.

Finally, we were sent on a plane to Japan, where we stopped to refuel before going on to Nam. We arrived in Cam Ranh Bay at a military holding base. We were put in a sorting barracks, waiting on our orders. Every evening we would assemble in the general assembly tent, where they would read off our names, telling us which part of the country and which units we were assigned to.

Frank and a number of guys from AIT were there. It was hot— eighty-five or ninety degrees—even though it was January. Oddly enough, the nights were a cool fifty degrees. During the night we would hear jets zooming by and explosions far away. The next day I saw Frank. We had a long talk. He told me of his home in Tucson and of his jobs playing as a drummer in a jazz band at a Tucson, Arizona night club. That night at the tent assembly they called my name. "Private Martin Glennon—I Corp—101st." This meant I was to go to the northernmost part of South Vietnam—I Corp—and be sent to the 101st Airborne Division, "The Screaming Eagles." Frank was also sent to the 101st. I had to laugh when I realized the song we sang in basic training, "I want to be an Airborne Ranger, I want to go to Vietnam" came true for me.

The next day Frank and I embarked on our journey to I Corp in South Vietnam. We took a C-130, a lumbering twenty-five to thirty seater prop plane. These leave a lot to be desired if one is looking for comfort. I was curious as to what I would find in Da Nang and finally, what I would be doing as a medic. As soon as we got to Da Nang we were taken by jeep to Camp Eagle, the 101st Airborne's main base. It was encircled by miles of barbed wire. I am sure the Viet Cong tried to infiltrate it.

Part of our training included being told about things we might encounter in the infantry companies in the jungle, things such as Viet Cong sappers armed with satchel charges—explosives that would give off flashes to cause confusion, allowing other VC to rush the position. They would rub mud and camouflage paint on their bodies so the GIs would not be able to see them very well in the dark. We were also informed of the possibility of running across bamboo vipers, which were very poisonous snakes found hanging on bamboo tree limbs. These snakes were small, only one to two feet long, but with a vehement bite. They called them Two-Steps, because in two steps you were affected by the bite. It did not take long for the poison to do a man in. Medics had no special snake-bite kits to fight the snake's deadly bite. Late that night, when we got back to Camp Evans, we were told we would soon be going to our medical battalion. As corpsmen, we would serve in platoons as Combat Infantry Medics.

"Headquarters HHC Company 2/506 Infantry!" the Sergeant yelled out. That was my destination. It was located on Camp Evans. Headquarters Company was a medical unit and we were then put in the infantry units. My friend Frank was also sent to the same company, but a recon unit, which went out in four- or five-man teams. I did not see Frank for a few months after that, and when we did meet later, he had many stories to share with me.

I was briefed by the lieutenant who was in charge of the medics about some basic procedures—sutures, medications, antibiotics and sick leave. He informed us about what would be a serious enough affliction for a man to come back to the base camp hospital and medical dispensary. All gunshot, grenade wounds and fevers that could not be broken for a few days were med-evaced back to Camp Evans.

On April 1, 1970, we were choppered in on CH-47 choppers, which carried about six men each. We came in on a hot LZ, meaning that our choppers were taking enemy small-arms fire by NVA soldiers. They were there, undoubtedly, to hold back re-entry to this abandoned firebase that we were to re-open.

My company, Alpha 2/506, was to secure a hill across from Ripcord so B Company could land on Ripcord. The NVA were waiting for us. They had their mortars zeroed in and when B Company landed they let them have it. B Company didn't have a chance. They couldn't even get their dead and wounded out because the NVA were shooting down the med-evacs. They were forced to bury their dead in old bunkers and leave them. My company got the job of recovering the dead and bringing them back to our position so that they could be picked up. From that day on, many men were either wounded or killed patrolling the area around Ripcord. Ripcord was north of Hamburger Hill, which in May of 1969, claimed many casualties of the 101st Airborne.

After the dead and wounded were taken out, we were to stay low and not give the enemy any ground. Our orders were to secure it for a few days until the company that was to stay on it for a while was safely inserted. Artillery was called in from a nearby firebase to where the sniper fire was thought to be coming from. The lieutenant had also asked for F-4 Phantom jets to air-strike surrounding hills. There was always a sense of security when these jets came in. Their rockets and bombs almost always caused the enemy to back off and re-group.

Ripcord was opened April 1, 1970 and by July 1, 1970 the NVA and VC were dug in so tight around Ripcord that there was a battle that lasted twenty-two days.

Word had gotten out at Firebase O'Reilly that Alpha Co. was moving to the AO (Area of Operation) around Firebase Ripcord, which was close to the A Shau Valley. As I got back to O'Reilly, some of the guys were smoking marijuana. They tried to hide it, knowing I did not approve. Although I drank beer, sometimes to excess, my view of any drugs was purely medicinal. They said to me, "Come on, Doc, try it. You won't have to worry about anything when you take a few puffs." I said, "No thanks. I'll stick to drinking." As I walked over to the bunker I was to guard, Bill greeted me. I saw he had his little New Testament in his left top shirt pocket, right over his heart. He undoubtedly had been reading it that day. I could tell because his countenance was bright and cheery. He had been drinking of another spirit—the Holy Spirit.

The next couple of days went by quickly. The choppers were scheduled to come in early morning. We packed up our gear and, as we were leaving, another company was replacing us on the firebase. Even though O'Reilly could not be termed a relaxation spot, it was certainly a break from the jungle warfare, and that is what it was being used for, as well as a security measure. The in-coming companies were definitely ready for a break.

We were helicoptered into a landing zone about five klicks away from Firebase Ripcord, close to the A Shau Valley. We were assigned to walk along a jungle ridge. We walked for what seemed miles, but no contact with the enemy. I was glad of that, but talk was going around that we would soon be in the heart of NVA territory.

That night we set up camp, traveling as a company of three platoons with our company commander, a captain, walking with the first platoon. Suddenly we heard a shot, but it was not the popping of the enemy rifles. No AKs or SKSs, but our own M-16 rifle fire. I asked what happened. The call for medic went out, but it wasn't my platoon, so the other medic took it. The pressure and tension was so great you could feel it on our back. Then it was confirmed, one of our own men shot himself, in the foot, by accident. Many of us knew this could not be an accident, but the fear of contact the next few days caused this. The soldier had shot himself in the foot to get out of the field. He was med-evaced out.

It was July 20, 1970. The night was restless, and during night guard duty I was apprehensive of the impending doom that seemed to be lurking. Nothing happened that night, though. When morning came, we woke up early, around 5 or 6, and were told we were moving our about 0700 hours.

On the morning of July 21, 1970, I quickly made my morning rounds with my platoon, giving out Dapsone, the anti-malaria pill. One was given every day. The other malaria pill I gave out every couple of days. Each were given to combat two different strains of malaria that were found to be in the region.

I had been in Vietnam six and a half months already and medics were only supposed to be out for six months unless a replacement could not be found, which was true in this case. The night and early morning of July 22 was restless. The platoon staff-sergeant had the night watch before me. He woke me up around 3 in the morning. As soon as I awoke, I was startled to smell a pungent fish odor. My first impression was that the gooks were so close I could smell them. After being in the jungle six months, I knew they were there. I sensed and smelled them. I told the platoon sergeant, but he did not believe me. I sensed the eyes of the enemy on our company. I believe we were being watched all night. First Platoon was sent out on a patrol at 0700. As the company commander and lieutenant-colonel discussed our next move, the radio they were talking on went out. As all the administrative part of the company gathered to talk, the rest of the company, which numbered about seventy-five at that time, were put on edge, wondering what was going on. We were east of Firebase Ripcord. I sensed something terrible was about to happen, yet for me this day would have a silver lining.

During this break I pulled out my pocket Gideon New Testament I had been reading the previous two months. Now, on this day of July 22, 1970, the words I read for some reason seemed to be alive. On the last couple of pages were written certain scripture passages such as John 3:16, Romans 10:9, and John 5:13. With these passages was a decision prayer to receive Christ as savior. I promptly said this prayer and wrote my name and date in this small Gideon New Testament. I sensed a tremendous release in my spirit and joy rose up in me and I vowed to serve God that day. Little did I know how soon my faith would be tested.

The break quickly ended. The lieutenant clued us in. We were going a different direction and my platoon (second) was to move out first. There was a great amount of tension in the air. We sensed the lieutenant might not be telling us all. Beads of sweat broke out on my forehead.

Our point element started moving out. In almost the direct opposite direction, far off in the background, we could hear faint explosions. Something was happening at Firebase Ripcord. Our point element had no sooner gotten 150 meters when an explosion ripped bark off a nearby tree trunk. An RPG was fired to stop the point element from going any further.

We all hit the jungle floor. The popping of AK-47 small-arms fire opened up on all sides of us. The rear two platoons were also getting hit. The call went out. "Medic! Medic!" Someone was calling for me to go up front. I was frozen. I just started calling upon Jesus. I said, "Jesus, Jesus, Jesus." I said his name over and over again. Later I found the verse in Proverbs 18:10. "The name of the Lord is a strong tower, the righteous runs into it and is deaf." I had unknowingly put myself in the tower of God's protection.

After a while one of the soldiers, Tom, with whom I'd become friends and whom Bill the communications man had led to the Lord, said to me, "Doc, I think its going to be all right." Tom obviously discerned my anxiety and distress. I know he was a sensitive person. Even though he looked to be tough on the outside, he was a kitten on the inside with a heart of gold. He said, "I think we're going to make it." These were the last words he said. The words of that infantry soldier had given me hope that my prayers were being answered.

I had decided to go forward to the front and patch up the point element's shrapnel wounds. A few men were wounded, but not seriously. Bill said, "Doc, wait. Don't go up now." I wondered why he said that. Now I believe he had a word of wisdom. The enemy knew the medic of the platoon gave the moral support. If the medic was out of commission, the soldiers would have to put their own patches on and tend to themselves, thus causing a less secure feeling.

The platoon staff-sergeant had decided to stand up and check the position. As he stood, he caught an enemy bullet that ripped through one side of his face and out the other, taking some teeth with it. I heard the repeated popping of AK-47 fire, then looked around and the sergeant was trying to say my name. "Doc," he whispered as best he could. But the blood was restricting him from talking. I gave him emergency treatment, a blood filler and a transfusion of dextrose. At one point he said, "Things are getting dark. I think I am going to die." I told him, "No you're not! You are going to make it." Although I did not really know how serious his wound was, the comment seemed to relieve him.

At approximately the same time, Third Platoon was edging it back to the hilltop. Second Platoon Lieutenant Widjeskog decided to go back and join up with the rest of the company. We started back. All of a sudden, small-arms fire blocked our path back. We were cut off from the other two platoons. It finally dawned on us ... we were surrounded and could not get back to them. So, we all regrouped where the point element had fallen back to. Slowly we crawled together and formed a circle. Each man held his M-16 rifle in front of him, watching his own perimeter in front of himself. We had one M-60 machine gun that could cut a mid-sized tree in half with enough concentrated fire. It was positioned to take care of approximately forty-five percent of the circle.

The NVA had a unit called sappers that just wore loin cloths and grenade belts. Often they would be found wearing heavy camouflaged paint, with their grenade belts full of satchel charge. These type of explosives gave off high flashes and caused confusion and fear. Little did we know a unit of sappers were creeping in on us.

We were in battle a solid seven hours. The head count was fifty-one wounded, twelve killed. The other two platoons' medics were killed. By the grace of God, I was spared. The medic that traveled with the company captain was also wounded. He and I were giving medical aid to all wounded.

The wounds varied from small amounts of shrapnel wounds to bullet wounds in the chest, arms, legs, and the worst was the abdomen. I could not stop the bleeding for that one. Alabama, the soldier who received the abdomen wound, died during the night or early morning, which mad it thirteen KIA. The captain had been wounded in the neck with shrapnel. The other platoon lieutenant was killed. Lieutenant Lee Widjeskog, from our Second Platoon, made it through. Third Platoon had no lieutenant. Thank God we had no MIAs.

On the morning of July 23, 1970 we received word by radio that help was on the way. This was a tremendous moral booster. By afternoon we were being airlifted out by Huey choppers. As my helicopter was leaving, we were cramped for space and a few of us sat on body bags in which our fellow comrades, who had died in valiant battle, were laid to rest. As I sat on a body bag the door-gunner looked at me with understanding as tears started to roll down my face. My mind was reeling with scenes of the previous twenty-four hours. I thought, "Well, God, you pulled me through, but I really cannot take much more. In fact, I certainly cannot take credit." At this point my sanity was at stake. I had seen enough in these last six months to last a lifetime.

We were taken to Camp Evans—C Co., 326 Medical Battalion. The doctors and medics had their work cut out for them when we arrived. Some were bandaged up and sent to the holding barracks and some went on to the hospital in Okinawa, Japan, and some all the way back to the States.

It took a couple of weeks before a new company was formed after that experience in the field July 22, when I made my commitment to Christ. A replacement was needed for almost every man. My six months as a medic were over in the field, but due to a shortage of medics, the headquarters company lieutenant in charge of the medics approached me about going back out into the jungle. I told them I would transfer to the medical evacuation hospital unit on Camp Evans, because I could not take anymore.

It was August, 1970 and I had four months to go in Nam. I worked in the camp hospital. We worked shift work—two men every shift worked on the ward. It held about forty beds, but we could make more room if it was needed.

Peter also worked on the ward. He was the same medic who was with us when we started to open Firebase Ripcord, in April. He had been getting letters from back home that deeply troubled him. He decided to end it all. He took his M-16 rifle, put it under his chin while in his hooch, and pulled the trigger. It blew out half of his face, but they saved him. They saved one eye, but the blast of the bullet took the other. They worked on him in the emergency room at 326 Evac, where the soldiers that are wounded from the field came in. The doctors worked for hours on him and sent him to a hospital stateside. I do not know of his whereabouts or what happened to him after that.

I had a lot of time on my hands and ended up thinking about life and death and why I had lived through the jungle experience. I went to church every evening at the base camp chapel, even though I worked at a club where everyone got drunk. I found myself wanting to do the right and good thing, but doing just the opposite. My friend Bill had come to visit me one night. In a polite way, he rebuked me for working in the club. But I was not ready for this and subsequently Bill visited me only one time more, though I know he prayed for me.

Soon after Bill's visit, a fellow soldier who was in from the field, and who was a drug user, tempted me to try some marijuana that had opium in it. After the first few puffs of his pipe I felt a woozy feeling. The walls seemed like they were melting a little. I decided I was going to go to sleep. That night I was awakened from a terrible nightmare. I dreamed the dark force of the Devil came through the backdoor of the hooch and was about to take me over. When I woke up, my legs were kicking him off. I immediately went to the ward where I worked and asked them to watch me. The rest of the night I slept all right. The next morning I made myself a promise not to take marijuana again.

When my R&R came, I went to Sydney, Australia. My R&R was taken with men I did not know from Camp Eagle. It took about eight to ten hours for us to reach our destination. Sydney was a big city, filled with shops, cafes and go-go bars. I became friends with a few guys and we stayed out till two or three in the morning, mostly getting drunk. There were girls that would start talking to you, to see how much they could get out of you. A few drinks, maybe a dinner or a night. I ended up going out with what in today's terms would be called a "teaser." When I saw her the next day, I almost got sick from disgust of my actions the previous night. This week's vacation was mixed with drunkenness and promiscuity. Finally, when I got back to Nam, I only had three months left to go. I was terribly nervous and the doctor prescribed Librium for me. It gave me more bad dreams and he switched it to Valium.

Finally my term in Nam was up and I was off. My friend Frank, who was also a medic, left at the same time. We rode back together and talked about our year's tour in the Republic of Vietnam, the sorrow and the joys. As I was gazing out the window I remembered that great battle on July 22 and the commitment I had made to God. I wondered what the future would hold when I got back home.

I was processed out through Oakland. When we arrived on the jet, there was a feeling of exhilaration and joy when we touched down and a cheer rang out from the GIs on the jet. We came off the bird, and were processed out opposite the boys who were going over to Nam and I remembered the previous year and how I looked into the faces of those coming back, just as these young men were looking at us. I wondered how many of these young men would be coming back? I was saddened by this thought.

We were all given about a three-week leave, which I was thankful for, because this was around Christmas and it was a family time of year. The excitement I felt at going home was dispelled with saddening news. Thomas, a high school friend, was killed on December 12, 1970 in Nam by a booby-trap. I had also lost my grandfather while I was gone. He was a very special person to me.

In January of 1971 I was serving out my final seven months at Fort Knox, Kentucky. Needless to say, my life was more or less a shambles. I had bad dreams of Vietnam, coupled with guilt over why I made it out of there alive while some other men did not. This all drove me to drinking, which I had previously done to forget the experience I had. One thing I held to was the commitment I had made to Christ for the rest of my life. How Jesus was going to do that was not my problem, because I could not do it on by own.

I enrolled back in the same college I had left when drafted. I had lost a lot of time. Two years, to be exact. Many of the people I was with when I first enrolled were ready to graduate college.

I did a lot of seeking amidst the 1972-73 peace movement. Pressure was really put on the Nixon Administration to pull out of Nam because too many young soldiers were being sent home in pine boxes. The horrible Communist atrocities to young men in Vietnam were not causing a righteous indignation of the American people, as it had done in previous wars. Rather, it caused a pressure to get out of the war—a non-involvement attitude that may be to the detriment of this country. Any way you look at it, Communist ideology is to conquer the world through any type of subversion they could use, by physically killing people or causing dissension among the ranks to the point of splitting opinions. May God help us to see their divisive actions and manipulation of public opinion to further their ungodly cause. The people who suffer will be our children, who find them on our shores with keys to our cities, given to them by our own people. God forbid, and may our eyes be opened, in Jesus' name.

I found the battle I had gone through was not totally over. I experienced a degree of delayed stress syndrome. This is defined as "Stress that cannot be expressed while the stressful situation is taking place." It is a reaction experienced by many survivors of catastrophic events, either man-made or natural. The nature of the catastrophe demands that the person does whatever is necessary for survival. There is no time for emotions. Emotions are delayed and emerge only after the stressful event has passed.

I had a guilt over surviving, while some of the other soldiers did not. A few of them even had families with children. I had a nervous anxiety. The nightmares I had when I first got out of the jungle and firefights, were subsiding. I filled my mind with the Word of God and memorized scriptures. Nevertheless, every so often I would have a flashback. The psychic aberrations of war were etched deeply into my mind. After these mental assaults, I would immediately get prayer from fellow believers. This includes many prayers for deliverance. At this time I was living at home and my father had persuaded me to go to the Veterans Administration. The VA doctors counseled me and prescribed a tranquilizer called Valium. I took it over a period of a year. I sensed the prayers were working more efficiently than the drug. Through continued prayer and many tears, Christ was put on top in my life. There are no more flashbacks now.

As gold is tried in the fire to bring forth the precious metal, so too we have been tried, fellow Vietnam veterans. We had accepted our responsibility to go where hostile forces were ready to devour us, the forces that would bring bondage to all freedom-loving peoples.

We have been spit upon and cursed at by people. Some of us have even had rocks thrown at us. But one fact still remains . . . we bore on our back the plight of freedom-desiring and loving people.

God, guts and guns has kept America free, and we are part of that. Vietnam veteran, you are America.

Jack Fidler

I went to grade school in Salem, Oregon, and junior high in Mackminville, where I am now living, and I graduated from St. Helen's Sr. High School in 1964.

I joined the Army in the middle of June 1964. I took my basic training at Fort Ord, California. That summer, about ninety-eight men died of spinal meningitis there. I had this strange feeling that I was in combat zone then, with what they called the Fort Ord "crit" going around there. After taking my basic, I also took pole lineman's school. I was in class 318, Training Company M.

One day I slid down a telephone pole, and because of the fact that spinal meningitis was going around, you didn't want to go on sick call. You wanted to avoid that place. It was said that if you weren't sick when you went there, you'd be sick when you got out. After about two days of suffering with splinters in my stomach and what not, I decided to go on sick call. I went down and the doctor patched me up and gave me medication. His closing remark to me was, "You boys over at the pole lineman's school sure keep us busy," like it was my fault and I did it on purpose just to keep him off the golf course.

From Fort Ord, California I went to Fort Gordon, Georgia and stayed there for about a month, learning how to install telephones, field phones, switchboard operation and patch panel work. After Fort Gordon, I went to Fort Polk, Louisiana, as a permanent party there. Interesting post. I thought I would be staying there for the rest of my three-year hitch. That's what most of the other men thought. I was there at Fort Polk, Louisiana in what they call the Ponderosa part of the camp, which was originally set up to be for the blacks in the military. We were to ride to Fort Hood, Texas. We went back to Fort Polk, Louisiana for about a month. It was a Friday when they called me down to the orderly room with ten other guys. They told us we had twenty-four hours to get off post, because we were going to be sent to Fort Hood Texas with 54th Signal Battalion and most likely we would be going to Vietnam. We didn't know what the big hurry was to get off post because they gave us a ten-day delay en route to go home and then report to Fort Hood. I reported there and for the next month packed gear up and got ready to go.

I only remember one protest upon leaving. We arrived in Oakland, California and got aboard the USS J.C.Brekenridge and we were delayed in leaving that port by two or three hours because someone attached their ski boat to our anchor and prevented us leaving. I don't know why they didn't bring in the anchor and the boat as well and teach them a lesson, but that was something else, sailing out under the Golden Gate Bridge. Then we sailed into Pearl Harbor in Hawaii. We were there about a day and a half before we set sail again. We then went to Japan. Just avoiding a typhoon, we stayed out at sea about three days and then sailed to Cam Ranh Bay in Vietnam. It took us twenty-three days to get from Oakland to Vietnam.

I remember when we first got there, we were unloaded onto the dock-personal gear—two duffel bags filled with equipment and combat gear. We were all combat dressed—helmets, backpack, M-14 rifle and four clips of ammo. Later on, after we unloaded, trucks came from a transport company to carry us and our gear to Nha Trang. We were just outside of Nha Trang about two miles. We climbed onto these trucks and I was up just behind the cab with a sergeant. We threw the duffel bags on first and then climbed on top of them. The sergeant next to me dragged out his dog tags and puts them on and proceeds to put a clip of ammo into his weapon. It was at that time I came to the realization that we must be in a combat zone. We proceeded on to Nha Trang, at which time I noticed the trucks were moving extremely fast—doing about fifty-five or sixty on those small narrow roads, and whenever we would come to a small community, the driver would blare on the horn and speed up. He wouldn't slow down through these little villages. Later on I realized why, and as we traveled to Cam Ranh Bay and back, someone in our outfit coined a phrase, "Big Raindrops"—slow vehicles make slow targets. We in turn picked up the pace whenever we were between Nha Trang and Cam Ranh Bay.

One other time I remember a fellow who came back from Cam Ranh Bay with some equipment he picked up—telephones and wire. Just outside of the camp about a mile, he got a flat tire at about 1 o'clock in the morning. He drove into camp on that flat tire, ruining the tire and rim. You know they tried to court martial him for that. It was probably smarter to do that than to stop and fix the tire at that time of the night. You would be taking a chance of getting your truck blown up or shot or both. The Army is very unique in its uniformity. It is ridiculous sometimes how we would put up these big GP tents and they were out there with transients. Imagine setting up tents in big sand docks using metal stakes about three feet long to put these things in. A little wooden stake wouldn't hold these tents up. While we were putting these tents up they had the engineer company out there sighting down the rows of tents making sure that everything is exactly straight and perfect and all the lines are exactly the same angle and so on. We got our tents up and lined up beautifully and then someone noticed that the instruction flap for our tent was at the front. After you rolled the sides up, it wouldn't make any difference, but somebody had to make note of it and somebody with authority had us take this GP large tent and turn it 180 degrees so the instruction flap was at the back end of the tent rather than the front end.

For the first few weeks that's about all that we had to do was beautify the area and load sandbags. We filled more sandbags than I could really count. We had to go out of the company area after a while because we were running out of sand. We would fill them, put them in the back of a two and a half ton truck, bring them back and stack them up around our tent. Then we finally got to doing what we were supposed to do. That was lay wire. One afternoon to evening, about a week after we got there, the officers rented a motel downtown in Nha Trang. They felt uncomfortable about being at that motel without communications. You know, a signal company without communications—to the officers maybe more of a disgrace than an inconvenience. At any rate, we set out about 6 o'clock that night to lay some cable—run a wire from FSC headquarters to the hotel, which the officers were staying in. They had it all fortified with two fifty-five-gallon drums of sand stacked one on top of the other, all around the hotel, and sandbags on top of that, and concertina wire on top of that. They then wanted communications.

Two squads went out to lay the wire and hang it down the streets. One group started at the FFV headquarters, the other started at the hotel. The group that started at the hotel ended up having a number of officers helping them. We who started at the headquarters made about two to three miles of wire when the squad that had the officers helping them only made a mile or so. We met in downtown Nha Trang, just on the outskirts, and we ended up having about a quarter mile of extra wire. I suggested that we just clip these cables together and splice them. They thought this would ruin the cables because they had big brass connectors that they thought would be better than splicing. What we ended up doing was stringing a couple hundred yards of this cable in between two telephone poles to take up the slack. Since it was getting dark and we didn't want to be up on telephone poles at night, this is what we proceeded to do. I didn't get stuck with that detail and I'm really glad. Later on they named the officers' hotel Cool Hall, which was after a pilot who was killed in a chopper along with his mechanic. His mechanic's name was John F. McDermott and he was killed and we named our tent city camp after him.

There were many times that we had action—mortars, that type of thing, all around us. I only recall one time our camp got hit or infiltrated by Viet Cong. One of our perimeter lights burnt out and they snuck in—clipped the wires at that the point, where the light was burned out—came in with satchel charges and proceeded to throw them around. They blew up a couple trucks. A lot of GP tents that we were staying in were blown up, or rather, just leveled. The satchel charges didn't do a lot of damage, just kind of scattered things. Their main objective seemed to be the officers' latrine because of the fact that it was the only real building on the compound. It had thatched walls and a tin roof. They must have thought it was something important, plus there were officers going in and out of it all day long. You've got to understand, the Vietnamese did not have bathroom facilities like we know them, or outhouses. I thought our military intelligence was slow, but theirs had to be really dragging to make your main objective to blow up an outhouse. They could have done some research and found out what that building was and done something more productive.

One day I got picked to go on the garbage detail, which is really interesting. We got a two-and-a-half-ton truck and proceeded to go around the company area and pick up garbage. We picked up these fifty-five-gallon drums and dumped them into the back of the truck. After completing that, we went and got a clip of ammo and our M-14 rifles and proceeded out to the Vietnamese garbage dump. Upon arrival we backed into the dump and, I swear, there must have been fifty to seventy-five Vietnamese who raced to the truck. They took down the tailgate and proceeded to unload all of our trash, at which point we stood on guard duty to see that they left things like tires, wheels, rims, radios—the equipment we were using. I don't know—I've never seen such a rush for garbage in all my life. They all had their friends, so they threw things out to them. We made it a policy not to dump our personal letters in the garbage but went into the burning pile.

I was there for probably three or four months and one day I was climbing a telephone pole and splicing some wires together and I mentioned to my sergeant down below that there was quite a view from up here, at which time he explained that anybody from out there can pretty much see you. I got to thinking about that and said that maybe climbing those poles and becoming so visible to the countryside was not such a good idea. I started volunteering for everything. At least in our outfit, if they asked for volunteers, chances it was a pretty good detail because somebody coming behind that person asking for volunteers wouldn't be asking for volunteers. He would be just taking bodies. I found it was a lot better to volunteer for something than to be just grabbed up for it. One day they came by and asked for people to serve on permanent guard duty. I volunteered for it and it turned out to be a pretty good deal. You had six hours of guard duty and then you had the rest of the day off. About every seven or eight days you had two days off, so it was a good amount of time for one to go around and take pictures and go to the beach swimming. We were in an R&R center, so it was basically pretty nice there. We grew pretty fond of each other.

We had special orders when we were pulling guard duty. One of those orders was that we had to have our helmets on. We found that when we were pulling guard duty in the daytime, the temperature inside those helmets would probably reach 150 degrees. So, one day we decided not to wear the helmets anymore; we would just wear the helmet liners. This relieved a little pressure, but not the heat. The heat is still intense when you are standing outside, the sun beating down on you and all that heat would just collect in those helmets. One day we all got together and discussed what we could do and we decided just to wear our ball caps. Just the regular Army utility cap at that time. So we did. We all proceeded to do it at the same time. We started out the day that way, wearing the ball cap, and you know, we got away with that because I think we all stuck together and the officers must have thought some special orders must have come down so we could wear the ball caps. We were convinced that the helmet might have saved our lives if we needed some sort of shield, but we knew it would kill us if we kept wearing it out there in the heat and sun.

With me it was always . . . if you have ever seen a fellow going down the street and he just got missed with a safe falling out the window or as he proceeds down the street a street car just misses him, and as he steps over a manhole it opens up after he passes. Well for the most part that is the way it was for my tour of duty. It seems like every time somebody mentioned something like that like, "Were you over at the Special Forces snack bar last night? Were you there when the hand grenade got thrown on the roof." "No, I left" at such and such a time and things like that happened just after I left.

I got into Vietnam the later part of August and had the opportunity to leave Vietnam the early part of August, not spending quite a whole year there, but it was close enough as far as I was concerned. However, I was considering staying another six months. If you came back from Vietnam with less than ninety days you would get automatic separation there in Oakland. They would not assign you to another post. But, I almost decided to do that when my orders came down and they let me pick from the wish list and I picked the midwestern part of the United States, which I was really surprised that I got. After Fort Carson, I came on home. My folks had moved to Salem, Oregon. I remember going down and trying to get a job. I tried to get a part-time summer job at this one place because I wanted to take advantage of the GI Bill and go to school. I was interviewed and I was frankly quite proud that I had served my country and went to Vietnam. I got to the part that talked about my obligation to my country and the draft and what not. I stated that I had already served my country and had been to Vietnam and he politely told me not to call him, that it was a "don't call us we'll call you" situation. I thought that was rather unusual, to be cut off like that. So, I went to school, thinking that an additional year of electronics school would make me more qualified to work for the phone company as a phone installer or technician, cable splicer or something like this—that I could be that much better trained to work for the phone company.

Well, about a month or so before school got out there was an ad in the "Statesman Journal" that Northwest Bell was advertising for some pole linemen telephone installers with or without experience. So I promptly went down and applied for the job. Upon applying for the job, there again it came out that I was a Vietnam veteran, and the lady that was interviewing me again promptly cut me off and said that all they had were openings for custodians at night. And there the interview ended and I caught on to what was in store for Vietnam veterans. I never did tell any potential employers that I was a Vietnam veteran, and after that I didn't have any trouble getting a job. I probably enjoyed my tour of duty over in Vietnam more than I enjoyed returning home and facing the misunderstandings from people. The people of Vietnam were quite warm and friendly, at least the ones that didn't have nicknames of Charlie, VC, and Viet Cong. Vietnam was a very lovely country. I enjoyed my tour of duty and enjoyed being there. I'm sorry that what we did there didn't mean more. It's a shame that the country had to be torn apart and had to be taken over by Communism. It's a shame that our country had to be torn apart also, or we couldn't go in and end the war in a matter of months or even years rather than decades. And now I see that their offering tours of Vietnam and you can go back there and visit Vietnam. I don't know, I think it would be interesting to do so.

Anyway, maybe I wasn't in a combat unit, but I was in a combat zone. I did see combat, and I did see not only the results of combat, but I did see the reasons for it. Whether it was a win, lose or draw situation there, I think we need to stand up to those governments that would particularly want to overthrow us and show them that whether we win or not, that there will be resistance wherever they go to try to inflict there ideologies upon us. I hope you can use some of these stories, and if not, I hope you've enjoyed listening to them. It's my story, maybe not much of one, but it's one that's meant something to me, and somehow, someway, I hope it changes some part of the world to make it a little bit better.

After getting out of the Army I got the GI Bill. On the GI Bill I went to what is now Schimecketty Community College for a year in electronics. I couldn't get a job in the electronics field because of being a vet—considering the Lieutenant Calley and My Lai Massacre at that time. It was a bad time for a Vietnam vet to be getting a job. My schooling was primarily in arts. Both mechanical drawing and the fine arts drawing, painting, sculpture, that type of thing, which slid me right into the graphic arts and printing.

Jerome Dingess Jr.

Throughout my high school days at Chapmanville High School, there were many things that were impressed upon me. A person must work hard and be willing to pay the price in order to obtain most things in life.

My morning began at 5 a.m., when I would be out of bed and ready to deliver the morning newspaper throughout the town of Chapmanville. It was fine during the spring, summer and fall. But, come winter, it became cold, walking through the snow to deliver the paper. Later on in my newspaper delivery career I switched to an evening paper route. It was better, but then again a price had to be paid. After school was football practice in the fall. So that meant that I had to hurry home and change clothes before delivery.

All the way through my high school years I worked at some type of job after school—from selling cards door to door, to trapping muskrats and selling their pelts.

One morning before going to school I went down to the riverbank to check my trap. I was holding onto one of the limbs, leaning over the bank, stretching. I was pulling my trap up, out of the water. Snap, the limb broke and into the water I went. Pulling myself onto the bank, I went back to the house, changed clothes and, off to school. My mother never found out about me falling into the river.

I would sell my pelts for five dollars each, provided that they were in good condition. Each week I caught about two. It was an exciting job. Trapping became an additional income to my paper route.

Involvement was the key phrase for me. Anything that was going on in the school, I would get involved, although it kept me busy. I always studied at night after supper was over. Many hours of studying, then to bed before the next day began all over.

My classes in high school included the following: English, Literature, Algebra, Geometry, Trigonometry, Latin, Chemistry, Physical Education, World History, and others. My future lay in store for me. I was trying to prepare for it the best way I knew how, by taking everything I could in school.

Leaving Los Angeles International Airport and heading for Da Nang, Vietnam on World Airways, we made stops at Hawaii and Japan before arriving at Da Nang. Approaching the airfield, the stewardess came over the intercom: "We hope your flight was an enjoyable one and we hope when your tour is over we can bring you back." I thought to myself, I sure hope so, too.

The first two weeks at Da Nang, I was sick. It was due to the climate change, jet lag, and knowing that I was in a hostile area. Physically, my throat stayed sore, my stomach was upset, and my head pounded. Around the third week in-country, I was okay. It was beginning to sink through, my daze wore off, and I came to realize that Vietnam was real.

"Okay, men, I don't want to see a piece of paper, cigarette butt, or anything that doesn't grow on the ground," came the voice of our sergeant. "Dingess," this was roll call. "Here," I said. Work schedule was six days a week, twelve hours a day. Being placed on night shift was par for the course. The first six months would be on day shift. Anyway you looked at it, twelve-hour shifts would keep a person busy.

Air cargo was a key to in-country supply. Our duties were to set up shipments and break down shipments from arrivals. Outside cargo was the duty that I was assigned. Night after night supplies were placed on pallets for flights to camps. C-130s would fly to these locations and off-load supplies for men in the field. We were a major link to mere existence.

Each night flares lit up the outer perimeter. Da Nang Air Base was very well protected. First, the Air Force had towers with men and weapons to help protect the base. Also, airmen and dogs patrolled the perimeter at night. There was a minefield in the outer perimeter. On the base were Marines, Army, Navy and Air Force personnel. This was the second largest base in-country, the other being at Saigon, in the southern part of South Vietnam.

Each week, generally at night, but sometimes during the day, rockets would hit our base. Charlie tried to hit our aircraft. By destroying the planes, supplies would be delayed to our camps. During my twelve months, I don't recall the Viet Cong ever hitting one of our planes on base.

One particular night, I was eating the second meal of my shift; the time was about midnight. Sitting at the table eating in the chow hall, rockets began hitting our base, one after the other. I hit the floor, counting the hits of eleven or twelve rockets. My heart was pounding so hard I thought it was coming out of my chest. I had never gone through an ongoing barrage of explosions. Sporadic explosions occurred during these days.

Being from Chapmanville, West Virginia, I had only viewed brief moments of war at the drive-in or from the local theater. Never in my wildest dreams did I expect to be a part of such action.

China Beach was a favorite place to go on our day off. It was a big beach not far from our base at Da Nang. One day a friend of mine and I were at the beach. Part of the beach area had a sign, "Keep Out—Strong Undercurrents." Well, I did not believe the sign and went into the water area anyway. After about twenty feet into the water I noticed that the current was pulling me out. I began swimming inward to the beach, swallowing water as I swam inward, yelling as much as my lungs would let me while continuing to swallow water. Two guys jumped into the water, swimming out to where I was and pulled me into shore.

Working, cleaning, sleeping, and drinking on occasion seemed a part of the life in Vietnam. Anxiety seemed par for the course. Rumors spread a great deal when the bombing was stopped on Hanoi by the president. We thought our base would be overrun by the VC. Our base was to be attacked by a rumored 10,000 VC. I don't know how the report began.

It was approximately 2 or 3 a.m. "Red Alert" was the command. We were preparing for a ground attack. Jumping up out of my bed, the entire base was on full alert. As my flak vest was put on and my boots laced up, we were going out the door of the barracks. Thoughts of our base being surrounded gave me a very cold chill. Moments later the alert was canceled. Sweat was coming down my face, my heart raced inside my body. Emotional outlets were limited in Vietnam; no one was supposed to be afraid. We were all military people.

Monkey Mountain was a very unusual name for a mountain. This is where we had our M-16 firing practice. One day on our way from base to Monkey Mt., Vietnamese were riding bikes, walking and sitting near their hooches. I watched as some of the mamasans hung their laundry on the outside lines. My thoughts went back to the base, when I saw some of the Vietnamese go through our garbage cans. Our cooks were throwing out our spoiled foods and other discarded foods. I wondered what was this war about. No one had ever told us, except that the war was to stop the Communists from taking over South Vietnam. But, was that the real reason? One theory had it that a large amount of oil was in South Vietnam and our large corporations wanted to own it.

Going back years before we became involved, the French were in Vietnam fighting and somehow our advisors slowly came into help the Vietnamese. Many questions were never answered and probably won't be until it is disclosed by whoever knows the answer. My knowledge was very limited to the main purpose. I was just an airman in a foreign country.

Each morning when I awoke, my mind would flicker back and forth, wondering if I would see tomorrow. The days turned into nights, and the nights to the next day. This would continue on for twelve months. Some days were better than others. Some nights would be short due to rocket attacks and sounds of gunfire in the distance.

Each week on my day off I would wonder what to do. For quite a few months I would just sleep late and go eat at the USO club. Or, I would read something, and maybe write some letters to my girlfriend in West Virginia. I wrote many letters; a lot of my emotional feelings went into these letters. My letters were an emotional escape for me and also for my buddies. We had feelings of frustration and rage. We wanted to *"come home"* when our tour ended.

Before arriving at Da Nang, I was stationed at Travis A.F.B. in California. I worked outside cargo, loading and off-loading planes every day, from C-141s to C-130s and occasionally, C-124s. Generally, various cargo shipments went and came. This included body transfer cases, which by the way, contained our military brothers from Vietnam, having given their lives for reasons they knew not, nor would they ever find out. After off-loading transfer cases every day for two years, it never dawned on me that I helped off-load a lot of our people who had given their lives for our country. Some came back in pieces, some in whole parts. Bodies and more bodies, where would it end?

I talked with guys coming back from Nam. The stories varied, but the experiences were similar, similar in that they were all glad they were back home. There were also comments about the parts they played in the war of politics.

On January 28, 1969 I celebrated my twenty-first birthday, a most talked about event of my past. When a person turned twenty-one, all was possible (I thought). Here I was at Da Nang, turning twenty-one and not knowing what to do with myself. I bought some brandy for the occasion and after work began sipping it from a cup. Later, going to another barracks, I played some cards with some friends until the early morning hours. The night lasted into the early morning hours. Fumbling to my barracks, weaving down the aisle, I found my bed and, falling into it, fell asleep. The morning woke me for the day's duty.

Another wonderful event that went by was Christmas. Christmas at Da Nang, where many of us felt the spirit that day—after work. There were no holidays taken off in Vietnam. We were at war, not at work. Then came New Year's Eve, 1968 passing into 1969. I wondered if I would ever see 1970.

Writing letters took the place of the telephone for most of us in Vietnam, although there was a MARS (Military Radio Stations) place to call home on some occasions when approved.

Shortly after arriving at Da Nang, I came across a friend of mine who lived not far from where I grew up, in "The Bottom" on 3rd Avenue in Chapmanville. He was a Marine, a "short timer," he told me. "Small world," I said. "You never know who you might run into over here," we both stated. Well, we talked for a while and he was scheduled for a watch on a nearby mountain. So that was the last I saw of him while in-country. Later I found out that he had made it back to the States okay.

The last ninety days in-country I shaded my short-timer calendar day by day. The last shaded area—next day was departure day. Going back to The World. That was the expression used. At last, a moment that surged upon my existence. My bags packed, I was all ready to leave. The time was about 1400 hours. Suddenly, an unexpected rocket hit our base. Anxiety, frustration, hate, fear, death, and life all surrounded me in that moment. Would I be leaving here after twelve months? Why was our base hit now? In the middle of the day, how did they know the plane was going back to The World?

Finally, we were permitted to board the World Airways plane. Lifting off the runway, airborne . . . clapping, yelling, whistling, cheering, joyful noise . . . those were the sounds coming form the inside of the plane. We were on our way back to The World. Landing in Los Angeles, and getting off the plane, I dropped to my knees and kissed the ground. Thank goodness—back in the U.S.A.

Standing in the airport waiting for a flight back to the East Coast, suddenly my eyes darted to the left, noticing a young woman in a mini-skirt. My mind began thinking back to my week in Sydney, Australia. The week in Sydney was filled with fun, frolic and adventure. Beautiful blue-eyed girls and bodies to match. I felt like I was in heaven that week. Arriving at the Sydney Airport turned out to be an experience. To start with, I was searched after going into the main terminal. What they were searching for was beyond me, but I didn't care because I was away from Vietnam for the present time anyway. Every night I went to various clubs and danced with a lot of different females. "Women everywhere," I thought. Oh, how I missed the softness and nice smelling perfume on them. After nine months, my senses became aware of what I had missed for nine months. Females.

When I arrived in Chicago, I took a taxi to the South Side, where my mother lived. As I was getting out of the taxi my eyes glanced up to the building in front of me. A big bold sign hanging down from the building read "WELCOME HOME SON." Tears came to my eyes, a lump to my throat.

I knocked on the door. Hugging my mother, she said, "Glad to have you home, son." I spent a week at her place before going on to West Virginia, where my father lived and where I would return after my military days were over.

Chicago was a big city and I did not know where anything was located. During the week in the Windy City I did see the Sears building and a few other places. It was a nice place to visit, with many places to go.

I was approaching the mountains of Charleston, where my dad was waiting to pick me up. He greeted me with a big handshake and a smile. "Glad to have you home, son," he said. I spent the next year with him and attended the Logan Branch of Marshall University.

From 1971 to 1981, many things took place. I had several part-time jobs, graduated from Marshall University with a bachelor's degree, got married and moved around to several states. Then, of course, my divorce.

Watching both of my sons being born was a big joy. Sharing their lives was also very delightful. The pain came when I had to part from their sight. The divorce in 1986 brought a personal crisis into my life. The hardest part of the divorce was yet to come. My ex-wife turned out to be a very vindictive person. She has refused to let my sons visit me during the summers at my place of residence, as was ordered in the divorce decree. She refuses to let me talk with them over the telephone. She stated once over the telephone, "I am not going to be inconvenienced." I had asked her to take them somewhere to use a telephone if she didn't have one. She does everything to prevent them from getting to know me.

Later I talked to a judge and a couple of lawyers concerning this matter. You must go to her place of residence and go through the court system again. The same thing, even though the judge in Florida gave me certain rights. My ex-wife now has me over a barrel until I can take her back to court. Meanwhile my two sons must suffer, not knowing why I don't call them, visit; nor am I able to bring them here to West Virginia for the summers.

Jason Eric Dingess was born January 15, 1982 at Charleston and Nathan Leon Dingess was born December 31, 1983, also in Charleston, West Virginia. Both boys were healthy at birth. Enjoying the four years with Jason and three with Nathan seems like such a short period of time. What I am hoping to do is to spend the entire summertime, each summer, with them and my wife Cecilia in West Virginia. They are probably wondering what has happened to me. But their mother could care less if they get to know me or not. She would prefer them to think I am dead.

During this past year we have moved to our present location at Christian. Moving takes a lot out of people and one never knows how much they have until they move. The military and college life helped prepare me for all of these changes in my life. My current position as a state probation and parole officer has opened a new realm in my life. It has combined my past experiences of counselling and teaching. Many new thoughts and ideas have come to me through my experiences.

If anything in life could prepare us for living a greater existence, it most certainly must be a tour in the military service. My feelings are that when the draft ended, so ended a vital link to our country's educational system. Also, to our country's protection for our future. So many people fail to realize the importance of a military experience to broaden one's self awareness.

Many years have passed since my Vietnam experience, but the memory lingers on. My twelve-month stay will always be a part of my total existence, as the other veterans who served over there will continue to live it too. No one ever forgets the events that took place. Some are unwilling to tell what happened, some try to forget what has happened, and some never will remember. Living with the pain may get to the point that some veterans want to scream, and others act out their anger. How do we cope with these past memories of the war in Vietnam?

Recalling my last year at Chapmanville High School, where I graduated in 1966, there were many fun times that took place. But, none prepared me for my time in Vietnam, except maybe the rigorous practice of football. Emotionally, I don't think anything can prepare a person for war except the actual experience of war. Maintaining a full schedule at high school certainly prepared me to keep myself occupied. The learning process did help me to cope with parts of my experience in Nam.

Today I think back as I write, about how fortunate I was to come back alive from Vietnam, when many of my Vietnam brothers didn't get this opportunity. Life is never the same for any of us, no matter what we may do. We are born, we learn and we die. It seems that life is full of wonderful things, when we realize what is going on in our lives. So many things take place in a person's life to change their direction, it seems. Decisions determine our directions, and our ability to make the best decisions will determine our place in life. Our belief in God does pull us through many of life's downfalls. I have often wondered why I was placed in a particular situation. My knowledge is limited, like everyone else's. Some people have gained more knowledge than others through formal education and life experiences. My feelings are that when a person combines their formal knowledge and their life experiences together, it forms a total picture. Then we become a better person.

Our hope for the future depends upon our daily activities and thoughts. We live with the hope of tomorrow and the wonders of our past, of how we made it through our experiences as we did. Without hope, all of us seem to lose sight of the future and lose the drive of the present. My determination is for self-improvement on a constant basis, although many mistakes are made daily. Hopefully, these will be limited.

Our actions today will determine our future, in that every action today will have some effect upon tomorrow. This will have an effect upon others in the community and the world.

Reflecting back to the past year and one-half, I must admit it has been the happiest spending it with my wife Cecilia. We were married May 21, 1988 in West Virginia. We went to Charleston on our honeymoon and then back to Verner. We only stayed a month before moving to Chapmanville. Cecilia has supported everything that I have wanted to do since we have been married. Without her, more than likely, I would not have written this chapter.

There are many more chapters of my life yet to be told. Maybe someday I will be able to share them with others.

Nicholas Cerreto

I attended Barringer High School and graduated in 1967. Like most guys my age, which was eighteen, I wasn't really too crazy about school but I managed to make it.

I was born and raised in Newark, New Jersey. It was a pretty wild time too, with the racial riots in the city, at times being under marshal law, with state police and National Guardsmen all over. You grew up fast at that time. You had to! The '60s were in full swing.

I got my first job at eighteen, at a company called Western Electric. I was assigned to the drafting department, and because I always did like to draw and sketch things, it was a good job for me. However, I only worked with them for one year. I could handle the job, but I couldn't handle the management. I guess being only eighteen and a city kid, I might have been a little too wild and maybe not ready to conform to the business world yet. I had a lot of things on my mind at that time—you know, the usual—girls, summers at the Jersey shore, the "war," being classified as "1A"—we all remember that. I guess I felt that I wanted to be a kid for a while. I didn't want to grow up so fast. Needless to say, I grew up very fast—a lot sooner than I expected.

I didn't date that many girls. However, it only took me a short time to know the one girl that I wanted. When I did meet and go out with her I knew that she was the one. We went together through that time, and she stayed beside me all through Vietnam. As a matter of fact, she got me through the damn war and to this day she still stands beside me, whatever I go through. To say that I love her forever doesn't really say it all.

On September 10, 1968 I came home from one of my many part-time jobs and I walked up the driveway to check the mail, like I'd done hundreds of times. Well, as soon as I saw the large yellow envelope, I knew immediately that it was for me. Uncle Sam had finally got me. I wasn't really thrilled, to say the least, but I figured I may as well get this thing over with—"I'm only eighteen now, I'll be out when I'm twenty." A lot of my family and friends, after hearing the news, reacted with mixed emotions. Some of the guys on the corner said "Don't go." My family was proud, but they were also worried. They tried not to show it, but I knew. My father and a lot of my uncles who were veterans of WW II and Korea used to say, "You'll be okay, just keep your head down," and we'd try to laugh it off, but I think that was just to try to hide the tears.

Donna, who was my girl then and is now my wife, was a little scared also. She was younger than me and I was probably the first person who she actually shared her life and emotions with and I was getting ready to go off to war. It was a lot for both of us to handle, especially at our young age. She wrote me all the time and used to send me those cassette voice tapes—I still have them—and in between all the letters and tapes, I got a lot of prayers.

That September I was off to Fort Dix, New Jersey for my basic training. I hated it, but like my high school days, I managed to graduate this too. I came home for a few days with my new uniform and my GI haircut. Everyone said I looked real good and they were all real proud of me, although not too many wanted to change places with me, even if they could look that good.

Regretfully, I returned to Fort Dix a few days later. I then received my orders with my MOS—13A10, Artillery and was to be sent to Fort Sill, Oklahoma, where I would receive my advanced training. I remember, through the whole nine weeks, I kept saying to myself, "What the hell am I doing here?" I felt like I was in a cowboy movie. Of course, it wasn't all work and no play. Every once in a while we were allowed to go into town, that rip-roaring garden spot of the world, Lawton, Oklahoma. This is when I really thought about going to Canada. I always remember that song by the Animals, "We Gotta Get Out of This Place." That was our theme song while in Oklahoma.

December 1968 came and we were all given a thirty-day leave. Most of us by now knew this would probably be the last leave we would get while in the States, so I'm sure we all made it a good one. The "Land of the Big Puddle" was getting to be more and more a reality.

On march 6, 1969 I received my new orders. I was to be at Oakland, California Army Base by March 8, and I would be processed and sent to the "Republic of Southeast Asia," as the Army put it. We knew it as "The Nam." They tried to dress it up, you know. I arrived in Vietnam on March 9, 1969 via Pan Am Airlines—never did like Pan Am. We exited the plane in our new green Army jungle fatigues, along with our pale faces and our rapidly beating hearts, I'm sure. We were put in these big green buses and I noticed that all the windows had this kind of "chicken wire" in front, with no glass in the actual window. I asked this army corporal what this was for and he told me it was in case we got mortared or some gooks tried to throw a grenade in the bus. The wire would stop it. Then he also said, "Then again, maybe it won't. Welcome to the Nam."

I did two weeks in Basic Jungle School in a town called Di An down in the Delta. I remember the first thing they told us was to forget everything we learned in the world. That's real good to know—sixteen weeks of training for nothing! After the two weeks, I received more orders. I was now permanently assigned to the 1st Inf. Division, "Big

Red One," 8 Battalion/6 Arty, 8-inch battery—the "big guns." I remember that I panicked a little when I heard "1st Inf. Div." I kept saying, "Hey, I'm artillery, not infantry."

Three other guys and I were choppered out to a little village base camp called Lai Khe. This was my home for my one-year tour. I thought it might not be too bad there. By the way it looked, it seemed quiet. Then I found out the camp was named "Rocket City" because the VC were always shooting rockets into the camp. I soon found out how right they were.

Our main function was to support infantry units out in the field when they needed us. Usually, they were all big operations. When you call in artillery from an eight-inch battery, you can bet that the shit is really hitting the fan out there in the boonies. In that year, we traveled to several firebases, mostly in the Mekong Delta area. There was Thunder 1, Thunder 2, Holiday Inn, and Firebase Kein. We lost a lot of guys at Firebase Kein, and some during our convoys out to the bush—mined roads, sniper fire, booby traps—you know, the whole nine yards. We also were involved in operations at Ben Cat, Tay Ninh, Xuan Loc, and Ben Luc. All in all I didn't have it too bad. I thank God for that. I lost a few friends, which I'll always remember, and I made a lot more. I still call and write my buddy from Philly, Eddie McKenna. It's funny all this happened twenty years ago, and I can still remember it like it was yesterday.

I started to process out of Nam on March 7, 1970. It was funny, you know—I walked through all the check-out points (finance, supply, medical) with my orders under one arm and my short-timer's stick under the other. I could almost feel other guys looking at me when I walked by them. I never said much to them, but they knew. I must have had that look on my face—"Hey world, I'm coming home!"

That night, before I was to be in Long Binh, all the guys in my section threw a party. We had our music tapes going, and beer and everything else was in abundance. It was great—sad, but great. Through the night, each of my buddies said good-bye in their own way. They looked at me with so much awe in their eyes, wishing they were me. We cried and laughed all in the same night. Sometime around 4:30 a.m. or so we all fell out. I woke up around 7 a.m. All my buddies were out cold. They were all on a three-day stand-down, so they had nothing else to do. I picked up my duffel bag and took one last look around the bunker, said a little prayer to everyone, and then left. I walked about two hundred yards to the main highway, Highway 1, we called it, and waited for the deuce-and-a-half to Long Binh to pick me up. It was about 8 a.m. by then and I looked back down at our base. It was so quiet and still. I looked out at the distant treeline, and I was wondering to myself if Charlie was looking at me, or if he knew I was going home that day. Charlie was always looking at us. I'm sure he was that day too. Well, tough luck, 'cause I made it.

I arrived at Long Binh, 90th Replacement, later that day. I started to process my paperwork. We all got a little speech from some colonel about how proud we should be, and how the United States thanks us for doing a fine job. I was thinking to myself, "Yeah, right. Next time, don't call me, I'll call you!" We spent the night at Long Binh, mostly in the Enlisted Men's club. It was a strange atmosphere in the club. On one side of the room were the "new guys," just arriving, and on the other side were "us," the vets, the ones who had made it. Again, as they stared at us, you could see the awe and the envy in their eyes. A few of them made their way to our table. They bought us some beers and we all talked about Nam, The World, and The World again. The two guys I was with were both grunts from the 1st Infantry Division's 1/28 Infantry—Black Lions. I remember them trying on purpose to keep the conversation light for the new guys—"Hell, why not? They'll find out soon enough."

Later that night we were advised that we would be leaving Nam on an earlier flight than expected. This would mean we'd arrive home a day earlier. Needless to say, we were one happy bunch. I don't think anyone slept that night. We all just laid in our bunks and stared at the ceiling, probably daydreaming our asses off.

Left Nam the next morning via United Airlines. We still couldn't believe it. As we became airborne, a loud cheer went up. We made it. We were finally getting out of the place. Everyone rushed to the windows to look out as the ground got farther and farther away. A lot of us were silent for a moment. We were looking down and remembering that some of us weren't going to make this trip on the Freedom Bird back to The World. How great it would have been if we all came home.

Nineteen-and-a-half hours later we arrived at San Francisco airport. As we flew over the Golden Gate Bridge, another loud cheer went up. We all started hugging each other and patting each other's backs—the whole works. At this time, the captain of the plane said over the intercom, "For those of you who don't remember, that's the U.S. down there."

We'd remembered, all right, and we cheered again. After landing we were bused to Oakland Army Base, where we were processed, given new uniforms, that famous steak dinner, and a ticket home.

I waited several hours and finally got a standby seat to the Newark airport. It was a little foggy and cold in Newark that day and it started to rain. I couldn't believe how cold it was but, you know, I didn't care. I was home—I made it—the kid was back!

I got a cab from the airport to where I lived in Newark. The cab driver was a WWII vet and we talked all the way to my street. He was a nice guy. As I was getting out of the cab I asked him how much I owed him. He replied, "Don't worry, pal. This ride is on the house. Take care and welcome home." I'll never forget that.

I walked down my block; it was early morning, real quiet and starting to drizzle again. I walked up the driveway and rang the first-floor bell. I stood out of sight so no one would notice me. My aunt answered the door and hugged me; we were both in shock. I told her to be quiet and I'd sneak up to the second floor, where my parents lived. As I was going up the stairs, all of a sudden the door opened and it was my mother. She was crying and yelling, "He's home, he's home. Butch is home!" My father came in the hall too, with my sister, and we were all hugging and kissing and crying. It was great. I was home. It was all over. We talked and talked, although they never really asked me too much and I never really told them, either. It was over. My dad was a WWII veteran and a POW in Germany. He knew what war was; no need to bring it home.

I rushed to see my girl that night. Naturally, we looked at each other like we were dreaming, but it wasn't any dream; it was real. We held onto each other for dear life, and to this day we've never let go. They gave me a big Welcome Home party the next week and everyone was there—all my family and friends. Everyone was happy, singing and dancing, eating and partying. It was beautiful, yet sometime during the night I had a private moment and wondered what the guys out in the bush were doing. I guess it never does leave you, does it?

As for myself, I was discharged from Fort Bragg, North Carolina on September 12, 1970 and was sent back to New Jersey a PFC. I managed to make it to Spec-4 in rank. After coming home I passed a civil service test for county corrections officer. I was employed from 1972 to 1984 as a corrections officer in the Newark City Jail. In 1984 I passed a test for Sheriff's Officer in Essex County, New Jersey and as of January 1985 I was promoted to detective and assigned to the Bureau of Narcotics, where I've been till the present time. My wife Donna and I have been married since October 1972 and reside in Newark, New Jersey.

As for my personal views about Vietnam, I have to confess that they have changed and have matured since 1969. One has to realize that back in 1969—and being only eighteen years old—I really wasn't too concerned about the political aspects of the war, or who was right or wrong. My main concern was to get the hell out of there in one piece. I would have to say that around 1979 or so, and when some of the POWs were sent home from North Vietnam, I started to really become concerned and even a little outspoken about the war. I started to write to newspaper

VIETNAM: OUR STORY—ONE ON ONE   PAGE 471

editorial columns, I joined the POW/MIA Association, the Society of the 1st Division, and the VFW. Then, in 1982, after visiting the memorial in Washington with my friend Jimmy Orr (4th Division, Infantry, Army) and marching in the "Homecoming" parade in New York City, I then started to really reflect on it. I went out and bought all the latest Vietnam movies—*Platoon, Hamburger Hill, Full Metal Jacket, Apocalypse Now*—and I even subscribed to a new magazine which comes out four times a year, dealing only with Vietnam.

The Wall really did it for me. Weeks later I could not get it off my mind. In the last few months I have even started to dream about it now and then. I realized that all these men, very young men, died for something that 'til this day, our government still can't come up with . . . a reason why they had to pay the "ultimate price." In a few books I have read, it said that both President Kennedy and Johnson were told that Southeast Asia was a bad idea and not to commit to it. Kennedy was told by, I believe, George Ball in 1961, that if he sent 5000 advisors over there that in ten years he would have 500,000 American troops there. How right he was! I remember at times being told by the South Vietnamese themselves that they wanted us to go home, to leave their country and them alone. To them, Communism was just another form of government. To be dominated by another people was nothing new to them. They were oblivious to it anyway. And through all that, we were dying one by one. Someone said that eighty percent of the KIAs were under twenty-five years old. They never got the chance to see what life is all about. To die for a cause is one thing, but to die for nothing is a shame. World War I, World War II and Korea had a cause. Someone tell me where or what was Vietnam's cause! I was there, and I don't know!

I think that sometimes other countries have to fend for themselves, and the United States is not and should not become the savior of the world. We should stand and fight when we are directly threatened, as we did in Europe and the Pacific, and that's when we should "kick butt." The next war, God forbid, has to be fought by the soldiers, not the politicians. The politicians lost Vietnam, not us! Those 58,000 are winners, not losers. You don't send men into battle to fight to a "draw." You fight to win, and as far as I'm concerned, we were never allowed to win!

Richard Carter

I guess my high school days were like many other kids' back in the middle '60s. There was rock 'n' roll music, long hair, beer busts, getting your first car and girls. It's amazing to me now, but I don't ever remember hearing about Vietnam until I was in the eleventh grade. I guess I had too many things on my mind back then. My parents were alcoholics, and the family was in a constant uproar. I wasn't like most kids. I really wasn't into rock 'n' roll music, I didn't have long hair, I had only been to one beer bust, I didn't have a car—but I did have a girl! Ah, yes. Rhonda was her name! And I was totally in love with her, as she was with me.

I was basically a good kid during my high school days. I never remember causing my parents any hardships like my older sister had. But I was having trouble in school. I got into a few fights and was kicked out of school for three days. But my downfall was passing all my subjects to acquire enough credits to go on to the next grade. It was really tough in the eleventh grade, but somehow I had enough credits to become a senior.

But the sixth week into my senior year it was found that I was a half-credit short—to be classified as a senior—and was informed that I had to go back into an eleventh grade homeroom. No way! I was not going to look like a complete idiot in front of all my friends and classmates! Well, I decided that I was just going to quit. A friend that I grew up with had quit school and he talked me into joining the Marine Corps with him on the buddy system. So, since I was only seventeen, I talked my parents into signing for me, and the rest is history.

After boot camp I was given my MOS—Infantry. I was going to be a grunt. The fighting force of the Marine Corps. Wow! Every Marine's dream! At least that's what I thought. Everyone in boot camp talked like, if you weren't a grunt, you were nothing but a pussy Marine. No glory just behind the lines filing paperwork, cooking chow and cleaning the heads. But a Marine grunt got all the glory, all the medals and all the women. But what I never heard, or even stopped to realize, was that they lived like animals (even worse). There were the insects, the heat, the lack of food and water, disease, lack of rest and sleep, and *death*. But, if I stop and think back to my training, this is what the Marines were preparing me for. And I guess I was probably told that a thousand times, if I heard it once.

It really didn't start to soak in until I received my orders to Vietnam. I was home on leave and my family and girlfriend seemed a little concerned about me going to Nam. We really didn't talk about it much, but the news on television painted a very clear picture of what I was headed for. This was the first time that I had watched television since entering the Marine Corps, and what I saw scared the living hell out of me. May 2, 1969, I landed at Da Nang about 2230 hours (10:30 p.m. civilian time) and was put up for the night in an old airplane hangar. It seemed to have hundreds of bunk beds, lined up and down in numerous rows and, with the size of the place, it seemed empty, although there were a lot of men lying down in the racks sleeping, reading and wandering around. What caught my attention the most was this one soldier about three racks away from me, sitting on the floor with his face in his hand and crying very hard. At times, I thought he was going to lose his breath and keel over. I thought of going over to him to see if I could help somehow, but I changed my mind, thinking he was better left alone with his problem.

I laid back in the rack to try and fall asleep and the first sounds of war brought me back to reality. I came out of the rack with a sudden jerk. What was that sound? As I opened my eyes, he said, "Mortar fire. What you hear, boy, is mortar fire!" I said, "Damn! I thought this was a secured area!" He said, "Boy, where you been? You're in Vietnam! There ain't nothin' secure about this place, just your chances of gettin' your ass shot off are a little less likely. Here in Da Nang you got a fifty-fifty chance, but once you're off this base, you're chances ain't so good!"

His name was Justin Willery, Spec-4, 82nd Airborne—World-bound! Without thinking, I asked him why he seemed so upset earlier if he was going back to The World. "Shouldn't you be thankful that you survived?" I asked. He said he was thankful and looking forward to seeing his family back in Georgia. But he was sad that he was leaving his family back here—the friends and buddies that he had lived with, fought with and suffered with these last thirteen months. He felt like he was letting them down, that he needed to be there for them when things got bad. He said, "You'll understand soon enough. But let me give you one piece of advice, boy. You're better off not gettin' too close to no one here, if you can do that—the hurt won't hurt as much." Although I really didn't understand exactly what he was talking about, I didn't ask for him to explain himself. I left it at that.

The next day I received my orders and boarded a convoy to join my unit at Quang Tri. About a half hour into the ride I noticed a lot of civilians on each side of the road, and at the same time saw two tanks on our right flank. Never really seeing a tank before, I was thinking to myself as I was watching them that I never stopped to realize tanks were used in Vietnam. At that split second the lead tank must have come off the ground ten feet—an explosion and debris was flying through the air. Then everyone started jumping off the trucks and crawling under them, with me not far behind.

I realized at that moment that I was really in deep shit. Tanks were exploding all around me and all hell could break loose at any moment, "And I haven't even been issued a goddamn weapon! Great! What am I supposed to do if the shit hits the fan? Throw rocks at the enemy?" Well, it was over about as quick as it had started. We were told to get back on the trucks. As everyone was getting back on the trucks, I noticed a large group of soldiers stopping all the civilians and I guess they were questioning them about the mine the tank had hit. They were talking awfully loud and you could tell by the tone of their voices that both the civilians and the soldiers were extremely upset. I learned later that the crew on the tank had all been killed.

Welcome to your first day in Nam.

I was assigned to Echo Company, Second Battalion, Fourth Marines, Third Marine Division. It was to be a few days before my unit was to come back into Quang Tri from the bush. Anyway, I had to go through what they called some sort of heat training. What it boiled down to was that they would walk, run and work the shit out of you in the hottest part of the day to see if you would die from heat exhaustion, how much you would puke your guts up and if you would sweat properly. It really didn't matter. Your ass was going out into the bush anyway, unless you did die first. Then it was to your advantage anyway; you'd get it over fast and avoid thirteen months of hell. This was supposed to get us used to the heat in Vietnam. Believe me, there was nothing in Vietnam that you ever get used to.

When my unit finally arrived I was assigned my M-16, helmet, web gear, flak jacket, pack and all the other things I would need on my year-long camping trip. From this moment on, you'll have to forgive me for not remembering names. It's not that my memory is failing me, it's more like it didn't matter at the time whose name was what. Because I was told it's best not to get close to anyone, it will hurt a lot less when they're not around. Although there are a few that I do remember, I will use them at that time, because even though I tried, I could not help but get close to them. Also remember, too, that even though their names may not stick in my mind, their faces, courage, leadership and determination to survive will never be erased from my mind. And I will consider every Marine that I fought beside my buddy, because every single day we were there we depended on each other to survive. And even though we felt like we had let them down at times when one would lose his life, we all felt like maybe there was something we could have done differently to change the outcome. It hurt and it hurt bad. Then you came back to reality and realized that if it's your turn, it's your turn, and you can't change fate.

My first day out in the bush, we were on patrol out of a firebase called the Rockpile. We had been humping for what seemed like hours when I looked up through the dense jungle and I could see this clearing up on a ridge about 500 yards away, and saw these figures walking across it. I was about to turn around and ask the guy behind me if he saw what I saw, when automatic weapons fire rang out! I hit the deck and in what seemed like only seconds these F-4 Phantoms were buzzing over head and started firing rockets. I swear, they were so close I could reach up and touch them as they flew over me. I could see the clearing on the ridge explode into a ball of fire and smoke and I also remember hearing over the radio—the radioman must have been only a few yards away—the conversation from the pilots to the ground. One pilot radioed that he had just put a rocket in the middle of at least twelve gooks.

Well, as luck would have it, my squad was elected to go across what turned out to be an old landing zone and check it out for any wounded or dead. This was suicide, I thought, to walk out in the open. We would be sitting ducks for any gooks who decided to fight it out, or were wounded and wanted to take a few Americans with them. I was scared shitless. We made it across with no trouble and found nothing. I mean nothing—no blood, no body parts, nothing. "What happened to the twelve gooks that pilot said he wiped out? Sarge said they carry off their dead. Okay, what if they were all dead? Who carries them off then? Oh well, what if . . . who gives a shit! I'm still here one more day!"

Things were pretty quiet for the next several weeks. We ran OPs during the day and listening post at night, along with our regular patrols out of base camp, sometimes lasting up to a week. It was on these long patrols that we encountered our most deadly firefights.

Operation Purple Martin lasted three months and was our most costly operation. On this particular operation we were to run a search and destroy from Quang Tri north to the DMZ. With base camp set up on LZ Carroll, we ran platoon-sized patrols. One night during my watch, I started feeling very dizzy and hot and I was sweating profusely. I went to see the corpsman. After checking me out he said that I had malaria and would med-evac me out, as soon as daylight broke. I spent the next thirty days in a hospital in Quang Tri.

After being released from the hospital I was choppered back to the bush to my unit. By this time they had moved out of LZ Carroll to LZ Stud. My platoon was out on a two-day patrol, so I filled sandbags and various other duties until they returned. I was helping sort out the company mail when I came across this letter with the name Tom Deterly on it. Surely this can't be the same Tom Deterly I went through boot camp, ITR and BITS with, and my closest friend during that time. No more than I was thinking this than my platoon returned from patrol, and as I greeted each one as they came over the LZ, my heart went straight up into my throat! There came Tom with a big fat grin on his face and an M-16 slung over his shoulder. We hugged, almost squeezing the breath out of one another! It was really him! What were the chances of us not only ending up in the same company, but the same platoon and the same squad! Ain't life grand, we said to each other. We had a lot to talk about, and God knows we would have plenty of time for that.

There was this black guy named Hucklebuck that became one of our best buddies. Hucklebuck was older than the rest of us. I guess he was at least twenty-four. He had only a fifth-grade education, but the kicker was that he had a wife and five kids back home in Georgia. I mean, what the hell is a man with a family doing in Vietnam? With five children at home? He said that there were no jobs back home so he joined the Marine Corps. At least they would have medical and financial help. Anyway, Hucklebuck's goal in life was to become a state trooper in Georgia. The whole squad got together and wrote the state of Georgia letters, telling them what an asset he would be to them and to please let us know what we could do to help him fulfill his dream. After about a month, an application came and we all got together and helped him fill it out. Another month passed and Hucklebuck—HQ—received a letter from the state informing him that after his discharge from the Corps, he would be accepted into their training program, providing he completed his high school GED before he graduated from the academy. You talk about one happy human being! We almost had to hold him down and gag him to keep him from letting every gook in Nam know where we were. HQ hugged each and every one of us and thanked us for helping make his dream come true. I don't think any of us felt as proud at that moment as we did in our whole lives. I know I was on cloud nine.

Dreams were all we had over there. We all talked about what we were going to do when we went back to The World. Everything from us all getting together, buying motorcycles and touring the whole United States, to marrying our girlfriends and settling down and having families. My plans were the latter.

August 1969: we were on Operation Dewey Canyon, running size patrols one klick south of the DMZ. I was walking point that day. I was about fifty meters ahead of the column. When I just came around a bend next to the trail, I froze dead in my tracks. There, about twenty-five meters ahead of me, was a gook in a tree, setting up a claymore mine facing the trail. He saw me about the time I saw him. I raised my M-16 and fired one shot, knocking him out of the tree. What I didn't see was another gook sitting against the same tree, and he had thrown a grenade towards me. In an instant there was this explosion and I was laying somewhere in the jungle and all hell was breaking loose. What seemed like an hour was but only minutes, rounds were buzzing over my head and there was movement all around me. I felt something warm between my legs and a great deal of pain. Afraid to move or make any sound, not knowing where I had landed or who was moving all around me, I just laid still and silent. I heard someone calling my name and I responded. It was my squad leader. After finding me, he immediately called for a corpsman. When the corpsman arrived, he said two words, "Oh shit." Well, that's all I had to hear. I really got scared and said, "Okay, Doc. Tell me straight. If I lost my family jewels, just finish me off!" He said he couldn't really tell, it was such a bloody mess, but it looked like everything was still there.

A chopper was called in for a med-evac. The jungle was so dense that a line had to be sent down to me while the chopper hovered 100 feet or so above. "Oh, great! While I'm being pulled up into the air to the chopper I'll make a great target for some gook who's decided to hang around and start some more shit!" I was assured that the area was secure and that it would be a safe trip. I believe that was the longest time in my life I had ever spent anywhere, but I made it safely. As I was settled into the chopper I noticed that they were lowering the cable down again. I thought to myself, who else is wounded? As they were pulling the cable back up, names and faces started running through my mind: "Please God, don't let it be Deterly, please." About the time the last thought went through my mind, the body appeared at the base of the doorway. I couldn't tell at first who it was because the chopper crew was blocking my view and they seemed to have trouble getting him inside. I decided I didn't want to look, so I closed my eyes.

After the chopper was making a forward motion and was flying, I slowly opened my eyes and focused them on the figure in front of me. My heart stopped pumping, and all the breath left my lungs, and I felt a sadness that I never felt before or experienced since. It was Hucklebuck. At first I thought he had been given some kind of pain medicine and had fallen asleep because he looked so peaceful and I couldn't see any wounds or blood. I stared at him for a few minutes, trying to figure out what was wrong with him. Finally, I asked a crewman what was wrong with him. He looked at me like I was some kind of nut and said, "He's a dead man. The guy bought the farm."

I lost my cool. I started screaming as loud as I could. "He ain't no slab of meat, man! At least you could cover him up with something!" The crewman said for me to calm down and get my shit together, he'd take care of it. He reached over and grabbed a poncho liner and covered my buddy Hucklebuck.

I spent twenty-six days in the hospital in Quang Tri, hoping every day that this was my ticket home. But no such luck. My wounds were only superficial and I'd be going back into the bush. When I returned to my unit, they were doing perimeter security at a firebase called the Rockpile, which was where all the heavy duty artillery was, and believe me, it was a lot quieter out in the bush. Deterly and I talked a lot about Hucklebuck and decided to write his family a letter and tell them what a great person he was and how much he loved his family and talked about them all the time.

All was quiet the next couple of days, and the night before we were to go back into the bush we all sat around cleaning our weapons and drinking hot beer. I had a funny feeling this time about the bush. I really couldn't put my finger on it, but I remember that I wasn't scared that I was going to be killed or injured. It was more like the feeling you have when you're going to play your first ball game. The score is tied, bottom of the ninth, two outs. It all depended on what the final outcome would be.

At 0600 hours we boarded the choppers to go to God-knows-where. Halfway into the flight we were informed that we were landing on a hot LZ. I could hear the distinct sound of AK-47 fire as we landed. As I exited the chopper and was running for cover I attempted to return fire and my M-16 would not fire. I laid low until the LZ was secure and then I checked my rifle. Come to find out, my firing pin was missing, and I distinctly remember replacing it the night before. After further investigation, someone in another platoon had switched rifles on me. I never found out who it was because he was transferred to another company, in fear of his life. The story was that he was cleaning his rifle and had lost his firing pin. Afraid of telling his platoon leader because he was a screw-up anyway, he crept over in the middle of the night and switched rifles. I guess mine was the first one he came to. The more that I thought about it the more angry I became. The man could have cost me my life, and other Marines, too! I guess to satisfy my anger I was told that he would be severely punished and would probably serve time in a military prison. After that, I checked my rifle daily, to make sure all parts were there and it was functioning properly. Something that I took for granted all these months.

Things were very peaceful the next few months. We ran daily patrols off firebases, daily OPs, and night LPs. Then in January we started hearing scuttlebutt about President Nixon pulling us out of Vietnam. We had heard bullshit like this before and were disappointed, and our morale would get very low. But any ray of hope was more than we had the day before. And hope had kept us alive this long, so we held on to all we could get.

February 1970: we were ordered to work our way back to Highway 1, to meet up with a convoy to Da Nang. We were going home! I'll never forget the mixed feelings that I had as we were walking down Highway 1 and tanks and other equipment were just left off to one side of the road for the South Vietnamese Army. I felt my chest swell up with pride that I had survived Vietnam. A war that I gave everything inside of me, to do my job and follow orders. I survived the heat, the bugs, the rains, the smell of death, the humping from dawn to dusk, the dysentery, the heartache of losing close friends. But most of all I won out over death, who many times tried to nail the coffin shut on me—everyday that I was there. I had survived and I was proud to be a human being again. Proud to be a United States Marine!

After reaching Da Nang, we spent a couple of days processing out. We were on our way to Okinawa, via the *USS Cleveland*. After reaching Okinawa we went to a Marine base called Camp Swab. There we were all given new orders. Most of Echo Co. 2/4 was sent to Japan for cold weather training to finish out their overseas tour, and anyone with less than two months was processed home.

I had three and a half months left, so I was Japan-bound. As we were standing outside the division headquarters to be processed, I passed out. Next thing I knew, I woke up in the hospital with malaria. I had to spend the next thirty days or so there, so my unit went on to Japan without me. Thinking I would join up with them after I got out, I enjoyed the bed rest.

After I was released from the hospital I was not allowed to join my unit in Japan. I was assigned to supply for the 9th Marine Division. It was a skate job for the next few months, and I enjoyed seeing all the sights of Okinawa. On May 2, 1970 I was on the Freedom Bird back to the States. We landed at Edwards Air Force Base in California and as the wheels touched down the aircraft shook with screaming servicemen. As I reached the bottom of the ramp and my feet were firmly planted on American soil, I dropped to my knees and kissed the ground with tears running down my face! I made it! I really made it! Thank you, God!

I returned home to Fort Worth, Texas, and on May 16, 1970 I married my high school sweetheart. While on leave, I received my orders to report to Camp Pendleton in California, to attend rifle marksmanship instructors school. After about two weeks, my wife joined me and we rented an apartment in Oceanside. We almost starved to death trying to pay for rent and food. I remember eating beans and bread everyday for weeks at a time then, when the next paycheck came, we would splurge and have some meat with our beans. We met some other Marine couples in the apartments and would somehow find something to do for entertainment.

Now, when my wife and I think back to that time, we both agree that it was the most fun and exciting time that we ever had.

The Marines came out with an early-out program three months after I was stationed at Edgon Range. I took it and my wife and I returned home to Fort Worth.

Since being released from the Marine Corps, I held various jobs the first couple of years. In January of 1972, my wife gave birth to our daughter Jennifer. In September of 1976, we had our second daughter, Cally. I worked for a wholesale plumbing supply house for twelve years. Always being a Marine at heart, I joined the Marine Corps Reserve in April of 1984. I'm sorry to say, but I hated it. It just wasn't what I thought it would be. There was no discipline with the younger Marines. Half were on drugs and the other half was just plain lazy. Of course there were a few exceptions, but they were generally older and had been in the Corps for ten or more years. In my reserve unit there were only about two other Marines who had served in Nam, and the older Marines that had not served in Vietnam were very envious of the ones who had, because the younger Marines would all gather around us and want to hear our war stories. My opinion is that to be a Marine and not have been in battle leaves a void that you had been trained for from the moment that you stepped on those yellow footprints. And I pray that no Marine, or anyone in any other branch of the service, will ever have to die in combat again. But to be honest, if I had to choose my death, giving my life for my country would be all right with me. And I'm sure, if you could go back and ask some of the servicemen who gave their lives, you would probably get the same answer.

Vietnam, to me, was a learning experience. First I learned that it doesn't take long for a seventeen-year-old boy to grow up quick. I learned how quick a man can die, and how quick a man can learn how to kill, what true comradeship was and how it kept you alive; and that depending on the other Marines in tough situations was what it was all about, because you can't survive by yourself in Vietnam—it takes team work. I learned how precious water and food were, something we all take for granted until there is none. I know to this day, every time I turn on the faucet to brush my teeth or get a drink of water; I'm reminded of all the times I had none to drink, and it seems such a waste to see it go down the drain.

When I returned home, I learned that being a Vietnam veteran wasn't something you went around bragging about. I learned that people were scared of you. They thought we were all baby killers, murderers, and were deranged in some way. My old friends from high school avoided me like I had some kind of disease. Here I thought that I had really accomplished something by surviving a war and serving my country. I was very proud to be a decorated war veteran, and the country and people that I fought for treated us lie we were lepers. And what about the many brave young men and women who gave their lives? Was it for nothing? In my opinion, no! Vietnam wasn't a popular war and we did leave without a confirmed victory. But that does not take anything away from the men and women who served and died there. We had a job to do, we followed orders, and we did it honorably. Of course, in the last few years the American people have let us Vietnam vets out of the closet. They have opened their minds and hearts and are beginning to understand the pain and suffering that we've gone through the last twenty years. That's nice. But for me, it's too late. I've already gotten over the rejection and the scars that the American people caused me some twenty years ago. I went on with my life without all the parades and glamor of war heroes. The hurt is still there, but so is my pride and honor, something that can never be taken away from me by anyone.

Now there's Panama! And it makes me sick to watch the television and read the newspapers, making such a big deal out of a two-week encounter with a few rebels. All the soldiers that fought and died there are heroes. Not taking anything away from these brave men and women that fought for the same cause as I did twenty years ago, but in my opinion America is trying to make up for that grave mistake twenty years ago, and is giving those soldiers recognition for a job well done, something Vietnam veterans did not get! It won't work, America. The damage is done and history cannot be changed!

I'm glad to see you learning from your mistakes. God knows we can't afford another Vietnam!

I'm happy with my life now. I've got a good and satisfying job. I'll be celebrating my twentieth wedding anniversary this year. My oldest daughter Jennifer gave birth to my grandson last February, so I finally have a boy in the family. And I am attending junior college next semester to finish up my degree in business.

I have a lot to be thankful for, and so do the American people! Please, America, be thankful that young men and women are willing to sacrifice their lives for the freedom you know and enjoy. And never forget: pray for the families that have lost loved ones in war, the missing in action and prisoners of war, for their fate is uncertain.

And to all my brothers and sisters that still carry the burden and scars of Vietnam, we are the only ones who know the feelings we feel. We are special! Let no one take that away! Semper Fi.

Joseph Csuk

I grew up in a little town called West Bend, Wisconsin, fifty-six miles north of Milwaukee as a crow flies. It's where the kettles and coffee pots come from that we or our parents use, stamped "West Bend Aluminum." It used to be that. Now it's just West Bend, because they make other items.

Well, I was a hell raiser most of my young life, and was headed for the Big House when I had a choice in my sophomore year to either take a life in the service or life in the Pen. I took service and never regretted it. I served the rest of my high school days in the Army. Most of my friends and relatives made bets that I'd get booted out.

But, I proved them wrong. I served and got an honorable discharge and I am proud of it. I remember when I was told to not hang it on my wall. It might cause trouble. To hell with that. "I served. I'll show it."

I went in at seventeen, turned eighteen in Fort Knox, Kentucky in 1964, where I took basic. We left Milwaukee by train in cattle-car confinement. I stayed at Antler Hotel while taking my indoctrination. All those who remember, say "Hi."

I went to signal school in Fort Gordon, Georgia. From there I went to Korea, wearing the patch of a skull called Vagabond in a Signal Battalion, and was attached to a lot of different units. I also learned a lot about not trusting the word of the Army or what those in rank have to say unless it is in writing.

From there to Fort Hood, Texas. There I met some good friends such as Henry Fields and David Mier—those that would be with me for our next orders. Those came after a short time—to Fort Lewis, Washington, 4th Infantry Division, on the way to Vietnam. That's how we got on the troop carrier, with my bald head . . . singing "Yellow Submarine" on deck until we saw the shore of Vietnam.

I hope all my friends made it.

To all my brothers that served: I write this letter and for those to come, that the mistakes of the past should never happen again.

Vietnam. Boy do I remember. It's all like a dream. Many fuzzy edges. Maybe too much booze or maybe too much war. But, I stepped off the troop carrier ship carrying Marines and Army—the last one to be used. We took an amphibious vehicle to shore in some sea that was not too steady. Then we flew in a box car and went to Pleiku. I remember my thoughts: "What the hell are we doing here?" And after a night on guard duty in the frontline bunker you would ask that question often. I was in Signal and came to Pleiku with the 4th Infantry Division. I had already served one hitch in Korea, but got orders to come here. "Luck holds, so I'll get home," I thought. "If not, make sure it's clean and not in pieces in a hospital." I knew I couldn't stand that. That scared me the most. Probably does us all. And so many of us would come home to all these fears.

Back to the bunker. My first impression was, "Hell stands between me and the enemy. . . . Light is a target. Be on guard of what you do. Horse sense, they call it. Try to stay alive."

Our boys were there before I got there. They seemed comfortable about being there. My first night of mortars, guns and bullets that ripped through the night made my knees knock and my jaw chatter. I'd say teeth, but it went deeper than that. I have never been that scared.

But after a time, you got used to it. Not over the fear, but accepting your fate. You went about filling sandbags over and over, building barracks and eating C-rations. Now, after it started to feel like a compound, you receive orders to go on convoy; move out by vehicle, a two-and-a-half-ton van loaded with big equipment from the 124th Signal Battalion Co. C. That was my office and home on the road. I was a 31M20 radio relay carrier operator. No, I didn't carry a radio in combat. I thought so in basic, but it meant radio airwaves and landline mobility unit. We used both radio and telephone. If you called from anywhere in Nam you came through our equipment.

To be on convoy was an earth shaking experience in itself, since you only have to contend with snipers. But dust three feet deep, and mined roadways. It was like coming face to face with a stone wall at sixty miles an hour. But you can't see it coming.

Sarg and I were told we would have the privilege of going to a fire support base. It was somewhere on a small hill overlooking the DMZ. The drive there was an experience! Dust as thick as fog. You could see not a foot around you, but just kept on pushing until you arrived. Every once in a while there was a truck on the side which hadn't been so lucky and the tanks just pushed them aside.

My first thought of this hill was, "You have to be kidding." It was no bigger than a small city block. There were little sandbagged adobe bunkers with guns on trailers and howitzers on or near them. We were told to wait to set up our equipment and raise the fifty-foot fly swatter antenna. It was like raising a marker for the Cong to set target at and it was used for that many times. Our guy lines were cut from shrapnel. But, since Charlie usually attacked at night, we lived to tell about it. It was like living through an earthquake every day. When the guns fired, the earth shook and dust left the ground around us like smoke. They fired continuously in different bursts so Charlie didn't know which were coming his way. It's an experience only those that have been there can know—what it feels like and sounds like.

There were a lot of things I heard while I was out there that I had never known of, such as Charlie digging holes in solid rock with air entrenching tools. There were not just holes, but whole caves-compounds underground. No matter how hard we pounded him with heavy artillery and Puff, he always came back fighting. A more determined enemy was probably never fought. To think of what he did with the shovel was amazing, since we used it mostly to fill sandbags, not to dig holes or create the mazes their human moles did. But before the rain came, they made us leave the fire station. That was good. For Charlie was building up every night and hitting heavier and more aggressively. It was a relief to move off of there.

There were other firebases. I remember Jackson Hole, for the Marine forces doing battle came through our equipment. Our Army forces were backed up by the Navy with artillery or cover fire. I also remember the exchanges of cold beer for the warm beer the foot soldiers had. We had the electricity and usually a small fridge, so we exchanged their warm beer for our cold beer. We never minded sharing our power with the troops if they didn't abuse it. If they did, I would pull the plug. It seemed the only ones I had trouble with were the officers. The higher the rank the more electrical appliances they had and the more juice they needed. I remember leaving the lights on for the 1st Cav. enlisted men so they could write letters, and then turning the juice off on their colonel. He had a hot plate and a coffee pot plugged in.

He had the nerve to threaten me with court-martial because he wore a bird. I told him to shove off. I gave the orders when it came to the use of electricity. Either you do as I say or I disconnect. Since communication is more important than hot coffee, I never could understand how some officers thought they were more important than their own men.

Well, from that point you get the idea. I didn't care much for the Army, for the ass-kissers who brown nose their way to rank, or officers and enlisted men who cheated the hard working and endangered officers and enlisted men who did their job. There were men who stole money and merchandise from us and sold it to the enemy for profit. That was the black market. There were four that were arrested for those deeds. They were entrusted with our mail then went through it and took what they wanted, maybe things bought at the PX, and then an empty box would be sent home. This happened in Pleiku. When I left they were still under armed guard. I don't know what happened to those individuals, but I hope they are still serving time. How can a man steal from a man he may need to depend on for his or his buddy's life. Those people were really low grade and not worthy of the right to be called Veteran or Soldier. They are as much the enemy as Charlie.

Sorry, I got carried away.

I remember a time—and maybe someone reading this will remember me—I was stationed near ROK Army. I got along real good with the Korean soldiers and officers. Even drank beer in their tents. Our troops didn't like them. Probably because they were different and looked a lot like the enemy, slant eyes and all, but they were not. They were tough fighting troops and they had lives like us, a family and homes to go home to if they survived. Besides, I spoke a little Korean from my last tour of duty and I liked the people. They are good hosts and the rice wines are great. Because they used Koreans on guard duty, I could go in and out of the compound pretty much as I pleased. This ticked off the people I was attached to, but it didn't matter to me for I'd never be a general anyway.

I remember one night sleeping on my cot when I was rudely interrupted and shaken awake. A bright light was on my eyes and then someone shouted, "You Joe?"

I said "Yeah, what about it?" and he told me he'd like to talk to me outside. When I asked what for, he just said "outside," and could I "get home to the village." Now he had my attention. It was the middle of the night and he wanted to go to the village. That was off-limits at night. This intrigued me, so I went with him.

He was an officer and said he had seven men that had just come off patrol. They had one night to make hay and lay some seed, then they would be going back out on patrol, not knowing if they would come back. Boy, I'll never know how or who spread the rumor that I could get them off base, but we did. I got them through the Korean guards, but we needed to be back by daybreak before the MPs, our guys, would go on duty. Fully loaded with our weapons and what we could carry, we went to town. I knocked on one of the mamasan's doors that served booze, beer and broads. We posted two guys on watch while the rest partied. The beer was great. The girl gave me clap.

We probably knew this was suicide, for Charlie was out there at night in those villages. But what the hell . . . "he owns that country and is here all the time."

So it was a little excitement and I'll never forget it. I just wish I had known the name of the guys that I was with and how the hell they came to me in the first place? This happened a few more times, but never like the first time.

As I have said, it was Charlie's country and his people. Sometimes those you trusted in the ARVNs' villages or those you called friends got you killed. If you were on med-evac helping the "Mountain Guards" and had an ARVN intercept it, it could be your last day. The bar you went to or the woman you had might lead to your end. I had a friend, a GI, that I came to Nam with on ship. He went AWOL for dope. Can you imagine going AWOL in Nam? Some did. I never knew if they found him or if he came back.

There are memories and bloody parts of the war that I haven't written about. I'd rather forget some of what I've seen. But not the War. For if it was a police action, why did so many of us die? And how could our government and the people pushing the peace movement have the idea that we weren't fighting for their right to be free? Our blood was being spilt on foreign soil and they were debating on what to call Vietnam, a police action or a war. Hell, it was WAR—ask us. We served and fought and died. Now, after twenty years, you want to honor us. Why didn't you celebrate when we came home? Honor us then, the living along with the brave. Why pardon the deserters, the noncombatants, those that fled to Canada, Mexico or anywhere else? What right did this government have to pardon them? We fought and some died and they put the bastards that were chicken shit or didn't respect the freedom that this country stands for in the same classification as those of us who served honorably. Not all of us wanted to be there, but did so out of honor to ourselves or fear of reprisal from our government. We served! Yet those that didn't got their names cleared and get some of our rights to benefits.

This war changed my life. For the longest time I fought with myself. What if I was right in taking the abuses that the people had in their heads about the Vietnam veteran. My parents said I was crazy and I was thrown out. I really lived with not knowing what I was or where I fit. When I went for a job I couldn't say I was a Vietman vet or they would think I was a loony. Since that time, when anyone killed someone or beat some one up, they said he came from Nam. The news was used to incite people and frighten them away from "us crazies."

I guess back in 1967 I didn't plan my career too well and no one cared. Lots of promises and shrinks that didn't understand the Vietnam entanglements—how can you talk to those that haven't been there? Even the VFW that I joined for a time didn't help. Us Baby Brothers didn't fit in with the WWII hero. I could tell their opinion of me by their actions.

So for fifteen years my life has been a mixed-up mess, trying to find the right path to follow. My wife has been with me through the worst, and some good times. I have two young adults now. One in college and one in the Navy. I always will love them, but I never really got close to them. None of the mushy affection like I saw in some families. I wonder how much of that relates back to this Nam?

"I'm proud of you two. I hope that because of what we went through, being a part of the Vietnam experience, you will never have to. Love, Dad."

Samuel Howard Jr.

I, Samuel Howard Jr., was born to Mr. Samuel Howard Sr. and Mrs. Myriah Howard, along with two sisters. At the young age of two years old I was too young to actually discern what was actually happening on a very dark day in our home. This tragedy would leave a permanent scar on me . . . for the rest of my life.

At two years of age, on this particular day, I heard my dad shouting at my mom really loud. My two sisters, one three years old and the other one year old, quickly gathered in a corner of the room and we saw our dad take out a gun and begin shooting our mom, and then turn on us. I could hear Mom screaming, "Please don't hurt them! Run and hide, children!"

Those were her last words. I ran into another room and hid in a closet. I heard screaming; my dad had shot my sisters also. My dad then went from room to room calling me: "Junior. Junior. Junior. Come here. I won't hurt you." I didn't answer, nor did I make a sound. After a long period of time the police arrived at our home, after neighbors alerted them. They found me in a fetal position in the closet, with clothes covering me. As the police brought me out of the closet I saw lots of blood and some of the policemen were crying in such a way that it frightened me even more. I yelled, "Mama! Mama!" but I got no answer. She was dead, along with one of my sisters, and although my remaining sister was shot, she didn't die. This would be the last time I would see any member of my family.

My dad was arrested and sentenced to prison for life. He died in prison in the state of Alabama.

I was raised by my Aunt Pinkie Williams in New York. For many years my new family kept all the facts from me. I often asked where were my mom and dad. On Father's Day and Mother's Day, while in grade school, I can remember making them cards like the other children in my class. However, when I got home I had no one to give them to. This was very sad and I began to think I was different from other children.

I was raised in a nice Christian home, yet I went astray because of the surrounding street gangs and peer pressure in which I got involved. I only wanted to be accepted and wanted things I saw other children with. I put all the good teaching I had behind and got involved with any and everything I thought would fill the void in my life. I quit high school and joined the United States Marine Corps because I had heard it to be for tough guys. I joined the Marines at seventeen years of age at the local recruiting center, in the downtown Flatbush section of Brooklyn, New York in January of 1968, during the peak of the Vietnam War. In July of 1968 I was in Da Nang, South Vietnam.

My MOS (duty), 1371, was combat engineer—land mine sweeping. Upon arriving in Vietnam I was ordered to Hill 10. On the route to my new base in a jeep, we were ambushed from a rice paddy. My first thought was that this was merely a ruse to see my reaction. I immediately got down on the floorboard of the jeep and buried my head between the sandbags. I thought, "Well, this is it. No way will I make it back to The World." I did make it to Hill 10, and after a brief orientation, we were informed not to trust any Vietnamese; no sex; and definitely no drugs—opium, etc.

My first serious combat experience was on my first operation called Oklahoma City. My duty was to put on the mine-sweeping metal detector and go out first before the pointmen—the grunts—and clear the path of mines. This job was so stressful that I had to result to any type of drug I could get, which was easy, because drugs grew in the fields of Vietnam. The mine sweeping then became a little easier because the frame of mind I was in after taking the drugs. Many times when the mine detector indicated metal, I laughed to myself and didn't even bother to check it out. I thought it only to be a C-ration can left long before now. Wrong! Many people were hurt because of my gross negligence, including myself. An anti-personnel mine exploded as a result of my state of mind.

After a few months of being in Vietnam, I found out that if I developed a "I don't care" attitude I would make it back to The World. And yes, it helped. A few of us Marines were ordered to guard a small village between Phu Bai and Hue. There I became friends with the Vietnamese people and I fell in love with a nice, sixteen-year-old girl named Vinh. To my surprise, their culture and traditions were much the same as ours. I met her mother. Her father was killed by Viet Cong. We all sat down on the floor and ate rice and dog meat with chop sticks. I didn't realize it was dog meat until Vinh told me. I didn't get sick, although I felt as though I would. Although Vinh, her mother and I had a language barrier, we just smiled for "Yes" and nodded for "No." They would always alert me when the enemy soldiers, Viet Cong and North Vietnamese Army, were planning an attack. In turn I would inform my superiors.

Vinh became pregnant by me and after the last warning that the Viet Cong were planning a major offensive, the brass pulled our unit out of the area and ordered us to a more secure area in the rear, Da Nang. I didn't want to go because of Vinh, however, I had no choice. A few months later I saw our Marine chaplain and told him I wanted to go back to the village to see this girl. I didn't tell him why. However, I think he knew I loved her. He said "No." Then I said I wanted to stay in Vietnam and not return to our country.

The chaplain then referred me to the unit psychiatrist, which I declined. I went AWOL to see Vinh. With only a magazine in my M-16 and two grenades, and no helmet, I arrived at the small village in which Vinh lived. The little Vietnamese children ran up to me and gave me the biggest hugs. And the others ran to get Vinh before I asked them to. After seeing Vinh for the first time in nearly four months, my heart dropped. There she stood, dressed in this black silk uniform, with this huge stomach. She walked up to me and said, "If me papasan was living, he would throw me in river." She then told me to go back to my unit and country because in Vietnam there's always fighting. She gave me pictures of her and, with tears in my eyes, and hers, I left. It would be the last time I saw Vinh. I love children and because of my childhood, I had planned to treat my children really good, and give them all the love I could.

On August 8, 1969, I returned to the good ol' U.S.A. Treasure Island, California. There I was asked if I wanted to re-enlist or be released. I chose the latter. After being released, I went to live with my Aunt Pinkie Williams, who raised me and now lived in the suburbs of New York. She didn't mind because I had saved money from Vietnam.

I began looking for a job, as my money began to run out. No luck in finding a job, so consequently, my aunt threw me out of her home. I slept in my car and showered in abandoned buildings. I eventually found a job as a clothing salesman for a prominent Jewish family in Jamaica, New York. They kind of felt sorry for me because of my duty in Vietnam, and I couldn't find a job. We all knew I had no skills or experience for the job they gave me. I worked for them for many years. I then began to develop problems from the Vietnam War. I often thought everyone was out to get me. So, I went to the Veterans Administration for help with my problems. However, the Veterans counselors always told me to come back or they would call me, which they never did.

I began drinking heavily because being drunk was the only way I could sleep or rest. The irony is, I never even once thought I was an alcoholic.

I became violent with my cousins, the only family I ever knew, and the ones who cared for me. I quit my job and went down to the Marine recruiting center in Jamaica, New York, and re-enlisted because I thought this would be best for everyone, and violence was the only way I knew how to perform and get a salary too.

However, the day I was supposed to report to Fort Hamilton in Brooklyn, New York, to be sent to my new duty station, I didn't show up. I just wanted away from everyone.

I then tried college, although it was very difficult for me to concentrate on my studies. I did graduate from LaGuardia Community College with an A.A. degree in Liberal Arts. I supported myself through college by driving taxi and college work-study programs, as I had no family to help. With all the stress I received from the lack of sleep, and the pressures from everyday life, my episodic problems began again. I was arrested for a violent crime against a friend of mine. Before I went to trial, I left town and came out to California to live with some distant relatives. They wanted no part of me.

I then left California for Las Vegas, Nevada. I had been told that in Las Vegas one could make quick, easy money. I was wrong again. I resorted to violence again to make ends meet. I became a suspect in a number of crimes. One in particular was the murder of a prominent doctor in Las Vegas. My fingerprints linked me to the crime. Although there were other, unidentified fingerprints found on the doctor's vehicle, I was a good candidate because of my violent acts and poverty.

I sought help from my cousins and they declined to get involved. They said I had changed since returning from Vietnam, and whatever I was charged with, I probably did it. My last recourse was my common-law wife, who left me in New York and returned to Tucson, Arizona because of my unpredictable actions. She did come to Las Vegas, Nevada, but to testify for the prosecution. There I sat, in the courtroom, all alone. I never felt so all alone in my life. I kept thinking, "Why is this happening to me?" I thought of mother, and "would things have been much different for me if she would have been alive." The only decent thing I thought I could do was to pray, as I had been taught by my Aunt Pinkie. I did pray, not to be set free from confinement, but for whatever God's will for me was. I felt as if I had ruined my life, and others' too. Within five months I was tried and convicted by a jury. The defense attorneys who represented me were the friends and clients of the deceased doctor. In no way do I blame the system, nor am I bitter, because this is all part of life, and never once did I think I would end up in a place like this.

I didn't come to prison to find religion or God. One has to be called by God. I could have been worse than I was before coming to prison. However, when God is in your life, you are a completely new person. I don't even like the things I used to do before, even beer. I don't need the false material things I thought would cause happiness and peace. The peace I have now is eternal, and I wish everyone could and would experience it. Years ago I even attempted suicide. Thank God I didn't. Now I counsel many people here who are so depressed and think there's no hope. We all go through life's turmoils even if one is in prison, with bars, or in a prison without bars.

Please take heed, and if you are headed in the wrong direction, stop, before you regret doing something you would never think you are capable of doing.

IT COULD HAPPEN TO YOU!

Update: after serving a thirteen-month tour in Vietnam, from July 1968 to August 1969, in which Samuel Howard received five medals for meritorious duty, he was honorably discharged from the United States Marine Corps, partially disabled. He is now on the state of Nevada's Death Row, awaiting execution pending appeals. He was sentenced in May, 1983.

R. E. "Dusty" Trimmer

I spent most of my childhood on Cleveland's eastside neighborhood, where you had to fight just to get home from school. My best friend was Butch, a tough, husky, black kid who taught me how to fight. We were in the first grade then and being a blond-haired blue-eyed Caucasian was not an advantage there.

What bothers me most is that it's usually another Nam vet, one of their relatives or their friends who ask us about Vietnam. Other people still just don't want to hear about it and think we should just put it out of our minds. Nam will be with those who experienced it forever, and . . . beyond.

Getting egged at Oakland when we came home in 1969 didn't bother me as much as when Cleveland's own Coming Home parade for us in 1988 was interrupted by, of all things . . . protestors of the Vietnam War. They were probably in kindergarten when my buddies and I were being ambushed in the Iron Triangle.

It made me sick when I read a newspaper article about how Cleveland's mega corporation wouldn't contribute to our twenty-year reunion and parade. Surely some of them were there, or people close to them had to be touched by Nam in some way. God, that depresses me to this day.

It didn't bother me too much that Jane Fonda took twenty years to apologize to us, but it did when she finally came forth with such a pitiful effort. If she could only see how she was being used back then.

I was a lonely child, subjected to divorce, a boarding home and beatings, neglect, a low-income family, separation from my sisters and brother (twice), a step-father who provided for me but didn't want me, a father who disowned me (his wife liked me less) but also a mother who tried her best, loved her kids and eventually succeeded in helping all five of us get out on our own.

I tried college for a couple of years after high school, had to work full-time and take night classes every day while trying to play sports too. Eventually the draft ended that and it was combat infantry all the way. Finally I was going to do something everyone would be proud of me for, especially Mom—I would go off to a war and fight for my country. I was, wasn't I? Wasn't I?!!

The 4th and 12th, 25th Infantry in Dau Tieng, was my first combat assignment after filling sand bags in Cam Ranh Bay for a week. The 4th and 12th had just been hit pretty hard along the Cambodian border where the Ho Chi Minh trail filtered into South Vietnam. Our area was to be the blocking force to prevent the NVA from getting to Saigon. Tet hit us hard. I spent only two and a half days with them. The 3rd and 22nd was nearly wiped out for the third time since January; it was not the first of April in 1968.

I hooked up with the 1st Platoon, Bravo Company of the 3rd and 22nd, same company as in the movie *Platoon*. We were to be the replacements for those guys who fought at Soui Trey, Soui Cut and the Battle of Good Friday before us.

We talked about our reunion as though all of us would surely be there ten or twenty years later. Only sparingly did we suffer a casualty from our platoon during April and May, until . . . an ambush! Fortunately I wasn't walking point that day. Paris walked it for the left squad, which would have mostly new faces after that day. I can say that on that day in June of 1968, I experienced the worst feelings of my entire life and also the best. My helmet was shot clean off my head from a tree sniper, so was Billy Loftis'. He and I pulled Paris out that day, had to crawl through a canal, guardedly, as his body was mangled, but he lived. Many more would have died that day if it wasn't for the platoon pulling together and refusing to pull back until every wounded man was saved; there were many. I never saw Paris again; would like to!

In 1973, I completely totalled a sports car at the estimated speed of 140 m.p.h. Since Nam, I was headed for self-destruction again, it seemed; almost accepted an offer to join the mercenaries. Now I had a lot of hospital time, some two months, to think about my life, where I was going, and where I had been. Nam came into my thoughts every day . . . why was I there, who sent me there, why weren't they there? Why had I given up on myself since coming home after fighting so hard, as I did most of my life, to stay in one piece? Why?! Why did so few care?

After more hospital time and plastic surgery, I quit my job of seven and a half years; gave them no reasons. I knew that another challenge was needed again. So, I jumped into another combat arena . . . selling advertising space.

The hospital, medical bills were never paid off and the insurance company reimbursed me some $4000 less than what I paid for the car. They told me to accept it or they would repair it rather than total it, and getting all of the parts could take a full year. Thanks a lot! So, five years after Nam I was backed into another ambush and had to fight my way out. Again I thought seriously about the mercenaries. I needed the money so bad.

From 1974-1979, I worked for eleven different companies, actually giving it my all each time. The favor was not returned at any of those eleven stops. One employer went bankrupt, another moved without notice, and one just plain cheated me out of $10,000. My next stop was personal bankruptcy in 1980. Once again I had to start from the bottom.

The girlfriends I had from 1969-1983 never could figure me out. I was here today and almost always gone tomorrow. I knew marriage would fail for me and no way could I bring a kid into this world, but I used to pick up a kid now and then at the Big Brothers organizations. It didn't always work out.

I started camping out in the Everglades for peace of mind back in 1977. Took four- or five-day excursions to recapture Nam, don't know why, just had to do it. But something more dangerous was needed. I wanted to go back to Nam. I really did. Not sure now, though.

In 1983, I took off for a three-day Everglades warm-up to get me ready for ten days in the heart of the Amazon jungle. This was nearly it, what I was looking for. I wrote about it to myself and my loving wife-to-be, Ginny.

The people down there were exactly like the poor bastards in Nam, without the slant eyes. There was even a revolution going on and the buildings in Iquitos, Peru were in rubble from sabotage. Still, it was like being back.

In the summer of 1988, members of the platoon and their wives somehow pulled off a twenty-year reunion for us. Unbelievably, fifteen members of the platoon and their families showed up. Most had not seen each other since 1968. Emotions were and have been since simply indescribable. Old friendships have been restrengthened . . . for life.

How do you forget a man who fought beside you every day for a lifetime? A lifetime is exactly what Vietnam seemed like twenty-two years ago to us, yet . . . it surely just happened yesterday, as I know almost every day over there can be remembered to some extent today.

It was only yesterday, wasn't it?

On January 1, 1988, I formed my own company called The Roland Group. The years since bankruptcy were good. Putting in fifteen- and twenty-hour workdays helped! We are an independent publishers' rep organization and I'm still selling advertising, just like the first sales job I embarked upon back in 1974.

Many of the techniques and strategies I use now are copied from our search and destroy missions near the Cambodian border in 1968. I have developed a promotion campaign that was also taken from the propaganda concept used against us by the North Vietnamese and Viet Cong. Funny, isn't it? It works.

In Vietnam, the enemy was everywhere; perception was one of their weapons. We have utilized the art of perception in our sales plans by making our competitors think we are everywhere and that they cannot beat us.

We soften our prospects up with the artillery (propaganda), then the infantry (salesperson) comes in to mop up and earn the order.

Vietnam has finally been good to me and my family. The memories are still sad, for they were made only yesterday, so tears still come to my eyes as they are right now during this writing. But, many of the tears are happy tears now. I remember more of the smiles and joking now than I used to. I have two step-daughters who are beautiful and treat me wonderfully.

I remember the bitching and moaning and, of course, we fought with each other. But many of us became stronger afterwards. I wish they all had, but one thing Nam taught me was that it's never too late to start building again. We had to build and re-build almost every day in the bush. That's sort of how real life is for me today . . . so maybe Vietnam was teaching me and preparing me for what was to come.

That bullet through my helmet (which only happened yesterday) carried a message for me back then. It's just that some of us don't quite get it for a while, but when you do . . . it's never too late, no matter what you have been through. . . . It's never too late, brothers!

Things like this have been said to me since coming back: "You're lucky it wasn't a big war like the other ones, so it couldn't have been too bad!"; "You were over there? No kidding! How long? Didn't know you were gone."; "Well, we're glad you're back; now it's time to forget that; what's done is done."; "That was a mistake, too bad you had to be involved with it."; "Want to go golfing tomorrow?!!"

I must dedicate my chapter to someone. It could easily be my entire platoon; it could easily be for my lovely mother or my wife; it could be for my two best friends, Mac and Jack. Three fallen comrades come to my mind for various reasons—John Victoryn, Dean Coldren and Alvin Robertson. To them I dedicate this chapter, and to their families.

I guess everything will be okay now. My step-father and I are okay; we talk more. My father still doesn't, but everything's okay. My wife, Ginny, is the most wonderful person I know, just like my mom was. They got along very well together while my mom was here. She's gone now.

Maybe there's only one thing left to say . . . DAMN THAT WAR!!!

David Andersen

I was a 1965 graduate of Duarte High School, thirty miles east of L.A. I was the son of the local mayor and my head was full of "*Hey*-all, Ally-Oop, oop, oop, oop-oop."

In 1966, sensing the psychic tidal wave of Vietnam, I joined the Navy Reserve, mainly to gain another year before active duty, time I used to keep dating someone while "going to college" for a year. I would come back to finish after Vietnam. But, the closer *it* got, the more I sensed that I'd being going into thick stuff with the Marines. It was a difficult sensation to ignore.

For a long time I said about the Navy reservist period that I became a hospital corpsman because I didn't like sailing or chipping paint, and that I didn't know I'd end up with the Marines. I knew. But I couldn't admit it: I wanted to see if I was as tough as a jarhead. By the time I went to Nam, I also considered myself a pacifist medic. Tough but peaceful (as in, most of my friends had long hair): a strange mental brew with which to jump into the thick of things in 1968 DMZland.

I spent the last half of 1968 with Fox Co., 2nd Bn. 3rd Marines as a "Doc," a Navy Hospital Corpsman. I can't remember much about that period. I don't want to think about it. I don't want to write about it anymore. I wrote a very long short story about it, even though I had to tone it down to make it believable. That fiction appears in *Adventures in Hell, Volume I*, the first book produced by Ritz Publishing.

In December 1968 I got a bad case of malaria. I med-evaced myself out of a ville where I lived with Lucky's squad. The pain from the malaria was incredible. It was a last straw, a last spiritual twist in me; I was crazy from the bush, and what was worse, I sensed it. Once I was well enough, if shaky, I went back to our rear in Phu Bai or Dong Ha, wherever it was. The E-6 who ran me must have known I could endure no more bush time, or maybe he just needed another piece of meat with some smarts attached. I was sent to the northern-most medical outpost (Vandergrift, if I recall) where several surgeons and several corpsmen acted as a kind of Marine MASH unit, treating the heavily wounded in I Corp. We were the first, emergency stop for severely wounded Marines.

I thought it was a reprieve. Another bad joke.

My mental condition was reflected in my daily diet: a piece of white bread, a strip of bacon (usually cooked), at least a case of beer, booze, etc. That brings me to the scenes about which Gary encouraged me to write.

I was by myself, on night duty. They brought in a wounded NVA (too much security to be ARVN). Eventually, there was just me, looking at him; and him, semicomatose on a waist-high stretcher, with an IV running. I remember watching him, then watching a moth fluttering, hitting a light bulb. I remember walking over to him and shutting off the IV. He turned his head and seemed to look at me—blank, semi-conscious stare—the enemy. . . I do not remember turning the IV back on. I should. But I can't. I remember watching the moth banging into the light bulb the rest of the night.

Looking backwards, I now understand that my feeling was natural: I was glad he died, for all the pain and suffering he caused people I served with. (Vengeance well earned, but tempered now.) But I was a corpsman. A medic. A healer. Right. After six months in the bush, there was only one appropriate, natural state for an NVA.

A morning not long after: I was still alive and had made it to one more sunup. I'd been up alone all night, on duty. I greeted my replacement with bloodshot eyes. I cracked open a brew. I ate my daily piece of bread with a daily "prayer," a slug of whiskey. I chugged on it, then tossed in two triple-whammy Thorazine capsules and finished the beer in a gulp. I hit my cot in a belly-dive, probably thinking about the people in Fox . . . and the dangers of GIs killing each other. I'd worked on guys who got the bad end of the deal that way. I'll never forget the "Blood" that came looking to shoot me, then took it out on another brother two hooches down. Weird war. (The night I was med-evaced out, some buddies put four sticks of C-4 explosive under some major's pillow with a grenade. The grenade was a dud. Lucky him.)

Next thing I recall that morning, another corpsman was shaking me, trying to wake me up from my sleep and dreams. He said something like, "Andy! Get up! Get up! We've got beau-coup cut-downs going, and more choppers up on the pad! Wake up!"

I stumbled into the cutting room, worn-smooth jungle boots unlaced, into absolute chaos. Dying Marines everywhere, even on the floor and in the foyer. It was a very bad dream in which I could do nothing rapidly. All my bush quickness was gone. Zip. Zero. I was on another planet, not from the drug or booze, but from the death and pain around me. I stooped down to help one guy in the foyer but then I kept walking, a nightmare somnambulist, up the oblique steps to the LZ. Bodies lying on the LZ. And more choppers hovering, with the distant thwak-thwak of chopper blades in the muggy air. Where to begin?

I went back to the guy I'd just knelt down by. He was dead, maybe because I'd walked on.

I started doing things, like stripping muddy pants' legs away from gross, shredded leg stumps. Whoa, I just can't write this part . . . .

People were hurt *real* bad. The place was full of that almost touchable presence in the air, of spirits leaving bodies. It reminded me of the aftermath of firefights with Fox Co., with that strange stillness of many deaths, fear and fatigue. But this threw me. Away from the bush,

I'd lost my "protective coating" of hard emotions. I felt human. I cared about these wounded guys, barely hanging on, suffering and dying. That was a bad, vulnerable state of mind for a corpsman to be in.

A deep, silent wailing began in me, from watching and hearing the moaning and pain-screaming. It was like an eerie dirge, or mumbled chant, like a siren only I and other Vietnam vets could hear, I guess.

All this took place in a few minutes, but it was dragged out in the same surrealistic way that happened during firefights.

I walked over to a guy who must have been all of eighteen years old, face just changing from cherub to grunt. I'd turned twenty-one in the jungles he'd just come out of. I knew him, even though I'd never met him. We were brothers of the bush. His leg was wrapped up by his head, attached only by some skin and ripped sinew. He was in shock. I started cutting away his fatigues with tape scissors. Someone else was replacing an IV bottle. The kid turned to me . . . looked into my eyes (like the "gook" did). He said, real *un*-shocklike, "How'm I doin', Doc?"

"No sweat, Marine." (I remember his words, not mine.)

"Where'm I hit, Doc?"

"Leg. Not bad."

A little smile spread across his face. He said, "Good, Doc. Just wanna get home . . . dance with my gal," then he went back into shock.

That kid won't ever dance again, America. It bothered me then, it bothers me still.

Later that day I lay down again and twilight dreams were my only rest: I remembered the animal camaraderie of the jungle . . . barely speaking from tiredness, one grunt to another after humping a last of too many klicks in the Z; opening a jungle-green can of pears after an insidious day and draining off the juice in a primal gulp, followed by a pause to reflect on the incredibly beautiful but violent world; and exchanging maybe five sentences in a whole twilight with a grunt that happened to be close, digging a foxhole; concentrating on getting ready for the next day's hump; and tired like sex on a bad hang-over.

Since leaving Vietnam, I have been successfully surviving as a professional communicator—publishing and public relations. Some vets who relate to my war experience ask how I'm doing? What had I learned?

From Vietnam, how about a motto for a corpsman while a Marine grunt? "Whether to save or to sever, always go for the jugular." From The World . . . I'm still learning. I believe it is called survival of the fittest, but if success is anything like it is in war, it has to do with determination and luck. And trying to be around good people.

Welcome home, Davey Boy. Your life is your homecoming parade.

"Gotta get home, Doc. . . . Dance with my gal."

"Gotta get home, Doc. . . . Dance with my gal."

David Crawley

I was born and raised in Rochester, Minnesota and graduated from Mayo High School in 1967. At that time the United States was involved in Vietnam. Because of the way that I was brought up, that every American owed his country something, I enlisted in the Marines. My Dad was injured in World War II, his brother served and their father was in World War I, so it was natural that I go, no questions asked. So in August 1967, I went into the Marine Corps, and by January I was on my way to Vietnam.

I served with 3rd Bn. 1st Marines, and was wounded twice, and also suffered with a bout of malaria. In November 1969 I was discharged after spending ten months in Great Lakes Naval Hospital for my second Purple Heart. When I came home, I tried to do what my father and his generation did after their war—get married, find a job, and have kids. But this was not that generation, and that lifestyle was not to be.

I tried joining the local VFW and was told, "We don't want Vietnam vets in our post." I went to college and wasn't accepted their either. Having been to Nam, us vets were labeled baby killers and drug addicts and nobody wanted us around. I finally married, had a couple of kids, and tried to settle down, but inside me was a restlessness—something I couldn't quite explain. Nowadays, the fancy term for it is called Post Traumatic Stress Disorder, but back then it hadn't been coined.

In 1975, America pulled out of Vietnam, and another stigma was attached to us vets. We had lost the first war in America's history. It's been twenty years now, and I'm getting tired of the stories and movies of how us vets have been portrayed. We've been analyzed these past twenty years as if we were lab rats. The thing that bothers me the most is that we have been written about by people who have no conception of what we went through, by people who seem to think it would be an exciting experience to camp out in their backyard. All these past years, the writers have tried to explain what's wrong with the vet. They say we need some adjustment, some fine tuning, and we have to get aligned to society. They say we have bad dreams, are alienated, and don't socialize well, and we are hostile, and aren't, to be frank, quite right in the head. But perhaps, it's in the veteran's head to be right or wrong. And maybe it makes a difference what memories are in that head.

For most writers, the war seemed to be domino theory, land reform, and civil war. I don't know; I seem to have missed that war by being away in Vietnam at the time. To me, Vietnam was midnight ambushes, no sleep, humping up and down mountains and valleys, waiting for the next firefight, putting friends on helicopters that were dead or had parts of their bodies missing.

I used to try to explain Vietnam to people, but I don't do that anymore. People would look at me at parties and you could see that they were thinking, "He's crazy." They couldn't understand phantom jets dropping napalm, no showers for months on end, or North Vietnamese running at you with explosives tied to their bodies, trying to kill you while they themselves died.

So we withdrew inside ourselves.

Now, all vets are different. Most came home and made productive lives for themselves. Some turned to alcohol, some turned to drugs. There were a few of us, because we were young, and life was intense, that got addicted to combat and the adrenaline high. So, we searched out more combat. I've been hunters of Nam vets in another war in another country called Rhodesia, where there was one last shot to avenge ourselves for America losing the Vietnam War.

To many of us the war was the best time of our lives. We loved it because we were alive and young. Then it was over; we came home. Everything seemed to just stop. All of a sudden, we were amongst so-called proper people who didn't know what we had done or seen, and truth to be told, didn't really care. Subconsciously, we didn't really like them either. We came home with wounds, and memories of dead friends to be greeted with sayings of baby killer, and drug addict. Slowly, we came to realize these were the people we were fighting for, and we didn't like it. It's not that we didn't try to fit in, it's just that what we saw to fit into wasn't for us. The only jobs we could get were the low-paying jobs, because after all, we were two years behind everyone else. Everyone else was in college while we were fighting for America.

So there we were. Portrayed as sullen and anti-social. We just hadn't made the trip back home. But they just didn't realize "home" means different things to different people. The home we grew up in and dreamed about while we were away, just didn't exist anymore. It's like the man in the movie said, "All we really asked, was for America to love us as we loved it."

So here we are. Society all of a sudden likes us and says to forget the past.

It's hard.

And for me, the bottom line is this:

"Vietnam. . . . if you haven't been there, *shut the fuck UP!*"

Gary Gullickson

My name is Gary Dean Gullickson. I was born May 25, 1949 in Red Wing, Minnesota. Most of my growing up was done in Mazeppa, Minnesota. I also lived in Zumbrota and Pine Island, small towns in southeast Minnesota. My parents are Lester and Delores from Mazeppa, known as Sis and Pete as long as I can remember. They are honest, hard working people. I love them both very much. I have three brothers and one sister. In order our names are Larry, Gary, Mary, Jerry and Terry.

Looking back, I was just what the military was looking for. A little rough around the edges, but with a little training, I would do whatever they asked—go anywhere they wanted and not ask many questions. I would try anything once, twice if I liked it.

I always had good grades in school. It seemed to come easy for me. I tried sports. I really enjoyed football. I think it was the contact. But after I got into high school I found things I liked better than studying. I had perfect attendance in the tenth grade, but even then, I was asked to take the grade over. The only time I missed was the night they gave out the award for attendance.

Going to a nearby town for a rumble was the most fun.

We moved to Pine Island. Things were tough there. You might say my reputation preceded me. Pine Island was one of the towns where we came for the Friday or Saturday night rumble. That made school and making friends very hard.

I was asked in class one day to make a belt out of paper clips. I told the teacher where to put those paper clips and left school right then. That was my last day of school.

It was time for me to see the real world. I left school with an attitude and a hunger to learn, my way.

I found work at the local meat market. I was very lucky to get that job. They were the greatest bunch of guys to work for I have ever met. They taught me many valuable lessons about life. We worked very hard together and had some good times. To this day I have a card in my scrap book signed by each of them. After a few months it was time for me to head on to another job—the United States Marine Corps. My boss at the meat market, Bob Owen, told me—and I can hear these words yet today—"I will not stop a man from going on as long as he betters himself." The guys told me my knife would be waiting in a drawer for me when I got home.

I suppose it was natural that I would end up in the military. My father served, as did his brothers. I watched my brother go into the Army in 1966 and saw how proud he was and the people were of the guys that were going in. I did not plan to go into the Marine Corps, but after the recruiter got hold of me and I saw that uniform—how could I say no?

July 1967—HOT! Marine Corps Recruit Depot, San Diego, California—Platoon 3027. Those yellow footprints. The words "better himself" were running over and over through my head. If I lived, maybe it would better me, but suddenly I was not so sure. With fear and doubt, I was ready to face whatever they were going to give me, and do it well. The training was hell, but after it was done I felt great. I was ready for the next challenge.

After more training and running up California hills that were too damn high to climb I was sent home on leave. My orders were for Okinawa. My brother, Larry, was in Vietnam by this time. I was married on this leave and already had a son, Billy Joe.

Okinawa was a hard place to do duty. Too small and not much to do. I did finish high school there. That was a big accomplishment for me. My brother Larry and a friend from high school came on their R&R to stay with me. They had seven days. We turned it into thirteen, with or without permission. Funny, I don't remember talking about Vietnam. I really did not know where it was. But we sure had a great time together. Even now, when I see Jerry Horning, we laugh about that time together.

Days passed and it was time to leave Okinawa. I returned home for a leave before reporting to Marine Air Base, Cherry Point, North Carolina. I hated it there and asked to be out as soon as it could be arranged. Eight months and a mountain of paper work later, I was on my way home again before heading to Vietnam, or so I thought. I had to sign a waiver to get orders to Nam because I had not been stateside long enough. In fact, I could have spent the rest of my time stateside, but as I said before, I'll try anything once.

I had sent my wife Sharon home ahead of me. In October of 1969, we had another son, Bobby Joe. Saying good-bye this time was one of the hardest things I ever had to do. It finally hit me. I was going to the place I had heard so much about and where so many had died. It was words from my dad and my uncle Gerald, who saw heavy combat in World War Two, that got me on the plane. I had an early flight out that day, but trouble with the plane made for a great day with my family. I finally got on the last plane that night and had no trouble sleeping from Minnesota to California.

The flight was long this time—it seemed much longer than the first overseas. We hit a storm just out of Hawaii that dropped the plane so far and fast it brought things like pillows off the shelf. A very scary ride, but what made it worse was a lot of the guys had gotten food poisoning.

Now, here is this plane with about 125 guys on it, it is hot and stinks anyway, with a storm that I felt was going to kill us, and then guys vomiting from food poisoning. It was, for sure, a ride I will never forget and is in some way one of the reason's I cannot get on a plane today, and will not. There are other reasons I don't like to fly.

We landed in Japan—I thought for fuel or to look around before we were on our way to Nam. My name was called and I was told this was where I would be. I told the person I had signed a waiver for Nam only. He said with a smile, what waiver? I knew then what the game was, and that there could be more than one player. I wrote a letter to Congressman Al Quie, telling him what had happened. It was not long after that that my CO called me into his office. He said he had received about forty-five letters from congressmen and wanted to know if I had written a letter. I told him, "Yes, Sir—Why?" He told me to sign a letter telling Mr. Quie that I was satisfied with what they were doing to get me out of Japan. I told him I would when I was satisfied. He told me to get out of his office. He said the only reason I wanted to go to Vietnam was for the money. What stupidity. Money was the last thing on my mind.

In a few days he called me back. He told me to sign the letter and pack my bags, that I was out of there. I signed the letter. He told me to get out of his office and on the way out he said, "Gullickson, I hope you get your fucking ass shot off in Nam." I said, "Thank you, Sir," and kept walking.

This really seems strange. I have had a long time to look at this situation. There were a lot of government people working to get me to Vietnam, but when we needed help they were no where to be found. When a veteran needs help now, where is his government? It's hard to get them to listen, let alone care.

In three days I was packed. I was put on a C-130 cargo plane. I was the only passenger in the back with all the boxes of supplies. It was a bad flight. It was freezing. I had time to think about a lot of things, but no one to share them with. Finally, I was going to the place I had wanted. People were talking about the Vietnam vet and protesting. I did not listen to anyone. America needed help and I was going to do my part. We had to stop the Communist there, before we were fighting them here. "Save our world and families." John Wayne did it and we had to do our part.

Boy, was I brainwashed.

March 26, 1970, Da Nang, South Vietnam. I can remember when the door opened. The heat, the smell, those faces waiting to leave. To this day I can see those faces. I saw every emotion in Websters Dictionary getting off that plane. Here was the place I wanted and still did not know where it was on the world map. As I got off the plane I heard remarks like, "You'll be sorry, boot," "You're in deep shit," "This place sucks," "We're on our way back to The World," "Good luck" and "War is a mother fucker."

Well, the stage was set. I was put on a truck with some others. It was really different from what I thought. It was pretty in a way, but the smell was terrible. Not a long ride and there I was—Marine Air Wing, Mag 16, Marble Mountain. I could see hundreds of helicopters. I checked in, found out what I would be doing and where I would spend the next nine months.

As I walked with my duffel bag in hand I looked around the area. The thing I remember most were the hooches. They were made of tin and wood, screen windows, and completely surrounded by sandbags. Between each hooch was a sandbag bunker. It did not take long to find out what they were. I can remember thinking as I walked that I saw no air conditioners and something told me they were going to be very hot because of the tin. I walked in and found my bunk and wall locker. There were just a couple guys there at the time. First question asked— "What's your name—where you from in The World?" After small talk they said, "You should have been here yesterday. Two Cobras collided in mid-air. We had to pick up body parts all over the place."

I knew this was not going to be a good time.

On June 16, 1990 I saw one of these guys for the first time in seventeen years—Richard Deubler. In 1973 I went to Lima, Ohio to see him. We lost touch for all those years, but in seeing each other, it was like we were never apart. We were still as close as we were in Nam.

The hooches slept eight people each. My area was by the rear door. I went to work in the pre-expended bin section of the unit. It contained parts for helicopters costing less than $35. I settled right in and was ready to get to work—stay busy so time would fly. I found the section a real mess. Parts were taking up to five days to get, which does not seem important until a chopper stays down because of one part. I spent day and night doing inventory in seven warehouses. I made a new system that only I could understand. At night my staff sergeant would come in to see what I was doing and look at the new system. He told our CO about it and in May I received a Meritorious Mast.

The day I stood in front of the whole Mag was one of the proudest in my life. I knew what I had done was going to make a big difference in the way the group was working. Before this job, I had no training as a supply clerk.

Shortly after the award, 1st MAW Mag 16 set a new flight record. A Marine record for total combat hours flown in a single month was set in June by the helicopters of Mag 16. The new mark of 11,580 flight hours was a feat never before accomplished in Marine history. The record was set by UH-1E gunships, AH-1G Cobras, CH-46 and CH-53 helicopters. I am sure the record still stands today. We were all very proud of it. I felt very good inside for the job I had done.

Days passed—hot, rain, cold. During this time my uncle was also in Nam. He was in the Army and stationed at Phu Bai, north of Da Nang. His unit would fly him down for a few days. We had some great times together. One of the worst hang-overs in my life. We laugh about it today. I could get some items his unit needed and would send them back with him. It was the trade for them bringing him to stay. I am thankful for that time together. I was glad he left Nam safe—memories we can share forever.

After some time in Nam, humor took on a whole new meaning. We did some crazy things to entertain ourselves. Richard Deubler and I were known as the Roach Patrol. We would go out at night with a can of rifle spray and a lighter. When we tipped over sandbags, hundreds of roaches would run like hell. One of us had the job of tipping the sandbags and the other would light up the roaches. We switched duties every now and then. The guys got a kick out of it.

The thing that really bothered me the most was when the radio was reporting that Marble Mountain would be a blood bath. Hanoi Hannah was telling us that the NVA had 5000 troops just waiting to overrun Marble Mountain. We heard it so much that at times we welcomed it. Everyone was on edge all the time and tired of it hanging over our heads. We spent many nights in the guard towers waiting for it to happen.

As time passed, I found myself wanting to see more and do more in direct action. As I said before, anything once. The day came. My staff-sergeant came to me and asked if I would like to fly on a CH-46 as a gunner. Well, my first thought was that I would be leaving Vietnam for flight school and then be coming back to really see firsthand what was going on out there. How wrong I was, in every way of thinking. I was told to be at the warehouse at 8 a.m.

From 8—12 I was told things about flight direction, smoke color, med-evac, resupply, left gunner, right gunner, and crew chief. I really did not know what they were talking about, and I did not listen closely, still thinking I would be sent out of there for school. We were told to come back at 1. I thought then for sure we would be sent out. WRONG. We had to load a 50-cal. machine gun with several cans of ammo on the chopper. We took off over the sea. They had a pallet set up with smoke on it. We got our class on how to fire the 50-cal. We took turns shooting at the pallet with long bursts of fire. I can remember when my turn came. I had ear plugs in and a helmet with a microphone in it to talk to the others in the chopper. It did feel great, but I was scared and I realized there would be no leaving for school. This was the United States Marine Corps crash course in welcome-to-the-big-time. When I took the box of ammo to the gun and set it down, I looked at that piece of death and destruction. What a shell! I took the string of shells, laid it in the gun, locked and loaded. When I grabbed onto the handles of the gun, a rush of fear and power went through me. To look down the barrel of a 50-cal with the shells hanging out the side is a real rush.

We were done with school.

Yes, that's it. Back to the warehouse area—unload and clean the gun real good.

There was a huge board with all sorts of numbers on it. I remember looking at it, looking for my name. It was there already. It gave flight and chopper number, or name, crew, and mission. None of it made much sense to me. I had to ask what it all meant. While I was standing there, a guy walked behind me and stopped at the board. He looked at it and then at me and said, "Oh shit," with a strange look on his face.

The next morning yours truly was on his way to the Que Son Mountains. To this day, those words send a chill up my spine. I will never forget the first day. I had an M-16, as did everyone else there. I had to go to the armory, check out a 38 pistol, go to the other armory and check out the 50-cal machine gun. I remember how heavy it was the first time I carried it. I got it mounted and then loaded my shells. Here I was, twenty-one years old, over 10,000 miles from home, a 38 pistol on my side, an M-16 rifle with two magazines taped end-to-end for quick use, and this 50-cal machine gun with *several* big shells. You could say I was equipped to kick some ass.

I can remember the flight to the Que Sons. We left with two CH-46 choppers and two Cobra gunships. I can remember meeting at the back of the chopper with the pilots and crew. When we took off it was a great feeling inside. It was my turn to see this place and war called Vietnam. The words from Bob Owen were really running in my head—to better himself. How did he know so much? On the way to our post, we met the choppers we were replacing.

We got to the base. It was located on top of the mountains, and we had to land on small pads. We waited in a hut with a table and cots. There was a field phone by the front door. I can hear that ring to this day. When it rang we all jumped up and ran to the choppers. One of the pilots stayed back and got all the information about where we were going and what the problem was. It is a really scary feeling when you do not know what sort of problem is going to come your way. You just know someone needs your help and it has to be done.

My first day was slow for Nam. Some minor wounds and some high fever med-evacs. The Que Sons were a bad place to pick people up. Most of the time you had to lower the chopper down to a trail and Charlie knew the 50-cal went back and forth, but not upward enough. He would wait for us to lower and he would shoot from above. You had to lean out of the chopper and watch up. Sort of like looking up so he could get a good shot or a good look at you before he blew your head off. I hated that feeling. The day passed and it was our turn to go back to the home base. I remember thinking as we met our replacement choppers, "I really do not want to do this at night." It was yet to come. On the way back we got a call for a permanent med-evac. Our pilot said he would be glad to help out. We changed direction and headed out to the spot to pick up the body. We circled around to pick the best way to come in. I stood behind the 50-cal and watched for anything. At the area, it was long grass with jungle-like terrain around it. I could see two Marines standing in the grass waiting for us. One was standing with his M-16 at the ready position and his T-shirt was torn and put around his head like a headband. The other stood and watched us land. He had sort of a beard, and longer hair. I was on the chopper that landed. As we landed the one Marine reached into the grass and picked up a body. He threw it into the chopper. I was watching the area, but from the corner of my eye I saw this body land and roll up next to me. When we were clear, the doc on board came over to examine. I looked down and got my first look at death from war. The hole in his back was very big. I could see right into the back of this lifeless person. The doc rolled the body over. He told the pilot it had been dead for awhile because rigor mortis had set in. When I saw that face, my body went numb. It was an NVA, but so young. The hole in the front was smaller. I can still see his face. My thought was, "What are we doing to these people? How can we do this?"

When I got back to the hooch that night all the guys had to hear about the day and check on me. We did care about each other. I did not want to talk much. I went up on top of the hooch with a warm beer and some grass. I could see the war going on not far away. It was pretty. The sunsets in Vietnam were very beautiful.

The next day was back to the mountains, but first we took troops to a few places, and mail, ammo, and supplies to several bases. It was interesting to see the differences in living conditions where we landed. I have a lot of respect for the ground fighter. I am not sure I could have done his job. The conditions they had to fight in were the worst anyone could imagine. No matter what anyone thinks, these were real brave men and I for one am very proud of them. I got the chance to see them work in their environment and no way would I want to do it. Unless you have seen the faces of men carrying a wounded or dead friend to a chopper, unless you have seen it, please do not say you know how they feel or how they should act. I am sure many of you can only guess what hell that really was. To me the Vietnam soldier was a great fighting force, but was never allowed to do what he was capable of doing. A shame to send a young man to fight and then not let him. It seemed too one-sided at times.

At the mountains this day I would get the chance to help one of my brothers. The call was for a wounded Marine. I can remember going in to get him. The fear was intense, but I shut it out and did my job. It is an awful feeling to see men carry someone on board that has just been hit. When I saw him, my whole attitude changed. I thought, "How dare you shoot one of us."

It all came to me. "Now I understood." At that moment I became very good at what I was doing. I felt like I wanted to get even for what I had just seen. Now I knew what this war was. I wanted to do my best and just get home, out of that fucking place. We got him to the hospital. When we came in the personnel there were waiting. With the doctors and corpsmen we had on board, he had good care. They are some more people I am very proud of. They were brave and had to do a lot with not much to work with. I have a high respect for the medical people in Nam. A great job done by some great people.

During the time I was flying, my thoughts kept returning to the last time I saw my friend Richard Seymore. He had flown as a gunner also, and stayed in the hooch next to me. In August, I walked into the supply headquarters and talked to Richard. I had just gone in to see how everyone was doing, and Richard was sitting at a desk with his feet up, reading a letter. He had his flight suit pulled down to his waist because of the heat. I went up to him and asked him how he was doing. He said good—he was just reading a letter from his girl in The World. I said, "I'll talk to you later," and he just looked up with a smile and said "Okay."

At the end of the day, I walked into the hooch and all eyes turned to me. The first thing the guys said was. "Richard is gone." I said, "What do you mean, 'gone'?" They said he had been killed in an accident. The chopper was shot down and he was shot before they landed.

I think at that time I had an out-of-body experience. I felt so weak, so numb, so useless. To this day I do not like telling anyone "I'll talk to you later." In Nam, death was so fast. We were close, so close for just a short time, but it would last a lifetime inside.

One guy from my hooch was with Richard at the time. He pulled him from the wreck. Last I heard, he was going to be in a hospital in Japan for quite a few months. I cannot remember his name but he was from Maine. We talked about Maine a lot. He had been in Nam for several months and extended to send money home to help his family. Richard and the pilot were killed. We had a memorial service for them.

I wish the assholes waiting to spit on us when we got home could have been at the service we had for them. Richard was twenty years, two months, and two days old. I only hope he can rest in peace. He gave the ultimate for a country that didn't understand, know, or care. Maybe after we all speak out he can rest easier. What a total waste of life that war became. Although his face has faded, his memory will be with me forever.

I usually flew left-side gunner. It just felt best to me. The unit I flew with was HMM 364, The Purple Foxes. I think it was one of the greatest chopper groups in Vietnam. Our insignia was a picture of a purple fox head in a circle, with the words "Give A Shit" around it, meaning, "We Care." We even gave out business cards.

I remember one big mission. We had to take a large group of Marines and a unit of Korean Marines into Arizona Territory. A *bad* place to go. The morning we were getting ready to leave, the flight line was full of choppers—The Foxes, Huey gunships, and Cobras. I can see the Marines we were taking in getting ready to go—getting their gear ready, loading ammo, shaking hands, hugging. You could feel in the air it was going to be one of those days. Our mission was for each chopper to take two loads. I got my 50-cal ready and lots of ammo on board. The fear and tension was so great I had to try and put it out of my mind. "Just do your job, get the men in, protect them as long as you can, and don't let Charlie put a hole in your head." The chaplain came out to the flight line to say a prayer.

The sound of all those choppers starting up at one time is a sound I will never forget. Sometimes I find myself missing it. I can see the sun rising and I can hear that song, "Sky Pilot." We lifted off to head into God only knew what. When we got to the area someone must have told Charlie we were coming to see him. We had to stay in the air for a very long time, maybe forty-five minutes or so, so the jets could demolish the area and show Charlie we were coming, ready or not. *He was.* Our Cobras broke off to help out. We circled above with the CO in a chopper above us directing the mission. It is some sight to be sitting in the air watching the fireworks below. Some of the thoughts in my head scare me today. With the flight helmet on you can hear everything that is being said. It was confusing to me at times. The thing I see most is when we got the word we were going down in five minutes. I gave the hand sign to the squad leader, and he gave it to the men.

What I saw then will be with me forever. The guys were sitting across from each other with rifles across their legs, loaded with gear, a look in their eyes you could not believe. When they got the sign, they all started stomping their feet together and pumping each other up. It was like they were off to the big football game for the championship. I was in disbelief at what I was seeing. I got so excited watching them I could not wait to get in and cover them while they got out of the chopper. Such brave boys they were.

When we went in Charlie was not going to give ground easy. It is a very scary time heading into a hot LZ not knowing what will happen. "Is this the one, is this the one that will take me home in a box? Had I seen everyone for the last time? I am sorry for so much, and if I make it out, I'll be different. I want to live, not die in this country." If you did not know God at all, at this time you were asking all kinds of things from him. The smell, the heat, the intense feelings inside. I have never felt such an intense high. As we went in I locked and loaded the 50-cal and made sure my ammo was ready for use. As we neared the ground I was watching for any sign of trouble. A short distance away I saw three puffs of smoke. It was at the edge of a small ditch. Enough of a sign for me. I cut loose with a burst that would have made John Wayne proud. I sighted by the way the grass and ground were flying. Even small trees did not stand a chance against the 50-cal. I hit my target and kept the fire in the area.

The shit was really flying now. The chopper landed, back door down, and the men were gone. I could hear the other gunners giving it hell. The smoke, dirt, noise, fire, voices, all this going on in my head. The barrel was so hot it turned red. I loaded again and kept shooting. "Give cover to the guys that are going to battle face to face, God protect them." As we lifted off I kept shooting. I know, inside, to this day, the enemy made one mistake. Three were laying too close together to face the 50-cal. The sight of what a 50-cal machine gun will do to a person will never leave me. At the time it does not matter. It is later that it gets to you. You just try to deal with it each day of your life. I have to think, "I did not want to do this, I only did as I was asked to do." We went back to the base and got another load of Marines. When we got back to The Arizona, it was about the same going in, but this time it was more controlled, with so many of the good guys in. We had to be careful. When it was over for us back at the base, it came to a stop. Time to reflect. We had several choppers hit, but none went down. The guys at the base were waiting for us to return, cheering, waving, running to meet us. It was a great feeling inside. The CO put on a party for us. Warm beer and beef. Back at the hooch the guys were all asking about it. It is amazing how close I got to those people. From all over America, so different in so many ways, but so close to each other. We made promises to stay in touch when we got to the world, but as things worked out, just wanting to forget, has left us so far apart. What a damn shame. I miss those guys. I hope we can unite again some day.

I would like to ask a favor here if I may. If any one reads this that did or knows anyone that served with me at these places please get in touch with me. Platoon 3027, July 1967 San Diego, CA; Camp Foster, Okinawa, 1967-68-69, Lot 10 (Raiders); H&S group Japan, 1969; Mag 16 Marble Mountain, Vietnam, 1970.

Night missions in Nam were scary. The darkness became an enemy as well. I could see the tracer rounds from ground fire, coming up towards me. It was like looking death in the face, only for me to say, "Fell short again. Maybe next time, if you're lucky." That Friday or Saturday night rumble back home would have been big fun compared to this. The color of a tracer coming at you in the dark—it definitely left an impression on me that will last a lifetime.

The most enjoyable time on a mission was one night when I was on twenty-four-hour duty. This was when we came in from the day's mission's and we had to stay close in case we were called out again. I spent most of the night on top of the hooch. It was a beautiful night. Full moon—warm—very quiet for Nam. Just sat and relaxed.

Let me start with the day. We were out on missions early. On one stop I found a guy I met on R&R. When we landed he looked over at the chopper. It was a fire base on top of a hill—don't know which one. When I saw him I gave a yell. He ran to the chopper and I hung out the window. We hugged. It was like finding a loved one. We did not get much time to talk, but I will never forget him. I can only hope he made it home safe. When we left there we got a call that we had to take ammo into the Marines that were engaged with Charlie and low on ammo. We stopped and got a pallet, lowered a hook and away we went. I was on the chopper that picked it up so it was us that would go in to drop it. This was for sure a HOT LZ. We went in and Charlie was pissed. We had a hell of a time getting in. The chopper got hit several times and the gunner behind me got hit in the shoulder. What a scary thing to do and see when you're leaving and headed back to the base.

When we got back I thought for sure I would be able to just lay back. WRONG again. I told the other gunner to hang in—"You're lucky. You're out of here for a while." We were told to head to another chopper. I took my 50-cal and ammo to the other chopper and got ready to go back to the WAR. God, I needed rest and time to sort this out. Maybe it is best the way it went. If I had time to think I would not have gone back.

The rest of the day was spent on routine missions. A fourteen-hour work day.

When I had just gotten in my bunk and started to dose, the door flew open and a voice screamed "Sergeant Gullickson!" My thought was "OH NO, this is the one—the other guys got shot down and we have to replace them. Back to the Que Sons. And at night. Of all times, night."

He told me to check in and had no idea why. I got all my gear and was putting my flight suit back on. The guys in the hooch were saying things like "It'll be all right," "Give 'em hell," "Good luck, man."

TO BETTER HIMSELF. Whoever said that was right. I got to the chopper, loaded and waited for the crew. When everyone got there no one would say what we had to do! We lifted off and in just a short ride started to land. We landed by the runway. I could not believe my eyes! Women! Americans! Round-eyes! It looked good! They had been at our Officers Club for the evening and our mission was to fly them out to the hospital ship. Our pilot said, "Watch this!" Instead of shutting the chopper down, he revved it up! Hats flew and dresses flew up, and the guys on the ground failed to see the humor in our gesture. We all just laughed. We got the young ladies on board and they were very grateful for the ride. The sight of American women and the smell of perfume! What a ride it was—the best one ever. During the flight, the pilot asked for one of them to come up front and sit. I went over to one and let her know that the pilot wanted her to come up and sit in front. She did so, immediately. She went up, and I saw her lift up her dress and take a seat on the control panel. I thought the view was probably good for all involved! She had a chance to see the South China Sea at night, and well, we all enjoyed the ride, too. To this day I have a lot of respect for the nurses. They did so much and gave a lot to save so many.

Landing on a ship at night is great. The ship was swaying with the motion of the sea, and we had to land on a small circle. When we went in the deck filled with people. It seemed they came from nowhere. There were guys on crutches, bandages all over, guys in wheel chairs, and guys standing. They were waving, applauding, giving peace signs. It was their way of saying "Thank you." Maybe it was our crew who had lifted them out of the bush. I felt very proud at that time. We waved, gave peace signs back, and lifted off. I was so proud of them. We went back to Da Nang for a load of blood, back to the ship and then back to the hooch. I had to tell the guys about how bad it was. They all met me at the door and wanted to know. They wanted to hear all the details. I miss that closeness with people. To this day I miss those guys.

The chopper pilots in Vietnam were definitely a different breed. Very brave and caring individuals. Every morning the crew had a meeting at the back end of the chopper. One pilot I remember very well. You either loved his style or you didn't! First time I met him he said, "I'm going to drive this thing like a '55 Chevy back in college. I fly low and fast. I know where every wire is in this country. We will go up and over them. I fly low to the ground because it would be hard for one of them to stand up and shoot us down when we're at the same level they are." This guy was very good at what he did. One day we did touch-and-go's on Highway 1, the busiest road in Vietnam (other than the Ho Chi Minh Trail).

You had to trust each other with your life in Vietnam. One of the scariest things with these guys was going on med-evacs in mountainous areas, such as the Que Sons. The trails were very small and narrow, and on the side of the mountain. You had to lower down into the valley, and back up to the trail. The crew chief would direct the chopper back, and watch the blades. The gunner's job would be to watch the area below, around, beside, and above the chopper. The idea was to get just the rear tires on the trail, and load as quickly as possible. Not a real comfortable feeling dangling hundreds of feet in the air, literally by a thread. So many little things could have sent us crashing down the side of the mountain—tree limb, wind change, one bullet. At the time I did not realize how dangerous it was.

One of the last missions I remember haunts me. We had to take a load of wounded Marines from the hospital by Da Nang to the hospital ship. We put the seats up on both sides of the chopper to have room for all the stretchers. We got the men on board and lifted off. On the way out, one of the guys touched my leg and pointed to the rear of the chopper. One of the long seats had fallen down right over one of the wounded at the back of the chopper. I walked back to the rear, stepping over them on the way. That was some sight, I bet, and some accomplishment in a moving CH-46. When I got to the back I reached down to put the seat back in place and secure it. As I picked it up, I looked into the face of one of the most horribly wounded men I had ever seen. This poor guy had a head wound and was stitched from one side to the other, all the way around this head. I looked at him and he smiled at me. I remember thinking, "You poor soul. You are hurt so bad and you can still smile at me." I will never forget the look on his face. I was so proud of him and I felt so bad. God, I hope he is okay now. Sometimes at night when I sleep, my breath gets fast, my heart speeds up and I wake up thinking of sights like this.

A short time later, I was done flying as a gunner. It was back to the warehouse. This time I really wanted to keep those $35 parts going. I had seen *firsthand* how important they were.

On October 25, 1970, Typhoon Kate struck the lowlands of Quang Nam Province. High winds and torrential rains lasted five days. From October 29 to October 31, 1970 the people at Marine Air Group 16 sought out and rescued over 11,000 Vietnamese civilians from sure death. This rescue mission was planned in a matter of hours. They flew in the worst possible conditions. There were fifteen helicopters hit by enemy ground fire during this mission. The Secretary of the Navy awarded a Meritorious Unit Commendation. Apparently, all the reporters were covering more important things. Why all the bad we did and not the good? Where are those people now that said we only killed women and kids?—that we were drug addicts, war mongers, just wasting the tax payers' money? When was the last time they helped an elderly person across the street or even took the time to think of the homeless people in this country? Their own country! Greed and politics still prevail.

It was not long and my good old staff sergeant came to see me again. This is the same guy who convinced me to be a gunner, and who showed skin flicks in the warehouse at night, for profit. This time it was for a new mission. The Army wanted a Marine sergeant to ride guard to Chu Lai on prisoner runs.

Anything once.

You bet I will! My reasons were simple. I did not know anything about it, and my best friend from high school was stationed at Chu Lai.

I met with the Army crew at the flight line. I walked up to them, 38 pistol at my side, looking good. We met. I asked, "What do we take on this trip?" They pointed to an airplane that looked like a "bush" plane. It was called the Otter. I asked, "What do you have for guns on her?" They just looked at me—I thought just because I looked so sharp. They looked down at the 38 and my thoughts were, "Oh, shit. Me and my 'Anything once.'" They said not to worry, they would fly over the sea so we would not be shot at. I did not really feel good about this, but off we went.

When we got to Chu Lai, I had to lay over for the day and night. I went to the motor pool to find Wes. He was almost in shock to see me there. It was great to see him, but so strange. Over 10,000 miles from home and together. It was a hell of a long way from Mazeppa, Minnesota. I can tell you that. We had a good time there. Got drunk as skunks, took pictures, raised some hell—the time was very special for us. It was suddenly time to go, and hard to say good-bye. In Nam you just never knew.

We flew off to get the prisoners. When we picked them up, I was not feeling so well and really did not want to get a bad time from any of them, and I made that very clear to them. We headed back to Marble Mountain. I sat behind them, hot, hung over, and *not* in a good mood. They would turn to look at me and I would just point to the front and tell them "pleasant" things. They had a very nice camp to stay in. When I saw the pictures of how our POWs had to live and were treated, it just really got to me. How could anyone treat another human being that way?

A short time later, Wes's unit got shipped out of Vietnam. He had a choice of places to go and chose Marble Mountain. Why, I will never know, but I was glad he did. We got to spend a lot of time together. I was proud of him and glad he was there. By the way, Wes married my sister, Mary. He was my brother in Nam, now he's my brother-in-law!

One day Wes and I went to the Air Force base. They had a very nice club there. That was also the club we would take one of the guys from our unit to. He would impress the Air Force guys by chewing the top off of a beer can in three seconds. We made bets on this guy and won several free drinks. We also had another guy that would eat cockroaches for free drinks.

We had to hitchhike to this club. We met a black guy there and commenced to get drunk, very drunk. We left the club and ended up in a ville that was really off-limits. This turned out to be one of the scariest nights of my tour. We could not get out of the ville because there were so many VC, and we got caught inside for the night. The VC were even running around, shooting up and down the ville, looking for us. Wes and I were in a small closet hiding out. The next day the black guy could not be found. When we asked about him, we were told, "Your friend is gone." That was the first time we had met him and the last time we saw him. I do not know what happened to him and I have no way to find out. I know three of us went into that ville and two of us came out. I hope he made it. I cannot even remember his name or his face, but that night haunts me yet.

My tour ended sooner than Wes's. I hated leaving him there. A very hard thing to do—leave someone you care for. The end of my time in Vietnam came December 9, 1970. Five days in Okinawa, two days in California; 180 days and "early out" of the Marine Corps!

I was honorably discharged from the United States Marine Corps on December 16, 1970. I was glad to get out because my orders were for Cherry Point, North Carolina again. NO WAY.

I can remember leaving Vietnam, and this time looking at the faces getting off the plane. In my head I thought, "MY GOD. You are so young! So white from lack of sun." The wide-eyed looks, scared, wondering "What now?" It seemed so long ago that I was one of them. I wanted to tell them, "This place will change you beyond your wildest dreams. For some of you, this is the place you will die." Even getting on the plane, I did not feel safe. Maybe Charlie was going to get just one more at us before we left.

One last look back and one more smell and I was on my Freedom Bird back to The World.

When I was flying back to Minnesota, I was really on my Freedom Bird. The landing was great. There was fresh snow and the lights made it shine like diamonds. The pilot circled a little longer for me so I could get a good look. I really felt good inside and very proud. My family was waiting at the airport.

Well, twenty years have passed since Vietnam. A long time to look back and see things as they really were. The good, the bad, and the ugly . . . the very ugly. It seems like yesterday.

In December 1968 I lost a very good friend in Vietnam. Buck was one of the nice guys that did not deserve what he got. When he came back, no one cared. I recently put this (below) on his grave in Pine Island, Minnesota. A flower pot and metal frame with a plaque that says:

"Buck, Much too soon, much too young you left us. Just one more talk on main street, one more party together. You are always with me, Buck. I can see us riding cycle on the highway. Me on my Jawa, you on your Honda Dream. The wind in your hair, the free look on your face. I miss you. DAMN THAT WAR. May you rest in peace my friend."

I got out of the Marines in December and was divorced in April of 1971. Lasting relationships have been a problem. I let people get as close to me as I feel they should. I do not think any of us will ever be the same after Vietnam. I have forgotten a large portion of my life. I think that in shutting out the bad, we shut out everything, not realizing it. Vietnam made young men grow up way too fast. How could a country send it's son's and daughter's to slaughter and just watch it happen. When the Vietnam veteran came home, he did not get the welcome all veterans should get. You made us feel guilty and put us into a shell. It took sixteen years for this country to realize it had Vietnam veterans. It was then that the welcome home began. The welcome home was very late. The damage was done and on a very large scale. It may seem funny, but I think just the words, "Thank you," could have saved a large number of lives. If The Wall in Washington, D.C. was to reflect the true number that died in Vietnam, and the thousands that have taken their own lives since Vietnam, it would be some wall to look at.

I feel as if I'm walking a fine line each day. I feel the line is between here and nowhere. I think what keeps me here is not knowing what is on the other side, and how to get back, if I cross. I think we all have this in our own way. There are more than physical wounds from war. None of the wounds will ever heal.

I have never known exactly what I should be doing. I did return to that meat market, and my knife was waiting in the drawer. Over the years I have held several jobs. I have been in business, lost at business, made money, lost money, but I keep trying.

Trying gets harder every year.

Sometimes I feel the ones that died in Vietnam were the lucky ones. They will be remembered. We that survived (?) are forgotten with our honor. Forgotten as have been our POW-MIAs. Our disabled and hospitalized veterans. The homeless veterans. How can a country just forget people that went to fight a war for them? It seems that if it does not happen to us, or very close to us, it just does not matter.

Take a good look at yourselves. Can you really just go on knowing of these problems?

As it is now, I feel as I did in Nam. All we ever had was each other. We have to help each other again. This is not the end, but hopefully a new beginning. Full circle will come. Walk proud, my brothers and sisters—you did only what you were asked to do. With peace and love, Gary.

Glossary

ABN	Airborne
Agent Orange	Chemicals used as a defoliant; in recent years, found to cause medical problems for Vietnam vets
AK-47	A Russian assault rifle
AIT	Advanced Individual Training
ARVN	Army Republic of Vietnam; a soldier of that army
Body Bags	Heavy-duty plastic zipper bags for corpses
Bush, the	Hostile land; also called The Boonies
CA	Moving from one place to another, usually by helicopter
CAP	Combined Action Platoon—usually two squads of Marines and one squad of South Vietnam civilian popular forces, living "permanently" in or near a ville.
CG	Commanding General
Chinook	Chinook/Army—CH-46/Marines, a large, twin-bladed helicopter used for transporting men and materials
Chopper	Helicopter
Claymore	Mine packed with plastique and rigged to spray hundreds of steel pellets
Cobra	Helicopter gunships heavily armed with rocket launchers and machine guns
Commo	Communications
CP	Command Post
C-4	Plastic explosive
C-7	A transport plane
C-130	A cargo plane used to transport men and supplies
DEROS	Date Estimated Return Overseas
DI	Drill Instructor
Division HQ	Command Headquarters
DMZ	Demilitarized Zone; misnomer for area separating North and South Vietnam in the same place as the 1954 Demarcation Line, taking in its narrow swath the South Ben Hai River that cut across and separated two nations.
Dust-off	Helicopter flight/landing for medical evacuation
ETS	Estimated Time of Separation from active military duty
Fast Movers	Jets with bombs—F-4s or F100s are classic examples
Firebase	Reinforced bases established to provide artillery fire support for ground units operating in the bush, often created in the jungle by blowing up a space with a bomb or C-4.

Firefight	Enemy forces engaging in an attempt to kill or maim one another with mobile weaponry, grenades, mortars, claymores, sticks, stones, and whatever else comes quickly into the fingertips
FNG	Fucking New Guy — "new" (beginning tour of duty) in Vietnam (used mainly in Army; see also, "Newby")
FO	Forward Observer
Freedom Bird	Jet aircraft departing South Vietnam for the U.S.A.
Free Fire Zone	An area agreed upon by most parties involved, with the understanding that anyone entering the zone will be more than fair game; a potential killing field
F-4s, F-100s	Jet fighter aircraft
Gooks	Slang for an Asiatic person, especially in reference to the enemy (NVA and VC)
Grunt	Slang for any Allied combat infantry soldier fighting in South Vietnam
Gunship	Helicopter armed with cannon, rockets, machine guns
HHCCo.	Headquarters Company
Hooch	Slang for any form of dwelling place
Howitzer	Large cannon
Huey	UH-1E—helicopter used for transporting troops, wounded and dead
Humping	Marching through enemy territory with heavy load; used by grunts in place of "marching"
IG	Inspector General
In-country	In the land of Vietnam, completing a tour of military duty
IV	Intravenous injection
KIAs	Killed In Action
Klick	One kilometer (0.62137 mile)
Kit Carson Scout	A former enemy soldier utilized as a guide in enemy territory
LBJ	Long Binh Jail; of secondary importance to most grunts, Lyndon Baines Johnson, U.S. President.
Legs	Army grunts; term applied by nongrunts
Lifer	Derogatory epithet for an individual making a twenty to thirty year career of the military and who followed the book to the perceived disadvantage of his subordinates
LP	Listening Post; often, in the bush, a two- to seven-man team set out, beyond a defensive perimeter, to listen for advance enemy troops, with the intention of holding fire on any observed enemy.

LT	Lieutenant; when acting as a savvy platoon leader in the bush, considered the most honorable officer by grunts
LZ	Landing zone (for helicopters)
Mad Minute	(Primarily U.S. Army) unit firing weapons en masse for a short period of time, to discourage enemy soldiers from attacking; recon by fire
Mamasan	Vietnamese woman, usually one with children ("mama")
Med-evac	Medical evacuation; evacuating the wounded by helicopter or airplane
MIAs	Missing In Action
MOS	Military Occupational Skill
MP	Military Police
M-16	Standard automatic weapon used by American forces.
M-60	A 30-caliber machine gun used by American troops
Nam	Vietnam (variant spelling: Viet Nam)
Napalm	Incendiary mixture of jellylike substance made from sodium palmitate added to gasoline or oil used in bombs and flame throwers; it fries everything that it touches
NCO	Non-Commissioned Officer (rank: E-4 through E-9)
NCOIC	Non-Commissioned Officer In Charge
NDP	Night defensive position
Newby	New Baby (pronounced NOO-BEE)—"new" (beginning tour of duty) in Vietnam (used mainly by Marines; see also "FNG")
NVA	North Vietnamese Army; a soldier of that army
OP	Observation Post
Ordnance	Military weapons collectively, along with ammunition and the equipment to keep them in good repair; secondary meaning, artillery
R&R	Rest and Recuperation; usually five to seven days in areas such as Sidney, Australia or Bangkok
Phantom	A jet fighter (F-4)
Pointman	The leading, scouting first man on an Allied patrol through the bush
ROK	Republic of South Korea Marine, a fierce warrior
Recon	Reconnaissance
RPG	Soviet-made enemy rocket
RSVN	Republic of South Vietnam
Rucks	Backpacks

Sappers	Viet Cong infiltrators whose job was to detonate explosive charges attached to their bodies within Allied positions, often crawling under barbed wire to reach their desired destination
Satchel charges	Explosive packs carried by VC sappers
Seabee	Member of U.S. Navy construction battalion, helped build naval aviation bases and facilities, and more
SERTS	Training for GIs when they got to Vietnam
SKs	Russian carbines
Tet	The lunar New Year as celebrated in Southeast Asia
TOC	Tactical Office Command Post
Tracer	A bullet with a phosphorus coating designed to burn and provide a visual indication of the bullet's trajectory; ammunition that traces its own course in the air with a trail of smoke or fire, which facilitates adjustment of aim ("and attitude," says Gary Gullickson)
VC	Viet Cong
Viet Cong	The local militias fighting Americans and other Allied troops in South Vietnam
Ville	Hamlet or village in South Vietnam; generic name applied by U.S. servicemen
The Wall	The Vietnam Veterans Memorial in Washington, D.C., located within sight of the Washington Monument; The Wall, as it is commonly referred to, is a black wall of stone set into the earth at a beautiful site, imprinted with the chiseled names of the more than 58,000 Americans who died in the Vietnam War; The Wall, in 1991, symbolizes and brings to the fore human-to-human stories and a healing process.
WIA	Wounded In Action
World, The	The United States of America/HOME
XO	Executive Officer
105mm	Howitzer (cannon size)
982mm	Recoil rifle
81mm	Mortar shell
50-cal	.50-caliber machine gun
45	.45-caliber pistol

"Jungle Boots," by Daniel J. Hunter, 1991, Rochester, Minnesota